The Special Education ALMANAC

The Special Education ALMANAC

EDITED BY

Elaine Fletcher-Janzen

Cecil R. Reynolds

John Wiley & Sons, Inc.

This book is printed on acid-free paper. ♾

Published by John Wiley & Sons, Inc., Hoboken, New Jersey.
Published simultaneously in Canada.

For general information on our other products and services please contact our Customer Care Department within the U.S. at (800) 762-2974, outside the United States at (317) 572-3993 or fax (317) 572-4002.

Wiley also publishes its books in a variety of electronic formats. Some content that appears in print may not be available in electronic books. For more information about Wiley products, visit our web site at www.wiley.com.

Library of Congress Cataloging-in-Publication Data:
The special education almanac / edited by Elaine Fletcher-Janzen & Cecil R. Reynolds.
p. cm.
Includes bibliographical references.
ISBN-13 978-0-471-67797-0 (paper)
ISBN-10 0-471-67797-3 (paper)
1. Special education—United States—Handbooks, manuals, etc. 2. Children with disabilities—Education—United States—Handbooks, manuals, etc. I. Fletcher-Janzen, Elaine. II. Reynolds, Cecil R., 1952–
LC3981.S577 2005
371.9—dc22

2005045773

Printed in the United States of America.

10 9 8 7 6 5 4 3 2 1

To our good friend and colleague Dr. Kathy Sullivan,
for all her good works with children.

Contents

Preface

One of the ways that *Webster's Dictionary* defines the word *almanac* is "annual publication containing statistical, tabular, and general information." This is a somewhat accurate descriptive statement about our goal to produce an almanac about special education (though we will not live up to the "annual" component, no doubt). After writing and editing encyclopedias and desk references for the past 20 years, we have amassed a huge amount of information that is usually filed in the reference sections of major libraries. It was our desire to redistribute some of the information garnered from these reference works into a handy single volume that would support the everyday professional needs of individuals working in the field of special education. After all, many questions pop up in the course of the day that allude to special education law, definitions, rules, and guidelines for professional practice and paperwork, and not everyone can run to the library to look up tiny nuggets of information. Of course, there is always the Internet, which is a vast source of information. However, the Internet sometimes is guilty of providing too much information and sometimes information that has not been adequately researched. Hence, the information in the *Special Educator's Almanac* is neatly bound and based on sound research, and so it comes to the professional instead of the other way round. Our hope is that it will be a ready reference for the student and the journeyman special education professional who want quick access to information about tests, disorders, laws, pediatric psychopharmacology, and even helpful web sites that concern the many and often unique children and adolescents they encounter.

As for the "annual" part of the definition of the word *almanac,* we are looking forward to seeing how the *Special Educator's Almanac* is received. This volume is full of up-to-date information. For example, a summary of the Individuals with Disabilities Education Improvement Act of 2004, signed into law a few days ago (as of the writing of this Preface), is included in Chapter 19. As the practice guidelines for the act unfold and translate in to everyday life, the shape and texture of special education practice will change and future editions of the *Almanac* will follow. Other examples of up-to-date information found in the *Almanac* are the sections on the different medications used by many special education children, the latest reviews of hundreds of tests, cutting-edge training materials for crisis intervention, and many resources for special education team members found on the Internet and in publications. It is unlikely that an annual revision of the *Almanac* will be necessary. However, we are looking forward to future updates as the field and market demand.

We would like to thank the usual suspects for their abiding support of our madcap schemes: Tracey Belmont, our editor at Wiley on so many projects, patiently supported the project from concept to fruition. Our contributing editors, Kimberley Applequist, Randall DePry, Ron Dumont, Sharon Hurst, James Kaufman, Larry Maheady, Anita Manning, Sam Ortiz, Denise Ortiz, Rachel Toplis, and John Willis, were cheerful, imaginative, and timely! We really appreciate their enthusiasm and excellent expertise.

We would also like to thank the usual suspects from our families. Elaine would like to thank David, Emma, and Leif for putting up with the usual manuscript deadline high jinks with humor and flexibility. Cecil never tires of expressing his gratitude and love to Julia, who makes it possible for him to work on so many projects that he enjoys and who makes him whole.

ELAINE FLETCHER-JANZEN
Colorado Springs, Colorado

CECIL R. REYNOLDS
Bastrop, Texas

January 2005

Contributing Editors

Kimberly Applequist
University of Colorado at
Colorado Springs
Colorado Springs, Colorado

Randall L. De Pry
University of Colorado at
Colorado Springs
Colorado Springs, Colorado

Ron Dumont
Fairleigh Dickinson University
Teaneck, New Jersey

James C. Kaufman
California State University at
San Bernadino
San Bernadino, California

Larry Maheady
SUNY Fredonia
Fredonia, New York

Anita P. Manning
School District 11
Colorado Springs, Colorado

Denise O. Ortiz
(Illustrations Editor)
South Huntington School District,
Long Island
East Yapank, New York

Samuel O. Ortiz
St. John's University
Jamaica, New York

Rachel Toplis
School District 49
Colorado Springs, Colorado

John O. Willis
Rivier College
Nashua, New Hampshire

Authors

Candace J. Andrews
California State University at San Bernadino
San Bernadino, California

Kimberly Applequist
University of Colorado at Colorado Springs
Colorado Springs, Colorado

Steve Axford
Falcon School District 49
Colorado Springs, Colorado

John Baer
Rider University
Lawrenceville, New Jersey

Randall L. De Pry
University of Colorado at Colorado Springs
Colorado Springs, Colorado

Gayle T. Dow
Indiana University
Bloomington, Indiana

Ron Dumont
Fairleigh Dickinson University
Teaneck, New Jersey

Elaine Fletcher-Janzen
University of Colorado, Colorado Springs
Colorado Springs, Colorado

Kathleen Gradel
SUNY Fredonia
Fredonia, New York

Sharon Hurst
Falcon School District 49
Colorado Springs, Colorado

Michael Jabot
SUNY Fredonia
Fredonia, New York

Allison Kaufman
Redlands, California

James C. Kaufman
California State University at San Bernadino
San Bernadino, California

Kathleen Magiera
SUNY Fredonia
Fredonia, New York

Larry Maheady
SUNY Fredonia
Fredonia, New York

Anita P. Manning
Colorado Springs School District 11
Monument, Colorado

Erica R. Mitchell
California State University at
San Bernadino
San Bernadino, California

Samuel O. Ortiz
St. John's University
Jamaica, New York

Jonathan A. Plucker
Indiana University
Bloomington, Indiana

Cecil R. Reynolds
Texas A&M University
College Station, Texas

Rachel Toplis
Falcon School District 49
Colorado Springs, Colorado

Julie Williams
University of Colorado at
Colorado Springs
Colorado Springs, Colorado

John O. Willis
Rivier College
Nashua, New Hampshire

1

Special Education Teaching Strategies

KATHLEEN GRADEL, MICHAEL JABOT, KATHLEEN MAGIERA,
AND LARRY MAHEADY

HISTORICAL PERSPECTIVE ON THE EVOLUTION OF SPECIAL EDUCATION TEACHING STRATEGIES

There have always been individuals who have special needs or who are currently known as having disabilities or being exceptional. However, there have not always been special education services to address their needs. Contemporary special education is a profession with roots in several academic disciplines—most notably medicine, psychology, sociology, and education. Historical accounts suggest that formal special education teaching strategies first appeared in the late eighteenth century, primarily involving children who were blind or deaf. By the early nineteenth century, attempts were made to educate children with significant cognitive and behavioral challenges—individuals who were labeled insane or idiotic at the time. Across subsequent centuries, special educators developed, evaluated, refined, and disseminated a wide variety of teaching practices. These instructional strategies extended beyond common academic subjects (e.g., reading, writing, and mathematics) and included perceptual and motor training, self-help skills, leisure and vocational preparation, and behavioral and social skill development.

Contemporary special education teachers, however, are now expected to do more than at any time in our brief history. They must ensure access to general education curriculum, expectations, materials, and outcomes, while also teaching functional skills needed for daily living and successful life transitions. They must collaboratively plan, implement, and evaluate teaching strategies with general education teachers in inclusive settings, manage mountains of paperwork, and help students prepare for high-stakes state and local exams. They must also coordinate with specialists in various therapies, ensuring that the skills focused on by these professionals are built into classroom and community practice. And they are expected to know about and use both educational and assistive technologies and services that will further empower their students in school and life.

What matters most, however, is that special educators provide their pupils with the highest-quality instructional services, day in and day out. As Heward (2006) suggests, special education is—first and foremost—purposeful and powerful intervention. Successful interventions prevent, eliminate, and/or overcome the obstacles that keep individuals with disabilities from learning and participating actively and fully in school and society.

THREE EXEMPLARS OF BEST-PRACTICE SPECIAL EDUCATION TEACHING STRATEGIES

Here, we highlight three exemplars of the high-quality teaching strategies that characterize effective special education service delivery: (1) best practices in literacy and content area instruction; (2) individual, classroom, and schoolwide behavior management, inclusive of self-management; and (3) vocational and life-oriented skill development. We offer these as examples of what special education has contributed to the larger literature and pool of best teaching practices.

Before proceeding, however, we must clarify a basic assumption. Contemporary special education teaching strategies are applied across a continuum of educational settings ranging from full-time inclusive general education classrooms to residential treatment facilities and community placements.

As seen in Figure 1.1, general education classrooms have emerged as the most common instructional arrangement for most students with special needs. Consequently, the distinctions among special and general educational goals, practices, and outcomes that persisted for years have become blurred. If we serve most children with special needs in inclusive educational settings, then we must be equally responsive to the needs of the normally developing peers who share their classrooms and communities. Whatever we promote as best practice or special education teaching strategies, therefore, must be effective for all students. It is our premise that—if special education is truly purposeful and powerful intervention—these strategies should be delivered on an equitable basis and must be assessed continually to monitor their ongoing effects on all pupils. Put simply, special education should be best-practice intervention for all. A more formal definition of best teaching practice is offered in Box 1.1.

Exemplar 1: Best Practice in Literacy and Content Area Instruction

The Individuals with Disabilities Education Act of 1997 (IDEA) mandates that school districts provide access to the general curriculum for students with special needs and align pupils' individualized education programs (IEPs)—exceptional students' educational blueprints—to state curriculum standards. This is often not an easy task, as both special and general education requirements have increased. Responding to external and internal criticisms regarding what is taught in our public schools, educational reformers have developed curricula that are purported to be more standards based, culturally and globally sensitive, and technologically

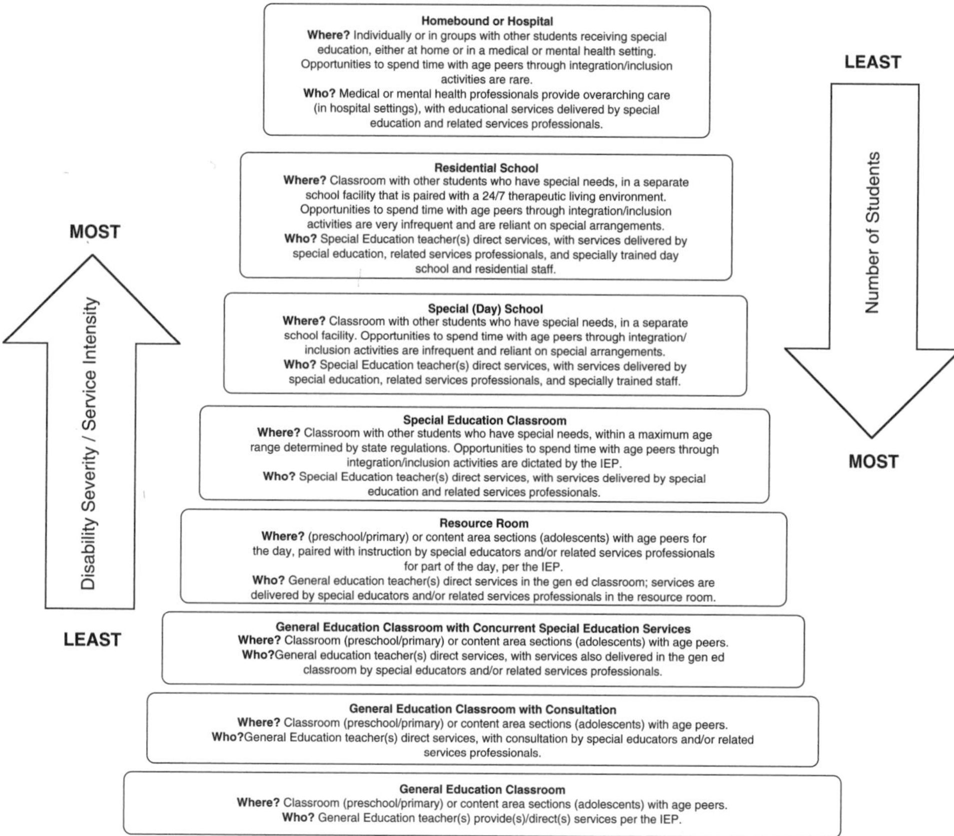

Figure 1.1 Continuum of Educational Services for Students with Disabilities (adapted from Heward, 2003).

infused. In the following sections, we highlight the qualities of best practices across three curricular areas: English language learning, mathematics, and science. We then discuss cross-content best practices.

Best Practice in English Language Learning

The ability to acquire competence in the English language is critical for success in American schools. Pupils who have clear understanding and competence in spoken and written English are likely to be successful in most other curricular areas. Yet reading, writing, and conversing in English are highly complex tasks at which a distressingly high proportion of our students continue to fail. Fortunately, broad

Box 1.1 Operational Definition of Best Teaching Practice

Best teaching practices refer to a curriculum, instructional intervention, systems change, or educational approach designed for use by families, educators, or students with the inherent expectation that its implementation will result in measurable educational, social, behavioral, and/or physical benefit. Practices may be considered evidence based or best practices when they are supported by a sufficient number of well-controlled, experimental, or quasi-experimental research studies (Odom et al., 2005).

Box 1.2 Operational Definition of Low-Risk Learning Environments

Low-risk learning environments refer to settings in which children take educational risks by making predictions and inferences about what they are learning and check their hypotheses against actual conclusions. Their teachers ask questions that elicit a wide range of possible answers, and students receive encouragement and recognition for engaging in such risky instructional activities (Vaughn, Bos, & Schumm, 2003).

levels of consensus have emerged recently regarding what constitutes effective literacy instruction (see, e.g., International Reading Association, 2003; National Council of the Teachers of English, 1996; National Reading Council, 1998). These professional organizations provide the following significant recommendations:

- Reading is a process that involves getting meaning from print.
- Students should use reading and writing actively as tools for learning.
- Teachers should provide daily opportunities for students to share and discuss what they read and write.
- Literacy assessment should match classroom practice.
- Instruction should include student choice and be provided in low-risk environments.

In Box 1.2, we provide a general description of a low-risk instructional environment.

Best Practice in Mathematics

Like literacy instruction, mathematics education has undergone substantial changes in recent years. Once more, an increased emphasis has been placed on pupils' deeper understanding of mathematical ideas and the use of an experiential and problem-solving approach to teaching and learning. Among the more significant recommendations offered by the National Council for the Teachers of Mathematics (NCTM; 1989, 1991, 1995) are the following:

- The ultimate goal of math instruction is to develop students' mathematical power.
- Students must investigate, problem solve, and communicate about mathematics.
- Understanding of math ideas is much more important than mathematical skills.
- Reasoning is fundamental to knowing and doing math.
- Mathematics is an integrated whole, not a set of discrete skills.

Best Practice in Science

It would be highly unlikely that science education would remain dormant at a time when rapid knowledge growth was occurring across the curriculum. Indeed, substantial curricular adaptations have been recommended by professional science education organizations (e.g., American Association for the Advancement of Science

[AAAS], 1989; 1993; National Research Council, 1996) responsible for determining what is taught in our science classrooms. As with literacy and math education, science educators have proposed an inquiry-based approach to science education that focuses on learning important concepts and principles within and across respective disciplines (e.g., biology, chemistry, geo-sciences, and physics). Among the more noteworthy recommendations are the following:

- Science study should involve doing science that is questioning and discovering—not just covering material.
- Hands-on inquiry involves a series of steps that builds pupils' investigative skills.
- Students should explore fewer topics but understand them in greater depth.
- Pupils outgrow misconceptions only by actively engaging in investigation.
- Good science teaching involves facilitation, collaborative group work, and limited use of information giving.

Cross-Discipline Best Instructional Practice

In addition to recommendations provided by discipline-specific professional organizations, educational researchers have provided valuable insights into best teaching practice across the curriculum. Here, we highlight the work of Doug Carnine, Ed Kame'enui, and their colleagues at the University of Oregon, as well as recent meta-analyses conducted by Robert Marzano and his colleagues. These researchers have examined the curricular and instructional conditions that promote the most effective and efficient learning of complex academic content for all pupils enrolled in inclusive educational settings. Several specific teaching strategies with strong empirical bases have generated from these efforts—all of which can be used across a range of academic content areas. Moreover, these strategies appear to work not only for those with diverse needs (i.e., those receiving special education services), but for all students.

First, Carnine, Kame'enui, and their colleagues have been clear that content area instruction should focus on big ideas. Big ideas are fundamental principles and concepts that are reflected across the curriculum and that provide the basis for more generalized learning. A focus on big ideas allows teachers to teach less content but at much greater depth, thereby resulting in more substantive learning by all students (Kame'enui, Carnine, Dixon, Simmons, & Coyne, 2002). Marzano, Pickering, and Pollock (2001) extended this emphasis by noting that clear and concise learning goals provide direction for learning yet permit flexibility to personalize accommodations for individual students. Well-planned objectives set criteria for performance that are clearly communicable to students, families, and others, and are designed so that the goals can be built into instructional feedback systems for students. Defining characteristics of big ideas are offered in Box 1.3.

Second, teachers should use nonlinguistic representations to help pupils learn content. Information is typically conveyed linguistically in most classrooms. That is, teachers talk about ideas and students listen and take notes, or pupils read and discuss what they have read with the teacher and/or peers. Research suggests, however, that, "the more we use nonlinguistic representations while learning, the better we can think about and recall our knowledge" (Marzano, Norford, Paynter, Pickering, & Gaddy, 2001, p. 143). Nonlinguistic strategies might include (1) graphic

Box 1.3 Defining Characteristics and Exemplars of Big Ideas

- Important concepts and principles reflected within and across the curriculum; for example, viewing history as a recursive process of individuals' addressing basic human rights problems, generating possible solutions, and then addressing the effects of each solution (problem—solution—effect); calculating volume of geometric shapes as a multiple of base times height; learning seven factors of the economy
- Teaching less content but at greater depth
- Using clear, concise, and measurable learning goals and objectives to guide your teaching

organizers, (2) pictographs or diagrams, (3) mental mapping, (4) physical models, (5) outlining, or (6) kinesthetic representations that allow students to manipulate their knowledge in meaningful ways. These varied visual and sometimes tactile displays illustrate key concepts and their relationships. Researchers refer to this as the use of conspicuous strategies. Conspicuous strategies promote pupils' understandings of the important connections that exist between concepts and big ideas. Research by Marzano, Pickering, et al. (2001) extends this idea by amplifying the importance of students' generating their own content visualizations, rather than responding by rote to templates constructed by their teachers.

In addition to seeing the important relationships among important big ideas within the curriculum, students must also link their newly acquired knowledge to existing understandings (i.e., prior knowledge). To assist in this process, teachers can prime students' prior knowledge by asking key questions that require them to draw comparisons between what they already know and the new concepts that they are learning. Instruction should be designed so that teaching materials provide access to the prior knowledge that we are encouraging them to use. Further, it is important that teachers—both special and general educators—systematically teach students to identify similarities and differences in concepts through various activities, including comparing, classifying, and using more complex analyses.

University of Oregon researchers also recommend the use of mediated scaffolding. These strategies provide students with instructional supports (e.g., visual cues and written prompts) that increase the likelihood that they will successfully learn new academic content. It is equally important that teachers gradually reduce support mechanisms (i.e., by fading) as students become more proficient with academic content and skills (Kame'enui et al., 2002).

A fifth recommended instructional strategy is strategic integration of academic content both within and across the curriculum. When learning new tasks or information, students must know and practice the steps that are needed to complete the tasks. Moreover, to become proficient in completing newly acquired skills, students need sufficient practice. Strategic review provides pupils with opportunities to practice the steps needed to successfully complete assigned tasks. Strategies are modeled initially by teachers who overtly display step-by-step procedures and then provide ample opportunities for pupils to apply these strategies in meaningful learning activities. Skill practice across relevant activities enables students to apply strategies whenever they encounter similar tasks. The importance of strategic integration for students with special needs is highlighted in a quotation in Box 1.4.

Judicious review, a sixth instructional strategy, gives students multiple additional opportunities to practice what they have learned and to receive constructive feedback on their performance. This strategy ensures that knowledge and skills are retained over time and can be applied in different situations. For students with spe-

Box 1.4 A Quotation Emphasizing the Importance of Strategic Integration for Students with Special Needs

For students with special needs, strategic integration is critical so that strategy and/or content learning is generalized, rather than mastered in isolated contexts, settings, or skill areas.

cial needs, systematic review of previously mastered skills and content has been referred to as *maintenance;* without ongoing opportunities to use prior skills and content, such abilities can be quickly lost, requiring reteaching and relearning.

In addition to forming these six research-based instructional strategies, special educators have played a significant role in the development of differentiated instruction, a concept that has taken hold nationwide as part of ongoing school reform movements (see, e.g., Tomlinson, 1999). *Differentiated instruction* refers to the modification of instruction and curricular content, processes, and products in response to individual student needs and abilities. In differentiated classrooms, teachers fashion instruction around essential concepts and principles, as well as around the diverse needs and skills of individual pupils.

Exemplar 2: Individual, Classroom, and Schoolwide Behavior Management

Remember when you started teaching and they told you "never smile until Christmas"? Remember when you thought that sending disruptive students to the principal's office (i.e., out of the classroom) was an effective way for reducing their misbehavior within your classroom? Did it really seem to work when we gave students who skipped school three additional days out of school on suspension? Does it really make sense to withhold positive attention from youngsters who rarely receive any positive attention outside of school? Is simply telling noncompliant and disruptive students that they should behave better the most effective way we have for getting them to do so? Shouldn't pupils be expected to know how to manage their own behavior and just do it?

Such questions, advice, policies, and practices have been evident in education for far too long. Not only have these perspectives and practices been ineffective, but in many cases they have been downright harmful. Fortunately, some of special education's strongest instructional practices have emerged from attempts to improve the individual, classroom, and schoolwide behavior of students who are least likely to comply naturally with school expectations. Six big ideas reflect special education's contributions to the improvement of pupil behavior: (1) recognize that behavior is learned, (2) identify socially important goals, (3) emphasize positive behavioral supports, (4) be proactive and with-it, (5) use self-management strategies, and (6) emphasize schoolwide implementation. These ideas are summarized in Box 1.5.

Recognize That Behavior Is Learned

Special educators recognized early on that most, if not all, human behavior was learned, typically through the complex interactions that occurred among individuals and their immediate learning environments. If most behaviors—both inappropriate and appropriate—are learned, then it followed logically that they can be unlearned or changed through systematic environmental analysis and adapta-

Box 1.5 Six Big Ideas for Influencing Student Behavior

- Recognize that behavior is learned.
- Identify socially important goals.
- Emphasize positive behavioral supports.
- Be proactive and with-it.
- Use self-management strategies.
- Emphasize schoolwide implementation.

tion. This concept was particularly important for special educators because many of their pupils had noticeable behavioral differences that set them apart from their peers and often resulted in negative educational outcomes (e.g., segregation in noninclusive classrooms, suspension, expulsion, and school dropout). The ability to change pupil behavior in a more socially appropriate manner empowered special educators to provide relief and support for children with behavioral difficulties, as well as for their teachers and caregivers. The special education and applied psychology literatures provide numerous examples of the wide range of behavior problems that have been improved through systematic behavioral interventions (e.g., self-injurious behavior, temper tantrums, social isolation, and aggression).

Identify Socially Important Goals

Special educators have also contributed significantly to the selection of functional or socially important behavioral goals: skills that will most likely help students succeed in school and society. Historically, the term *discipline* has become synonymous with punishment in our schools (see Box 1.6 for more details).

Consequently, the goals of many traditional classroom and behavior management approaches were to suppress misbehavior and produce quiet and docile yet attentive students. Indeed, the picture of a classroom of children sitting straight up in their desks with their feet firmly on the floor and staring attentively at the teacher was the hallmark of good classroom management for many educators. While there is nothing inherently wrong with quiet, seated pupils who pay attention, research has found this to be an insufficient educational outcome. Instead, students must be actively involved in their own learning, and they must acquire more socially responsible behaviors if they are to succeed in school and life. They must, for example, learn to treat themselves and others with respect, cooperate with peers and adults, and try to do their best academically. Good behavior management simply replaces inappropriate behavior with more responsible social actions.

Box 1.6 Objective and Inferred Definitions of Discipline

According to *Webster's Dictionary,* discipline is (1) training that develops self-control, (2) orderly conduct, (3) a system of rules, as for a monastic order, or (4) strict control to enforce obedience. The word *discipline* is actually a derivative of the word *disciple,* or follower of a positive image or way. However, very different meanings have been attached to the term *discipline* within America's public schools. Most often, discipline has been equated with punishment, and many educators have assumed that in order to develop good discipline one must rely on negative consequences such as reprimands, loss of privileges, or exclusion.

Box 1.7 Examples of Teacher Comments When Catching Pupils Being Good

- "I see LaChandra has her desk cleaned off and is ready to line up for gym."
- "Thank you, Janeil, for raising your hand and waiting for me to call on you before responding."
- "I see everyone is keeping their hands and feet to themselves. Very well done."
- "Yes, Jamaal, thanks for putting your completed assignment in the in box before the bell rang."
- "Armando and Daritza, you are doing a great job of taking turns and sharing your materials."

Emphasize Positive Behavioral Supports

A third best practice emphasizes the use of positive over negative or reductive consequences to teach pupils new academic and interpersonal skills more effectively and efficiently. Rather than waiting until Christmas to smile—or withholding positive attention from students who rarely receive it at home—effective educators catch pupils being good early and often throughout the school year. Moreover, they use a ratio of three or four positive comments to each reductive consequence (e.g., reprimand). When one notices pupils being good it is very important to recognize their behavior or what they are doing rather than making more global positive statements. Box 1.7 provides a few examples of appropriate praise statements.

A ratio of three or four positive comments to each reprimand not only creates a more positive learning environment but also provides frequent opportunities for students to be recognized for the many good things that they do during the school day. In school, the key lies in finding positive consequences that are natural and meaningful for students, that require little time to use, and that are relatively inexpensive.

The extensive research of Marzano, Pickering, et al. (2001) also indicates that feedback, particularly explicit information about what students are doing well compared to a performance standard, is an essential ingredient of effective instruction. Notably, they advise teachers to provide recognition for effort and accomplishments while teaching students to discriminate between their effort and personal results. This tweaking of the traditional catch-'em-being-good advice can foster self-responsibility and self-management in schools. John Hattie (1992) reported, after reviewing 8,000 studies, that "The most powerful single modification that enhances achievement is feedback. The simplest prescription for improving education must be dollops of feedback" (p. 9).

Be Proactive and With-It

Special educators also emphasize a proactive rather than reactive approach to behavior management. Instead of waiting for pupils to misbehave and then reacting by applying a reductive consequence (e.g., verbal reprimand), smart educators prevent behavior problems by structuring their classrooms for academic and behavioral success. They do so by following the tips in Box 1.8.

Highly effective special educators anticipate and prepare themselves for possible aberrant behaviors (e.g., noncompliance, disruption, bullying, and aggression) and develop preplanned strategies for responding to such occurrences. Preplanned strategies include any activities that make it less likely that pupils will misbehave

Box 1.8 Tips for Structuring Your Classroom for Success

- Use functional rules, procedures, and routines that clearly articulate classroom and school expectations and responsibilities.
- Place pupils appropriately into academic materials and engage them actively in meaningful learning tasks.
- Model prosocial behavior through your daily interactions with students and other staff.
- Offer numerous opportunities for pupils to engage in socially appropriate actions.
- Recognize students regularly and genuinely for their accomplishments and efforts.
- Use functional behavioral assessments and unique information about the student, the classroom, the school, and the family to individualize behavior support plans for your most challenging learners.

in the first place. Effective teachers also use an instructive approach when student misbehavior does occur. That is, rather than punishing students' behavioral mistakes, they treat such behaviors as legitimate opportunities to reteach pupils how to behave more appropriately in the future (Rhode, Jenson, & Reavis, 1996; Sprick, Howard, Wise, Marcum, & Haykin, 1998).

This "with-it" mindset and action orientation allows one to intervene in challenging behaviors without stigmatizing students as unteachable (Marzano, Marzano, & Pickering, 2003). Smart educators use a critical blend of technically and contextually appropriate instructional procedures to meet the needs of children as well as the desires and values of their families and teachers.

Use Self-Management Strategies

Special educators also use self-monitoring and self-management strategies to help pupils take responsibility for their own performance. Independent learning requires students to check their own behavior, to decide if it is effective, and, if necessary, to make changes to meet an expected standard. Self-management can be as simple as students' reducing the number of times they talk out in class or can extend to more complex reflections requiring them to adjust their own behaviors to an explicit set of school rules and standards. One critical component involves self-monitoring—teaching students to identify and measure their own performance. Some basic tips for using self-monitoring strategies effectively can be found in Box 1.9.

Researchers have found that simply teaching students to keep track of their own behavior often has a therapeutic effect. Individuals who eat or smoke too much usually do so less frequently when taught to count how often they do such things. Similarly, teaching students to make marks each time they interact appropriately with peers tends to increase the likelihood that they will do so in the future. If just counting does not produce desired behavior change, then students must learn to do something about it without being prompted by a teacher. Self-management is feasible for students with diverse learning needs and is applicable to both academic and behavioral expectations (Cole & Bambara, 2000; Korotitsch & Nelson-Gray, 1999; Shapiro, Durnan, Post, & Skibitsky-Levinson, 2002).

Self-monitoring and self-evaluation strategies were used initially with students' noncompliant behaviors (e.g., Rhode, Morgan, & Young, 1983). Students were taught to recognize when they were doing something inappropriate (e.g., leaving their seats, being off task) and then to record and track these incidents. By self-recording, students became more aware of their behavior, and they either self-

Box 1.9 Some Tips for the Appropriate Use of Self-Monitoring Strategies

- The primary purpose of self-monitoring strategies is to make pupils more aware of their behavior so that they can learn to control it themselves.
- Explicitly define the behavior to be self-monitored, provide examples and nonexamples, and role-play each occurrence.
- Provide a simple sheet for students to record each occurrence of the target behavior (some excellent examples are available from the Tough Kid Toolbox; Jenson, Rhode, & Reavis, 1996).
- Set a specific time limit for monitoring. A period of 15, 30, or 60 minutes per day is more than sufficient. Monitoring one's behavior indefinitely is too overwhelming for most individuals. Select the time when the problem is most prevalent and gradually increase monitoring times.
- Check your students' accuracy on a random basis and reinforce them for correctly matching your independent recordings.
- Give students frequent opportunities to self-monitor, use positive feedback for doing so, and gradually begin to fade.

modified or participated in a contingency that was teacher mediated. Teacher consequences were then faded over time as students learned to self-regulate or self-manage.

More recently, Mitchem and Young (2001) described how self-monitoring can be combined with peer-assisted learning strategies to create the Classwide Peer-Assisted Self-Management (CWPASM) program. This program, which teaches all students within a classroom to monitor their own behaviors simultaneously, would appear to be very functional for inclusive educational settings. The need to maintain orderly classroom behavior and teach children how to manage their own behavior is a critical outcome for general and special educators alike.

Schoolwide Implementation

Finally, special educators have learned most recently that they are more likely to achieve generalized behavior changes when they work on a school- or system-wide basis. Schoolwide approaches involve faculty and staff working collaboratively to identify a common set of behavioral expectations for all children, adopting a consistent set of beliefs for managing student behavior (e.g., a proactive approach), and then implementing similar practices in response to pupils' appropriate and inappropriate behavior. Research on schoolwide behavior plans and positive behavioral support systems provide two shining examples of the type of behavioral change that is possible when educational professionals are on the same page and work collaboratively to meet common educational goals (e.g., Sprick et al., 1998; Sugai & Horner, 2005). Such systems promote social responsibility among all pupils and minimize disruptive and significant behavior problems among our most challenging students. Schoolwide behavior plans are used increasingly within highly effective school districts. Positive behavioral supports are put into place for individual students (e.g., those receiving or at risk for special education services) and for schoolwide challenges such as bullying, acts of disruption, and violence. Today, the special education–born emphasis on self-management has grown significantly into schoolwide directions for fostering self-regulation, a natural blend of the special and general education worlds.

Exemplar 3: Vocational and Life-Oriented Skill Development

Our third and final exemplar of special education teaching practice is vocational and life skills instruction. In the 1970s, special educators began to look critically at their outcomes and realized that many students with special needs were leaving high school without a repertoire of functional life skills. That is, they (1) were not prepared adequately to acquire entry-level jobs, (2) required maximum assistance to get around the community, and (3) had not learned even the most essential young adult social skills (e.g., appropriate greeting and conversational skills). This realization co-occurred with the mainstreaming and community inclusion movements in which individuals with disabilities were being expected to participate more fully in school and community life. While these integration movements were well intended and had a strong philosophy of equality, they failed to provide a sound foundation for translating what we knew about good teaching into routine instructional practice. Thus, special educators began to prepare students for fuller participation outside the classroom, in areas including community mobility, prosocial skill development, job preparation, household management, and sexuality. Special educators expanded their instructional toolbox, therefore, by developing four critical knowledge bases and skill sets. Inherent in these instructional domains are teaching strategies that do the following:

- Identify knowledge and skills with lifelong functionality
- Instruct individuals in natural settings
- Use real-world jobs, training, and support
- Treat transition seriously

Identify Knowledge and Skills with Lifelong Functionality

The notion of looking at what life demands of students and then directly teaching them to do such things has set special educators apart from many of their educational peers. Making decisions about whether people with disabilities should feed, toilet, and/or dress themselves was certainly not difficult; nor were decisions about teaching appropriate language skills. Yet decisions became more complex when individuals were approaching graduation without being fully independent in even these most basic skills. Although special education had prided itself in teaching life skills, many youth were graduating without the ability to ride commercial buses, cross streets, buy groceries, prepare meals independently, or interact with the general public in socially appropriate ways (Heward, 2006). To adjust existing curricula, special educators examined real-world expectations and developed environmental inventories (see, e.g., Snell, 1987). These inventories involved careful analyses of what normally developing adults did when they engaged in community-related activities. The result was new lists of teachable goals and a functional curriculum for older exceptional students.

Special educators also had to prioritize what needed to be learned because for many students receiving special education services there simply was not enough time to teach them everything they needed to prosper outside of school. Therefore, the primary functionality question became "What is most critical for this student to learn now?" This question, in turn, required special educators to make other challenging decisions about whether to (1) bypass planned instruction and complete the task in another way, (2) use substitutes to complete activities (e.g., peers, paraprofessionals, or technology), (3) teach specific skills, or (4) teach generalized skill sets (see Snell, 1987).

Instruct in Natural Settings

It soon became obvious that if special educators were going to deliver a functional, community-oriented curriculum then they would have to do so in more natural settings. In the old days, special education classrooms were equipped with beds and stoves and students would practice basic housekeeping skills right there in school. Similarly, special education students learned about safely crossing streets, sexuality, and engaging in appropriate leisure activities through the use of photos, videos, and/or models within the classroom. Full community participation, however, required students to apply their newly acquired skills in real-life settings, and to do so they had to be taught in community-based settings.

The complexities associated with community-based instruction greatly surpassed those involved with occasional field trips to parks, museums, and local restaurants. Indeed, special educators were required to conduct in-depth analyses of community placements, identify and teach critical prerequisite skills for success in each setting, and then determine the least number of settings or conditions required to maximize skill generalization. For example, if students were taught only to make and answer telephone calls on push-button desk phones, then they would be unlikely to independently use cell phones. Similarly, if they were taught to cross streets controlled solely by traffic signals, then they would likely have difficulty crossing intersections without signals. Community-based instruction, therefore, took into account both the "teaching sets" of exemplars (i.e., what is taught) and the explicit instruction required to teach these skills in naturalistic settings (i.e., how to teach). Using systematic instructional practices such as task analysis, error correction, shaping, prompting, and chaining, community-based instruction provided the necessary ingredients that many special needs youth needed for success outside of the classroom.

As special educators became more adept at teaching functional skills, modifications were made in their community-based instructional practices. For example, think about teaching appropriate language skills. Functional communication skills require individuals to use language in the context of relating to other people, irrespective of whether they are in school or the community. Special educators and related service professionals (e.g., speech/language, physical, and occupational therapists) recognized, therefore, that they must change their language instruction from more artificial conditions—repeating words and phrases in massed trials outside the context of real social interactions—to more naturally occurring contexts like saying what one wants to eat during meals and snacks and engaging in verbal turn taking during real-life conversations and games.

Use Real-World Job Training and Support

Special educators were also prompted to adapt their teaching practices when they saw what happened to their high school graduates during the 1970s. Even under the best conditions, most special education graduates were spending their days in sheltered workshops or day treatment centers, segregated sites where they did either subcontracts from real work (e.g., parts assembly) or made-up "busy" work (e.g., sorting buttons). This often translated into meaningless work for little or no pay, certainly not the goal of a meaningful life for young adults with special needs. To rectify the situation, special educators sought out more meaningful vocational alternatives.

Initially, they identified potential work opportunities earlier in students' careers and created appropriate instructional contexts for teaching such work-related skills within the school continuum. Students with special needs were given real work opportunities in their early teens and then received more demanding and natural work-related experiences as they approached graduation. In our best special education programs, students with special needs actually worked at real-life jobs that they eventually transitioned into upon graduation.

Second, special educators used similarly smart functional decision-making skills when they designed employment programs. That is, they carefully examined what skills—social, mobility, academic, and/or motoric—were required by specific jobs, conducted in-depth environmental analyses to identify the conditions under which such skills had to be performed, and then provided direct instruction in authentic employment settings. Students with special needs were learning to do real jobs in real contexts. On-the-job training became the primary instructional vehicle. Special educators used explicit instruction to teach critical job skills, important social skills required for interacting with coworkers and supervisors, and relevant community survival skills (e.g., getting to and from work, handling pay, and eating meals on the job). Box 1.10 provides some excellent resources for facilitating employment opportunities for individuals with special needs.

Box 1.10 Additional Resources for Facilitating Employment Opportunities

Professional Journals

Career Development for Exceptional Individuals
Journal of Vocational Rehabilitation
Mouth: The Voice of Disability Rights

Books

Bellamy, G. T., Rhodes, L. E., Mank, D. M., & Albin, J. M. (1988). *Supported employment: A community implementation guide.* Baltimore: Brookes.

Benz, M. R., & Lindstrom, L. E. (1997). *Building school-to-work programs: Strategies for youth with special needs.* Austin, TX: PRO-ED.

Rusch, F. R. (1990). *Supported employment: Models, methods, and issues.* Pacific Grove, CA: Brooks/Cole.

Wehman, P., & Kregel, J. (Eds.). (1998). *More than a job: Securing satisfying careers for people with disabilities.* Baltimore: Brookes.

Web sites

Ability Network Magazine. http://www.ability.ns.ca/anet
Association of Disability Advocates. http://www.icanect.net/fpa/
The Disability Rights Activist. http://www.disrights.org
The National Home of Your Own Alliance. http://www.alliance.unh.edu

Treat Transition Seriously

Transition refers to a coordinated set of activities that promote movement from school to postschool settings. This typically includes facilitating student adjustment in three primary domains: (1) the quality of residential environment, (2) the adequacy of social and interpersonal networks, and (3) meaningful employment (Halpern, 1985; Heward, 2006). Transition planning usually begins in youths' early teens and is outlined within their respective individualized transition plans (Heward, 2006). Transition plans must be highly individualized and incorporate (1) what and where individuals will work, live, and recreate; (2) what intervention steps will be taken to promote successful postgraduation performance; and (3) how supports will be coordinated so that individuals succeed as young adults.

FUTURE DIRECTIONS FOR SPECIAL EDUCATION TEACHING STRATEGIES

Obviously, special educators have developed and refined a variety of high-quality instructional strategies over the years. They have done so partly because their students have become more challenging and partly because the requirements for living a well-rounded and independent life in a complex society have increased noticeably. As special educators persevere in their efforts to assist individuals in this regard, we see at least three constructive directions for improved teaching practice:

- Bridging the gap between research and practice
- Increasing the availability and intensity of early intervention and prevention programs
- Enhancing the general and special education partnership

While in-depth analyses of such issues are beyond the scope of this chapter, we can comment briefly on their relevance. First, although special education research has produced a significant and reliable knowledge base about effective teaching strategies (e.g., Cook & Schirmer, 2003; Lovitt, 2000; Vaughn, Gersten, & Chard, 2000), ample evidence suggests that few of these best teaching practices ever find their way into routine classroom use (e.g., Carnine, 1997; Greenwood & Maheady, 2001; Wilson, Floden, & Ferrini-Mundy, 2002). Even the most powerful teaching practices available will be of little value to individuals with special needs if their teachers do not use them. Minimally, a concerted and systematic effort must be undertaken to identify the conditions under which evidence-based teaching practices will be used and sustained in our public schools. Similarly, although we have learned that it is better to intervene earlier rather than later with individuals with special needs, we have not always done so. To the maximum extent possible, therefore, we must focus our teaching and intervention efforts on the prevention of academic and behavioral failure rather than its remediation. Early childhood special education intervention and schoolwide behavioral prevention programs come to mind in this regard. Finally, it has become increasingly clear that there are simply too many children with too many diverse needs in our classrooms for any one professional, in either special or general education, to meet all of their needs. Thus, general and special educators must learn to work more collaboratively to meet mutual defined educational goals. We believe that we can accomplish such goals by these means:

- Using common, explicit language to discuss teaching practices that make a noticeable difference in pupil performance
- Translating evidence-based research findings into teacher-friendly products (guidebooks, curriculum maps, etc.) and making them readily available to our primary consumers (e.g., teachers, parents, and administrators; see, e.g., www.sopriswest.com)
- Developing and using common formative assessment measures (e.g., curriculum-based assessment) that are sensitive to ongoing rates of pupil progress and representative of important educational outcomes; see, e.g., Fuchs & Fuchs, 1999; Shinn, Shinn, Hamilton, & Clarke, 2002)
- Implementing and sustaining effective professional development strategies that cross disciplines and address important classroom and schoolwide needs

REFERENCES

American Association for the Advancement of Science (AAAS). (1989). *Science for all Americans.* New York: Oxford University Press.

American Association for the Advancement of Science (AAAS). (1993). *Benchmarks for science literacy.* New York: Oxford University Press.

Carnine, D. (1997). Bridging the research to practice gap. *Exceptional Children, 63,* 513–521.

Cole, C. L., & Bambara, L. M. (2000). Self-monitoring: Theory and practice. In E. S. Shapiro & T. R. Kratochwill (Eds.), *Behavioral assessment in schools* (2nd ed., pp. 202–232). New York: Guilford Press.

Cook, B. G., & Schirmer, B. R. (2003). What is special about special education? Overview and analysis. *The Journal of Special Education, 37,* 202–204.

Fuchs, L. S., & Fuchs, D. (1999). Monitoring student progress toward the development of reading competence: A review of three forms of classroom-based assessment. *School Psychology Review, 28,* 659–671.

Greenwood, C. R., & Maheady, L. (2001). Are future teachers aware of the gap between research and practice? *Teacher Education and Special Education, 24,* 333–347.

Halpern, A. A. (1985). Transition: A look at the foundations. *Exceptional Children, 51,* 479–486.

Hattie, J. A. (1992). Measuring the effects of schooling. *Australian Journal of Education, 36*(1), 5–13.

Heward, W. L. (2006). *Exceptional children: An introduction to special education* (8th ed.). Upper Saddle River, NJ: Merrill/Prentice Hall.

International Reading Association. (2003). *Standards for reading professionals: A reference for the preparation of educators in the United States* (revised). Newark, DE: International Reading Association. Available online at http://www.reading.org/advocacy/standards/standards03_revised/

Jenson, W. R., Rhode, G., & Reavis, H. K. (1996). *The tough kid tool box.* Longmont, CO: Sopris West.

Kame'enui, E. J., Carnine, D. W., Dixon, R., Simmons, D. C., & Coyne, M. D. (2002). *Effective teaching strategies that accommodate diverse learners* (2nd ed.). Upper Saddle River, NJ: Prentice Hall.

Korotitsch, W. J., & Nelson-Gray, R. O. (1999). An overview of self-monitoring research in assessment and treatment. *Psychological Assessment, 11,* 415–425.

Lovitt, T. C. (2000). *Preventing school failure: Tactics for teaching adolescents* (2nd ed.). Austin, TX: PRO-ED.

Marzano, R., Marzano, J. S., & Pickering, D. J. (2003). *Classroom management that works: Research-based strategies for every teacher.* Alexandria, VA: Association for Supervision and Curriculum Development.

Marzano, R., Norford, J. S., Paynter, D. E., Pickering, D. J., & Gaddy, B. B. (2001). *A handbook for* Classroom Instruction That Works. Alexandria, VA: Association for Supervision and Curriculum Development.

Marzano, R., Pickering, D. J., & Pollock, J. E. (2001). *Classroom instruction that works: Research-based strategies for increasing student achievement.* Alexandria, VA: Association for Supervision and Curriculum Development.

Mitchem, K. J., & Young, K. R. (2001). Adapting self-management programs for classwide use. *Remedial and Special Education, 22,* 75–88.

National Council of Teachers of English (NCTE). (1996). *Standards for the English language arts.* Urbana, IL: NCTE.

National Council of Teachers of Mathematics (NCTM). (1989). *Curriculum and evaluation standards for school mathematics.* Reston, VA: Commission on Standards for School Mathematics.

National Council of Teachers of Mathematics (NCTM). (1991). *Professional standards for teaching mathematics.* Reston, VA: National Council of Teachers of Mathematics.

National Council of Teachers of Mathematics (NCTM). (1995). *Assessment standards for school mathematics.* Reston, VA: National Council of Teachers of Mathematics.

National Reading Council. (1998). *Preventing reading difficulties in young children.* Washington, DC: National Academy Press.

National Research Council. (1996). *National science education standards.* Washington, DC: National Research Council.

Rhode, G., Jenson, W. R., & Reavis, H. K. (1996). *The tough kid book.* Longmont, CO: Sopris West.

Rhode, G., Morgan, D. P., & Young, K. R. (1983). Generalization and maintenance of treatment gains of behaviorally handicapped students from resource rooms to regular classrooms using self-evaluation procedures. *Journal of Applied Behavior Analysis, 16,* 171–188.

Shapiro, E. S., Durnan, S. L., Post, E. E., & Skibitsky-Levinson, T. (2002). Self-monitoring procedures for children and adolescents. In M. R. Shinn, H. M. Walker, & G. Stoner (Eds.), *Interventions for academic and behavior problems II: Preventive and remedial approaches* (pp. 433–454). Bethesda, MD: NASP Publications.

Shinn, M. R., Shinn, M. M., Hamilton, C., & Clarke, B. (2002). Using curriculum-based measurement in general education classrooms to promote reading success. In M. R. Shinn, H. M. Walker, & G. Stoner (Eds.), *Interventions for academic and behavior problems II: Preventive and remedial approaches* (pp. 113–142). Bethesda, MD: NASP Publications.

Snell, M. E. (1987). *Systematic instruction of persons with severe handicaps.* Columbus, OH: Charles E. Merrill.

Sprick, R., Howard, L., Wise, B. J., Marcum, K., & Haykin, M. (1998). *Administrator's desk reference of behavior management.* Longmont, CO: Sopris West.

Sugai, G., & Horner, R. H. (2005). Schoolwide positive behavior supports: Achieving and sustaining effective learning environments for all students. In W. L. Heward, T. E. Heron, N. A. Neef, et al., *Focus on behavior analysis in education: Achievements, challenges, and opportunities* (pp. 90–102). Upper Saddle River, NJ: Pearson.

Tomlinson, C. A. (1999). *The differentiated classroom: Responding to the needs of all learners.* Alexandria, VA: Association for Supervision and Curriculum Development.

Vaughn, S., Bos, C. S., & Schumm, J. S. (2003). *Teaching exceptional, diverse, and at-risk students in the general education classroom* (3rd ed.). Boston: Allyn & Bacon.

Vaughn, S., Gersten, R., & Chard, D. J. (2000). The underlying message in LD intervention research: Findings from research syntheses. *Exceptional Children, 67,* 99–114.

Wilson, S. M., Floden, R. E., & Ferrini-Mundy, J. (2002). Teacher preparation research: An insider's view from the outside. *Journal of Teacher Education, 53,* 190–204.

2

An Introduction to Educational and Psychological Measurement and Testing

CECIL R. REYNOLDS

All measurements in education and psychology have conceptual and mathematical properties, and those who use tests and other assessments, whether teacher-made or standardized commercial procedures, and those who must use them will use them more effectively with an understanding of the basic concepts on which they are based. This predicate to the listing and description of various educational and psychological tests will introduce these concepts and explain the most fundamental differences among types of educational and psychological tests (e.g., intelligence tests versus achievement tests). The conceptual understanding of these issues rather than technical or mathematical computations is emphasized.

WHAT IS MEASUREMENT AND WHAT ARE TESTS?

Measurement is a set of rules for assigning numbers to represent objects, traits, attributes, or behaviors. A ruler or yardstick is a measuring device for length and is designed based on standard instructions (rules) set by an official government office that designates rules and standards for all weights and measures. An educational or psychological test is a measuring device, and as such it involves rules (e.g., administration and scoring instructions) for assigning numbers to an individual's performance on the test. These numbers are then thought to represent some trait, behavior, or attribute of the individual, such as intellectual level, skill at performing two-digit multiplication, or reading comprehension. When we measure something, the units of measurement have a mathematical property called the *scale of measurement.* A scale is a system or scheme for assigning values or scores to the characteristic being measured. There are four scales of measurement, and the different scales have distinct properties and convey unique types of information. The four scales of measurement are named *nominal, ordinal, interval,* and *ratio.* The scales form a hierarchy, and as we progress from nominal to ratio scales we are able to perform increasingly sophisticated measurements that capture more detailed information. It is important to know the underlying scale of measurement when looking at a test score because the type and amount of information revealed by each is quite different. In particular, ordinal scales and interval scales, which are quite common in education and psychology, are often confused, leading to common misinterpretations of scores on these two scales.

SCALES OF MEASUREMENT

Nominal Scales

Nominal scales are the simplest of the four scales. Nominal scales provide a qualitative system for categorizing people or objects into categories or groups. These categories typically are mutually exclusive. For example, gender is a nominal scale that assigns individuals to mutually exclusive categories. Another example is assigning people to categories based on their college academic major (e.g., education, psychology, chemistry). Numbers can be assigned to nominal scales, but the numbers are simply used to identify or label the categories; the categories are not ordered in a meaningful manner. For example, we might use the number 1 to represent a category of students who list their academic major as education, the number 2 if their academic major is psychology, the number 3 if their academic major is chemistry, and so on. Herein, 3 is not greater than 2, and 2 is not greater than 1. The numbers are simply used to label or identify the categories. We could just as easily call them red, blue, green, and so on. Another individual might assign a different set of numbers. Because of the arbitrary use of numbers in nominal scales, nominal scales do not actually quantify the variables under examination. Numbers assigned to nominal scales should not be added, subtracted, ranked, or otherwise manipulated. As a result, many common statistical procedures cannot be used with these scales and their usefulness is limited.

Ordinal Scales

Ordinal scale measurement allows you to rank people or objects according to the amount or quantity of a characteristic they display or possess. As a result, ordinal scales allow us to quantify the variables under examination and provide substantially more information than nominal scales. For example, ranking the children in a classroom according to height from the tallest to the shortest is an example of ordinal measurement. In this example the tallest person in the class would receive the rank of 1, the next tallest would receive a rank of 2, and so on. While ordinal scale measurement provides quantitative information, it does not ensure that the intervals between the ranks are consistent. That is, the difference in height between the children ranked 1 and 2 might be 3 inches, while the difference between those ranked 3 and 4 might be 1 inch. Ordinal scales indicate the rank-order position among individuals or objects, but they do not indicate the extent by which they differ. All the ordinal scale tells us, then, is who is taller, number 5 or number 7; it tells us nothing about how much taller. Ordinal scales are somewhat limited in both the detail they provide and the statistical procedures that can be applied. Nevertheless, the use of these scales is fairly common in educational settings. Percentile rank, age equivalents, and grade equivalents are all examples of ordinal scales. It remains improper to add, subtract, multiply, or divide ordinal scale scores.

Interval Scales

Interval scales provide more information than either nominal or ordinal scales. Interval scale measurement allows you to rank people or objects like an ordinal scale, but on a scale with equal units. This means the difference between adjacent units on the scale is equivalent. The difference between scores of 75 and 76 is the same as the difference between scores of 80 and 81 (or 82 and 83, 97 and 98, etc.). Many educational and psychological tests are designed to produce interval level scores. If, on a test using interval scales, individual A receives a score of 100, individual B receives a score of 110, and individual C receives a score of 120, we know that person C scored the highest, followed by B, then A. Given that the scores are on an interval scale, we also know that difference between individuals A and B (i.e., 10 points) is equal to the difference between B and C (i.e., 10 points). Interval scale data can be manipulated using common mathematical operations (e.g., addition, subtraction, multiplication, and division), while lesser scales (i.e., nominal and ordinal) cannot.

Interval scales represent a substantial improvement over ordinal scales and provide considerable information. There is a major limitation, however; interval scales do not have a true zero point. On an interval scale a score of zero does not reflect the total absence of the attribute. For example, if an individual was unable to answer any questions correctly on an intelligence test and scored a zero, it would not indicate the complete lack of intelligence, only that he or she was unable to respond correctly to any questions on this test. Most likely, the test chosen was just too difficult to allow us to measure the individual's level of intelligence. Likewise, even though an IQ of 100 appears to be twice as large as an IQ of 50, it does not mean that the person with a score of 100 is twice as intelligent as the person with a score of 50. In educational settings, interval scale scores are most commonly seen in the form of standard scores (scores that have been set to a specific mean and standard deviation, not unlike IQ scaling, which is, by convention, typically set to a mean of 100 and a standard deviation of 15).

Ratio Scales

Ratio scales have the properties of interval scales plus a true zero point that reflects the complete absence of the characteristic being measured. Miles per hour, length, and weight are all examples of ratio scales. As the name suggests, with these scales we can interpret ratios between scores. For example, 50 miles per hour is twice as fast as 25 miles per hour, 20 feet is twice as long as 10 feet, and 60 pounds is three times as much as 20 pounds. Ratios are not meaningful or interpretable with interval scales. A child with a math achievement test score of 100 does not know

Table 2.1 Common nominal, ordinal, interval, and ratio scales

Scale	Example	Sample scores
Nominal	Gender	Female = 1
		Male = 2
	Place of birth	Northeast = 1
		Southeast = 2
		Midwest = 3
		Southwest = 4
		Northwest = 5
		Pacific = 6
Ordinal	Preference desserts	1 = Most preferred (chocolate)
		2 = Intermediate preferred (fruit)
		3 = Least preferred (cheese)
	Graduation class rank	1 = Valedictorian
		2 = Salutatorian
		3 = 3rd rank
		Etc.
	Percentile rank	99th percentile
		98th percentile
		97th percentile
		Etc.
Interval	Intelligence scores	IQ of 100
	Behavior rating scale scores	Aggression score of 75
	SAT	Verbal score of 550
Ratio	Height in inches	60 inches tall
	Weight in pounds	100 pounds
	Percent correct on classroom test	85%

twice as much as one with a score of 50. With the exception of percent correct on classroom achievement tests and the measurement of behavioral responses (e.g., reaction time), there are relatively few ratio scales in educational and psychological measurement. However, even the number of correct responses on a classroom test can be interpreted in ways that are misleading and just incorrect. If one student answers 50% of the questions correctly and another answers 75% correctly, while it is true that the second student answered 50% more questions correctly, one still cannot infer accurately that the second student knows 50% more about the subject of the test than the first student does. Fortunately, we are able to address most of the measurement issues in education adequately using interval scales.

Table 2.1 gives examples of common nominal, ordinal, interval, and ratio scales found in educational and psychological measurement. There is a clear hierarchy among the scales, with nominal scales being the least sophisticated and providing the most information.

THE DESCRIPTION OF TEST SCORES

A student's test score alone provides little information. For example, if you know that a student's score on a test of reading achievement is 79, you know very little about the student's reading skills. Even if you know the scale of measurement represented by the test (e.g., an interval scale), you still know very little about the student's reading abilities. To interpret or describe test scores meaningfully you need to have a frame of reference. For a norm-referenced test, the frame of reference is how specified groups of other people performed on the test. If you knew that in a class of 25 children, a score of 79 was the highest score achieved, you would describe it as reflecting above-average (or possibly superior) performance. In contrast, if 79 were the lowest score, you would know the score reflects below-average performance. The following sections provide information about test score distributions and common statistics used to describe them.

Distributions

A distribution is simply a set of scores. These scores can be scores earned on a math test, scores on an intelligence test, or scores on a measure of anxiety. We can also have distributions reflecting physical characteristics like weight, height, or strength. Distributions can be represented in a number of ways, including tables and graphs. There are two important characteristics of test score distributions that are particularly important in understanding them. The first characteristic is central tendency and the second is variability.

Measures of Central Tendency

The scores in many distributions tend to concentrate around a center (hence the term *central tendency*), and there are three common descriptive statistics used to summarize this tendency. These are the mean, median, and mode. These statistics are frequently referenced in mental and in physical measurement and all teachers should be familiar with them.

Mean

Most people are familiar with the mean as the simple arithmetic average. Practically every day you will hear multiple discussions involving the concept of the average amount of some entity. Students may be very concerned about their grade point average (GPA). The GPA is the mean level of your academic performance, where your grade in each class is a score. Formally, the mean of a set of scores is defined by the equation

$$\text{Mean} = \frac{\text{Sum of Scores}}{\text{Number of Scores}}$$

The mean has several important characteristics that make it useful as a measure of central tendency. The mean is meaningful for distributions containing ordinal, interval, and ratio level scores (though it is not applicable for nominal scores). Second, the mean of a sample is a good estimate of the mean for the population from which the sample was drawn. This is useful when developing standardized tests in which standardization samples are tested and the resulting distribution is believed to reflect characteristics of the entire population of people with whom the test is expected to be used. The mean also is essential to the definition and calculation of other descriptive statistics useful in the context of measurement.

An undesirable characteristic of the mean is that it is sensitive to extreme scores. By this we mean a score that is either extremely high or extremely low relative to the rest of the scores in the distribution. An extreme score, either very large or very small, tends to pull the mean in its direction, and so it may not fairly represent typical values. The tendency for the mean to be affected by extreme scores is especially problematic when there are a small number of scores.

Consider the following circumstance. An economist is interested in the average wage of workers at a local widget factory employing 100 people. Of these, 98 are in manufacturing and earn $50,000 each. The engineer who designs the widgets earns 2 million per year, and the head of the factory earns 4 million per year. If we include all of these salaries, the average salary is $109,000 per year—more than double the salary of 98% of the workers. When we see such unusual distributions that have what are often called *outliers* (in this case, the two folks with the million-dollar-plus salaries), we use other statistics to help us understand the distribution of the scores (in our example, each person's salary is in essence a score). These other two useful measures of the central tendency of a distribution of scores are known as the median and the mode.

Median

The median is the score or potential score that divides the distribution in half. Half of the scores are above it and half below. When the number of scores in a distribution is an odd number, the median is simply the score that is in the middle of the distribution. For an even number of scores, the median is the average of the two scores that come closest to dividing the distribution into two equal numbers of scores. In our example of salaries, the median is $50,000. This seems a more accurate reflection of what is paid to workers at the widget plant than does the average.

Mode

The mode of a distribution is the most frequently occurring score. Again in our economic example, the mode is $50,000, the most frequently occurring salary and again a better representation of what is typically paid than is the mean. To attract job applicants, the factory head might advertise the mean salary of $109,000, which, although technically correct, is a poor choice of statistics in this instance and misleading. However, the mode does have significant limitations as a measure of central tendency. First, some distributions have two scores that are equal in frequency and higher than other scores. This is referred to as a *bimodal distribution,* and in this case the mode is ineffective as a measure of central tendency. Second, the mode is not a very stable measure of central tendency, particularly with small samples. As a result of these limitations, the mode is often of little value as a measure of central tendency, but knowledge of all three measures gives us a good view of the central tendency of a distribution.

Measures of Dispersion or Variability Around the Central Tendency

Two distributions can have the same mean, median, and mode yet differ considerably in the way the scores are distributed around the measures of central tendency. Therefore, it is not sufficient to characterize a set of scores solely by measures of central tendency. A measure of dispersion (the spread or variability) of a set of scores helps describe the distribution more fully. There are three measures of variability commonly used to describe distributions: range, standard deviation, and variance.

Range

The range is the distance between the smallest and largest score in a distribution. The range is calculated simply by subtracting the lowest score from the highest. The range thus considers only the two most extreme scores in a distribution and tells us about the limits or extremes of a distribution. It does not provide information about how the remaining scores are spread out or dispersed within these limits. We need other descriptive statistics, namely the variance and standard deviation, to provide information about the spread or dispersion of scores within the limits described by the range.

Standard Deviation

The mean and standard deviation are the most widely used statistics in educational and psychological testing as well as research in the social and behavioral sciences. The standard deviation is computed by subtracting each score from the mean, squaring the result (to eliminate negative numbers), and then adding all of the squared difference values. Once we have this sum (called the *variance of the distribution*), we find its square root (this is in order to undo our trick of squaring the differences to eliminate negative numbers). This value, the square root of the sum of the squared difference scores, is called the standard deviation.

The standard deviation is a measure of the average distance of scores from the mean of the distribution. The larger the standard deviation, the more scores differ from the mean and the more variability there is in the distribution. If scores are widely dispersed or spread around the mean, the standard deviation will be large. If there is relatively little dispersion or spread of scores around the mean, the standard deviation will be small.

Variance

In calculating the standard deviation we first calculate the variance. The standard deviation is actually the positive square root of the variance. Therefore, the variance is also a measure of the variability of scores. The reason the standard deviation is more frequently used when interpreting individual scores is that the variance is in squared units of measurement and this complicates interpretation. While the variance is in squared units, the standard deviation (i.e., the square root of the variance) is in the same units as the actual scores and more easily understood. Although the variance is difficult to apply when describing individual scores, it does have special meaning as a theoretical concept in measurement theory and in statistics.

NORMS AND REFERENCE GROUPS

To understand the individual's performance as represented by a score on a psychological or educational measurement device, it is necessary, except with certain very specific tests, to evaluate the individual's performance relative to the performance of some preselected group. To know simply that an individual answers 60 out of 100 questions correctly on a history test, and 75 out of 100 questions correctly on a biology test, conveys very little information. On which test did this individual earn the better score? Without knowledge of how a comparable or other relevant group of persons would perform on these tests, the question of which score is better cannot be answered.

Raw scores on a test, such as the number or percentage of correct responses, take on meaning only when evaluated against the performance of a normative or reference group of individuals. For convenience, raw scores are typically converted to a standard or scaled score and then compared against a set of norms. The reference group from which the norms are derived is defined prior to the standardization of the test. Once the appropriate reference population has been defined, a random sample is tested, with each individual tested under as nearly identical procedures as possible. Many factors must be considered when developing norms for test interpretation. Some of these conditions place requirements on the test being normed, some on the trait being measured, and others on the test user.

1. The psychological trait being assessed must allow the ranking of individuals along a continuum from high to low; that is, it must be amenable to at least ordinal scaling. If a nominal scale was employed, only the presence or absence of the trait would be of interest and relative amounts of the trait could not be determined; norms, under this unusual condition, would be superfluous, if not distracting or misleading.
2. The content of the test must provide an adequate operational definition of the psychological trait under consideration. With a proper operational definition, other tests can be constructed to measure the same trait and should yield comparable scores for individuals taking both tests.
3. The test should assess the same psychological construct throughout the entire range of performance.
4. The normative reference group should consist of a large random sample representative of the population on whom the test is to be administered later.
5. The normative sample of examinees from the population should have been tested under standard conditions.
6. The population sampled to provide normative data must be appropriate to the test and to the purpose for which the test is to be employed.

The last point is often misinterpreted, especially with regard to evaluation of exceptional children. Many adequately normed psychological tests are inappropriately maligned for failure to include significant numbers of handicapped children in their normative sample. This is really not an appropriate criticism. For example, if knowledge of an emotionally disturbed child's level of intellectual functioning relative to age mates in the United States is desired, comparing the child's performance to that of other similarly emotionally disturbed children makes no sense.

A large, cumulative body of evidence demonstrates clearly that test scores predict most accurately (and equally well for a variety of subgroups) when based on a large representative random sample of the population, rather than highly specific subgroups within a population.

The normative or reference group most often used to derive scores is the standardization sample, a sample of the target population drawn using a set plan. The best tests, and most publishers and developers of tests, aspire to a standardization sample that is drawn using population-proportionate stratified random sampling. This means that samples of people are selected based on subgroups of a larger group to ensure that the population as a whole is represented. In the United States, for example, tests are typically standardized via a sampling plan that stratifies the sample by gender, age, ethnicity, socioeconomic background, region of residence, and community size based on population statistics provided by the U.S. Bureau of the Census. If the Census Bureau data were to indicate, for example, that 4% of the U.S. population consisted of African American males in the middle range of socioeconomic status residing in urban centers of the south region, then 4% of the standardization sample of the test would be drawn to meet this set of characteristics.

UNITS OF MEASUREMENT

Raw scores such as number correct are tedious and difficult to interpret properly. Raw scores are thus typically transformed to another unit of measurement. Scaled scores are preferred, but other units such as age and grade equivalents are common. Making raw scores into scaled scores involves creating a set of scores with a predetermined mean and standard deviation that remain constant across some preselected variable such as age.

Once the mean and standard deviation of test scores are known, an individual's standing relative to others on the attribute in question can be determined. The normal distribution or normal curve (also known as the bell curve, Gaussian distribution, or unit normal distribution) is most helpful in making these interpretations. A person whose score falls 1 standard deviation above the mean performs at a level exceeding about 84% of the population of test takers. Two standard deviations will be above 98% of the group. The relationship is the same in the inverse below the mean. A score of 1 standard deviation below the mean indicates that the individual exceeds only about 16% of the population on the attribute in question. Approximately two-thirds (68%) of the population will score within 1 standard deviation of the mean on any psychological test.

Virtually all tests designed for use with children along with most adult tests standardize scores and then normalize them within age groups so that a scaled score at one age has the same meaning and percentile rank at all other ages. Thus, a person age 10 who earns a scaled score of 105 on the test has the same percentile rank within his or her age group as a 12-year-old with the same score has in his or her age group. That is, the score of 105 will fall at the same point on the normal curve in each case.

Not all scores have this property. Grade and age equivalents are very popular types of scores that are much abused because they are assumed to have scaled-score properties when in fact they represent only an ordinal scale. Grade equivalents ignore the dispersion of scores about the mean although the dispersion changes from age to age and grade to grade. Under no circumstances do such equivalen scores qualify as standard scores. Consider the calculation of a grade equiv When a test is administered to a group of children, the mean raw scor lated at each grade level, and this mean raw score then is called the *lent* score for a raw score of that magnitude. If the mean raw score for beginning fourth graders (grade 4.0) on a reading test is 37, then any person earning a score of 37 on the test is assigned a grade equivalent score of 4.0 regardless of the person's age. If the mean raw score of fifth graders (grade 5.0) is 38, then a score of 38 would receive a grade equivalent of 5.0. A raw score of 37 could represent a grade equivalent of 4.0, 38 could be 5.0, 39 could be 5.1, 40 could be 5.3, and 41 could be 6.0. Thus, differences of one raw score point can cause dramatic differences in the grade equivalents received, and the differences will be inconsistent across grades with regard to the magnitude of the difference in grade equivalents produced by constant changes in raw scores.

Grade equivalents tend to become standards of performance as well, which they clearly are not. Contrary to popular belief, grade equivalent scores on a test do not indicate what level of reading text a child should be using. Grade equivalent scores on tests simply do not have a one-to-one correspondence with reading series placement or the various formulas for determining readability levels.

Grade equivalents have many other problems as well.

1. The growth curve between age and achievement in basic academic subjects is nonlinear and flattens at upper grade levels.
2. Grade equivalents assume that the rate of learning is constant throughout the school year and that there is no gain or loss during summer vacation.
3. Grade equivalents involve an excess of extrapolation, especially at the upper and lower ends of the scale. However, since tests are not administered during every month of the school year, scores between the testing intervals (often a full year) must be interpolated on the assumption of the constant growth rates. Interpolation between sometimes extrapolated values on an assumption of constant growth rates is a somewhat ludicrous activity.
4. Different academic subjects are acquired at different rates, and the variation in performance varies across content areas so that "two years below grade level for age," for example, may be a much more serious deficiency in math than in reading comprehension.
5. Grade equivalents exaggerate small differences in performance between individuals and for one individual across tests.

Age equivalents have many of the same problems. The standard deviation of age equivalents varies substantially across tests, subsets, abilities, or skills assessed, and exists on an ordinal, not interval scale. It is inappropriate to add, subtract, multiply, or divide age or grade equivalents or any other form of ordinal score.

The principal advantage of standardized or scaled scores lies in the comparability of score interpretation across age and content.

Standard scores are more accurate and precise. Scaled scores can be set to any desired mean and standard deviation. Fortunately, a few scales can account for the vast majority of standardized tests in psychology and education.

What has been said thus far about scaled scores and their equivalency applies primarily to scores that have been forced to take the shape of the Gaussian or bell curve. When test-score distributions derived from a standardization sample are examined, the scores frequently deviate significantly from normal. Often, test developers will then transform scores, using one of a variety of statistical methods to take a normal distribution. Despite what is often taught in early courses in psychological statistics and measurement, this is not always appropriate. It is commonplace to read that psychological variables, like most others, are normally distributed within the population; many are. Variables such as intelligence, memory skills, and academic achievement will closely approximate the normal distribution when well measured. However, many psychological variables, especially behavioral ones such as aggression, attention, and hyperactivity, deviate substantially from the normal curve within the population of humans.

When a score distribution then deviates from normality, the test developer is faced with the decision of whether to create normalized scores via some transformation or to allow the distribution to retain its shape with perhaps some smoothing to remove irregularities due to sampling error. In the later case, a linear transformation of scores is most likely to be chosen.

To make this determination, the test developer must ascertain whether the underlying construct measured by the test is normally distributed or not and whether the extant sample is adequate to estimate the distribution, whatever its shape. For applied, clinical devices, the purpose of score transformations that result in normalization of the distribution is to correct for sampling error and presumes that the underlying construct is, in fact, normally or near-normally distributed. Normalization of the score distribution then produces a more accurate rendition of the population distribution and improves the utility of the standardized scaled scores provided. If the population distribution of the construct in question is not normal—for example, aggressive behavior—then a different form of transformation, typically linear, is required to be accurate. This decision affects how clinicians best interpret the ultimately scaled scores.

MODELS AND METHODS OF TESTING AND ASSESSMENT

A variety of assessment methods are available for evaluating exceptional children. Some of these methods grew directly from specific schools of psychological thought, such as the psychoanalytic view of Freud (projective assessment techniques) or the behavioral schools of Watson, Skinner, and Bandura (applied behavior analysis). Other methods have grown out of controversies in and between existing academic disciplines, such as personality theory and social psychology. New and refined methods have come about with new developments in medicine and related fields, whereas other new testing methods stem from advances in the theory and technology of the science of psychological measurement. Unfortunately, still other new techniques stem from psychological and educational faddism with little basis in psychological theory and little if any empirical basis. Any attempt to group tests by characteristics such as norm-referenced versus criterion-referenced, traditional versus behavioral, maximum versus typical performance, and so on, is doomed to criticism. As will be seen in the pages that follow, the demarcations between assessment methods and models are not as clear as many would contend. In many cases, the greatest distinctions lie in the philosophical orientation and intent of the user. As one prominent example, many "behavioral" assessment techniques are as bound by norms and other traditional psychometric concepts as are traditional intelligence tests. Even trait measures of personality end up being labeled by some as behavioral assessment devices. The division of models and methods of assessment to follow is based in some part on convenience and clarity of discussions but also with an eye toward maintaining the most important conceptual distinctions among these assessment methods.

TRADITIONAL NORM-REFERENCED ASSESSMENT

Intelligence, Achievement, and Special Abilities

These assessment techniques have been grouped together primarily because of their similarity of content and, in some cases, their similarity of purpose. There are, however, some basic distinctions among these measures. Intelligence tests tend to be broad in terms of content; items sample a variety of behaviors that are considered to be intellectual in nature. Intelligence tests are used to evaluate the current intellectual status of the individual, to predict future behavior on intellectually demanding tasks, and to help achieve a better understanding of past behavior and performance in an intellectual setting. Achievement tests measure relatively narrowly defined content, sampled from a specific subject matter domain that typically has been the focus of purposeful study and learning by the population for whom the test is intended. Intelligence tests, by contrast, are oriented more toward testing intellectual processes and use items that are more related to incidental learning and not as likely to have been specifically studied as are achievement test items. Tests of special abilities, such as memory, mechanical aptitude, and auditory perception, are narrow in scope as are achievement tests but focus on process rather than content. The same test question may appear on an intelligence, achievement, or special ability test, however, and closely related questions frequently do. Tests of intelligence and special abilities also focus more on the application of previously acquired knowledge, whereas achievement tests focus on testing just what knowledge has been acquired. One should not focus on single items; it is the collection of items and the use and evaluation of the individual's score on the test that are the differentiating factors.

Intelligence Tests

Intelligence tests are among the oldest devices in the psychometric arsenal of the psychologist and are likely the most frequently used category of tests in the evaluation of exceptional children, especially in the cases of mental retardation, learning disabilities, and intellectual giftedness. Intelligence and aptitude tests are used frequently in adult assessment as well and are essential diagnostic tools when examining for the various dementias. They are used with adults in predicting a variety of other cognitive disorders and in the vocational arena. Since the translation and modification of Alfred Binet's intelligence test for French schoolchildren was introduced in the United States by Lewis Terman (of Stanford University, hence the Stanford-Binet Intelligence Scale), a substantial proliferation of such tests has occurred. Many of these tests measure very limited aspects of intelligence (e.g., Peabody Picture Vocabulary Test, Columbia Mental Maturity Scale, Ammons and Ammons Quick Test), whereas others give a much broader view of a person's intellectual skills, measuring general intelligence as well as more specific cognitive skills (e.g., the Reynolds Intellectual Assessment Scales and the various Wechsler Intelligence scales).

Intelligence tests in use today are for the most part individually administered (i.e., a psychologist administers the test to an individual in a closed setting with no other individuals present). For a long time, group intelligence tests were used throughout the public schools and in the military. Group tests of intelligence are used more sparingly today because of their many abuses in the past and the limited amount of information they offer about the individual. There is little of utility to the schools, for example, that can be gleaned from a group intelligence test that cannot be obtained better from group achievement tests. Individual intelligence tests are far more expensive to use but offer considerably more and better information. Much of the additional information, however, comes from having a highly trained observer (the psychologist) interacting with the person for more than an hour in a quite structured setting, with a variety of tasks of varying levels of difficulty.

Intelligence testing, which can be very useful in clinical and vocational settings, is also a controversial activity, especially with regard to the diagnosis of mild mental retardation among minority cultures in the United States. Used with care and compassion, as a tool toward understanding, such tests can prove invaluable. Used recklessly and with rigidity, they can cause irreparable harm. Extensive technical training is required to master properly the administration of an individual intelligence test (or any individual test, for that matter). Even greater sensitivity and training are required to interpret these powerful and controversial devices. Extensive knowledge of statistics, measurement theory, and the existing research literature concerning testing is a prerequisite to using intelligence tests. To use them well requires mastery of the broader field of psychology, especially differential psychology, the psychological science that focuses on the psychological study and analysis of human individual differences and theories of cognitive development.

Achievement Tests

Various types of achievement tests are used throughout the public schools with regular classrooms and exceptional children. Most achievement tests are group tests administered with some regularity to all students in a school or system. Some of the more prominent group tests include the Iowa Test of Basic Skills, the Metropolitan Achievement Test, the Stanford Achievement Test, and the California Achievement Test. These batteries of achievement tests typically do not report an overall index of achievement but rather report separately on achievement in such academic areas as English grammar and punctuation, spelling, map reading, mathematical calculations, reading comprehension, social studies, and general science. The tests change every few grade levels to accommodate changes in curriculum emphasis. Group achievement tests provide schools with information concerning how their children are achieving in these various subject areas relative to other school systems throughout the country and relative to other schools in the same district. They also provide information about the progress of individual children and can serve as good screening measures in attempting to identify children at the upper and lower ends of the achievement continuum. Group-administered achievement tests help in achieving a good understanding of the academic performance of these individuals but do not provide sufficiently detailed or sensitive information on which to base major decisions. When decision making is called for or an in-depth understanding of a child's academic needs is required, individual testing is needed.

Tests of Special Abilities

These are specialized methods for assessing thin slices of the spectrum of abilities for any single individual. These measures can be helpful in further narrowing the field of hypotheses about an individual's learning or behavior difficulties when used in conjunction with intelligence, achievement, and personality measures. The number of special abilities that can be assessed is quite large. Some examples of these abilities include visual-motor integration skills, auditory perception, visual closure, figure-ground distinction, oral expression, tactile form recognition, and psychomotor speed. While these measures can be useful, depending on the questions to be answered, one must be particularly careful in choosing an appropriate, valid, and reliable measure of a special ability. The use and demand for these tests are significantly less than those for the most popular individual intelligence tests and widely used achievement tests. This in turn places some economic constraints on development and standardization procedures, which are very costly enterprises when properly conducted. One should always be wary of the "quick and dirty" entry into the ability testing market. There are some very good tests of special abilities available, although special caution is needed. For example, simply because an ability is named in the test title is no guarantee that the test measures that particular ability.

To summarize, norm-referenced tests of intelligence, achievement, and special abilities provide potentially important information in the assessment process. Yet each supplies only a piece of the required data. Equally important are observations of how the student behaves during testing and in other settings, and performance on other measures.

Norm-Referenced, Objective Personality Measures

Whereas tests of aptitude and achievement can be described as maximum performance measures, tests of personality can be described as typical performance measures. When taking a personality test, one is normally asked to respond according to one's typical actions and attitudes and not in a manner that would present the "best" possible performance (i.e., most socially desirable). Faking or deliberate distortion of responses is certainly possible, to a greater extent on some scales than others, and is a more significant problem with personality scales than cognitive scales. Papers have even been published providing details on how to distort responses on personality tests in the desired direction. Although there is no direct solution to this problem, many personality measures have built-in "lie" scales or social desirability scales to help detect deliberate faking to make one look as good as possible and F or infrequency scales to detect the faking of the presence of psychopathology.

The use and interpretation of scores from objective personality scales also have implications for this problem. Properly assessed and evaluated from an empirical basis, response to the personality scale is treated as the behavior of immediate interest and the actual content conveyed by the item becomes nearly irrelevant. As one example, there is an item on the Revised Children's Manifest Anxiety Scale (RCMAS), a test designed to measure chronic anxiety levels in children, that states "My hands feel sweaty." Whether the child's hands actually do feel sweaty is irrelevant. The salient question is whether children who respond "true" to this question are in reality more anxious than children who respond "false" to such a query. Children who respond more often in the keyed direction on the RCMAS display greater general anxiety and exhibit more observed behavior problems associated with anxiety than children who respond in the opposite manner. Although face validity of a personality or other test is a desirable quality, it is not always a necessary one. It is the actuarial implications of the behavioral response of choosing to respond in a certain manner that holds the greatest interest for the practitioner. Scales developed using such an approach are empirical scales.

Another approach is to devise content scales. As the name implies, the item content of such scales is considered more salient than its purely empirical relationship to the construct. Individuals with depression, especially men, may be edgy and irritable at times. Thus, the item "I sometimes lash out at others for no good reason" might show up on an empirically derived scale assessing depression, but is unlikely to find its way onto a content scale. "I am most often sad" would be a content-scale item assessing depression. Content scales are typically derived via expert judgments, but from an item pool that has passed muster at some empirical level already.

The emphasis on inner psychological constructs typical of personality scales poses special problems for their development and validation.

Objective personality scales are probably the most commonly used of all types of tests by clinical psychologists. They provide key evidence for the differentiation of various forms of psychopathology, including clinical disorders and especially personality disorders. Omnibus scales such as the Minnesota Multiphasic Personality Inventory (revised; MMPI-2) are common with adult populations and also have adolescent versions. Omnibus scales directed at children and adolescents specifically, however, may be more appropriate for these younger age ranges. Among the many available, the self-report of personality from the Behavior Assessment System for Children-2 (BASC-2) is the most commonly used.

Projective Assessment

Projective assessment of personality has a long, rich, but very controversial history in the evaluation of clinical disorders and the description of normal personality. This controversy stems largely from the subjective nature of the tests used and the lack of good evidence of predictive validity coupled with sometimes fierce testimonial and anecdotal evidence of their utility in individual cases by devoted clinicians.

The subjectiveness of projective testing necessarily results in disagreement concerning the scoring and interpretation of responses to the test materials. For any given response by any given individual, competent professionals would each be likely to interpret differently the meaning and significance of the response. It is primarily the agreement on scoring that differentiates objective from subjective tests. If trained examiners agree on how a particular answer is scored, tests are considered objective; if not, they are considered subjective. Projective is not synonymous with subjective in this context, but most projective tests are closer to the subjective than objective end of the continuum of agreement on scoring of responses. Projective tests are sets of ambiguous stimuli, such as ink blots or incomplete sentences, and the individual responds with the first thought or series of thoughts that come to mind or tells a story about each stimulus. Typically no restrictions are placed on individuals' response options. They may choose to respond with anything they desire; in contrast, on an objective scale, individuals must choose from a set of answers provided by the test or at least listed for the examiner in a scoring manual. The major hypothesis underlying projective testing is taken from Freud. When responding to an ambiguous stimulus, individuals are influenced by their needs, interests, and psychological organization and tend to respond in ways that reveal, to the trained observer, their motivations and true emotions, with little interference from the conscious control of the ego. Various psychodynamic theories are applied to evaluating test responses, however, and herein too lie problems of subjectivity. Depending on the theoretical orientation of the psychologist administering the test, very different interpretations may be given. Despite the controversy surrounding these tests, they remain very popular.

Projective methods can be divided roughly into three categories according to the type of stimulus presented and the method of response called for by the examiner. The first category calls for the interpretation of ambiguous visual stimuli by the patient with an oral response. Tests in this category include such well-known techniques as the Rorschach (the famous so-called ink blot test) and the Thematic Apperception Test (TAT, wherein patients look at an ambiguous picture and make up a story about it). The second category includes completion methods, whereby the patient is asked to finish a sentence when given an ambiguous stem or to complete a story begun by the examiner. This includes the Despert Fables and a number of sentence completion tests. The third category includes projective art, primarily drawing techniques, although sculpture and related art forms have been used. In these tasks, the child is provided with materials to complete an artwork (or simple drawing) and given instructions for a topic, some more specific than others. Techniques such as the Kinetic Family Drawing, the Draw-a-Person, and the Bender-Gestalt Test (which also has other uses, especially as a measure of visual-motor integration skills) fall in this category.

Criterion-related and predictive validity have proven especially tricky for advocates of projective testing. Although techniques such as the TAT are not as amenable to study and validation through the application of traditional statistical and psychometric methods as objective tests may be, many clinical researchers have made such attempts with less than heartening results. None of the so-called objective scoring systems for projective devices has proved to be very valuable in predicting behavior, nor has the use of normative standards been especially fruitful. This should not be considered so surprising; however, it is indeed the nearly complete idiographic nature of projective techniques that can make them useful in the evaluation of a specific patient. It allows for any possible response to occur, without restriction, and can reveal many of a patient's current reasons for behaving in a specific manner.

Behavioral Assessment

The rapid growth of behavior therapy and applied behavior analysis has led to the need for tests that are consistent with the theoretical and practical requirements of these approaches to the modification of human behavior. Thus, the field of behavioral assessment has developed and grown at an intense pace. The general term *behavioral assessment* has come to be used to describe a broad set of methods including some traditional objective personality scales, certain methods of interviewing, physiological response measures, naturalistic observation, norm-referenced behavior checklists, frequency counts of behavior, and a host of informal techniques requiring the observation of a behavior with recording of specific responses. Behavioral assessment will be discussed here in its more restricted sense to include the rating (by self or others) of observable behavioral events, primarily taking the form of behavior checklists and rating forms that may or may not be normed. Although we would certainly include psychophysiological assessment within this category, the scope of the work simply will not allow us to address this aspect of behavioral assessment except to say that it is indeed a most useful one in the treatment of a variety of clinical disorders.

The impetus for behavioral assessment comes not only from the field of behavior therapy but also from a general revolt against the high level of inference involved in such methods of assessing behavior as the Rorschach and the TAT. The greatest distinguishing characteristic between the behavioral assessment of psychopathological disorders and most other techniques is the level of inference involved in moving from the data provided by the assessment instrument to an accurate description of the patient and the development of an appropriate intervention strategy. This is a most useful strength for behavioral assessment strategies but is their greatest weakness when it is necessary to understand what underlies the observed behaviors. Behavioral assessment grew from a need to quantify observations of a student's current behavior and its immediate antecedents and consequences, and this is the context within it that remains most useful today.

There are a number of formal behavior rating scales or behavior checklists now available. These instruments typically list behaviors of interest in clearly specified terms and have a trained observer or an informant indicate the frequency of occurrence of these behaviors. Interpretation can then take on a normative or a criterion-reference nature depending on the purpose of the assessment and the availability of norms. Clusters of behaviors may be of interest that define certain clinical syndromes, such as Attention-Deficit/Hyperactivity Disorder. On the other hand, individual behaviors may be the focus (e.g., hitting other children). More frequently, behavioral assessment occurs as an informal method of collecting data on specific behaviors being exhibited by a patient and is dictated by the existing situation into which the psychologist is invited. An informal nature is dictated by the nature of behavioral assessment in many instances. Part of the low level of inference in behavioral assessment lies in not generalizing observations of behavior across settings without first collecting data in multiple settings. In this regard, behavioral assessment may for the most part be said to be psychosituational. Behavior is observed and evaluated under existing circumstances, and no attempt is made to infer that the observed behaviors will occur under other circumstances. Comprehensive systems that are multimethod and multidimensional and that assess behavior in more than one setting have been devised and provide a good model for the future (BASC-2).

Another area of assessment that stems from behavioral psychology and is considered by many to be a subset of behavioral assessment is task analysis. Whereas behavioral assessment typically finds its greatest applicability in dealing with emotional and behavioral difficulties, task analysis is most useful in evaluating and correcting learning problems. In task analysis, the task to be learned (e.g., brushing one's teeth or multiplying two-digit numbers) is broken down into its most basic components, is observed, and those skills specifically lacking are targeted for teaching to the child. In some cases, hierarchies of subskills can be developed, but these have not held up well under cross-validation. Task analysis can thus be a powerful tool in specifying a learner's existing (and needed) skills for a given learning problem. Task analysis could, for example, form an integral part of any behavioral intervention for a child with specific learning problems. The proper use of these procedures requires a creative and well-trained individual conversant with both assessment technology and behavioral theories of learning, since there are no standardized task analysis procedures. Those involved in task analysis need to be sensitive to the reliability and validity of their methods. As with other behavioral assessment techniques, some contend that behavioral assessment techniques need only demonstrate that multiple observers can agree on a description of the behavior and when it has been observed. Though not having to demonstrate a relationship with a hypothetical construct, behavioral techniques must demonstrate that the behavior observed is consistent and relevant to the learning problems. For behavior checklists and more formal behavioral assessment techniques, most traditional psychometric concepts apply and must be evaluated with regard to the behavioral scale in question.

Other Types and Models of Tests

There are certainly many other ways of assessing or measuring student performance. Becoming more popular are, for example, techniques known as curriculum-based assessment (CBA) or curriculum-based measurement (CBM). However, these are typically not standardized, nor do they have national norms; instead, they are developed locally for use in specific schools. Such tests take direct samples of the local curriculum and test kids on such factors as reading speed. They are quite useful in many regards but are not covered in our section on tests since they are not available commercially and are locally developed measures.

Specialized psychologists such as neuropsychologists and vocational psychologists will use some other forms of specialized tests as well, but these typically fall under one of the subsets of types of tests already described—for example, neuropsychological tests and tests of special aptitudes and skills that simply emphasize the integrity of brain systems in their design. Measures of vocational interest will follow the model of objective personality tests already noted as well.

Accessing Critical Commentary on Standardized Psychological Tests

Not every educator or other practitioner can be or should be an expert on the technical adequacy and measurement science underlying each and every standardized test that might be useful in a school or clinical practice. With a clear understanding of the fundamentals of measurement, however, individuals can make intelligent choices about test selection and test use based on the test manuals and accompanying materials in most cases. However, when additional expertise or commentary is required, critical reviews of nearly every published test can be accessed with relative ease.

Many journals in psychology routinely publish reviews of new or newly revised tests, including such publications as the *Archives of Clinical Neuropsychology, Journal of Psychoeducational Assessment, Journal of Learning Disabilities, School Psychology Review, Applied Neuropsychology,* and the *Journal of Personality Assessment.* Another source of critical information on published tests is the publications of the Buros Institute of Mental Measurement.

In the late 1920s, Oscar Krisen Buros began to publish a series of monographs reviewing statistics texts. He noted the rapid proliferation of psychological and educational tests beginning to occur at the same time and rapidly turned his attention to obtaining high-quality reviews of these tests and publishing them in bound volumes known as the *Mental Measurements Yearbook* (MMY). The first MMY was published by Buros in 1938, and the series continues today. Buros died in 1978, during the final stages of production of the eighth MMY (although they are called "yearbooks," they are not published annually), and his spouse, art director, and assistant Luella Buros saw the eighth MMY to completion. Subsequently, she opened a competition for proposals to adopt the institute and continue the work of her late husband. A proposal written by one of the editors of this volume (Cecil R. Reynolds, then on the faculty of the University of Nebraska at Lincoln) was chosen, and the Buros Institute of Mental Measurement was established in 1979 at the University of Nebraska at Lincoln, where it remains permanently due to a generous endowment from Luella Buros.

The institute continues to seek out reviewers to evaluate and provide critical commentary on all educational and psychological tests published in the English language although applying less rigor than its founder in selecting reviewers. These reviews are collected in an ongoing process, as tests are published or revised. The collected reviews are published on an unscheduled basis approximately every 5 to 8 years. However, as reviews are written and accepted for publication, they are added to the Buros Institute database, which may be searched online by subscription to the master database or through most major university libraries. Information on how to access current reviews in the Buros database can be obtained from nearly any reference librarian or through a visit to the Buros Institute website.

3

Test Descriptions and Reviews

RON DUMONT AND JOHN O. WILLIS

The following test descriptions and reviews are meant to be a source of general information regarding each test. Given the vast number of tests currently published, and the speed at which tests are revised or edited, it would be impossible to provide in-depth reviews of each of these tests. We have attempted, wherever possible, to provide information about where the reader can go to get more information. Where appropriate we have listed articles, reviews, and web sites that may be useful to the reader.[1]

One well-known and well-regarded source of test review material is the Buros Center for Testing (http://www.unl.edu/buros/), publisher of the *Mental Measurements Yearbook* (MMY) and *Tests in Print* (TIP) series. Introduced in 1938, the series has become the recognized standard for objective information on commercially available tests.

Two books often used as a source of information about tests and testing are Jerome M. Sattler's *Assessment of Children: Cognitive Applications,* fourth edition, published by Sattler (www.sattlerpublisher.com), and Salvia and Ysseldyke's *Assessment In Special and Inclusive Education,* ninth edition, published by Houghton Mifflin (www.houghtonmifflinbooks.com).

1. The following is a list of contributors (all affiliated with Fairleigh Dickinson University except Leah Doughlin Rogove) who kindly assisted with the preparation of the test review and test descriptions: Annie Petrossian, Brie Insalaco, Cara Nicolini Hilton, Carlea Alfieri, Debbie Mattei, Eric Klein, Jennifer Hajinlian, Jessica Ippolito, Joe Breshnahan, Jon Kurtyka, Jon Rogove, Leah Doughlin Rogove (Yeshiva University), Julie Blundon, Kate Hogkins, Laura Matelfy, Laura Richardson, Lisa Hahn, Mia Downing, Mia Hernandez, Rachel Kandel, Rachel Wieder-Blank, Shira Freundlich, Shira Kaufman, Shira Kurtz, and Syreeta Washington.

Several online databases are also very useful when reviewing tests and searching for articles related to test use. Two of these databases are the Educational Resource Information Center and PsycInfo.

The Educational Resource Information Center (ERIC) is a national information system supported by the U.S. Department of Education, the National Library of Education, and the Office of Educational Research and Improvement. It provides access to information from journals included in the Current Index of Journals in Education and Resources in Education Index. The ERIC web site (http://www.eric.ed.gov/) provides full text of more than 2,200 digests along with references for additional information and citations and abstracts from over 1,000 educational and education-related journals.

PsycInfo contains more than 1 million citations and summaries of journal articles, book chapters, books, dissertations, and technical reports, all in the field of psychology. Journal coverage, which spans from 1887 to the present, includes international material selected from more than 1,700 periodicals in over 35 languages. More than 60,000 records are added each year. It also includes information about the psychological aspects of related disciplines such as medicine, psychiatry, nursing, sociology, education, pharmacology, physiology, linguistics, anthropology, business, and law. Examples of titles offered in PsycInfo (http://www.apa.org/psycinfo/) include *Academic Medicine, Academic Psychiatry, Behavior Genetics, Behavioral Disorders, Journal of Abnormal Child Psychology, Journal of Applied Social Psychology, Journal of Behavioral Medicine, Journal of Psychiatry & Neuroscience, Journal of Psychology, Psychoanalytic Psychology, Psychological Assessment,* and *Psychological Medicine.*

Journals are also often very useful for gathering information about tests and their use. The following are several very useful journals.

- *Assessment* (http://www.sagepub.co.uk/journal.aspx?pid=105477) presents information of direct relevance to the use of assessment measures, including the practical applications of measurement methods, test development and interpretation practices, and advances in the description and prediction of human behavior.
- *Journal of Psychoeducational Assessment* (JPA; http://www.psychoeducational.com/) provides current information regarding psychological and educational assessment practices, legal mandates, and instrumentation. The JPA is known internationally for the quality of assessment-related research, theory and position papers, interviews with leaders in the field, and book and test reviews that it publishes.
- *Psychology in the Schools* (http://www3.interscience.wiley.com/cgi-bin/jhome/32084) is a bimonthly peer-reviewed journal devoted to research, opinion, and practice. The journal welcomes theoretical and applied manuscripts focusing on the issues confronting school psychologists, teachers, counselors, administrators, and other personnel workers in schools and colleges, public and private organizations.

The following tests are reviewed in varying depth at the University of Oregon web site (http://idea.uoregon.edu/assessment/analysis_results/assess_results_by_test.html).

Auditory Analysis Test
Clinical Evaluation of Language Fundamentals—Third Edition (CELF-3)

Comprehensive Test of Phonological Processing (CTOPP)
Curriculum-Based Measurement (CBM): Oral Reading Fluency
Degrees of Reading Power (DRP)
Dynamic Indicators of Basic Early Literacy Skills—Fifth Edition (DIBELS)
Early Reading Diagnostic Assessment (ERDA)
Gray Oral Reading Test IV (GORT-IV)
Iowa Test of Basic Skills (ITBS)
Letter Sound Fluency
Lindamood Auditory Conceptualization Test
An Observation Survey of Early Literacy Achievement
Peabody Picture Vocabulary Test—Third Edition (PPVT-3)
Phonological Awareness Test
Qualitative Reading Inventory (QRI)
Roswell-Chall Auditory Blending
Slosson Oral Reading Test—Revised (SORT-R)
Stanford Achievement Test—Ninth Edition (SAT-9)
TerraNova—CAT (Second Edition TerraNova; Sixth Edition CAT)
Test of Language Development—primary: Third Edition (TOLD-P:3)
Test of Phonological Awareness (TOPA)
Test of Word Knowledge (TOWK)
Test of Word Reading Efficiency (TOWRE)
Texas Primary Reading Inventory (TPRI)
Wechsler Individual Achievement Test II (WIAT-II)
Woodcock-Johnson III Test of Achievement
Woodcock-Johnson III Test of Cognitive Abilities
Woodcock Reading Mastery Test—Revised (WRMT-R)
Yopp-Singer Test of Phoneme Segmentation

Some tests are reviewed at our web site, Dumont/Willis on the web (http://alpha.fdu.edu/psychology).

The test reviews in this chapter have been grouped by the following broad categories and, within those categories, arranged in alphabetical order: behavior scales, cognitive ability, early childhood development, visual motor, and language. Although it is clear that some test batteries cover more than one broad category, tests were placed based upon these authors' best estimate of what the test measures.

BEHAVIOR SCALES

American Association on Mental Retardation (AAMR) Adaptive Behavior Scales—Residential and Community: Second Edition

Authors: Kazuo Nihira, Henry Leland, and Nadine Lambert
Ages: 18 through 80
Administration Time: 15 to 30 minutes
Publisher: PRO-ED

The AAMR Adaptive Behavior Scales—Residential and Community: Second Edition (ABS-RC:2, 1993) is intended to assess adaptive behaviors and gauge how people cope with natural and social demands of their environment. The ABS-RC:2 measures skills and abilities necessary to perform tasks of daily living and to participate in social activities. This measure is intended to assess the behavior of institutionalized persons with mental retardation and those in community settings who previously had been classified at different adaptive behavior levels according to the AAMR's *Classification in Mental Retardation* (Grossman, 1983). It is also intended to be used to assess the adaptive behavior levels in public school populations. Designed for mentally handicapped persons aged 18–80, this measure is individually administered in an interview format based on the informant's knowledge of the individual being assessed. Testing time is estimated at 15–30 minutes.

Originally published in 1969, the ABS-RC has undergone many alterations and intensive item analyses. Items that were carried over from the previous version were identified on the basis of their interrater reliability and their ability to discriminate between the two groups mentioned (i.e., those previously classified in an institutionalized setting and those classified in a public school population).

Domain raw scores are converted to standard scores (mean [M]=10, standard deviation [SD]=3) and percentiles. Factor raw scores are used to generate quotients (M=100, SD=15) and percentiles. The normative sample for the ABS-RC:2 consists of over 4,000 persons with developmental disabilities in the community or in residential settings. It was selected to represent the national population with developmental disabilities. Persons included in the sample had additional disabilities (e.g., blindness, deafness, emotional disturbance, learning disability, physical impairments, and speech/language impairments; Carey, 1998). Internal consistency reliabilities and stability for all scores exceed .80. Further evidence supporting the scale's statistical adequacy is provided in the manual.

The manual is clearly written. It provides appendixes that include norm tables for converting raw scores to standard scores, percentiles ranks, and age equivalents. A software-based scoring and reporting system is available from the publisher. Some reviewers have criticized the ABS-RC:2 for being overly similar to the AAMR Adaptive Behavior Scales—School: Second Edition (Harrison, 1998). This point may be important to consider if questions exist regarding the more appropriate measure for a particular individual.

Additional Information

Carey, K. T. (1998). Review of the AAMR Adaptive Behavior Scale—Residential and Community, Second Edition. In J. C. Impara & B. S. Plake (Eds.), *The thirteenth mental measurements yearbook.* Lincoln, NE: Buros Institute of Mental Measurements.

Grossman, H. J. (Ed.). (1983). *Classification in mental retardation.* Washington, DC: American Association on Mental Retardation.

Hatton, C., Emerson, E., & Robertson, J. (2001). The Adaptive Behavior Scale—Residential and Community (Part I): Towards the development of a short form. *Research in Developmental Disabilities, 22,* 273–288.

Harrison, P. L. (1998). Review of the AAMR Adaptive Behavior Scale—Residential and Community, Second Edition. In J. C. Impara & B. S. Plake (Eds.),

The thirteenth mental measurements yearbook. Lincoln, NE: Buros Institute of Mental Measurements.

Lambert, N., Nihira, K., & Leland, H. (1993). *AAMR Adaptive Behavior Scale—Residential and Community: Second Edition.* Austin, TX: PRO-ED, Inc.

http://www.uab.edu/cogdev/mentreta.htm

http://gri.gallaudet.edu/~catraxle/ADAPTSOC.html

http://216.239.39.104/search?q=cache:QZMoXvKL7gQJ:www.dualdiagnosis ontario.org/pdf/EnglishPublication/Chapter5.pdf+abs-rc:2+review&hl=en (Measures of Adaptive Functioning- Pg.19)

AAMR Adaptive Behavior Scales—School: Second Edition

Authors: Nadine Lambert, Kazuo Nihira, and Henry Leland
Ages: 3 through 18
Administration Time: 15 to 30 minutes
Publisher: PRO-ED

The AAMR Adaptive Behavior Scales—School: Second Edition (ABS-S:2, 1993) was designed to assess the current functioning of children being evaluated for evidence of mental retardation, for evaluating adaptive behavior characteristics of children with autism, and for differentiating children with behavior disorders who require special education assistance from those with behavior problems who can be educated in regular class programs (Harrington, 1998).

The ABS-S:2 was developed in its first-edition original form by Kazuo Nihira et al. and was revised and standardized in 1974 by Nadine Lambert, Myra Windmiller, and Linda Cole. It was revised and standardized once again in 1981 by Nadine Lambert and Myra Windmiller. This second and most recent edition was published in 1993. It is intended for use with children and adolescents ages 3:0 through 18:11. The ABS-S:2 is administered individually in an interview format. Testing time is estimated at 15–30 minutes.

The current scale is divided into two parts. In Part One skills are grouped into nine behavior domains: Independent Functioning, Physical Development, Economic Activity, Language Development, Numbers and Time, Prevocational/Vocational Activity, Self-Direction, Responsibility, and Socialization. These skills focus on personal independence and evaluate the coping skills considered important to independence and responsibility in daily living.

The behaviors in Part Two are grouped into seven domains, which assess adaptive behaviors that relate to the manifestation of personality and behavior disorders: Social Behavior, Conformity, Trustworthiness, Stereotyped and Hyperactive Behavior, Self-Abusive Behavior, Social Engagement, and Disturbing Interpersonal Behavior.

Domain raw scores are converted to standard scores (M=10, SD=3) and percentiles. Factor raw scores are used to generate quotients (M=100, SD=15) and percentiles. The standardization sample for the ABS-S:2 included 2,000 persons with developmental disabilities attending public schools and 1,000 with no disabilities (Harrington, 1998).

Stinnett, Fuqua, and Coombs (1999) examined the construct validity of the AAMR Adaptive Behavior Scale—School:2 (ABS-S:2; Lambert, Nihira, & Leland,

1993) through exploratory factor analyses and reported that "results indicated the ABS-S:2 is a two-factor instrument both for children with and without mental retardation." Factor I items were related to Personal Independence, and Factor 2 items were related to Social Behavior. "Because the data strongly indicated a 2-factor model for both the MR and Non-MR samples, users should be cautious in interpreting ABS-S:2 results in terms of the 5-factor model presented by the test's authors" (Stinnett et al.).

Additional Information

Harrington, R. L. (1998). Review of AAMR Adaptive Behavior Scales—School: Second Edition. In J. C. Impara & B. S. Plake (Eds.), *The thirteenth mental measurements yearbook.* Lincoln, NE: Buros Institute of Mental Measurements.

Lambert, N., Nihira, K., & Leland, H. (1993). *AAMR Adaptive Behavior Scale—School: Second Edition.* Austin, TX: PRO-ED, Inc.

Stinnett, A. T., Fuqua, D. R., & Coombs, W. T. (1999). Construct validity of the AAMR Adaptive Behavior Scale—School: 2. *School Psychology Review, 28,* 31–43.

Watkins, M. W., Ravert, C. M., & Crosby, E. G. (2002). Normative factor structure of the AAMR Adaptive Behavior Scale—School (2nd ed.). *Journal of Psychoeducational Assessment, 20,* 337–345.

http://www.uab.edu/cogdev/mentreta.htm

http://gri.gallaudet.edu/~catraxle/ADAPTSOC.html

Achenbach Child Behavior Checklist

Authors: Thomas M. Achenbach and Leslie A. Rescorla

Ages: 6 to 18

Time: 15 to 20 minutes

Publisher: Achenbach System of Empirically Based Assessment (ASEBA) Child Behavior Checklist

The purpose of the Child Behavior Checklist (CBCL 6–18, 2001) is to quickly collect standardized ratings on a broad spectrum of competencies and problems for children aged 6 to 18 years as reported by the child's parent or others that are involved with the child within the home environment. For the 120 behavioral, emotional, and social problem statements, the respondent is directed to answer all items as best as possible even if they do not seem applicable to the child. The instructions to the respondent are located on the CBCL booklet and are written on a fifth-grade reading level. If the respondent cannot read, the CBCL can be administered in an alternate format where the examiner reads the items and records the responses of the respondent.

The CBCL measures competencies using a Total Competence Score, which represents a parent's perception of the child's performance on an Activities scale, a Social scale, and a School scale.

Problems are measured on the CBCL's Syndrome Scales. These represent the parents' perception of their child's behavior based on eight statistically derived categories (factors): Anxious/Depressed, Withdrawn/Depressed, Somatic Complaints, Social Problems, Thought Problems, Attention Problems, Rule-Breaking Behavior, and Aggressive Behavior.

The Anxious/Depressed, Withdrawn/Depressed, and Somatic Complaints scales constitute the Internalizing Problems scale score, and the Rule-Breaking Behavior and Aggressive Behavior scales combine to yield the Externalizing Problems scale scores. Adding the Social Problems, Thought Problems, and Attention Problems scales to the Internalizing and Externalizing Problem scales generates a Total Problem scale score.

In addition, problems on the CBCL have been categorized into six DSM-Orientated Scales: Affective Problems, Anxiety Problems, Somatic Problems, Attention-Deficit/Hyperactivity Problems, Oppositional Defiant Problems, and Conduct Problems.

Scoring the CBCL is easy, and responses are directly recorded from the CBCL booklet. Scoring can be done in one of three ways: by hand, by computer, or by scanner. The hand-scoring method is time consuming, and the many calculations leave room for frequent errors. Although the computer-scoring and scanning methods are initially more costly, they reduce time spent scoring and are more accurate.

Males and females have separate norms based on age. The two age ranges used for each gender are 6–11 and 12–18. Normative data are provided only on the hand-scoring profiles. No other printed norm tables are available at this time. The computer-generated profile does not provide the examiner with such data.

T-scores and percentiles are calculated for each scale for comparative purposes. For each scale T-scores are further categorized as being within normal limits, within the borderline range, or within the clinical range. The value of T-scores for each range varies depending on the scale. On the Competence Scales and Total Competence scale, higher T-scores are associated with normal functioning. On the syndrome scales, Internalizing, Externalizing, Total Problem, and DSM (*Diagnostic and Statistical Manual*)-Orientated scales, lower T-scores are associated with normal functioning.

The CBCL also allows for multiple respondent comparisons to be made using another CBCL, TRF (Teacher Report Form), or YSR (Youth Self Reports).

The CBCL sample consisted of 1,753 children. The demographics in the manual indicate that 914 boys and 839 girls were used. There were 387 boys in the 6–11 age group and 527 boys in the 12–18 age group. There were 390 girls in the 6–11 age group and 449 girls in the 12–18 age group. The number of participants for each year (i.e., number of 6-year-olds, number of 7-year-olds, etc.) was not presented in the manual. For the sample, socioeconomic status was broken down to three levels with the following results: upper (33%), middle (51%), and lower (16%). In terms of ethnicity, 60% were non-Latino White, 20% were African American, 9% were Latino, and 12% were mixed/other. There were 100 sampling sites in 40 states and the District of Columbia. Of the participants, 17% were from the Northeast, 20% were from the Midwest, 40% were from the South, and 24% were from the West. Overall the sample procedures appear to be adequate and fairly representative.

Internal consistency or "split-half reliability" were moderately high and ranged from .55 to .75. For the empirically based problem scales (syndromes, Internalizing, Externalizing, and Total Problem) reliabilities were high, ranging from .78 to .98. In all cases, Total scores have the highest internal consistency. For the DSM-Orientated Scales, alphas were high as they ranged from .72 to .91. Test-retest reliability was high for most of the scales with a range of .80 to .94. The test-retest interval was 8–16 days, and the sample included children who had been referred for mental health services and those who had not.

The CBCL is very user friendly. It is easy to administer and take. A big drawback for the examiner is the time requirement and inaccuracy of hand-scoring procedures. If the computer-scoring system is used, scoring is also relatively easy.

Additional Information

Impara, J. C., & Plake, B. S. (Eds.). (1998). *The thirteenth mental measurements yearbook.* Lincoln, NE: Buros Institute of Mental Measurements.

Belter, R. W., Foster, K. Y., & Imm, P. S. (1996). Convergent validity of select scales of the MMPI and the Achenbach Child Behavior Checklist—Youth Self-Report. *Psychological Reports, 79,* 1091–1100.

Biederman, J., Monuteaux, J. C., Greene, R. W., Braaten, E., Doyle, A. E., & Faraone, S. V. (2001). Long-term stability of the Child Behavior Checklist in a clinical sample of youth with Attention-Deficit/Hyperactivity Disorder. *Journal of Clinical Child Psychology, 30,* 492–502.

Behavior Assessment System for Children—2

Authors: Cecil R. Reynolds and Randy W. Kamphaus

Ages: 2:0 to 21 (TRS and PRS); 8 to 21 (SRP). Separate SRP for college attendees available for ages 18 to 25.

Testing Time: 10 to 20 minutes

Publisher: AGS Publishing

The Behavior Assessment System for Children—2 (BASC-2, 2004) is a multimethod, multidimensional system that is used to evaluate the behavior and self-perceptions of children of ages 2 years 0 months to 21 years 11 months. It is made up of five components, each of which may be used individually or in any combination.

The Teacher Rating Scales (TRS) are a comprehensive measure of both adaptive and problem behaviors in the school setting that is intended to be filled out by teachers or others who fill a similar role. The respondent rates descriptors of behaviors on a four-point scale of frequency, ranging from Never to Almost Always. It takes 10 to 20 minutes to complete and has three forms with items targeted at three age levels: preschool (2–5), child (6–11), and adolescent (12–21). The composite scores include Externalizing Problems, Internalizing Problems, School Problems (6–21), Adaptive Skills, and a broad composite, the Behavioral Symptoms Index (BSI). The TRS has various optional content scales that assist in the interpretation of the primary BASC-2 scales and also broaden the assessment to include recent concerns in behavioral assessment (e.g., Bullying, Anger Control, evaluation of Bipolar Disorder, etc.). The TRS includes a validity check to detect a negative response set on the part of the teacher doing the rating, and a validity check that evaluates the consistency of item responses.

The Parent Rating Scales (PRS) are a comprehensive measure of a child's adaptive and problem behaviors in community and home settings. The PRS uses the same four-choice response format as the TRS and also takes 10 to 20 minutes to complete. The PRS assesses the same clinical problems and adaptive behavior domains as the TRS; however, it does not include the School Problems composite or the Learning Problems and Study Skills scales, and it includes an additional adaptive scale (Activities of Daily Living). The PRS also includes the same validity scales offered on the TRS.

The Self-Report of Personality (SRP) is a personality inventory that consists of true/false statements and four choice rating items. It takes about 20 to 30 minutes to complete and has three forms: child (ages 8–11), adolescent (ages 12–21), and college (18–25). The composite scores include School Problems, Internalizing Problems, Inattention/Hyperactivity, Personal Adjustment, and an overall composite score, the Emotional Symptoms Index (ESI), which is composed of both negative (clinical) scales and positive (adaptive) scales. Multiple indexes are incorporated to assess the validity of the child's responses. The SRP has various optional content scales to assist in the interpretation of the primary BASC-2 scales and also broaden the assessment to include recent concerns in behavioral assessment (e.g., Anger Control, Ego Strength, etc.). A version of the SRP normed in an interview format for ages 6–7 is scheduled for release in spring of 2005 (SRP-I).

The Structured Development History (SDH) is an extensive survey of a child's social and medical information. The SDH, completed by a clinician during an interview with parent or guardian, is useful in the diagnostic and treatment process. It may also be completed by the parent or other knowledgeable caregiver independently as a questionnaire.

The Student Observation System (SOS) is a form for recording a direct observation of the classroom behavior of a child. Children's positive and negative behaviors are recorded using the technique of momentary time sampling during 3-second intervals spaced 30 seconds apart over a 15-minute period. It can be used when initially assessing the child as part of the diagnostic process, and also repetitively to evaluate the effectiveness of treatment programs. An electronic version of the SOS, known as the BASC Portable Observation Program (POP) is available for PDA applications.

Parent Feedback Forms are provided for each form of the PRS, TRS, and the SRP. These explain the purpose and use of the instruments in lay language and provide a parent-oriented summary and explanation of the child or adolescent's scores along with directions for obtaining additional information.

The BASC-2 Parent Ratings Scales, Self-Report of Personality, and Structured Developmental History are available in Spanish as well as English. Audio CDs are provided in English and Spanish for the PRS and the SRP as well.

The BASC-2 composite scores are converted to T-scores that have a mean of 50 and a standard deviation of 10. The manual that accompanies the BASC-2 contains instructions for administering and scoring the TRS, PRS, and SRP, and provides information for using the SDH and SOS. It also has information on the development, appropriate uses, validity, reliability, and interpretation of all components of the BASC-2. There are three formats available for the TRS, PRS, and SRP: hand scoring, computer entry, and scannable forms. The hand-scoring forms are printed in a convenient self-scoring format, which allows them to be scored rapidly without using templates or keys. The computer-entry forms are designed to allow users to key item responses into a personal computer in about 2 to 5 minutes. The scannable forms are designed for use with mark-read (bubble) scanners.

The standardization sample was collected from over 375 testing sites that were selected to provide diversity in geographic region, socioeconomic status, and culture and ethnicity. The sample included 4,650 TRS ratings, 4,800 PRS ratings, and 3,400 SRP ratings. These samples were representative of the population according to the 2001 Current Population Survey. General education classrooms in public and private schools were targeted for data collection. Parental permission was obtained for each form collected. PRS ratings included in the norm samples were obtained from only one of the child's parents or guardians. Teachers were assigned up to four TRS ratings per classroom. This data-gathering technique resulted in substantial overlap between the norm samples for the TRS, PRS, and SRP.

The internal consistency reliability for the PRS and SRP averaged in the low to mid .80s for all three levels—preschool (P), child (C), and adolescent (A). The internal consistency was in the middle to upper .80s for the TRS. The test-retest reliability of the TRS had median values of .82, .86, and .81, and the PRS had median values of .77, .84, and .81 for the scales at the three age levels, respectively. The test-retest reliability for the SRP had median values of .71, .75, and .84 at each level.

Impressive evidence of convergent validity of the BASC-2 is based on its correlations with several other measures, including the Achenbach System of Empirically Based Assessment (ASEBA) Youth Self-Report Form (ASEBA; Achenbach & Rescorla, 2001), the Conners-Wells Adolescent Self-Report Scale (CASS; Conners, 1997), the Children's Depression Inventory (CDI; Kovacs, 2001), the Revised Children's Manifest Anxiety Scale (RCMAS; Reynolds & Richmond, 2000), the Brief Symptom Inventory (BSI; Derogatis, 1993), the Beck Depression Inventory—II (BDI-II; Beck, Steer, & Brown, 1996), and the Minnesota Multiphasic Personality Inventory—2 (MMPI-2; Butcher, Graham, Ben-Porath, Tellegen, Dahlstrom, & Kaemmer, 2001).

To aid evaluators with the interpretation of the BASC-2 results, the manual provides information regarding the profiles for the following groups: Attention-Deficit/Hyperactivity Disorder, Bipolar Disorder, Depression Disorders, Emotional/Behavioral Disturbance, Hearing Impairment, Learning Disability, Mental Retardation or Developmental Delay, Motor Impairment, Pervasive Developmental Disorders (including Asperger's and Autism), and Speech or Language Disorder.

Additional Information

Adams, C. D., & Drabman, R. S. (1994). BASC: A critical review. *Child Assessment News, 4,* 1–5.

Clausen, H. H. (2003). The clinician's guide to the Behavior Assessment System for Children. *Child Neuropsychology, 9,* 234–236.

Doyle, A., Ostrander, R., Skare, S., Crosby, R. D., & August, G. (1997). Convergent and criterion-related validity of the Behavior Assessment System for Children—Parent Rating Scales. *Journal of Clinical Child Psychology, 26,* 276–284.

Flanagan, D. P., Alfonso, V. C., Primavera, L. H., Povall, L., & Higgins, D. (1996). Convergent validity of the BASC and SSRS: Implications for social skills assessment. *Psychology in the Schools, 33,* 13–23.

Flanagan, R. (1995). A review of the Behavior Assessment System for Children (BASC): Assessment consistent with the requirements of the Individuals with Disabilities Education Act (IDEA). *Journal of School Psychology, 33,* 177–186.

Gladman, M., & Lancaster, S. (2003). A review of the Behavior Assessment System for Children. *School Psychology International, 24,* 276–291.

Kline, R. B. (1994). Test review: New objective rating scales for child assessment, I. Parent- and teacher-informant inventories of the Behavior Assessment System for Children, the Child Behavior Checklist, and the Teacher Report Form. *Journal of Psychoeducational Assessment, 12,* 289–306.

Kline, R. B. (1995). Test review: New objective rating scales for child assessment, II. Self-report scales for children and adolescents: Self-Report of Personality of the Behavior Assessment System for Children, the Youth Self-Report, and the Personality Inventory for Youth. *Journal of Psychoeducational Assessment, 13,* 169–193.

McCloskey, D. M., Hess, R. S., & D'Amato, R. C. (2003). Evaluating the utility of the Spanish version of the Behavior Assessment System for Children—Parent Report System. *Journal of Psychoeducational Assessment, 21,* 325–337.

Sandoval, J. (1998). Review of the Behavior Assessment System for Children. In J. C. Impara & B. S. Plake (Eds.), *The thirteenth mental measurements yearbook* (pp. 128–131). Lincoln, NE: Buros Institute of Mental Measurements.

Wilder, L. K., & Sudweeks, R. R. (2003). Reliability of ratings across studies of the BASC. *Education & Treatment of Children, 26,* 382–399.

Witt, J. C., & Jones, K. M. (1998). Review of the Behavior Assessment System for Children. In J. C. Impara & B. S. Plake (Eds.), *The thirteenth mental measurements yearbook* (pp. 131–133). Lincoln, NE: Buros Institute of Mental Measurements.

Behavioral and Emotional Rating Scale

Authors: Michael H. Epstein and Jennifer M. Sharma
Ages: 5:0 through 18:11
Testing Time: 10 minutes
Publisher: PRO-ED

The Behavioral and Emotional Rating Scale: A Strength-Based Approach to Assessment (BERS, 1998) is an individually administered 52-item scale that assesses children's (ages 5:0 through 18:11) emotional and behavioral strengths in five factor-analytically derived subscales. The first subscale, Interpersonal Strengths (e.g., "Uses anger management skills"; 15 items), assesses a child's ability to control emotions or behavior in a social situation. The second subscale, Family Involvement (e.g., "Participates in family activities"; 10 items), focuses on a child's participation and relationship with his or her family. The third subscale, Intrapersonal Strengths (e.g., "Demonstrates a sense of humor"; 11 items), assesses a child's outlook on his or her competence and accomplishments. Subscale four, School Functioning (e.g., "Completes homework regularly"; 9 items), focuses on a child's competence in school and classroom tasks. The fifth subscale, Affective Strengths (e.g., "Asks for help"; 7 items), addresses a child's ability to express feelings toward others and to accept affection from others.

A teacher, caregiver, or any adult knowledgeable about the child can complete the BERS, although there is only one form. The adult reads a phrase (e.g., "participates in family activities") and chooses the number on a Likert-type scale from 0 to 3 (0 = not at all like the child; 1 = not much like the child; 2 = like the child; 3 = very much like the child) that best represents the child's emotions or behaviors in the past 3 months. Respondents are also asked to complete eight open-ended questions about the child's personal and situational resiliencies and protective factors (e.g., "What are the child's favorite hobbies or activities?", "Who is this child's favorite teacher?"). Information obtained from the BERS is useful in the development of individualized education programs (IEPs), treatment or intervention planning, and evaluation of a program or treatment plan.

Raw scores from the five subscales can be converted to percentile ranks and to standard scores with a mean of 10 and a standard deviation of 3. Summing the standard scores of the five subscales and converting the sum into a quotient derives an overall "Strength Quotient" with a mean of 100 and a standard deviation of 15.

The BERS was normed on students between the ages of 5:0 and 18:11 using data collected from February to November 1996. Separate norms were produced for 2,176 students without disabilities and 861 students with emotional and behavioral disorders. The manual reports demographics of this standardization sample based on age, gender, geographic location, race, ethnicity, and socioeconomic status. Based on these data, separate male and female norms for children without disabilities and separate male and female norms for children with emotional and behavioral disorders were calculated. Although the BERS covers the age range of 5 to 18, there are no separate age-based norm tables in the manual.

The interrater reliability of the BERS was tested on nine pairs of teachers and classroom aides who were asked to complete the BERS on 96 students previously diagnosed with emotional or behavioral disorders. Correlations between the two raters on the five subscale and overall BERS scores were between .83 and .98. Content sampling revealed that items on the BERS correlate above .80, making it a highly reliable scale. The test-retest reliability was tested on seven special education teachers who were asked to complete the BERS on 10 of their students and then, approximately 2 weeks later, again asked to complete the BERS on the same students. Correlations between the two sets of ratings on the five subscale and overall BERS scores were between .85 and .99. Evidence for criterion validity is moderate to high based on the relationship between the BERS and the Teacher Report Form (Achenbach, 1991), the Self-Perception Profile for Children (Harter, 1985), and the Walker-McConnell Scale of Social Competence and School Adjustment (Walker & McConnell, 1988). Construct validity was confirmed through statistically different scores on the mean scores of the nondisordered and disordered children used to norm the scale.

Additional Information

Achenbach, T. M. (1991). *Manual for the Teacher Report Form and 1991 profile.* Burlington, VT: University of Vermont, Department of Psychiatry.

Dumont, R., & Rauch, M. (2003). Test review: Behavioral and Emotional Rating Scale by M. Epstein & J. Sharma (PRO-ED, 1998). *NASP Communiqué, 28,* article 7. Retrieved May 22, 2004, from www.nasponline.org/publications/cq287Test.html.

Epstein, M. H. (1998). Assessing the emotional and behavioral strengths of children. *Reclaiming Children and Youth, 6,* 250–252.

Epstein, M. H., Harniss, M. K., Pearson, N., & Ryder, G. (1999). The Behavioral and Emotional Rating Scale: Test-retest and inter-rater reliability. *Journal of Child and Family Studies, 8,* 319–327.

Epstein, M. H., & Sharma, J. (1998). *Behavioral and Emotional Rating Scale: A strength based approach to assessment.* Austin, TX: PRO-ED.

Friedman, P., Friedman, K. A., & Weaver, V. (2003). Strength-based assessment of African-American adolescents with behavioral disorders. *Perceptual & Motor Skills, 96,* 667–673.

Harter, S. (1985). *Manual for the Self-Perception Profile for Children.* Denver, CO: University of Denver.

Quay, H., & Peterson, D. R. (1996). *Revised Behavior Problem Checklist: Professional manual.* Odessa, FL: Psychological Assessment Resources.

Trout, A. L., Ryan, J. B., & La Vigne, S. P. (2003). Behavioral and Emotional Rating Scale: Two studies of convergent validity. *Journal of Child & Family Studies, 12,* 399–410.

Walker, H. M., & McConnell, S. R. (1988). *Manual for the Walker-McConnell Scale of Social Competence and School Adjustment.* Austin, TX: PRO-ED.

http://www.air.org/cecp/interact/expertonline/strength/transition/3.htm (Test review and case study by Mark Epstein and Susan Randolph at the Center for Effective Collaboration and Practice)

Conners Parent Rating Scales—Revised, Conners Teacher Rating Scales—Revised, and Conners-Wells Adolescent Self-Report Scale

Author: C. Keith Conners

Ages: 3 to 17

Testing Time: 15 to 25 minutes

Publisher: Multi-Health Systems

The revised Conners rating scale follows the original aims of the earlier version in assessing Attention-Deficit/Hyperactivity Disorder (ADHD; Conners, 1997). Both the Conners Parent Rating Scales Revised (CPRS-R:L and CPRS-R:S) and the Conners Teacher Rating Scales Revised (CTRS-R:L and CTRS-R:S) are designed to assess ADHD and related behavioral problems, including cognitive problems, family problems, emotional problems, anger control problems, and anxiety problems for children aged 3 to 17. These measures should be used as an ancillary source of information rather than the sole means of diagnosing ADHD. Because ADHD treatments have differential efficacy depending on the *Diagnostic and Statistical Manual of Mental Disorders,* fourth edition (DSM-IV) subtype (Inattentive, Hyperactive, or Combined), the ability of the Conners scales to assist in this differential is important. They have been shown to be usable as screening tools but not as the primary methods of diagnosis or of distinguishing between ADHD subtypes (Hale, How, Dewitt, & Coury, 2001).

Both the parent and teacher measures are available as a long form and a short form. The long forms for both parent (CPRS-R:L) and teacher (CTRS-R:L) scales include Oppositional, Cognitive Problems, Hyperactivity, Anxious-Shy, Perfectionism, Social Problems, the Conners Global Index, Restless-Impulsive, Emotional Lability, *DSM-IV* symptom subscales including *DSM-IV* Inattentive and *DSM-IV* Hyperactive-Impulsive. For the parent scale, there is an additional Psychosomatic scale. The CPRS-R:L contains 80 items, and the CTRS-R:L contains 59 items. Each takes approximately 20 minutes to complete.

The short forms of the parent (CPRS-R:S) and teacher (CTRS-R:S) scales include Oppositional, Cognitive Problems, and Hyperactivity scales and the ADHD Index. The CPRS-R:S contains 27 items, and the CTRS-R:S contains 28 items. Each takes under 10 minutes to complete. Both the short and long forms have questions in a Likert 4-point scale (from "never" to "very often").

The CPRS-R:L was normed on parents or guardians of 2,482 children ages 3 to 17. Eighty-three percent of the children were Caucasian, but the normative sample also included African Americans, Hispanics, Asian Americans, Native Americans, and others. Gender distribution was approximately equal. Internal reliability (Cronbach's alpha coefficient) is reported for each scale by gender and ranged from .73 to .94. Test-retest intervals between 6 and 8 weeks were studied for each subscale using 49 children (average age 11.8) and ranged from .47 to .85.

The CTRS-R:L was normed on teachers of 1,973 children ages 3 to 17. Seventy-eight percent of the adolescents were identified by teachers as Caucasian. Test-retest intervals between 6 and 8 weeks were studied for each subscale using 50 children (average age 11.2) and ranged from .47 to .88. CTRS-R:L internal reliability (Cronbach's alpha coefficient) is reported for each scale, divided by gender, and ranged from .77 to .96. Test-retest reliability ranged from .62 to .87 (Danforth & DuPaul, 1996).

The validity of this measure was determined by its ability to discriminate between clinically referred and nonreferred children (Miller, Koplewiccz, & Klein, 1997). Correlations (concurrent validity) between parent and teacher ratings for individual subscales ranged from .12 to .47 for males and .21 and .55 for females, indicating that teacher and parent raters often perceived the same children quite differently.

The Conners-Wells Adolescent Self-Report Scales (CASS-L and CASS-S) are new additions to the parent and teacher rating scales. The long form (CASS-L) contains 10 subscales including Family Problems, Emotional Problems, Conduct Problems, Cognitive Problems, Anger Control Problems, Hyperactivity, ADHD Index, and *DSM-IV* Subscales including *DSM-IV* Inattentive and *DSM-IV* Hyperactive-Impulsive, and takes approximately 20 minutes to complete.

The CASS-L contains 87 items that are rated using an adapted Likert 4-point scale (from "never" to "very often") by adolescents between 12 and 17 years of age. The CASS-L was normed on 3,394 adolescents between the ages of 12 and 17 (1,558 males and 1,846 females). Sixty-two percent of this sample was Caucasian. Internal reliability (Cronbach's alpha coefficient) is reported for each scale by gender and ranged from .75 to .92. Test-retest intervals between 6 and 8 weeks were studied for each subscale using 50 children (mean age 14.8) and ranged from .73 to .89.

The CASS-S contains 27 items and takes under 10 minutes. It contains subscales that closely follow the short forms for parents and teachers and include Conduct Problems, Cognitive Problems, Hyperactive-Impulsive, and an ADHD Index.

Additional Information

Reviewed in Plake, B. S., & Impara, J. C. (Eds.). (2001). *The fourteenth mental measurements yearbook.* Lincoln, NE: Buros Institute of Mental Measurements.

Conners, C. K. (1997). *Conners Rating Scales—Revised technical manual.* North Tonawanda, NY: Multi-Health Systems.

Conners, C. K. (1999). Conners Rating Scales—Revised. In M. E. Maruish, *Use of psychological testing for treatment planning and outcomes assessment* (2nd ed.; pp. 467–495). Mahwah, NJ: Lawrence Erlbaum Associates.

Danforth, J. S., & DuPaul, G. J. (1996). Interrater reliability of teacher rating scales for children with Attention-Deficit/Hyperactivity Disorder. *Journal of Psychopathology & Behavioral Assessment, 3,* 227–237.

Hale, J. B., How, S. K., Dewitt, M. B., & Coury, Daniel L. (2001). Discriminant validity of the Conners Scales for ADHD Subtypes. *Current Psychology, 20,* 231–250.

Miller, L. S., Koplewiccz, H. S., & Klein, R. G. (1997). Teachers' ratings of hyperactivity, inattention, and conduct problems in preschoolers. *Journal of Abnormal Child Psychology, 2,* 113–119.

Devereux Behavior Rating Scale—School Form

Authors: Jack A. Naglieri, Paul A. LeBuffe, and Steven I. Pfeiffer
Ages: 5 to 18
Testing Time: 5 minutes
Publisher: The Psychological Corporation

The Devereux Behavior Rating Scale—School Form (DSF) is based on federal criteria and is designed to evaluate behaviors of children and adolescents that may be indicative of moderate to severe emotional disturbances. This instrument is also useful for providing normative comparisons of behavior and for comparative results from different informants (e.g., parents and teachers). It is used for assessing a child or adolescent in a variety of settings. The information derived from the DSF can be used for treatment planning and for the evaluation of pre/post measures of treatment. It is effective in evaluating progress during educational interventions and can be helpful in determining whether a child or adolescent should be placed in a special education program due to a serious emotional disturbance. The DSF has two forms that include separate sets of items appropriate for children ages 5 to 12 and for adolescents ages 13 to 18. The scale includes 40 items consisting of four subscales that address areas identified in the federal definition of Serious Emotional Disturbance. The areas are Interpersonal Problems, Inappropriate Behaviors/Feelings, Depression, and Physical Symptoms/Fears. It takes approximately 5 minutes to administer.

The DSF results are compared to a nationally standardized sample of more than 3,000 cases that are approximated closely to the 1990 census data on all demographic variables. There are separate norms for age and sex for both parent and teacher raters. The form is easy to administer and score, with items and directions written at the sixth-grade reading level. There is multilevel analysis and interpretation, with the Total Scale Score and Subscale Scores assisting the evaluator in eligibility determination. The Subscale Scores help facilitate IEP planning and the design of preferred intervention. The Problem Item Scores help to identify specific behavioral problems for treatment.

The DSF internal consistency estimates are calculated according to age and gender, age and rater, and age, rater, and gender. The DSF Total Scale internal reliability coefficients range from .92 (parent ratings for females aged 13–18) to .97 (teacher ratings for males and females aged 5–12). The median Total Scale reliability coefficients by age are .96 (ages 5–12) and .94 (ages 13–18), by gender, .95 (males) and .94 (females), and by rater, .93 (parents) and .96 (teachers). The median internal reliability coefficients for the four subscales across rater, gender, and age are .85 (Interpersonal Problems), .84 (Inappropriate Behaviors/Feelings), .84 (Depression), and .82 (Physical Symptoms/Fears). The median reliability coefficient across all subscales, age, rater, and gender is .84. The DSF has very good test-retest reliability (24 hours, 2 weeks, and 4 weeks) and interrater reliability.

The construct-related validity of the DSF indicate that all item total correlations are significant ($p < .01$) and clearly indicate that the items are highly correlated to the total score. A considerable amount of data was collected and evaluated by the authors to determine the criterion-related validity of the DSF. The examination included ratings of regular education children and adolescents compared to seriously emotionally disturbed children and adolescents from a number of different settings. In addition, another study examined whether the criterion-related validity of the DSF could be generalized to racial or ethnic subpopulations. Results based on this study support the DSF's usefulness in screening for serious emotional disturbances and suggest that the criterion-related validity is generalizable to Caucasian, African American, and Hispanic children (Goh, 1997).

Additional Information

Reviewed in Impara, J. C., & Plake, B. S. (Eds.). (1998). *The thirteenth mental measurements yearbook.* Lincoln, NE: Buros Institute of Mental Measurements.

Floyd, R. G., & Bose, J. E. (2003). Behavior rating scales for assessment of emotional disturbance: A critical review of measurement characteristics. *Journal of Psychoeducational Assessment, 21,* 43–78.

Gimpel, G. A., & Nagle, R. J. (1996). Factorial validity of the Devereux Behavior Rating Scale—School Form. *Journal of Psychoeducational Assessment, 14,* 334–348.

Goh, D. S. (1997). Clinical utility of the Devereux Behavior Rating Scale: School Form among culturally diverse children. *Psychology in the Schools, 34,* 301–308.

Naglieri, J. A., LeBuffe, P. A., & Pfeiffer, S. I. (1993). *Devereux Behavior Rating Scale—School Form test manual.* San Antonio, TX: The Psychological Corporation.

Naglieri, J. A., & Gottling, S. H. (1995). Use of the Teacher Report Form and the Devereux Behavior Rating Scale—School Form with learning disordered/emotionally disordered students. *Journal of Clinical Child Psychology, 24,* 71–76.

Nickerson, A. B., & Nagle, R. J. (2001). Interrater reliability of the Devereux Behavior Rating Scale—School Form: The influence of teacher frame of reference. *Journal of Psychoeducational Assessment, 19,* 299–316.

Devereux Scales of Mental Disorders

Authors: Jack A. Naglieri, Paul A. LeBuffe, and Steven I. Pfeiffer

Ages: 5 to 18

Testing Time: 15 minutes

Publisher: The Psychological Corporation

The Devereux Scales of Mental Disorders (DSMD, 1994) are designed to assess whether a child or adolescent is experiencing, or is at risk for, psychopathology, including externalizing disorders (attention/delinquency and conduct scales), internalizing disorders (anxiety and depression scales), and critical pathology disorders (acute problems and autism scales). It is useful for evaluating treatment effectiveness and in analyzing information for treatment planning. The DSMD has two levels: a 111-item child form for ages 5 to 12 and a 110-item adolescent form for ages 13 to 18. The content of the items is based on the diagnostic criteria of the *DSM-IV*. The DSMD takes 15 minutes to complete, and the rater can be any adult who has known the child for at least 4 weeks. Parent and teacher raters use the same form, with separate norms provided for each. The scales are easily completed, scored, and interpreted and are written at the sixth-grade reading level. Items are rated on a 5-point Likert-type scale ranging from 0 ("never") to 4 ("very frequently").

The DSMD can be hand scored or computer scored, and it helps professionals assess behavior in a variety of settings. The results are compared to a national standardized sample of more than 3,000 cases approximated closely to the 1990 census. There are separate norms for females and males. The DSMD scoring method allows professionals to compare DSMD scores of the same child or adolescent at different points in time during treatment.

The DSMD Total Score internal consistency coefficients were .98 by age, .98 by gender, and .97 (parents) and .98 (teachers) by rater. The median reliability coefficients for the composite scales on the child form are .97 (Externalizing), .94 (Internalizing), and .90 (Critical Pathology). For the six scale scores on the child form, the median reliability coefficients are .96 (Conduct), .84 (Attention), .88 (Anxiety), .89 (Depression), .90 (Autism), and .78 (Acute Problems). The median reliability coefficients for the composite scales on the adolescent form are .94 (Externalizing), .96 (Internalizing), and .92 (Critical Pathology). For the six scale scores on the adolescent form, the median reliability coefficients are .96 (Conduct), .75 (Delinquency), .84 (Anxiety), .93 (Depression), .88 (Autism), and .90 (Acute Problems). The DSMD has good test-retest (24-hour and 1-week intervals) and interrater reliability.

The DSMD authors have cited in the test manual numerous studies that provide support for the DSMD's differential validity including adolescents diagnosed with anxiety disorders, conduct disorders, and depressive disorders. In addition, the DSMD T-scores are distinguished between children and adolescents with psychiatric diagnoses and nonclinical children and adolescents. Other studies have found the DSMD to be able to differentiate between inpatient children and adolescents diagnosed with ADHD and those with a Conduct Disorder diagnosis, and the DSMD Composite and Subscales Scales accurately differentiate between inpatient children and adolescents diagnosed with depressive disorders, disruptive disorders, and psychotic disorders. The DSMD has been reported to produce greater classification accuracy than the REIS Scales and the Teacher Report Form (TRF) in finding behavioral and emotional disturbances in children and adolescents with mental retardation. The DSMD also has been found to have higher specificity and positive predictive power than the TRF when evaluating serious emotional problems in children and adolescents (Smith & Reddy, 2000). The DSMD was also compared to the Child Behavior Checklist (CBCL) for diagnostic classification accuracy in adolescents. The DSMD and CBCL were comparable in classifying oppositional or conduct disorder, the CBCL was superior for classifying major depression, and the DSMD was superior for classification of substance abuse (Curry & Ilardi, 2000).

Additional Information

Reviewed in Plake, B. S., & Impara, J. C. (Eds.). (2001). *The fourteenth mental measurements yearbook.* Lincoln, NE: Buros Institute of Mental Measurements.

Curry, J. F., & Ilardi, S. S. (2000). Validity of the Devereux Scales of Mental Disorders with adolescent psychiatric inpatients. *Journal of Clinical Child Psychology, 29,* 578–588.

Gimpel, G. A., & Nagle, R. J. (1999). Psychometric properties of the Devereux Scales of Mental Disorders. *Journal of Psychoeducational Assessment, 17,* 127–144.

Naglieri, J. A., LeBuffe, P. A., & Pfieffer, S. I. (1994). *The Devereux Scales of Mental Disorders test manual.* San Antonio, TX: Psychological Corporation.

Smith, S. R., & Reddy, L. A. (2000). A test review of the Devereux Scales of Mental Disorders. *Canadian Journal of School Psychology, 15,* 85–91.

Smith, S. R., & Reddy, L. A. (2002). The concurrent validity of the Devereux Scales of Mental Disorders. *Journal of Psychoeducational Assessment, 20,* 112–127.

Smith, S. R., Reddy, L. A., & Wingenfeld, S. A. (2002). Assessment of psychotic disorders in inpatient children and adolescents: Use of the Devereux Scales of Mental Disorders. *Journal of Psychopathology & Behavioral Assessment, 24,* 269–273.

Smith, S. R., Wingenfeld, S. A., & Hilsenroth, M. J. (2002). The use of the Devereux Scales of Mental Disorders in the assessment of Attention-Deficit/Hyperactivity Disorder and Conduct Disorder. *Journal of Psychopathology & Behavioral Assessment, 22,* 237–255.

Scale for Assessing Emotional Disturbance

Authors: Michael H. Epstein and Jennifer M. Sharma
Ages: 5:0 through 18:11
Testing Time: 10 minutes
Publisher: PRO-ED

The Scale for Assessing Emotional Disturbance (SAED) is an individually administered, 52-item measure of emotional and/or behavioral disturbance in children ages 5 through 18. The four-page response form can be completed in approximately 10 minutes by caregivers, counselors, teachers, or other persons knowledgeable about the child. The scale has three sections. The first is Student Competence

Characteristics, in which the adult rater compares this child to other students of the same age on a scale of 0 to 4 (0 = far below average, 4 = far above average) in categories such as family support, level of academic achievement, and motivation. The second section is Student Emotional and Behavioral Problems, in which the rater reads a statement (e.g., "makes threats to others") and chooses the number on a scale from 0 to 3 (0 = not at all like the child, 3 = very much like the child) that best represents the child's emotions and behaviors in the past 2 months. The final section is Adversely Affects Education Performance, in which the rater judges the extent to which the student's educational performance is affected by emotional and behavioral problems on a scale of 0 to 5 (0 = not adversely affected, 5 = affected to an extreme extent). The SAED also includes eight open-ended questions that address the child's situational and personal resiliencies and protective factors (e.g., "In what school subject[s] does the child do best?" or "What job[s] or responsibilities has this student held in the community or in the home?"). The scale provides an overall emotional and behavioral functioning SAED Quotient and percentile rank, and seven subscale scores measuring Inability to Learn, Relationship Problems, Inappropriate Behavior, Unhappiness or Depression, Physical Symptoms or Fears, Social Maladjusted, and Overall Competence. Information obtained from the SAED is useful in identifying children with emotional disturbance; in developing IEPs, treatment, or intervention planning; and in evaluation of a program or treatment plan.

The SAED was normed on students between the ages of 5:0 and 18:11 using data collected from January 1996 to May 1997. Separate norms were produced for 2,266 students without disabilities and 1,371 students with emotional and behavioral disorders. (No explanation whatsoever is given about how these 1,371 children came to be classified as emotionally disordered.) The manual reports demographics of this standardization sample based on age, gender, geographic location, race, ethnicity, and socioeconomic status.

Scores on the seven subtests are presented in standard scores with a mean of 10 and standard deviation of 3. The overall SAED quotient score has a mean of 100 and a standard deviation of 15.

The interrater reliability of the SAED was tested on six pairs of teachers who were asked to complete the SAED on 44 students previously diagnosed with emotional or behavioral disorders. Correlations between the two raters on the seven subscales and overall SAED scores were around .80. Content sampling revealed that items on the SAED correlate above .75, making it a highly reliable scale. The test-retest reliability was determined by SAED scores for special education children whose teachers rated them twice with about 2 weeks between each rating. Correlations between the two sets of ratings on the seven subscales and overall SAED quotient were between .84 and .94. The SAED was deemed to have criterion validity based on the positive relationships between the SAED and the Teacher Report Form (Achenbach, 1991) and the SAED and the Revised Behavior Problem Checklist (Quay & Peterson, 1996). Construct validity was confirmed through statistically significant differences between the mean scores of the nondisordered and disordered children used to norm the scale.

Additional Information

Achenbach, T. M. (1991). *Manual for the Teacher Reports Form and 1991 profile.* Burlington, VT: University of Vermont, Department of Psychiatry.

Cullinan, D., Evans, C., & Epstein, M. H. (2003), Characteristics of emotional disturbance of elementary school students. *Behavioral Disorders, 28,* 94–110.

Dumont, R., & Rauch, M. (2000). Test review: Scale for Assessing Emotional Disturbance by M. Epstein & D. Cullinan (PRO-ED, 1998). *NASP Communiqué, 28,* article 8. Retrieved May 22, 2004, from http://www.nasponline.org/publications/cq288SAED.html

Epstein, M. H., Cullinan, D., & Ryser, G. (2002) Development of a scale to assess emotional disturbance. *Behavioral Disorders, 28,* 5–22.

Epstein, M. H., & Cullinan, D. (1998) *The Scale for Assessing Emotional Disturbance.* Austin, TX: PRO-ED.

Floyd, R. G., & Bose, J. E. (2003) Behavior rating scales for assessment of emotional disturbance: A critical review of measurement characteristics. *Journal of Psychoeducational Assessment, 21,* 43–78.

Quay, H., & Peterson, D. R. (1996). *Revised Behavior Problem Checklist: Professional manual.* Odessa, FL: Psychological Assessment Resources.

COGNITIVE ABILITY

Beta III

Authors: C. E. Kellogg and N. W. Morton
Ages: 16 through 89
Testing Time: 30 minutes
Publisher: The Psychological Corporation

The Beta III (1999) provides a quick assessment of adults' (aged 16–89) nonverbal intellectual capabilities, including visual information processing, spatial and nonverbal reasoning, processing speed, and aspects of fluid intelligence. It is easily administered and hand scored either individually or in a group and requires only 30 minutes to complete. It is useful for screening large populations of people for whom administering comprehensive test batteries would be difficult, including low-functioning or low-skilled individuals, and is ideal for use in prison systems, companies, and schools. Administration instructions for the Beta III are available in English or Spanish, making it one of the most comprehensive of language-free and culture-fair tests.

Beta III is the updated version of the Revised Beta Examination, Second Edition, which was published in 1974. It features new norms, contemporary and larger artwork, new items, new subtest (Matrix Reasoning), extended age range, low floors for individuals with average and lower cognitive abilities, and higher ceiling with more challenging items. Five subtests make up the Beta III: Coding, which contains code symbols with numbers that are assigned to the symbols at the top of the page; Picture Completion, which requires the subject to draw in what is missing to complete the picture; Clerical Checking, which entails circling an "equal" or a "not equal" symbol depending on whether pairs of pictures, symbols, or numbers are the same or different; Picture Absurdities, where the subject is asked to place an "X" on the one picture out of four that shows something wrong or foolish; and Matrix Reasoning, which requires the subject to choose the missing symbol or picture that best completes a set of symbols or pictures.

Extensive reliability and validity studies have been conducted with Beta III. The test was normed on a sample of 1,260 adults, including people with Mental Retardation and more than 400 prison inmates. The sample was representative of the 1997 U.S. census data with respect to age, gender, race/ethnicity, educational level, and geographic region. Beta III was validated using other well-known tests, including the WAIS-III, ABLE-II, Raven's Standard Progressive Matrices, Revised Minnesota Paper Form Board Test (RMPFBT), Personnel Tests for Industry—Oral Direction Test (PTI-ODT), Bennett Mechanical Comprehensive Test (BMCT), and Revised Beta Examination, Second Edition (Beta II).

Additional Information

Reviews of this test are pending for *The Sixteenth Mental Measurements Yearbook.*

McCallum, S., Bracken, B., & Wasserman, J. (2000). *Essentials of nonverbal assessment.* New York: Wiley.

Bilingual Verbal Ability Tests

Authors: Ana F. Muñoz-Sandoval, Jim Cummins, Criselda G. Alvarado, and Mary L. Ruef

Ages: 5 to adult

Testing Time: 30 minutes

Publisher: Riverside Publishing

The Bilingual Verbal Ability Tests (BVAT) are designed to provide a measure of overall verbal ability and a unique combination of cognitive/academic language abilities for bilingual individuals.

The BVAT comprises three individually administered subtests: (1) Picture Vocabulary, in which the subject is required to name a pictured object with gradually increasing degrees of difficulty; (2) Oral Vocabulary, which is broken into two tasks: Synonyms, where the subject is required to make a synonymous word association with gradually increasing difficulty; and Antonyms, where the subject is required to make an opposite word association with gradually increasing degrees of difficulty; and (3) Verbal Analogies, where the subject is required to recognize the analogous relationships between two words and to find a third word that bears the same relationship.

All the subtests are administered first in the English language. Each item failed in English is readministered in the native language. If the child answers correctly in his or her native language, that score is added to the score for that subtest. The overall subtest score is based on the child's knowledge or reasoning skills using both languages, thus reflecting the nature of the bilingual ability.

These tests are drawn from the Woodcock-Johnson—Revised (WJ-R; 1989) Cognitive (COG) Battery and translated into 15 different languages, presumably the most widely used languages in the United States: Arabic, Chinese (Simplified and Traditional), English, French, German, Haitian-Creole, Hindi, Hmong, Italian, Japanese, Korean, Navajo, Polish, Portuguese, Russian, Spanish, Turkish, and Vietnamese. These three subtests have been translated from English into 18 languages.

There are two basic options for the BVAT interpretation: age based or grade based. In addition to standard scores, the Relative Proficiency Index (the same indicator as the Relative Mastery Index in the WJ-R), and percentile ranks, the BVAT offers an "instructional zones" index, five levels of English-language proficiency (Negligible, Very Limited, Limited, Fluent, and Advanced), and aptitude/achievement discrepancies in relation to the WJ-R Achievement Tests. All scoring is automated through the Scoring and Reporting Program software, which is a standard feature of the BVAT kit. The BVAT Comprehensive Manual contains the Examiner Training and Practice Exercises. A training videotape, prepared by the publisher, accompanies the test.

The BVAT provides an overall score (BVA) that can be used to determine an individual's overall level of verbal ability. Raw scores are converted to standard scores, percentile ranks, age and grade equivalents, relative proficiency index, instructional ranges, and cognitive-academic language proficiency (CALP) levels.

U.S. normative data for the BVAT on 5,602 subjects was obtained during WJ-R COG standardization (1988–89). Reliability was calculated through a split-half procedure corrected for length by the Spearman-Brown formula and resulted in reliability coefficients in the high .80s for the subtests and in the mid-.90s for the clusters. Construct validity was reported within the .7 to .9 range.

Some of the 15 languages have deleted items (sometimes up to four items) because of the "untranslatable" nature of these items (see Table 8-5, p. 71 in the test manual). It is not clear what effect it may have on the scores obtained if they are based on norms that include all items. Another aspect of the content validity is the issue of uneven complexity (from a relatively easy naming task in Picture Vocabulary to a much more difficult verbal reasoning task in Verbal Analogies).

Additional Information

Reviewed in Plake, B. S., & Impara, J. C. (Eds.). (2001). *The fourteenth mental measurements yearbook.* Lincoln, NE: Buros Institute of Mental Measurements.

http://www.bgcenter.com/BVAT1.htm

http://ldn.tamu.edu/archives/studprojs/BVAT.ppt

http://www.utpjournals.com/jour.ihtml?lp=product/cmlr/572/Bilingual4.html

http://www.iapsych.com/bvatrr.pdf

Cognitive Assessment System

Authors: Jack Naglieri and J. P. Das
Ages: 5:0 to 17:11
Testing Time: 45 to 60 minutes
Publisher: Riverside Publishing

The Cognitive Assessment System (CAS; Naglieri & Das, 1997a) is a test of cognitive ability. It is administered individually and was created for children ages 5 years through 17 years and 11 months. The test comprises a total of 12 subtests and can be administered in two forms. The Standard battery consists of all 12 subtests, while the Basic battery is made up of 8 subtests. Administration time is 60 minutes and 45 minutes, respectively.

The CAS was created as a tool for professionals to complete clinical, psychoeducational, and neuropsychological evaluations and is based on the PASS model. The PASS theory is represented by four scales on the CAS, specifically Planning, Attention, Simultaneous, and Successive cognitive processes (PASS). The first process, Planning, is an individual's ability to conceptualize and then apply the proper strategies to successfully complete a novel task. Essentially, the individual must be able to determine, select, and then use a strategy to efficiently solve a problem. Attention is a cognitive process by which an individual focuses on one cognitive process while excluding extraneous competing stimuli. The third process, Simultaneous processing, is the integration of stimuli into a coherent whole. Fourth is Successive processing, which involves organizing various things into a specific sequential order. A Full Scale score can also be obtained from the data.

Standard scores are provided for all subtests, with a mean of 10 and a standard deviation of 3. The four scales, along with the Full Scale score, are also reported as standard scores, and have a mean of 100 and a standard deviation of 15.

The CAS was standardized on a stratified random sample of 2,200 American children and adolescents aged 5 years 0 months to 17 years 11 months, using the 1990 census data. Strata included race, gender, region, community setting, educational classification, classroom placement, and parent education. A total of 240 examiners were utilized for standardization, along with 68 sites.

Reliability data are impressive. Median internal consistency reliabilities for the Full Scale are .96 on the Standard battery and .87 on the Basic battery. Internal consistency for the scales is also very good; reliability coefficients range from .88 to .93. Median test-retest reliability coefficients for the Basic and Standard batteries are .82. Studies investigating the criterion validity of the CAS have generally shown that the CAS does not sufficiently correlate with other measures of cognitive ability. Because many of these measures are based on the Cattell-Horn-Carroll theory, these results are seen by some as lending evidence to the assertion that the CAS is an alternative way of validly conceptualizing intelligence.

Overall, the CAS is a well-standardized instrument. Because the test is based on the PASS theory and differs from other assessment tools, it may offer a different context through which measures of intelligence can be measured and thought of. It has also been suggested that the CAS has implications that are important in the learning environment. Although the CAS demonstrates assets, it does have limitations. In particular, caution must be exercised when using the data for interpretation. There is much overlap within the Attention scale and the Planning scale, so it may be difficult to separately interpret their results. Despite the fact that Naglieri and Das provide factor analytic evidence to support the CAS and the PASS model, further validation is needed.

Additional Information

Reviewed in Plake, B. S., & Impara, J. C. (Eds.). (2001). *The fourteenth mental measurements yearbook.* Lincoln, NE: Buros Institute of Mental Measurements.

Hildebrand, D. K., & Sattler, J. M. (2001). Cognitive Assessment System. In

J. M. Sattler, *Assessment of children: Cognitive applications* (4th ed., pp. 548–550). San Diego, CA: Jerome M. Sattler.

Keith, T. Z., Kranzler, J. H., & Flanagan, D. P. (2001). What does the Cognitive Assessment System (CAS) measure? Joint confirmatory factor analysis of the CAS and the Woodcock-Johnson Tests of Cognitive Ability (3rd Edition). *School Psychology Review, 30,* 89–119.

Kranzler, J. H., & Keith, T. Z. (1999). Independent confirmatory factor analysis of the Cognitive Assessment System (CAS): What does CAS measure? *School Psychology Review, 28,* 117.

Naglieri, J. A. (1999). How valid is the PASS theory and CAS? *School Psychology Review, 28,* 145.

Naglieri, J. A., & Das, J. P. (1997a). *Cognitive Assessment System.* Chicago: Riverside Publishing.

Naglieri, J. A., & Das, J. P. (1997b). *Cognitive Assessment System: Interpretive handbook.* Chicago: Riverside Publishing.

Comprehensive Test of Nonverbal Intelligence

Authors: Donald D. Hammill, Nils A. Pearson, and J. Lee Wiederholt
Ages: 6:0 through 90
Administration Time: 1 hour
Publisher: PRO-ED

The Comprehensive Test of Nonverbal Intelligence (CTONI, 1997) measures nonverbal reasoning abilities of individuals aged 6 through 90 for whom other tests may be inappropriate or biased. Because CTONI contains no oral responses, reading, writing, or object manipulation it is particularly appropriate for students who are bilingual, speak a language other than English, or are socially or economically disadvantaged, deaf, language disordered, motor impaired, or neurologically impaired. The CTONI should not be administered to people with vision problems. It is easy to administer and score and requires only 1 hour to complete. The CTONI instructions can be administered orally to students who speak English or in pantomime for those who speak languages other than English or who are deaf, aphasic, or neurologically impaired. One criticism has been that the CTONI manual does not provide information about whether the test was standardized using pantomime, oral, or computerized administration.

The CTONI measures analogical reasoning, categorical classifications, and sequential reasoning in two different contexts: pictures of familiar objects (people, toys, and animals) and geometric designs (unfamiliar sketches, patterns, and drawings). There are six subtests in total. Three subtests use pictured objects while three use geometric designs. Each subtest contains 25 items. Examinees indicate their answers by pointing to alternative choices. In addition to raw scores, standard scores, percentiles, and age equivalents, CTONI also provides three composite IQ scores: Nonverbal Intelligence Quotient, Pictorial Nonverbal Intelligence Quotient, and Geometric Nonverbal Intelligence Quotient. Items have been carefully reviewed to protect against bias in regard to race, gender, ethnicity, and language.

The CTONI was normed on a sample of over 2,901 individuals from America in two samples (2,129 in 1995 and 772 in 1996) and is representative of the 1990 *Statistical Abstract of the United States* with respect to age, gender, race/ethnicity, educational level, and geographic region. Reliability studies of the CTONI provide evidence for content sampling, time sampling, and interscorer reliability and have yielded reliability coefficients of .80 or greater. Studies have reported content, criterion-related, and construct validity as well.

This nonverbal intelligence test is also available in a computer-administered format, the CTONI-CA. It is an interactive multimedia test that can easily be completed on a computer. Instructions are given in a clear human voice, and the examinee simply points the mouse and clicks on the answer. When the test is completed, the examinee can see comprehensive results on the screen or print up a report.

Additional Information

Reviewed in Impara, J. C., & Plake, B. S. (Eds.). (1998). *The thirteenth mental measurements yearbook.* Lincoln, NE: Buros Institute of Mental Measurements.

Athanasiou, M. S. (2000). Current nonverbal assessment instruments: A comparison of psychometric integrity and test fairness. *Journal of Psychoeducational Assessment, 18,* 211–229.

Bradley-Johnson, S. (1997). Test review: Comprehensive Test of Nonverbal Intelligence. *Psychology in the Schools, 34,* 289–292.

Drossman, E. R., Maller, S. J., & McDermott, P. A. (2001). Core profiles of school-aged examinees from the national standardization sample of the Comprehensive Test of Nonverbal Intelligence. *School Psychology Review, 30,* 586–598.

Lassiter, K. S., Harrison, T. K., & Matthews, T. D. (2001). The validity of the Comprehensive Test of Nonverbal Intelligence as a measure of fluid intelligence. *Assessment, 8,* 95–103.

http://alpha.fdu.edu/psychology/ctoni_comments.htm

Detroit Tests of Learning Aptitude—Fourth Edition

Author: Donald D. Hammill
Ages: 6:0 through 17:0
Testing Time: 40 minutes to 2 hours
Publisher: PRO-ED

The Detroit Tests of Learning Aptitude—Fourth Edition (DTLA-4, 1998) is intended for use with children and adolescents ages 6:0 to 17:0. There is also an adult version for ages 16:0 through 79:0 and a primary version for children aged 3:0 to 9:11. It was designed to (1) measure both general intelligence and discrete ability areas; (2) show the effects of language, attention, and motor abilities on test performance; and (3) allow interpretation in light of current theories of intellect.

The DTLA-4 consists of 10 subtests, which take between 40 minutes and 2 hours to administer. Administration time varies by individual, as none of the subtests are timed. To administer the test, an examiner's manual, two color picture books for the subtests, profile and summary forms, examiner's record booklets, response forms, story sequence chips, and design sequence cubes are needed. Percentiles, standard scores, and age equivalents can be derived from this test. A computerized scoring program is available to convert raw scores to the three types of scores, as well as to calculate intra-ability differences.

The 10 subtests of the DTLA-4 include Word Opposites, Design Sequences, Sentence Imitation, Reversed Letters, Story Construction, Design Reproduction, Basic Information, Symbolic Relations, Word Sequences, and Story Sequences. The Picture Fragments subtest found in previous editions has been removed to shorten the length of administration. These subtests measure a variety of specific cognitive abilities, including vocabulary, auditory and visual memory, and visual problem solving. Scoring of the subtests results in scaled scores (M = 10; SD = 3), which are then compiled into 16 composite scores (M = 100; SD = 15), including the Overall Composite, Optimal Level Composite, Domain Composites, and Theoretical Composites. The Overall Composite is formed from the scaled scores of all of the subtests in the battery. The Optimal Level Composite is calculated from the four highest subtest scores, giving an estimate of the individual's potential or highest level of performance possible when any inhibiting influences are disregarded. Domain Composites are given for language, attention, and manual dexterity, while Theoretical Composites allow for interpretation in terms of major theories proposed by Horn and Cattell, Jensen, Das, and Wechsler.

The DTLA-4 was standardized on 1,350 students in 37 states, stratified by age. This sample was representative of the 1996 U.S. census with respect to gender, race, ethnicity, residence (urban or rural), family income, educational attainment of parents, and geographic distribution. With respect to reliability, test-retest studies range from .71 to .96 for the subtests, while coefficients for the composites exceed .90. Internal consistency was shown to exceed .80 for the subtests and .90 for the composites. Scorer reliability coefficients were in the .90s for all tests. Several factor analyses have been completed regarding the validity of the DTLA-4 showing intercorrelation between the subtests, chronological age, and tests of academic achievement. Criterion prediction validity has been examined through the comparison of the DTLA-4 with various aptitude tests, including the TONI3, WISC, KABC, PPVT, and WJPEB.

Test bias was considered throughout test construction. The effects of bias in terms of culture, race, and gender were controlled and minimized by the inclusion of minority and disabled groups within the normative sample. Internal consistency was seen throughout these subgroups. Differential item functioning analysis was used to reduce item bias, and delta score values were used to identify potential bias.

Additional Information

Reviewed in Plake, B. S., & Impara, J. C. (Eds.). (2001). *The fourteenth mental measurements yearbook.* Lincoln, NE: Buros Institute of Mental Measurements.

Hammill, D. (1998). *Detroit Tests of Learning Aptitude—4.* Austin, TX: PRO-ED.

Differential Ability Scales

Author: Colin Elliott

Ages: 2:6 through 17:11

Administration Time: 45 to 80 minutes

Publisher: The Psychological Corporation

The Differential Ability Scales (DAS; Elliott, 1990a) is an individually administered measure of cognitive ability and achievement designed to measure specific abilities and assist in determining strengths and weaknesses for children and adolescents aged 2 years 6 months through 17 years 11 months. The DAS is composed of 17 cognitive subtests and three tests of achievement. The cognitive subtests include 12 core subtests and five diagnostic subtests. The core subtests are used to calculate a high-level composite score called the General Conceptual Ability (GCA) score ("the general ability of an individual to perform complex mental processing that involves conceptualization and transformation of information" [Elliott, 1990b, p. 20]) and three lower-level composite scores: Verbal Ability, Nonverbal Reasoning Ability, and Spatial Ability cluster scores. With lower g-loadings, the diagnostic subtests are used predominantly to assess strengths and weaknesses and do not contribute to the composite scores. Finally, the DAS includes three tests of achievement: Basic Number Skills, Spelling, and Word Reading. Administration time is estimated to be 45 to 65 minutes for the full cognitive battery and 15 to 25 minutes for the achievement tests.

Three batteries comprise the DAS: a lower preschool-level battery for ages 2:6 to 3:5, an upper preschool-level battery for ages 3:6 to 5:11, and a school-age-level battery for ages 6:0 to 17:11. These batteries differ with regard to subtests included and the number of abilities measured. The lower preschool level is made up of four core cognitive subtests, which yield the GCA score and a "Special Nonverbal Composite," and two diagnostic cognitive subtests. In comparison, the upper preschool level comprises six core cognitive subtests, which yield a GCA score and Verbal Ability and Nonverbal Ability cluster scores, and four to six diagnostic cognitive subtests. The school-age-level battery consists of six core cognitive subtests, three or four diagnostic cognitive subtests, and three achievement tests, and it yields a GCA score and three cluster scores: Verbal Ability, Nonverbal Ability, and Spatial Ability. The DAS, like many other standardized cognitive ability tests, uses the Deviation IQ (M = 100, SD = 15) for the Verbal, Nonverbal, Nonverbal Reasoning, Spatial, and General Conceptual Ability composite scores and T scores (M = 50, SD = 10) for the 17 individual subtests.

The DAS was standardized on a stratified sample of 3,475 American children and adolescents. Data from the 1988 U.S. census was used to stratify the sample. Strata included age, sex, ethnicity, parental education, educational preschool enrollment, and geographic location. Between the ages of 2:6 and 4:11, age groups consisted of 175 children; between the ages of 5:0 and 17:11, age groups consisted of 200 children. In order to prevent bias related to item-scoring rules, an additional 600 African American and Hispanic American children and adolescents were tested, and study item bias and prediction bias were studied.

Reliability and validity data are very good. Average internal consistency reliability coefficients for the GCA are .90 for the lower preschool level, .94 for the upper preschool level, and .95 for the school-age level (Elliott, 1990b). Internal consistency of the clusters is also very good; reliability coefficients range from .88 for the Verbal Ability cluster in both the upper preschool and school-age levels to .92 for the Spatial Ability cluster in the school-age level. Median test-retest reliability coefficients for the GCA are .90 for the lower preschool level, .94 for the upper preschool level, and .91 for the school-age level. With regard to clusters, reliability coefficients range from .82 for the Spatial Ability cluster in the school-age level to .88 for the Verbal Ability in the school age level. Finally, with regard to concurrent validity, the GCA correlates well with other measures of intelligence (M = .76).

Overall, the DAS is a well-standardized instrument with strong psychometric properties. Additional strengths are that the GCA is highly g-saturated, that the time of administration is relatively short, that the test is adaptive in nature, and that children as young as 2 and 3 years of age can be assessed. Despite these assets, the DAS has some limitations. In particular, caution must be exercised when scoring Word Definitions, Similarities, Recall of Designs, and Copying, as these subtests require considerable judgment by the examiner. In addition, the range of possible GCA scores varies from age group to age group, and GCA scores are derived from different combinations of subtests in each of the three batteries.

As of June of 2004, the second edition of the DAS was being developed (C. D. Elliott, personal communication, June 28, 2004). While the style, format, and methods of administration of the DAS-II will be very similar to those of its predecessor, there will be several changes: the three brief achievement tests will not be included, outdated items will be replaced, floors and ceilings of existing subtests will be improved, matrices will probably be downwardly extended into the preschool level battery, and Spanish instructions for administration will be included. In addition, it is expected that three new subtests will be added to the school-age-level battery (i.e., subtests measuring phonological awareness and rapid naming or speed of lexical access, as well as a new working memory subtest). With these changes, the DAS-II may be able to detect both fluid reasoning and spatial abilities at the upper preschool level. Finally, the DAS-II will be linked to the WIAT-II. It is anticipated that the DAS-II will be published in 2006.

Additional Information

Aylward, G. P. (1992). Review of the Differential Ability Scales. In J. J. Kramer & J. C. Conoley (Eds.), *Eleventh mental measurements yearbook* (pp. 281–282). Lincoln, NE: Buros Institute of Mental Measurements.

Bain, S. K. (1991). Review of the Differential Ability Scales. *Journal of Psychoeducational Assessment, 9,* 372–378.

Braden, J. P. (1992). The Differential Ability Scales and special education. *Journal of Psychoeducational Assessment, 10,* 92–98.

Dumont, R., Cruse, C. L., Price, L., & Whelley, P. (1996). The relationship between the Differential Ability Scales (DAS) and the Wechsler Intelligence Scale for Children—Third Edition (WISC-III) for students with learning disabilities. *Psychology in the Schools, 33,* 203–209.

Dumont, R., Willis, J., & Sattler, J. M. (2001). Differential Ability Scales. In J. M. Sattler, *Assessment of children: Cognitive applications* (4th ed., pp. 507–545). San Diego, CA: Jerome M. Sattler.

Elliott, C. D. (1990a). *DAS administration and scoring manual.* San Antonio, TX: The Psychological Corporation.

Elliott, C. D. (1990b). *DAS introductory and technical handbook.* San Antonio, TX: The Psychological Corporation.

Keith, T. Z. (1990). Confirmatory and hierarchical confirmatory analysis of the Differential Ability Scales. *Journal of Psychoeducational Assessment, 8,* 391–405.

Youngstrom, E. A., Kogos, J. L., & Glutting, J. J. (1999) Incremental efficacy of the Differential Ability Scales factor scores in predicting individual achievement criteria. *School Psychology Quarterly, 14,* 26–39.

http://alpha.fdu.edu/psychology/DAS.html

http://cps.nova.edu/~cpphelp/DAS.html

Kaufman Adolescent and Adult Intelligence Test

Authors: Alan S. Kaufman and Nadeen L. Kaufman

Ages: 11 through 85

Testing Time: 60 minutes

Publisher: AGS Publishing

The Kaufman Adolescent and Adult Intelligence Test (KAIT, 1993) is an individually administered measure of general intellectual ability for use with persons between the ages of 11 and 85 years or over. The KAIT consists of Crystallized and Fluid Scales that yield a Composite IQ. The Crystallized Scale assesses a general store of knowledge acquired through education and sociocultural experience and includes Definitions, Auditory Comprehension, Double Meanings and an alternate subtest—Famous Faces. The Fluid Scale, primarily a measure of problem solving ability in novel situations, is composed of Rebus Learning, Logical Steps, Mystery Codes (Core Battery Subtests) and an alternate Memory for Block Designs subtest. The two alternate subtests are provided in the event that a Core Battery subtest is spoiled or if a measure should be substituted for other clinical reasons. In addition to the Core Battery subtests, the Expanded Battery includes memory measures that allow for interpretation of immediate and delayed recall (Rebus Delayed Recall and Auditory Delayed Recall). There is also a supplemental Mental Status subtest that is composed of 10 items assessing examinees' attention and orientation. The Core Battery takes a little over an hour to administer, while the Expanded Battery typically takes an additional half hour to complete.

Subtests' raw scores are converted to scaled scores that have a mean of 10 and a standard deviation of 3. The Fluid, Crystallized, and Composite IQ scales yield scores with a mean of 100 and a standard deviation of 15. The score for the Mental Status subtest produces raw scores that are translated into descriptive categories.

While the Cattell-Horn concept of Fluid (Gf) and Crystallized (Gc) intelligence (1966, 1967) is the predominant theory on which the KAIT is founded, the test also draws upon neuropsychological and cognitive developmental models, specifically Golden's (1981) concept of planning ability as related to pre–frontal lobe development and Piaget's (1972) highest stage of cognitive development, formal operations.

The test kit includes a manual, two easels, a Mystery Codes booklet, six wooden blocks, test record, and an audiocassette tape. For ease of administration, examiner instructions are printed on the test easel pages. Most subtests provide "teaching" items, which give the examinee an opportunity to become familiar with the task. The start points for each subtest do not vary according to age of the examinee.

The KAIT was standardized between 1988 and 1991 on a U.S. sample of 2,000 participants from the ages of 11 to 94 years old. The sample was representative of the 1990 U.S. census, although the western region of the United States was slightly overrepresented and the northeast was underrepresented. The sample was stratified by gender, age, geographic region, race/ethnic group, and socioeconomic status. Items were subjected to analyses of difficulty and discrimination along with Rasch item analysis. Extensive data regarding reliability and validity of the test are presented in the manual. Internal consistency is excellent for the three IQ scales (average .95). The six Core subtests also have adequate split-half reliability (about .90). Test-retest reliability was ascertained utilizing a sample of 153 individuals who were retested after 6 to 99 days (X = 31 days). The reliability coefficients for all three scales are good (Crystallized and Composite = .94 and Fluid = .87). Construct and concurrent validity for the KAIT is also adequate. Factor analysis supports the delineation of a crystallized factor and a fluid factor. Concurrent validity was established by comparing scores for the KAIT to established intelligence measures (WISC-R, WAIS-R, S-B: IV, and the KABC). While individual interpretation of subtests is discouraged, McGrew, Untiedt, and Flanagan (1996) found all of the subtests (except Memory for Block Designs) to be good measures of Spearman's *g*. As reported in the manual, diagnostic validity studies were carried out with a variety of clinical samples; however, Dumont and Hagberg (1994) note that mentally retarded and gifted populations were not included in the comparisons.

The KAIT is a useful measure of intelligence that can be utilized with a variety of populations. The use of Fluid and Crystallized Scales is consistent with the multiple factor theory of intelligence and allows for administration to people with diverse backgrounds. A particular strength of the test is its potential for use with the geriatric population. Furthermore, given the broad age range of the test, it could easily be substituted for the WISC-IV (for children aged 11 through 16 years 11 months) or WAIS-III. The auditory and visual nature of the subtests is also a strength and may add to examinee interest. It has been noted that "both children and adults found the test to be non-threatening and for some it was enjoyable and challenging" (Dumont and Hagberg, 1994, p. 195). However, these authors also noted that caution should be taken when using the KAIT with those possessing symptoms of dementia or memory or reading problems. While more research is needed with specific populations (e.g., gifted and learning disabled students), the KAIT is an innovative and valid alternative to traditional intelligence tests.

Additional Information

Brown, D. T. (1994). Review of the Kaufman Adolescent and Adult Intelligence Test (KAIT). *Journal of School Psychology, 32,* 85–89.

Dumont, R., & Hagberg, C. (1994). Test reviews: Kaufman Adolescent and Adult Intelligence Test. *Journal of Psychoeducational Assessment, 12,* 190–196.

Dumont, R., & Whelley, P. (1995). The KAIT (Kaufman Adolescent and Adult Intelligence Test): Some thoughts from two practicing school psychologists. *Communiqué, 24,* 22–23.

Flanagan, D. P., Alfonso, V. C., & Flanagan, R. (1994). A review of the Kaufman

Adolescent and Adult Intelligence Test: An advancement in cognitive assessment? *School Psychology Review, 23,* 512–525.

Golden, C. J. (1981). The Luria-Nebraska Children's Battery: Theory and formulation. In G. W. Hynd & J. E. Obrzut (Eds.), *Neuropsychological assessment and the school age child: Issues and procedures* (pp. 277–302). New York: Grune & Stratton.

Horn, J. L., & Cattell, R. B. (1966). Refinement and test of the theory of fluid and crystallized general intelligences. *Journal of Educational Psychology, 57,* 253–270.

Kaufman, A. S., & Kaufman, N. L. (1993). *Kaufman Adolescent and Adult Intelligence Test.* Circle Pines, MN: American Guidance Service.

Keith, T. Z. (1995). Review of the Kaufman Adolescent and Adult Intelligence Test. In J. C. Conoley & J. C. Impara (Eds.), *Twelfth mental measurements yearbook* (pp. 530–532). Lincoln, NE: Buros Institute of Mental Measurements.

Lassiter, K. S., Matthews, T. D., & Bell, N. L. (2002). Comparison of the General Ability Measure for Adults and the Kaufman Adolescent and Adult Intelligence Test with college students. *Psychology in the Schools, 39,* 497–506.

McGrew, K. S., Untiedt, S. A., & Flanagan, D. P. (1996). General factor and uniqueness characteristics of the Kaufman Adolescent and Adult Intelligence Test. *Journal of Psychoeducational Assessment, 14,* 208–219.

Piaget, J. (1972). Intellectual evolution from adolescence to adulthood. *Human Development, 15,* 1–12.

Kaufman Assessment Battery for Children—Second Edition

Authors: Alan S. Kaufman and Nadeen L. Kaufman
Ages: 4 through 18:11
Testing Time: 30 to 70 minutes
Publisher: AGS Publishing

The Kaufman Assessment Battery for Children—Second Edition (KABC-II, 2004) contains a total of 18 subtests grouped into Core or Supplemental tests. The Core subtests are those used to compute either the Fluid-Crystallized Index (FCI) or Mental Processes Index (MPI) and separate scale scores, while the Supplemental subtests provide expanded coverage of the abilities measured by the Core KABC-II subtests and allow for the computation of a Nonverbal Index (NVI). Some subtests are labeled Core at some ages and Supplementary at other ages The battery for ages 3:0 to 3:11 consists of five (MPI) or seven (FCI) Core subtests that combine to yield the global score and five Supplemental or Out-of-Level subtests that may be administered. The battery for ages 4:0 to 5:11 includes nine (FCI) or seven (MPI) Core subtests and an additional three to nine Supplementary or Out-of-Level subtests. From ages 6:0 to 18:11 the battery includes 10 (FCI) or 8 (MPI) Core subtests and an additional six or seven Supplementary or Out-of-Level subtests. At all ages except 3 to 3:11, the subtests not only combine to produce the Global Index scores (FCI or MPI) but also yield up to four (Luria model) or five (CHC model) indexes. These index scores represent Sequential Processing/Short-

Term Memory, Simultaneous Processing/Visual Processing, Learning Ability/Long-Term Storage and Retrieval, Planning Ability/Fluid Reasoning, and Crystallized Ability. This last (Crystallized Ability) is only represented in the CHC model. Although the typical battery is given to children based upon their chronological age, several subtests were also normed at overlapping age range. This overlap provides the examiner flexibility when testing children aged 3 through 7 years. In these cases, subtests appropriate for the individual's abilities are available.

The KABC-II was standardized on 3,025 children selected to be representative of noninstitutionalized, English-proficient children aged 3 years 0 months through 18 years 11 months living in the United States during the period of data collection (September 2001 through January 2003). The demographic characteristics used to obtain a stratified sample were age, sex, race/ethnicity, parental educational level, educational status for 18-year-olds, and geographic region.

In the standardization sample, there were 18 age groups: 3:0–3:5, 3:6–3:11, 4:0–4:5, 4:6–4:11, 5, 6, 7, 8, 9, 10, 11, 12, 13, 14, 15, 16, 17, and 18 years. In each 6-month age group between 3 years 0 months and 3 years 11 months, there were a total of 100 children, while from ages 4 years 0 months to 4 years 11 months and at age 18, there were 125 children. For ages 5 through 14 there were 200 children at each 1-year age group, and for ages 15 through 17 there were a total of 150 children at each 1-year age group. In each of the 18 age groups, there were approximately equal numbers of males and females. This sampling methodology was excellent.

The KABC-II, like many other standardized cognitive ability tests, uses the Deviation IQ (M = 100, SD = 15) for the five Scale Indexes (Sequential Processing/Short-Term Memory, Simultaneous Processing/Visual Processing, Learning Ability/Long-Term Storage and Retrieval, Planning Ability/Fluid Reasoning, and Crystallized Ability), and the three Global Indexes (FCI, MPI, NVI) and scaled scores (M = 10, SD = 3) for the 18 individual subtests. The calculation of the KABC-II scores involves a three-step process. After each subtest is scored, raw point totals are converted to a scaled score with a range from 1 to 19. From the sums of the scaled scores for the subtests that create Scale Indexes, the examiner obtains the standard scores for the index of the test. Finally, the standard scores obtained for the respective Scale Indexes are added and this sum is used to obtain the FCI or MPI score. Age groups are 3-month intervals for children 3 years, 0 months to 5 years, 11 months; 4-month intervals for children 6 years 0 months through 14 years 11 months; and 6-month intervals for 15 years and older.

Extensive data regarding reliability and validity of the test are presented in the manual. Internal consistency is excellent for the index scales (average in mid- to upper .90s). The subtests also have adequate reliability, with only 4 of the 18 subtests having reliability below .80. Test-retest reliability was ascertained utilizing a sample of 205 individuals who were retested after 12 to 56 days. The reliability coefficients for all scales are good (mid-.80s to mid-.90s). Construct and concurrent validity for the KABC-II is also adequate. While individual interpretation of subtests is discouraged, the loadings on the first unrotated factor provide information about *g*, or general intelligence. The KABC-II subtests form three *g*-related clusters: The Knowledge/Gc subtests have the highest *g* loadings in the test. On average, the proportion of variance attributed to *g* is 56 percent for the Knowledge/Gc subtests, 43 percent for the Planning/Gf subtests, 31 percent for the Learning/Glr subtests, 30 percent for the Sequential/Gsm subtests, and 26 percent for the Simultaneous/Gv subtests. Subtests with the highest proportion of variance attributed to *g* are Riddles, Verbal Knowledge, and Expressive Vocabulary, all subtests of the Knowledge/Gc Scale Index. None of the Planning/Gf, Learning/Glr subtests, Sequential/Gsm subtests, or Simultaneous/Gv subtests are good measures of *g*.

Additional Information

Test has been recently released, therefore there were no published studies available at the time of this review.

http://alpha.fdu.edu/psychology/kabc_index.htm

Kaufman Brief Intelligence Test

Authors: Alan S. Kaufman and Nadeen L. Kaufman
Ages: 4 through 90
Testing Time: 15 to 30 minutes
Publisher: AGS Publishing

The Kaufman Brief Intelligence Test (K-BIT, 1990) is an individually administered test of verbal and nonverbal ability. The test can be administered to persons aged 4 through 90. The K-BIT takes approximately 15 to 30 minutes to administer. The K-BIT consists of two subtests, Vocabulary (which is meant to measure verbal memory) and Matrices (nonverbal memory). The Vocabulary subtest comprises two sections: Expressive Vocabulary and Definitions. In the first part, the individual is asked to name a pictured object, and in the second the individual has to supply the correct word given written clues. Both the Vocabulary and Matrices subtests are administered using an easel. Matrices is a nonverbal test in which the individual looks at visual stimuli and chooses the one that best completes the relationship. Starting points on the K-BIT are determined by the examinee's age. The K-BIT must be hand scored using the manual. The raw scores obtained are converted to standard for both the subtests and the resulting IQ Composite scores (M=100, SD = 15).

The K-BIT was conormed with the Kaufman Adolescent and Adult Intelligence Test (KAIT) on a sample of 2,022 individuals that ranged in age from 4 to 90 years. The standardization sample was representative of U.S. census data from 1985 and 1990 with respect to race, geographic region, and socioeconomic status.

K-BIT internal consistency scores ranged from .88 to .98 for the IQ Composite, and from .89 to .98 and .74 to .95 for the Vocabulary and Matrices subtests, respectively. Test-retest reliability coefficients ranged from .92 to .95 for the IQ Composite. The subscale coefficients were .86 to .97 for Vocabulary and .80 to .92 for Matrices. The K-BIT also demonstrated good content, construct, and concurrent validity. In a 1997 study, the K-BIT IQ Composite was found to correlate well with the Full Scale IQ on the Wechsler Intelligence Scale for Children (WISC-III) among 6- to 15-year-olds (Douglas, Wessels, & Riebel, 1997). The K-BIT is easily administered to a wide range of individuals and is a good screening tool for intellectual aptitude. The K-BIT is not a substitute for a comprehensive intelligence measure, nor does it give any projective information.

Additional Information

Reviewed in Conoley, J. C., & Impara, J. C. (Eds.). (1995). *The twelfth mental measurements yearbook.* Lincoln, NE: Buros Institute of Mental Measurements.

Boyd, C. L., & Dumont, R. (1996). Inquiring psychologists want to know: How well does the K-BIT predict WISC-III results? *Communiqué, 24,* 24.

Canivez, G. L. (1996). Validity and diagnostic efficiency of the Kaufman Brief Intelligence Test in reevaluating students with learning disability. *Journal of Psychoeducational Assessment, 14,* 4–19.

Childers, J. S., Durham, T. W., & Wilson, S. (1994). Relation of performance on the Kaufman Brief Intelligence Test with the Peabody Picture Vocabulary Test—Revised among preschool children. *Perceptual & Motor Skills, 79,* 1195–1199.

Donovick, P. J., Burright, R. G., Burg, J. S., & Gronendyke, S. J. (1996). The K-BIT: A screen for IQ in six diverse populations. *Journal of Clinical Psychology in Medical Settings, 3,* 131–140.

Friedberg, P., & Hildman, L. (1992). Test review: Kaufman Brief Intelligence Test (K-BIT). *Communiqué, 20,* 10–11.

Hays, J. R., Reas, D. L., & Shaw, J. B. (2002). Concurrent validity of the Wechsler Abbreviated Scale of Intelligence and the Kaufman Brief Intelligence Test among psychiatric inpatients. *Psychological Reports, 90,* 355–359.

Kaufman, A. S., & Kaufman, N. L. (1990). *Manual for the Kaufman Brief Intelligence Test.* Circle Pines, MN: American Guidance Service.

Smith, D. K., Wessels, R. A., & Riebel, E. M. (1997). *A correctional correlational? Study of the K-BIT and the WISC-III.* Paper presented at Annual Meeting of the American Psychological Association, Chicago, IL.

Kaufman Brief Intelligence Test, Second Edition

The Kaufman Brief Intelligence Test, Second Edition (KBIT-2, 2004) will be available fall 2004. The KBIT-2 is an individually administered test of verbal and nonverbal ability. The test is suitable to be administered to persons aged 4 through 90 and takes approximately 20 minutes to administer. The KBIT-2 consists of two scales, verbal and nonverbal. The verbal scale is composed of two parts: Verbal Knowledge and Riddles. The nonverbal scale contains the Matrices subtest. Unlike the K-BIT, the verbal scale on the second edition does not require the examinee to read or spell words.

Both the Vocabulary and Matrices subtests are administered using an easel. The items are in color and are designed to appeal to children. Starting points on the KBIT-2 are determined by the examinee's age. The raw scores obtained are converted to standard scores (M=100, SD = 15) for both the subtests and the resulting IQ Composite.

The KBIT-2 was conormed with the Kaufman Test of Educational Achievement, Second Edition—Brief Form for individuals aged 26 to 90. The norming sample was representative of U.S. census data with respect to race, geographic region, and socioeconomic status. Studies conducted on the KBIT-2 demonstrated high reliability and validity. The exact data from these studies were not available at the time of publication.

The KBIT-2 may be used as an intellectual screening tool and/or to assess disparity between verbal and nonverbal intelligence.

Leiter International Performance Scale—Revised

Authors: Gale H. Roid and Lucy J. Miller

Ages: 2:0 to 20:11

Time: 90 minutes

Publisher: Stoelting

The Leiter International Performance Scale—Revised (Leiter-R, 1997) is an individually administered nonverbal test designed to assess intellectual ability, memory, and attention functions in children and adolescents. The Leiter-R consists of two groupings of subtests: the Visualization and Reasoning (VR) Battery (10 subtests), and the Attention and Memory (AM) Battery (10 subtests). It also includes four social-emotional rating scales (Examiner, Parent, Self, and Teacher) that provide information from behavioral observations of the examinee. For initial screening purposes, four subtests in the VR Battery can be used to measure the child's global intellectual level as part of a battery of other tests and assessments. The full VR Battery (six subtests for children ages 2 to 5) can be used for identification, classification, and placement decisions. Examiners have the option of using the VR and AM Batteries separately. The manual also cautions that IQ scores from the Leiter-R should never be used in isolation and should be evaluated in the context of a wide variety of information about the child. The manual includes an extensive discussion of the interpretation of Leiter-R results and provides case studies to demonstrate the interpretation of scores.

The Leiter-R includes the following 20 subtests.

Reasoning

Classification: Examinees categorize objects or geometric designs.

Sequencing: Examinees identify the stimulus that comes next in a sequence.

Repeated Patterns: Examinees identify which of several stimuli fill in missing parts in repeated sequences of pictures or figures.

Design Analogies: Examinees identify geometric shapes that complete matrix analogies.

Visualization (Spatial)

Matching: Examinees match response cards to easel pictures.

Figure—Ground: Examinees identify designs embedded in complex backgrounds.

Form Completion: Examinees see randomly displayed parts of designs and must select the whole design from alternatives.

Picture Context: Examinees use visual-context clues to identify a part of a picture that has been removed from a larger picture.

Paper Folding: Examinees view an unfolded object in two dimensions and match it to a picture of the whole object.

Figure Rotation: Examinees identify rotated pictures of original nonrotated objects.

Memory

Immediate Recognition: Examinees are shown five pictures for 5 seconds, and after items are removed and re-presented they must identify the one item that is missing.

Delayed Recognition: Examinees, after a 20-minute delay, identify the objects presented in the Immediate Recognition subtest.

Associated Pairs: Examinees are shown pairs of objects for 5 to 10 seconds, and after objects are removed, students must make meaningful associations for each pair.

Delayed Pairs: Examinees, after a 20-minute delay, identify the items in the Associated Pairs subtest.

Forward Memory: Examinees remember pictured objects to which the examiner points and must repeat the sequence in which the examiner points to the objects.

Reversed Memory: The examiner points to pictures or figures in order, and the student must point to the same pictures in reverse order.

Spatial Memory: Examinees are shown increasingly complex stimulus displays, arranged in matrix format, and the examinees must then place cards in order on a blank matrix display.

Visual Coding: Examinees match pictures and geometric objects to numbers.

Attention

Attention Sustained: Examinees are given large numbers of stimuli and must identify those that are alike.

Attention Divided: Examinees divide attention between a moving display of pictures and the sorting of playing cards.

The majority of Leiter-R items require the examinee to move response cards into slots on the easel tray. Some items require arranging foam rubber shapes and pointing to responses on the easel pictures. Subtest starting points are determined by the child's age (there are three age groups for administration of the Leiter-R: 2–5, 6–10, and 11–20). The manual contains detailed scoring instructions, and for most subtests responses are scored as 0 or 1. Scoring criteria for each item are noted on the instruction page for each subtest. For some subtests, scoring requires counting the number of correct responses and the number of errors.

Raw scores on the subtests and rating scales are converted to scaled scores (M = 10, SD = 3) using tables in the manual. IQ scores are calculated from sums of subtest scaled scores and converted to IQ standard scores (M = 100, SD = 15). Composite scores can also be obtained for Fluid Reasoning, Fundamental Visualization, Spatial Visualization, Attention, and Memory. In addition, the raw scores for each subtest and IQ can be converted to growth-scale scores that express a child's abilities in a metric that can reflect growth and be useful for treatment planning and measuring change over time.

The Leiter-R Visualization and Reasoning battery was standardized between 1993 and 1995 on 1,719 typical children and adolescents, while the Attention and Memory battery was standardized on a subset of 763 of the same typical children. An additional 692 atypical children were tested to provide data for comparison studies. Data collection used a national stratification plan based on 1993 U.S. census statistics for age, gender, and socioeconomic status. Nationally representative proportions of children who are Caucasian, Hispanic American, African American, Asian American, and Native American were included.

The manual provides internal-consistency reliability coefficients for the Visualization/Reasoning Battery, the Attention/Memory Battery, and the Attention/Memory Battery Special Diagnostic Scales. Fewer than half the coefficients are above .80. Reliabilities are also provided for IQ and composite scores. Most of these exceed .80. Evidence is also provided for test-retest reliability. Coefficients are high for composites and (except above age 11) low for subtests.

Evidence of content validity is based on mapping of the test to theoretical models of intelligence. Evidence of construct validity is based on completion of factor analyses showing a match between the scale and the theoretical model that guided its development. Concurrent validity between the Leiter-R (Brief and Full Scale IQ) and the Wechsler Intelligence Scale for Children (WISC-III; Performance and Full Scale IQ) on children ages 6 to 16 resulted in correlations of .85 and .86.

Additional Information

Reviewed in Plake, B. S., & Impara, J. C. (Eds.). (2001). *The fourteenth mental measurements yearbook.* Lincoln, NE: Buros Institute of Mental Measurements.

Athanasiou, M. S. (2000). Current nonverbal assessment instruments: A comparison of psychometric integrity and test fairness. *Journal of Psychoeducational Assessment, 18,* 211–229.

Farrell, M. M., & Phelps, L. (2000). A comparison of the Leiter-R and the Universal Nonverbal Intelligence Test (UNIT) with children classified as language impaired. *Journal of Psychoeducational Assessment, 18,* 268–274.

McCallum, S., Bracken, B., & Wasserman, J. (2000). *Essentials of Nonverbal Assessment.* New York: Wiley.

Roid, G., Nellis, L., & McLellan, M. (2003). Assessment with the Leiter International Performance Scale—Revised and the S-BIT. In R. S. McCallum, *Handbook of nonverbal assessment* (pp. 113–140). New York: Kluwer Academic/Plenum.

Tsatsanis, K. D., Dartnall, N., & Cicchetti, D. (2003). Concurrent validity and classification accuracy of the Leiter and Leiter-R in low-functioning children with autism. *Journal of Autism & Developmental Disorders, 33,* 23–30.

Naglieri Nonverbal Ability Test

Author: Jack A. Naglieri
Ages: 5 through 17

Testing Time: 30 minutes, group or individually administered
Publisher: The Psychological Corporation

The Naglieri Nonverbal Ability Test (NNAT, 2003) is a test of ability that can be used to predict academic achievement for children ages 5 through 17 years. The test, based on earlier forms of the Matrix Analogies Tests (MAT-SF; Naglieri, 1985b; MAT-EF; Naglieri, 1985a), has two forms: one that can be administered individually (NNAT-I) and a group-administered measure (the NNAT-MLF). The nonverbal nature of the test means that the examinee is not required to speak, read, or write, which may be especially appropriate for children with diverse linguistic and educational backgrounds. Administration time is approximately 30 minutes and test booklets may be hand scored or scored by machine.

The NNAT-I has two parallel forms consisting of 75 items each, while the multilevel group-administered test (NNAT-MLF) is organized into 38 items in each of seven levels. Item levels demarcate corresponding grades, starting with A = kindergarten and ending with G=grades 10–12. Examinees are presented with visual stimuli in the form of shapes and geometric designs and may respond by filling in a circle corresponding to the selected answer. The items are divided into four types: Pattern Completion, Reasoning by Analogy, Serial Reasoning, and Spatial Visualization. For each item category, examinees are required to use logic and reasoning to determine relationships between the stimuli. The Nonverbal Ability Index (NAI) reflects overall general ability and utilizes scaled scores with a mean of 100 and a standard deviation of 10 and can yield age or grade based scores. Percentile Ranks, stanine scores, and normal curve equivalent scores may also be obtained.

A strength of the NNAT is the large and representative sample on which it was standardized. Fall (1995) samples included 22,600 children, and spring (1996) samples consisted of 67,000 students from kindergarten to twelfth grade. Based on 1994 National Center for Education Statistics, stratified, random sampling was employed to ensure adequate geographic, socioeconomic, and ethnic representation. However, Midwestern, suburban, and rural students were slightly overrepresented.

The psychometric properties of the test are adequate, with internal consistency of grade-based and age-based cluster scores ranging from .83 to .93 and .81 to .88 (KR-20). Yet cluster score internal consistency reliability yielded more variability and lower coefficients. The test was standardized concurrently with the established Stanford Achievement Test Series, Ninth edition (SAT-9). Consistent with data reported in the manual, Naglieri and Ronning (2000) found strong correlations between the SAT-9 and the NNAT. The manual also reports minimal correlations (.07–.51) to the Aprenda2, a Spanish normed test of achievement. The authors controlled for bias by subjecting items to statistical analyses, whereby statistical differences between groups determined an item's elimination.

Given the growing diversity of the United States, culture fair measures of ability and intelligence are a necessity. It has been noted that Black and Hispanic students typically score lower on traditional tests, and while some of these students may lack academic skills, there may be strengths that the most popular tests do not assess. Recent work by Naglieri and Ford (2003) highlights a potential important use of the NNAT. The authors demonstrate that the NNAT may be an effective tool in the identification of gifted ethnic minority children. Furthermore, it is suggested that the nonverbal nature of the test provides children with the opportunity to demonstrate abilities when other measures relying more heavily on verbal abilities may place these groups at a disadvantage.

Additional Information

Reviewed in Plake, B. S., & Impara, J. C. (Eds.). (2001). *The fourteenth mental measurements yearbook.* Lincoln, NE: Buros Institute of Mental Measurements.

Naglieri, J. A. (1985a). *Matrix Analogies Test—Expanded Form.* San Antonio; TX: The Psychological Corporation.

Naglieri, J. A. (1985b). *Matrix Analogies Test—Short Form.* San Antonio, TX: The Psychological Corporation.

Naglieri, J. A. (1997). *Naglieri Nonverbal Ability Test.* San Antonio, TX: The Psychological Corporation.

Naglieri, J. A., & Ford, D. Y. (2003). Addressing underrepresentation of gifted minority children using the Naglieri Nonverbal Ability Test (NNAT). *Gifted Child Quarterly, 47,* 155–160.

Naglieri, J. A., & Ronning, M. E. (2000). The relationship between general ability using the Naglieri Nonverbal Ability Test (NNAT) and Standard Achievement Test (SAT) reading achievement. *Journal of Psychoeducational Assessment, 18,* 230–239.

Pictorial Test of Intelligence—Second Edition

Author: Joseph L. French
Ages: 3 through 8
Testing Time: 30 minutes
Publisher: PRO-ED

The Pictorial Test of Intelligence—Second Edition (PTI-2, 2001) is an individually administered measure of intelligence designed for use with children with and without disabilities. Its multiple-choice format and lack of time constraints make it useful for children with motor or speech delays or both. No vocalization is required on the part of examinees: they need only point to the correct response. Motorically impaired children can respond by fixing their eyes on the correct response, since the stimulus cards and the space between the choices are large enough to allow this accommodation.

PTI-2 is composed of three subtests. Verbal Abstractions measures the child's ability to demonstrate word knowledge, verbal comprehension, and verbal reasoning using pictorial stimuli. Form Discrimination measures the child's ability to match forms, differentiate between similar shapes, and reason about abstract shapes and patterns. Quantitative Concepts measures the child's ability to perceive and recognize size and number symbols, count, and solve simple arithmetic problems.

Scores on these three subtests (M=10, SD=3), are combined to yield a composite score (M = 100, SD = 15) referred to as a Pictorial Intelligence Quotient (PIQ). The choice of the abbreviation PIQ may lead to some confusion with Wechsler's PIQ (performance IQ).

Directions for subtests are provided both on the examiner's side of the easel and in the record book. Basal and ceiling rules, as well as starting and stopping points, are simple to understand. The manual provides raw score to standard score and percentile conversions. Age equivalents are also supplied, but the author discourages users from reporting them.

The PTI-2 was standardized on 970 children from 15 states who were selected to correspond to the 1997 census report. Stratification variables included age, gender, race, ethnicity, residence (urban or rural), disability status, family income, and parental education. The average number of children tested at each age level was 162, with the smallest numbers at ages 3 (N=136) and 8 (N=144). While the school age norms approximate the U.S. population, the demographic characteristics of the preschool sample are not described.

Split-half, test-retest, and interscorer reliability statistics presented in the manual reflect excellent internal consistency and stability as well as agreement between raters. Internal consistency was addressed through split-half procedures for the entire normative sample. Coefficient alphas for PIQ exceed .90 at every age, with an average reliability of .94. The reliabilities for the three subtests exceed .80 at every age. Stability data are limited to a study of 27 Wyoming children between the ages of 5 and 8. Evidence for criterion-related validity is limited to one study examining the correlation between the PTI-2 PIQ, the Cognitive Abilities Scale—Second Edition (CAS-2; Bradley-Johnson & Johnson, 2001) and the Wechsler Preschool and Primary Scale of Intelligence—Revised (WPPSI-R; Wechsler, 1989) in a small group (N=32) of 8-year-olds.

The PTI-2 is an objective and quickly administered measure of general cognitive ability. The manual is clear, thorough, and well organized. Overall, the psychometric properties of the PTI-2 are very good, though the standardization sample could be better defined. Additional validation studies with other, larger, and more representative samples are needed.

Additional Information

Reviewed in Plake, B. S., Impara, J. C., & Spies, R. A. (Eds.). (2003). *The fifteenth mental measurements yearbook.* Lincoln, NE: Buros Institute of Mental Measurements.

Bradley-Johnson, S., & Johnson, C. M. (2001). Cognitive Abilities Scale—Second Edition. Austin, TX: PRO-ED.

Stavrou, E. (2002). Test Review: Pictorial Test of Intelligence—Second Edition (PTI-2). *Communiqué, 31,* 8.

Wechsler, D. (1989). Wechsler Preschool and Primary Scale of Intelligence—Revised. San Antonio, TX: The Psychological Corporation.

Reynolds Intellectual Assessment Scales

Authors: Cecil R. Reynolds and Randy W. Kamphaus

Ages: 3 to 90

Testing Time: 20 to 35 minutes

Publisher: Psychological Assessment Resources

The Reynolds Intellectual Assessment Scales (RIAS, 2003) is an individually administered test of intelligence assessing two primary components of intelligence, verbal (crystallized) and nonverbal (fluid). Verbal intelligence is assessed with two tasks (Guess What and Verbal Reasoning) involving verbal problem solving and verbal reasoning. On the Guess What (GWH) subtest, the examinee attempts to identify an object or concept from verbal clues (e.g., "What is made of wood, plastic, or metal and makes graphite marks on paper?" or "What is circular or semicircular, is marked with degrees, and is used to measure angles?" or "Who discovered the moons of Jupiter, discovered laws of motion, and was imprisoned for one of his publications?"). On the Verbal Reasoning (VRZ) subtest the examinee completes spoken analogies (e.g., "Stroll is to slow as sprint is to ________" or "Circumnavigate is to perimeter as traverse is to ________"). Nonverbal intelligence is assessed by subtests (Odd-Item Out and What's Missing) that utilize visual and spatial ability tasks. On the Odd-Item Out (OIO) subtest the examinee is given 20 seconds to determine which of six objects or abstract designs does not belong with the others. If the examinee chooses incorrectly, there is a second, 10-second chance to earn partial credit. On the What's Missing (WHM) subtest the examinee is given 20 seconds to tell what part has been removed from a drawing. If the examinee chooses incorrectly, there is a second, 10-second chance to earn partial credit. These two scales combine to produce a Composite Intelligence Index (CIX). In contrast to many existing measures of intelligence, the RIAS eliminates dependence on motor coordination, visual-motor speed, and reading skills.

A Composite Memory Index (CMX) can be derived from two supplementary subtests (Verbal Memory and Nonverbal Memory) that assess verbal and nonverbal memory. However, these memory measures do not contain delayed recall components.

The Verbal Memory (VRM) subtest provides a basic, overall measure of short-term memory skills (e.g., working memory, short-term memory, learning) and measures recall in the verbal domain. The examinee attempts to repeat as precisely as possible several sentences or two short stories that have been read aloud by the examiner. The Nonverbal Memory (NVM) subtest measures the ability to recall pictorial stimuli in both concrete and abstract dimensions. The examinee is given 20 seconds to choose one of six pictures that matches a model that was exposed for 5 seconds and removed. If the examinee chooses incorrectly, there is a second, 10-second chance to earn partial credit. These short-term memory assessments require approximately 10 minutes of additional testing time.

The makeup of the battery also allows for the completion of the Reynolds Intellectual Screening Test (RIST). The RIST consists of only two RIAS subtests (one verbal and one nonverbal) that were selected on the basis of theoretical, empirical, and practical considerations. The RIST index is highly correlated with the full scale IQs of both the WISC-III and the WAIS-III. The RIST was designed to be used as a measure for reevaluations or in situations where the full RIAS may not be warranted.

A variety of scores, including T scores, Z scores, normal curve equivalents (NCE), stanines, and age equivalent (age 3 to 14 only) scores are provided.

The RIAS was standardized on a normative data sample of 2,438 individuals, from 41 states, aged 3 to 94 years. The normative sample was matched to the 2001 U.S. census on age, ethnicity, gender, educational attainment, and geographical region. During standardization an additional 507 individuals, in 15 different clinical groups, were administered the RIAS to supplement validation of RIAS.

Mean reliability coefficients ranged from .94 to .96 for the four RIAS indexes and from .90 to .95 for the six RIAS subtests. Test-retest reliability of the four index scores ranged from .83 to .91.

The RIAS Manual reports high correlations with the Wechsler Intelligence Scale for Children (WISC-III; $r = .76$), Wechsler Adult Intelligence Scale (WAIS-III; $r = .79$), and Wechsler Individual Achievement Test (WIAT; $r = .69$ for total achievement).

The manual is impressive in its organization and breadth and depth of content and is written in a style that makes it appropriate for psychologists.

Additional Information

Reviews of this test are pending for *The Sixteenth Mental Measurements Yearbook.*

Slosson Intelligence Test Revised—Third Edition for Children and Adults

Authors: Richard L. Slosson; revised by Charles L. Nicholson and Terry L. Hibpshman; supplementary manual: Sue Larson

Ages: 4 through 65

Testing Time: 10 to 20 minutes

Publisher: Slosson Educational Publications

The Slosson Intelligence Test Revised—Third Edition for Children and Adults (SIT-R3, 2002 with 1998 calibrated norms) provides a quick and reliable individual screening test of Crystallized Verbal Intelligence. This revision has adapted score sheets for scannable or electronic readers and offers a supplementary manual for the blind or visually impaired. The SIT-R3 has minimal performance items and features embossed materials, allowing for one of the only measures of intelligence for the visually challenged population of both children and adults.

The SIT-R3 test items are derived from the following subtests: Vocabulary (33 items), General Information (29 items), Similarities and Differences (30 items), Comprehension (33 items), Quantitative (34 items), and Auditory Memory (28 items).

The test has been nationally restandardized and developed with the American Psychological Association criteria clearly in mind. Multiple statistical procedures were used to assure that there is no significant gender or racial bias. Every item on the test was reevaluated using classical item analysis to choose "good" statistical items and new differential item functioning analysis to find and eliminate biased items. SIT-R3 users may continue to administer and score the SIT-R3 with the 1998 Calibrated Norms Tables as usual and just order the supplementary manual when testing persons with low visual acuity.

Administration time for the SIT-R3 is about 10–20 minutes. The SIT-R3 correlated .827 with the WISC-R Verbal Intelligence Quotient, even though the SIT-R3 does not cover Fluid Reasoning performance. The calibrated norms reflect a high .828 correlation between the SIT-R3 total standard score (TSS) and the WISC-III Full Scale Intelligence Quotient.

Computer Report aids educators in determining expected achievement and finding levels of ability or weakness. It scores and prints an individual three-page report using the TSS and computes the Severe Discrepancy Level to determine learning disabilities under federal guidelines. Computer Report is noncompliant with Windows XP.

Additional Information

No reviews for the 2002 edition are anticipated by the Buros Institute of Mental Measurements; however, a review of earlier editions of the test is available in Conoley, J. C., & Impara, J. C. (Eds.). (1995). *The twelfth mental measurements yearbook.* Lincoln, NE: Buros Institute of Mental Measurements.

Stanford-Binet Intelligence Scale: Fifth Edition

Author: Gale H. Roid
Ages: 2 to 85+
Testing Time: 45 to 75 minutes (full test), 15 to 20 minutes (abbreviated)
Publisher: Riverside Publishing

The Stanford-Binet Fifth Edition (SB5, 2003) is an individually administered test of cognitive abilities. The Full Scale IQ (FSIQ) is derived from the administration of 10 subtests (five Verbal and five Nonverbal). Subtests, including the two routing subtests, are designed to measure five factors: Fluid Reasoning, Knowledge, Quantitative Reasoning, Visual-Spatial Processing, and Working Memory. The first two subtests (contained in Item book 1) are routing subtests and are used to determine start points for the remaining Nonverbal (Item book 2) and Verbal (Item book 3) subtests. The two routing subtests contained in book 1 may also be used as a brief measure of intellectual ability. The SB5 also provides examiners the option of calculating Change-Sensitive Scores (CSS)—a method of criteria-referenced scoring rather than normative-referenced, which avoids truncation at high and low ends, as well as an extended IQ (EXIQ)—a special-case application for evaluating subjects with extremely high (or low) IQs.

SB5 subtests are composed of testlets—brief minitests at each level (1 through 6) of difficulty. Testlets typically have either six items or a total of six points at each of the six ability levels for a given subtest.

The SB5 has a mean of 100 and a standard deviation of 15 (in contrast to the prior edition's standard deviation of 16). Individual subtests are now scaled with a mean of 10 and a standard deviation of 3.

The SB5 was standardized on a sample of 4,800 individuals. Each of the early years (ages 2 through 4) was divided into half-year groupings (doubling the sample size at that age period) to account for the instability and rapid cognitive change of the very youngest age group. Using variables identified in the U.S. Census Bureau publications (2001), norm group individuals were stratified according to race/ethnicity, sex, parental education level, and geographic region.

The technical manual provides strong evidence for reliability and validity. Average internal consistency reliabilities were in the .90s for all scales and indexes, while the individual subtest reliabilities were all in the .80s. Concurrent validity evidence is strong.

The SB5 has an initially steep administration learning curve. While the materials at the lower levels are very child friendly, examiners may consider some difficult to manipulate and administer. Test administration sequence follows the examinee's ability level across all subtests. Testlets, starting at a particular ability level, are administered individual subtests. If an examinee does not obtain a specified basal for any subtest, the examiner immediately drops back one ability level and administers the specific testlet until a basal is reached.

Scoring of the SB5 test items is relatively easy and consistent with the scoring criteria of other standardized intelligence measures.

Additional Information

http://www.riverpub.com/products/clinical/sbis5/resource.html:

SB5 Assessment Service Bulletin #2: Accommodations on the Stanford-Binet Intelligence Scales, Fifth Edition

SB5 Assessment Service Bulletin #3: Use of the Stanford-Binet Intelligence Scales, Fifth Edition in the Assessment of High Abilities

SB5 Assessment Service Bulletin #4: Special Composite Scores for the Stanford-Binet Intelligence Scales, Fifth Edition

http://alpha.fdu.edu/psychology/SB5_index.htm

Test of Nonverbal Intelligence—Third Edition

Authors: Linda Brown, Rita J. Sherbenou, and Susan K. Johnsen
Ages: 6:0 through 89:11
Testing Time: 15 to 20 minutes
Publisher: PRO-ED

The Test of Nonverbal Intelligence—Third Edition (TONI-3, 1998) was created as a language-free measure of intelligence, aptitude, abstract reasoning, and problem solving for persons ages 6:0 through 89:11. It does not require the subject to read, write, speak, or listen. The test is entirely nonverbal and does not involve much movement more than a point, nod, or other symbolic gesture indicating a response decision. It is particularly useful for individuals who are deaf, language disordered (both expressive and receptive), non-English speaking, or culturally different, and those with conditions resulting from Mental Retardation, developmental disabilities, Autism, cerebral palsy, stroke, traumatic brain injury, or other neurological impairment.

The two equivalent forms of the TONI-3 make it ideal for use in situations dependent upon pre- and post-testing. Each form contains 45 items arranged to become progressively more difficult. Raw scores are converted to percentile ranks and to deviation quotients that have a mean of 100 and a standard deviation of 15 points.

The abstract or figural subject matter of the test ensures that each item presents a novel problem. There are no words, numbers, familiar pictures, or symbols within the test. The drawings in the Picture Book have been significantly improved in the TONI-3.

The test was normed in 1995 and 1996 on a sample of 3,451 people whose demographic characteristics matched those of the 1990 U.S. census for both school-age and adult populations. The normative group was stratified by age across the variables of geographic region, gender, race, residence (urban or rural), ethnicity, presence of a disabling condition, family income, and educational level achieved by the adult participants and parents of minor participants.

Close to 20 years of research established the test's reliability and validity. The manual reports extensive research, including the authors' own and studies conducted by independent investigators since the original test was first published in 1980. Substantial validity data are also reported, documenting the TONI-3's relationship to other measures of intelligence, achievement, and personality, its efficiency in discriminating groups appropriately, its factor structure, and other important estimates of test validity for samples of children, adolescents, and adults.

Additional Information

Reviewed in Plake, B. S., & Impara, J. C. (Eds.). (2001). *The fourteenth mental measurements yearbook.* Lincoln, NE: Buros Institute of Mental Measurements.

Brown, L. (2003). Test of Nonverbal Intelligence: A language-free measure of cognitive ability. In R. Steve McCallum (Ed.), *Handbook of nonverbal assessment* (pp. 191–221). New York: Kluwer Academic/Plenum.

Brown, L., Sherbenou, R. J., & Johnsen, S. K. (1997). *Test of Nonverbal Intelligence—Third Edition, examiner's manual.* Austin, TX: PRO-ED.

Universal Nonverbal Intelligence Test

Authors: B. A. Bracken and R. S. McCallum

Ages: 5:0 through 17:11

Testing Time: 15 to 45 minutes

Publisher: Riverside Publishing

The Universal Nonverbal Intelligence Test (UNIT, 1998) is an individually administered instrument designed for use with children and adolescents from ages 5:0 through 17:11. It is intended to provide a fair assessment of intelligence for those who have speech, language, or hearing impairments, different cultural or language backgrounds, those who are unable to communicate verbally, and those with Mental Retardation, Autism, giftedness, and learning disabilities.

The UNIT measures intelligence through six culture-reduced subtests that combine to form two Primary Scales (Reasoning [RQ] and Memory [MQ]), two Secondary Scales (Symbolic [SQ] and Nonsymbolic [NQ]), and a Full Scale (FSIQ). Each of the subtests (Symbolic Memory, Cube Design, Spatial Memory, Analogic Reasoning, Object Memory, and Mazes) are conducted using eight reasonably universal hand and body gestures, demonstrations, scored items that do not permit examiner feedback, sample items, corrective responses, and transitional checkpoint items to explain the tasks to the examinee. The entire process is nonverbal but does require motor skills for manipulatives, paper and pencil, and pointing.

Three administrations are available for use depending on the reason for referral. These are an Abbreviated Battery containing two Subtest Scores (10–15 minutes), the Standard Battery containing four Subtest Scores (30 minutes), and the Extended Battery containing six Subtest Scores (45 minutes).

Standardized through a carefully generated stratified random sampling plan, the UNIT resulted in a sample that closely matched the U.S. population according to the 1995 census. Normative data were collected from a thorough nationwide sample of 2,100 children and adolescents, ranging in age from 5:0 through 17:11. An additional 1,765 children and adolescents were added to the standardization sample to participate in the reliability, validity, and fairness studies. This gives a total of 3,865 participants across the variables of age, sex, race, Hispanic origin, region, community setting, classroom placement, special education services, and parental educational achievement.

Technical qualities appear to be quite strong. Reliabilities are high for both standardization and clinical samples. Validity studies show strong concurrent validity with many other measures of intelligence. The UNIT has also been acknowledged as a moderately good predictor of academic achievement. Discriminant validity evidence is cited, demonstrating that the UNIT differentiates between those with mental retardation, learning disabilities, speech-language impairments, and giftedness. Some concern has been raised about the criterion-related validity and the factor analysis for minority and clinical samples (Young & Assing, 2000), but overall this test is a theoretically and psychometrically sound measure of nonverbal intelligence.

Additional Information

Reviewed in Plake, B. S., & Impara, J. C. (Eds.). (2001). *The fourteenth mental measurements yearbook.* Lincoln, NE: Buros Institute of Mental Measurements.

Athanasiou, M. S. (2000). Current nonverbal assessment instruments: A comparison of psychometric integrity and test fairness. *Journal of Psychoeducational Assessment, 18,* 211–229.

Bracken, B. A., & McCallum, R. S. (1998). *Universal Nonverbal Intelligence Test, examiner's manual.* Itasca, IL: Riverside Publishing.

Caruso, J. C., & Witkiewitz, K. (2001). Memory and reasoning abilities assessed by the Universal Nonverbal Intelligence Test: A reliable component analysis (RCA) study. *Educational & Psychological Measurement, 61,* 5–22.

Drossman, E. R., & Maller, S. J. (2001). Core profiles of school-aged examinees in the national standardization sample of the Universal Nonverbal Intelligence Test. *School Psychology Review, 20,* 567–579.

Farrell, M. M., & Phelps, L. (2000). A comparison of the Leiter-R and the Universal Nonverbal Intelligence Test (UNIT) with children classified as language impaired. *Journal of Psychoeducational Assessment, 18,* 268–274.

Fives, C. J., & Flanagan, R. (2002). A review of the Universal Nonverbal Intelligence Test (UNIT): An advance for evaluating youngsters with diverse needs. *School Psychology International, 23,* 425–448.

Maller, S. J. (2000). Item invariance in four subtests of the Universal Nonverbal Intelligence Test across groups of deaf and hearing children. *Journal of Psychoeducational Assessment, 18,* 240–254.

Maller, S. J., & French, B. F. (in press). UNIT factor invariance across deaf and standardization samples. *Educational and Psychological Measurement.*

Young, E. L., & Assing, R. (2000). Test review: The Universal Nonverbal Intelligence Test (UNIT). *Journal of Psychoeducational Assessment, 18,* 280–288.

Wechsler Abbreviated Scale of Intelligence

Author: David Wechsler
Ages: 6 to 89
Administration Time: Approximately 15 to 30 minutes
Publisher: The Psychological Corporation

The Wechsler Abbreviated Scale of Intelligence (WASI) is an individually administered test that measures the intelligence in clinical and nonclinical populations. The test can be administered in approximately 30 minutes to individuals between the ages of 6 and 89 years.

The WASI consists of four subtests: Vocabulary, Similarities, Block Design, and Matrix Reasoning. All WASI items are new and parallel to their full Wechsler counterparts. Block Design consists of a set of 13 modeled or printed two-dimensional geometric patterns that the examinee replicates within a specified time limit using two-color cubes. Matrix Reasoning is similar to the WAIS-III and WISC-IV Matrix Reasoning subtest. Similarities is parallel to the WISC-IV and WAIS-III subtests and includes low-end picture items. Vocabulary has both oral and visual presentation of words and also has picture items that were designed to extend the floor of the test. The four subtests result in a Full Scale IQ score (FSIQ) and can also be divided into Verbal IQ (VIQ) scores and Performance IQ (PIQ) scores. The PIQ score comprises the performances on Matrix Reasoning, which measures nonverbal fluid ability, and on Block Design, which measures visuomotor and coordination skills. The VIQ score assesses performance on the Vocabulary and Similarities subtests of the WASI. An estimate of general intellectual ability can also be obtained from just a two-subtest administration that includes Vocabulary and Matrix Reasoning and provides only the FSIQ score.

Nationally standardized with 2,245 cases, the WASI has reliability coefficients for both the children and adolescent subtests, and FSIQs range from .81 to .98. The WASI subtests have significant correlations with the corresponding subtests of the WISC-III. Additionally, it has been evidenced that the WASI measures constructs similar to those measured by its WAIS-III counterparts.

Reviews of the WASI have been generally positive. However, Axelrod (2002) did note that, for a clinical sample he examined, "the WASI did not consistently demonstrate desirable accuracy in predicting scores. . . . The results suggest that clinicians should use the WASI cautiously, if at all, especially when accurate estimates of individuals' WAIS-III results are needed."

Additional Information

Reviewed in Plake, B. S., & Impara, J. C. (Eds.). (2001). *The fourteenth mental measurements yearbook.* Lincoln, NE: Buros Institute of Mental Measurements.

Axelrod, B. N. (2002). Validity of the Wechsler Abbreviated Scale of Intelligence and other very short forms of estimating intellectual functioning. *Assessment, 9,* 17–23.

Hays, J. R., & Shaw, J. B. (2003). WASI profile variability in a sample of psychiatric inpatients. *Psychological Reports, 92,* 164–166.

Ryan, J. J., Carruthers, C. A., & Miller, L. J. (2003). Exploratory factor analysis of the Wechsler Abbreviated Scale of Intelligence (WASI) in adult standardization and clinical samples. *Applied Neuropsychology, 10,* 252–256.

Wechsler Adult Intelligence Scale—Third Edition

Author: David Wechsler
Ages: 16 to 89
Testing Time: 60 to 90 minutes
Publisher: The Psychological Corporation

The Wechsler Adult Intelligence Scale—Third Edition (WAIS-III, 1997) is an individually administered measure of intellectual ability for ages 16 to 89. The WAIS-III contains 14 subtests, which provide a Verbal Scale IQ (VIQ), Performance Scale IQ (PIQ), and a global Full Scale IQ (FSIQ). Each of these IQ scores is a standard score with a mean of 100 and a standard deviation of 15. On the other hand, each of the 14 subtests is a scaled score with a mean of 10 and a standard deviation of 3.

The Verbal IQ is composed of six subtests: Vocabulary, Similarities, Arithmetic, Digit Span, Information, and Comprehension. Letter-Number Sequencing is a new supplementary subtest that may replace Digit Span when it has been spoiled. The Performance IQ is composed of five subtests: Picture Completion, Digit Symbol-Coding, Block Design, Matrix Reasoning, and Picture Arrangement. Symbol Search and Object Assembly are both supplementary subtests. Symbol Search may substitute for Digit Symbol-Coding when it has been spoiled. Object Assembly is an optional subtest that does not count toward the IQ or Index scores. It can be used to replace any spoiled Performance subtest, but only for individuals younger than 75 years of age. Verbal and Performance subtests alternate to maintain the examinee's interest. The WAIS-III also groups its subtests into four indexes: Verbal Comprehension (VCI), Perceptual Organization (POI), Working Memory (WMI), and Processing Speed (PSI).

The Index scores are also standard scores with a mean of 100 and a standard deviation of 15. It is not necessary to administer all subtests in order to obtain IQ and Index scores. The examiner can administer subtests according to what scores are required (IQ scores, Index scores, or both).

The administration time of the WAIS-III varies according to what subtests are given and the level of ability of the examinee. Administration of the 11 subtests required to obtain the three IQ scores ranges from 60 to 90 minutes, averaging about 75 minutes. Administration of the 11 subtests required for the four indexes takes approximately 60 minutes, with a range of 45 to 75 minutes. The 13 subtests needed to obtain both IQ and Index scores take about 80 minutes, ranging from 65 to 95 minutes. Object assembly takes an additional 10 to 15 minutes.

The WAIS-III was standardized on a U.S. sample of 2,450 English-speaking subjects. The normative sample was stratified by age, gender, ethnicity, geographic region, and educational level, and was consistent with the 1995 U.S. census data. This sample was divided into 13 age groups that ranged from 2 to 10 years. The sample consisted of individuals from all intellectual ability levels. For the purpose of performing item bias analyses, the WAIS-III was administered to an additional 200 African American and Hispanic individuals without discontinue rules (The Psychological Corporation, 1997).

Reliability for the WAIS-III is strong. The average split-half reliability coefficients were 0.97 for the Verbal IQ, 0.94 for the Performance IQ, and 0.98 for the Full Scale IQ, with average coefficients for the factor indexes ranging from 0.88 for Processing Speed to 0.96 for Verbal Comprehension. Average split-half reliabilities for the subtests ranged from 0.70 for Object Assembly to 0.93 for Vocabulary. Three hundred ninety-four individuals from the standardization sample were retested an average of 5 weeks after initial testing, and their data provided test-retest data for the WAIS-III. The IQs and Indexes have test-retest reliability coefficients ranging from 0.88 to 0.96.

The four-factor structure of the WAIS-III has been validated. However, there was not strong support for the Perceptual Organization factor for the oldest age group, ages 75 to 89 (Kaufman & Lichtenberger, 1999). Criterion validity was performed by correlating the WAIS-III with the WAIS-R (Wechsler, 1981). The correlations between the two tests were high, with a correlation of 0.94 for the Verbal IQ, 0.86 for the Performance IQ, and 0.93 for the Full Scale IQ (Kaufman & Lichtenberger, 1999). On average, individuals obtained about 2.9 points less on the Full Scale IQ on the WAIS-III than on the WAIS-R. This is what would be expected given the Flynn effect (Flynn, 1984). In his work, Flynn found a similar pattern between the WAIS and WAIS-R.

Many improvements were made in the third edition of the WAIS, but the major features of the WAIS-R were retained. The floor of the WAIS-III IQ scores was extended down to 45 and the ceiling was extended to 155. The age range was extended to 89 years.

The norms of the test were updated, and the test no longer relies on a reference group (ages 20–34) for calculating all scaled scores. A number of items were modified in other subtests, and the artwork was updated on Picture Completion, Picture Arrangement, and Object Assembly. Three subtests were added to the WAIS-III: Letter-Number Sequencing, Matrix Reasoning, and Symbol Search. The addition of Matrix Reasoning and Letter-Number Sequencing has enhanced the measurement of fluid reasoning and working memory (Kaufman & Lichtenberger, 1999). In addition, the WAIS-III relies less than the WAIS-R on timed performance when calculating the Performance IQ. According to Kaufman and Lichtenberger, the addition of the four index scores is the major structural change in the WAIS-III, and these four-factor indexes are helpful in interpretation. Although criticisms have been made of the WAIS-III, its strengths appear to be greater than its weaknesses (Kaufman & Lichtenberger).

Additional Information

Reviewed in Plake, B. S., & Impara, J. C. (Eds.). (2001). *The fourteenth mental measurements yearbook.* Lincoln, NE: Buros Institute of Mental Measurements.

Donders, J., Zhu, J., & Tulsky, D. (2001). Factor index score patterns in the WAIS-III standardization sample. *Assessment, 8,* 193–203.

Flynn, J. R. (1984). The mean IQ of Americans: Massive gains 1932 to 1978. *Psychological Bulletin, 95,* 29–51.

Jeyakumar, S. L. E., Warriner, E. M., & Raval, V. V. (2004). Balancing the need for reliability and time efficiency: Short forms of the Wechsler Adult Intelligence Scale—III. *Educational & Psychological Measurement, 64,* 71–87.

Kaufman, A. S., & Lichtenberger, E. O. (1999). *Essentials of WAIS-III assessment.* New York: Wiley.

Kennedy, J. E., Clement, P. F., & Curtiss, G. (2003). WAIS-III Processing Speed Index scores after TBI: The influence of working memory, psychomotor speed and perceptual processing. *Clinical Neuropsychologist, 17,* 303–307.

Taub, G. E., McGrew, K. S., & Witta, E. L. (2004). A confirmatory analysis of the factor structure and cross-age invariance of the Wechsler Adult Intelligence Scale—Third Edition. *Psychological Assessment, 16,* 85–89.

Taylor, M. J., & Heaton, R. K. (2001). Sensitivity and specificity of WAIS-III/WMS-III demographically corrected factor scores in neuropsychological assessment. *Journal of the International Neuropsychological Society, 7,* 867–874.

Tulsky, D. S., & Ledbetter, M. F. (2000). Updating the WAIS-III and WMS-III: Considerations for research and clinical practice. *Psychological Assessment, 12,* 253–262.

Tulsky, D. S., Saklofske, D. H., Chelune, G. J., Heaton, R. K., Ivnik, R. J., Bornstein, R., et al. (Eds.). (2003). *Clinical interpretation of the WAIS-III and WMS-III.* San Diego, CA: Academic Press.

Wechsler, D. (1981). Wechsler Adult Intelligence Scale—Revised. San Antonio, TX: The Psychological Corporation.

Zhu, J., Tulsky, D. S., Price, L., & Chen, H. (2001). WAIS-III reliability data for clinical groups. *Journal of the International Neuropsychological Society, 7,* 862–866.

Wechsler Intelligence Scale for Children—Fourth Edition

Author: David Wechsler
Ages: 6:0 through 16:11
Administration Time: 65 to 80 minutes
Publisher: The Psychological Corporation

The Wechsler Intelligence Scale for Children—Fourth Edition (WISC-IV, 2003) is an individually administered clinical instrument for assessing the cognitive ability of children of ages 6 years 0 months through 16 years 11 months. It is composed of 15 subtests, 10 of which have been retained from the WISC-III and five of which are new subtests. Administration takes approximately 65 to 80 minutes for most children. The test provides a composite score (Full Scale IQ) that represents general intellectual ability as well as four factor index scores (Verbal Comprehension, Perceptual Reasoning, Working Memory, and Processing Speed). Each of the IQs and factor indexes are standard scores with a mean of 100 and a standard score of 15 for 33 age bands. The subtests on the WISC-IV provide scaled scores with a mean of 10 and a standard deviation of 3.

Three subtests comprise the Verbal Comprehension Index: Similarities, Vocabulary, and Comprehension. In addition, two supplementary verbal subtests, Information and Word Reasoning, are also available and may substitute for any of the other Verbal Comprehension subtests if needed. These subtests assess verbal reasoning, comprehension, and conceptualization.

Three subtests comprise the Perceptual Reasoning Index: Block Design, Picture, Concepts, and Matrix Reasoning. Picture Completion is a supplementary subtest that can be used as a substitution if necessary. These subtests measure perceptual reasoning and organization.

Two subtests comprise the Working Memory Index: Digit Span and Letter-Number Sequencing. There is also one supplementary subtest, Arithmetic, that can be used to replace either of the Working Memory subtests. These subtests measure attention, concentration, and working memory.

Two subtests comprise the Processing Speed Index: Coding and Symbol Search. Cancellation is a supplementary subtest and can be used as a substitute for either subtest of the Processing Speed Index. These subtests measure the speed of mental and graphomotor processing.

There are two manuals that accompany the WISC-IV. The Administration and Scoring Manual contains all of the information needed to administer subtests, score responses, and complete the Record Form. The Technical and Interpretive Manual contains psychometric, technical, and basic interpretive information. During revision from the WISC-III to the WISC-IV, the Stimulus Book artwork was updated to be more attractive and engaging for children. Outdated items were revised or removed and new items were incorporated to reflect more contemporary ideas and situations. The Record Form was redesigned to reduce the occurrence of administration and scoring errors, and includes an abbreviated version of the administration and scoring rules for each subtest. Administration procedures were simplified to improve the user-friendliness of the scale. Instructions to examiners are more succinct and understandable, and similar wording is used across subtests to provide consistency and clarity. There are teaching, sample, and/or practice items along with queries and prompts incorporated within every subtest that should enhance the child's understanding and retention of the subtest task.

The standardization sample for the WISC-IV included 2,200 children divided into 11 age groups ranging from 6 to 16, with 200 participants in each age group. (Note that the Arithmetic subtest was normed on only 1,100 children—100 per age). The sample was representative of the 2000 U.S. census with respect to age, sex, race, parent education level, and geographic region.

The overall internal consistency reliability for the subtests ranges from .79 to .90. For the composite scales, the internal consistency reliability ranges from .88 to .97. The test-retest reliability ranges from .76 to .92 for the subtests and from .86 to .93 for the composite scales, with a mean time interval of 32 days. Research on the Wechsler scales has provided strong evidence of validity based on the scales' internal structure. Intercorrelations among subtests provide initial evidence of both the convergent and discriminant validity of the WISC-IV. Evidence of criterion validity was also shown by moderate to high correlations between the WISC-IV and the WISC-III, WPPSI-III, WAIS-III, WASI, WIAT-II, CMS, and GRS.

Additional Information

Flanagan, D. P., & Kaufman, A. S. (2004). *Essentials of WISC-IV assessment.* New York: Wiley.

Sattler, J. M., & Dumont, R. P. (2004). *Assessment of children: WISC-IV and WPPSI-III supplement.* San Diego, CA: Jerome Sattler.

Wechsler, D. (2003a). *Wechsler Intelligence Scale for Children—Fourth Edition:*

Administration and scoring manual. San Antonio, TX: The Psychological Corporation.

Wechsler, D. (2003b). *Wechsler Intelligence Scale for Children—Fourth Edition: Technical and interpretative manual.* San Antonio, TX: The Psychological Corporation.

http://alpha.fdu.edu/psychology/WISCIV_Index.htm

Wechsler Preschool and Primary Scales of Intelligence—Third Edition

Author: David Wechsler

Ages: 2:6 through 7:3

Administration Time: 2:0 through 3:11, approximately 30 to 35 minutes; 4:0 through 7:3, approximately 40 to 50 minutes

Publisher: The Psychological Corporation

The Wechsler Preschool and Primary Scales of Intelligence—Third Edition (WPPSI-III, 2002) is an individually administered instrument that assesses cognitive functioning and global intelligence for early childhood. The WPPSI-III is widely utilized in clinical and school settings as a means to identify potential delays or intellectual giftedness in early childhood development. It is frequently used to aid in decision making for special education preschool placement. The instrument can provide information pertaining to a child's cognitive strengths and weaknesses related to language, visual-perceptual skills, visual-motor integration, and reasoning.

The instrument covers a broad age range where advances in development are typical for youngsters. Therefore, the instrument is divided into two separate batteries (the first for ages 2 years 6 months through 3 years 11 months and the second for ages 4 years through 7 years 3 months). The test consists of 14 subtests that combine into four or five composites: Verbal IQ (VIQ), Performance IQ (PIQ), Processing Speed Quotient (PSQ, for upper ages only), General Language Composite (GLC), and a Full Scale IQ (FSIQ).

The FSIQ is a general measure of global intelligence reflecting performance across various subtests within the VIQ and PIQ domains. In general, the VIQ contains subtests that measure general fund of information, verbal comprehension, receptive and expressive language, attention span, and degree of abstract thinking. The PIQ is composed of subtests that collectively assess visual-motor integration, perceptual-organizational skills, concept formation, speed of mental processing, nonverbal problem solving, and graphomotor ability.

Composite scores are derived by combining scores from selected subtests as follows:

Ages 2:6 to 3:11

VIQ: Receptive Vocabulary and Information

PIQ: Block Design and Object Assembly

GLC: Receptive Vocabulary and Picture Naming

FSIQ: VIQ and PIQ combined

Ages 4:0 to 7:3

- VIQ: Information, Vocabulary, and Word Reasoning (Comprehension and Similarities may be substituted)
- PIQ: Block Design, Matrix Reasoning, and Picture Concepts (Picture Completion and Object Assembly may be substituted)
- PSQ: Coding and Symbol Search
- GLC: Receptive Vocabulary and Picture Naming
- FSIQ: VIQ, PIQ, and Coding.

Note that there are guidelines when deciding to utilize a substitution in replace of a core subtest. Only one substitution is allowed for a core subtest from either VIQ or PIQ. Overall, no more than two substitutions can be made when deriving a FSIQ.

The WPPSI-III was standardized on a sample of 1,700 children who were selected as being representative of the 2000 U.S. census data stratified on age, gender, geographic region, ethnicity, and parental education levels. The standardization sample was divided into nine age groups: eight of the groups contained 200 children, and one group (ages 7:0–7:3) consisted of 100 children.

There are age-specific starting points for each subtest as well as practice items to allow the child to become familiar with each task. Some subtests are scored as pass-fail, and others are scored based on the quality of response. The child receives full credit for all items prior to the starting point and does not receive credit for items after the discontinue rule is met. In general, the points are tabulated to formulate a raw score, which is converted into standard scores. The instrument also includes reverse and discontinue rules to eliminate unnecessary fatigue or extended testing time. Reverse rules are designed to tap into items prior to the child's age-specific starting point to allow the examiner to extend the floor for children who experience difficulty with the first couple of items. The discontinue rules vary for each subtest but follow the same underlying principle, which governs the examiner to discontinue administration after the child fails to correctly respond to a set number of items.

Scores provided include scaled scores, standard scores, percentiles, and qualitative descriptors. All raw scores are converted to allow a child's performance to be compared to his or her same-aged peers from the normative sample. Scaled scores have a mean of 10 and a standard deviation of 3. The composite standard scores have a mean of 100 and a standard deviation of 15. Percentile ranks are used to describe the child's performance relative to the normative sample as being better than or equal to the calculated percentage. Descriptors include Extremely Low, Borderline Intellectual Functioning, Low Average, Average, High Average, Superior, and Very Superior range.

Internal consistency values for each subtest ranged from .75 to .96. The test-retest coefficients ranged from .86 to .92. The average internal consistency values and test-retest coefficients exceeded .80. Correlations were obtained comparing the WPPSI-III FSIQ with other global measures; when compared with alternate assessment instruments such as the Differential Ability Scales, Bayley Scales of Infant Development-II, and WPPSI-R, coefficients ranged from .80 to .89.

Additional Information

Reviews of the WPPSI-III are pending for the upcoming *Sixteenth Mental Measurements Yearbook.*

Hamilton, W., & Burns, T. (2003). WPPSI-III: Wechsler Preschool and Primary Scale of Intelligence (3rd ed). *Applied Neuropsychology, 10,* 188–190.

Lichtenberger, E., & Kaufman, A. (2004). *Essentials of WPPSI-III Assessment.* Hoboken, NJ: Wiley.

Sattler, J. M., & Dumont, R. P. (2004). *Assessment of Children: WISC-IV and WPPSI-III supplement.* San Diego, CA: Jerome Sattler.

The Psychological Corporation. (2002). *WPPSI-III technical and interpretive manual.* San Antonio, TX: The Psychological Corporation.

Wechsler, D. (2002). *WPPSI-III administration and scoring manual.* San Antonio, TX: The Psychological Corporation.

http://alpha.fdu.edu/psychology/WPPSIIII.htm

Woodcock-Johnson III Tests of Cognitive Abilities

Authors: Richard W. Woodcock, Kevin McGrew, and Nancy Mather
Ages: 2 to 90
Testing Time: 15 minutes to 2 hours (depending upon test selection)
Publisher: Riverside Publishing

Unlike many individual ability tests, the Woodcock-Johnson III Tests of Cognitive Abilities (WJ III COG, 2001) are explicitly designed to assess a student's abilities on many specific Cattell-Horn-Carroll Gf-Gc (CHC) cognitive factors, not just a total score or a few factors. The General Intellectual Ability (GIA) score of the WJ III is based on a weighted combination of tests that best represent a common ability underlying all intellectual performance. Examiners can get a GIA (Std) score by administering the first seven tests in the Tests of Cognitive Abilities or a GIA (Ext) score by administering all 14 cognitive tests. Each of the cognitive tests represents a different broad CHC factor. A Brief Intellectual Ability (BIA) score is available, which takes about 10 to 15 minutes to administer and is especially useful for screenings and reevaluations. The BIA score is derived from three cognitive tests: Verbal Comprehension, Concept Formation, and Visual Matching. Examiners are permitted to select the tests they need to assess abilities in which they are interested for a particular student.

The WJ III Tests of Cognitive Abilities provides interpretive information from 20 tests to measure cognitive performance.

Comprehension-Knowledge (Gc)

Verbal Comprehension: Naming pictures, giving antonyms or synonyms for spoken words, and completing oral analogies

General Information: Answering "where" and "what" factual questions

Long-Term Retrieval (Glr)

Visual-Auditory Learning: The student is taught rebus symbols for words and tries to read sentences written with the symbols.

Retrieval Fluency: The student tries to name as many things as possible in one minute in each of three specified categories (e.g., fruits)

Visual Processing (Gv)

Spatial Relations: The student tries to select by sight alone, from many choices, the fragments that could be assembled into a given geometric shape.

Picture Recognition: The student is shown one or more pictures and tries to identify it or them on another page that includes several similar pictures.

Auditory Processing (Ga)

Sound Blending: The student tries to identify dictated words broken into separate sounds.

Auditory Attention: The student tries to recognize words dictated against increasingly loud background noise.

Fluid Reasoning (Gf)

Concept Formation: For each item, the student tries to figure out the rule that divides a set of symbols into two groups.

Analysis-Synthesis: The student tries to solve logical puzzles involving color codes similar to mathematical and scientific symbolic rules.

Processing Speed (Gs)

Visual Matching: As quickly as possible, for 3 minutes, the student circles two identical numbers in each row of six numbers.

Decision Speed: As quickly as possible, for 3 minutes, the student tries to find the two pictures in each row that are most similar conceptually (e.g., sundial and stopwatch).

Short-Term Memory (Gsm)

Numbers Reversed: The student repeats increasingly long series of dictated digits in reversed order.

Memory for Words: The student tries to repeat dictated random series of words in order.

Additional Tests

Incomplete Words: The student attempts to recognize words dictated with some sounds omitted.

Auditory Working Memory: The student tries to repeat randomly dictated words and numbers (e.g., cow 9 up 3 5) with the words first and then the numbers in the order they were dictated. This test also measures Gsm, working memory, or division of attention.

Visual-Auditory Learning—Delayed: The student tries again to read sentences written with the rebuses learned in Visual-Auditory Learning. There are norms from one half-hour to 8 days. This is an additional measure of Glr.

Rapid Picture Naming: The student tries to name simple pictures as quickly as possible for 2 minutes. This test measures Gs and naming facility or Rapid Automatized Naming (RAN).

Planning: The student tries to trace a complex, overlapping path without lifting the pencil, retracing any part of the path, or skipping any part. Gf and Gv are involved in this test.

Pair Cancellation: The student scans rows of pictures and tries, as quickly as possible for 3 minutes, to circle each instance in which a certain picture is followed by a certain other picture (e.g., each cat is followed by a tree). This test also measures Gs.

The WJ III provides raw scores that are converted, using age- or grade-based norms, to Standard Scores, Percentile Ranks, W scores, age and grade equivalents (AE and GE), relative proficiency index (RPI), Instructional Ranges, and Cognitive-Academic Language Proficiency (CALP) levels. All score transformation is performed through the use of the computer program (WJ III Compuscore). The program can also generate several "discrepancy" analyses: intra-ability discrepancies (intracognitive, intra-achievement, and intra-individual) and ability achievement discrepancies (predicted achievement vs. achievement, general intellectual ability vs. achievement, and oral language ability vs. achievement).

The WJ III was normed on 8,818 children and adults (4,783 in grades kindergarten through 12) in a well-designed national sample. The same persons also provided norms for the WJ III tests of academic achievement, so the ability and achievement tests can be compared directly and cognitive and achievement tests can be combined to measure CHC factors. The technical manual provides extensive coverage of reliability and validity areas. The median reliability coefficient alphas for all age groups for the standard battery of the WJ III COG for tests 1 through 10 ranged from .81 to .94. For the extended battery, median coefficients ranged from .74 to .97. The reliability scores for the WJ III meet or exceed standards. The median cluster reliabilities are mostly .90 or higher, and the individual test reliabilities are mostly .80 or higher and can be used for decision-making purposes with support from other sources. The manual presents considerable evidence supporting the validity of scores from the test, noting that the earlier versions of the battery have also been shown to have validity. Test content on the WJ III COG has emerged from previous versions, is similar to the content found on other well-established cognitive measures, or is based on sound experimental instruments.

Additional Information

Reviewed in Plake, B. S., Impara, J. C., & Spies, R. A. (Eds.). (2003). *The fifteenth mental measurements yearbook.* Lincoln, NE: Buros Institute of Mental Measurements.

Mather, N., & Jaffe, L. (2002). *Woodcock-Johnson III: Reports, recommendations, and strategies.* New York: Wiley.

Rizza, M. G., McIntosh, D. E., & McCunn, A. (2001). Profile analysis of the Woodcock-Johnson III Tests of Cognitive Abilities with gifted students. *Psychology in the Schools, 38* (special issue: New perspectives in gifted education), 447–455.

Schrank, F. A., Flanagan, D. P., Woodcock, R. W., & Mascolo, J. T. (2001). *Essentials of WJ III cognitive abilities assessment.* New York: Wiley.

http://alpha.fdu.edu/psychology/woodcock_index.htm

http://www.iapsych.com/wj3delrecall_files/frame.htm

EARLY CHILDHOOD DEVELOPMENT

Bayley Scale for Infant Development, Second Edition

Author: Nancy Bayley

Ages: 1 month through 42 months

Testing Time: 15 to 60 minutes

Publisher: The Psychological Corporation

The BSID-II (1993) is an individually administered measure of developmental functioning of infants and children between 1 and 42 months of age that includes three scales: Mental, Motor, and Behavior Rating. It was designed to (1) produce observable behavioral responses in infants; (2) assess children's level of cognitive, language, personal-social, and gross-motor development; (3) identify areas of impairment or delay; (4) develop curricula for interventions; and (5) assess interventions. The BSID-II presents infants with situations and tasks designed to produce an observable set of behavioral responses. The observed responses are scored on complementary development scales—Mental Scale, Motor Scale, and Behavior Rating Scale.

The test takes 15 to 35 minutes to administer to children less than 15 months of age and up to 60 minutes for children older than 15 months of age. The Mental Scale assesses cognitive, language, and personal-social developments, and the Motor Scale assesses fine and gross motor development. The Behavior Rating Scale is completed by the assessor throughout the testing situation and allows for greater interpretation of the Mental and Motor Scales. Typical areas of assessment within the Behavior Rating Scale are attention, arousal, orientation, engagement, emotional regulation, and motor quality. The manual provides scoring instructions for each item as well as information for interpretation of the results using case studies as examples. The Bayley Infant Neurodevelopmental Screener, which contains 11 to 13 items selected from the BSID-II, allows programs with high caseloads to screen infants 3 to 24 months for neurological impairment or developmental delay in 10 to 20 minutes.

The BSID-II was standardized on a stratified random sample of 1,700 children (850 boys and 850 girls). The sample was stratified in terms of age, sex, region, race/ethnicity, and parent education. Seventeen age groups were created ranging in age from 1 month to 42 months, each with 100 children. Internal consistency has been shown to be .88 for the Mental Scale, .84 for the Motor Scale, and .88 for the Behavior Rating Scale using Cronbach's alpha. Test-retest reliability has shown coefficients for children aged 1 to 12 months of .83 for the Mental Scale and .77 for the Motor Scale. On the Behavior Rating Scale, for children aged 1 month, the test-retest reliability was seen to be .55, and at 12 months of age it was .90. For children aged 24 and 42 months, test-retest reliability was seen to be .91 for the Mental Scale, .79 for the Motor Scale, and .60 for the Behavior Rating Scale. The overall test-retest reliability coefficients were .78 for the Motor Scale and .87 for the Motor Scale. Original interrater reliability coefficients for the BSID-II were .96 for the Mental Scale, .75 for the Motor Scale, and between .47 and 1.00 for the Behavior Rating Scale. Chandlee, Heathfield, Salganik, Damokosh, and Radcliffe (2002) found similar interscorer reliability when 60 items from the BSID-II Mental Scale were administered to 29 children between the ages of 12 and 39 months.

Agreement between scorers was generally 90 percent or above, but 23 percent of the items showed reliability below 90 percent.

Concurrent validity studies have been performed on the BSID-II and the BSID. For the Mental Development Index, the correlation was .62, and for the Psychomotor Development Index, the correlation was .63. Goldstein, Fogle, Wieber, and O'Shea (1995) compared administrations of the BSID and BSID-II to high-risk preterm infants and found that the two tests correlated very highly. Mean scores from the BSID-II were lower than those from the BSID, as was expected.

The Mental Development Index has been correlated with the McCarthy Scales of Children Abilities (MSCA) and the Wechsler Preschool and Primary Scale of Intelligence—Revised (WPPSI-R) Full Scale IQ, Verbal IQ, and Performance IQ. Results showed correlations of .79, .73, .73, and .63, respectively. The Psychomotor Development Index has also been correlated with the same instruments, and correlations were .45, .41, .39, and .37, respectively. Tests have shown the BSID-II as a whole to be in 80 percent agreement with the Denver Developmental Screening Test II when classifying children.

Additional Information

Reviewed in Impara, J. C., & Plake, B. S. (Eds.). (1998). *The thirteenth mental measurements yearbook.* Lincoln, NE: Buros Institute of Mental Measurements.

Bayley, N. (1993). *Bayley Scales of Infant Development, Second Edition.* San Antonio, TX: The Psychological Corporation.

Black, M. M., & Matula, K. (1999). *Essentials of Bayley Scales of Infant Development II assessment.* New York: Wiley.

Chandlee, J., Heathfield, L. T., Salganik, M., Damokosh, A., & Radcliffe, J. (2002). Are we consistent in administering and scoring the Bayley Scales of Infant Development II? *Journal of Psychoeducational Assessment, 20,* 183–200.

Glenn, S. M., Cunningham, C. C., & Dayus, B. (2001). Comparison of the 1969 and 1993 standardizations of the Bayley Mental Scales of Infant Development for infants with Down's syndrome. *Journal of Intellectual Disability Research, 45,* 56–62.

Goldstein, D. J., Fogle, E. E., Wieber, J. L., & O'Shea, T. M. (1995). Comparison of the Bayley Scales of Infant Development—Second Edition and the Bayley Scales of Infant Development with premature infants. *Journal of Psychoeducational Assessment, 13,* 391–396.

Niccols, A., & Latchman, A. (2002). Stability of the Bayley Mental Scale of Infant Development with high risk infants. *British Journal of Developmental Disabilities, 48,* 3–13.

Boehm Test of Basic Concepts—Third Edition

Author: Ann E. Boehm
Ages: 5 to 7 years
Testing Time: 30 to 45 minutes
Publisher: The Psychological Corporation

The Boehm Test of Basic Concepts—third edition (BTBC-3, 2000) was developed to assess the understanding of basic concepts in young children. The test can be administered individually or in group format in kindergarten, grade 1, and grade 2. Children are asked to correctly identify a picture from among several choices when presented with verbal cues incorporating such terms as *over, least, left,* and so on. Based on these results, children can be identified as deficient in conceptual development and assessed for school readiness.

The BTBC-3 assesses 50 basic concepts most frequently occurring in kindergarten and first- and second-grade curricula. These include size (e.g., medium-sized), direction (away), quantity (as many), time (first), classification (all), and general (other).

Two parallel forms, E and F, allow for pre- and posttesting to help determine whether the student's comprehension of the concept is consistent across multiple contexts. The results can be used to demonstrate progress as a result of teaching or intervention. The manual includes directions for administration in English and Spanish.

Boehm-3 gives raw scores and percentile ranks. It was normed on two samples in the fall of 1999 (Form E, N=2,866; Form F, N=3,189) and in the spring of 2000 (Form E, N=2,348; Form F, N=2,196). Reliability studies yielded coefficients alpha between .80 to .91. An alternate-forms reliability study showed that nearly 94 percent of students had a difference of 4 or fewer raw score points from one form to the other.

Additional Information

Review is forthcoming in *The Sixteenth Mental Measurements Yearbook.*

Boehm, A. E. (2000). Assessment of basic relational concepts. In B. A. Bracken, *Psychoeducational assessment of preschool children* (3rd ed., pp. 186–203). Needham Heights, MA: Allyn & Bacon.

Bracken Basic Concept Scale—Revised

Author: Bruce A. Bracken

Ages: 2:6 to 7:11

Administration Time: 30 minutes

Publisher: The Psychological Corporation

The Bracken Basic Concept Scale—Revised (BBCS-R, 1998) is a developmentally sensitive measure of children's basic concept acquisition and receptive language skills. It can be used as a language measure, a school readiness screener, and an intelligence screener, although its primary purpose is to measure basic concept acquisition. This latest version contains colorful artwork, new items, and improved norms. The BBCS-R measures basic concept acquisition and receptive language skills. It comprises items relating to 301 basic concepts in 11 distinct conceptual categories: Colors, Numbers/Counting, Comparisons, Quantity, Direction/Position, Textiles/Materials, Time/Sequence, Letters, Sizes, Shapes, and Self/Social Awareness.

The BBCS-R was normed on a nationally representative sample of 1,100 children, 200 at each age group. Included in the sample were proportionate samples of children with disabilities (e.g., developmentally delayed, learning disabled). Separate samples of Spanish-speaking children (e.g., Caribbean, Mexican, Puerto Rican) were also tested to provide technical data for using the BBCS-R with Hispanic youth. For English-speaking children, the average subtest reliability coefficient ranged from .73 to .98, while the total test reliabilities ranged from .96 to .99 across age spans. Reliability for the Spanish-speaking children was very similar. The technical manual for the BBCS-R provides several sources of validity data, including content, construct, and criterion-related validity. The BBCS-R is linked directly to remedial and instructional interventions though the Bracken Concept development program (Bracken, 1986).

Additional Information

Reviewed in Plake, B. S., & Impara, J. C. (Eds.). (2001). *The fourteenth mental measurements yearbook.* Lincoln, NE: Buros Institute of Mental Measurements.

Bracken, B. A. (1998). *Examiner's manual for the Bracken Basic Concept Scale—Revised.* San Antonio, TX: The Psychological Corporation.

Panter, J. E. (2000). Validity of the Bracken Basic Concept Scale—Revised for predicting performance on the Metropolitan Readiness Test—Sixth Edition. *Journal of Psychoeducational Assessment, 18,* 104–110.

Wilson, P. (2004). A preliminary investigation of an early intervention program: Examining the intervention effectiveness of the Bracken Concept Development Program and the Bracken Basic Concept Scale—Revised with Head Start students. *Psychology in the Schools, 41,* 301–311.

Developmental Assessment of Young Children

Authors: Judith K. Voress and Taddy Maddox

Ages: Birth through 5:11

Testing Time: 1 hour 40 minutes for comprehensive battery

Publisher: PRO-ED

The Developmental Assessment of Young Children (DAYC, 1998) is designed for children between birth and 5 years 11 months. It is an individually administered test of developmental abilities in the adaptive, cognitive, communication, physical, and social-emotional domains. Each of the five domains reflects areas that are required for assessment and intervention for young children according to IDEA. This particular measure can be tailored to the specific assessment needs of each child, or all domains may be administered. The DAYC has four uses: the identification of children with developmental delays, recognition of strengths and weaknesses, documentation of a child's progress, and measurement of children's developmental abilities for research purposes.

The Cognitive subtest consists of 78 items that assess concept development. The Communication subtest consists of 78 items measuring receptive/expressive language and verbal/nonverbal abilities. The Social-Emotional subtest consists of 58 items that assess social awareness in relationships and social competence. The

Physical Development subtest consists of 87 items measuring motor development. The last subtest, Adaptive Behavior, consists of 62 items that assess independent functioning in self-help.

Administration time is approximately 1 hour and 40 minutes for the comprehensive battery. Each subtest requires about 20 minutes to complete. Testing may occur over more than one session; however, it should be completed as soon as possible. Administration is fairly straightforward. Items passed receive 1 point and those failed receive 0 points. Basal and ceilings are utilized for each subtest. Data are recorded on the subtest scoring forms. The DAYC provides standard scores, percentile scores, and age equivalents as well as a General Development Quotient (GDQ) if all five subtests are completed.

Normative data were collected on a national sample of 1,269 individuals consistent with the 1996 U.S. census. The sample also includes an "at-risk" category of children with no present disability but an identified risk factor. Internal consistency reliability coefficients range from .90 to .99, and test-retest reliability was good (r = .90). Three types of validity were reported in the manual. Content-description validity correlations range from .94 to .99. Criterion-related validity was examined through comparison with the Battelle Developmental Inventory Screening Test and the Revised Gesell and Amatruda Developmental and Neurologic Examination. Coefficients were significant at the .01 level with the Battelle (range from .47 to .61) and at the .05 level with the Gesell (range from .41 to .53). Construct validity was assessed, but statistical data were not reported in the available reviews.

Reviews state that the DAYC is well organized, easy to understand, and simple to use. One limitation of the DAYC is the lack of research regarding treatment effects. It is suggested that the DAYC is not appropriate for evaluating change after a program intervention.

Additional Information

Reviewed in Plake, B. S., & Impara, J. C. (Eds.). (2001). *The fourteenth mental measurements yearbook.* Lincoln, NE: Buros Institute of Mental Measurements.

Miller Assessment for Preschoolers

Author: Lucy Miller
Ages: 2:9 through 5:8
Testing Time: 30 to 40 minutes
Publisher: The Psychological Corporation

The Miller Assessment for Preschoolers (MAP, 1982) is a comprehensive measure of developmental abilities for children ages 2 years 9 months to 5 years 8 months. The MAP identifies children who show moderate preacademic problems that may affect development. The protocols are clearly labeled for each age group and indicate the child's level of development based on a color-coded system. Twenty-seven performance items create the core of the MAP. The performance indexes are Sensory and Motor, Coordination, Verbal and Nonverbal, Foundations and Coordination, and Complex Abilities. Administration time is approximately 30 minutes. All 27 performance items must be administered to calculate the total MAP score.

Normative data were collected using five different editions of the MAP. The final edition was normed on 1,200 preschoolers. The MAP adequately differentiates children in the lowest 25 percent of abilities but does not adequately identify those in the upper 75 percent. Interrater reliability ranges from .84 to .99 for the performance indexes and is .98 for the total MAP score. Internal consistency reliability is .79. Construct validity was examined between the indexes and the MAP total score and ranges from .65 to .78.

The test materials are clearly organized in marked containers for efficient administration. The examiner's administration binder is also clearly marked with chapter tabs.

Additional Information

Reviewed in Mitchell, J. V., Jr. (Ed.). (1985). *The ninth mental measurements yearbook.* Lincoln, NE: Buros Institute of Mental Measurements.

Daniels, L. E. (1998). The Miller Assessment for Preschoolers: Construct validity and clinical use with children with disabilities. *American Journal of Occupational Therapy, 52,* 857–865.

Humphry, R., & King-Thomas, L. (1993). A response and some facts about the Miller Assessment for Preschoolers. *Occupational Therapy Journal of Research, 13,* 34–49.

Kirkpatrick, L. A., & Schouten, P. G. (1993). "Questions and concerns about the Miller Assessment for Preschoolers": Reply. *Occupational Therapy Journal of Research, 13,* 50–61.

Miller, L. J. (1993). "Questions and concerns about the Miller Assessment for Preschoolers": Comment. *Occupational Therapy Journal of Research, 13,* 29–33.

Parush, S., Winokur, M., & Goldstand, S. (2002a). Long-term predictive validity of the Miller Assessment for Preschoolers. *Perceptual & Motor Skills, 94,* 921–926.

Parush, S., Winokur, M., & Goldstand, S. (2002b). Prediction of school performance using the Miller Assessment for Preschoolers (MAP): A validity study. *American Journal of Occupational Therapy, 56,* 547–555.

Schouten, P. G., & Kirkpatrick, L. A. (1993). Questions and concerns about the Miller Assessment for Preschoolers. *Occupational Therapy Journal of Research, 13,* 7–28.

Mullen Scales of Early Learning, AGS Edition, 1995

Author: Ellen M. Mullen
Ages: 0 to 68 months
Testing Time: 25 to 40 minutes
Publisher: American Guidance Service (AGS)

The Mullen Scales of Early Learning: AGS Edition (MSEL:AGS; Mullen, 1995) is an individually administered test of cognitive functioning that may be used with children from birth to 68 months. The MSEL:AGS consists of four cognitive scales, Visual Reception, Receptive Language, Expressive Language, and Fine Motor, as well as a Gross Motor Scale. Scores on the four cognitive scales are combined to yield the Early Learning Composite (ELC).

The Visual Reception Scale attempts to measure visual processing, visual discrimination, and visual memory, by requiring the child to respond by pointing to objects or pictures or by manipulating objects. Item examples include fixating on and tracking a silver triangle, looking for a toy when covered and then displaced, and sorting blocks and spoons by category.

The Receptive Language Scale purports to assess a child's auditory comprehension and auditory memory skills. This scale places the emphasis on a child's ability to decode verbal input while reducing output requirements. Examples of questions on this item include "What is your name?" and "What do we wash our hands with?"

The Expressive Language Scale was constructed to measure speaking ability and language formation. This scale assesses a child's spontaneous utterances, verbal responses to items, and concept formation. Children can receive points for jabbering with inflection, naming objects, or repeating numbers or sentences back to the examiner.

The Fine Motor Scale purports to measure a child's ability to manipulate small objects and use control and coordination skills. As on the Visual Reception Scale, vocalization is not required. This scale requires the child to manipulate objects using one hand (unilaterally) and two hands (bilaterally).

The Gross Motor Scale attempts to assess the range of gross motor abilities from 0 to 33 months with 35 items. Given that the data for the Gross Motor Scale are available only for children aged 34 months to 68 months, this scale is not included in the ELC. The scale asks the child to perform such tasks as support self on forearms, walk with one hand held, and walk on a line with arms at side.

The raw scores for each scale can be converted into age-adjusted normalized scores. The T score for the four cognitive skills can be further converted into a normalized ELC score (M=100, SD=15). In addition, the scores can be used to obtain the child's percentile rank and age equivalent score, the age at which the child's raw score is the median score.

The MSEL:AGS was standardized on a nationally representative sample of 1,849 children aged 2 days to 69 months with no known physical and mental disabilities and parents who spoke primarily English. Data on children were collected during two different periods—1981 to 1986 and 1987 to 1989—for the south, west, north, and north central regions. Approximately 40 percent of the sample came from the earlier norming period and included children only in the Northeast region. Although the standardization sample included 1,849 individuals, with at least 200 individuals per 1-year interval, the sample approximated the U.S. population, as indicated by 1990 census data, only on gender. There was limited correspondence between U.S. population estimates and the standardization sample on race/ethnicity, community size, and socioeconomic status (i.e., fathers' occupation). Users should be extremely cautious in interpreting an individual's performance using the MSEL:AGS norms given that the data were collected during two different time periods and later combined to form the current standardization sample data.

The total test (i.e., ELC) internal consistency reliability coefficients of the MSEL:AGS range from .83 to .95 (median = .91) and are considered at least adequate. However, the test-retest reliability coefficients for the ELC cannot be assessed because they are not available. That is, test-retest reliability data are based on an earlier version of the scales that did not contain the ELC. Specific construct validity evidence consists of the developmental trend of the raw scores, intercorrelations of the scales, and factor analysis. Although this analysis provides some evidence for the ELC approximation of *g*, there is limited empirical evidence to support the placement of items on their respective scales or for the inclusion of the scales themselves. In addition, no confirmatory factor analyses were conducted with the AGS version of the MSEL. The limited construct validity evidence of the MSEL:AGS may be a major quantitative weakness of this instrument because interpretation of an individual's performance on the various scales is rendered tentative at best.

Additional Information

Reviewed in Plake, B. S., & Impara, J. C. (Eds.). (2001). *The fourteenth mental measurements yearbook.* Lincoln, NE: Buros Institute of Mental Measurements.

Bradley-Johnson, S. (2001). Cognitive assessment for the youngest children: A critical review of tests. *Journal of Psychoeducational Assessment, 19,* 19–44.

Dumont, R., Cruse, C., Alfonso, V., & Levine, C. (2000). A test review: The Mullen Scale of Early Learning: AGS Edition (MSEL:AGS). *Journal of Psychoeducational Assessment, 18,* 125–132.

VISUAL MOTOR

Beery-Buktenica Developmental Test of Visual-Motor Integration—Fifth Edition

Authors: Keith E. Beery, Norman A. Buktenica, and Natasha A. Beery

Ages: 2 through 18

Administration Time: 10 to 15 minutes

Publisher: Pearson Assessments

The Beery-Buktenica Developmental Test of Visual-Motor Integration (Beery VMI, 2004) is a measure of visual and motor integration for ages 2 through 18. The Short Format and Full Format tests present individuals with drawings of geometric forms arranged in order of increasing difficulty, which they are asked to copy on the record form. The Beery VMI includes supplemental tests of visual perception and motor coordination that are generally administered when results show that further testing is necessary. With these supplemental tests, a comparison of the individual's test results with relatively pure visual and motor performances can be obtained. The test can be administered individually or to groups, although individual administration is recommended for the supplemental tests. The authors suggest that these tests should be given in the following order, in which they were normed: VMI, Visual Perception, and Motor Coordination. Administration time varies from 10 to 15 minutes for the Short Form and Full Form tests and is approximately 5 minutes for the supplemental tests. The record form provides the examinee with instructions, and the manual contains administration guidelines and examples of correct and incorrect responses for each item.

This measure was normed in 2003 on a national sample of 2,512 individuals between 2 and 18 years of age. The sample was representative of the 2000 U.S. census data with respect to gender, ethnicity, and geographic location. Results are reported as standard scores (with a mean of 100 and a standard deviation of 15), scaled scores (with a mean of 10 and a standard deviation of 3), percentiles, or other equivalents. In the newest edition of the VMI, the manual also provides approximately 600 Stepping Stones, or milestones, derived from age-specific norms from birth through 6 years of age.

The internal consistency of the items on the Beery VMI was determined to be .96, and interrater reliability coefficients ranged from .92 to .98 for the VMI and its supplemental Visual Perception and Motor Coordination tests. Test-retest reliability ranges from .85 to .89 for a mean time interval of 10 days. Past versions of the test have been frequently correlated with the original Bender-Gestalt, with a median correlation of .56. In particular, significant correlations have been demonstrated for the Bender Visual Motor Gestalt Test and the VMI with a sample of gifted elementary school students (Knoff & Sperling, 1986), and the VMI showed more developmental sensitivity than the Bender-Gestalt Test when used in a sample of emotionally and behaviorally disturbed adolescents (Shapiro & Simpson, 1994). The Beery VMI has also demonstrated correlations ranging from .62 to .75 with the Copying, Position in Space, and Eye-Hand Coordination subtests of the Developmental Test of Visual Perception (DTVP-2), whereas the correlation between the Beery VMI and the Drawing subtest of the Wide Range Assessment of Visual Motor Abilities (WRAVMA) was only .52. Past editions of the VMI have been found to be a good predictor of academic or other problems when used in combination with other measures, although correlations decline as children progress through grade levels.

Additional Information

Although no review of the Beery VMI-Fifth Edition was available at the time of this writing, the fourth edition was reviewed in Plake, B. S., & Impara, J. C. (Eds.). (2001). *The fourteenth mental measurements yearbook.* Lincoln, NE: Buros Institute of Mental Measurements.

Beery, K. E., Buktenica, N. A., & Beery, N. A. (2004). *The Beery-Buktenica Developmental Test of Visual-Motor Integration: Administration, scoring and teaching manual.* Minneapolis, MN: NCS Pearson.

Knoff, H. M., & Sperling, B. L. (1986). Gifted children and visual-motor development: A comparison of Bender-Gestalt and VMI test performance. *Psychology in the Schools, 23,* 247–251.

Marr, D., & Cermak, S. (2002). Predicting handwriting performance of early elementary students with the Developmental Test of Visual-Motor Integration. *Perceptual & Motor Skills, 95,* 661–669.

Shapiro, S. K., & Simpson, R. G. (1994). Patterns and predictors of performance on the Bender-Gestalt and the Developmental Test of Visual Motor Integration in a sample of behaviorally and emotionally disturbed adolescents. *Journal of Psychoeducational Assessment, 12,* 254–263.

Bender Visual-Motor Gestalt Test, Second Edition

Authors: Gary Brannigan and Scott Decker

Ages: 4 to 85

Testing Time: 10 to 20 minutes

Publisher: Riverside Publishing

The original Bender-Gestalt test was a frequently administered and thoroughly researched drawing test. Originally developed as a measure of visual-motor maturity in children, the test has come to be used as a projective personality technique, as well as being used with children as an indicator of school readiness, emotional problems, and learning difficulties. It has also become widely used as a screening measure for neurological impairment in both adults and children. The Bender-Gestalt II (2003) is an individually administered assessment used to evaluate visual-motor integration skills in children and adults ages 4 to 85. It consists of 16 geometric designs, printed on stimulus cards. These designs include the original nine designs from the Bender-Gestalt Test and seven new designs that have been included to enhance its utility in educational, psychological, and neuropsychological assessment. The Bender-Gestalt II also includes an Observation Form as well as two supplemental tests, the Motor Test and the Perception Test, which aid in evaluating the examinee's performance on the Bender-Gestalt II. Administration involves two phases: the Copy phase and the Recall phase. In the Copy phase, the examinee is asked to copy each of the designs onto a blank sheet of paper. In the Recall phase, the examinee is asked to redraw the designs from memory. Although the test has no time limits, the examiner records how long it takes the examinee to reproduce the designs. The Bender-Gestalt II Examiner's Manual contains administration and scoring guidelines; information on the standardization and norming process; normative tables; reliability and validity test data; and a new, easy-to-use global scoring system.

The standardization sample of the Bender-Gestalt II was based on a stratified, random sampling plan of 4,000 individuals, ages 4 to 85, devised to match the percentages of the stratification variables from the U.S. 2000 census (U.S. Census Bureau, 2001). The normative sample was designed to be nationally representative and matched to percentages of the U.S. population for demographic variables including age, sex, race/ethnicity, geographic region, and socioeconomic level (educational attainment). In addition, large numbers of individuals from clinical or special populations were collected to study the differential effects of group inclusion on test performance. These populations included individuals with Mental Retardation, specific learning disabilities, Attention-Deficit/Hyperactivity Disorder, serious emotional disturbances, Autism, Alzheimer's disease, and giftedness. After all normative data were collected, z-scores were transformed into a standard score scale (M=100, SD=15). Scores were rounded and truncated to limit the standard score range to 4 standard deviations above and below the mean, providing a range of standard scores from 40 to 160.

A variety of methods was used to estimate the reliability of the Bender-Gestalt II Copy and Recall phases. When using the Global Scoring System, the average interrater reliability was .90 for the Copy phase and .96 for the Recall phase, both impressive given its ease of use and diverse applications. Using the split-half procedure to measure internal consistency, the overall reliability for the standardization group was .91 with an average standard error of measurement of 4.55, indicating consistent and stable measurement. In test-retest reliability studies, the average corrected coefficient was .85 for the Copy phase and .83 for the Recall phase. These coefficients were well within the acceptable range. Evidence also suggests high validity. Several studies demonstrated a high correlation between the Bender-Gestalt II and intelligence, achievement, and visual-motor ability measures, which are often used in comprehensive psychoeducational assessment. The results also suggest that the Bender-Gestalt II is related to, yet distinct from, other constructs. The Bender-Gestalt II measures a single underlying construct that is sensitive to maturation and/or development, and scores are highly influenced by and sensitive to clinical conditions. This dimensionality provides added utility to the test.

Additional Information

Reviews for this edition are pending for *The Sixteenth Mental Measurements Yearbook.*

Brannigan, G. G., & Decker, S. L. (2003). *Bender Visual-Motor Gestalt Test—Second Edition: Examiner's manual.* Itasca, IL: Riverside Publishing.

Wide Range Assessment of Visual Motor Abilities

Authors: Wayne Adams and David Sheslow

Ages: 3 to 17

Testing Time: 4 to 10 minutes per subtest

Publisher: Wide Range

The Wide Range Assessment of Visual Motor Abilities (WRAVMA, 1995) provides a Visual-Motor Integration Composite resulting from separate subtest assessments of Fine-Motor, Visual-Spatial, and Visual-Motor abilities. These three areas can be measured individually or in combination.

Administration time for each subtest of the WRAVMA takes about 4–10 minutes. The Fine-Motor (peg board) test has the individual insert as many pegs as possible into a waffled, roughly square peg board. The examinee has 90 seconds to complete this task. Norms are provided for both dominant and nondominant hands. In the Visual-Spatial (matching) test, the child is asked to mark the option that goes best with the standard presented. Correct selection depends on visual-spatial skills such as perspective, orientation, rotation, and size discrimination. The Visual-Motor (drawing) subtest requires children to copy designs that are developmentally arranged to increase in difficulty. The manual supplies examples of acceptable and unacceptable responses for the 24 drawing items, as well as justifications for each. The test booklets are colorful and appealing.

Performance on the subtests can be interpreted both qualitatively and quantitatively to create a more complete evaluation of visual-motor abilities. Scaled scores, standard scores, age equivalents, and percentiles may be obtained for each subtest.

The WRAVMA was normed on a representative sample of over 2,600 children, ages 3–17, stratified according to gender, geographic region, socioeconomic standing, and race/ethnic group. This sample reflected the 1990 U.S. census data.

Reliability measures of the three subtests show internal consistency coefficients exceeding .90 and test-retest reliability coefficients ranging from .81 to .91. Construct validity is supported by item separations of .99. Concurrent validity varies from .67 for the WRAVMA Visual-Spatial test with the Motor Free Visual Perception Test, to .81 for the WRAVMA Fine-Motor test with the grooved peg board, and .87 for the WRAVMA Visual-Motor test with the Beery-Buktenica Developmental Test of Visual-Motor Integration (VMI).

Additional Information

Reviewed in Plake, B. S., & Impara, J. C. (Eds.). (2001). *The fourteenth mental measurements yearbook.* Lincoln, NE: Buros Institute of Mental Measurements.

Adams, W., & Sheslow, D. (1995). *Wide Range Assessment of Visual Motor Abilities.* Wilmington, DE: Wide Range.

LANGUAGE

Clinical Evaluation of Language Fundamentals, Third Edition

Authors: Eleanor Semel, Elisabeth H. Wiig, and Wayne Secord
Ages: 6 through 21
Testing Time: 45 to 60 minutes
Publisher: The Psychological Corporation

The Clinical Evaluation of Language Fundamentals, Third Edition (CELF-3, 1995) is an individually administered battery of tests that can be used to diagnose language disorders. The battery is designed to be administered to individuals ages 6 through 21 and takes approximately 45 to 60 minutes to administer. There are two stimulus easels that contain visual stimuli. Examinee responses are recorded on the record form.

The CELF-3 consists of subtests that are categorized into either Expressive or Receptive domains. Subtests include Formulated Sentences (subject is given target word and picture stimulus and asked to form sentence), Sentence Assembly (subject produces two semantically and syntactically intact sentences from visually and orally presented words or word clusters), Word Structure (subject completes orally presented sentences with picture stimuli), Word Associations (subject lists as many words within given category as possible in 1 minute), Recalling Sentences (imitation of orally presented sentences), Sentence Structure (subject points to one of four pictures in response to an orally presented stimulus), Semantic Relationships (subject listens to four facts, then selects two of four visually presented options), Word Classes (subject picks two out of three or four orally presented words that go together), and Concepts and Directions (subject identifies pictures of geometric shapes in response to orally presented direction). The scores in each domain produce Receptive and Expressive Language Composites that together are used to obtain the Total Language Score. Each provides standard scores, percentile ranks, and age equivalents.

The norms are based on a sample of 2,450 students that ranged in age from 6 to

21 years. The standardization sample consisted of normally achieving students; however, a number of cases of individuals with language disorders were collected to add to the battery's clinical validity. The sample was representative of U.S. children with respect to sex, race, geographic region, family income, and highest education achieved by primary caregiver.

Internal consistency tests for the Standard Scores ranged from .83 to .95 and from .54 to .95 for the subtests (Semel, Wiig, & Secord, 1995). Test-retest reliability was calculated using 152 individuals from the norming sample. Semel et al. reported that reliability results for the Receptive Language Scores and Expressive Language Scores were .80 and .86, respectively, and that the mean correlation for the Total Language Score was .91. Reliability scores on the subtests ranged from .52 to .90. Semel et al. performed a discriminant analysis to determine the extent to which the CELF-3 would discriminate between individuals who did and did not have a learning disorder. Results indicated a 71.3 percent concurrence between the CELF-3 and school system classification requirements. Validity was further examined by comparing the CELF-3 to the Wechsler Intelligence Scale for Children (WISC-III). Correlations ranging from .56 to .75 were found. Research is supportive of the CELF-3 as a measure of verbal ability, but its role as an effective predictive instrument or as one legitimate for the language-disabled population is questionable due to the normative sample used.

Additional Information

Reviewed in Impara, J. C., & Plake, B. S. (Eds.). (1998). *The thirteenth mental measurements yearbook.* Lincoln, NE: Buros Institute of Mental Measurements.

Biddle, A., Watson, L., Hooper, C., et al. (2002). *Criteria for determining disability in speech-language disorders: Evidence report / technology assessment no. 52.* Rockville, MD: Agency for Healthcare Research and Quality.

Semel, E. M., Wiig, E. H., & Secord, W. A. (1995). *Clinical Evaluation of Language Fundamentals, Third Edition.* San Antonio, TX: The Psychological Corporation.

Comprehensive Assessment of Spoken Language

Author: Elizabeth Carrow-Woolfolk

Ages: 3:0 through 21:11

Testing Time: 30 to 45 minutes depending on what scale(s) are used

Publisher: AGS Publishing

The Comprehensive Assessment of Spoken Language (CASL, 1999) is an individually administered, norm-referenced test that provides an assessment of the oral language skills of children and young adults. Only a verbal or nonverbal (pointing) response is required of the examinee, and reading or writing ability is not needed to respond to test items. Each of the 15 CASL tests is a highly reliable, stand-alone test. The clinician is free to give one test or several and can report the score(s) with confidence. A subtest must be given in conjunction with other subtests to form a composite score.

The CASL provides an in-depth assessment of four language categories.

- *Lexical / Semantic Language,* assessed using the following tests

  Basic Concepts: Examiner reads a sentence aloud while examinee looks at four pictures and points to the picture or part of the picture that represents the correct response.

  Antonyms: Examiner says a stimulus word, and the examinee must respond orally with a single word that means the opposite of the stimulus word.

  Synonyms: Examiner says a stimulus word and four synonym options, then repeats the stimulus word. The examinee chooses the option that means the same as the stimulus.

  Sentence Completion: Examiner reads the stimulus sentence, which is missing the last word, and the examinee must respond with a single word that meaningfully completes the sentence.

  Idiomatic Language: Examiner reads the stimulus idiom, which is missing its final part, and the examinee must complete the phrase with an acceptable form of the idiom.

- *Syntactic Language,* assessed using the following tests

  Syntax Construction: Examiner reads the stimulus item while the examinee looks at a picture. The examinee must respond with a word, phrase, or sentence that is grammatically and semantically appropriate.

  Paragraph Comprehension: Examiner reads a stimulus paragraph twice, then reads a series of items relating to the paragraph while the examinee looks at a set of pictures for each item and responds by pointing to or giving the number of the correct response.

  Grammatical Morphemes: Examiner reads one pair of words or phrases that demonstrates an analogy, then reads the first word or phrase of a second pair. The examinee must complete the analogy of the second pair.

  Sentence Comprehension: For each item, examiner reads two pairs of stimulus sentences, one pair at a time. The examinee must determine whether both sentences in each pair mean the same thing.

  Grammaticality Judgment: Examiner reads a stimulus sentence that is grammatically either correct or incorrect. The examinee must judge the correctness of the sentence and, if it is incorrect, must correct it by changing only one word.

- *Supralinguistic Language,* assessed using the following tests

  Nonliteral Language: Examiner reads the stimulus item and the accompanying question, and the examinee must answer by explaining the nonliteral meaning of the item.

  Meaning from Context: Each item contains a very uncommon word. The examiner reads the item, and the examinee must explain the meaning of the uncommon word by using context clues.

  Inference: Examiner describes a situation in which part of the information is omitted, then asks an accompanying question. The examinee must answer the question using world knowledge to infer the missing information.

Ambiguous Sentences: Examiner reads the stimulus item, and examinee must respond with two possible meanings for the item.

- *Pragmatic Language,* assessed using the following test

  Pragmatic Judgment: Examiner reads a situation that represents some aspect of everyday life that requires communication or a pragmatic judgment on the part of the examinee. The examinee responds with the appropriate thing to say or do in the situation.

The CASL was standardized on 1,700 persons between 3:0 and 21:11 selected to match the 1994 U.S. census data. The manual provides evidence for strong reliability. Internal reliability ranged from .64 to .94 depending on the subtest. Core composites and indexes also showed high reliability, with most being in the low to mid-.90s. Test-retest reliability is reported as ranging from .92 to .93 for core composites and .88 to .96 for indexes. The manual also provides adequate evidence for content, construct, and criterion-related validity. Intercorrelations among the test components ranged from .30 to .79 and provide evidence to suggest that each test is measuring something unique but high enough to support their combination to produce the core composite and index scores. Age-based and grade-based standard scores (M = 100, SD = 15), grade and test-age equivalents, percentiles, normal curve equivalents (NCEs), and stanines are available.

Additional Information

Reviewed in Plake, B. S., Impara, J. C., & Spies, R. A. (Eds.). (2003). *The fifteenth mental measurements yearbook.* Lincoln, NE: Buros Institute of Mental Measurements.

Comprehensive Receptive and Expressive Vocabulary Test—Second Edition

Authors: Gerald Wallace and Donald D. Hammill
Ages: 4:0 through 89:11
Testing Time: 20 to 30 minutes
Publisher: PRO-ED

The Comprehensive Receptive and Expressive Vocabulary Test—Second Edition (CREVT-2) provides an efficient measure of both receptive and expressive oral vocabulary. It is used predominantly to identify students who fall significantly below their age group in oral vocabulary proficiency and to note discrepancies between levels of receptive and expressive skill.

Administration time for the CREVT-2 takes about 20 to 30 minutes. All words in the CREVT-2 are appropriate for children and adults and were found to be unbiased. The Receptive Vocabulary Subtest requires the examinee to point to the picture of the word said by the examiner. The 61 items are thematic, full-color photographs representing concepts with which most people are familiar, such as animals, transportation, household appliances, recreation, and clerical materials. The Expressive Vocabulary Subtest asks the examinee to define words said by the examiner, encouraging the individual to discuss in detail each stimulus word. The

25 items of this subtest relate to the same 10 common themes used in the Receptive Vocabulary Subtest (animals, transportation, occupations, etc.), allowing for easy transition from subtest to subtest. The applications of basals and ceilings allow this test to be given quickly and make it appropriate for a wide age range.

To quantitatively measure performance, the raw scores obtained on each subtest are converted to standard scores and percentile ranks. Age equivalents are also given.

The CREVT-2 was normed on a representative sample of 2,545 persons, ages 4:0 through 89:11. Norms were stratified by age according to gender, socioeconomic standing, disability, ethnicity, and other critical variables. This sample reflected the 2000 U.S. census data.

Reliability coefficients are provided for subgroups of the normative sample. New validity studies have been conducted paying close attention to how the CREVT-2 would generalize to the population.

Additional Information

Reviewed in Plake, B. S., Impara, J. C., & Spies, R. A. (Eds.). (2003). *The fifteenth mental measurements yearbook.* Lincoln, NE: Buros Institute of Mental Measurements.

Smith, T., Smith, B. L., & Eichler, J. B. (2002). Validity of the Comprehensive Receptive and Expressive Vocabulary Test in assessment of children with speech and learning problems. *Psychology in the Schools, 39,* 613–619.

Wallace, G., & Hammill, D. D. (1994). *Comprehensive Receptive and Expressive Vocabulary Test.* Austin, TX: PRO-ED.

Comprehensive Test of Phonological Processing

Authors: Richard Wagner, Joseph Torgesen, and Carol Rashotte
Ages: 5:0 through 24:11
Testing Time: 30 minutes
Publisher: PRO-ED

The Comprehensive Test of Phonological Processing (CTOPP, 1999) assesses phonological awareness, phonological memory, and rapid naming. The CTOPP's principal uses are to identify individuals who are significantly below their peers in important phonological abilities, to determine strengths and weaknesses among developed phonological processes, and to document an individual's progress in phonological processing as a result of special intervention programs.

Because the test spans such a wide range of ages and abilities, it was necessary to develop two versions of the test. Version 1 is designed primarily for kindergartners and first graders (ages 5–6) and contains seven core subtests and one supplemental test. Version 2 is designed for persons in second grade through college (ages 7–24) and contains six core subtests and eight supplemental tests.

The CTOPP contains the three composites: Phonological Awareness Quotient (PAQ), which measures awareness of and access to phonological structure of oral language; Phonological Memory Quotient (PMQ), which measures the ability to code information phonologically for temporary storage in working or short-term memory; and Rapid Naming Quotient (RNQ), which measures efficient retrieval of phonological information from long-term or permanent memory, as well as the examinee's ability to execute a sequence of operations quickly and repeatedly.

The test contains the following subtests: Elision, Blending Words, Sound Matching, Memory for Digits, Nonword Repetition, Rapid Color Naming, Rapid Digit Naming, Rapid Letter Naming, Rapid Object Naming, Blending Nonwords, Phoneme Reversal, Segmenting Words, and Segmenting Nonwords.

Composite scores are reported by combining scores from the following tasks for each construct listed.

- Ages 5 and 6:

  Phonological Awareness: Elision, Blending Words, and Sound Matching
  Phonological Memory: Memory for Digits and Nonword Repetition
  Rapid naming: Rapid Color Naming and Rapid Object Naming

- Ages 7 to 24:

  Phonological Awareness: Elision and Blending Words
  Phonological Memory: Memory for Digits and Nonword Repetition
  Rapid naming: Rapid Digit Naming and Rapid Letter Naming

All subtests begin with item 1. The ceilings are uniform on all subtests—three missed items in a row, except for the sound matching (four out of seven items are missed) and the rapid naming tasks (measure time; if names more than four items incorrectly, no score for the subtest). If items are given above the ceiling and any of these items are passes, they are scored as incorrect.

Scores provided include percentiles, standard scores, and age and grade equivalents. Subtest standard scores have a mean of 10 and a standard deviation of 3. The composite quotients have a mean of 100 and a standard deviation of 15. The manual also provides information relating the CTOPP standard scores to NCE scores, T scores, *z*-scores, and stanines.

The CTOPP was normed on 1,656 individuals ranging in age from 5 through 24 and residing in 30 states. The total school-age population was 1,544. Over half of the norming sample came from children in elementary school (through grade 5), where the CTOPP is expected to have its widest use. The demographic characteristics of the normative sample are representative of the U.S. population as a whole with regard to gender, race, ethnicity, residence, family income, educational attainment of parents, and geographic regions. The sample characteristics were stratified by age and keyed to the demographic characteristics reported in the 1997 *Statistical Abstract of the United States.*

Most of the average internal consistency or alternate forms reliability coefficients exceed .80. The test-retest coefficients range from .70 to .92.

Additional Information

Bhat, P., Griffin, C. C., & Sindelar, P. T. (2003). Phonological awareness instruction for middle school students with learning disabilities. *Learning Disability Quarterly, 26,* 73–87.

Havey, J. M., Story, N., & Buker, K. (2002). Convergent and concurrent validity of two measures of phonological processing. *Psychology in the Schools, 39,* 507–514.

Hintze, J. M., Ryan, A. L., & Stoner, G. (2003). Concurrent Validity and Diagnostic Accuracy of the Dynamic Indicators of Basic Early Literacy Skills and the Comprehensive Test of Phonological Processing. *School Psychology Review, 32,* 541–556.

Lennon, J. E., & Slesinski, C. (2001). Comprehensive Test of Phonological Processing (CTOPP): Cognitive-Linguistic Assessment of Severe Reading Problems. http://www.nasponline.org/publications/cq296CTOPP.html

http://alpha.fdu.edu/psychology/tests_measuring_PA.htm

http://idea.uoregon.edu/assessment/analysis_results/aram/ctopp_aram.pdf

Expressive Vocabulary Test

Author: Kathleen T. Williams

Ages: 2:6 to 90+

Testing Time: 15 minutes

Publisher: AGS Publishing

The Expressive Vocabulary Test (EVT, 1997) is an individually administered measure of expressive vocabulary and word retrieval. Younger children are required to label pictures or body parts presented, while older examinees are required to provide a synonym for the word and picture provided. The labeling items (1–38) are designed for younger examinees because labeling is one of the first stages of expressive language development. The synonym task was chosen for older subjects because it allows sampling of a variety of vocabulary and because of the labeling task's early ceiling effect. Both labeling and synonym items are presented with pictures. The examinee responds to each item with a one-word answer. The presentation easel includes colorful pictures that are balanced for gender and ethnic representation. The record form indicates both the correct and the most frequently given incorrect answers, which facilitates the scoring process. The record form also indicates to the examiner which responses require further prompting. A computer scoring program called ASSIST is also available. The program provides graphs of repeated testing results and suggests vocabulary-building exercises. A variety of scores are reported, including standard scores (with a mean of 100 and standard deviation of 15), percentile ranks, and age equivalents.

The EVT was conormed with the Peabody Picture Vocabulary Test III (PPVT-III), a receptive vocabulary measure, on a population of 2,725 examinees ages 2 years 6 months to 90+ years of age. The sample was representative of the 1994 U.S. census with respect to gender, race/ethnicity, region, and socioeconomic status. Because the EVT and the PPVT-III were conormed, scores from these measures are directly comparable.

The EVT reliability analyses indicate a high degree of internal consistency. Median spilt-half reliability is .91, while the median internal alpha reliability is .95. Test-retest reliability coefficients derived from four studies of different aged samples ranged from .77 to .90. Concurrent validation studies found EVT scores more correlated with the Verbal than the Performance scale on the Wechsler Intelligence Scale for Children—Third Edition. The EVT was also correlated with the Oral Expression Scale and Written Language Scales (OWLS). The EVT was not more highly correlated with crystallized than with fluid intelligence on the Kaufman Adolescent and Adult Intelligence Test (KAIT), a finding opposite of what was expected.

Additional Information

Reviewed in Plake, B. S., & Impara, J. C. (Eds.). (2001). *The fourteenth mental measurements yearbook.* Lincoln, NE: Buros Institute of Mental Measurements.

Carlson, J. F. (2001). Expressive Vocabulary Test. *Journal of Psychoeducational Assessment, 19,* 100–105.

Gray, S., Plante, E., & Vance, R. (1999). The diagnostic accuracy of four vocabulary tests administered to preschool-age children. *Language, Speech, & Hearing Services in Schools, 30,* 196–206.

Smith, T., Smith, B. L., & Eichler, J. B. (2002). Validity of the Comprehensive Receptive and Expressive Vocabulary Test in assessment of children with speech and learning problems. *Psychology in the Schools, 39,* 613–619.

Ukrainetz, T. A., & Blomquist, C. (2002). The criterion validity of four vocabulary tests compared with a language sample. *Child Language and Teaching Therapy, 18,* 59–78.

Williams, K. T. (1997). *Expressive Vocabulary Test manual.* Circle Pines, MN: American Guidance Service.

Illinois Test of Psycholinguistic Abilities—Third Edition

Authors: Donald D. Hammill, Nancy Mather, and Rhia Roberts
Ages: 5 to 12:11 years
Testing Time: 45 to 60 minutes
Publisher: PRO-ED

The Illinois Test of Psycholinguistic Abilities, Third Edition (ITPA-3, 2001) measures spoken and written language. All of the subtests measure some aspect of language, including semantics, grammar, phonology, reading comprehension, word identification, and spelling. The ITPA-3 uses the following subtests to assess a child's specific linguistic ability:

Spoken Analogies: Examiner says a four-part analogy, with the last part missing. The child gives the missing part (e.g., "Dogs bark, cats ________").

Spoken Vocabulary: Examiner says a sentence or phrase that describes a noun, and the child must provide the correct word (e.g., "I am thinking of something with wheels").

Morphological Closure: Examiner gives an oral prompt with the last part missing and the child completes the phrase by saying the missing part (e.g., "big, bigger, ________").

Syntactic Sentences: Examiner says a sentence that is syntactically correct but semantically nonsensical and the child repeats the sentence (e.g., "Purple hammers are smart").

Sound Deletion: Examiner asks the child to delete words, syllables, and phonemes from spoken words (e.g., say "weekend" without the "end").

Rhyming Sequences: Examiner says strings of rhyming words that increase in length, and the child repeats them (e.g., "noon," "soon," "moon").

Sentence Sequencing: Child reads sentences silently and then puts them in order to form a plausible sequence (e.g., rearrange: I go to school, I get up, I get dressed).

Written Vocabulary: After reading an adjective the child writes a noun that is closely associated with the stimulus word (e.g., complete this: "A broken ________").

Sight Decoding: The child pronounces a list of printed words that contain irregular parts (e.g., "would," "laugh," "height").

Sound Decoding: The child reads aloud phonically regular names of make-believe animal creatures (e.g., Flant, Yang).

Sight Spelling: Examiner reads aloud irregular words from a list. The child is given a printed list in which the irregular part of the words and one or more phonemes are missing. The child writes in the omitted part of the words (e.g., Examiner reads "said," and the child sees s__d and fills in the missing letters).

Sound Spelling: The examiner reads aloud phonically regular nonsense words, and the child writes the word or the missing part.

These ITPA-3 subtests can be combined to form the following composites: General Language, Spoken Language, Written Language, Semantics, Grammar, Phonology, Comprehension, Spelling, Sight Symbol Processing, Sound Symbol Processing.

Subtest raw scores are transformed into standard scores, percentile ranks, and age equivalents.

Normative data for a sample of 1,522 children were collected in 27 states during the years 1999 and 2000 and reflected the population characteristics of the United States for 1999. Data were stratified according to ethnicity, race, gender, disability status, geographic region, parental education, residence (rural/urban), and family income, and the results were a close match to projected percentages. In each of the 1-year age groups, the number in the samples exceeded 100 (ranging from 138 at age 12 to 239 at age 10).

Internal consistency, stability, and interscorer reliability for all subtests and composites are high (greater than .90).

Additional Information

Reviewed in Plake, B. S., Impara, J. C., & Spies, R. A. (Eds.). (2003). *The fifteenth mental measurements yearbook.* Lincoln, NE: Buros Institute of Mental Measurements.

Oral and Written Language Scales

Author: Elizabeth Carrow-Woolfolk

Ages: 3:0 through 21:11

Testing Time: 5 to 60 minutes depending on what scale(s) are used

Publisher: AGS Publishing

The Oral and Written Language Scales (OWLS; 1996) are an individually administered assessment of receptive and expressive (oral and written) language for children and young adults. The OWLS Listening Comprehension and Oral Expression Scales and the Written Expression (WE) Scale can be purchased and used alone. The OWLS are intended for children aged 3 years to 21 years 11 months on the Listening Comprehension and Oral Expression scales and for children 5 years to 21 years 11 months on the Written Expression scale. Neither Oral Language scale requires reading; in Listening Comprehension, responding verbally is not required—the child may point to the correct answer.

The Listening Comprehension Scale (LCS) of the OWLS is a measure of receptive language. It contains three examples and 111 items and takes approximately 5 to 15 minutes to administer, depending upon the examinee's age. The examiner reads a verbal stimulus aloud. The examinee responds by indicating a picture on the examinee's side of the easel. Correct responses are indicated on the examiner's side of the easel and on the record form.

The Oral Expression Scale (OES) is a measure of expressive language. It consists of two examples and 96 items and takes approximately 10 to 25 minutes to administer, depending upon the examinee's age. The examinee answers a question, completes a sentence, or generates one or more sentences in response to a visual or verbal stimulus. Common correct and incorrect responses are included on the record form.

The Written Language Scale is designed to assess writing skills. It consists of 39 items divided into four overlapping item sets, each designed for a specified age level, and takes approximately 10 to 40 minutes to administer, depending upon the examinee's age. There is a variety of item types, including copying printed words and sentences; writing letters, words, and sentences from dictation; and writing sentences and paragraphs according to specific oral instructions. The OWLS Written Expression scale may be administered in small groups "with examinees 8 years and older who are being assessed for reasons other than placement decisions" (Carrow-Woolfolk, 1996, p. 33), as was done in some cases during the standardization. The OWLS Written Expression Scale does not have subtests but does provide reproducible Descriptive Analysis Worksheets, which permit calculation of percentile ranks and determination of strengths and weaknesses for 9 of the 15 Skills Areas at each year of age.

For each OWLS Scale, age-based standard scores (M = 100, SD = 15), grade-based standard scores (WE only), percentiles, NCEs, stanines, test-age equivalents, and grade equivalents (WE only) are provided.

The standardization group contained a representative national sample of 1,373 students stratified to match the U.S. census data for 1991 on the basis of age, sex, and four categories each of mother's education, race/ethnicity, and geographic region.

Internal consistency reliabilities range from .84 to .93. Test-retest reliabilities were .73 and .90. Interrater reliability averaged .95. Construct validity of the OWLS is based on extensive development efforts to match the content and format of the test to language theory (e.g., Carrow-Woolfolk, 1988, 1996; Carrow-Woolfolk & Lynch, 1981).

The OWLS offers a brief but comprehensive assessment of receptive and expressive language. The manuals for the tests are clear, explicit, and helpful. After a little practice, scoring and interpretation quickly become efficient. The OWLS manuals include data on statistical significance and base rates of differences among the three scales.

Additional Information

Reviewed in Plake, B. S., & Impara, J. C. (Eds.). (2001). *The fourteenth mental measurements yearbook.* Lincoln, NE: Buros Institute of Mental Measurements.

Carrow-Woolfolk, E. (1988). *Theory, assessment and intervention in language disorders: An integrative approach.* Philadelphia: Grune & Stratton.

Carrow-Woolfolk, E. (1996a). *Oral and Written Language Scales: Listening Comprehension and Oral Expression Scales manual.* Circle Pines, MN: American Guidance Service.

Carrow-Woolfolk, E. (1996b). *Oral and Written Language Scales: Written Expression Scale manual.* Circle Pines, MN: American Guidance Service.

Carrow-Woolfolk, E., & Lynch, J. I. (1981). *An integrative approach to language disorders in children.* San Antonio, TX: The Psychological Corporation.

Goldblatt, J., & Friedman, F. (1998–1999). Oral and Written Language Scales (OWLS). *Diagnostique, 24,* 197–209.

http://www.agsnet.com/assessments/owls_worksheets.asp

http://www.slpforum.com/faq/owls.asp

http://alpha.fdu.edu/psychology/oral_and_written_language_scales.htm

Peabody Picture Vocabulary Test—Third Edition

Authors: Lloyd M. Dunn, Leota M. Dunn, Kathleen T. Williams, and Jing-Jen Wang

Ages: 2:6 through 90+

Administration Time: 10 to 20 minutes

Publisher: American Guidance Service

The Peabody Picture Vocabulary Test—Third Edition (PPVT-III, 1997) is an individually administered test of listening comprehension in the English language for children and adults ages 2 years 6 months to 90. This test is an achievement test of receptive vocabulary as well as a screening test of verbal ability for individuals who use the English language as their dominant language. The test consists of two forms, Form III A and Form III B. Each form contains four training items and 204 test items. The test items are broken down into 17 sets of 12 items each. Most examinees complete 5 sets, or 60 items. This untimed test takes an average of 11 to 12 minutes to complete.

Examinees are shown four black-and-white pictures and are instructed to point to the picture that best represents the meaning of the stimulus word said by the examiner. Examinees are only required to use nonverbal responses. The starting point is determined by the age of the test taker. However, if the examinee's level of functioning is found to fall below the 25th percentile or above the 75th percentile, he or she can begin the test at the more appropriate level. Test descriptions and history, testing and scoring procedures, and standardizations or statistics can be found in the examiner's manual. A norms booklet is also included in the test for scoring purposes. Test responses and scores are recorded on performance record forms that are included with the test (there are separate forms for Form III A and Form III B).

Standardization data for the PPVT-III were collected in 1995–96. The sample of 2,725 individuals represented the U.S. census data from March 1994. The sample consisted of 1,441 females and 1,284 males as well as 2,000 children and 725 adults over the age of 19. All persons in the sample were between the ages of 2.5 and 90. The following disability categories were represented in normative sample: learning disabled, 5.5 percent; speech impaired, 2.3 percent; Mentally Retarded, 1.2 percent; hearing impaired, .13 percent; gifted and talented, 2.9 percent. Raw scores are converted to age equivalents, percentiles, normal curve equivalents, w-scores, and stanines using a scoring table in the test kit.

The alternate forms reliability coefficients computed from standard scores for the PPVT-III ranged from .88 to .96 with a median of .94. Internal consistency ranged from .86 to .97 with a median reliability of .94. Test-retest reliability among all forms and age groups for the PPVT-III were in the .90s. Criterion validity was examined by looking at the correlations between the PPVT-III and other tests of intelligence and verbal abilities. The correlations between standard scores of the Peabody and the WISC-III ranged from .82 to .92 for children between the ages 7 years 11 months and 14 years 4 months. The correlations between the PPVT-III and the Kaufman Adolescent and Adult Intelligence Test were .76 to .91 for ages 13 to 17 years 8 months, and .62 to .82 using the Kaufman Brief Intelligence Test for ages 18 to 71 years 1 month. The correlations between the Oral and Written Language Scales and the PPVT-III ranged from .63 to .83 for ages 3 to 5 years 8 months and 8 years 1 month to 12 years 10 months.

The PPVT-III appears to be a reliable and valid test of receptive vocabulary. The easy administration and short testing time also add to its appeal.

Additional Information

Reviewed in Plake, B. S., & Impara, J. C. (Eds.). (2001). *The fourteenth mental measurements yearbook.* Lincoln, NE: Buros Institute of Mental Measurements.

Bell, N. L., Lassiter, K. S., & Matthews, T. D. (2001). Comparison of the Peabody Picture Vocabulary Test—Third Edition and Wechsler Adult Intelligence Scale—Third Edition with university students. *Journal of Clinical Psychology, 57,* 417–422.

Campbell, J. (1998). Test reviews. *Journal of Psychoeducational Assessment, 16,* 334–338.

Campbell, J. M., Bell, S. K., & Keith, L. K. (2001). Concurrent validity of the Peabody Picture Vocabulary Test—Third Edition as an intelligence and achievement screener for low SES African American children. *Assessment, 8,* 85–94.

Dunn, L. M., & Dunn, L. M. (1997). *Examiner's manual for the Peabody Picture Vocabulary Test—Third Edition.* Circle Pines, MN: American Guidance Service.

Washington, J., & Craig, H. (1999). Performances of at-risk, African American preschoolers on the Peabody Picture Vocabulary Test-III. *Language, Speech, and Hearing Services in Schools, 30,* 75–82.

Phonological Awareness Test

Authors: Carolyn Robertson and Wanda Salter

Ages: 4 through 9

Testing Time: 40 minutes

Publisher: Linguisystems

The Phonological Awareness Test (PAT, 1997) is an extension of the Phonological Awareness Profile, which was first published in 1995. The profile proved useful in planning instruction; however, users of the profile hoped for a standardized version of the assessment. Thus, the authors developed the PAT. This test was designed to assess students' awareness of the oral language segments that make up words. It comprises four sections:

1. *Rhyming:* Discrimination—identify rhyming words presented in pairs; Production—provide a rhyming word given a stimulus word
2. *Deletion:* Compounds and Syllables—say a word and say it again deleting a root word or syllable; Phonemes—say a word and say it again deleting a phoneme
3. *Substitution:* With Manipulatives—using colored blocks, isolate a phoneme, then change it to another phoneme to form a new word; Without Manipulatives—isolate a sound in a word, then change it to another sound to form a new word
4. *Isolation:* Final—identifies final phoneme in a word; Medial—identifies medial phoneme in a word

The PAT provides opportunities for analysis of student performance on each subtest. Performance can be classified according to four developmental levels: word, syllable, phoneme, and grapheme. Depending on student performance on the PAT, sample activities for instruction are presented to increase students' sound awareness. The manual recommends beginning instruction at the earliest level in which the student demonstrates difficulty. The Phonological Awareness Kit and the Phonological Awareness Kit—Intermediate provide a program of activities for each level of phonological awareness and phoneme-grapheme correspondence. The manual specifies that this test should be administered by a professional trained in analyzing the phonological structure of speech. It further indicates that it is unlikely that support personnel or paraprofessionals can adequately administer, interpret, and score the test.

The PAT was standardized from September to November 1996 on a sample of 1,235 students from five U.S. states.

Test for Auditory Comprehension of Language—Third Edition

Author: Elizabeth Carrow-Woolfolk
Ages: 3:0 through 9:11
Testing Time: 15 to 25 minutes
Publisher: PRO-ED

The Test for Auditory Comprehension of Language—Third Edition (TACL-3, 1999) is an individually administered measure of receptive spoken language that assesses a subject's ability to understand the following categories of English language forms: Vocabulary, Grammatical Morphemes, and Elaborated Phrases and Sentences.

The TACL-3 consists of 142 items, divided into three subtests.

Vocabulary: assessing the literal and common meanings of word classes (nouns, verbs, adjectives, and adverbs) and of words that represent basic percepts and concepts

Grammatical Morphemes: assessing the meaning of grammatical morphemes (prepositions, noun number and case, verb number and tense, noun-verb agreement, derivational suffixes) and the meaning of pronouns, tested within the context of a simple sentence

Elaborated Phrases and Sentences: assessing the understanding of syntactically based word relations and elaborated phrase and sentence constructions, including the modalities of single and combined constructions (interrogative sentences, negative sentences, active and passive voice, direct and indirect object), embedded sentences, and partially and completely conjoined sentences

It uses the popular point-to-the-picture-of-the-word-I-say technique. This simple procedure eliminates the external influences that are present in a less structured format. At the beginning of each subtest the phrase "Show me" is used to introduce each stimulus item. The examiner begins at the first item in each of the three subtests and stops when the examinee has three consecutive correct responses. Each item is composed of a word or sentence and a corresponding picture plate that has three full-color drawings. One of the three pictures for each item illustrates the meaning of the word morpheme or syntactic structure being tested. The other two pictures illustrate either two semantic or grammatical contrasts of the stimulus, or one contrast and one decoy. The examiner reads the stimulus aloud and directs the subject to point to the picture that he or she believes best represents the meaning of the item. No oral response is required on the part of the examinee. The test takes approximately 15 to 30 minutes to administer.

All scoring is dichotomous: 1 for correct and 0 for incorrect. Correct responses are noted in the profile/examiner's record book as A, B, or C.

Percentile ranks, standard scores, and age equivalents are available for children ages 3:0 through 9:11. The TACL-3 provides a variety of norm comparisons based on a standardization sample of 1,102 children, relative to socioeconomic factors, ethnicity, gender, and disability that are the same as those estimated for the year 2000 by the U.S. Bureau of the Census. Studies have shown the absence of gender, racial, disability, and ethnic bias. Reliability coefficients are computed for subgroups of the normative sample (e.g., individuals with speech disabilities, African Americans, European Americans, Hispanic Americans, females) as well as for the entire normative group.

Earlier editions of the TACL were reviewed extensively; references for the newest edition of this instrument are unavailable because of its recent publication date. A review of the TACL-R by Schmitt (1987) concluded that the instrument can be considered both a valid and a reliable test for determining an individual's knowledge of the test's constructs. Bankson (1989) reported that the TACL-R could be particularly useful as part of a comprehensive language evaluation of children referred for language disorders. Haynes (1989) felt the test was a well-designed and psychometrically sound instrument for evaluating limited aspects of comprehension.

Additional Information

Bankson, N. W. (1989). Review of the Test for Auditory Comprehension of Language—Revised. In J. C. Conoley & J. J. Kramer (Eds.), *The tenth mental measurements yearbook* (pp. 822–824). Lincoln, NE: Buros Institute of Mental Measurements.

Carrow-Woolfolk, E. (1999). *Test for Auditory Comprehension of Language—Third Edition.* Austin, TX: PRO-ED.

Haynes, W. O. (1989). Review of the Test for Auditory Comprehension of Language—Revised. In J. C. Conoley & J. J. Kramer (Eds.), *The tenth mental measurements yearbook* (pp. 824–826). Lincoln, NE: Buros Institute of Mental Measurements.

Schmitt, J. F. (1987). *Test critiques,* Volume VI (pp. 586–593). Austin, TX: PRO-ED.

http://www.med.unc.edu/wrkunits/syllabus/distedu/childas/publish/refsupp/tacl3.pdf (retrieved 6-14-04)

Test of Adolescent and Adult Language—Third Edition

Authors: Donald D. Hammill, Virginia Brown, Stephen C. Larsen, and J. Lee Wiederholt

Ages: 12:0 through 24:11

Testing Time: 1 to 3 Hours

Publisher: PRO-ED

The Test of Adolescent and Adult Language—Third Edition (TOAL-3; 1994) is a revision of the Test of Adolescent Language originally published in 1981 and revised in 1987. The TOAL-3 has extended the norms to include 18- through 24-year-old persons enrolled in postsecondary education programs. This improvement required that the name of the test be changed to indicate the presence of the older population in the normative sample.

The TOAL-3 is used to assess the linguistic aspects of listening, speaking, reading, and writing of adolescents and adults. The TOAL-3 consists of eight subtests, which combine to create the Overall Language Ability as well as 10 composite quotients: Listening (the ability to understand the spoken language of other people); Speaking (the ability to express one's ideas orally); Reading (the ability to comprehend written messages); Writing (the ability to express thoughts in graphic form); Spoken Language (the ability to listen and speak); Written Language (the ability to read and write); Vocabulary (the ability to understand and use words in communication); Grammar (the ability to understand and generate syntactic and morphological structures); Receptive Language (the ability to comprehend both written and spoken language); and Expressive Language (the ability to produce written and spoken language).

The Overall Language Ability quotient and the other 10 composite quotients have a mean of 100 and a standard deviation of 15.

The normative sample exceeded 3,000 persons in 22 states and three Canadian provinces. It was representative of the U.S. population according to 1990 U.S. census percentages for region, gender, race, and residence; the sample is stratified by age. Unfortunately, the normative data were collected from only a subset of the entire young adult population. Specifically, approximately 70 percent of individuals 18 to 25 years old were described as those "who seek some form of postsecondary education following their years in high school" (Hammill et al., 1994, p. 47). It may be assumed that individuals who seek postsecondary education have better language abilities than those who do not. Moreover, young adults with a history of speech or language impairments do not pursue postsecondary education as often as do their peers without such impairments (Felsenfeld, Broen, & McGue, 1994; Records, Tomblin, & Freese, 1992). Thus, young adults who might have scored in the lower portion of the full range of language performance were unfortunately excluded from the TOAL-3 normative sample, thereby restricting the range of scores (particularly low scores) included in the norms.

All reliability coefficients exceed .80. Content, criterion-related, and construct validity have been thoroughly studied. Correlations between the TOAL-3 and other tests of language (TOLDI:2, PPVT, DTLA3, TOWL2) show a considerable relationship. The TOAL-3 is also related to IQ and age. The provision of a factorial analysis has enhanced the construct validity of the test. Studies showing the absence of racial and gender bias have been added. Most important, the TOAL-3 scores distinguished dramatically between groups known to have language problems and those known to have normal language. In addition, the TOAL-3 scores distinguished between groups known to have language problems and those known to have normal language. Evidence is also provided to show that TOAL-3 items are not biased with regard to race or gender.

Most reviewers have praised the test's statistical properties, theoretical base, and clearly written manual (McLoughlin & Lewis, 1990; Roberts & Mather, 1998, Shapiro, 1989; Stinnett, 1992; Williams, 1985). Several reviewers, however, think the test is too long, yields too little useful information, and has old normative data (Richards, 1998; MacDonald, 1998).

Additional Information

Reviewed in Impara, J. C., & Plake, B. S. (Eds.). (1998). *The thirteenth mental measurements yearbook* (pp. 1018–1019). Lincoln, NE: Buros Institute of Mental Measurements.

Felsenfeld, S., Broen, P. A., & McGue, M. (1994). A 28-year follow-up of adults with a history of moderate phonological disorder: Educational and occupational results. *Journal of Speech and Hearing Research, 37,* 1341–1353.

Johnson, C. J., Taback, N., Escobar, M., Wilson, B., & Beitchman, J. H. (1999). Local norming of the Test of Adolescent/Adult Language—3 in the Ottawa Speech and Language Study. *Journal of Speech, Language, & Hearing Research, 42,* 761–766.

MacDonald, J. (1998). Review of the Test of Adolescent Language—Third Edition. In J. C. Impara & B. S. Plake (Eds.), *The thirteenth mental measurements yearbook* (pp. 1018–1019). Lincoln, NE: Buros Institute of Mental Measurements.

McLoughlin, J. A., & Lewis, R. B. (1990). *Assessing special students* (3rd ed.). Columbus, OH: Merrill.

Records, N. L., Tomblin, J. B., & Freese, P. R. (1992). The quality of life of young adults with histories of specific language impairment. *American Journal of Speech-Language Pathology, 1,* 44–53.

Richards, R. A. (1998). Review of the Test of Adolescent Language—Third Edition. In J. C. Impara & B. S. Plake (Eds.), *The thirteenth mental measurements yearbook* (pp. 1019–1021). Lincoln, NE: Buros Institute of Mental Measurements.

Roberts, R., & Mather, N. (1998). Test review: Test of Adolescent and Adult Language—Third Edition (TOAL-3). *Journal of Psychoeducational Assessment, 16,* 75–83.

Shapiro, D. A. (1989). Review of the Test of Adolescent Language—2. In J. C. Conoley & J. J. Kramer (Eds.), *The tenth mental measurements yearbook* (pp. 828–830). Lincoln, NE: Buros Institute of Mental Measurements.

Stinnett, T. A. (1992). Test reviews. *Journal of Psychoeducational Assessment, 10,* 182–189.

Williams, R. T. (1985). Review of the Test of Adolescent Language. In J. V. Mitchell (Ed.), *The ninth mental measurements yearbook* (pp. 1549–1551). Lincoln, NE: Buros Institute of Mental Measurements.

Test of Language Development—Primary, Third Edition

Authors: Phyllis Newcomer and Don Hammill

Ages: 4:0 through 8:11

Testing Time: 1 hour

Publisher: PRO-ED

The Test of Language Development—Primary, Third Edition (TOLD-P:3, 1997) is an individually administered, norm-referenced test for use with children ages 4 years 0 months to 8 years 11 months. This test takes approximately 1 hour and is composed of nine subtests that measure different components of spoken language. Picture Vocabulary, Relational Vocabulary, and Oral Vocabulary assess the understanding and meaningful use of spoken words. Grammatic Understanding, Sentence Imitation, and Grammatic Completion assess differing aspects of grammar.

Word Articulation, Phonemic Analysis, and Word Discrimination are supplemental subtests that measure the abilities to say words correctly and to distinguish between words that sound similar. Each subtest contains sample items and between 14 and 30 test items presented orally by the examiner. Children must either point (Picture Vocabulary and Grammatic Understanding) or respond orally to each subtest. The TOLD-P:3 provides scores in the form of standard scores, percentile ranks, and age equivalents for interpretation.

The TOLD-P:3 was standardized in 1996 on a sample of more than 1,000 children in 28 states representative of the U.S. population. An additional 519 children were administered the test for use in reliability and validity studies. The sample was stratified by age and was found to be representative of the nation's school-age population as reported in the Statistical Abstract of the United States (U.S. Bureau of the Census, 1990) regarding gender, race, ethnicity, family income, education of parents, and disability. Test reliability, which was investigated by the coefficient alpha and test-retest methods, is high enough to warrant the use of the test with individual children. Content validity was established by relating the test's contents to the individuals' actual language and by item analysis. Criterion-related validity was established by correlating subtests with two commonly used tests (Bankson Language Test, Second Edition, and the Comprehensive Scales of Student Abilities). Construct validity was determined by studying the relationship of TOLD-P:3 to age, IQ, and school achievement, as well as by factor analysis of the scores. The TOLD-P:3 scores distinguish between groups of children who have language problems (mental retardation, learning disability, reading disability, speech delay, and articulation problems) and those who do not. Reliability and validity studies were computed separately for minority and disability groups, as well as the general population.

Additional Information

Reviewed in Plake, B. S., & Impara, J. C. (Eds.). (2001). *The fourteenth mental measurements yearbook.* Lincoln, NE: Buros Institute of Mental Measurements.

Bell, S. K. (2000). Test review: Test of Language Development—Primary, Third Edition. *Journal of Psychoeducational Assessment, 18,* 167–176.

Test of Phonological Awareness

Authors: Joseph K. Torgesen and Brian R. Bryant
Grades Kindergarten to 2
Testing Time: 20 minutes
Publisher: PRO-ED

The Test of Phonological Awareness (TOPA, 1994) measures young children's awareness of the individual sounds in words. The TOPA Kindergarten version (measuring same and different beginning sounds) can be used to identify children in kindergarten who may profit from instructional activities to enhance their phonological awareness in preparation for reading instruction. The Early Elementary version (measuring same and different ending sounds) can be used to determine if first- and second-grade students' difficulties in early reading are associated with delays in development of phonological awareness.

The elementary version assesses final sounds of words. This is a 20-item test, comprising two subtests, and is administered in large groups, in small groups (six to eight students) or individually. In the kindergarten version, items on the first subtest require students to compare the initial sound of a stimulus word to the initial sounds of three response choices and identify the response choice with the same sound. Items of the second subtest are structured similarly except that students identify the response choice with a different initial sound. At the early elementary level, the two subtests are structured in the same manner except that students identify final sounds. At the beginning of the second semester of kindergarten, students scoring in the lowest quartile are deemed at risk for poor reading development. For first- and second-grade students scoring below the lowest 15th percentile, reading problems are deemed likely due to phonological deficits.

Both versions can be administered either individually or to groups of children. The test has been standardized on a large sample of children (857 from kindergarten, 3,654 from elementary grades) representative of the population characteristics reported in the U.S. census. The TOPA Kindergarten version does not have national representation, but the early elementary version does. The TOPA Kindergarten sample was gathered from 10 schools, while the TOPA Elementary was gathered from 38 schools.

Raw scores are calculated by adding the number of items answered correctly. The manual states that the three main types of scores obtained are raw, standard, and percentile scores. Percentiles and standard scores are obtained based on the student's raw score. The manual also provides conversions for stanines and normal curve equivalents.

The manual provides information to generate percentiles and a variety of standard scores. Internal consistency reliabilities range from .89 to .91 at different ages. Evidence of content, predictive, and construct validity also is provided in the manual.

Long (1998) finds the TOPA test format simple and reports that administration should be completed rapidly in most instances. McCauley (1998) feels that the TOPA makes a substantial contribution to the group assessment of phonological awareness in young school-age children. She states that evidence of reliability and validity is generally quite adequate.

Additional Information

Reviewed in Impara, J. C., & Plake, B. S. (Eds.). (1998). *The thirteenth mental measurements yearbook.* Lincoln, NE: Buros Institute of Mental Measurements.

Dohan, M. (1996). The Test of Phonological Awareness: A critical review. *Journal of Speech-Language Pathology & Audiology, 20,* 22–26.

Long, S. H. (1998). Review of the Test of Phonological Awareness. In J. C. Impara & B. S. Plake (Eds.), *The thirteenth mental measurements yearbook* (pp. 1049–1050). Lincoln, NE: Buros Institute of Mental Measurements.

McCauley, R. (1998). Review of the Test of Phonological Awareness. In J. C. Impara & B. S. Plake (Eds.), *The thirteenth mental measurements year-*

book (pp. 1050–1052). Lincoln, NE: Buros Institute of Mental Measurements.
http://alpha.fdu.edu/psychology/tests_measuring_PA.htm
http://idea.uoregon.edu/assessment/analysis_results/aram/topa_aram.pdf

Test of Word Finding—Second Edition

Author: Diane J. German
Ages: 4:0 through 12:11
Testing Time: Less than 60 minutes
Publisher: PRO-ED

Test of Word Finding—Second Edition (TWF-2, 2000) assesses an important expressive vocabulary skill. An examiner can diagnose word-finding disorders by presenting five naming sections: Picture Naming (Nouns), Picture Naming (Verbs), Sentence Completion Naming, Description Naming, and Category Naming. The TWF-2 includes a special sixth comprehension section that allows the examiner to determine if errors are a result of word-finding problems or are due to poor comprehension. The instrument provides formal and informal analyses of two dimensions of word finding: speed and accuracy. The formal analysis yields standard scores, percentile ranks, and grade standards for item response time. The informal analysis yields secondary characteristics (gestures and extra verbalization) and substitution types. Speed can be measured in actual or estimated item response time.

The TWF-2 was developed to be administered to children. Three forms are provided: a pre-primary form for preschool and kindergarten children, a primary form for the first and second grades, and an intermediate form for the third through sixth grades.

The TWF-2 uses four different naming sections to test a student's word-finding ability: Picture Naming (Nouns) assesses a student's accuracy and speed when naming compound and one- to four-syllable target words. Sentence Completion Naming assesses a student's accuracy when naming target words to complete a sentence read by the examiner. Picture Naming (Verbs) assesses a student's accuracy when naming pictures depicting verbs in the progressive and past tense forms. Picture Naming Categories assesses a student's accuracy and speed when naming objects and the distinct categories to which they belong.

Five supplemental analyses are provided to allow the examiner to gain critical information to enhance the interpretation of a student's test performance and help formulate a word-finding intervention plan. Three of the informal analyses (Phonemic Cueing Procedure, Imitation Procedure, Substitution Analysis) probe the nature of students' word-finding errors. The two other analyses (Delayed Response Procedure and Secondary Characteristics Tally) contribute to interpreting students' Word Finding Quotient.

Standard scores and percentile ranks are provided. The instrument was nationally standardized on 1,836 individuals from 26 states. Characteristics of the sample matched the national population in 1997. Reliability coefficients for typical-performing students and students with word-finding difficulties exceeded .84. Correlations between TWF-2 and other tests of vocabulary showed a considerable relationship.

Additional Information

Reviewed in Plake, B. S., Impara, J. C., & Spies, R. A. (Eds.). (2003). *The fifteenth mental measurements yearbook.* Lincoln, NE: Buros Institute of Mental Measurements.

ACHIEVEMENT

Diagnostic Assessments of Reading with Trial Teaching Strategies

Authors: Florence G. Roswell and Jeanne S. Chall
Grades: Multilevel, ungraded format
Testing Time: 20 to 30 minutes
Publisher: Riverside Publishing

The DARTTS program is a two-component program comprising the Diagnostic Assessment of Reading (DAR) and Trial Teaching Strategies (TTS) and designed for reading teachers, classroom teachers, special education and Title I teachers, and other professionals.

The DAR component is an individually administered criterion-referenced assessment of reading. The six subtests that make up the scale are Word Recognition (reading words from graded word lists), Word Analysis (letter knowledge, matching letters and words, and letter-sound correspondence knowledge), Oral Reading (graded reading passages), Silent Reading Comprehension (graded reading passages with comprehension assessed with multiple-choice questions), Spelling (writing dictated words), and Word Meaning (providing a definition for each word from graded word lists presented orally). For the DAR, the examiner simultaneously administers and scores the tests, marking students' responses as correct, incorrect, or omitted. A mastery criterion has been established for each test, and the student continues with each test until the highest mastery level has been established.

The Trial Teaching Strategies (TTS) component identifies how each student learns best through microteaching sessions. The TTS procedures are suitable for all teaching approaches and are used flexibly to aid any student reading at any level.

Raw scores can be converted to national percentile ranks. This assessment was standardized nationally on 1,664 students, and validity measures were determined using the Gates-MacGinitie Vocabulary Test. During the 1990–91 school year, a validation study was conducted with about 4,000 students on the DARTTS program. Participating students were tested with a nationally standardized reading test immediately before and then again after the use of the DARTTS materials to measure short-term gains. Then they were retested at the end of the school year to assess long-term stability of gains. Data from the validation study are included in the DARTTS technical manual.

Additional Information

Reviewed in Conoley, J. C., & Impara, J. C. (Eds.). (1995). *The twelfth mental measurements yearbook.* Lincoln, NE: Buros Institute of Mental Measurements.

Gates-MacGinitie Reading Test

Authors: Walter H. MacGinitie, Ruth K. MacGinitie, Katherine Maria, and Lois G. Dreyer

Ages: Kindergarten through grade 12 and adult reading

Testing Time: 35 to 105 minutes (group administered)

Publisher: Riverside Publishing

The Gates-MacGinitie Reading Test (GMRT) is a formal assessment of balanced reading skills across grade levels. These levels encompass Pre-Reading, Beginning Reading, Level 1, and Level 2. Skills tested include phonemic awareness, decoding skills, phonological awareness, vocabulary, comprehension, word knowledge, and fluency.

Materials required are student test booklets or answer sheets, teacher directions for administering the test, and the manual for scoring and interpretation, which is optional. These tests are also machine scorable.

This instrument is designed to be given to a group of children. The various subtests are timed. The instrument is a multiple-choice test for all grade levels. It is a thorough assessment of reading skills and can be used by the teacher to assess areas of strength or weakness, for both individual students and an entire class. Raw scores are translated into percentile rankings, stanine scores, grade equivalency scores, extended scale scores, and normal curve equivalency scores.

Internal consistency along with means and standard deviations for total scores and subscales for each level of the GMRT are evident for both spring and fall administrations. These are quite satisfactory and fall in the upper .80s and .90s for grades 1–12 (Swerdlik, 1992). Validity data support the intercorrelations among subtests. Validity data also provide evidence that the GMRT is a powerful test for assessing reading achievement at the lower and upper levels.

The bulk of the validity evidence relates to providing data that support substantial relationships between the GMRT and other instruments that are assumed to measure the same constructs of reading vocabulary and comprehension. These tests include general achievement screening batteries such as the Iowa Test of Basic Skills (ITBS), Tests of Achievement and Proficiency (TAP), the Comprehensive Tests of Basic Skills (CTBS), California Achievement Test (CAT), Metropolitan Achievement Test (MAT), the Survey of Basic Skills (SBS), the Verbal and Mathematics sections of the Preliminary Scholastic Aptitude Test (PSAT) and the Scholastic Aptitude Test (SAT), and the English, Math, Social Science, Natural Science, and Composite sections of the American College Test Program (ACT; Swerdlik, 1992).

Additional Information

Reviews of the fourth edition of this test are pending for the *Sixteenth Mental Measurements Yearbook*.

Swerdlik, M. (1992). Review of the Gates-MacGinitie reading tests, third edition. In J. Kramer and J. Conoley (Eds.), *The mental measurements yearbook* (Vol. 12, pp. 352–353). Lincoln, NE: University of Nebraska.

http://alpha.fdu.edu/psychology/a_sampling_of_reading_tests.htm

Gray Diagnostic Reading Tests—Second Edition

Authors: Brian R. Bryant, J. Lee Wiederholt, and Diane P. Bryant
Ages: 6:0 to 13:11
Testing Time: 45 to 60 minutes
Publisher: PRO-ED

The Gray Diagnostic Reading Tests—Second Edition (GDRT2), a revision of the Gray Oral Reading Tests Diagnostic (GORTD), assesses students who have difficulty reading continuous print and who require an evaluation of specific abilities and weaknesses. Two parallel forms are provided to allow examiners to study a student's reading progress over time.

The GDRT2 has four core subtests, each of which measures an important reading skill. The four subtests are Letter/Word Identification, Phonetic Analysis, Reading Vocabulary, and Meaningful Reading. Three supplemental subtests, Listening Vocabulary, Rapid Naming, and Phonological Awareness, measure skills that many researchers and clinicians think have important roles in the diagnosis or teaching of developmental readers or children with dyslexia.

The GDRT2 was normed in 2001–2 on a sample of 1,018 students ages 6 through 13. The normative sample was stratified to correspond to key demographic variables (i.e., race, gender, and geographic region). The reliabilities of the test are high; all average internal consistency reliabilities for the composites are .94 or above. Among other major improvements, studies showing the absence of culture, gender, race, and disability bias have been added, and several new validity studies have been conducted, including a comparison of the Wechsler Intelligence Scale for Children—Third Edition (WISC-III) to the GDRT2.

Gray Oral Reading Tests—Fourth Edition

Authors: J. Lee Wiederholt and Brian R. Bryant
Ages: 6 to 18
Testing Time: 20 to 30 minutes
Publisher: PRO-ED

The Gray Oral Reading Tests, Fourth Edition (GORT-4) provide an objective measure of growth in oral reading. Five scores give information on a student's oral reading skills in terms of the following factors:

Rate—the amount of time taken by a student to read a story
Accuracy—the student's ability to pronounce each word in the story correctly
Fluency—the student's Rate and Accuracy Scores combined
Comprehension—the appropriateness of the student's responses to questions about the content of each story read
Overall Reading Ability—a combination of a student's Fluency (i.e., Rate and Accuracy) and Comprehension Scores

The test consists of two parallel forms, each containing 14 sequenced reading passages with five comprehension questions following each passage. For each reading passage, raw scores are calculated for Accuracy and Rate by calculating the number of words read correctly and the length of time it takes the student to read the passage. Between 0 and 5 points are provided for each Accuracy and Rate score, depending on how quickly and accurately the student reads the passage. Those points are then summed to obtain a Fluency score. A Comprehension score is calculated by summing the number of Comprehension items (between 0 and 5) answered correctly for each passage. Raw scores for all four subtests (Accuracy, Rate, Fluency, Comprehension) are then used to compute standard scores, percentile ranks, and age and grade equivalents for the subtests. The sum of the Fluency and Comprehension standard scores are converted to percentile ranks and an Overall Reading Quotient. Error analysis can be completed by recording incorrect words students substitute for words in the passage and categorizing them according to the type of error, including Meaning Similarity, Function Similarity, Graphic/Phonemic Similarity, Multiple Sources, and Self-Correction. A checklist is also provided for an overall analysis of the student's reading behavior, including additions, deletions, prosody, and attitude toward reading. Fluency and Comprehension scores are calculated for each passage read.

The GORT-4 was normed on a sample of 1,677 students aged 6 through 18. The normative sample was stratified to correspond to key demographic variables including race, gender, ethnicity, and geographic region. Race in the manual was divided into White (85 percent), Black (12 percent), and other (3 percent). Educational attainment of parents included less than a bachelor's degree (72 percent), bachelor's degree (21 percent), and master's, professional, or doctoral degree (7 percent) categories. The disability status of the sample included the following categories: no disability (92 percent), learning disability (2 percent), speech-language disorder (<1 percent), Attention-Deficit Disorder (2 percent), and other handicap (2 percent).

The reliabilities of GORT-4 are high, with average internal consistency reliabilities being .90 or above. The validity is extensive and includes studies that illustrate that GORT-4 may be used with confidence to measure change in oral reading over time. Throughout the validity section of the manual, the authors reference studies correlating earlier versions of the GORT. The authors are assuming that the content of the GORT-4 is similar enough to that of earlier versions to allow such comparisons. No evidence is provided to support this assumption, however.

Additional Information

Reviewed in Plake, B. S., Impara, J. C., & Spies, R. A. (Eds.). (2003). *The fifteenth mental measurements yearbook.* Lincoln, NE: Buros Institute of Mental Measurements.

Kaufman Functional Academic Skills Test

Authors: Alan S. Kaufman and Nadeen L. Kaufman
Ages: 15 to 85+
Testing Time: 15 to 25 minutes
Publisher: AGS Publishing

The Kaufman Functional Academic Skills Test (K-FAST, 1994) is a two-subtest measure of an individual's ability to perform typical life tasks that demand mathematical reasoning or reading comprehension. Normed for ages 15–85+, the items on the K-FAST relate to daily activities that occur outside of the traditional academic setting.

Administration time for both subtests of the K-FAST is about 15–25 minutes. The Arithmetic subtest measures reasoning and computation skills as well as mathematical concepts, using pictorial stimuli to reduce the influence of reading ability. The Reading subtest assesses the ability to recognize and understand certain rebuses, abbreviations, and phrases.

Performance on the subtests can be interpreted using age-based standard scores with a mean of 100 and standard deviation of 15, as well as percentile ranks and descriptive categories for Arithmetic, Reading, and a Functional Academic Skills Composite.

The K-FAST was normed on a representative sample of 1,424 subjects, stratified by age according to gender, geographic region, socioeconomic standing, and race/ethnic group. This sample reflected the 1988 U.S. census data. It has good reliability and validity.

The K-FAST was developed, field-tested, and standardized with the Kaufman Adolescent and Adult Intelligence Test (KAIT), the Kaufman Brief Intelligence Test (K-BIT), and the Kaufman Short Neuropsychological Assessment Procedure (K-SNAP). These four tests provide a range of cognitive assessment options.

Most adaptive behavior inventories rely on subjective information supplied by parents, teachers, guardians, and others to determine a client's ability level. However, the K-FAST directly and objectively tests adaptive functioning. Further, the K-FAST includes many items that allow for accurate and stable measurement over a wide age range for individuals with low cognitive ability.

The K-FAST should not be interpreted as an intelligence test or used as the only measure of adaptive functioning.

Additional Information

Reviewed in Impara, J. C., & Plake, B. S. (Eds.). (1998). *The thirteenth mental measurements yearbook.* Lincoln, NE: Buros Institute of Mental Measurements.

Flanagan, D. P., McGrew, K. S., & Abramowitz, E. (1997). Improvement in academic screening instruments? A concurrent validity investigation of the K-FAST, MBA, and WRAT-3. *Journal of Psychoeducational Assessment, 15,* 99–112.

Kaufman, A. S., & Kaufman, N. L. (1994). *Kaufman Functional Academic Skills Test manual.* Circle Pines, MN: American Guidance Service.

Klimczak, N. C., Bradford, K. A., & Burright, R. G. (2000). K-FAST and WRAT-3: Are they really different? *Clinical Neuropsychologist, 14,* 135–138.

Process Assessment of the Learner—Test Battery for Reading and Writing

Author: Virginia Berninger

Ages: Grades kindergarten through 6

Testing Time: 15 to 60 minutes

Publisher: The Psychological Corporation

The Process Assessment of the Learner—Test Battery for Reading and Writing (PAL-RW, 2001), uses a variety of tasks to assess children's development of reading and writing processes. According to the author, the PAL-RW can be used to screen by identifying students at risk for reading or writing problems, monitor by tracking student progress in early intervention and prevention programs, and diagnose by evaluating the nature of reading- or writing-related processing problems.

The PAL-RW includes the following subtests (with examples given):

Alphabet Writing (speed of writing lowercase letters of the alphabet from memory in 15 seconds)

Receptive Coding

Task A: Student is shown a word (AT) for 1 second, then shown IT. Are the words the same?

Task B: Student is shown a word (BAT) for 1 second, then shown C. Is the letter in the word?

Task C: Student is shown a word (ATE) for 1 second, then shown ET. Are the two letters in the word in the correct order?

Task D: Student is shown a word (MOTHER) for 1 second, then shown L. Is the letter in the word?

Task E: Student is shown a word (SOCIETY) for 1 second, then shown EI. Are the two letters in the word in the correct order?

Expressive Coding

Task A: Student is shown a word (QAST) for 1 second, then must write the word.

Task B: Student is shown a word (LADFUST) for 1 second, then must write the third letter.

Task C: Student is shown a word (POGDUS) for 1 second, then must write the last three letters.

Rapid Automatic Naming (RAN)

Rapid Letter Naming: Name these letters as fast as you can (Item 1: m t g k b h r a n; Item 2: fi ps er ou).

Rapid Word Naming: Name these words as fast as you can (dog eat of sit over).

Rapid Digit Naming: Name these numbers as fast as you can (Item 1: 3 7 8 1 9 6 2; Item 2: 67 89 45 73).

Rapid Word and Digit Naming: Name these words and digits as fast as you can (tea eat 56 of 89 over).

Note-Taking Task A: Listen to a story and take notes as it is read.

Rhyming

Task A: Listen to three words and tell which one does not have the same sound (ball call help).

Task B: The word is PIG. Tell me all the real words you can that rhyme with PIG.

Syllables: Hear a word (both real and made-up), say the word, and now say it with a sound left out (PUTTING. Say PUTTING. Now say it without the PUT.).

Phonemes: Hear a word (both real and made up), say the word, then say it with a sound left out, and then say what sound was left out. (SIT. Say SIT. Now say IT. What sound is missing?)

Rimes: Say a word (real or made up) with a sound left out. (Say BIKE without /b/.)

Word Choice: Student is shown three words and must indicate the one that is spelled correctly (PIG PAG PIZE).

Pseudoword Decoding: Read some words that are not real words (DRIY HAFFE STROC).

Story Retell: After being read a short story, student must answer questions and then retell story in own words.

Finger Sense

Repetition (1 and 2): Touch thumb to index finger 20 times (right and left hands; scored for completion time).

Succession (1 and 2): Touch thumb to each finger five complete times (right and left hands; scored for completion time).

Localization: After having one finger touched out of sight, tell which finger was touched.

Recognition: Each finger is assigned a number. After having one finger touched out of sight, tell what number of the finger was touched.

Fingertip Writing: After having a letter "written" onto a fingertip, tell which letter was written.

Sentence Sense: Read three sentences and tell which one makes sense.

I ATE THE CAKE.
I EIGHT THE CAKE.
I ATE THE CAPE.

Copying: Here is a sentence (or paragraph). Copy it as fast as you can.

Task A: THE LAZY BOY JUMPED OVER A BALL.
Task B:a paragraph

Note-Taking Task B: Take the notes created earlier (Note-Taking Task A) and write a paragraph based on the notes.

The PAL-RW was normed in 1999–2000 on 868 individuals in grades K–6 from around the United States and stratified for sex, race/ethnicity, parental education, and geographic region. Normative sampling is adequate (>100 at each grade, ranging from 105 in grade 6 to 142 in grade 1). All scores are based upon the grade of the child tested, not the chronological age.

Test-retest comparisons based on 86 children in grades 1, 3, and 5 tested a second time 14 to 49 days later show reliabilities that ranged from .61 to .92. Five measures had reliabilities below .70. Of the 14 tests, 7 had lower scores on retest.

Criterion-related validity studies with individually administered tests varied greatly in sample size (WIAT-II, $N = 120$; PPVT-III, $N = 19$–43; VMI, $N = 7$–12; and CELF-III, $N = 14$). Despite the relatively small sample sizes in some of the validity studies, the PAL-RW generally did show expected correlations with other reading, decoding, and language tests. Comparison between clinical and nonclinical samples suffer somewhat from limitations in sample size. For example, of 18 measures assessed and compared, the samplings range from an N of 3 to an N of 23.

The PAL-RW attempts to measure the emerging skills needed for the complicated tasks of reading and writing. As a diagnostic tool for early grade school children, it appears to be quite useful. Its use with older children may be hampered by the limited number of items on certain subtests. The scores obtained by older children may accurately reflect the problems they may have in the specific area, but the lack of sufficient numbers of items limits any diagnostic or interpretive statements that can be made. The use of the PAL-RW to "monitor students' progress during and after intervention" (a stated use of the test) seems problematic given the poor test-retest statistics provided in the manual.

Additional Information

This test will be reviewed in *The Sixteenth Mental Measurements Yearbook.*
http://alpha.fdu.edu/psychology/PAL.htm

Test of Early Mathematical Ability—Second Edition

Authors: Herbert P. Ginsburg and Arthur J. Baroody
Ages: 3:0 through 8:11
Testing Time: 20 minutes
Publisher: PRO-ED

The Test of Early Mathematical Ability—Third Edition (TEMA-3, 1990) measures the mathematics abilities of children between the ages of 3:0 and 8:11. The test measures informal and formal (school-taught) concepts and skills in the following areas: numbering skills, number comparison facility, numeral literacy, mastery of number facts, calculation skills, and understanding of concepts. It has two parallel forms, each containing 72 items. The items of the instrument were chosen based on existing research and national norms. Almost every item is linked to an empirical research study. The items are sequenced in order of increasing difficulty.

The TEMA-3 standardization sample was composed of 1,219 children. The characteristics of the sample approximate those in the 2001 U.S. census. The results of the test, which takes approximately 20 minutes to administer, may be reported as standard scores (M = 100, SD = 15), percentiles, and age or grade equivalents. Reliabilities are in the .90s; validity has been experimentally established. Also provided is a book of remedial techniques (Assessment Probes and Instructional Activities) for improving skills in the areas assessed by the test. Numerous teaching tasks for skills covered by each TEMA-3 item are included. After giving the test, the examiner decides which items need additional assessment information and uses the book to help the student improve his or her mathematical skills.

A separate Probes guide (Ginsburg, 2003) provides a series of follow-up questions to be used after the standard testing to examine children's methods of solution and their "zone of proximal development" with respect to key items failed during standard administration. For each item, the Probes session begins with reworded questions designed to determine if the child did not understand the original question. A strategy question then follows to identify the child's method of solution (e.g., tell me what you are thinking about this problem). Next, a justification question is asked (e.g., can you prove to me that 2 and 2 is 5?). Finally, the examiner gives a hint (e.g., how about using your fingers to count?) to determine whether the child can solve the problem with some adult assistance. Conducting this sequence of questioning may reveal the source of the child's difficulty, which could directly inform a teacher's instruction or a clinician's intervention.

Additional Information

Ginsburg, H. P. (2003). *Assessment probes and instructional activities for the Test of Early Mathematics Ability—3.* Austin, TX: PRO-ED.

Ginsburg, H. P., & Baroody, A. J. (2003). *The Test of Early Mathematics Ability: Third Edition.* Austin, TX: PRO-ED.

Test of Early Reading Ability—Third Edition

Authors: D. Kim Reid, Wayne P. Hresko, and Donald D. Hammill
Ages: 3:6 to 8:6
Testing Time: 30 minutes
Publisher: PRO-ED

The Test of Early Reading Ability—Third Edition (TERA-3, 2002) measures the actual reading ability of young children. The test consists of three subtests: Alphabet (29 items) measures knowledge of the alphabet and its uses, Conventions (21 items) measures knowledge of the conventions of print, and Meaning (30 items) measures the construction of meaning from print.

There are five identified purposes of the TERA-3: (1) to identify children who are below their peers in reading development; (2) to identify strengths and weaknesses of individual children; (3) to document progress as a result of early reading intervention; (4) to serve as a measure in reading research; and (5) to serve as one component of a comprehensive assessment. To their credit, the authors clearly state that the TERA-3 is not to be used as a sole basis for instructional planning.

Each subtest has a mean of 10 and a standard deviation of 3. An overall Reading Quotient is computed using all three subtest scores. Performance is reported as a standard score (M = 100; SD = 15); percentile rank is provided. Age equivalents and grade equivalents are also given, although the authors provide cautionary remarks about their use in the manual. The TERA-3 has two alternate, equivalent forms. Answers receive a score of 1 for correct or 0 for incorrect, and expected answers are clearly indicated in the examiner's record booklet.

The TERA-3 was standardized on a relatively small stratified national sample of 875 children. These children were well matched on several critical demographics projected by the U.S. Bureau of the Census for 2000. Normative data are given for every 6-month interval. Both internal consistency and test-retest reliability are reported in the test manual. Reliability is consistently high across all three types of reliability studied. All but 2 of the 32 coefficients reported approach or exceed .90.

Additional Information

Reviewed in Plake, B. S., Impara, J. C., & Spies, R. A. (Eds.). (2003). *The fifteenth mental measurements yearbook.* Lincoln, NE: Buros Institute of Mental Measurements.

Test of Early Written Language—Second Edition

Authors: Wayne Hresko, Shelly Herron, and Pamela Peak

Ages: 3:0 to 10:11

Testing Time: 30 to 50 minutes

Publisher: PRO-ED

The Test of Early Written Language—Second Edition (TEWL-2, 1996) measures early writing ability in children from ages 3 years, 0 months, to 10 years, 11 months. It consists of 57 untimed items, presented in developmental sequence, which assess the use of conventions, linguistics, and conceptualization. The Basic Writing subtest requires responses to specific items (spelling, capitalization, punctuation, sentence construction, and metacognitive knowledge), while the Contextual Writing subtest depends on the authentic assessment (story format, cohesion, thematic maturity, ideation, and story construction) of a writing sample. Subtests may be given independently or combined to provide a Global Writing Quotient.

The Basic Writing Subtest requires the administrator to establish a starting point for the child using suggested beginning items provided in the manual. Items for young students, for example, require them to draw a picture of a favorite TV character and tell about him or her, identify writing instruments, indicate directionality of printed text, and write their name. Older students are asked to construct sentences from haphazardly presented words, combine sentences, identify writing conventions, and complete similar tasks. These items, scored 1 or 0, are recorded in an individual profile or record booklet.

The Contextual Writing Subtest requires the child to write a story about a visual stimulus. For younger students a simple scene is used; older students respond to a more complete scenario (e.g., a detailed playground scene). With the aid of a key, the student's story is scored on a 0 to 3 scale for 14 specific criteria, including sentence structure, ideation, thematic maturity, structure, sequence, use of dialogue, cohesion, and elaboration. Unlike many published writing tests, the TEWL-2 gives the student the opportunity to review and edit the story prior to scoring.

The test can be used as a diagnostic device for children ages 4:0 to 10:11 and as a research tool for children 3:0 to 3:11.

Three quotients (Basic Writing, Contextual Writing, and Global Writing) are provided, each based on a mean of 100 and a standard deviation of 15. Percentile ranks, age equivalents, standard score quotients, and normal curve equivalents are also provided. The TEWL-2 norms represent more than 1,400 children from 33 states. Normative information generally conforms to population characteristics for gender, race, ethnicity, geographic region, and residence (urban or rural) relative to the 1990 U.S. census data. Internal consistency and reliability coefficients all exceed .90. Substantial content description procedures, criterion prediction procedures, and construct identification procedures are presented.

The materials are well prepared; the manual is particularly useful, especially for scoring the Contextual Writing Subtest. Administering both tests is relatively time consuming, but as the measure is to be used diagnostically with at-risk students only, large numbers should not be involved. The provision of comparable forms permits the alternate form's use in assessing the impact of any interventions.

The TEWL-2 possesses an excellent conceptual framework and content-appropriate tasks. However, assessing a student's writing abilities from one sample of expressive writing using a single stimulus may impose serious limitations on the scope, and probably on the quality and dependability, of the diagnostic information generated by the task.

Additional Information

Hresko, W. P., Herron, S. R., & Peak, P. K. (1996). *Test of Early Written Language, Second Edition.* Austin, TX: PRO-ED.

Hurford, D. P. (1998). Review of the Test of Early Written Language, Second Edition. In J. C. Impara & B. S. Plake (Eds.), *The thirteenth mental measurements yearbook* (pp. 1027–1030). Lincoln, NE: The Buros Institute of Mental Measurement.

Trevisan, M. S. (1998). Review of the Test of Early Written Language, Second Edition. In J. C. Impara & B. S. Plake (Eds.), *The thirteenth mental measurements yearbook* (pp. 1027–1030). Lincoln, NE: The Buros Institute of Mental Measurement.

Test of Reading Comprehension—3

Authors: Virginia Brown, Donald Hammill, and J. Lee Wiederholt
Ages: 7:0 through 17:11
Testing Time: 30 minutes
Publisher: PRO-ED

The Test of Reading Comprehension—3 (TORC-3, 1995) comprises eight subtests grouped under either the General Reading Comprehension Core, which yields a Reading Comprehension Quotient, or the Diagnostic Supplements. The General Reading Comprehension Core includes General Vocabulary (the understanding of sets of vocabulary items that are all related to the same general concept), Syntactic Similarities (the understanding of meaningfully similar but syntactically different sentence structures), Paragraph Reading (the ability to answer questions related to storylike paragraphs), and Sentence Sequencing (the ability to build relationships among sentences, both to each other and to a reader-created whole).

Four Diagnostic Supplements subtests are available for use in a more comprehensive evaluation of relative strengths and weaknesses. Three of the subtests are measures of content-area vocabulary in mathematics, social studies, and science. The final subtest, Reading the Directions of Schoolwork, measures the student's understanding of written directions commonly found in schoolwork.

Raw scores can be converted into standard scores, grade-equivalent scores, age-equivalent scores, and percentiles. The TORC-3 was standardized on 1,962 students from 19 states between 1993 and 1994. Data are provided supporting test-retest and internal consistency reliability. Information on the normative sample of students is provided by geographic region, gender, residence, race, ethnicity, and disabling condition stratified by age and keyed to the 1990 census data. Criterion-related and content validity has been updated and expanded, and test-retest reliability has been reworked to account for age effects. Studies also have been added showing the absence of gender and racial bias.

Additional Information

Reviewed in Impara, J. C., & Plake, B. S. (Eds.). (1998). *The thirteenth mental measurements yearbook.* Lincoln, NE: Buros Institute of Mental Measurements.

Test of Word Reading Efficiency

Authors: Joseph K. Torgesen, Richard K. Wagner, and Carol A. Rashotte

Ages: 6:0 to 24:11

Testing Time: 5 to 10 minutes

Publisher: PRO-ED

The Test of Word Reading Efficiency (TOWRE, 1999) is an individually administered timed test of word reading efficiency in the English language for children and adults ages 6:0 to 24:11. This test is a measure of an individual's ability to pronounce printed words fluently and accurately. The test focuses on two main abilities: the ability to sound out words with quickness and accuracy and the ability to recognize familiar words as whole units or sight words. The goal of the TOWRE is to quantify an individual's level of skill with regard to word identification. Research shows that this is critical for ultimate reading success.

The test consists of two subtests, each with alternate forms. The Sight Word Efficiency (SWE) subtest assesses the number of real printed words that can be identified accurately within 45 seconds. There is a total of 104 words in subtest one; however, not all testees will finish the list within the allotted time. The Phonetic Decoding Efficiency (PDE) subtest measures the number of printed nonwords that can be pronounced accurately within 45 seconds. This test has 63 nonwords. When giving only one test form, the test should take about 5 minutes, including directions and practice items. Implementing both forms can take between 7 to 8 minutes to complete.

Forms A and B for both subtests are of equal difficulty. The tester first administers the practice items to the individual. If both forms are given, directions may be omitted for the second form. After the practice items are completed, test takers are asked to read the list of words or nonwords printed on the card as quickly as possible. If they cannot read a word, they may skip it and go to the next word. They must stop reading after 45 seconds. Each test taker starts at the first word regardless of age. There are no basals or ceilings for this test.

Test descriptions and history, testing and scoring procedures, standardizations, and statistics can be found in the examiner's manual. Normative tables used for scoring purposes can be found in the appendix of the examiner's manual. Test responses and scores are recorded on profile or examiner record booklets that are included with the test (separate forms for Form A and Form B).

Standardization data for the TOWRE were collected from fall 1997 to spring 1998. The sample consisted of 1,507 individuals from 30 states. The sample was not a complete representation of the current population at the time. The geographic distribution of adults was uneven, there was a lack of representation of Native Americans for children and adults, and the Hispanic population was underrepresented for the school-age child.

The alternate-form reliability coefficients computed from standard scores for the TOWRE (total word reading) ranged from .94 to .98. The alternate-form reliability for subtest one ranged from .86 to .97 and from .91 to .97 for subtest two. Test-retest reliability among all forms and age groups for the TOWRE ranged from .82 to .97. Concurrent validity was examined by looking at the correlations between the TOWRE and other reading tests. The correlation between the phonemic decoding efficiency subtest and the word attack subtest of the Woodcock Reading Mastery Tests—Revised (WRMT-R) was .85, and the correlation between sight word efficiency subtest and the word identification subtest of the WRMT-R was .89.

Predictive validity was examined by looking at the correlations between the TOWRE and the Gray Oral Reading Tests—Third Edition (GORT-3). The correlation between the sight word efficiency subtest and the GORT-3 ranged from .75 to .87, and the correlation between the phonemic decoding efficiency subtest and the GORT-3 ranged from .47 to .68. These correlations show that the TOWRE can be a strong predictor of reading ability. Its predictive validity is much higher than that of the WRMT-R.

The TOWRE appears to be a reliable and valid test of word reading efficiency. The easy administration and short testing time also add to its appeal. However, this test was not normed using the Native American population or using an accurate representation of Hispanic children. This should be taken into consideration when choosing this testing tool.

Additional Information

Reviewed in Plake, B. S., Impara, J. C., & Spies, R. A. (Eds.). (2003). *The fifteenth mental measurements yearbook.* Lincoln, NE: Buros Institute of Mental Measurements.

Rashotte, C. A., Torgesen, J. K., and Wagner, R. K. (1999). *Examiner's Manual for the Test of Word Reading Efficiency.* Austin, TX: PRO-ED.

Test of Written Language—Third Edition

Authors: Donald D. Hammill and Stephen C. Larsen
Ages: 7:6 through 17:11
Testing Time: 1.5 hours
Publisher: PRO-ED

The Test of Written Language—Third Edition (TOWL-3, 1996) was designed to (1) identify students who perform significantly more poorly than their peers in writing and who as a result need special help, (2) determine a student's particular strengths and weaknesses in various writing abilities, (3) document a student's progress in a special writing program, and (4) conduct research in writing.

The TOWL-3 contains eight subtests (with two equivalent forms, A and B) that measure student's writing competence through body essay-analysis (spontaneous) formats and traditional test (contrived) formats. The TOWL-3 is untimed. Using a pictorial prompt, the student writes a passage that is scored on Contextual Conventions (capitalization, punctuation, and spelling), Contextual Language (vocabulary, syntax, and grammar), and Story Construction (plot, character development, and general composition). The contrived subtests (Vocabulary, Spelling, Style, Logical Sentences, and Sentence Combining) measure word usage, ability to form letters into words, punctuation, capitalization, ability to write conceptually sound sentences, and syntax. Composite quotients are available for overall writing, contrived writing, and spontaneous writing.

The TOWL-3 was standardized on a 26-state sample of more than 2,000 public- and private-school students in grades 2 through 12. These students have the same characteristics as those reported in the 1990 *Statistical Abstract of the United States.* Normative sample is stratified and representative relative to gender, residence, region, disabling condition, and income and education of parents.

Composite quotients are available for overall writing, contrived writing, and spontaneous writing. Percentiles, standard scores, and age and grade equivalents are provided. Internal consistency, test-retest with equivalent forms, and interscorer reliability coefficients approximate .80 at most ages, and many are in the .90s. The validity of the TOWL-3 was investigated, and relevant studies are described in the manual, which has a section that provides suggestions for assessing written-language informally and that gives numerous ideas for teachers to use when remediating writing deficits. In addition, the TOWL-3 is shown to be unbiased relative to gender and race and can be administered to individuals or small groups. Because two equivalent forms (A and B) are available, examiners can evaluate student growth in writing using pretesting and posttesting that is not contaminated by memory.

As a diagnostic and formative evaluation tool, it is most useful in identifying students who are performing substantially below their peers. The TOWL-3 contains a strong conceptual model of writing and good evidence of validity and subtest reliability although it may be "too difficult for younger students (7- and 8-year-olds)." Scoring and interpretation procedures are also a bit complex and time consuming.

Additional Information

Bucy, J. E., & Swerdlik, M. E. (1998). Review of the Test of Written Language—Third Edition. In J. C. Impara & B. S. Plake (Eds.), *The thirteenth mental measurements yearbook.* Lincoln, NE: Buros Institute of Mental Measurements.

Geist, E. A., & Boydston, R. C. (2002). The effect of using written retelling as a teaching strategy on students' performance on the *TOWL-2. Journal of Instructional Psychology, 29,* 108–118.

Hansen, J. B. (1998). Review of the Test of Written Language—Third Edition. In J. C. Impara & B. S. Plake (Eds.), *The thirteenth mental measurements yearbook* (pp. 1070–1072). Lincoln, NE: Buros Institute of Mental Measurements.

http://alpha.fdu.edu/psychology/test_descriptions.htm#Achievement

Wechsler Individual Achievement Test—Second Edition

Author: David Wechsler
Ages: 4 through adult
Testing Time: Approximately 45–120 minutes
Publisher: The Psychological Corporation

The Wechsler Individual Achievement Test—Second Edition (WIAT-II, 2001) is a measure of academic achievement skills and problem-solving abilities for ages 4 through 85. Administration time varies depending on the age of the examinee and the number of subtests administered, but the test usually takes 45 minutes to complete for children in kindergarten or prekindergarten, 90 minutes for grades 1 through 6, and approximately 90 to 120 minutes for grades 7 through 16 (four-year college). An individual's performance is compared to others in the appropriate age range or grade level. Two stimulus books include information regarding appropriate starting points, reversals, discontinuation rules, and appropriate prompting and querying for each of the subtests. The WIAT-II presents one item at a time without time limits, except for the Written Expression subtest. The WIAT-II has four content areas (Reading, Mathematics, Written Language, and Oral Language) assessed using the following subtests:

Word Reading: naming letters, phonological skills (working with sounds in words), and reading words aloud from lists. Only the accuracy of the pronunciation (not comprehension) is scored.

Pseudoword Decoding: reading nonsense words aloud from a list (phonetic word attack).

Reading Comprehension: matching words to pictures, reading sentences aloud, and orally answering oral questions about reading passages. Silent reading speed is also assessed.

Spelling: written spelling of dictated letters and sounds and words that are dictated and read in sentences.

Written Expression: writing letters and words as quickly as possible, writing sentences, and writing a paragraph or essay.

Numerical Operations: identifying and writing numbers, counting, and solving paper-and-pencil computation examples with only a few items for each computational skill.

Math Reasoning: counting, identifying shapes, and solving verbally framed "word problems" presented both orally and in writing or with illustrations. Paper and pencil are allowed.

Listening Comprehension: multiple-choice matching of pictures to spoken words or sentences and replying with one word to a picture and a dictated clue.

Oral Expression: repeating sentences, generating lists of specific kinds of words, describing pictured scenes, and describing pictured activities. Content of answers is scored, but quality of spoken language is not for most items.

Depending on the subtest, items are either scored dichotomously or assigned a score of 0, 1, or 2. A composite score for reading is the total of the raw scores obtained on the word reading, reading comprehension, and pseudoword reading subtests. A composite score for written language is the total of the raw scores obtained on spelling and written expression subtests. Finally, a composite score for oral language is the total of the raw scores obtained on listening comprehension and oral expression subtests. There are qualitative descriptions for the scores: extremely low, borderline, low average, average, high average, superior, very superior. The WIAT-II also provides scoring guidelines and additional scoring examples. Optional scoring includes Reading Comprehension: Target Words; Reading Comprehension: Reading Speed; Written Expression: paragraph or essay word count; Written Expression: paragraph or essay holistic score.

The WIAT-II provides standard scores (with a mean of 100 and a standard deviation of 15), percentiles, stanines, normal curve equivalents (NCEs), and age and grade equivalents for each of the subtests. Scores are based either on the student's age (4-month intervals for ages 4 through 13, 1-year intervals for ages 14 through 16, and one interval for ages 17 through 19) or on the student's grade (fall, winter, and spring norms for prekindergarten through grade 8, full-year norms for grades 9 through 12, and separate college norms).

This measure was normed on a sample of 5,586 individuals between 4 and 85 years of age. The sample was representative of the 1998 U.S. census data with respect to grade, age, geographic region, gender, ethnicity, and parent education level. About 8–10 percent of the sample at each grade level had either a learning disability, speech-language impairment, emotional disturbance, mild mental impairment, ADHD, or a mild hearing impairment. About 3 percent of the population at each grade level was gifted and talented. All students spoke English. A sample of 1,069 students was given both the WIAT-II and a Wechsler Intelligence Scale so that examinees' WIAT-II scores could be compared to achievement scores predicted from their intelligence scale scores on the basis of actual test scores from the sample.

The average interitem reliability coefficients range from .80 to .98, and WIAT-II scores demonstrate adequate stability across time, ages, and grades. Studies have indicated that the subtests that are more likely to result in variability, such as Reading Comprehension, Written Expression, and Oral Expression, produce overall interrater correlations of .94, .85, and .96 respectively. Also, the pattern of correlations among the subtests provides discriminant evidence of validity. Correlation coefficients among the scores on the reading-related, mathematics, and spelling subtests of the WIAT-II and those on corresponding subtests of the WIAT, Wide Range Achievement Test—Third Edition (WRAT-3), and Differential Ability Scales (DAS) are highly consistent. Correlation coefficients between the WIAT-II and the Wechsler scales range from .25 to .82.

Additional Information

Reviewed in Plake, B. S., Impara, J. C., & Spies, R. A. (Eds.). (2003). *The fifteenth mental measurements yearbook.* Lincoln, NE: Buros Institute of Mental Measurements.

Glutting, J. J., & McDermott, P. A. (1994). Core profile types for the WISC-III and WIAT: Their development and application in identifying multivariate IQ-achievement discrepancies. *School Psychology Review, 23,* 619–630.

Konold, T. R. (1999). Evaluating discrepancy analyses with the WISC-III and WIAT. *Journal of Psychoeducational Assessment, 17,* 24–35.

Ward, T. J., Ward, S. B., Glutting, J. J., & Hatt, C. V. (1999). Exceptional LD profile types for the WISC-III and WIAT. *School Psychology Review, 28,* 629–643.

Wechsler, D. (2001). *Wechsler Individual Achievement Test—Second Edition: Manual.* San Antonio, TX: The Psychological Corporation.

http://alpha.fdu.edu/psychology/WIAT_mainpage.htm

http://idea.uoregon.edu/assessment/analysis_results/aram/wiat_aram.pdf

Wide Range Achievement Test—Third Edition

Author: Gary Wilkinson

Ages: 5 to 75

Testing Time: 15 to 30 minutes

Publisher: Wide Range

The Wide Range Achievement Test—Third Edition (WRAT-3, 1993) is an instrument used to measure the development of basic academic skills in the areas of reading, spelling, and arithmetic for ages 5 through 75. There are two alternate test forms, the Blue and Tan version, providing three subtests that may be given in any order: (1) reading (recognizing and naming letters and pronouncing printed words), and (2) spelling (writing names, letters, and words from dictation), and (3) arithmetic (counting, reading number symbols, computing oral problems). For the Reading subtest, the phonetic guide for each reading item is printed on the test form and the individual being tested reads from the Reading Card included with the materials. The instructions for each test and the correct answers for items are located in the manual, though there is also an optional Spelling Card. Administration time varies depending on the age and ability of the examinee but usually takes between 15 to 30 minutes to complete and approximately 5 minutes to score. The Blue and Tan forms may be administered together in order to provide a more comprehensive analysis of the individual's skills.

This measure was normed in 1992 and 1993 on a sample of 4,433 individuals between 5 and 75 years of age. The sample was representative of the 1990 U.S. census data with respect to age, geographic region, gender, ethnicity, and socioeconomic level. The WRAT-3 yields standard scores (mean of 100 and standard deviation of 15), grade scores (kindergarten to 12th grade), absolute scores, percentiles, and normal curve equivalents.

The internal consistency of the items on the WRAT-3 ranges from .85 to .95 over the nine WRAT-3 subtests, and coefficient alpha scores for the three combined tests range from .92 to .95. Test-retest reliability ranges from .91 to .98. Content validity was measured by the Rasch statistic of item separation, and the highest separation score possible was found for each test of the WRAT-3. Moderate positive correlations have been demonstrated with the Full Scale Score on the WISC-III and higher correlations were noted with the Verbal score. Weaker correlations have been demonstrated with the WRAT-3 and other standardized group tests of achievement, and the authors have stated that this is the result of significant differences in the test formats. Studies have indicated moderate to strong correlations with the Kaufman Functional Academic Skills Test (K-FAST), the Woodcock-McGrew-Werder Mini-Battery of Achievement (MBA), and the Kaufman Brief Intelligence Test (K-BIT; Klimczak et al., 2000; Flanagan et al., 1997). Also, strong correlations, ranging from .72 to .98, have been demonstrated between the WRAT-3, K-BIT, and Peabody Picture Vocabulary Test—Revised (PPVT-3) for adults with developmental disabilities (Powell et al., 2002).

Additional Information

Reviewed in Conoley, J. C., & Impara, J. C. (Eds.). (1995). *The twelfth mental measurements yearbook.* Lincoln, NE: Buros Institute of Mental Measurements.

Flanagan, D. P., McGrew, K. S., Abramowitz, E., Lehner, L., Untiedt, S., Berger, D. & Armstrong, H. (1997). Improvement in academic screening instruments? A concurrent validity investigation of the K-FAST, MBA, and WRAT-3. *Journal of Psychoeducational Assessment, 15,* 99–112.

Klimczak, N. C., Bradford, K. A., Burright, R. G., & Donovick, P. J. (2000). K-FAST and WRAT-3: Are they really different? *The Clinical Neuropsychologist, 14,* 135–138.

Powell, S., Plamondon, R., & Retzlaff, P. (2002). Screening cognitive abilities in adults with developmental disabilities: Correlations of the K-BIT, PPVT-3, WRAT-3, and CVLT. *Journal of Developmental & Physical Disabilities, 14,* 239–246.

Wilkinson, G. S. (1993). *Wide Range Achievement Test—Third Edition: Administration manual.* Wilmington, DE: Wide Range, Inc.

Woodcock-Johnson III Tests of Achievement

Authors: Richard W. Woodcock, Kevin McGrew, and Nancy Mather

Age range: 2 to 90

Testing Time: 15 minutes to 2 hours (depending upon test selection)

Publisher: Riverside Publishing

The WJ III measures a great many aspects of academic achievement with a wide variety of relatively brief tests. Many of these achievement tests can be used with the WJ III Tests of Cognitive Abilities to assess a student's abilities on many specific Cattell-Horn-Carroll (CHC) Gf-Gc "cognitive factors." Examiners are permitted to select the tests they need to assess abilities in which they are interested for a particular student.

The WJ III Tests of Achievement provide interpretive information from 22 tests to measure cognitive performance.

Reading

Letter-Word Identification: naming letters and reading words aloud from a list.

Reading Fluency: speed of reading sentences and answering "yes" or "no" to each.

Passage Comprehension: orally supplying the missing word removed from each sentence or very brief paragraph (e.g., "Woof," said the ________, biting the hand that fed it.).

Word Attack: reading nonsense words (e.g., plurp, fronkett) aloud to test phonetic word attack skills.

Reading Vocabulary: orally stating synonyms and antonyms for printed words and orally completing written analogies (e.g., elephant : big :: mouse : ________).

Written Language

Spelling: writing letters and words from dictation.

Writing Fluency: writing simple sentences, using three given words for each item and describing a picture, as quickly as possible for seven minutes.

Writing Samples: writing sentences according to directions. Many items include pictures; spelling does not count on most items.

Editing: orally correcting deliberate errors in typed sentences.

Spelling of Sounds: written spelling of dictated nonsense words.

Punctuation and Capitalization: formal writing test of these skills.

Mathematics

Calculation: involves arithmetic computation with paper and pencil.

Math Fluency: speed of performing simple calculations for 3 minutes.

Applied Problems: oral math "word problems," solved with paper and pencil.

Quantitative Concepts: oral questions about mathematical factual information, operations signs, and so on.

Oral Language

Story Recall: The student answers oral questions about stories that were dictated to the student.

Understanding Directions: The student follows oral directions to point to different parts of pictures.

Picture Vocabulary: The student points to named pictures or names pictures.

Oral Comprehension: The student provides antonyms or synonyms to spoken words and completes oral analogies (e.g., elephant is to big what mouse is to _____).

Supplemental

Story Recall—Delayed: The student answers questions about the stories heard earlier.

Sound Awareness: rhyming, deletion, substitution, and reversing of spoken sounds.

Academic Knowledge: oral questions about factual knowledge of science, social studies, and humanities.

The WJ III provides raw scores that are converted, using age- or grade-based norms, to Standard Scores, Percentile Ranks, w-scores, age and grade equivalents (AE and GE), relative proficiency index (RPI), Instructional Ranges, and Cognitive-

Academic Language Proficiency (CALP) levels. All score transformation is performed through the use of the computer program (WJ III Compuscore). The program also can generate several "discrepancy" analyses: intra-ability discrepancies (intracognitive, intra-achievement, and intra-individual) and ability achievement discrepancies (predicted achievement versus achievement, general intellectual ability versus achievement, and oral language ability versus achievement).

The WJ III was normed on 8,818 children and adults (4,783 in kindergarten through grade 12) in a well-designed national sample. The same persons also provided norms for the WJ III tests of academic achievement, so the ability and achievement tests can be compared directly and cognitive and achievement tests can be combined to measure CHC factors. The technical manual provides extensive coverage of reliability and validity areas. The median reliability coefficient alphas for all age groups for the standard battery of the WJ III ACH for tests 1 through 12 ranged from .81 to .94. For the Extended battery, median coefficients ranged from .76 to .91. The reliability scores for the WJ III meet or exceed standards. The median cluster reliabilities are mostly .90 or higher, and the individual test reliabilities are mostly .80 or higher, and can be used for decision-making purposes with support from other sources. The technical manual presents a considerable amount of evidence supporting the validity of scores from the test, noting that the earlier versions of the battery have also been shown to have validity. The WJ III ACH content is similar to that of other achievement tests. Growth curves of cluster scores illustrate expected developmental progressions. Extensive data focus on validity evidence from confirmatory factor analyses of test scores from participants aged 6 to adult. The internal correlations of the entire battery are consistent with relations between areas of achievement and between areas of achievement and ability clusters.

Additional Information

Reviewed in Plake, B. S., Impara, J. C., & Spies, R. A. (Eds.). (2003). *The fifteenth mental measurements yearbook.* Lincoln, NE: Buros Institute of Mental Measurements.

Mather, N., & Jaffe, L. (2002). *Woodcock-Johnson III: Reports, recommendations, and strategies.* New York: Wiley.

Mather, N., Wendling, B. J., & Woodcock, R. W. (2001). *The Essentials of WJ III Tests of Achievement Assessment.* New York: Wiley.

http://alpha.fdu.edu/psychology/woodcock_index.htm

Young Children's Achievement Test

Authors: Wayne P. Hresko, Pamela K. Peak, Shelley R. Herron, and Deanna L. Bridges

Ages: 4:0 through 7:11

Testing Time: 25 to 45 minutes

Publisher: PRO-ED

The Young Children's Achievement Test (YCAT, 2000) is an individually administered measure designed to determine early academic abilities and document educational progress. Its main purpose is to help identify young children who are at risk for school failure. The test was designed for English-speaking preschoolers, kindergartners, and first-graders (ages 4:0 through 7:11). The YCAT yields an overall Early Achievement Standard Score and individual subtest standard scores for the following five subtests: General Information, Reading, Mathematics, Writing, and Spoken Language. The YCAT allows for flexibility in administration because the subtests can be administered in any order or be given independent of each other. A variety of scores are reported for both the subtests and composite score, including standard scores (with a mean of 100 and standard deviation of 15), percentiles, and age equivalents.

The YCAT materials include an examiner's manual, picture book, examiner record booklets, and student response forms. The examiner record booklet indicates multiple examples of correct responses, which facilitates the scoring process. Items are either scored as correct (1) or incorrect (0), and there are approximately 20 items per subtest.

The YCAT was normed on 1,224 children. The sample was representative of the U.S. population as reported in the 1997 *Statistical Abstract of the United States.* Overall, the YCAT appears to be a reliable measure. Test-retest reliability was calculated over a 2-week period and ranged from .97 to .99. Interrater reliability ranged from .97 to .99 for the individual subtests. Internal consistency as measured by Cronbach's coefficient alpha ranged from .74 to .92, with the majority of subtest values in the mid- to high .80s. The Early Achievement Composite Score yielded high internal consistency values of .95 to .97. With respect to validity, criterion-related validity has been demonstrated with the Comprehensive Scales of Student Abilities (1994), the Kaufman Survey of Early Academic and Language Skills (1993), the Metropolitan Readiness Tests (1995), and the Gates-MacGinitie Reading Tests (1989).

Additional Information

Reviewed in Plake, B. S., Impara, J. C., & Spies, R. A. (Eds.). (2003). *The fifteenth mental measurements yearbook.* Lincoln, NE: Buros Institute of Mental Measurements.

4

Crisis Intervention and Students with Special Needs

ANITA P. MANNING

Ann was a great teacher. The students in her fourth-grade class loved her, their parents trusted her, and her colleagues respected her. Ann had a heart problem. When she left school early in the spring to complete a necessary medical procedure, the children hugged her tightly and talked about the party they would have when she returned. But Ann didn't come back. An unexpected complication arose from which she could not recover. When the announcement was made to her class, all the students were understandably distraught, but some were additionally impacted due to their individual characteristics: One student had learning disabilities. Another had a history of depression. A third had cognitive impairments. This chapter is for Ann, her colleagues, and, especially, her students.

Following major acts of school violence epitomized by tragedies of the magnitude of Jonesboro, Paducah, and Columbine, the topic of crisis intervention captured the attention of a nation of educators. These traumatic, almost incomprehensible, events activated policymakers, school administrators, and entire communities to tackle the tasks of creating safer schools, developing sound crisis response plans, and providing ongoing support for victims. While events of rarity, these tragedies served another important function. They caused those who work with children and adolescents to pause and consider the frequencies with which students face more common traumatic events. Certainly deaths on school grounds, particularly homicides with multiple victims, are rare. But every day students in schools face personally devastating circumstances in the absence of media cameras and advice from experts on high-profile trauma. The people who help them during these times are the educators who are with them every day.

In a small community in Colorado, the cumulative effects of crisis are illustrated by the experiences of the graduating class of 2002. The freshman class started its high school experience in the fall of 1999 on the heels of the Columbine shooting. Graduation occurred in the spring following 9/11. In between those two large-scale tragedies, the class lost four of their members as the result of car accidents and health complications. The impact of trauma on this group of students increased with each subsequent event. Were it not for the capable and sensitive way in which they were supported in the aftermath of each crisis, the long-term effects would have been much more debilitating. The positive role that their teachers, principal, and other district staff played in their ability to cope is without question. Clearly, all educators must become more knowledgeable and skilled in crisis intervention.

It makes perfect sense to provide crisis intervention activities in schools. Schools are where students spend a large number of their waking hours. At school, students have access to professionals with specialized training and extensive experience in working with children and adolescents. Staff members know their students well and understand the unique demographics and idiosyncrasies of their community. They are also familiar with local community resources and can serve as reliable referral sources when outside assistance is required.

When a crisis occurs, however, administrators and other staff are often faced with inadequate information, limited time, and insufficient resources with which to make crucial decisions (Office of Safe and Drug-Free Schools, 2003). Staff members often have little or no formal training in crisis response. Until the late 1990s, few mental health practitioners in schools came from programs that included coursework on crisis intervention. Of those who chose to pursue specialized training on their own, the diversity in available models made communication difficult in the throes of a crisis.

While there has been a national movement to introduce crisis intervention into the curriculum of training programs for school psychologists, school counselors, school social workers, and school nurses, the need for assistance at the time of a crisis often extends well beyond those with a mental health background. Administrators, classroom teachers, support staff, and paraprofessionals are often called upon to assist. It is imperative that educators know what to expect and how to collaboratively use the skills they have to ensure the greatest positive impact on their students. It is also important for educators to recognize the limits of their competencies in dealing with varying aspects of crisis intervention.

It is also essential that a carefully considered plan for crisis intervention be developed and that there exist opportunities to create and test critical aspects of those plans before they are needed. Plans should contain clearly defined guidelines for the timely response of student intervention. While the best time for providing crisis intervention services is within 24 to 36 hours, it is important for school crisis responders to remember that symptoms of emotional shock may emerge months or even years after the loss (Poland, Pitcher, & Lazarus, 2002; Young, 2002; National Association of School Psychologists [NASP], 1992). Therefore, not only must plans address the immediate aftermath of a particular crisis, but they must also contain guidance for dealing with the long-term effects of that event.

Crisis intervention resources contain much information with regard to establishing crisis response teams, creating effective crisis plans, and providing psychological first aid to impacted students (Poland & McCormick, 1999; Newgass & Schonfeld, 2000; Brock & Poland, 2002). However, little has been written about how

Box 4.1 Excerpt from *Tear Soup*

"I've learned that grief, like a pot of soup, changes the longer it simmers and the more things you put into it."

these recommendations apply to students with disabilities (Lavin, 1998; Jimerson & Huff, 2002). The document "Practical Information on Crisis Planning: A Guide for Schools and Communities" (Office of Safe and Drug-Free Schools, 2003) recommends that schools plan for the diverse needs of children and staff. However, in a review of crisis plans completed prior to the development of that document, researchers found that few schools had addressed children or staff with physical, sensory, motor, developmental, or mental challenges in their crisis plans. While some elements of crisis intervention require few modifications for use with students with special needs, other aspects may require additional and specific accommodations in order for interventions to be most effective.

This chapter was written to assist staff whose experience with crisis response may be limited. This chapter is especially for those who work with students with special needs and/or disabilities. The following guidelines are not about crisis intervention related to large-scale acts of school violence, terrorism, or war, nor do they contain all information that the uniqueness of an individual crisis might require. This chapter was written to provide educators with a quick reference guide to which to refer when a crisis occurs in their school. It also provides reminders and thinking points to assure that the requirements of students with special needs are included in those efforts.

WHAT IS A CRISIS?

A crisis is defined as "an unstable or crucial time or state of affairs in which a decisive change is impending, especially one with the distinct possibility of a highly undesirable outcome" (*Webster's Ninth Collegiate Dictionary,* 1987). The American Psychiatric Association (2000) describes an extreme traumatic stressor as the "direct personal experience of an event that involves actual or threatened death or serious injury, or other threat to one's physical integrity; or witnessing an event that involves death, injury, or a threat to the physical integrity of another person; or learning about unexpected or violent death, serious harm, or threat of death or injury experienced by a family member or other close associate" (p. 463).

According to Judith Herman (1992), "Traumatic events are extraordinary, not because they occur rarely, but rather because they overwhelm the ordinary adaptations to life." School crises or traumatic events vary widely in their impact and can include highly diverse events such as severe illness or injury, violent or unexpected death, threatened death or injury, acts of war, natural disasters, and manmade or industrial disasters (Brock, Sandoval, & Lewis, 2001).

CRISIS TEAMS

Many of us have experienced situations in which crisis teams were established in ineffective ways. For example, at the first staff meeting of the school year, a clipboard may be passed and the staff instructed to sign up for at least two functions.

Somewhere on the list, one will inevitably find "crisis team." Two types of individuals are likely to respond. The first group consists of those who have training, experience, competency, and interest in this area. The second group consists of those who have none of those qualities but attempt to hedge their bets by signing up for a committee that may not be active or activated.

A preferred method of creating crisis teams is through invitation (Colorado Society of School Psychologists Statewide Crisis Response Team, 2003; Ruof & Harris, 1988). It is important that members be selected based not only on their training and experience but also on the personal qualities they possess. The following personal characteristics may identify potential crisis team members for consideration:

- Excellent communication skills
- Compassionate
- Confident
- Respected and trusted by students and colleagues
- Stable and mature
- Remains calm and focused amidst chaos
- Exercises good judgment
- Works cooperatively without territorialism
- Initiates conversation easily
- Sensitive to diversity and cultural differences
- Good problem solver

Teams may be created from the staff of individual buildings, staff across a school district, or a combination of these. Regardless of the approach, the team should include at least one member who has knowledge of the field of special education. This is important in assuring that the needs of students with disabilities are considered in all aspects of crisis intervention. Just as individual education plans (IEPs) describe the learning needs and accommodation requirements of students with special needs, crisis plans should identify modifications and accommodations that may be necessary when those students are faced with the task of understanding and coping with a school crisis.

While these general guidelines may establish a pool of individuals to whom invitations are issued, those individuals should be free to decline the invitation. Even when a team has been established, individual team members should have the option to choose or decline participation in a specific response based upon their own personal crisis history. Consider an example in which, unknown to members of a crisis team, a team member had a personal history that included the loss of a parent in a manner similar to the way in which the student victim died. Midway through the response, the team member became overwhelmed with emotion. Not only was he or she unable to continue to assist others, but the attention of the team was divided as they attempted to support both the students and their colleague. Had team members been told initially that they could decline participation in any specific response, much personal duress could have been avoided and intervention effectiveness maintained.

Crisis teams work together best when they receive common training in crisis response, which leads to a consistent vocabulary and framework. It is essential that the team update and refresh their skills on a regular basis (Colorado Society of School Psychologists, 2003). Practice activities do not have to be comprehensive reenactments. Tabletop exercises in which team members discuss how they would respond to crisis situations in a particular scenario can be helpful and often fit into the limited amounts of time that crisis teams have in which to meet. Another effective activity involves a discussion of how the team would have responded to actual crisis events found in newspapers or magazine articles. A third exercise includes a trial of specific elements of the existing plan such as activation of a calling tree, contact of crisis team members, and so on.

It is critical that teams meet regularly and not just at the time of a crisis. Meeting regularly ensures that team relationships develop and strengthen. Communication improves, and healthy discussions about team roles and expectations can occur. Teams should use interim periods to discuss and strengthen preventative efforts. Such activities may include the evaluation and selection of preventative programs, the design and facilitation of training activities for other staff, and the development of collaborative relationships with community-based crisis response agencies.

DEVELOPING A CRISIS PLAN

At the time of a crisis, the best-laid plans are subject to flaws. It is important to develop plans prior to their need and to test such plans through regular practice activities. However, effective crisis plans are never finished and must be frequently updated based upon feedback from their review and use as well as on the availability of new information in the field of crisis intervention.

Strong crisis plans address both the physical and psychological safety of students. They address those aspects in relationship to all crises that schools are likely to encounter. The physical component may address, but is not limited to, topics such as building safety, evacuation and lockdown plans, class size, and traffic flow. The psychological component may address, but is not limited to, topics such as the process for activating a crisis team, team member role descriptions, guidelines for direct intervention, and a list of approved community-based resources for assistance.

Effective plans address all levels of intervention: prevention (efforts being used to prevent crises from happening), intervention (activities in the immediate aftermath of a crisis), and postvention (long-term treatment and follow-up). In each phase of the plan, it is essential to address how students with special needs have access to each level. For example, physical safety plans should address the specifics of how students with physical disabilities will be managed during intervention (i.e., physical moves to a safe area inside or outside the building). Psychological safety components should address issues such as early identification and support of students with emotional needs, recommendations regarding disciplinary procedures in the aftermath of a crisis, and procedures for working collaboratively with all professionals who support students with mental health issues.

DETERMINING THE IMPACT OF A CRISIS

In determining the impact of a particular event, crisis teams should consider the following factors identified by Poland and McCormick (1999):

- Whether the crisis involved death or injury: A crisis resulting in death has a greater impact than one resulting in injury.

- How well-known and well-liked the victim was: In general, the more familiar and popular the victim, the greater the impact.
- How the person died and whether the death was expected: Unexpected deaths generally have a greater impact than deaths that were expected due to terminal health conditions or old age.
- Where the death occurred (on or off school grounds): Deaths on school grounds have a greater impact than deaths away from school grounds.
- The crisis history of the school and/or community: Crises in schools and communities that have experienced a number of tragedies have a greater level of impact.
- If a perpetrator was responsible for the death, whether the perpetrator is a member of the school and/or community: Crises in which perpetrators are known to the school and/or community have a greater impact than crises in which the perpetrator was a stranger.

Newgass and Schonfeld (2000) noted that certain risk factors increase the likelihood that students will require additional assistance in the aftermath of trauma:

- Group affiliations with the victim
- Shared characteristics, attributes, or interests with the victim
- History of poor coping
- Atypical or more intense reactions not explained by the relationship to the victim
- Personal history related to trauma

Based upon these factors, students with disabilities may be at increased risk for high levels of impact. A student with significant emotional disabilities, for example, may have close and frequent contact with a student victim through shared related services or center-based programming. The two students may struggle with similar internalizing problems (such as depression or anxiety). A history of poor coping may be common to both. Their educational history may contain multiple instances of interpersonal relationship difficulties, disciplinary referrals, and academic struggles. Students with emotional disabilities may also possess fewer of the resiliency factors necessary to adequately cope with the disruptions created by a crisis event.

Following a crisis, a student with a history of emotional and behavioral difficulties may demonstrate the symptoms of their disability with increased intensity. For example, the child who has Attention-Deficit/Hyperactivity Disorder (ADHD) is likely to have increased difficulty with attention and concentration in the aftermath of trauma. The child who has difficulty establishing or maintaining peer relationships may become more resistant, combative, or withdrawn. Students who are easily upset may have increased difficulty calming. Students who are depressed or anxious may exhibit greater levels of withdrawal, depression, and anxiety following the event and may be at increased risk for self-harm.

The impact of trauma on students with disabilities is affected not only by social and emotional characteristics such as those noted but also by a student's level of cognitive functioning. Although impairments in cognitive ability may initially serve an important protective function, students with such impairments may be poorer problem solvers, have more difficulty dealing with threatening situations, and fail to learn from previous experiences (Masten & Coatsworth, 1998). Students with learning disabilities may have distortions in their perceptions or in their ability to discriminate between essential and non-essential information (Hillman, 2002). Students whose disabilities affect their understanding and/or ability to cope with change are especially vulnerable to the effects of trauma. Even students who have limited comprehension of the event may demonstrate significant behavioral changes in response to a disruption in routine created by the crisis or to the general reactions shown by teachers and parents.

Children's developmental levels also affect their understanding of a traumatic event and how they cope with the resulting changes. Developmental levels do not necessarily correspond with chronological age. For example, a child with a disability may have a chronological age of 13 but the developmental age of a much younger child. A typical crisis reaction for a preadolescent may include withdrawal from others, while a child functioning at a younger developmental level may respond with separation difficulties.

Just as a child's response to a traumatic event is directly impacted by the response of his or her parent (Aptekar & Boore, 1990), the response of school staff and students to a tragedy is affected by the response of the administrator involved. In situations where administrators acknowledge accurately the impact of the trauma, model appropriate reactions to the situation, and allow others to express their reactions as well, the sooner the entire school population will adjust and adapt to the new situation. Effective crisis planning begins with leadership at the top (Office of Safe and Drug-Free Schools, 2003).

WHEN A CRISIS OCCURS

The following sections discuss essential steps in crisis response.

What to do when Information Regarding a Crisis Becomes Known

Contact the building administrator. When death or significant injury occurs, it is important that the building administrator be contacted immediately (even if the individual is out of state). The administrator will then either assume the duty of crisis coordinator or designate someone to act in that capacity. It is important that a representative from central administration be notified as well because they will often be contacted by parents, community members, and the media for information pertaining to the crisis. Should the victim be a student with a disability, a special education teacher or para-educator is often the first to learn of the incident. That person should contact the building administrator before taking any other steps. The administrator may then designate the special education professional as the official contact for the family.

Confirm the facts. If death is involved, it should be confirmed via resources such as the county coroner or the appropriate law enforcement agency. Although the victim's family is also an obvious resource for confirmation and information, other avenues may be pursued out of respect for the privacy of the family. The interaction

Box 4.2 Essential Steps in Crisis Response

Contact administrators
Confirm facts
Contact staff
Gather crisis team
Develop announcements
Meet with staff
Make announcement
Conduct class meetings
Debrief with staff
Reestablish routine
Identify postvention activities and timelines

between school and family should focus on consolation and support. Once the death has been verified, the crisis intervention can proceed.

Never make an assumption about the cause of death or injury based upon the individual's personal history or disability (e.g., depression, anxiety, impulsivity, etc.) without confirming it with the appropriate authorities. For example, suppose a young man attending a center-based program for students with significant emotional issues died as the result of strangulation from a rope around his neck. School staff immediately began to refer to the death as a suicide. However, because no suicide note was found, the death was ruled by the local coroner's office as accidental. The family also reported to the school that the death was accidental.

In another example, during a domestic dispute the father of a student aimed a gun toward his wife in the front yard of their home. Police were called, shots were fired, and the man died. Initial reports from the family suggested that the man was killed by police fire; however, the coroner's office ruled the death a suicide based upon the location of the fatal wound.

In situations such as these, the crisis team must provide truthful and accurate information to students even when it is in conflict with the wishes of the family or the official ruling of the medical examiner or coroner. It has been suggested that terms such as "suicide-equivalent behavior" or discussion about the difficulty of accepting suicide may be viable options (Liebermann, 1999).

Contact staff. All members of the school staff should be contacted as soon as possible in order to give them time to begin to manage their own reactions before being asked to assist students. Staff members include teachers, administrators, and support personnel (secretaries, custodial workers, bus drivers, attendance office clerks, lunchroom staff, etc.). Special efforts should be made to contact staff in other buildings who may have had prior experience with the student. Community members who should be contacted include athletic club coaches, private music instructors, and the like. Students with disabilities often have relationships outside the school that may be overlooked, including private therapists, physicians, mentors, tutors, and so on.

When contacting building staff, a calling tree or snow chain may be used. However, the fewer the number of people delivering the information, the less the opportunity for error in sharing facts. Unless a very large number of people must be contacted, callers should be limited to a small number of administrators and mental health staff.

When delivering a message, staff members should have a scripted statement that they can use to make sure that no important details are overlooked. Staff members should be requested to go through a designated contact person to deliver messages of condolences, support, and so on, until the family's wishes concerning visitors and phone calls can be determined. In the message, preliminary details of the school intervention should be shared. This is a good time to relay to staff that the school administrator has given permission for them to set aside the curriculum.

If an answering machine is in use, do not leave specifics on the answering machine. Instead, tell the person that you have important information for them and ask them to return the call as soon as possible. Always follow up to make sure that staff members and others are not taken by surprise when returning to school because contact was not made.

Call the crisis team together. The building administrator, who often serves as the crisis coordinator, sets the time of the initial crisis team meeting and notifies team members. It is critical that contact information for crisis team members be kept current and readily available. When the crisis team meets, members will have opportunities to discuss with administrators any specific recommendations that will assist with the intervention process. This is an excellent opportunity for team members who have knowledge of students with special needs to identify additional considerations such students may require.

Resource needs will be determined by the extent of the impact resulting from the injury or death of a student, staff member, or parent. If the victim is a student with special needs, the degree of school impact increases as the amount of exposure to typical peers increases. For example, if the victim has a high-incidence disability (such as a learning disability), he or she is likely to have been involved in the regular education setting for a large portion of the day. Familiarity with greater numbers of students increases the level of impact. Even if the victim's educational services were delivered in a more restrictive setting and familiarity with overall student population is low, the impact may continue to be high based upon the vulnerability created by the special needs of other students in that program.

The greater the impact, the more support during intervention will be needed. For high-impact deaths, additional assistance from a district or community-based crisis team should be requested.

Develop announcements for students and parents. The student announcement should contain a brief statement of factual information regarding the crisis. Keep language within the announcement simple. Information about memorial or funeral services, if known, may be included.

A parent letter may be similar to the student announcement previously created. In some instances, the crisis team may choose to identify the student by characteristics rather than name (such as "a fourth-grade male"). Also provide parents with a list of professional resources (giving names of professionals within and outside the school) that parents may contact if they have questions about their child's reactions and needs.

Include written information regarding typical child or adolescent reactions to crisis, how parents can support their children, how to talk to children about death, and so on, making sure that documents are also available in languages other than English if necessary. For parents of students with special needs, include the contact information for members of the special education team who have specific training and knowledge about how crisis affects students with special needs as well as an understanding of the child's particular needs.

On the Day of the Crisis Intervention

Hold a joint meeting with all participating crisis response teams and staff. This meeting is usually held at the beginning of the school day. The building-level crisis team is introduced along with any responders from outside the building who will be present during the day.

Prior to or immediately following this meeting, allow staff members time to be with one another to address some of their own reactions. Advise the staff of the procedure for requesting support both for their students and for themselves. Explain any employee assistance programs that are available and how they can be accessed. If possible, have a representative from those groups at the meeting. Recognize that some staff members may have significant reactions to the crisis based upon their relationships with particular students and/or their personal crisis history. Advise them of the availability of substitute teachers or others who can cover their class if necessary.

Review the plan for the day. Discuss how the needs of students will be met during the day. For example, during first period, an announcement may be made in the classroom to all classes, followed by a class meeting to process the information. For those students who require additional assistance, identify the locations where that will take place and outline the procedure for getting students there, particularly if they are upset. Note that some students prefer to meet with a group of their friends and should be allowed to do so to provide maximum support for one another. If there is to be a location for large numbers of students to gather and support each other, identify that location as well.

The staff should be reminded that students with special needs often require special methods of intervention. If modifications or accommodations create significant changes in the way crisis interventions will be delivered to these students (e.g., led by special education staff and others who know the students well or provided within a smaller setting), explain that procedure. Additionally, the school may contact the families of those students directly to describe the support being given and to offer additional resources.

Discuss potential options for activities that teachers may wish to provide during upcoming days. Emphasize variety. Some students may wish to continue to work on their assignments. Some may choose to read. Some may prefer to sit quietly or listen to music. Opportunities to draw or to journal may be helpful. Review disciplinary procedures to ensure that structure and support continue to be provided appropriately within the context of the crisis intervention.

Predict behavioral reactions. Typical crisis reactions typically fall into four main areas (Poland & McCormick, 1999) but may vary in expression based upon the child's developmental level:

- Fear of the future
- Academic regression
- Behavioral regression
- Sleep disturbances, nightmares, and night terrors

Offer printed information to teachers and staff regarding crisis reactions based upon developmental levels. Emphasize the importance of observing children with special needs carefully to watch for comprehension and perceptual concerns or difficulties expressing thoughts and reactions. Describe the ways that the behavioral characteristics of students with mental health and medical issues may increase in intensity. Individually discuss with teachers any appropriate accommodations necessary to address the individual needs of specific students in their classroom.

Identify students requiring special interventions. Start a list that identifies students known to be close to the victim or who, for some other reason, may require special assistance. Discuss ways for staff to keep records of students who have required small-group or individual intervention. One option that has been successfully used is to have students place their names (individually or with others if they choose to come with close friends) on a list in the main office. Responders can then document names of students seen, critical observations, and recommendations for follow-up. The list also gives a method of recognizing those students who appear to be most impacted as indicated by multiple requests for assistance. This is particularly helpful when different responders may be seeing the same students at different times.

Decide if and when a parent meeting will be held. It is very helpful to have parents included in intervention efforts. On such occasions, parents (especially those of students in a highly impacted class) can be notified of the crisis by phone and invited to attend a parent meeting at the school. Such meetings give parents the opportunity to support each other and to ask vital questions about how to assist their children. This is a good time to provide parents with written information concerning typical childhood reactions to trauma, referral sources, and so on. Do not overlook the value of books on death and grief written especially for children. Parents appreciate the opportunities to view examples that they may purchase on their own.

When Students Arrive

Make the student announcement. The announcement should be read aloud in each classroom at approximately the same time. Announcements should not be made to large groups or over the intercom. If teachers are upset, team members may wish to come to the classroom to read the announcement. If the general education classroom contains students believed to be at increased risk for specialized intervention, those students may be dismissed and taken to a different location for small-group or individual intervention immediately after the announcement. Be prepared for extreme variability in reactions. Make sure to record any students who are absent so that phone calls to parents can be made to share the announcement so that no students will be taken by surprise when they return to school.

Conduct class meetings and group crisis interventions. Class meetings should generally be limited to 30 minutes, with extension based upon the needs of the class (e.g., if the victim is a student in that particular classroom or if class members have a special relationship with the victim). These meetings serve both supportive and educational functions. Facts are presented and rumors dispelled.

Students are often relieved to hear that their classmates have similar thoughts and reactions. Opportunities to share the things that trouble them currently and to predict the areas that may pose difficulty for them in the future provide them with the chance to brainstorm coping strategies. When told that responses like sleeping difficulties, appetite decreases, and poor concentration are common in sit-

Box 4.3 Helping Children Cope

Use developmentally appropriate language
Model a healthy expression and management of feelings
Help reestablish a sense of security and safety
Encourage an open discussion of reactions to the crisis
Listen
Validate concerns and fears
Reassure
Educate about the "normal" reactions to crisis
Help predict upcoming problems or situations
Help develop solutions
Maintain a routine
Keep your promises

uations similar to the one in which they find themselves, students learn important lessons about grief and are reassured about the normalcy of their reactions.

While the topic of group crisis intervention is beyond the intent of this chapter, it should be noted that it has been effectively used in the school setting. When this form of intervention is used, it is essential for facilitators to have received adequate training and practice in its use. Group crisis interventions are most effective when homogeneous groups are identified. In schools, where established classes are often used to provide interventions, the heterogeneity of the class with respect to the relationship between individual students and the victim sometimes affects the usefulness of such a technique. If relationships with the victim are too diverse, students are often reluctant to participate openly.

One perception often held by students is that their behavior directly or indirectly contributed to the death or injury of the victim. Often, this thought will be relayed in rather indirect statements such as "Our class was really awful at times. I knew we should have been nicer to our teacher." Should those kinds of statements surface, it is important to reassure students that, especially in the case of unexpected deaths, it is typical for people to feel guilty about things that they did or didn't do. Reassure them that such behaviors did not cause the tragedy.

Other points of discussion that often arise involve the issues of entitlement and equity. Students frequently argue that others should not be so emotional because they weren't friends with the victim, they had been mean to the victim in the past, and the like. It may be helpful to teach or remind students that reactions to situations may be determined by the personal history of an individual—a history of which they may have no knowledge. Students may also express concerns about the differences in crisis response for different crisis events. For example, they may question why seemingly more things were done for a particular student who died than for another. Even though method and intensity of intervention are determined by impact, crisis teams should carefully consider these issues in advance.

Follow up with crisis team members and staff at the end of the day. Discuss the events of the day, noting what went well, what didn't go well, and what should happen the next day. Document the special needs of students who may need long-term assistance. Designate individuals to make telephone contact with the parents of those students to discuss concerns and provide additional resources. Contact should also be made with any outside therapists and/or physicians who may be working with students who have special needs.

Leave time in this meeting for staff to address their own reactions and concerns. While this can be uncomfortable for some, required staff meetings often provide unexpected benefits when individuals recognize similarities between their own reactions and those of others. Value from this type of activity does not require active participation; individuals gain much information and comfort by simply listening. Informal support groups for staff frequently arise from this experience. It is the well informed administrator or crisis coordinator who continues to provide opportunities for staff to meet in the days and weeks following a crisis.

In the Days and Weeks Following the Intervention

Reestablish routine. Returning to well-known routines can be comforting and helpful to students. While keeping the needs of individual students in mind, experienced crisis responders will validate that some students prefer to immerse themselves in academic work even on the day of the crisis response. Others prefer alternate activities such as those previously discussed.

The key to successful intervention is variety. However, as soon as possible, a daily schedule should be resumed with accommodations for students who may need support during the day. Should the crisis occur in close proximity to major academic events such as American College Test (ACT) or Scholastic Assessment Test (SAT) testing, it may be necessary to remind organizers of such events of the importance of rescheduling. While educators intuitively recognize the necessity of this, the cost of rescheduling in terms of time and trouble can sometimes cloud otherwise rational decision making.

Identify timelines for appropriate postvention activities. Such activities are critical in helping students cope with issues such as anniversary dates, media reminders, and legal issues that reintroduce and prolong the effects of traumatic events. With special populations, it is important to remember that the collage of factors that often accompanies special needs (such as shared characteristics with the victim, personal trauma histories, and emotional and learning problems) makes this group particularly susceptible to disruptions in healing created by intermittent reminders of the tragedy.

Removal of belongings. One of the most difficult decisions following the death of a student or staff member involves the decision of when to remove their belongings (classroom desk, locker contents, posted schoolwork, etc.). A common mistake is removing belongings too quickly. While this is a topic that elicits a diverse range of opinions, an important element with which most appear to agree is the inclusion of students in the decision-making process. Some schools have identified a school holiday or vacation close to the time desired that is useful for the purpose of transition. Others have allowed students to formalize the process by gathering and boxing belongings and creating a class letter to send to parents of the deceased.

Establish memorials. Almost immediately, students, families, and community members request to do something to honor the victim. Often, the victim's desk or locker becomes an impromptu memorial. Requests may range from creation of memory books for the family (staff should be sure to monitor contents before sending home) and the dedication of a sports event to more permanent memorials such as the planting of a tree, the creation of a rock garden, or the dedication of a high school yearbook. Generally, consumable memorials such as scholarship funds or donations to prevention programs are recommended. The more permanent the suggested memorial, the more time should elapse before decisions are made that are unchangeable. Remember that if the death was by suicide, a school memorial is advised against in order to prevent contagion effects.

WHEN SUICIDE IS INVOLVED

When a death results from suicide, some important differences in crisis response should be noted (Poland & McCormick, 1999; Poland & Lieberman, 2002; Lieberman & Davis, 2002). Students should be told that the death was a suicide, but specific details pertaining to the method should not be discussed. The emphasis of the discussion should be on the fact that suicide is a bad choice and can be prevented. Give students specific examples of steps they can take to help a friend or themselves if talk or thoughts of suicide are encountered. Parents and staff should be educated about suicide contagion and the steps required in order to prevent it.

To avoid glorifying the suicide, school should not be dismissed and a normal schedule should be maintained. Permanent or physical memorials should not be allowed. "Living memorials" such as suicide prevention efforts or other worthy causes that shift the focus to survivors are recommended if memorials are requested. Contact with the victim's family is encouraged to provide them with support as well as to assist in identifying other students who may be at increased risk for contagion due to their personal history with the victim.

SUMMARY

While high-profile school shootings in recent years have heightened the awareness of the need for effective crisis intervention in the school setting, students are significantly more likely to be affected by a common crisis during their school years. On those occasions, staff will be asked to provide support even though many have had no formal training or experience in crisis response. While there have been an increasing number of resources developed to assist educators with school-based crisis response, little attention has been given to the considerations of students with special needs. These students may be particularly vulnerable in times of crisis and should be given the highest priority for intervention. Administrators and staff should take care to assure that all aspects of crisis intervention address students with special needs.

Crisis response literature frequently notes that the symbols of crisis and opportunity are interchangeable in some cultures. This fact serves as a reminder that crisis affords educators the opportunities to help all students as they process the inevitable yet unpredictable events of life. With appropriate assistance and support, students will develop greater resiliency and stronger coping strategies.

I was in Ann's class at the end of the school year. Once again, there were smiles and laughter. But something new was there as well. There was a relationship between the students that I had not seen before—a caring and supportive aura not always found in classrooms at the elementary level. I knew it was due to the efforts of the parents, staff, and community. And I knew that, through her death, Ann had taught all of us one more extremely valuable lesson.

Box 4.4 Excerpt from *Tear Soup*

"And most importantly, I've learned that there is something down deep within all of us ready to help us survive the things we think we can't survive."

The contents of this chapter are based upon conventional or common wisdom found throughout the literature in the area of crisis intervention and response. The interested reader is encouraged to access the following resources for additional information:

American Psychological Association: www.apa.org
National Association of School Psychologists: http://nasponline.org
National Education Association: http://www.nea.org
National Organization for Victim Assistance: http://www.try.nova.org
U.S. Department of Education: www.ed.gov

REFERENCES

American Psychiatric Association. (2000). *Diagnostic and statistical manual of mental disorders* (4th ed., text rev.). Washington, DC: Author.

Aptekar, L., & Boore, J. A. (1990). The emotional effects of disaster on children: A review of the literature. *International Journal of Mental Health, 19,* 77–90.

Brock, S., & Poland, S. (2002). School crisis preparedness. In S. Brock, P. Lazarus, & S. Jimerson (Eds.), *Best practices in school crisis prevention and intervention* (pp. 273–288). Washington, DC: National Association of School Psychologists.

Brock, S. E., Sandoval, J., & Lewis, S. (2001). *Preparing for crises in the schools: A manual for building school crisis response teams* (2nd ed.). New York: Wiley.

Colorado Society of School Psychologists Statewide Crisis Response Team. (2003). *Developing consistency in school-based crisis response.* Denver, CO: Author.

Herman, J. (1992). *Trauma and recovery.* New York: Basic Books.

Hillman, J. L. (2002). *Crisis intervention and trauma: New approaches to evidence-based practice.* New York: Kluwer Academic/Plenum.

Jimerson, S., & Huff, L. (2002). Responding to a sudden, unexpected death at school: Chance favors the prepared professional. In S. Brock, P. Lazarus, & S. Jimerson (Eds.), *Best practices in school crisis prevention and intervention* (pp. 449–485). Washington, DC: National Association of School Psychologists.

Lavin, C. (1998). Helping individuals with developmental disabilities. In K. Doka & J. Davidson (Eds.), *Living with grief: Who we are, how we grieve* (pp. 161–180). Philadelphia: Brunner & Mazel.

Lieberman, R., & Davis, J. (2002). Suicide intervention. In S. Brock, P. Lazarus, & S. Jimerson (Eds.), *Best practices in school crisis prevention and intervention* (pp. 531–551). Washington, DC: National Association of School Psychologists.

Masten, A. S., & Coatsworth, J. D. (1998). The development of competence in favorable and unfavorable environments: Lessons from research on successful children. *American Psychologist, 53,* 205–220.

National Association of School Psychologists (NASP). (1992). Helping children grow up in the 90s: A resource book for children and families. Silver Spring, MD: Author.

Newgass, S., & Schonfeld, D. (2000). School crisis intervention, crisis prevention, and crisis response. In A. R. Roberts (Ed.), *Crisis intervention handbook: Assessment, treatment and research* (pp. 209–228). Boston: Oxford University Press.

Office of Safe and Drug-Free Schools, U.S. Department of Education. (2003). *Practical information on crisis planning: A guide for schools and communities.* Washington, DC: Author.

Pfohl, W., Jimerson, S., & Lazarus, P. (2003). Developmental aspects of psychological trauma and grief. In S. Brock, P. Lazarus, & S. Jimerson (Eds.), *Best practices in school crisis prevention and intervention* (pp. 309–331). Washington, DC: National Association of School Psychologists.

Poland, S., & Lieberman, R. (2002). Best practices in suicide intervention. In *Best Practices in School Psychology IV* (Vol. 2, pp. 1151–1165). Washington, DC: National Association of School Psychologists.

Poland, S., & McCormick, J. S. (1999). *Coping with crisis: Lessons learned.* Longmont, CO: Sopris West.

Poland, S., Pitcher, G., & Lazarus, P. (2002). Best practices in crisis prevention and management. In A. Thomas & J. Grimes (Eds.), *Best practices in school psychology IV* (Vol. 2, pp. 1057–1079). Washington, DC: National Association of School Psychologists.

Ruof, S., & Harris, J. (1988). How to select, train, and supervise a crisis team. *Communique, 17* (4), 19.

Webster's Ninth Collegiate Dictionary. (1987). Springfield, MA: Merriam Webster.

Young, M. (2002). *The community crisis response team training manual.* Washington, DC: National Organization for Victim Assistance.

5

Childhood Disorders

CECIL R. REYNOLDS

AARSKOG SYNDROME

Aarskog syndrome, or Aarskog-Scott syndrome, is a genetic disorder characterized by short stature and musculoskeletal, facial, and genital abnormalities. This inherited disorder of unknown etiology involves either an autosomal recessive or semidominant X-linked transmission. Aarskog syndrome is a rare condition.

Although there is no treatment for Aarskog syndrome itself, genetic counseling is recommended for affected families as a preventive measure. Trials of growth hormone have not been found effective to treat short stature in this disorder. Specific treatments will depend upon individual symptoms and may include surgery for cryptorchidism and inguinal hernia, orthodontic treatment for facial abnormalities, and ophthalmologic consultation. Children with Aarskog syndrome will likely have multiple X rays to examine for musculoskeletal abnormalities. In some cases, cystic changes in the brain and generalized seizures may occur, resulting in a need for referral to a neurologist and pharmacotherapy.

Special education considerations include the possibility of cognitive impairment and Attention Deficit Disorder with or without hyperactivity. Although estimates vary across studies, 70 to 90% of affected individuals can be expected to have normal or low normal intelligence. Children with Aarskog syndrome may be eligible for special education services, with the specific handicapping condition depending upon the nature and severity of symptoms. Findings from the literature suggest that the most likely handicapping conditions are Mentally Retarded or Other Health Impairment.

The text of this chapter was adapted from *The Childhood Disorders Diagnostic Desk Reference* edited by Elaine Fletcher-Janzen and Cecil Reynolds published by John Wiley & Sons in 1993.

ACALCULIA (ACQUIRED DYSCALCULIA)

Acalculia, also known as acquired dyscalculia, is the loss of arithmetic skills due to brain injury. The arithmetic difficulties may involve the reading or writing of numbers or arithmetic signs and misaligning or rotating digits or numbers, as well as inaccurately solving problems requiring calculation. Traumatic brain injury and cerebrovascular disease are the most common causes; however, demyelinating disease, neoplasm, and degenerative disease can also produce acalculia.

Youth with acalculia may receive special education services under the classification of Traumatically Brain Injured if a physician can provide eligibility documentation of a brain injury. If this documentation is not possible, a student may qualify as Mentally Retarded or Learning Disabled in the areas of mathematics calculation, mathematics reasoning, or both, depending on the severity of his or her brain injury. Modifications implemented in the classroom may involve the use of a calculator, mathematical fact tables, or computer technology. Instructional techniques should include numerous repetitions of basic mathematical concepts and calculations.

ACHONDROPLASIA

Achondroplasia is the most common form of skeletal dysplasia or chondrodystrophy. It is a bone disorder that is characterized by a defect in the formation of the cartilage of the long bones. People with achondroplasia often refer to themselves as dwarfs or little people. Achondroplasia usually results from a spontaneous mutation (chemical change) within a single gene. The condition may be passed on to future generations. For example, a couple with one achondroplasic spouse and an average-statured spouse has a 50% chance of having an average-statured child (Telzrow, 2000).

Achondroplasia occurs in all races and with equal frequency in females and males. It affects approximately 1 in 25,000 children in the United States.

Although intelligence is not usually affected by this condition, children with achondroplasia may qualify for special services within the physical disability category. Children with this condition may require adaptive equipment to accommodate their short stature. Older children may require pain management techniques to adjust to the pain often experienced in the lower back with spinal cord and nerve problems. Ear infections need to be recognized and treated promptly, and frequent hearing checks may be necessary to avoid hearing problems.

ACROCALLOSAL SYNDROME

Acrocallosal syndrome (ACS) is a genetic disorder that is apparent at birth. The disorder is typically characterized by underdevelopment or absence of the corpus callosum and by mental retardation. However, other associated symptoms may be variable, even among affected members of the same family.

ACS is believed to be a rare condition, but prevalence is unknown and has not been studied in detail. Considered at first to be sporadic, the syndrome has more recently been ascribed to an autosomal recessive gene, on the basis of its observation in two siblings. True and confirmed etiology remains unknown.

Special education approaches 100% in cases of ACS, but learning and academic skills vary across individuals with the disorder. A child with ACS typically qualifies for special education services under multiply handicapped due to health problems and speech and language delays accompanied by mental retardation. In addition, occupational therapy is often required. Prognosis is poor for children with ACS.

ACROMEGALY

Acromegaly is characterized by excessive growth due to oversecretion of growth hormone, which is produced in the liver and other tissues and is secreted by the anterior pituitary gland. Oversecretion of growth hormone is often caused by the presence of a benign pituitary tumor (adenoma) but can also be caused by lung and pancreas tumors that stimulate the excessive production of substances similar to growth hormone.

Characteristics include:

1. Enlarged hands, feet, jaw, facial features, and internal organs.
2. Coarsening facial features and deeper voice.
3. Excessive perspiration.
4. Amenorrhea.
5. Sweaty handshake.

Treatment of acromegaly is primarily medical.

Acromegaly, referred to as gigantism when seen in children, is not necessarily accompanied by cognitive deficiencies. Special education issues are most often related to physical accommodations or services such as occupational therapy.

ADDISON'S DISEASE

First described by Dr. Thomas Addison in the mid-1800s, Addison's disease (adrenocortical insufficiency, hypocortisolism) is an endocrine disorder characterized by a lack of production of the hormones *cortisol* and *aldosterone,* both of which are produced by the adrenal cortex. Each individual has two adrenal glands, one above each kidney. Each adrenal gland has two parts. The inner part is called the medulla, and the outer part is called the cortex. Thus, the outer part of the adrenal gland is responsible for producing the hormones cortisol and aldosterone. Cortisol has many effects on the body, including maintaining blood pressure, maintaining cardiovascular functions, and slowing the immune system's inflammatory response. In addition, cortisol balances the effects of insulin in breaking down sugar for energy and regulating the metabolism of proteins, carbohydrates, and fats. Aldosterone helps the body maintain blood pressure, water, and salt balance. Together these two hormones have a role in the proper functioning of our major organs. Thus, Addison's disease has a significant impact on the body's functions.

Children with this disorder may be classified under Other Health Impairment. They may need a school schedule that includes rest periods, a shortened school day, or both. Peer helpers may be needed to assist students during the day. Also, easy access to restrooms and the health or nurse's office should be available to the student. In addition, psychological services may be needed to deal with chronic health concerns and other mental health issues. Parents should consult with the school psychologist in their district to discuss any academic needs with respect to chronic illness.

The prognosis for Addison's disease is good, and patients can lead a normal, crisis-free life as long as replacement hormones are taken properly and absorbed.

ADRENOCORTICOTROPIC HORMONE (ACTH) DEFICIENCY

Adrenocorticotropic hormone (ACTH) deficiency, sometimes referred to as secondary adrenal insufficiency, is a rare (affecting fewer than 1 in 100,000) and potentially life-threatening form of adrenocortical failure in which there is partial or complete lack of ACTH production and secretion by the anterior pituitary gland. ACTH acts to stimulate release of cortisol from the adrenal cortex during both the diurnal rhythm and exposure to stressors. Onset may occur throughout the life span.

ADRENOLEUKODYSTROPHY

Adrenoleukodystrophy (ALD) is an inherited, serious, progressive neurological disorder affecting the adrenal gland and white matter of the nervous system.

The results of treatment of ALD have been disappointing. There are ongoing attempts to evaluate the efficacy of preventative treatment via Lorenzo's oil in presymptomatic affected individuals.

It is difficult to know how best to provide education to children with a severe degenerative neurological disease. Identification is currently important for genetic purposes and presumably will ultimately be important for treatment. Overt, persistent deterioration (loss) in skills and behavior requires medical evaluation. It is important to remember that after the genetic abnormality associated with ALD is identified, the outcome is not clear or predictable.

AGENESIS OF THE CORPUS CALLOSUM

Agenesis of the corpus callosum (ACC) is a congenital disorder characterized by partial to complete absence of the corpus callosum. The incidence of the disorder is difficult to estimate because many individuals with ACC are relatively asymptomatic and may never present for evaluation.

When ACC occurs in isolation (Type I), it is relatively asymptomatic. Often, the diagnosis is made as a coincidental finding. However, on very detailed cognitive tasks, subtle difficulties with bimanual coordination and interhemispheric transfer of sensorimotor information occurs.

ACC can also occur in combination with a variety of other congenital anomalies (Type II). In general, the constellation of neurological and neuropsychological findings in the Type II group is more dependent on the comorbid abnormalities than on ACC per se.

ACC and associated anomalies can be identified prenatally by transvaginal sonography and CT scan. After ACC is identified, genetic testing and counseling are recommended. Children identified with ACC in isolation have an excellent prognosis for normal intellectual development and for living a normal and productive life. Treatment and special education considerations of ACC are largely dependent on the nature and severity of the associated anomalies in a given individual.

AGORAPHOBIA

Agoraphobia (Greek for *fear of the market*) is fear of being alone in places or situations in which the individual believes that escape might be difficult or embarrassing or in which help may not be available in the event that the individual experiences panic-like symptoms. The fear leads to an avoidance of a variety of situations that could include riding a bus, going into a school building, maintaining attendance for the complete school day, being on a bridge or in an elevator, and riding in cars or attendance at special events like field trips or performances. Children in particular may come up with their own "treatment" for the disorder, in the form of rules—not riding in other people's cars, not waiting in lines, not going to birthday parties, and so on—that are difficult for family members to accommodate.

The most widely used treatments for phobias consist of behavioral, cognitive-behavioral, and pharmacological interventions. Recently, a parent-training component added to CBT intervention significantly enhanced treatment outcomes when compared with cognitive-behavioral therapy (CBT) alone.

Special education services may be available to students diagnosed with agoraphobia under specific categories of Other Health Impaired, Severe Emotional Disturbance, or Behavior Disorder if an impact on the child's education can be established; this may be particularly important if the disorder is chronic in nature. Accommodations may also be requested and provided under Section 504 of the Rehabilitation Act of 1973. Due to the nature and scope of the disorder, school attendance may become problematic.

AGRAPHIA

Agraphia is the loss or impairment of the ability to produce written language and is the result of acquired central nervous system dysfunction. The term *agraphia* is often used interchangeably with dysgraphia. Agraphia may occur in isolation, but more often it is associated with disorders such as aphasia (disordered speech), dyslexia (disorder of reading), and acalculia (disorder of mathematical calculation).

Treatment of agraphia should be tailored to the needs of each child according to a thorough assessment of linguistic, sensorimotor, visuospatial, and cognitive abilities, as well as psychosocial and environmental factors that may affect writing ability. It should be determined whether the written language disorder parallels similar oral speech or language problems and whether individual children learn more effectively with phonemic or whole-word approaches.

AICARDI SYNDROME

Aicardi syndrome is a very rare genetic disorder that was first identified and reported in 1965 by Jean Aicardi, a French neurologist. It was originally described as consisting of a triad of primary features: infantile spasms, chorioretinal lacunae, and agenesis of the corpus callosum. Modern imaging techniques have revealed that corpus callosum agenesis does not occur in all cases and that the presence of several other brain abnormalities (see characteristics) are more characteristic of the disorder than is isolated agenesis of the corpus callosum. Severe mental and motor developmental delays usually occur, with only a limited number of affected children able to develop some language or to ambulate independently or with assistance. There is currently no specific treatment for Aicardi syndrome. Special education services are often needed for severe developmental delays. These services may include physical and occupational therapy, provision of adaptive equipment, and instruction for skill development at the appropriate developmental level for the individual child. Prognosis for children with Aicardi syndrome varies with the severity of the disorder.

Characteristics

1. Classic triad.
   - Infantile spasms
   - Chorioretinal lacunae
   - Agenesis of the corpus callosum (complete or partial)

2. New major features (present in most patients studied by magnetic resonance imaging).
   - Cortical malformations (mostly microgyria)
   - Periventricular and subcortical heterotopia
   - Cysts around the third ventricle, choroid plexuses, or both
   - Papillomas of choroid plexuses
   - Optic disc and nerve coloboma

3. Supporting features (present in some cases).
   - Vertebral and costal abnormalities
   - Microphthalmia and other eye abnormalities
   - Split-brain electroencephalogram (dissociated suppression-burst tracing)
   - Gross hemispheric asymmetry

Source: Aicardi (1999)

ALBINISM

Albinism refers to a group of inherited conditions. Individuals with albinism have a deficiency or absence of pigment in the skin, hair, and eyes (or eyes only) due to an abnormality in production of a pigment called melanin. Albinism affects individuals from all races.

One of the primary treatment concerns regarding albinism is vision rehabilitation. Surgery may be carried out to improve strabismus (crossed eyes or lazy eye). However, because surgery does not correct the misrouting of the optic nerves from the eyes to the brain, surgery does not provide fine binocular vision.

Individuals with albinism are sensitive to glare. Sunglasses or tinted contact lenses help with outdoor light. It is helpful to place indoor light sources for reading behind rather than in front of the individual. There are a variety of optical aids for individuals with albinism.

Other medical problems may affect the individual with albinism. People with albinism are at increased risk for skin cancers because of the lack of the protective melanin pigment.

Also, individuals with albinism are at risk for social isolation because the condition is often misunderstood. Social stigmatization can occur, especially within communities of color, where the race or paternity of a person with albinism may be questioned.

The child with albinism may qualify for special education services under the category of Visually Handicapped. Due to the vision problems previously noted, the child with albinism may require certain individual accommodations in order to meet his or her educational needs. These accommodations may include large-print text, adequate lighting, books on tape, low-vision aids, and extended test-taking time. In addition, supportive counseling and sensitive education of the school community may be needed if social ostracization is observed.

ALEXANDER DISEASE

Alexander disease is a rare, genetic, degenerative disorder of the nervous system. It is one of a group of genetic disorders called the leukodystrophies that affect growth of the myelin sheath on nerve fibers in the brain. This disease can occur at any age, including adulthood. The most frequent form of Alexander disease is the infantile form. It has an average onset at 6 months of age.

There is neither a cure nor a standard course of treatment for Alexander disease; however, much support care is necessary, including good nutrition and generous use of antibiotics and antiepileptics. The treatment of Alexander disease is thus symptomatic and supportive.

Children with this disease would probably initially qualify for Early Childhood services (special education services for children under the age of 3). Depending on the extent of mental retardation and their life span, they may then qualify as Mentally Retarded and enter life skills classes. They may also qualify as Other Health Impaired for the seizures, Physically Handicapped, or Speech Impaired depending on the areas of delay. The prognosis for patients with Alexander disease is generally poor.

ALEXIA

Alexia is an acquired neurological disorder characterized by a partial or complete inability to read. The etiology of alexia is typically associated with a lesion behind and beneath the left occipital lobe, which damages the visual pathways within the hemisphere. Alexia can also be caused by the combination of a lesion on the corpus callosum, which disconnects the right-to-left visual information transfer, or a lesion in the left occipital lobe, which disconnects the left visual association cortex from the left language cortex. This results in a disconnection of visual information in the right hemisphere from the word-recognition system in the left hemisphere.

ALPORT SYNDROME

Alport syndrome is an inherited (usually X-linked) disorder. It involves damage to the kidneys, blood in the urine, and loss of hearing in some families—and in some cases, loss of vision. In cases in which there is no family history of kidney disease, Alport syndrome is caused by a mutation in a collagen gene.

Alport syndrome is classified by mode of inheritance, age, and features other than kidney abnormalities. Treatment of Alport syndrome includes vigorous treatment of the chronic renal failure. Hemodialysis may be used to treat this problem. This treatment would involve removing blood from the patient's artery, cleaning it of unwanted substances that would be normally excreted in the urine, and returning the cleansed blood to a vein. It is also important to aggressively treat urinary tract infections and control blood pressure; this can be done through diet by restricting salt and protein intake. High blood pressure can also be controlled with medication. Cataracts may be surgically repaired. Genetic counseling is also recommended.

Hearing loss may be permanent. If diagnosed during school age, the child may be eligible for special education services under the classification of Hearing Impaired, Visually Impaired, or Other Health Impaired. Prognosis for females is that they usually have a normal life span with little or no manifestation of the disease. Some complications may arise during pregnancy. Males, however, are likely to develop permanent deafness, a decrease in or total loss of vision, and chronic renal failure.

ALSTRÖM SYNDROME

Alström syndrome is an autosomal recessive genetic disorder characterized primarily by retinitis pigmentosa beginning during infancy and progressive sensorineural hearing loss beginning in early childhood. There is typically infant or childhood obesity that may normalize somewhat later, and individuals with this disorder frequently develop diabetes mellitus by early adulthood. In contrast to Bardet-Biedl syndrome, which shares several symptoms, in Alström syndrome there are normal intelligence and normal extremities.

AMBLYOPIA

Amblyopia is a term used to describe a loss of vision in an eye that appears to be physically healthy. It is commonly known as lazy eye. Amblyopia can occur for a variety of reasons, including strabismus (crossed or turned eye), congenital cataracts, cloudy cornea, droopy eyelid, nearsightedness, farsightedness, or astigmatism. Amblyopia may occur in various degrees depending on the severity of the underlying problem. The visual system is fully developed between approximately the ages of 9 and 11. If it is caught early, amblyopia can be corrected—however, after age 11 it is difficult if not impossible to train the brain to use the eye normally.

AMNESIA

The term amnesia refers to memory loss, either partial or total. Classification of amnesia types may be according to temporal factors, etiology, or extent of memory loss. Amnesia may occur after a neurological injury or illness, or it may represent a psychological reaction to a traumatic event. Amnesia may occur after head injury, electroshock therapy, drug or alcohol intoxication, anoxia, or other conditions affecting the memory systems of the brain. It may also occur as a symptom of psychological disorders such as Major Depression, Posttraumatic Stress Disorder, or Dissociative Identity Disorder. Children who have been physically or sexually abused, survivors of war or other catastrophe, or victims of violence may develop psychological amnesia.

ANENCEPHALY

Anencephaly is a neural tube defect (NTD) resulting in the incomplete development of part of the neural tube that usually develops between the 23rd and 26th days of pregnancy. Specifically, the cephalic or head end of the neural tube does not close, which results in a failure to form major portions of the brain, skull, and scalp. Infants with anencephaly are born without a forebrain, and the rest of the brain tissue is often exposed. Etiology is unknown.

Prognosis is poor because most infants do not survive infancy; many are miscarried, are stillborn, or die within a few hours or days after birth.

ANGELMAN SYNDROME

Angelman syndrome, formerly known as happy puppet syndrome due to a resemblance of children with the disorder to the movement and appearance of a marionette, is a rare congenital neurodevelopmental disorder with complex genetic etiology. It is manifested by mental retardation, speech impairment, movement disorder, and easily-provoked laughter. Dysmorphic facial features frequently occur. The condition is usually not recognized at birth or in infancy due to nonspecific features. Average age of diagnosis is 6 years.

There is no specific treatment for Angelman syndrome at this time other than management of symptoms. Severe developmental delay necessitates intensive education and rehabilitation efforts. Managing hyperactivity and inattention improves opportunities for learning.

ANXIETY DISORDERS

Anxiety disorders are very common in children. There are nine major disorders that have anxiety as a salient feature: Separation Anxiety, Obsessive-Compulsive Disorder, Panic Disorder, Generalized Anxiety Disorder, Posttraumatic Stress Disorder (PTSD), and Social Phobia. Anxiety disorders contain many common features like fears, irritability, nervousness, insomnia, inattentiveness, and hypervigilance. Special education placement will vary. Because anxiety is an internalizing disorder, children with anxiety disorders may go unnoticed in the classroom. Children who do receive special education services are most likely to be diagnosed with severe emotional disturbance.

APHASIA, BROCA'S

Often called expressive or motor aphasia, Broca's aphasia is characterized by difficulties with the motor production of speech, problems with articulation, and a paucity of spoken language. Broca's aphasia can vary in severity from a slight difficulty in the reproduction of a spoken word to a complete inability to produce spoken language.

Broca's aphasia occurs in children who either fail to or have difficulty in expressing themselves despite normal cognitive abilities and normal linguistic comprehension. Developmental language disorders and mental retardation should be ruled out when screening for this disorder. The main cause is a traumatic brain injury resulting in a lesion to the left hemisphere of the brain in either the frontal operculum or the corticocortical association pathways in the white matter of the temporal, parietal, and frontal lobes that relate to the motor speech areas.

APHASIA, WERNICKE (SENSORY APHASIA)

Wernicke aphasia is characterized by the inability to comprehend speech or to produce meaningful speech following lesions to the posterior cortex. Individuals with Wernicke aphasia rarely experience muscular weakness affecting one side of the body, or hemiparesis. In most cases, its etiology involves a lesion affecting the dominant temporal lobe, particularly the auditory association cortex of the posterior-superior portion of the first temporal gyrus.

ARACHNOID CYSTS

Arachnoid cysts are benign cerebrospinal fluid-filled sacs that develop between the surface of the brain and cranial base or attach to the arachnoid membrane. Although most are slow growing and asymptomatic at first, if untreated, they can have devastating effects as a result of increased intracranial pressure.

ASPERGERS SYNDROME

Aspergers syndrome (AS) is a pervasive developmental disorder considered to be at the higher end of the autistic spectrum. The main distinction between a child with autism and a child with AS is in cognitive ability. Children with AS typically have an IQ within the normal to very superior range. Children with AS often have normal basic language skills but will have problems with pragmatic-social language. Children with AS typically have impairments in three areas of functioning: social skills, language, and behavior. With respect to behavior, children with AS display repetitive routines and compulsions that can be confused with a diagnosis of Obsessive-Compulsive Disorder (OCD). The difference between AS and OCD would be in the purpose it serves the child. For a child with AS, the repetitive routines and compulsions may serve as self-stimulatory behavior or high arousal. Aspergers syndrome is considered to be more common than autism. The syndrome is also more common in boys than girls.

Children with AS are eligible for special education services under the Autism category, but these services might not be necessary for children with mild symptoms. In fact, many children can function well in general education classrooms without the need of special education services. For those children who do need special education services, speech services can be extremely beneficial, as can receiving instruction in a resource room for those children with significant learning difficulties or behavior problems.

ASTHMA

Asthma is the most common chronic disease of childhood and the leading cause for pediatric hospitalization and school absenteeism. An estimated 4.8 million children in the United States experience asthma attacks ranging from mild to severe, with the highest rate found among African Americans. Asthmatic symptoms are manifest in 80% of children by age 5. Despite new knowledge about the pathophysiology and treatment of asthma, the morbidity and mortality rates continue to climb. Mortality is often associated with the lack of proper diagnosis of asthma severity and lack of adequate treatment due to limited funds for access.

Asthma is a chronic respiratory disease caused by reversible airflow obstruction. The obstruction of the airway is attributed to several factors, including bronchospasm, swelling of the airway, increased mucus secretion, and lymphocytic invasion of the airway walls. Characteristic symptoms include wheezing, coughing, and shortness of breath. Asthma can also be triggered by exercise, cold air, tobacco smoke, sudden changes in barometric pressure, pollutants, foods, and chemicals. Aspirin has not been known to cause an asthma attack in children, but it has with adults. Some conditions that exacerbate asthma in children, however, include sinusitis, gastroesophageal reflux, and psychosocial factors. Psychologists, teachers, and other professionals need to help educate parents and children about ways to prevent and treat asthma and to collaborate to ensure adequate educational opportunities. Home-school partnerships can be used to improve the child's health and school attendance. This may serve not only to enhance achievement but also to improve the child's self-esteem (e.g., enable him or her to interact more with peers both in and outside the classroom).

ATAXIA, FRIEDREICH

Friedreich ataxia is the most common of the hereditary ataxias and results in degeneration of the spine and cerebellum.

There is currently no treatment for Friedreich ataxia.

A few studies have looked at cognitive functioning in patients with Friedreich ataxia, and these have been conducted with adult populations. Patients with Friedreich ataxia appear to have a disturbance in the speed and efficiency of information processing, and this is independent of motor abnormalities. There is no consistent evidence of global cognitive impairment. Educational services to children with Friedreich ataxia should recognize the progressive nature of the disease, the sensory abnormalities that may develop, and the need for assistive technology. These children will require help with motor performance in all domains.

ATTENTION-DEFICIT/HYPERACTIVITY DISORDER

It is estimated that approximately 3 to 6% of children have some form of attention-deficit/hyperactivity disorder (ADHD); approximately three times as many males are identified as females. Although diagnosis of ADHD may occur at any age, most often diagnosis is made in elementary school–aged children. Subtyping of ADHD is made based on the extent to which symptoms are present in areas of inattention and hyperactivity/impulsivity with resulting subtypes of predominantly inattentive (PI), predominantly hyperactive-impulsive (PHI), and combined type (CT). By middle childhood, the majority of children with ADHD also present with some co-occurring disorder. Comorbid disorders with ADHD are most likely to be learning disabilities, language disabilities, Oppositional Defiant Disorder, and Conduct Disorder.

Treatment options for ADHD include the use of medication, strategies and modifications within the classroom, behavior management (e.g., contingency management, self-management), cognitive behavior therapy (e.g., self-talk), and parent training and education about ADHD. Research suggests that the most effective treatments include multiple components (e.g., medication, behavior management, and parent training) as opposed to any single approach to treatment. Children with ADHD may be eligible for special education or related services if (1) they have a co-occurring disorder that meets eligibility criteria or (2) the ADHD symptoms are significantly and adversely affecting their educational progress.

Not only is it evident that differential diagnosis of ADHD, learning disability, and Conduct Disorder is needed, but also the research on subtypes of ADHD (PI, PHI, CT) indicates that a view of ADHD as unidimensional is questionable. It may be most appropriate to view ADHD as a cluster of different behavioral deficits (attention, hyperactivity, impulsivity), each with a specific neural substrate of varying severity, of variable etiology, occurring in variable constellations, and sharing a common response to treatment.

AUTISM

Autism, more recently referred to as Autism Spectrum Disorder, is classified under the umbrella of pervasive developmental disorders, which also includes Aspergers syndrome, Retts, Childhood Disintegrative Disorder, and pervasive development disorder not otherwise specified. Autism cannot be diagnosed by physiological symptoms or medical testing, but rather is determined by how closely the child's condition fits behavioral criteria.

Characteristics include:

1. Child does not respond to name.
2. Child does not make eye contact.
3. Child resists cuddling and holding.
4. Child appears to be unaware of others' feelings.
5. Child has abnormal social interaction and prefers to play alone.
6. Child starts speaking later than other children, if at all.

7. If child does speak, there is abnormal tone and rhythm in speech.
8. Child fails to initiate or maintain conversation.
9. Child may repeat words or phrases verbatim but does not know how to use them.
10. Child uses repetitive movements, such as rocking or hand twisting.
11. Child develops specific routines or rituals and becomes very upset if there is a change in routine.
12. Child may engage in self-injurious behaviors, such as head banging.
13. Child is usually hyperactive.
14. Child may be fascinated by parts of an object.

To date, there is no cure for autism. The effects of autism, however, can be overcome or reduced through a combination of treatment modalities, such as behavioral, dietary, and biomedical interventions.

A diagnosis of autism qualifies for special education services. The amount of support required would depend on the severity of the characteristics that the child exhibits, ranging from full, one-on-one support to minimal support at various times of the day.

BATTEN DISEASE

Batten disease is one of a group of degenerative encephalopathic diseases known as the neuronal ceroid-lipofuscinoses (NCLs). In all the NCLs ceroid or lipofuscin accumulates within neurons and cells in other body systems.

Classical juvenile NCL is the most common of the NCLs, accounting for 49% of the patients with NCL and has an incidence of 1 in 25,000. Batten disease produces a slowly progressive dementia, visual loss, and behavioral changes. Initially, cognitive impairment is mild and is observable only at school. Later, psychomotor problems, including extrapyramidal, pyramidal, and cerebellar findings develop, followed by seizures. Death occurs by 20 years of age.

Educational interventions should be aimed at maintaining the highest level of functioning. The anticipated deterioration must be acknowledged in educational plans. There is no current medical treatment.

BATTERED-CHILD SYNDROME

Battered-child syndrome describes children who are chronically exposed to physical, sexual, or psychological abuse or neglect. The physical abuse may range from moderate injuries to severe ones that require hospitalization. Owing to unknown numbers of unreported cases of child abuse, incidence is difficult to estimate.

Due to chronic abuse and maltreatment, battered infants tend to form insecure attachment styles that often hinder their adaptation to the preschool environment. Battered children usually hide their feelings and view themselves in negative ways, which could also interfere with adapting to a school environment because the child may have deficits in achievement motivation and self-efficacy. Problems may also arise when a battered child must form peer relationships in a school setting.

Prognosis obviously depends on the nature and extent of the abuse and consequent damage.

BELL'S PALSY

Bell's palsy is an acute unilateral facial nerve paralysis resulting from injury or viral or spirochete infection (e.g., mumps, Lyme disease), or from postinfectious allergic or immune demyelinating facial neuritis that may have an abrupt onset of clinical manifestations about 2 weeks after infection. The age of onset can be anywhere from infancy to adolescence, and the incidence is common.

BIPOLAR AFFECTIVE DISORDER

Bipolar Affective Disorder (BAD) is a mood disorder that is characterized by distinct periods of depression and manic episodes. Manic episodes are characterized by elevated mood, grandiosity, pressured speech, racing thoughts, distractibility, decreased need for sleep, increased goal-directed behavior, and extreme involvement in pleasurable (but reckless) activities. Depressive episodes are often characterized by diminished interest, sadness, disturbed sleep and appetite, feelings of guilt and hopelessness, and problems with concentration and performance. During periods of depression, suicidal thoughts are common. In fact, among adolescents diagnosed with BAD, around 20% make serious suicide attempts; males are more likely to complete these.

Frequently reported comorbid conditions include Attention-Deficit/Hyperactivity Disorder, Conduct Disorder, and substance abuse. Children and adolescents with BAD are likely to require special accommodations at school—in some cases, special education (e.g., services under the category Emotional Disturbance). Regardless of the need for special service, the school psychologist should be contacted to ensure appropriate services, including home-school collaborations regarding behavior and schoolwork (e.g., implementing strategies such as home notes to improve work completion). Education about BAD is also important for the child, parent, and teacher.

BRUXISM

Bruxism is the medical term for unintentional, forcible grinding and clenching of the jaw and teeth. Etiology is not known, but certain anatomical and psychological factors may lead to the onset of bruxism. Bruxism usually occurs at night during sleep and is often associated with stress. It also commonly occurs in children with cerebral palsy.

BULIMIA NERVOSA

The word *bulimia* translates to "oxen appetite" or gorging. There are two types of bulimia nervosa. One involves a recurrent pattern of binge eating followed by purging, either by vomiting or using diuretics or laxatives; the non-purging type involves engagement in a strenuous exercise routine or other inappropriate compensatory behaviors to avoid weight gain. The hallmark of bulimia nervosa is eating a larger amount of food than most people would eat under similar circumstances and experiencing the eating as out of control. Although a small percentage of those diagnosed with bulimia are male, the disorder is most commonly diagnosed in females. Most bulimics are within 10 to 15 pounds of their normal weight range and have struggled with weight fluctuation. Bulimia usually develops during late adolescent or early adult years.

CAFE AU LAIT SPOTS

Cafe au lait spots refer to hyperpigmented areas of the skin. The spots are flat, sharply demarcated, more or less oval patches that are light to medium brown in color. The coffee-stain appearance is reflected by the name, which means "coffee with milk" in French. The long axis of the cafe au lait spot or oval is situated along a cutaneous (skin) nerve tract. The spots are usually present at birth but may become apparent in the first few years of life. Cafe au lait spots are prevalent in approximately 10% of the normal population.

Cafe au lait spots often represent benign birthmarks; however, they can be a manifestation of other underlying disorders. Most commonly, they are associated with neurofibromatosis, which is a genetically transmitted neurocutaneous disorder.

CARDIOFACIOCUTANEOUS SYNDROME

Cardiofaciocutaneous (CFC) syndrome, also known as cardio-facial-cutaneous syndrome and facio-cardio-cutaneous syndrome, affects both males and females. It is a rare genetic disorder found in children that is diagnosed based on specific physical appearances of the head, face, chest, hands, skin, and/or heart, in addition to visual impairment, growth delays, and/or varying degrees of mental retardation. This rare disorder has an autosomal dominant inheritance and, in circumstances where no family history of CFC syndrome is found, is thought to be the result of random sporadic mutations.

Many symptoms are associated with CFC syndrome. The head of a CFC patient may have one or more of the following characteristics: macrocephaly (unusually large in size); a prominent forehead with abnormal narrowing of both sides; a short, upturned nose with a low nasal bridge; and prominent external ears (pinnae) abnormally rotated toward the back of the head. Distinctive facial characteristics may consist of extremely sparse and brittle curly hair, a lack of eyebrows and eyelashes, palpebral fissures (downwardly slanting eyelid folds), ocular hypertelorism (widely spaced eyes), and esotropia (inward deviation of the eyes). There is also a greater chance of difficulties with oral motor/feeding/swallowing because of the increased incidence of craniofacial abnormalities. Congenital heart defects are common among individuals with CFC syndrome. Children with CFC may need special care in the classroom. They may fall behind in their lessons due to mental retardation or to missing large amounts of classes. Additionally, these children may be on pain management techniques that interfere with their schooling.

CARPENTER SYNDROME (ACROCEPHALOPOLYSYNDACTYLY, TYPE II)

Carpenter syndrome (acrocephalopolysyndactyly, Type II) is a congenital condition that was first described in 1901 by George Carpenter, a British pediatrician.

Although Carpenter syndrome presents with marked phenotypical variability, defining characteristics of this disorder include acrocephaly (peaked head), craniosynostosis (premature closure of the cranial sutures), craniofacial asymmetry, soft tissue syndactyly (webbing of the fingers and toes), and preaxial polydactyly, primarily of the toes.

Psychoeducational interventions for the child with Carpenter syndrome will depend on the degree of involvement as well as on its severity. Most of these children will qualify for special educational services under the handicapping conditions of physical disabilities or multiple disabilities; as such, the Individualized Educational Plan (IEP) must offer comprehensive and aggressive treatment efforts designed to address the whole range of each child's needs. As children with Carpenter syndrome age, they may exhibit developmental delays and increasing difficulty with daily tasks. The prognosis for individuals with Carpenter syndrome is variable, given its expression.

CENTRAL AUDITORY PROCESSING DISORDER

Central auditory processing disorder (CAPD) is the term used to describe audiological difficulties that are characterized by reduced abilities to process auditory information in individuals with normal peripheral hearing. CAPD includes difficulties in locating the source and direction of sounds, discriminating between sounds, recognizing patterns of sounds, ordering sounds that are presented in close temporal proximity, and discerning sounds in background noise. This will, in turn, produce poor listening skills, difficulty hearing in situations with background noise, difficulty with localization of sounds, difficulty following directions, high distractability by irrelevant noise, inattention, and academic difficulties, particularly in reading and spelling.

There are no research-supported treatments at this time for CAPD, but there are some effective management techniques. Addressing the individual needs of a child with CAPD would include modifications to the environment, remediation, and development of compensatory abilities. Special education or services under Section 504 of the Americans with Disabilities Act may be appropriate for a child with CAPD.

CEREBELLAR DISORDERS

The cerebellum, meaning "little brain," lies beneath the cerebral cortex and is attached to the brain stem. The cerebellum consists of three lobes; the middle (or vermis) and the outer (right and left) lobes. The cerebellum regulates muscle coordination and balance; therefore, damage to the area often leads to jerky and uncoordinated movements, as well as poor balance. Recent research also associates abnormalities in the cerebellum with cognitive and social deficits, even autistic-like behaviors.

Disorders involving the cerebellum may be present from birth or acquired later in life and may produce uncoordinated muscle movements (sometimes jerky) and poor balance, dysmetria, or difficulty judging distances, headaches, vomiting, seizure, vision changes, drowsiness, and confusion.

Special education, if needed at all, is typically provided under the category

Other Health Impairment. If a brain injury, however, is the cause of the cerebellar abnormality, a classification of TBI may be more appropriate.

CEREBRAL INFARCT

Cerebral infarct refers to the sudden insufficiency of blood flow to the brain causing decreased oxygen and subsequent tissue death. A partial or complete occlusion causes the disruption of venous or arterial blood flow.

CEREBRAL PALSY

Cerebral palsy (CP) is a neurological movement disorder associated with brain damage occurring before, during, or soon after birth. This disorder is not progressive, although symptoms may not be evident until a child fails to meet, or shows delays in meeting, developmental milestones. CP is divided into four subtypes: spastic, athetoid, ataxic, and mixed. Spastic CP is characterized by severe muscle contractions in arms and legs. Athetoid CP involves writhing movements of the extremities (athetosis). Ataxic CP involves the cerebellum, and lack of balance and coordination while standing or walking predominates. Spastic CP is the most common. Severity of symptoms ranges from mild to severe.

Special education issues will vary widely depending on the severity of CP symptoms. These services will be available to children with CP under the handicapping condition of Other Health Impairment or Physical Disability.

CHILDHOOD DISINTEGRATIVE DISORDER

Childhood Disintegrative Disorder (CDD) is classified as a pervasive developmental disorder and is characterized by at least 2 years of normal early development followed by profound loss of previously acquired skills in the areas of cognition, communication, motor control, and bowel and bladder control. Once established, behaviors manifested as a result of CDD are indistinguishable from those of autism. Previously, CDD has been referred to as Heller's syndrome, dementia infantilis, and disintegrative psychosis.

CHILDHOOD SCHIZOPHRENIA

Childhood schizophrenia is a syndrome with psychotic features that may include auditory and visual hallucinations, delusions, disorganized and incoherent speech, disorganized or catatonic behavior, flat affect, and loss of interest in current activities. The characteristics of childhood schizophrenia mimic those of adult schizophrenia in many ways; however, hallucinations are usually less organized and more likely to be visual in children. Childhood schizophrenia can be divided further into several subtypes: paranoid, disorganized, catatonic, and undifferentiated. Children with paranoid schizophrenia have frequent hallucinations and delusions of a persecutory nature. Those with the disorganized type have unclear and disorganized speech and behavior. Children with the catatonic type suffer from motor problems, echolalia, and rigidity of motion. Those with the undifferentiated type of schizophrenia have the primary symptoms of schizophrenia, but they do not meet the criteria for the paranoid, disorganized, or catatonic types. Childhood schizophrenia is a rare condition, but it has been found to occur more in children with a familial connection to this disorder.

Special education placement will vary with this disorder. Children who do receive services are most likely to be diagnosed with severe emotional disturbance. Unfortunately, because this condition is rare, children may be diagnosed with other conditions prior to an accurate diagnosis of childhood schizophrenia. Pervasive Developmental Disorder, Autism, Attention-Deficit/Hyperactivity Disorder, and other disorders of speech and motor skills may be the initial diagnoses. For those in need of special education placement, services again can vary from behavioral monitoring in the classroom to residential placement. Children who remain in the public school setting often need supplementary aids and services such as speech therapy, occupational and physical therapy, counseling, and social and life-skills training. Because of the cognitive and memory skill problems that are associated with the disorder, children also may need extra academic support in the form of resource or content mastery services. Properly medicated children or those with milder forms of schizophrenia can function well with minimal support.

CHOREA

Chorea refers to an irregular, nonrhythmic, rapid, and unsustained involuntary movement that flows from one body part to another. The timing, direction, and distribution of movements stemming from chorea are unpredictable in nature.

CHRONIC FATIGUE SYNDROME

Chronic fatigue syndrome (CFS) or chronic fatigue immune dysfunction syndrome in children and adolescents is characterized by debilitating fatigue, neurological problems, and a variety of symptoms. It is defined by a thorough medical examination that excludes other medical and psychiatric diagnoses and by unexplained, persistent chronic fatigue that exists for at least 6 months and is of new onset resulting in reduced occupational, educational, social, or personal activities. Second, at least four of the following symptoms co-occur: substantial impairment in short-term memory or concentration, multijoint pain without swelling or redness, headaches, sore throat, tender lymph nodes, muscle pain, unrefreshing sleep, and postexertional malaise lasting for more than 24 hours. Etiology is unconfirmed.

Treatment for CFS is generally symptomatic, resulting in medical-oriented therapies and pharmacological enhancement of symptoms. Physical therapy is often employed to reduce pain through gentle stretching techniques, myofacial release, and heat or cold applications.

Special education placement under Other Health Impairment may be warranted if students are diagnosed with CFS by a physician and if it is educationally significant. Students may benefit from a modified schedule that allows for some social periods during the day at school but also accommodates their fatigue. Homebound instruction may help minimize academic difficulties and provide ongoing tutorial support. Most children do recover from CFS with a mean out-of-school duration of one year.

CLEFT LIP AND PALATE

Cleft lip and palate are congenital malformations affecting the jaw region. The most severe forms include disconfiguration of the lips, nose, upper jaw, teeth, and palate. These defects generally result from the palatal shelves failing to join together during the sixth to eighth week of fetal development. The resulting opening, known as a cleft, may occur in the upper lip, alveolus, and palate. Major treatment for both cleft lip and cleft palate is reconstructive surgery.

Children with cleft palate may need special education services owing to residual hearing and articulation problems that may exist after surgery. They should receive early and frequent hearing tests and may also require speech therapy for articulation and tone (hypernasal) problems. Speech therapy is generally effective only in cases where the affected child has adequate speech mechanisms. Prognosis with successful surgery is now very good.

COCKAYNE SYNDROME

Cockayne syndrome is characterized by growth retardation, microcephaly, photosensitivity, and a prematurely aged appearance. In the classical and most common form of Cockayne syndrome (Type I), growth and development generally proceed at a normal rate in infancy, with symptoms becoming apparent after 1 or 2 years of age. An early-onset or congenital form of Cockayne syndrome (Type II) is apparent at birth. This form of the syndrome generally involves more severe symptoms and earlier death. There is some recent evidence that there may be a third form, Cockayne syndrome Type III, which involves a late onset of symptoms. It is a progressive and debilitating disease.

Children with Cockayne syndrome may qualify for special education services under the handicapping conditions of Infant Disability, Preschool Disability, Significantly Limited Intellectual Capacity, or Multiple Disabilities. Because of the progressive nature of this disease, frequent assessment of cognitive functioning, language ability, and psychomotor functioning may be indicated to ensure that appropriate interventions are provided. The symptoms of Cockayne syndrome are progressive, and most children with the disease die in early childhood, although some live into their late teens or early 20s.

COHEN SYNDROME

Cohen syndrome is characterized by truncal obesity, hypotonia, mental retardation, and ocular and craniofacial abnormalities. Characteristic craniofacial features include microcephaly, small jaw, prominent incisors, small philtrum, and high-arched palate. Children with Cohen syndrome usually qualify for special education services due to mental retardation, health problems, or visual impairments that affect learning.

CONDUCT DISORDER

Conduct Disorder is a behavior pattern in which an individual violates societal norms or the basic rights of others. Conduct Disorder is generally defined by age of onset as during childhood or during adolescence and tends to be earlier for boys than for girls. Boys are diagnosed with conduct disorder four to five times more frequently.

CONDUCTIVE HEARING LOSS

Diseases or obstructions in the outer or middle ear cause conductive hearing losses. A conductive hearing loss is the impairment of hearing due to a failure of sound pressure waves to reach the cochlea through normal air conduction channels; at the same time, the inner ear is usually normal. Etiology of a conductive hearing loss varies, including the following: (1) foreign body obstruction; (2) bacterial infections of the external ear canal (otitis externa), growths of the bony external canal (osteoma, hyperostosis, exotosis); (3) congenital atresia, middle ear infections (acute, serous, or chronic otitis media); (4) hardening of the middle ear system (otosclerosis); or (5) trauma to the outer or middle ear system that causes a blockage of sound to the inner ear. Sensitivity to sound is diminished, but clarity (interpretation of the sound) is not changed in a person with a conductive hearing loss. Conductive losses usually affect all frequencies of hearing evenly and do not result in severe losses. A person with a conductive hearing loss usually is able to wear a hearing aid or can be helped medically or surgically. If volume is increased to compensate for the loss, hearing is usually normal.

CONGENITAL WORD BLINDNESS

Congenital word blindness is an archaic term used to describe poor readers. It was first used by W. P. Morgan in the late 19th century to explain unexpected reading failures in otherwise intelligent children.

CORNELIA DE LANGE SYNDROME

Cornelia de Lange syndrome (CdLS) is a rare genetic disorder characterized by prenatal and postnatal growth retardation, facial abnormalities, cognitive deficits or mental retardation, and developmental delays. Physical characteristics and symptoms vary in severity and presentation from case to case.

The abnormalities characteristic of CdLS may be detected prenatally through the use of ultrasound imaging; in most cases, however, it is diagnosed at birth. A diagnosis of CdLS should be considered if the child exhibits the distinctive facial characteristics listed along with the limb anomalies, mental retardation, and growth retardation. Associated abnormalities include cardiac defects, gastroesophogeal reflux, glue ear, intestinal obstruction due to gastrointestinal problems, and respiratory infection.

Treatment is directed toward the noted symptoms and may involve the collaborative efforts of numerous health care professionals including pediatricians, orthopedic surgeons, heart specialists, urologists, speech pathologists, and occupational therapists. Surgery may be performed to correct cleft palate, and orthopedic techniques may be used to treat limb deformities. Plastic surgery may also be helpful in reducing excessive hair. Antibiotic drug therapy may help fight associated respiratory infection. Anticonvulsant medication may be needed for patients who experience seizure episodes.

Early intervention is important in ensuring that children with CdLS reach their highest potentials. Special education services may be available to children with CdLS under the handicapping condition of Other Health Impairment. Services that may be beneficial include special remedial education, vocational training, speech therapy, and other medical and social services.

CRETINISM

Cretinism is a syndrome caused by hypothyroidism (underactivity of the thyroid gland) at birth. Two types of cretinism have been distinguished. Endemic cretinism is essentially an iodine deficiency disorder. Insufficient levels of iodine cause maternal hypothyroidism, which increases the incidence of fetal hypothyroidism in the neonate. Endemic cretinism is characterized by severe developmental delays, deaf-mutism, and spasticity of the arms and legs. Endemic cretinism has been virtually eradicated in the United States and in many developed nations with the addition of iodine to table salt.

For individuals with frank cretinism, special education placement will most likely be necessitated. Admission under the qualifying condition of multiply handicapped may be appropriate to address the hearing impairments, mutism or speech difficulties, and mental retardation that are associated with this disorder. Occupational and physical therapies may also be necessary to address coordination and gait disorders, as well as spasticity.

With early detection and intervention, the prognosis for infants with congenital hypothyroidism is good. Recent studies emphasize that early treatment is essential and have demonstrated that most optimal development is achieved if thyroid deficiencies are corrected before the third week of life. Children who receive early treatment can achieve normal mental and psychomotor development.

CRI DU CHAT SYNDROME (CRY OF THE CAT SYNDROME)

Cri du chat syndrome is a congenital disorder characterized at birth by the infant's high-pitched, cat-like cry. This specific cry has been linked to a small larynx and is present immediately following birth, lasting for several weeks. Cri du chat syndrome is also known as Cat's cry or 5p- syndrome.

There is no treatment for cri du chat syndrome. Educational intervention should include physical therapy as well as language therapy, should be consistent, and should begin early. Children with the syndrome often have significant language difficulties: Some children are able to use short sentences, but others use basic words, gestures, or sign language. Many individuals with cri du chat syndrome also experience retarded physical and mental development, resulting in a small stature and varied levels of cognitive handicaps.

CROUZON SYNDROME

Crouzon syndrome, also known as craniofacial dysostosis, is characterized by premature closure of the cranial sutures between certain bones in the skull and distinctive facial abnormalities. Crouzon syndrome is commonly characterized by facial features, including a flat, broad forehead, widely spaced eyes with a reversed slant, a high palate, a beak-like nose, and occasionally malformations of auditory canals. The cranial and facial malformations can vary in severity from case to case, including differences seen between individuals within the same family. The degree of cranial malformation may be variable depending on the specific cranial sutures involved as well as the order and rate of progression. Limb abnormalities are rarely seen. Often, however, individuals with Crouzon syndrome experience dental abnormalities due to underdevelopment of the upper jaw. The degree of cranial malformation may be variable, depending on the specific cranial sutures involved as well as the order and rate of progression.

Studies have shown that neurological deficits include as many as 30% affected by headaches and about 12% affected by uncontrolled seizures. Mental retardation was present only in approximately 3% of the cases.

Early intervention is important with infants diagnosed with Crouzon syndrome. Diagnosis is often based on a variety of clinical evaluations, identification of characteristic physical findings, and specialized tests. Treatment will depend on the specific symptoms affecting the individual. Although only a small percentage are affected by mental retardation, special educational services may prove useful to mediate any potential learning disabilities as well as help the child maintain studies due to potential frequent absences from doctors' appointments and other medical interventions.

CRYPTOPHASIA

Cryptophasia was historically described as a secret language between twins that they invent themselves and that is unintelligible to others. It has been found that some words are indeed invented, but for the most part the words come from the adult language to which they are exposed. At least 90% of the vocabulary in cryptophasia can be directly related to the language of the parents.

Eventually, these children adopt the proper structure in their language; it just takes longer for children who use cryptophasia. Specific treatments have not been discussed because the general consensus in the literature is that these children will outgrow this unintelligible language. It is important for parents to encourage regular language usage in their children. If the children do not begin using regular language, it would be crucial to contact a speech therapist.

CYSTIC FIBROSIS

Cystic fibrosis (CF) is an inherited disease that causes malfunction of the exocrine system. CF primarily affects gastrointestinal and respiratory functions; however, it can also impact hepatic, pancreatic, gastrointestinal, and reproductive systems. Chronic upper respiratory infections are often the first symptom of CF, followed by frequent and severe infections involving the accumulation of mucus. This creates opportunities for bacterial infections in the mucus membranes throughout the body, which is why the disease is associated with progressive and irreversible lung damage, pancreatic insufficiency, cirrhosis of the liver, sterility, and megacolon.

CF is not commonly associated with learning problems, and most children with the disease will not require special education services. Problems engaging in physical exercise due to difficulties breathing (e.g., shortness of breath) and proper nutrition (e.g., poor appetite and weight loss) can, however, seriously impact learning and social interactions. Accommodations in the classroom and in physical education courses are often sufficient, but when needed, children with CF can receive special education under the category Other Health Impairment.

CYTOMEGALOVIRUS, CONGENITAL

Cytomegalovirus (CMV) is a communicable DNA virus in the herpes family that when contracted in later childhood or adulthood is generally either asymptomatic or causes a short, mild illness with a fever and other flulike symptoms.

If contracted by a pregnant woman, CMV may cross the placental barrier and cause fetal death or serious deformities in her offspring. It is a member of the STORCH (syphilis, toxiplasmosis, varicella, and other infections, rubella, cytomegalovirus, and Herpes) complex, a group of maternal infections that have similar effects on offspring. It is the most common such infection, occurring in some 5 to 25 per 1,000 births.

About 10% of fetuses infected in early prenatal development will be born with CMV and show symptoms at birth. Of infants asymptomatic at birth, about 5 to 15% will develop hearing loss, low intelligence, or behavior problems during the first few years of life.

No effective treatment is available for congenital or perinatal CMV. A variety of supportive care and special education services will be required, depending on the extent and variety of symptoms.

DARIER DISEASE

Darier disease is a skin disorder in which a red rash appears on parts of the body, particularly the forehead, ears, neck, chest, groin, and back. This rash often has a foul odor and is accompanied by weakening of the fingernails causing V-shaped indentations. The rash may also itch. Darier disease is not contagious. Darier disease normally manifests itself in the teenage years, and symptoms are gradually progressive.

DEMENTIAS OF CHILDHOOD

Dementia refers to a global cognitive decline that impacts more than one component of cognitive functioning and involves a memory impairment. The term *decline* indicates deterioration in cognitive functioning from a previous higher level of functioning. The etiology of dementia may be traced to a general medical condition, persistent effects of a substance, or multiple causes. The acquired nature of dementia suggests that it results in decreased mental functioning over time, as compared to an acute or sudden onset.

Dementias in children can be classified similar to how they are identified in adults. They are the result of general medical conditions, persistent substance exposure, or a mixture of the two. Medical conditions that may cause dementia include brain tumors or neoplasms, which can lead to changes in cognitive functioning. Children treated with chemotherapy for acute lymphocytic leukemia or childhood leukemia have also been known to suffer from neuropsychological impairments. Dementia resulting from kidney dialysis affects less than 1% of individuals undergoing dialysis.

Cerebrovascular disease, or strokes, can produce impairments in cognitive ability and are referred to as vascular dementia. Dementia may also be associated with traumatic brain injuries. The juvenile type of Huntington's disease can cause cognitive impairments, memory retrieval deficits, and difficulties with planning and attention. Lastly, medical conditions such as brain lesions (hydrocephalus), endocrine disorders (hypothyroidism), nutritional deficiencies (Vitamin B_{12} deficiency), immune conditions, and metabolic diseases can produce symptoms of dementia.

Children infected with HIV may develop symptoms of progressive neurodevelopment degeneration termed HIV encephalopathy, neuroaids, or AIDS dementia complex. This condition initially consists of mild symptoms such as depression, forgetfulness, or difficulty sustaining attention, but can develop into complete dementia.

Children with dementias may be eligible to receive services under the classification Other Health Impairment. If they are eligible to receive special education services, academic support could be beneficial. Treatment typically consists of cognitive rehabilitation techniques to compensate for memory impairment (e.g., the use of visual imagery and verbal encoding strategies). External memory aids, such as tape recorders and notebooks, also can be helpful. Pharmacological interventions, such as cholinergically active drugs that are known to impact memory and cognition positively, may also be useful.

DEPRESSION

Depression in childhood and adolescence encompasses a variety of specific diagnoses, including Major Depressive Disorder, Dysthymic Disorder, Cyclothymic Disorder, and Bipolar Disorder. This entry focuses specifically on Major Depressive Disorder, which is an affective disorder characterized by one or more episodes of depressed (or irritable) mood or loss of interest and pleasure in most activities for periods of at least 2 weeks.

Major Depressive Disorder is rare in preschool children but increases in frequency at school age and again in adolescence. The average age of onset of Major Depressive Disorder is 11 years, and prevalence rates in the general population range from 1% in childhood to 6 to 8% in adolescence. Episodes of major depression in youth typically last for 6 to 8 months or longer, and the risk for subsequent episodes is high. In children, males and females are equally affected, but Major Depressive Disorder is twice as common in adolescent females as in adolescent males.

Children with Major Depressive Disorder may qualify for special education services under the category Serious Emotional Disturbance. Due to the negative impact of episodes of major depression on academic functioning and the increased likelihood of concomitant behavior disorders, these children may also qualify for special education services under the categories Specific Learning Disability and Behavior Disorders. Impaired social interaction skills are a prominent characteristic of Major Depressive Disorder, so social skills training may be one component of the special education services that these children require. Comorbidity rates for youth diagnosed with Major Depressive Disorder are high for disruptive behavior disorders, anxiety disorders, and attention-deficit disorders, as well as for substance abuse disorders in adolescence. Early onset of Major Depressive Disorder is associated with an increased likelihood of recurrence into adulthood and sustained impairments in academic and social functioning.

DIABETES INSIPIDUS

Diabetes insipidus (DI) is a syndrome that is characterized by an inability to conserve water and maintain the body's essential water homeostasis. Onset of this condition occurs when there is an insufficient level of antidiuretic hormone (ADH) or when the kidneys have a decreased sensitivity to ADH. When a deficiency in ADH occurs, the kidneys cannot reabsorb water and concentrate urine. Subsequently, an excessive volume of dilute urine is produced and excreted. In response to such unregulated loss of water, individuals with diabetes insipidus experience constant thirst and must increase their fluid intake substantially to prevent dehydration.

Many children with diabetes insipidus can be expected to participate in a regular education setting. However, classroom accommodations under Section 504 will likely be required to allow the child to have adequate access to fluids during the school day and unrestricted passes to the restroom.

DIABETES, INSULIN-DEPENDENT (TYPE I, JUVENILE DIABETES)

Insulin-dependent diabetes mellitus (IDDM), also known as Type I diabetes or juvenile diabetes, is a chronic metabolic disorder characterized by pancreatic failure and resulting inability to produce insulin and metabolize glucose. The etiology of IDDM is unknown. Genetic factors appear to be related to disease onset, but environmental and individual factors are also implicated. Although it is not known what initiates the disease course, the mechanism responsible for IDDM is considered to be an autoimmune process. In IDDM the immune system produces antibodies that attack and destroy the insulin-producing pancreatic beta cells, causing severe insulin deficiency. IDDM is one of the most common chronic disorders of children in the United States.

Because there is no known cure for IDDM, lifelong treatment is required. Treatment focuses on keeping blood glucose levels within a target range that closely approximates the normal range of blood glucose levels found in nondiabetic individuals. Children with IDDM have been found to have weaknesses in visuospatial processing, verbal ability, visuomotor abilities, memory, attention, and specific learning disabilities in reading, spelling, and arithmetic. Therefore, eligibility for special education services will vary considerably depending on the specific nature and severity of neuropsychological and educational dysfunction. Children with IDDM who do not qualify for special education services may be considered for accommodations under Section 504. Because poor diabetes control can significantly interfere with learning, educational plans should include instructions for managing the child's diabetes during the school day (e.g., frequency and timing of insulin injections and blood glucose monitoring).

DIABETES, TYPE II

Diabetes is a collection of diseases that takes on different forms. All forms of diabetes involve the hormone insulin. Diabetes mellitus (diabetes means "to siphon," and mellitus means "honey") results either when the body does not produce enough insulin or when an excess of insulin is present. The latter is known as Type II diabetes, or non-insulin-dependent diabetes.

Approximately 80% of those with diabetes have Type II. Results of several research studies over the past 20 years indicate that Type II diabetes in children is perhaps growing to epidemic proportions, especially among minorities. This phenomenon coincides with the increase in obesity in young children.

Children diagnosed with Type II diabetes will most likely qualify for special education services under the category of Other Health Impairment or Physical Disability. They are also protected under Section 504 of the Rehabilitation Act. Ideally, a Diabetes Health Care Plan should be developed as a joint effort of the parent, the student's health care team, and the school. The plan should address the specific needs of the child and outline instructions and responsibilities of each party (parents, student, school personnel).

DIPLOPIA (DOUBLE VISION)

Diplopia, also known as double vision, is a vision impairment in which the eye sees two images. There are two types of diplopia: monocular and binocular. In monocular, the double vision is present at all times, even when one eye is occluded or closed. Monocular diplopia is caused by defects to the front of the eye, such as cataracts or a need for glasses. In binocular, it is due to the misalignment of the images that are reflected to the brain. For example, one eye may aim higher or lower than the other so that they cannot fuse into one image. This problem can be remedied by closing one eye or occluding it. Binocular diplopia often occurs secondary to other disorders.

In children there is a tendency to attempt unconsciously to compensate for the binocular double vision by suppressing one of the images. When this occurs, the child begins to favor one eye. Although this strategy is effective, eventually the child will have difficulty perceiving three-dimensionally. With time, it will lead to a condition known as strabismus, in which one eye turns inward or outward. Depending on the child, both eyes can become involved, or the child can alternate eyes. If the brain continues to compensate for one eye, the unused eye loses its ability to function, and there will be a permanent vision impairment.

DOWN SYNDROME

Down syndrome is a relatively well-known genetic disorder that is strongly associated with mental retardation. It is usually identified at birth and is confirmed by a karyotype showing trisomy of Chromosome 21. Down syndrome usually is caused by an error in cell division called *nondisjunction.* However, two other types of chromosomal abnormalities, *mosaicism* and *translocation,* also are implicated in Down syndrome, although to a much lesser extent. Regardless of the type of Down syndrome that a person may have, all people with Down syndrome have an extra, critical portion of the Chromosome 21 present in all, or some, of their cells.

Down syndrome affects people of all ages, races, and economic levels. Women age 35 and older have a significantly increased risk of having a child with Down syndrome. The most frequently occurring chromosomal abnormality, Down syndrome occurs once approximately every 800 to 1,000 live births. Approximately 5,000 children with Down syndrome are born each year, and over 350,000 people have Down syndrome in the United States.

There is no genetic or pharmacological therapy available at present to cure Down syndrome. The primary methods of diminishing the effects of retardation associated with Down syndrome are psychoeducational: working directly with the individual; providing advice, support, and training to parents and others in the immediate environment; and altering the more distal social and physical environment to increase the roles and activities for which individuals with Down syndrome are suitable candidates. Early intervention programs are usually individualized, systematic, and highly structured, following curricula based on developmental milestones. The emphasis in those programs is usually placed on cognitive and language development.

Under the Individuals with Disabilities Education Act, comprehensive services (e.g., family training, home visits, special instruction, medical services for diagnosis and evaluation, case management) are provided for infants, toddlers, and school-aged children with Down syndrome and their families on the basis of need as established in the individualized family service plan (IFSP) and the individualized education plan (IEP). The inclusion of students with Down syndrome in typical classrooms represents the latest effort to provide children with this disability with the best education possible in their neighborhood schools.

In spite of significant advances in the quality of life for children with Down syndrome, prognosis is not so optimistic. One of the most robust findings about cognitive development in Down syndrome is a decline in developmental rate as children get older.

DYSCALCULIA

Dyscalculia is a widely used term for disabilities in mathematics. Whereas the term *acalculia* is reserved for the total inability to do math, dyscalculia refers to a less severe problem performing math problems. Dyscalculia can be developmental or acquired (e.g., traumatic brain injury), and the problem can range from mild to severe. Specific math computation and comprehension difficulties include problems with counting, recognizing numbers, manipulating math symbols (mentally or in writing), sequential memory for numbers and math operations, and reversing numbers (e.g., while reading, writing, and recalling numbers).

DYSGRAPHESTHESIA

Dysgraphesthesia is the inability to recognize symbols drawn on parts of the body. Often referred to as a neurological "soft sign," dysgraphesthesia is more common in children with learning disabilities or behavior disorders, although a direct causal relationship has not been found.

Dysgraphesthesia is assessed through the use of tests of sensory perception, specifically skin writing procedures, most often with symbols or numbers traced on the palm of the hand or on the fingertips. Fewer errors on these kinds of assessment measures are expected as children become older, and reliability of soft neurological signs such as dysgraphesthesia is greater in 8- to 11-year-olds than it is in 5- to 6-year-olds.

DYSGRAPHIA

Dysgraphia is a disorder characterized by writing difficulties. More specifically, it is defined as difficulty in automatically remembering and mastering the sequence of muscle motor movements needed in writing letters or numbers. The difficulty in writing is incongruent with the person's ability and is not due to poor instruction. The disorder varies in terms of severity, ranging from mild to severe.

DYSKINESIA

Dyskinesia is a collection of movement disorders involving impairment of central nervous system motor control. It is thought to be due to damage or abnormal development of the basal ganglia, the deep subcortical nuclei in the cerebral cortex. Involuntary movement, irregular motions, or lack of coordinated voluntary movement characterizes dyskinesia. Dyskinetic movement disorders include dystonia, tremor, chorea, tics, and myoclonus. Each movement disorder is uniquely characterized. For example, dystonia is characterized by involuntary, sustained posturing. Small oscillating movements at rest or with effort characterize tremor. Random, excessive, irregularly timed movements characterize chorea. Tics are brief, repetitive, involuntary movements. Involuntary movements that are rapid, shock-like, and arrhythmic (unpatterned) characterize myoclonus.

Each movement disorder is unique in regard to the somatic distribution and quality of movement, the age of onset, and etiology. Dyskinesia may be the primary sign or symptom or may be included with the other signs or symptoms of a syndrome.

DYSLEXIA, DEVELOPMENTAL

Dyslexia, or reading disability, is characterized by low reading achievement, as measured by an individually administered standardized test of reading accuracy or comprehension that is substantially below what would be expected given an individual's chronological age, measured intelligence (IQ), and age-appropriate education. It should be noted, however, that recent studies have demonstrated that the same component processes and underlying neuropsychological deficits are present in poor readers, regardless of their general cognitive potential.

Dyslexia is the most common learning disability, with a prevalence rate ranging from 4 to 10% depending on the criteria used to define the disorder. There is evidence from behavioral genetic studies that dyslexia is 50 to 60% heritable.

Fortunately, dyslexia is one of the more treatable learning disorders, and many affected individuals learn to read and obtain high school and college degrees. However, spelling ability, reading fluency, and phonological awareness tasks may still pose varying degrees of difficulty for the compensated dyslexic. Theoretically sound methods of treatment acknowledge the primary deficits in phonemic awareness and phonological decoding (the ability to translate letters in words to sounds) and typically use a multisensory approach to facilitate these skills in early readers. Treatment methods also target secondary problems in comprehension, motivation, attention, and self-esteem, as necessary.

DYSMETRIA

Dysmetria is defined as an aspect of ataxia in which the ability to control the distance, power, and speed of an act is impaired. Individuals with dysmetria have problems judging the extent to which they must move their body to reach a desired goal and often have difficulty stopping their movement in a precise manner to reach the goal. Movements, therefore, undershoot (hypometria) or overshoot (hypermetria) the distance. Individuals with dysmetria may have difficulty raising their arms parallel to the floor (i.e., arms extended at the shoulder level). Some may also have problems moving their arms above their heads from their shoulders and back down while keeping their eyes closed.

DYSPHONIA

Dysphonia is a general term referring to any voice disorder of phonation. Dysphonia is a deviation in pitch, intensity, and quality resulting primarily from the action of the vocal folds. Included in this definition are characteristics of the voice that consistently interfere with communication, draw unfavorable attention, adversely affect the speaker or listener, or are inappropriate to the age, sex, or perhaps the culture or class of the individual. Dysphonia is inclusive of over 30 specific types and can be organic, psychogenic, or functional in nature.

ECHOLALIA

Echolalia is defined as the spontaneous repetition of words or phrases spoken by another person. The repetition, or echo, of verbal utterances can be either immediate or delayed. Although echolalia may occur to some degree in young children as a normal process of speech development, its presence is generally symptomatic of a functional disorder if occurring after the age of 2:6 to 3 years old.

ECHOPRAXIA

Echopraxia is defined as the involuntary and spasmodic imitation of movements made by another person. The imitation or repetition of body movements characteristic of echopraxia may be concomitant with a variety of disorders. Echopraxia serves as a diagnostic marker for specific developmental, psychiatric, and neurological disorders because of the frequent incidence of involuntary movement or gesture imitation associated with certain disorders.

ELECTIVE MUTISM

Elective mutism (also known as selective mutism) is a psychiatric condition occurring primarily during childhood that is characterized by the refusal or failure to speak in specific situations (in school or with classmates) despite speaking in other situations.

The condition is rare, affecting less than 1% of individuals in the United States, and is slightly more common in males than females. Although children with elective mutism generally have normal language skills, they occasionally have associated communication disorders or a medically based articulation problem. The diagnosis of elective mutism may be confirmed by an extensive evaluation to rule out other possible causes, such as a hearing or speech impairment. Cultural factors should also be considered. Immigrant children who may be uncomfortable with or unfamiliar with the social communication norms may be reluctant to speak in social situations, but they should not receive a diagnosis. The diagnosis of elective mutism is appropriate if the child has the *ability* to understand and speak language but does not speak in social situations.

The duration of the disorder is highly variable, ranging from a few months to several years. Often associated features of anxiety or social phobia may be chronic.

EMOTIONAL DISTURBANCE

Emotional disturbance represents a broad category of psychological difficulties that have also been referred to as internalizing or externalizing disorders. Emotional disturbance usually includes symptoms of anxiety and depression, but it can include symptoms consistent with a psychotic disorder, such as sensory hallucinations. It is characterized by an emotional disturbance of sufficient severity to interfere significantly with a child's academic, social, and emotional functioning.

ENDOCRINE DISORDERS

The endocrine system consists of the pituitary, thyroid, parathyroid, adrenal, pancreas, gonads, and placenta. The general function of the endocrine system is to control growth and reproduction and to maintain chemical homeostasis in the body.

Disorders associated with the endocrine system may result from partial or total insensitivity of tissue to endogenous hormones, hypersecretion of hormones, or hyposecretion of hormones. Endocrine disorders may have a variety of etiologies including chromosomal abnormalities, prenatal deficiencies, maternal hormonal deficiencies during gestation, and a variety of environmental variables (e.g., toxins, traumatic brain injury, brain tumors, and viruses).

Endocrine disorders also vary in prevalence and in the age at which symptoms appear. Commonly, endocrine disorders in children are detected because a child's development is premature or delayed. Relatively common endocrine disorders of childhood include Turner's syndrome, Klinefelter syndrome, congenital adrenal hyperplasia, hyperthyroidism, diabetes mellitus, and obesity. Rarer forms of the disorders may include hypothyroidism, which rarely appears as a birth defect, and multiple endocrine neoplasia Type 2 (MEN 2), which involves an overactivity and enlargement of the endocrine glands.

Medical treatment for the hormonal imbalance is the standard defense against endocrine disorders. Hormone replacement therapy is widely used for disorders of hyposecretion or tissue insensitivity such as Turner's syndrome or hypopituitary syndromes. Estrogen replacement therapy is used to supplement the underproductive gonads of females with Turner's syndrome. In hypopituitary syndromes, growth-hormone replacement therapy is used to stimulate growth. For disorders involving hypersecretion of endocrine glands, medical treatment seeks to reduce hormone levels through the use of natural or synthetic hormones (e.g., gonadatropin-releasing hormone for overactive pituitary glands).

The psychoeducational sequelae of endocrine disorders vary as widely as do the etiology and symptoms. Disorders associated with under- or overactive pituitary glands are typically not associated with cognitive deficits. At the other extreme, global deficits in cognitive functioning can result from endocrine disorders such as hypothyroid disorders. Furthermore, domain-specific deficits may also be associated with endocrine problems. For example, chromosomal disorders such as Klinefelter syndrome and Turner's syndrome are associated with average intelligence but with specific deficits in reading and visual-spatial processing respectively.

The psychological sequelae of endocrine disorders are also important to consider in managing these conditions. Behavioral and emotional problems may result from hormonal imbalances, reactions to treatments, or reactions to looking and feeling different from peers.

FETAL ALCOHOL SPECTRUM DISORDERS

Fetal alcohol spectrum disorders (FASD) is a group of birth defects or abnormalities occurring in children who are born to women who have histories of relatively high levels of periodic or consistent alcohol consumption during pregnancy. The defects, which can include physical, mental, and behavioral problems, are irreversible. FASD is not a single birth defect; rather, it is a cluster or pattern of related problems. The severity of symptoms varies, with some children experiencing problems to a far greater degree than others.

Doctors cannot diagnose FASD before a baby is born, and even after birth, FASD shares many of the same physical or behavioral characteristics as other syndromes and is therefore difficult to diagnose. Doctors often rely on certain manifestations such as a growth deficiency, facial malformations, or the presence of heart defects in order to diagnose FASD. Evaluations of a child's development may also assist doctors in making a diagnosis. There is no cure for FASD and the physical defects and mental deficiencies persist for a lifetime.

Depending on the severity of the symptoms, a child with FASD could qualify for special education services under several different categories, including Mental Retardation, Emotional Disturbance, Other Health Impairment, or specific Learning Disability. The school psychologist would work with the multidisciplinary team to provide appropriate services to the child with FASD that are consistent with the specified disability.

FETAL HYDANTOIN SYNDROME

Fetal hydantoin syndrome (FHS) is caused by the anticonvulsant drug (AED) phenytoin (Dilantin). Phenytoin is a prenatal teratogen, causing a variety of physical defects, including infant failure to thrive, dysmorphic facies and other physical abnormalities, growth deficiency, and mental retardation, usually mild. The effects, particularly craniofacial, of prenatal exposure to phenytoin are so similar to those of several other AEDs, including carbamazepine, valproic acid, mysoline, and phenobarbital, as to have led to the general descriptive term *fetal antiepilep-*

tic drug syndrome. As with most teratogens, major damage occurs from exposure early in prenatal development.

Treatment and education of children with FHD or other AED syndrome needs to be individualized, owing to wide variations in the degree and type of resulting problems. Intervention may be needed as early as infancy to deal with potential failure to thrive. The major problems in childhood that call for special services are low intelligence and mental retardation.

FRAGILE X SYNDROME

Fragile X syndrome (FXS), a genetic disorder, involves a mutation of the FMR1 gene (fragile X mental retardation 1 gene), located at the bottom end of the X chromosome. A mutation in this gene lowers the production of the FMR protein. Variations in the amount of the FMR protein account for the wide range of behavioral and physical features displayed by persons with FXS. This sex-linked condition affects males more than females, because males only have one X chromosome, whereas females, with two X chromosomes, will generally have one chromosome without the mutation. FXS is the most common cause of inherited mental retardation and accounts for 30% of cases of mental retardation associated with the X chromosome.

Treatment for those affected by FXS emphasizes medical, developmental, educational, and behavioral concerns. Medically, interventions are aimed at treating recurrent otitis media, seizures, and problems associated with loose connective tissue (i.e., gastroesophageal reflux, sinus infections, mitral valve prolapse, joint dislocations, and hernias). Medications are sometimes prescribed for the treatment of attention deficit and hyperactivity, mood lability, aggression, anxiety, and obsessive-compulsive behaviors.

Delays in language and motor development are best addressed through speech and language therapy and occupational therapy. Speech language interventions should address auditory processing problems, deficits in pragmatic communication, and motor dyspraxia. Speech intervention should also capitalize on language strengths that include humor, imitation, and memory skills and empathy. Occupational therapy generally emphasizes sensory integration dysfunction as well as development of fine and gross motor skills and motor planning abilities.

Children with FXS will have varying educational needs depending on the degree of involvement related to the FMR1 mutation. Some children may experience learning disabilities and will require support from a resource room. Others will be more profoundly affected and may require special education services through a program designed for students with significantly limited intellectual capacity. Special education eligibility is often through a physical disability or a multihandicapped classification. In general, because students with FXS are strong visual and imitative learners, they will benefit from inclusion in the general education classroom for some part of their school day.

Educational interventions and accommodations in the regular or special education classroom will require a multimodal approach that combines visual and auditory input. Using behavioral reinforcement, predictable routines, preparation for transitions, and calming techniques will facilitate the ability of the student with FXS to adapt to classroom demands. Issues related to poor sensory integration will require that distractions be minimized, that seat breaks are given, and that oral-motor and physical activities are integrated into the school day (e.g., allow a break to chew gum, wrap a bungee cord around the legs of the desk). Interventions useful for those with attentional problems are also appropriate; for instance, it will be helpful to provide visual, verbal, and physical prompts and to use a behavioral management approach to promote compliance with behavioral and educational goals.

FRYNS SYNDROME

Inherited as an autosomal recessive trait, Fryns syndrome is characterized by many abnormalities present at birth. These characteristics include abnormalities of the head and face, protrusion of part of the stomach and the small intestines into the chest cavity, underdeveloped lungs, cleft palate, underdevelopment of the fingers and toes, and some degree of mental retardation. Fryns syndrome normally results in stillbirths for the children who have inherited this disorder. In the children who live with Fryns syndrome, their existence is meager, with severe cognitive and physical deficits, the former the result of brain malformations.

Special education issues specifically relate to multiple handicaps due to health problems and mental retardation. Prognosis is poor, and chronic management through assisted living is necessary.

GALACTOSEMIA

Galactosemia is an inborn error of metabolism that results in an accumulation of galactose in the blood, tissue, and urine. Galactosemia is caused by an autosomal recessive gene, and heterozygotes for the trait exhibit reduced enzyme activity. Three types are known, each due to a specific enzyme deficit: (1) Classic galactosemia, the most prevalent and most severe form, occurs in approximately 1 in 70,000 births and is attributed to a marked deficiency of galactose-1-phosphate uridyl transferase; (2) Galactokinase deficiency, less severe, occurs in 1 in 155,000 births and leads to the development of cataracts; (3) A rare form, with no clear clinical abnormalities, is attributed to a deficit of EDP-glucose-4-epimerase. Classic galactosemia accounts for approximately 95% of cases.

Symptoms of classic galactosemia begin within 2 weeks after birth. Without treatment, the disorder is usually lethal, and many affected infants die during the first few weeks of life. Even among treated children, mental retardation, learning disabilities, and a variety of other serious problems are common.

Treatment consists of elimination of galactose and lactose from the diet as early as possible. All milk products, including mother's milk, butter, cheese, and yogurt, must be avoided because galactose is mainly formed by digestion of disaccharide lactose found in animal milk. Strict adherence to diets generally based on soybeans is critical. Shortly after the beginning of dietary intervention, most physical symptoms subside. The infant gains weight; vomiting, diarrhea, and liver anomalies disappear; and cataracts regress, although any brain damage is permanent.

Unfortunately, prognosis for cognitive development in treated individuals is not as good as initially thought, and those involved in special education should be aware of the many and varied problems that treated galactosemic children may have. Even early dietary intervention generally only partially reduces the degree and severity of cognitive damage. IQs cluster in below normal to low-normal range. Other specific difficulties may interfere with the education of treated galactosemic children and call for additional special education services. About 50% of treated children are developmentally delayed, and learning difficulties increase with age. These effects apparently owe to progressive neurological disease or to brain damage sustained at an earlier age that becomes more apparent with age. Treated galactosemic children may also show visual-perceptual, motor function-balance, spatial-mathematical relationship, attention, and speech-language deficits. They generally present no significant behavior problems except for occasional apathy and withdrawal.

GENDER IDENTITY DISORDER

Gender Identity Disorder (GID) represents a profound disturbance in a child or adolescent's individual sense of identity with regard to maleness or femaleness. Children with GID feel as though they have been born as the wrong gender and express a strong desire to be the opposite gender. This feeling may be expressed in many ways, such as dressing as the opposite sex, discomfort with same-sex peers, and verbal statements of dissatisfaction with gender to a marked degree, accompanied by distress. Onset is usually between the ages of 2 and 4 years. Only a very small number of these children will later meet the adolescent and adult criteria for the disorder.

The cause of GID remains unknown. Because children (especially boys) with GID are often ridiculed by peers, they may be prone to school avoidance and are at especially high risk for school dropout. Hence, children with GID may require special support in the school setting in order to develop coping skills to deal with social issues. It is unlikely that special education services would be needed for these children.

GLIOBLASTOMA

A glioblastoma is a malignant astrocytoma, or brain tumor. A brain tumor is defined as a new growth of tissue in which cells multiply uncontrollably. Like all brain tumors, glioblastomas have no physiological use and are independent of surrounding tissue. One specific type of glioblastoma is a glioblastoma multiforme. These tumors are usually located in the cerebral hemispheres and grow very rapidly. Glioblastomas, regardless of the type, are always malignant and account for approximately 8 to 12% of all pediatric brain tumors. Like other pediatric brain tumors, glioblastomas are usually primary site tumors—that is, they are not metastases. The 5-year survival rate in children is approximately 35%, or about one in three children.

HEARING IMPAIRMENT

Hearing impaired is a term used to describe individuals who have a significant hearing loss. Hearing loss can be classified into four types: conductive, sensorineural, mixed, or central. Sensorineural loss, or nerve deafness, is the most common hearing impairment. Hearing impairment can also be defined by severity of loss. A decibel (dB) is the unit used to measure the loudness of sound. The higher the dB, the louder the sound. *Mild loss* refers to sounds less than 40 dB; these individuals are often referred to as hard of hearing and have difficulty with quiet or distant speech. *Moderate loss* involves sounds between 41 and 70 dB; individuals with this degree of loss typically require a hearing aid but can hear when facing the speaker within 3 to 5 feet. *Severe loss* includes sounds between 71 and 90 dB; persons suffering this degree of loss require a hearing aid but may hear loud noises one foot from their ear. *Profound loss* refers to the sounds over 90 dB; a hearing aid and specialized training are necessary for individuals with this degree of loss. The term *deaf* refers to individuals with a loss above 70 dB.

The etiology of hearing impairments is multifaceted, and may include (1) congenital or hereditary factors; (2) obstruction or blockage of the sound pathways; (3) accidental damage to a part of the hearing mechanism; (4) otosclerosis, a spongy bony growth that immobilizes or causes malfunction of the middle-ear bones or cochlea; (5) presbycusis, or age-related hearing impairment; (6) Meniere's disease, which involves the symptoms of vertigo, tinnitus, and hearing loss; and (7) ototoxic drugs or allergies. Exposure to loud noise for extended periods is also a cause of hearing impairment.

As the type and amount of hearing loss vary, so must the degree of educational interventions. The main goal of intervention is to teach the child to communicate. Children with hearing impairment may be eligible for special education services under the category of Hearing Impaired. The extent of special education services will vary greatly, depending upon the degree of impairment and the utilization and impact of assistive devices. Training in speech and language is typically a critical component of school-based interventions. There can be profound emotional and social ramifications of hearing impairments that are left untreated.

Although some evidence suggests that hearing loss may be accompanied by additional learning deficits, hearing loss has not been identified as the primary etiology of additional learning problems. Early identification and intervention are important in the determination of prognosis. Outcome is good because multiple interventions are available. Researchers are currently investigating the impact of hearing loss on learning, behavior, and communication.

HUNTER SYNDROME

Hunter syndrome (mucopolysacchridosis II, or MPS II), a progressive disorder arising from a deficiency in the enzyme iduronate sulfatase, is a sex-linked inborn error of metabolism (IEM) affecting only males. The enzyme's absence or deficiency prevents complete breakdown of the mucopolysaccharides heparen sulphate and dermatan sulfate, which then accumulate in bodily cells. One of a group of lycosomal storage disorders that arise from altered mucopolysaccharide metabolism, Hunter syndrome is of two types, MPS IIA, having severe effects commonly leading to death by age 10 to 15 years, and MPS IIB, having milder effects and a life span of about 50 years.

Boys with Hunter syndrome need extensive special education interventions. Having recurrent problems and a progressive disease, they need teachers who are skilled in basic medical care. These boys can have problems chewing and swallowing their food, so caretakers must ensure that they have easily managed food such as soft puddings or pureed food. Their progressive stiffening of joints will call for physical therapy. Boys with severe Hunter syndrome may never speak or have a very small vocabulary and be prone to repetition of words or short phrases and will benefit from speech therapy to improve basic communication. Because their hyperactive and aggressive behavior may be disruptive, their instructors should be skilled in working with profoundly impaired students. Boys with the milder form of Hunter syndrome may be placed in a more normal school setting, although they may still need services for mild retardation and disruptive behavior disorders. The prognosis for boys with the severe form is poor. Their progressive deterioration leads to increasing dependency, physical problems, and early death. Boys with the less severe form can be expected to live a more normal life but will still need considerable medical and educational intervention.

HUNTINGTON'S CHOREA

Huntington's chorea (HC), also referred to as Huntington's disease, is an autosomal dominant disorder that causes deterioration of the central nervous system, in particular, the basal ganglia. HC has a 100% penetrance, and offspring have a 50–50 chance of developing the disease. Huntington's is characterized by repetitive rapid jerking of the face, trunk, and limbs. The chorea can be unilateral or bilateral and can move from one side of the body to another. The motions are involuntary but can be incorporated into voluntary movements to provide a disguise.

HC is estimated to occur in 5 to 10 individuals out of 100,000. The age of onset is typically between 35 and 55 years of age; however, in approximately 10% of cases the disease begins before the age of 20; and in 5% before the age of 14. When the onset is before age 20, the disease is referred to as juvenile Huntington's chorea (JHC).

Compared to adult-onset HC, JHC has a greater paternal inheritance pattern, less prominent choreiform movements, greater rigidity, facial grimacing, and dysfluent speech. Unlike the adult who exhibits hyperkinetic movement patterns, children present more like Parkinson's patients, that is, with rigid musculature and slowed movements. With JHC there is also a propensity to develop epilepsy, often in the form of generalized myoclonic seizures. Although the disease progresses more slowly than when it begins in adulthood, it is often more severe in children and adolescents. Psychological problems, especially depression and paranoid ideations, are fairly common among individuals with JHC, and the disease eventually causes dementia and death.

Children and adolescents with JHC often require special education services (e.g., as Other Health Impairment). Psychological services are also likely to be needed, given the degenerative nature and severity of the disease. Supportive therapy for both the child and family should be offered, as well as help making contact with community agencies. Treatment for the disease itself consists of symptom relief, that is, drugs that improve movements by reducing the impact on the dopaminergic and cholinergic systems and drugs that treated associated problems (e.g., valproic acid, baclofen, haloperidol, and phenothiazine). Neuroleptics have the advantage of treating both abnormal movements and psychiatric symptoms. Prognosis for HC is poor. Not only is quality of life compromised, but life span is also shortened. On average individuals with HC live 8 years from the time of onset.

HYPERTELORISM

Hypertelorism refers to the physical finding of wide separation of the eyes. This diagnosis is made by measuring the inner canthal distance (ICD), which is the space between the junctions of the eyelids along either side of the bridge of the nose. When ICD equals or exceeds three standard deviations above normal for the child's age, one can be confident of the diagnosis. To confirm their clinical impression, clinicians consult genetics textbooks, which contain graphs of various facial measurements, including ICD. Hypertelorism is often associated with other eye abnormalities. The most common of these are exotropia (external deviation of the eye) and optic atrophy (underdevelopment of the optic nerve).

Hypertelorism is a frequent feature of nearly 50 syndromes and genetic disorders. It is occasionally seen in about 20 more. It can be a minor morphologic variation, such as a familiar trait. Finally, hypertelorism may be a developmental abnormality secondary to an underlying brain anomaly or the persistence of a midline cleft, which separates rapidly growing blocks of tissue that form an embryo's face and head.

KERNICTERUS

Kernicterus is a neurologic syndrome that results from the accumulation of bilirubin in the newborn brain. The symptoms of kernicterus begin during the first week of life and are nonspecific because they are also consistent with many other abnormalities in the neonate (infection, low blood sugar, brain hemorrhage, etc.).

For children who survive kernicterus, an early childhood intervention (ECI) program should be initiated to help the child reach developmental milestones. For those children who have sustained a hearing loss, speech therapy may be necessary. Continued special education services will be required as the child enters the school setting. Evaluation and treatment from occupational and physical therapy also may be needed to help with the muscle spasms and increased muscle tone.

Discussing the prognosis for infants with kernicterus is difficult because of the wide array of symptomatic severity it may cause. Infants with ominous neurological signs have a very poor outlook. There is a 75% mortality rate in this group. Of those patients who survive beyond the first few months, 80% have profound neurological sequelae (muscle spasms, mental retardation, hearing loss, and increased muscle tone in all four extremities).

KLINEFELTER SYNDROME (XXY)

Klinefelter syndrome (KS) results from a chromosomal abnormality in which at least one extra X chromosome is present in males (i.e., XXY). Obvious signs of KS often do not appear until adolescence or adulthood, when males with KS often show hypogonadism, delayed puberty, and excessive growth of lower extremities. Although the chromosomal abnormality can be diagnosed in infancy or childhood, it is most often diagnosed in adulthood when questions of fertility arise.

Effective treatment of KS is dependent on diagnosis made through genetic testing. Treatment consists of hormone replacement therapy (i.e., testosterone), usually in injection form. Even if treatment does not begin until adulthood, some benefit can be obtained, including increased facial and pubic hair, increased energy and strength, and increased libido. Positive effects on mood are also common. Testicular size, gynecomastia, and sterility are not affected.

Children with KS may qualify for special education services under Other Health Impairment or by qualifying with language impairments or learning disabilities. KS is associated with developmental delays, particularly in language and motor domains. There is also an increased incidence of learning disabilities, behavioral and social problems, and language impairments. For these reasons, it is important to complete a comprehensive neuropsychological and psychological evaluation with children diagnosed with KS to determine what Special Education services are necessary (if any). Although these children often show normal intellectual functioning, a decreased verbal IQ is common. Other neuropsychological difficulties may include poor attention span, poor short-term auditory memory, and problems with memory retrieval. Special education services may be needed for the problems just mentioned. Children with KS may also require special education services due to behavioral and emotional difficulties such as impaired social skills, depression, or behavioral problems. Special education services can help remediate learning difficulties and manage behavior in the classroom. These children may also require speech and language therapy and occupational therapy. They may need specific classroom accommodations such as increased frequency of breaks and shorter assignments due to increased fatigue. In addition, accommodations to compensate for weak verbal skills are likely to be appropriate.

KRABBE DISEASE

Krabbe disease is a rare, degenerative disorder of the central and peripheral nervous systems. It is one of a group of genetic disorders called the leukodystrophies. The disorder involves a genetic anomaly that interferes with the development of nerves in the brain, and particularly with the development of the myelin sheath that surrounds the nerve. It is identified by the presence of characteristic globoid cells in the brain tissue. Krabbe disease is inherited in an autosomal recessive pattern and occurs equally as often in boys and girls. The gene involved has been identified as 14q31. If more than one person in a family is diagnosed with Krabbe disease, they may not have the same form or express the same symptoms.

Because the nerves affected are central to the brain, Krabbe disease affects respiration, body temperature, and other involuntary (automatic) functions of the body, as well as voluntary movements and muscle control. Because of the neural involvement, digestion is impaired, seizures are common, and areas within the brain atrophy.

Individuals with the late onset of Krabbe disease may be learning disabled and may require special education services. Because some of the first signs of the disease are loss of vision and deterioration of fine motor movements, there may be a need for specialized services for individuals who are vision impaired and fine motor movement impaired. Services may need to be extended throughout high school because symptoms may last 20 years or more in the very rare cases of juvenile and adult forms. Whenever there is a history of Krabbe disease in a family, it is strongly recommended that nonaffected family members receive genetic counseling prior to having children because they may be carriers. There is no cure for Krabbe disease.

LANDAU-KLEFFNER SYNDROME

Landau-Kleffner syndrome (LKS)—also called acquired epileptiform aphasia, infantile acquired aphasia, or aphasia with convulsive disorder—is a rare, childhood neurological disorder characterized by the sudden or gradual development of aphasia (loss of language) and an abnormal electroencephalogram (EEG).

LKS affects the parts of the brain that control speech and comprehension. The disorder usually occurs in children between the ages of 3 and 7. Typically, these children develop normally; then, for no apparent reason, they lose the ability to understand others and to speak. Although many of the affected individuals have seizures, some do not. The disorder is difficult to diagnose and may be misdiagnosed as autism, Pervasive Developmental Disorder, hearing impairment, learning disability, auditory-verbal processing disorder, Attention Deficit Disorder, mental retardation, childhood schizophrenia, or emotional-behavioral problems. The cause of LKS is unknown.

Treatment of LKS usually consists of medication to control the seizures and abnormal brain wave activity (anticonvulsants) and has very little effect on language ability. Corticosteroid therapy has improved the language ability of some children. Sign language instruction has benefited others.

Special education programming will most likely be needed for children with LKS. Special education assessments can assist with the diagnosis and management of the condition. Speech and language therapy will also help with management and assessment. It is probable that the family and child would benefit from counseling due to the seriousness and uncertain onset of the disorder. Adjustments to chronic illness will need education and understanding on the part of the special and regular education team. School personnel can also be instrumental in the monitoring of seizure activity and sensitivity to side effects from anticonvulsant medications.

LEARNING DISABILITIES

Although there has been disagreement in the field regarding a specific operational definition, the term *learning disabilities* generally refers to a group of disorders that are characterized by learning problems to the degree that academic achievement or daily functioning is significantly impaired. The three primary diagnoses include reading disorder, mathematics disorder, and disorder of written language.

Symptoms of learning disabilities may occur as early as kindergarten, but a diagnosis typically is not made before the end of first grade and may not be apparent until later grades. Learning disabilities are three to four times more common in males than in females. Prevalence rates in the general population range from 2% to 4%. Reading disorder is estimated to affect 60 to 80% of students identified with learning disabilities. There are wide interindividual differences among children with learning disabilities, although there are some shared characteristics.

Due to the heterogeneity of this population, treatment is typically comprised of individualized education plans that outline instructional activities specifically tailored to meet the learning needs of each individual student. The general approaches to treatment include remediation of skill deficits, as well as accommodations in instruction, assignments, and evaluation methods. Unfortunately, there is a lack of research supporting the long-term efficacy of any specific instructional method, intervention technique, or combination thereof. The majority of research has focused on reading disabilities, with findings suggesting that phonological approaches to intervention are most efficacious.

Comorbidity rates for students with learning disabilities are high for disruptive behavior disorders, attention-deficit disorders, and depressive disorders. The school dropout rate for these students is nearly 40%, and learning disorders are likely to persist into adulthood, potentially affecting employment opportunities as well as social adjustment. There is a substantial need for methodologically sound research exploring the efficacy of intervention strategies for well-defined subgroups of children with learning disabilities, particularly research that examines long-term outcomes.

LEUKEMIA, ACUTE LYMPHOCYTIC

Acute lymphocytic leukemia (ALL) is a malignant condition in which immature white blood cells are produced in abnormally large quantities and disrupt normal blood cell growth. The blood cells, also referred to as blasts, accumulate in bone marrow, blood, and lymphatics, and they circulate throughout the blood and lymphatic system. Vital organs, including the lungs, kidney, spleen, and liver, are often damaged as a result of the condition. Leukemic cells can also affect tissue of the brain and spinal cord.

ALL is responsible for approximately 85% of leukemia in patients under the age of 21. The disease, which is more common in Caucasian males, is usually diagnosed during the preschool years.

Treatment for ALL primarily consists of cranial radiation therapy and intrathecal chemotherapy using methotrexate. These treatments have been credited with the tremendous increase in long-term survival over the past three decades, but they have also been blamed for certain medical and cognitive problems; these include growth problems associated with endocrine problems and reduced abilities and learning capacity associated with central nervous system assault. Neuropsychological problems include poor attention and memory, slowed processing speed and motor performance, and visual-spatial deficits.

Not all children with ALL require special education services; however, many will require some type of accommodation in the classroom (especially around the time of treatment). Some students may require extra time to complete missed assignments, tutoring to catch up on work, or both. In cases in which special education is needed, services under the category of Other Health Impaired may be appropriate; this includes assistance from the school nurse as well as from the school psychologist. Often, interventions include supportive counseling and education (i.e., of the school staff and peers). Schools are often a refuge for parents and children struggling to cope with a serious medical condition—especially a life-threatening disease. At times, parents have little information as to where to turn for help and are not even aware of resources in the community.

LISSENCEPHALY

Lissencephaly is a disorder of brain maturation in which the brain has limited or absent gyri and sulci, resulting in a smooth brain surface. It results when early migration patterns of neurons are disrupted. The cause is not certain, but both genetic and nongenetic explanations have been hypothesized, such as viral infections during the first trimester of pregnancy, insufficient blood supply to the brain during the first trimester, damage on Chromosome 17, and recessive inheritance of a recessive gene.

There are many options for schooling, depending on the severity of the lissencephaly. All children with lissencephaly suffer from severe mental retardation and poor muscle control similar to that of children with cerebral palsy and will require special accommodations and additional aides.

MACROGLOSSIA

Macroglossia is defined as enlargement of the tongue. Diagnosing macroglossia is a judgment call on the part of the examiner. Unlike the case in numerous assessments of body proportions (height, weight, head circumference, distance between the pupils of the eye, etc.), there are no charts or graphs to assist physicians in determining when the tongue is large. However, certain clinical clues may be present. The tongue may protrude from the mouth or cause symptoms of upper airway obstruction (noisy breathing, snoring, or cessation of breathing). Feeding difficulties may also be present.

MARASMUS

Marasmus, which is sometimes referred to as protein calorie malnutrition, is a severe disorder of malnutrition. This disorder develops when an individual does not take in a sufficient amount of protein or an adequate number of calories.

Although marasmus can occur in individuals of any age, it is generally observed in children under 1 year of age in urban areas of developing countries. Research has shown that malnutrition during critical periods of brain development can lead to decreased myelinization, fewer neurons and glial cells, less dendritic branching, fewer-than-normal synaptic connections, and lower velocity of impulse conduction. When school-aged children were examined, they were found to have significant differences on measures of full-scale IQ and on verbal IQs.

Findings suggest that assessments of cognitive abilities, achievement, memory, sensory integration, hyperactivity, attention, motor activity, and adaptive functioning are suggested for a child who has had marasmus. Assessments may need to be performed throughout development because some brain damage may not be apparent until late childhood or early adolescence. Schools should also be ready to provide social and developmental rehabilitation, special education services if needed (typically for children with mental retardation or learning disabilities), and long-term intervention for the family addressing the underlying issues related to the child's malnutrition. Behavioral interventions may also be required while the child is recovering and could address lethargy, apathy, eating habits, and motor problems. With younger children, delays in achieving developmental milestones may also need to be addressed.

MENTAL RETARDATION, MILD TO MODERATE

Mental retardation is defined as a disorder in which the overall intellectual functioning of a person is well below average, he or she has a significantly impaired ability to cope with common life demands, and he or she lacks the daily living skills required of others within their same age group. Mental retardation is a particular state of functioning that begins in childhood and may interfere with one's ability to learn, communicate, provide self-care, live independently, have meaningful social interactions, and be aware of one's own safety. Mental retardation is neither a medical nor a mental disorder, but rather is a disorder defined by society that is based on a statistical concept and not on the qualities inherent in those who have the disorder. There are four degrees of severity of mental retardation: mild, moderate, severe, and profound.

Although mental retardation is a lifelong, irreversible disorder, treatment is related to the system of supports one will require in order to overcome limits in adaptive skills. The support required falls into four levels of intensity. Intermittent support refers to support on an as-needed basis and does not necessarily require continuous or daily support. Limited support occurs over a limited time span, such as during transition from school to work. Extensive support provides for assistance on a daily basis and may be required at home and at school or work. Pervasive support is constant support across all environments and may include life-sustaining measures.

Mental retardation is one of the 14 categories of disabilities outlined in the Individuals with Disabilities Education Act. As such, members of the special education team will likely need to assess, identify, and provide services for those students in the school with mental retardation. It is important for the team to keep in mind that the label should not prevent school personnel from viewing the child as an individual, just like any other child. Although assessment may be difficult, the focus should be on the child's strengths and abilities, rather than on the child's limitations.

During the past 30 years, significant advances in research in the areas of newborn screening for phenylketonuria, congenital hypothyroidism, Rh disease, and other screenings have prevented many cases of mental retardation. Research is also being conducted on the development and function of the nervous system and on gene therapy to correct defective genes that may cause mental retardation.

MENTAL RETARDATION, SEVERE TO PROFOUND

Severe and profound mental retardation (SMR, PMR) are characterized by a below-average level of intellectual functioning that affects 3 to 4% of individuals diagnosed with mental retardation. An IQ range of below 20 to 25 and 20 to 40 respectively generally typifies individuals with SMR and PMR.Corresponding severe impairments in adaptive functioning are also apparent in these individuals.

During early childhood years, individuals with SMR and PMR often fail to acquire normal speech and are slow to develop motor skills. They are usually diagnosed in infancy due to the significant impairment in early development. During school-age years individuals with SMR and PMR may learn to talk and can be trained in elementary self-care skills. Communicative abilities, however, remain limited throughout their lives.

Most children with SMR are served in special education programs under the Individuals with Disabilities Education Act's classification of Intellectual Disabilities, whereas individuals with PMR may need residential placement. Educational services can begin as early as birth and continue until young adulthood. Home-based services are often provided until the child is of school age. These include speech and language services and physical therapy. School services are typically provided in self-contained classrooms with inclusion in certain nonacademic regular education activities. It is not uncommon for these children to receive assistance from a number of related services personnel. Children with cerebral palsy, for example, often require the services of the speech and language pathologist as well as the occupational and physical therapist. School nurses may also be necessary to attend to the medical needs of children with critical medical needs. Although direct services by the school psychologist and school counselor may be less frequent, consultations with teachers and parents regarding behavior management and transition issues (e.g., post–high school) are often needed. Guidance personnel may also be in the best position to provide support to the family and information about community agencies and resources (e.g., respite care, financial assistance, and long-term life planning).

Interventions with the child tend to be intensive and behavioral. Approximately 20 to 35% of individuals with SMR have significant behavior problems or psychiatric diagnoses. For children in residential settings the rate may be as high as 60%. There are some behavior problems that do appear to be specific to mental retardation, including self-injurious behaviors such as hair pulling, hitting, biting, and head banging. Medication is often used to control behaviors (e.g., mood stabilizers and anticonvulsants). Single drugs, however, are often ineffective, and a polydrug approach is often needed. Unfortunately, this has its own unwanted side effects, including sedation and reduced singular drug potency.

The prognosis for individuals with SMR and PMR is poor. Not only is the life span shortened by the various concomitant medical problems (e.g., coronary disease and respiratory conditions), but quality of life is also limited by these and other conditions (e.g., sensory handicaps that limit exposure to the environment).

MICROCEPHALY

Microcephaly refers to a smaller than normal head circumference, with the presumption that the smaller size reflects a smaller-sized brain. Rather than a disorder or disease entity, microcephaly is viewed as a sign of cerebral malformation. Microcephaly does not have a single cause, but rather can result from a number of different factors. Microcephaly can occur as a result of genetics, both in autosomal recessive form and in autosomal dominant form. The autosomal recessive form is more likely to occur if parents are cousins. A third form of genetic transmission of microcephaly is X-linked: The mother is a carrier for the disorder, but only sons are affected. Other genetic causes of microcephaly are directly related to other disorders that result from chromosomal defects (e.g., Trisomy 21). Syndromes that include microcephaly as a marker are continuously being identified.

MUNCHAUSEN SYNDROME BY PROXY

Munchausen syndrome by proxy (MSBP), a member of the family of factitious disorders, shares certain features with Munchausen syndrome and is considered a special form of child abuse. The most common element is the tendency for people to fabricate or produce physical or psychological symptoms in order to assume the patient role and gain the attention, care, and special grace that may come with this role. The name itself derives from Baron von Münchausen, a notorious 18th-century teller of tall tales.

Most case reports of MSBP identify the mother as the primary perpetrator (90 to 95%), although some rare cases may involve the father, babysitter, or other relative. The victim is typically a toddler or infant, although elderly adults and animals have also suffered the abuse. Although there is no established profile of perpetrators of MSBP, there is the underlying motivation to gain primary attention from the medical or mental health community. The parent is driven to gratify his or her own needs at the expense of the child. Doctor shopping may be a hallmark sign of possible MSBP, and with basic medical information readily available on the Internet, many perpetrators can develop a great deal of knowledge about specific symptoms sufficient to fabricate convincingly or induce a diagnosis in their offspring.

There are no known special education concerns, although teachers may become aware of recurrent medical conditions that suggest this form of abuse. As a special form of child abuse, teachers may become required to report their suspicions to child protective services. Prognosis remains guarded at best. Case studies are common, although empirical research remains sparse at best concerning characteristics of the victims or perpetrators or addressing treatment outcomes.

MYOCLONUS

Myoclonus is a symptom and not a diagnosable disease. It is defined as a sudden, brief, jerky, shock-like, and usually irregular, involuntary movement emanating from the central nervous system. Five distinguishing traits characterize myoclonus: positivity or negativity, distribution, regularity, its relation to motor activity, and synchronization. When the myoclonic jerk is the result of a muscular contraction, it is called positive myoclonus, but if it is the result of a temporary suspension in muscular activity, it is called negative myoclonus. Myoclonic jerks can be distributed across one area (focal), two or more adjacent areas (segmental), or in various areas of the body (generalized). The regularity with which these myoclonic jerks present themselves allows clinicians to classify them as rhythmic (very regular), arrhythmic (irregular), or oscillatory (in the presence of a sudden stimulus).

NEUROFIBROMATOSIS, TYPE 1

Neurofibromatosis (NF) is one of a series of disorders described as neurocutaneous syndromes (phakomatoses). Neurofibromatosis is an autosomal dominant genetic disorder that affects the development and growth of ectodermal tissues. There are two distinctive forms of NF, Type 1 (NF-1) and Type 2 (NF-2). NF-1 is characterized by multiple hyperpigmented areas and peripheral neurofibromas. NF-2 is characterized by the development of acoustic (8th cranial nerve) neuromas and other intracranial and/or intraspinal tumors. NF is associated with variable medical and neurologic conditions, and different individuals with the same diagnosis experience variable symptoms and severity of symptoms. Although some affected individuals have minimal involvement that has no substantial impact on their lives, others encounter disfigurement secondary to multiple neurofibromas, life-threatening tumors.

The complications of NF are multisystem. Individuals with NF have an increased risk for malignancy, particularly of the skin and nervous system, although these patients are also at increased risk for developing leukemia. Hypertension, kyphosis, and scoliosis, contributing to pulmonary compromise, gastrointestinal bleeding secondary to gastrointestinal neurofibromata, and neurologic abnormalities occur. Learning difficulties, speech problems, attentional disorders, and seizures are common.

The learning needs of children with NF-1 have been extensively evaluated. Intellectual ability is generally in the normal range, although the curve is shifted to the left, with mean reported IQs generally in the low 90s. There is a disproportionate requirement for special education with as many as 73% of those children with NF-1 evaluated requiring special services.

Treatment of patients with NF is symptomatic. Neurofibromas of the peripheral nerves are generally not a problem unless they are regularly irritated or present a cosmetic impediment. Intracranial tumors are managed with neurosurgical and oncologic intervention. The treatment of optic gliomas is controversial and generally expectant. Anticipatory counseling to deal with psychosocial and educational issues is important, and parent support groups may be helpful. Educational intervention is the most pressing need for many children with NF. Children with a diagnosis of NF should be carefully monitored and their educational needs met in an expeditious and energetic fashion.

NEUROFIBROMATOSIS, TYPE 2

Neurofibromatosis Type 2 (NF-2) is a less common type of neurofibromatosis. Neurofibromatoses are genetically transmitted disorders of the nervous system that often have an autosomal dominant pattern of transmission. These disorders may cause tumor growth on nerves and other abnormalities, such as multiple skin changes (e.g., café au lait spots) and bone deformities. Neurofibromatosis Type 1 (NF-1) is the more common type of neurofibromatosis.

NF-2 is characterized by bilateral tumors on the 8th cranial nerve. It was thought to be primarily associated with tumors on a branch of the 8th cranial nerve associated with hearing and formerly was known as bilateral acoustic neurofibromatosis or central bilateral acoustic NF. These names are no longer technically correct because tumors also are known to occur on the vestibular nerve branch of the 8th cranial nerve in NF-2.

Most individuals with NF-2 do not become symptomatic until they are teenagers. If they are still in school, they may qualify for special education assistance under the categories of Hearing Impaired or Visually Handicapped. Depending on the severity of these sensory impairments, the student may require certain classroom accommodations. The child with vision problems may require large-print text or extended time in order to meet his or her individual needs. Similarly, the child with hearing impairment may need preferential seating or classroom amplification.

NEURONAL MIGRATION DISORDERS

Neuronal migration disorders (NMDs) are a group of disorders caused by the abnormal migration of nerve cells (neurons) very early in the development of the fetal nervous system. Neuronal migration is the process in which neurons move from their place of origin to their permanent location. When this process is disrupted, the result is a structurally abnormal brain involving the cerebral hemispheres, cerebellum, brain stem, and/or hippocampus.

NMDs may include schizencephaly, porencephaly, lissencephaly, agyria, macrogyria, pachygyria, microgyria, micropolygyria, neuronal heterotopias (including band heterotopia), agenesis of the corpus callosum, and agenesis of the cranial nerves. These disorders may be associated with other abnormalities, including other NMDs. NMDs may be associated with early death. Most individuals with NMDs have a normal physical appearance, but there may be variations in facial appearance that can be detected by trained professionals.

NOONAN SYNDROME

Noonan syndrome is a rare genetic disorder that causes a wide range of clinical features of varying severity, most commonly involving distinctive facial features, cardiac abnormality, chest deformity, and short stature. It is named for Jacqueline A. Noonan, a pediatric cardiologist, who identified the clinical and genetic characteristics of the syndrome. The syndrome is transmitted as an autosomal dominant trait, with some cases attributed to spontaneous mutation. As with many other autosomal dominant disorders, there is widely variable expressivity, which can make mildly affected individuals difficult to recognize. It is identified by clinical characteristics, and there is currently no diagnostic test for it. Chromosome studies are normal. Several other conditions have symptoms similar to those of Noonan syndrome, including cardiofaciocutaneous syndromes, Turner syndrome, Costello syndrome, Noonan-like multiple giant cell lesion syndrome, neurofibromatosis-Noonan syndrome, Watson syndrome, and LEOPARD syndrome.

Noonan syndrome is usually apparent at birth. Birth weight is usually normal but may be increased due to subcutaneous edema or peripheral lymphedema. The head appears large, long, narrow, and pointed at the top (turricephalic). Eye abnormalities are common, including ocular hyperteliorism, ptosis, strabismus, epicanthal folds, an antimongoloid slant, and amblyopia. Feeding problems in early infancy and failure to thrive are also common. Facial features frequently follow predictable changes over time. In later childhood, the face appears more triangular, the neck lengthens such that pterygium colli appears more pronounced, trapezii appear more prominent, and wispy scalp hair becomes wooly or curly. In adolescence, the nasal bridge becomes higher and thinner, the eyes become less prominent, and development of secondary sexual characteristics may be delayed or reduced. Some males are infertile; most females have normal fertility. In later adulthood, there are high forehead hairline, wrinkled and unusually transparent skin, and prominent nasolabial folds.

The incidence of Noonan syndrome is approximately 1 in 1,000 to 2,500 newborns. There is speculation that the true incidence may be higher because wide variability in expressivity may result in mild cases being seen as a normal variant. Males and females are equally affected. No variability has been found related to race or geographic location.

Special education services are likely to be needed for a child with Noonan syndrome, to remediate possible cognitive, language, and motor developmental delays. Specific services required depend on the individual case. Interventions for learning disabilities and mental retardation, as well as physical and occupational therapy services, psychological and vocational counseling, and genetic counseling for the patient and family may be necessary. Early detection is important due to the range and severity of symptoms that may require treatment and is medically essential due to the large number of potential health problems and unusual risks that may be present. For example, some individuals with Noonan syndrome show unusual anesthetic and medication sensitivities, requiring special care. Awareness of blood abnormalities is important to reduce the risk of excessive bleeding.

Prognosis in Noonan syndrome depends on the severity of the condition and availability of treatment. A team of specialists is often required, including those specializing in cardiology, hematology, pediatrics, and others. Current research includes exploration of recombinant human growth hormone as a treatment for short stature. Future genetic research may lead to the discovery of the causes of Noonan syndrome, from which methods of earlier detection, prevention, and treatment may be possible.

OPPOSITIONAL DEFIANT DISORDER

Children with Oppositional Defiant Disorder (ODD) exhibit noncompliant behaviors in excess of what is normal for similarly aged children. Symptoms often include temper tantrums, irritability, and difficulty controlling anger. In order to distinguish clinical behavior from normal limit-testing, behaviors must markedly interfere with social and academic functioning.

Treatment of ODD often includes parent training and social skills training. Parent training involves teaching parents to give effective commands, reward compliance, deal with noncompliance, and improve parenting skills. Social skills training addresses cognitive distortions (e.g., assuming negative intentions by others) and cognitive deficiencies (e.g., not knowing how to approach others). Researchers also have been studying pharmacological treatments such as anticonvulsants, nontricyclic antidepressants such as buproprion, and tricyclic antidepressants; however, further research must be conducted before conclusive recommendations can be made.

ODD is not a special education category as defined by the Individuals with Disabilities Education Act. However, if a student meets requirements in his or her state under the definition of emotional disturbance or has a comorbid disability, he or she may receive special education services. Although services and placement must be individualized for each child, the most restrictive placement is usually a classroom for children exhibiting behavior problems. Services dependent on comorbid conditions as well. For instance, many children with ODD also have ADHD. Therefore, these children may require services that address attention and hyperactivity as well.

Prognosis for children with early-onset ODD often includes academic problems, poor peer relations, risk of head injury due to violent behavior, distorted arousal and reactivity patterns, and for some, development of Conduct Disorder.

OTITIS MEDIA

Otitis Media (OM) is characterized by an inflammation of the middle ear and is typically associated with an accumulation of fluid. This fluid may or may not be infected. Infection is usually a bacterial or viral infection secondary to a cold, sore throat, or other respiratory problem. When the fluid is not infected, it results in a condition called otitis media with effusion (OME). Another name for this condition is Serous otitis media. If the fluid in the middle ear becomes infected, then the condition is referred to as acute otitis media (AOM). In both cases, there is fluctuating loss in hearing, which returns to normal. Rarely can a permanent hearing loss occur.

Consultation or evaluation by an audiologist and speech-language pathologist should be sought to further define the scope of the effects of recurrent OM. In some cases, delays in articulation and language development are sufficient enough to warrant speech-language therapy services in the school setting. These services generally produce positive results.

Research linking recurrent OM to later developmental difficulties is controversial. Further research is needed to clarify this relationship. Until then, medical management combined with collaboration with other allied health care professionals, caregivers, and teachers can minimize the effects of OM.

PANDAS (PEDIATRIC AUTOIMMUNE NEUROPSYCHIATRIC DISORDER ASSOCIATED WITH STREPTOCOCCI)

PANDAS, or pediatric autoimmune neuropsychiatric disorder associated with streptococci, has been used to describe a group of disorders—in particular, Obsessive-Compulsive Disorder (OCD) and tic disorder or Tourette syndrome. PANDAS has been associated with Group A beta-hemolytic streptococcus (GABHS), as well as Sydenham chorea, a condition that results from rheumatic fever following strep infection. Although PANDAS share certain features of Sydenham—in particular, OCD and tics—it is not clear whether PANDAS represents acute rheumatic fever.

The course of PANDAS is episodic—that is, periods of partial or complete remission are interspersed between periods of exacerbated symptoms. It is not clear whether the condition is chronic or if total remission can be achieved. There is no indication, however, that prophylactic treatments to prevent recurrences of the GABHS infection is indicated as it is with Sydenham chorea. Symptoms of PANDAS can, however, be improved with therapy—specifically, plasmapheresis and intravenous immunoglobulin.

There is no indication that children who have PANDAS require special education services. Some children, however, may benefit from assistance and classroom accommodations during periods of symptom exacerbation. School psychological services may be particularly important in order to identify what the child's needs are and what intervention would be most appropriate to address these needs. Given the abrupt onset of the condition and its episodic nature, it is likely that the child and his or her family will need supportive therapy. Parents may be especially open to suggestions about ways to manage the variety of psychiatric and neurological problems that accompany PANDAS. A psychiatric evaluation is therefore critical to determine whether medications will benefit the child and reduce associated problems (e.g., tics, obsessions and compulsions, anxiety, lability, and hyperactivity).

PANIC DISORDER

A Panic Disorder is characterized by recurrent, unexpected panic attacks. A panic attack is a discrete period of intense fear or terror that has a sudden onset and reaches a peak within 10 minutes or less. Panic attacks fall within three general categories defined by the presence or absence of triggers. Uncued panic attacks occur unexpectedly and out of the blue, with no apparent situational context. In contrast, both cued or situationally bound panic attacks occur whenever a person encounters or anticipates encountering a feared object or situation. At least one of the aforementioned panic attacks must be followed by at least a month of one or more of the following consequences: persistent concern about additional attacks, worry about the meaning of the attacks, and an appreciable change in behavior related to the attacks. Panic Disorder often occurs along with agoraphobia. The child or adolescent may refuse to leave his or her home or may refuse to go to school. Although agoraphobia may develop at any point in conjunction with a Panic Disorder, it usually occurs within 1 year of recurrent panic attacks.

The most efficacious treatments for childhood anxiety disorders include behavior therapy, cognitive-behavioral treatments, and pharmacological treatments. Behavioral treatments include contingency management, response prevention, systematic desensitization involving graduated exposure to feared stimuli, modeling (using self or live or symbolic models) and self-control strategies. Empirical validation of the effectiveness of traditional psychotherapy for this disorder has been inadequate.

Pharmacological interventions for anxiety-based disorders include the use of serotonin reuptake inhibitors (SRIs) such as Prozac, Paxil, Zoloft, Luvox, or Celexa with initial dosages lower than recommended and slowly adjusted for maximum therapeutic effect. Benzodiazepines such as Xanax and Ativan as well as trycyclic antidepressants have shown minimal to modest benefit and in some cases have been no more effective than placebo in children. These treatments are usually provided as an adjunct to psychological treatments.

Special education services may be available to children or adolescents diagnosed with Panic Disorder under specific categories of Other Health Impaired, Emotional Disturbance, or Behavior Disorder; this may be particularly important if the disorder is chronic in nature. Accommodations may also be requested and provided under Section 504 of the Rehabilitation Act of 1973. Due to the nature and scope of the disorder, school attendance may become problematic. Families can benefit from additional counseling and support to effectively implement a treatment plan across both school and home settings.

Adolescents who present with panic disorders are likely to have a family history of panic attacks or related anxiety symptoms. These children or adolescents also tend to exhibit other problems and may meet diagnostic criteria for depression or other types of internalizing disorders. Some individuals may experience episodic outbreaks, with several years of remission between panic episodes. The high proportion of children diagnosed with Panic Disorder who also report a history of separation anxiety problems has led to speculation that separation anxiety is a precursor to the development of a panic disorder.

PERSEVERATION

Perseveration is defined as the involuntary and pathological persistence of the same verbal response or motor activity regardless of the stimulus or its duration. A child exhibiting perseverative behavior will often continue a task beyond the normal end point and may have difficulty making the transition to another task. Perseveration is typically considered a subtle indicator or soft sign of neurological abnormalities and is often associated with brain damage or organic mental disorders. Within the school-age population, this condition is thought to be most common among children who have a learning disability or brain injury. Perseveration may also be present in schizophrenia as an association disorder.

PERVASIVE DEVELOPMENTAL DISORDER

The category of Pervasive Developmental Disorders (PDD) includes Autistic Disorder, Rett Disorder, Childhood Disintegrative Disorder (CDD), Asperger's Disorder, and Pervasive Developmental Disorder Not Otherwise Specified (PDDNOS; American Psychiatric Association [APA], 1994). PDD is characterized by impairment during the first few years of life in social, affective, communicative, and cognitive development. It is difficult to estimate an overall prevalence rate for the five disorders due to disagreement regarding different diagnosis. For example, there is some research to suggest that autism and PDDNOS are different points on a continuum.

In conjunction with the need for differential diagnosis, several disorders may be comorbid with the PDD, such as mental retardation, ADHD, Obsessive-Compulsive Disorder, anxiety disorders, and Tourette syndrome. The need for additional diagnosis for children with PDD is debated.

Individual prognosis varies greatly depending on severity and the specific diagnosis. A child with autism or Aspergers who has few cognitive deficits may live independently as an adult with few noticeable symptoms. In contrast, a child who develops Rett syndrome will need long-term care, and 26% die prematurely.

PFEIFFER SYNDROME

Pfeiffer syndrome is one of the acrocephalosyndactyly syndromes (Apert syndrome, Apert-Crouzon syndrome, Chotzen syndrome) characterized by craniosynostosis, mild syndactyly of the hands and feet, and newborn dysmorphic facial features.

The major diagnostic criteria in Pfeiffer syndrome are craniosynostosis and syndactyly, plus malformations of the thumb and great toe (coarse, broad, short, and usually deviated medially); there is a wide range of expressivity of phenotypes.

There is essentially no treatment for the underlying disorder, and treatments such as craniotomy, corrective surgery, and cosmetic surgery are obviously individualized. Genetic counseling is recommended because the recurrence risk is not elevated with unaffected parents but is 50% with one affected parent.

Special education programming may be required due to occasional incidence of seizures and mental retardation with certain subtypes of Pfeiffer syndrome. An individualized assessment and individual education plan would address the sequelae of these conditions. The craniofacial appearance tends to improve with age with this syndrome.

PHENYLKETONURIA

Phenylketonuria (PKU) is the most common of all aminoacidopathies and is caused by autosomal recessive deficiency of the hepatic phenylalanine hydroxylase system. This metabolic abnormality results from a markedly reduced activity (< 2% of normal) of phenylalanine hydroxylase, the hepatic enzyme that converts phenylalanine to tyrosine. The deficiency of this enzyme results in toxic levels of phenylalanine in the blood and a potential deficiency of the amino acid tyrosine. If treatment is not begun in the early days following birth, mental retardation, microcephaly, epilepsy, tremors, hypopigmentation of skin, and hyperactivity can occur.

When dietary treatment with phenylalanine restriction is started early, the child can achieve close-to-normal development. It has long been recommended that individuals with PKU follow dietary restrictions during the first 5 to 6 years of life, when brain growth is most rapid. Continuation of the diet after this time also appears to be beneficial because loss of IQ, behavioral changes, or both have been reported in older children and adolescents who did not adhere to the diet.

Special education may not be necessary in well-controlled cases. However, school personnel may have to support dietary restrictions because recent research now supports lifelong dietary restrictions as opposed to former practice that discontinued the diet at around age 8. Special education programming will be necessary for those children who have been identified late or children whose diets may have been less than adequate.

PHOBIAS

Specific phobias are persistent fears of clearly identified circumscribed objects or situations, usually leading to an immediate anxiety response and avoidance of the stimulus. Common specific phobias in children include fears of the dark; weather-related phenomena such as thunder and lightning; doctors, dentists, or medical procedures requiring physical contact; and insects or other animals. The focus of the fear may be some expected harm from the object or situation (e.g., fear of dogs associated with a fear of being bitten). The diagnosis is not warranted unless the child's fears reflect clinically significant impairment—for example, school refusal or excessive fear of going out to play because an encounter with an animal may occur. To differentiate between specific phobias and other anxiety disorders in children, the child's fear may not be related to other fears, such as panic attacks, social humiliation-embarrassment, or separation from a parent. Specific phobias may also vary as a function of beliefs associated with different cultures and ethnic groups. Fears of supernatural phenomena (i.e., spirits, etc.) should be considered a specific phobia only if they are obviously in excess of cultural norms and cause significant impairment. Specific phobias may provoke panic attacks, especially if the person perceives that there is no escape. Anxiety is invariably experienced immediately when encountering the feared stimulus and may be expressed by crying, tantrums, or freezing or clinging behavior. Children often do not recognize that the fears are excessive or unreasonable and typically do not verbally express distress about the phobias.

Special education support services may be available to children diagnosed with a specific phobia under specific categories of Other Health Impaired, Severe Emotional Disturbance, or Behavior Disorder, if an impact on the child's education can be established. Such services may be particularly important if the disorder is chronic in nature. Accommodations may also be requested and provided under Section 504 of the Rehabilitation Act of 1973. Families can benefit from additional counseling and support to effectively implement a treatment plan across both school and home settings.

PICA

Pica as a disorder is characterized by habitual ingestion of inedible substances. Frequently associated with mental retardation, it also occurs in normal young children (younger than age 3) and in pregnant women in certain cultural groups. For example, in infancy and early childhood, children often chew on their cribs, wood, sand, and grass as a method of early exploration. Pica sometimes continues into adolescence and adulthood.

Pica can be life threatening or can contribute to the development of other disorders, depending on the items eaten, and its risks should not be underestimated. Paint chips, dirt and sand, paper, fabric, feces, cigarette stubs, and bugs are among materials commonly eaten. Of particular concern is eating of dirt or paint that contains lead—pica is the major route for exposure to lead.

The cause of pica remains unknown, even after hundreds of years of study. Pica is a learned behavior that may be initially acquired through normal exploration of the environment or imitation. Its maintenance may owe to a number of factors.

Those in special education may have to implement treatment programs for developmentally disabled children with pica. All those who work with young children should be alert to pica behavior and make appropriate referrals.

POSTCONCUSSION SYNDROME

Postconcussion syndrome is an acquired disorder of the brain, most commonly caused by mild to moderate head trauma. It is defined by a constellation of somatic complaints, cognitive difficulties, and emotional changes beginning after significant cerebral concussion and persisting for a minimum of 3 months.

Effective treatment of postconcussion syndrome is dependent on accurate diagnosis. Compared to adults, children are less likely to be able to understand the cognitive and emotional changes they are experiencing following a head injury. They also often lack the vocabulary to accurately describe these changes to parents or physicians. As a result, they may be misdiagnosed as having Attention-Deficit/Hyperactivity Disorder or Oppositional Defiant Disorder based on outward behavioral changes.

Research indicates that postconcussion syndrome may be caused by a combination of the physical effects of the brain injury as well as anxiety about the symptoms caused by the injury. Environmental stressors such as family changes (e.g., moves or divorce) or difficulty with peers are also likely to exacerbate the symptoms of postconcussion syndrome. Research also indicates that subsequent head injuries are more likely to worsen symptoms of postconcussion syndrome and may in some cases lead to more serious cognitive deficits or even death.

It has been suggested that children who experience a mild to moderate head injury may be more likely to be aware of changes in their cognitive and emotional functioning than are children who experience a more severe injury. Similarly, they may be more likely to be distressed by these changes. This increased awareness-distress has in turn been hypothesized to explain why children with mild to moderate head injury are more likely to develop postconcussion syndrome than are more severely injured children. These same children are also likely to be rapidly returned to a regular academic and social schedule because they display few outward signs of their injury. This rapid return to normal activities may be overwhelming due to changes in cognitive and emotional functioning. Consequently, children's academic and social progress should be closely monitored in the first months following a concussion, and academic modifications should be considered for children and adolescents in the first year after injury. These modifications may include a quiet work area, extended time for tests and assignments, reduced class load, tutoring, or special education placement.

The prognosis for children with postconcussion syndrome is generally good. Most children make a full recovery following a concussion; however, approximately 33% of children will meet criteria for postconcussion syndrome 3 months after the injury, and 10% will continue to meet criteria for diagnosis 1 year after their injury. For those with symptoms enduring for more than 1 year, the prognosis is more mixed. These children are likely to do more poorly academically, limiting their employment possibilities. The emotional and somatic difficulties they experience may lead them to miss school and work and seek medical attention more often than do their peers.

POSTTRAUMATIC STRESS DISORDER

Posttraumatic Stress Disorder (PTSD) is a constellation of symptoms resulting from severe anxiety following exposure to a catastrophic event. The child may have either witnessed or directly experienced an event that involved actual or potential death or serious injury to him- or herself or others. Such events may include physical assault, domestic violence, sexual abuse, natural disaster, automobile accidents, and so on. The child reexperiences the traumatic event in nightmares and flashbacks or may engage in repetitive play regarding the event. Intense psychological distress, physiological responses, or both when the child is exposed to an event resembling or symbolizing the traumatic event is common. Increased arousal and symptoms of severe anxiety are characteristic, as are avoidance of reminders and emotional numbing.

In order to diagnose PTSD, symptoms must last for at least 1 month and cause significant distress or impairment in important areas of functioning (e.g., school and social interactions). PTSD may occur immediately following a traumatic event or after a delay. Children who have been exposed to trauma, regardless of when they manifest the problems, are at risk for the development of serious psychological problems, including dissociative symptoms and identity disorder, depression, drug abuse, conduct disorder, anxiety disorders, and personality disorders (e.g., Borderline Personality Disorder).

Children with PTSD may be eligible for special education services under the classification of Emotional Disturbance. Support by the school psychologist may be necessary to help the child cope with and reduce anxiety as well as memory and cognitive problems caused by anxiety secondary to stimulation of traumatic memories. In some cases, hospitalization may be needed.

Children who are exposed to one traumatic event that does not involve abuse are less likely to suffer long-term psychological symptoms. However, when a child is exposed to repeated, abusive, or multiple traumas, psychological symptoms are likely to persist into adulthood.

PRADER-WILLI SYNDROME

Prader-Willi syndrome is a multisystem disorder characterized by neonatal hypotonia, onset of obesity in later childhood, hyperphagia, small hands and feet, short stature, and mental retardation. Although it arises from a genetic defect, it is not inherited and is instead a rare birth defect. It is caused by the partial deletion of the paternal Chromosome 15 in 70% of patients or by the inheritance of two copies from one parent (usually termed maternal disomy) in the remaining patients. The exact gene that causes Prader-Willi syndrome has not been discovered.

Prader-Willi syndrome is a rare birth defect that occurs in about 1 in 15,000 births. It affects both genders and all races. However, there is a paucity of cases reported among African Americans.

Obesity and related problems (which can lead to death) are treated through strict monitoring of food intake and regular exercise. Medication such as selective serotonin reuptake inhibitors have been found to improve behavioral problems. Psychotropic medication has also been found to be helpful in treating psychological problems.

Patients with Prader-Willi syndrome are infertile. Hormones can be used to treat sexual development; however, side effects such as increased weight gain and exacerbated oppositional behavior may occur, and treatment should be monitored on an individual basis.

If possible, children with Prader-Willi syndrome should be incorporated into the normal classroom. Food may be used cautiously as a reinforcer for good behavior and learning. It is important to provide clear and consistent messages as well as structure to control temper tantrums as well as eating habits. Children with Prader-Willi may require occupational therapists, speech pathologists, orthopedic surgeons, dietitians, and exercise therapists, in addition to other pediatric medical professionals. Special education services may be available to children with Prader-Willi syndrome under the handicapping condition of Other Health Impaired, Speech Impaired, or Mental Retardation. There is no known cure for Prader-Willi syndrome. With weight control, life expectancy can be normal.

PROGEROID SYNDROMES (PROGERIA)

Progeria is a rare genetic disorder characterized by an appearance of accelerated aging. Its name is derived from the Greek, meaning *prematurely old.* The classic type is the Hutchinson-Gilford Progeria syndrome, which was first described in England in 1886 by Dr. Jonathan Hutchinson and again in 1886 and 1904 by Dr. Hastings Gilford. Some progeroid syndromes manifest symptoms of premature aging at birth, such as Bamatter-Francescetti syndrome, Berardinelli-Seip syndrome, De Barsy syndrome, Hallerman-Streiff syndrome, Von Lohuizen syndrome, and Wiedemann-Rautenstrauch syndrome. Others become clinically apparent later in life, such as Cockayne syndrome, Hutchinson-Gilford progeria syndrome, and Werner syndrome. Progeroid syndromes occur in about 1 per 4 million births. They affect both sexes in equal proportion and have been observed in all races.

There is no specific treatment or cure for progeria. However, there are progeria support groups, as well as a foundation devoted to progeria research accessible via the Internet, which may be useful to children and their families, both in monitoring medical developments and in increasing social support.

Although children with progeria have normal intellectual functioning, their medical condition may present challenges in an educational context. Frequent medical attention may be needed by children with progeria, resulting in loss of school time. Moreover, their unusual appearance may be a source of unwanted attention from others who are not familiar with the disorder. This attention sometimes takes the form of stares, teasing, or intrusive questions. A sense of isolation has also been reported among individuals with progeria and their families, due to the extreme rareness of the illness. If these issues are addressed, however, there is no reason that children with progeria cannot function in a mainstream educational context.

RETINOPATHY OF PREMATURITY

Retinopathy of prematurity (ROP) is the most common cause of retinal damage in infancy. Incidence has recently been stable, but prevalence is increasing because of the increased survival of infants with very low birth weight—about 67% of infants who weigh less than 3 pounds (1,251 g) and about 80% of infants who weigh less than 2.2 pounds (1,000 g) at birth will manifest some degree of ROP. Exposure to excessive or prolonged oxygen is the major risk for ROP, but presence of other medical complications also increases risk. Unfortunately, threshold safe levels or durations of oxygen are not known.

Development of the inner retinal blood vessels occurs across the second half of pregnancy. Thus, their growth is incomplete in premature infants. If they continue growth abnormally, ROP results. Incidence and severity of ROP vary with the proportion of retina that is avascular at birth.

Vision loss ranges from myopia (correctible with glasses) to strabismus, glaucoma, and blindness. Children with moderate, healed ROP but who have cicatrices (dragged retina or retinal folds) have increased risk for retinal detachments later in life.

RETT SYNDROME

Rett syndrome (RS) is a pervasive neurodevelopmental disorder that affects almost solely females. It is marked by a period of apparently normal development for 6 to 18 months, followed by rapid physical and mental deterioration. The discovery in 1999 of the X-linked methyl-CpG-binding protein 2 gene (MeCP2) mutation confirmed RS's long-inferred genetic basis.

No cure or effective treatment for RS is available, although some symptoms can be managed. Treatment is specific to the individual and the severity of symptoms at any particular time. A multidisciplinary approach is necessary, typically beginning with treatment from a neurologist, developmental pediatrician, or both. Lifelong physical, occupational, and speech therapy are often necessary, as are academic, social, vocational, and supportive services. Each symptom needs a specific treatment for alleviation, such as medication for seizures and agitation and braces, surgery, and physical therapy for scoliosis.

Patients with RS may benefit from special education. A thorough communication evaluation is crucial in guiding special education efforts. Exposure to enriching environments and situations that are strongly motivating and allowing adequate time for processing and responding can be helpful. Alternative communication techniques (e.g., augmentative communication) should be employed specifically to individual strengths and weaknesses.

A child diagnosed with RS will live well into her 40s, but quality of life is at best severely compromised. Some functioning may show brief spontaneous recovery, but prognosis is poor and the progressive course of the disorder is currently irreversible. Affected girls will require lifelong close care and supervision, placing a heavy burden on their caretakers. Families may benefit from early and maintained counseling.

RUSSELL-SILVER SYNDROME

Russell-Silver syndrome is a rare disorder characterized by retarded growth, asymmetry of the body and face, and a triangular face. There is no known etiology for this disorder; most cases occur from sporadic gene changes. This very rare genetic disorder has a wide variation of characteristics.

Shoe lifts, limb-lengthening surgery, and corrective surgery are methods used to correct asymmetry and other physical abnormalities.

Children with Russell-Silver syndrome may qualify for special education services for physical therapy for the physical disabilities associated with asymmetry and growth retardation. Speech therapy may be needed for speech difficulties due to a hypoplastic mandible. The developmental delays can result in learning disabilities that merit special education services as well. Low self-esteem and emotional problems may arise with appearance, requiring psychological assessment and services. Prognosis for Russell-Silver syndrome is good because most of the characteristics minimize with time.

SCHMIDT SYNDROME

Schmidt syndrome is an endocrine disorder that is diagnosed when there are several different malfunctions in the endocrine glands, which are responsible for the production of hormones. Hypothyroidism and Addison's disease are the main characteristics of Schmidt syndrome, although problems with the functioning of other endocrine glands such as the gonads, parathyroids, and pancreas, insulin-dependant diabetes, and autoimmune disorders are common in those with Schmidt syndrome.

Addison's disease specifically refers to the malfunction of the adrenal glands and in most cases a diminished amount of cortisol in the body. This deficiency in turn leads to weakness, fatigue, low blood pressure, and weight loss.

Children with Schmidt syndrome are at risk for several different health problems. Addison's disease will cause children to be especially weak and fatigued, and they may not have the energy to attend a full day of school or to keep up with peers at play. Hypothyroidism may lead to problems with weight gain and may make the child susceptible to teasing. Diabetes must be monitored closely—including while the child is in school—and proper instructions for care must be available at all times. Other glandular failure may cause a decrease in the production of various hormones, which may lead to delayed development and other associated health risks, depending on the particular hormones that are lacking. Finally, autoimmune disorders make the child more susceptible to catching colds and more serious diseases from his or her peers.

SEIZURES, ABSENCE

An absence seizure, formerly known as a petit mal, is defined as a sudden, involuntary, transient alteration in cerebral function due to abnormal discharge of neurons in the central nervous system (CNS). Absence seizures fall into the category of generalized seizures, of which there are two types: primary and secondary. Primary generalized seizures are characterized by synchronous bilateral epileptic discharges. The first sign of seizure appears simultaneously in both hemispheres. A secondary generalized seizure is one that begins in one hemisphere and then spreads throughout the brain. In some cases, generalized tonic-clonic seizures develop; in fact, approximately 50% of children with absence seizures have at least one generalized tonic-clonic seizure during their lifetimes.

Antiepileptic drug therapy is the recommended treatment for absence seizures—in particular, valproate, clonazepam, and ethosuximide. With antiepileptic drug treatment, prognosis for absence seizures is highly favorable, with complete remission in 70 to 80% of cases. Although prognosis for absence seizures is good, many children who have this type of seizure will need to be seen for psychological assessments to determine service needs.

Special education services are not necessarily indicated. Regular classroom accommodations and disability services, however, may be needed to ensure that the child has access to the educational environment (e.g., tutoring by a peer or classroom aide to catch up on work that was missed and allowance for extra time to complete assignments). When special education services are needed, they are likely to be provided for associated conditions rather than for the absence seizure itself (e.g., genetic syndromes and CNS insults causing seizure activity). Educators still need to be aware that untreated recurrent seizures put children at risk for cognitive impairments and psychological disturbance. Depression, anxiety, and behavior problems are not that uncommon. These problems may be explained in part by the fact that the child is the recipient of negative reactions from peers as well as from teachers who mistake the seizure for daydreaming or inattention. Educating school staff and peers may be as critical as any other treatment—that is, aside from medication therapy.

SEIZURES, ATONIC

Atonic seizures are also referred to as drop attacks and epileptic fall. Hughlings Jackson first described "sudden epileptic falls" in 1886. Unlike most epileptic seizures that involve either positive motor behavior (e.g., tonic, clonic, and myoclonic) or the absence of motor behavior (e.g., absence seizures), atonic seizures involve negative motor phenomena. The primary characteristic of an atonic seizure is a sudden loss of muscle tone that lasts 1 to 2 s. In a small number of cases, myoclonic jerks precede the loss of muscle tone; however, in most cases there is no warning (or aura). As a result, falls and injuries are common. The seizure is accompanied by a brief period of unconsciousness lasting 300 ms to 3 s and has an electroencephalogram (EEG) pattern of bilateral synchronous polyspike wave and spike wave. The atonic seizure typically occurs shortly after awakening and continues throughout the day.

Children who have atonic seizures with associated conditions such as Lennox-Gaustaut syndrome (LGS) will likely receive special education services in the schools (e.g., self-contained classrooms for students with intellectual disabilities). For children without LGS or other similar syndromes (e.g., Doose syndrome), Other Health Impaired services may be needed—in particular, services provided by the school nurse (e.g., medication management and consultation with treating physicians) and therapists (e.g., occupational or physical therapists if falls have resulted in injuries that prevent the child from accessing an education). Given the frequency of atonic seizures (i.e., sometimes 100 or more episodes a day) and the attentional problems that some of these children have, the resource teaching staff may be needed to ensure adequate exposure to learning material and adequate help completing assignments. Tutoring may also help; such tutoring could be provided by peer tutors or by paraprofessionals in the classroom. Children with atonic seizures should also be provided with counseling to help them to develop mechanisms to cope with their condition. The unexpected nature of the seizures and the safety risks seriously limit some of the activities in which these children can engage, including recreational and social activities.

Unfortunately, antiepileptic drugs have not been found to be particularly helpful in treating atonic seizures. Some of the drugs that are effective in treating associated seizures have in fact been shown to exacerbate atonic seizures (e.g., valproate and clonazepam, both of which have been shown to improve myoclonic seizures). Other drugs have also been found to increase falling, including carbamazepine. Felbamate has shown some promise with children who have LGS; however, the drug is indicated more for partial or generalized seizures associated with LGS, not the atonic seizure. Treatment of atonic seizures remains a challenge.

SEIZURES, GENERALIZED TONIC-CLONIC

Generalized tonic-clonic seizures are one of the most common childhood neurological disorders. The seizure involves synchronous bilateral electrical epileptical discharges; therefore, the first signs reflect involvement of both hemispheres of the brain. The seizure, however, can begin in a focal area of the brain (or one hemisphere) as a partial seizure and spread to other areas and become a generalized seizure. Seizures are defined as a sudden, involuntary, transient alteration in neurological function resulting from excessive electrical discharge of neurons. Generalized tonic-clonic seizures, formerly known as grand mal seizures, are the most common and dramatic of childhood seizure manifestations.

Characteristic features include loss of consciousness followed by repetitive rapid (but rhythmic) jerking of the limbs. These movements are followed by slower irregular movements, eyes rolling back, rapid breathing causing saliva to froth, and sometimes incontinence (urinary and bowel). Following the seizure is a postictal sleep phase in which the individual is difficult to awaken. These seizures are often considered to be idiopathic; however, fever, central nervous system infections, and genetic transmission are possible causes.

Anticonvulsant drug therapy is the recommended form of treatment for children with generalized tonic-clonic seizures. Drugs used for tonic-clonic seizures include phenobarbital, phenytoin, carbamazepine, and primidone, to name a few. Treatment of generalized seizures with partial onset is the same as that for primary generalized seizures. If the child does not respond to antiepileptic drug therapy, however, surgery may be used to remove damaged tissue.

Depression and anxiety as well as behavior problems are common among children with tonic-clonic seizures. These children are subject to peer rejection and teasing, and some even receive negative reactions from adults. These situations serve only to exacerbate the problems these children have adjusting to their seizure condition and functioning in daily life (e.g., academically and socially). School nurses can help to educate peers and teachers alike about seizures. The child may also need this information, as well as information as to how to best handle others' reactions. In some cases, it will be necessary to provide psychological therapy for the child. Such therapy may include supportive insight-oriented treatments, as well as assertiveness training and social skills tips. Including parents is critical, not only to keep them and the child's physician informed about the response to treatment, but also to ensure ample social opportunities outside of school and adequate assistance with homework. Special education services are probably not needed; however, in some cases services for students with other health impairments will be necessary to ensure adequate learning. Section 504 plans are likely to suffice in providing adequate accommodations in the classroom, including reduced workload and peer tutoring to help the child catch up on material missed (e.g., school absences or postictal sleep).

SEIZURES, MYOCLONIC

Myoclonic seizures, formerly called minor motor seizures, are characterized by brief, involuntary muscle contractions and may affect one or many muscles bilaterally, although not necessarily symmetrically. A hand may suddenly fling out, a shoulder may shrug, a foot may kick, or the entire body may jerk. It can occur as a single event or as a series of jerks. The abrupt jerking may affect the legs, causing the child to fall, or it may cause the child to drop or spill what he or she is holding. Myoclonic seizures should not be confused with tics, tremors, chorea, or startle responses. Tics can usually be suppressed—at least temporarily—by an effort of will, whereas myoclonus cannot; and myoclonus does not have the characteristic continuous flow of movements as in chorea or the smooth to-and-from movements of tremors.

Special education services or classroom accommodations may be needed for children whose seizures are concomitant with CNS disorders or whose cognitive functioning has been diminished as a result of the seizures (e.g., severe myoclonic epilepsy). Educators need to be aware that untreated seizures put children at risk for cognitive impairments and psychosocial or psychological maladjustment. Social isolation and poor peer relationships are particularly problematic for school-aged children and adolescents with epilepsy. Depression and anxiety as well as behavior problems are common.

SEIZURES, PARTIAL

Partial seizures, like all other seizures, result from excessive synchronous discharge of neuronal activity. Among children with epilepsy, 40% have partial seizures, which include temporal lobe seizures and seizures that have specific focuses of abnormal electrical discharge (e.g., focal motor seizures).

The etiology of partial seizures varies, but they are often associated with an underlying disease or trauma. Possible causes include cerebral scars, central nervous system infection (i.e., meningitis), vascular lesions, porencephalic cysts, neoplasms, developmental cerebral anomalies, and traumatic brain injury. Clinical manifestations of a partial seizure vary depending on the focuses of the abnormal electrical activity (e.g., posturing and jerky movements with motor strip focuses), including the degree to which the seizure spreads and affects other areas of the brain. As a result, partial seizures are classified as one of three categories: simple partial, complex partial, and partial seizure with secondary generalization.

Children who have simple partial seizures will not have impairment of consciousness or an aura. The seizure is more likely to manifest as a motor and sensory response. For example, the child may complain of numbness and tingling, have a bad taste sensation, and experience changes in auditory and visual perception (e.g., distortions of sound and seeing objects as being larger or smaller than they actually are). With complex partial seizures, there is an impairment of consciousness as well as an aura that precedes the seizure. This aura can include fear, déjà vu, abdominal pain, and unusual taste or odor. Automatisms, or repeated purposeless activities, often occur after a brief period of staring (e.g., playing with buttons on clothing, facial grimacing, lip smacking, and making irregular hand movements). Mental confusion and lethargy are also common, as is temporary aphasia (or difficulty communicating). In some cases, partial seizures develop into generalized seizures, in which the electrical activity spreads throughout the brain, causing tonic-clonic and myoclonic movements and brief episodes of staring and loss of consciousness (see entries on generalized tonic-clonic, myoclonic, and absence seizures).

Treatment of choice for seizures is drug therapy. Anticonvulsant drugs are used to keep the level of neuronal excitability below seizure threshold. Although it is preferred, single-drug use is often ineffective, resulting in polydrug use. Drug treatment for partial seizures includes carbamazepine, phenytoin, and primidone, to name a few. Felbamate is also used for children who have partial seizures associated with Lennox-Gaustaut syndrome.

Many of the medications used to prevent seizures can negatively affect learning. Phenobarbital, for example, depresses psychomotor speed and diminishes cognitive speed in memory tasks. Often children treated with this drug develop hyperactivity, motor slowing, and impairment in memory, concentration, and cognitive processing. As a result of negative side effects of antiepileptic medications, some have tried alternative treatments such as the ketogenic diet.

Many children with seizures are absent from school several days a year, thereby missing instructional opportunities and time to complete assignments. It is difficult for these children to compete with unaffected peers. Given the long-term risk of learning problems, special education services may be needed to help the child with seizures learn the expected amount of information. Services for this population are often provided under the category of Other Health Impaired; however, depending on the specific deficits, services may be more appropriately provided under Specific Learning Disabilities or Emotional Disturbance. Regardless of category, children with partial seizures need to be closely followed to ensure that adequate assistance is provided. School nursing and psychological services will be important to monitor progress and identify areas where services are needed (e.g., speech and language and occupational therapy). Counseling may also be important to help the child cope with this medical problem and deal with the frustration that is often experienced. Working with families, especially educating parents and siblings, will also be important and may be an important area on which school psychologists can focus their attention.

SICKLE CELL DISEASE

Sickle cell disease is a chronic hemolytic anemia occurring almost exclusively in those of African American descent, characterized by sickle-shaped red blood cells

(RBCs) due to homozygous inheritance of hemoglobin S (HbS). In HbS, valine is substituted for glutamic acid in the sixth amino acid of the b-chain. Due to this molecular change, this form of hemoglobin is less soluble and can form rodlike tactoids that cause red blood cells to sickle at sites of low oxygen pressure. Distorted, inflexible RBCs plug small arterioles and capillaries, which leads to occlusion and infarction. Because sickled RBCs are too fragile to withstand the mechanical trauma of circulation, hemolysis occurs after they enter the circulation.

Due to the increased risk and prevalence of clinical and silent strokes in this population, many children with sickle cell disease manifest a number of neurological and cognitive deficits that may make them eligible for special education services. Children with clinically evident strokes are generally more impaired, with the potential of having motoric as well as cognitive sequelae. Those children with silent strokes (those not clinically evident on neurological exam) have also been shown to perform more poorly than children with sickle cell disease who have not had any CNS pathology.

A number of prophylactic and symptomatic interventions have decreased the morbidity of this disorder. The life span of homozygous sickle cell patients has steadily increased to over 40 years of age.

SOTOS SYNDROME (CEREBRAL GIGANTISM)

Sotos syndrome is characterized by prenatal onset of excessive size that persists through at least the first 4 years of life with macrocrania, a high forehead (dolichocephalic), hypertelorism, prominent jaw, premature eruption of teeth, and a narrow palate with prominent, lateral palatine ridges.

Treatment of Sotos syndrome is entirely symptomatic, and in addition to the previous characteristics, there are more than 40 other occasional abnormalities that occur on an occasional basis in Sotos syndrome. These may require special treatment consideration and may include various seizure disorders, complete to partial callosal agenesis, hypoplasia of the septum pellucidum, septum interpositum, and the cerebellar vermin, glucose dysregulation, increased incidence of at least nine cancers, and multiple orthopedic abnormalities.

Special education placement will approach 100% in cases of Sotos syndrome, but learning and academic skills vary greatly. Individual psychoeducational testing and revisions of educational plans should both occur at least annually between the ages of 4 years and 1 year postpuberty. Qualification for special education services is most often as multiply handicapped due to health problems, behavioral problems, and speech and language delays that are often accompanied by mental retardation. (However, as many as 10% of these children may have IQs within the normal range.) Occupational therapy services are often required due to coordination deficits.

Behavior problems evident in Sotos syndrome include very poor overall social adjustment, increased aggressiveness, temper tantrums, and related difficulties with the self-regulatory systems of the brain producing attention, concentration, and impulse control problems. Social adjustment and emotional problems characterized as emotional immaturity persist into adulthood. Prognosis is poor, and some form of supervised living throughout the individual's life along with chronic management via psychopharmacotherapy occurs in nearly all cases. Future research is focusing on etiology and prevention of this serious and pervasive disorder.

SPASTICITY

Spasticity, a type of muscle hyperactivity, is a disorder associated with a lesion of the central nervous system. Most commonly the lesion is in the sensorimotor area of the cerebral cortex or associated pathways. Spasticity is a diagnostic sign of an upper motor neuron syndrome such as cerebral palsy. It is defined as a velocity-dependent increase in muscle tone (hypertonia) with hyperactive deep tendon reflexes (DTRs). Clinically, spasticity is manifested by an increase in resistance to passive movement (i.e., muscle stiffness). Conversely, the presence of spasticity may impair voluntary motor control, thereby impacting specific functions such as gait, upper extremity tasks such as reaching, and self-help skills. Spasticity may be rated as mild, moderate, or severe. Prolonged spasticity may lead to muscle and joint contractures, bone deformities, and muscle atrophy.

SPINA BIFIDA

Spina bifida is a neural tube defect that results from the spine's failure to close during the first month of pregnancy. This disorder can range from generally asymptomatic (occulta) with a very small spinal opening to a completely open spinal column (rachischisis) with severe neurological damage. The partially exposed spinal cord is susceptible to both infection and direct injury, resulting in loss of function. Spina bifida is the most common neural tube defect, occurring in approximately 0.5 to 1 in 1,000 births in the United States.

The mildest cases may not require medical treatment, but surgery to close any openings in the spinal cord may be performed during infancy (often during the first 24 hr following birth). Early intervention may help to prevent further damage to the spinal cord and limit the risk of infection. When hydrocephalus is present, a shunt is placed to drain excess cerebrospinal fluid (CSF). Physical and occupational therapy are often necessary to improve mobility, flexibility, and adaptive functioning. People with spina bifida may require assistive devices such as crutches, walkers, wheelchairs, and braces.

Special education issues will differ among children depending on the severity of symptoms. These services will be available to children with spina bifida under the handicapping condition of Other Health Impairment or Physical Disability. Children with spina bifida are likely to require assistance to cope with physical limitations. The type of assistance may include occupational therapy, physical therapy, and adapted physical education. Children with spina bifida are at increased risk for learning disabilities, language impairment, and attentional difficulties. About 30% have mild to severe mental retardation.

STUTTERING

Stuttering is a speech fluency disorder characterized by disruption of the normal flow of speech with frequent repetitions or prolongations of speech sounds, syllables, or words, or by an individual's inability to start a word. Other facial tremors or movements may also be present as the individual attempts to speak. Stuttering may be exacerbated by specific situations, such as speaking on the telephone or in front of a group of people. In contrast, speech fluency may improve when singing or speaking aloud. The onset of the disorder may be sudden or gradual.

Stuttering is a disorder distinct from two other speech fluency disorders, cluttering and spasmodic dysphonia. Cluttering is characterized by excessive interruptions of the flow of speech due to disorganized speech planning, talking too fast, or a lack of awareness of what one wants to say. The voice disorder, spasmodic dysphonia, involves interruption of phonation due to overadduction of the vocal folds. Other speech problems, such as cluttering and disordered phonology, may occur with stuttering and should be evaluated. The etiology of stuttering may be genetic, although the specific cause is unknown; nor has a specific gene for stuttering been identified.

There is no formal cure for stuttering, but a variety of treatments are available to improve speech fluency. Evaluation and possible intervention by a speech therapist are suggested for children who stutter for more than 6 months. When stuttering is determined to be developmental in nature, recommendations are often aimed at assisting parents and modifying the environment and interactions relating to communication. Programs have been developed to assist individuals in relearning speaking skills and addressing emotional factors that may arise from the stuttering problem.

Special education services are unlikely to be provided when stuttering is a transient problem. Conversely, for children whose stuttering persists for more than 6 months, an evaluation by a speech-language therapist and consideration of possible treatment may be warranted. Children whose stuttering negatively impacts their educational performance may be eligible to receive special education services under the category of Speech and Language Impairment (SLI). School psychologists sometimes help with relaxation training, social skill development, and self-esteem building. The prognosis for a child who stutters is generally quite good.

TOURETTE SYNDROME

Tourette syndrome (TS) is a neurological disorder that is characterized by motor and vocal tics. The tics are repetitive, rapid, involuntary movements that vary in the age of onset, severity, and complexity but must be present before age 18. The tics often wax and wane over time.

TS needs to be differentiated from other disorders such as Huntington disease, stroke, Lesch-Nyhan syndrome, Wilson's disease, multiple sclerosis, head injury, Syndenham chorea, postviral encephalitis, Obsessive-Compulsive Disorder, Attention-Deficit/Hyperactivity Disorder (ADHD), mental retardation, autism, and effects from medications. There is a complex and controversial relationship between TS and ADHD, with a high rate of comorbidity and a correlation between stimulant use and the onset of tics. It is currently thought that a genetic predisposition to TS may be triggered by some stimulants used to treat ADHD.

There is no known cure for TS. The disorder often improves with age, and the majority of children cope without medication. Neuroleptics such as Haldol are sometimes prescribed to reduce symptoms; however, careful monitoring of side effects is needed. Side effects may include excessive fatigue, weight gain, intellectual dulling, memory problems, and school or social phobia. Phobias would generally appear in the first few weeks of treatment with medication. Secondary problems, including depression, anxiety, and antisocial behaviors may worsen with age and require treatment. Educating families, schools, and fellow students and providing counseling may prevent or reduce the need for medication and the development of secondary problems associated with TS.

Given the variety in the severity of symptoms and comorbid disorders, education programs need to be designed to best meet the individual's needs. Consideration of tic frequency, attention problems, social adjustment, learning disabilities, and other problems related to TS should be addressed. Although there is great variability in TS severity, most children fall into the mild to moderate range of symptoms, and often students with TS function well in regular education settings.

Modifications can include breaking assignments into shorter tasks, numbering sequential tasks, providing models, giving written and verbal directions with visual cues, preferential seating, and reducing distraction in the environment. The student may benefit from assistance with organizational and time management skills. In addition, the teacher and child may locate a designated private place such as a study carrel where a student can go if tics become severe. Promoting understanding in the schools regarding the nature of TS also may reduce the social problems associated with TS.

TRAUMATIC BRAIN INJURY

Traumatic brain injury (TBI) refers to any class of mechanical injury to the brain. Approximately 100,000 children and adolescents are hospitalized annually for TBI. It is estimated that an additional 100,000 children sustain TBI annually but either do not seek medical treatment or are treated and released by emergency facilities. TBI is one of the leading causes of hospitalization and mortality throughout childhood and adolescence, with the incidence peaking sharply between the ages of 15 and 24 years. Males are two to four times more likely than females to sustain a head injury, particularly during adolescence.

The typical etiology of head injury and associated pathological findings vary over the course of childhood. Children aged 5 years or younger are most likely to sustain TBI in accidents and falls. Because children's skulls are not fully fused and the physical force in this type of injury is more focal, younger children are more likely to sustain skull fracture and delayed intracranial hematoma than are older children. School-aged children are more likely to be injured in pedestrian-motor vehicle accidents, bicycle accidents, and sports activities. These injuries are most often associated with concussion. Older children and adolescents, aged 10 to 19, most often sustain TBI in motor vehicle accidents.

Neuropsychological assessment is recommended to assist in treatment planning. Speech, occupational, and physical therapies are often necessary early in rehabilitation. Psychotherapy for the child and his or her family is also recommended to assist them in adjusting to the effects of TBI. Specific behavioral therapy may be necessary to help with problems with temper modulation, frustration tolerance, and task persistence. Formal social skills training may also be indicated. Academic accommodations are usually necessary in cases of moderate to severe TBI. Special education programs for these children should include an environment designed to minimize stress, with a low pupil-to-teacher ratio. Academic programs should utilize intensive, repetitive instruction with an emphasis on integrating classroom instruction with real-life situations by including parents and physicians in the academic process.

TRICHOTILLOMANIA

Trichotillomania is an impulse disorder characterized by recurrent pulling of hair. Sufferers can pull hair from any part of the body, including the scalp, eyebrows, eyelashes, and pubic region. However, in children, the most common areas affected are the scalp and eyelash-eyebrow areas.

The cause of trichotillomania is currently unknown. It has been linked to inheritance, diet, hormonal changes, and stress. Trichotillomania is sometimes informally classified in the same family of disorders as Obsessive-Compulsive Disorder, although it is actually classified with compulsive disorders such as compulsive gambling or stealing.

Children diagnosed with trichotillomania will usually require extra assistance in school to alleviate the hair-pulling behaviors. Additionally, these children may experience very low self-esteem and may develop issues with body image and sexuality. Peer education may be needed in classes where a student has trichotillomania, as it can be very visually apparent.

TRISOMY 18

Trisomy 18 is an autosomal dominant chromosome abnormality. There are three types of Trisomy 18. In the full form, every cell in the body has three number 18 chromosomes instead of the normal pair. With the mosaic form, there is a mixture of abnormal cells (three number 18 chromosomes) and normal cells (pairs of number 18 chromosomes). In the third condition (partial form), either the long arm (18q+) or the short arm (18p+) of Chromosome 18 is duplicated.

The special education accommodations and services for Trisomy 18 full form and severe mosaic type are provided under the diagnostic rubric of mental retardation or communication or motor skills disorders. These services will need to be individually tailored. For example, if the child is nonambulatory, all instructional environments including restrooms need to be wheelchair accessible, and educational personnel should be familiar with the student's daily care needs. Educational instruction should be multisensory, and supportive communication devices such as soundboards should be employed where appropriate.

Because children with Trisomy 18 mild mosaic and partial form who possess normal intellectual functioning are at increased risk for learning difficulties, neuropsychological and psychoeducational assessment is important. Careful attention should be paid to the acquisition of early reading and mathematics skills when the child is enrolled in prekindergarten through Grade 2 so that intervention can begin immediately. If the child meets formal criteria, special education services are provided under the learning disability category.

TURNER SYNDROME

Turner syndrome is a noninherited, genetic disorder found in females that is caused by the complete absence (classic karyotype) or abnormal presentation (mosaicism) of the second X chromosome. Turner syndrome can also occur when there is structural abnormality or rearrangement of one or both of the X chromosomes.

Although there is great variability of symptom expression among affected persons, the total absence of the second X chromosome is strongly associated with increased skeletal, cardiac, and renal anomalies. Ongoing medical assessment throughout the life span is essential to monitor and/or provide treatment for 35 possible physical abnormalities. Any number of these difficulties have potential long-term deleterious impact. For example, abnormalities of facial bone structures predispose the development of middle ear infections that can lead to hearing loss and increase the possibility of language delay or disorder. A comprehensive listing of the physical anomalies associated with Turner syndrome and the American Academy of Pediatrics policy guidelines regarding health care for individuals with Turner syndrome are available online at http://www.aap.org.

Treatment for two of the most common symptoms associated with Turner syndrome (short stature and infertility) now includes administration of growth hormone, hormone replacement therapy to facilitate secondary sexual development, and assisted reproduction. Although these treatment regimens provide an increased quality of life, it is also equally important to address issues of self-esteem and relationships with peers through therapy and social skills intervention.

Although not typically identified as a central feature of Turner syndrome, parent and teacher behavioral checklists often reveal problems with hyperactivity and impulsivity, although children with Turner syndrome evidence wide variability in symptom expression and often meet the criteria for atypical attention disorder. A comprehensive treatment regimen may need to include a medication referral and will need to examine the impact of behavioral difficulties on the child's intellectual and academic progress.

Given the wide range of physical and neurocognitive difficulties that may be associated with Turner syndrome, a comprehensive educational assessment is essential to ensure the timely and appropriate delivery of special education services for these children. Included in a comprehensive psychoeducational battery should be measures of intelligence, achievement, executive functioning, language, attention, memory, visual perception, and personality.

It is important to obtain an in-depth assessment of mathematics functioning because individuals with Turner syndrome on average perform two grade levels below current placement.

Children with Turner syndrome often qualify for special education services under a learning disability category and if significant attentional difficulties are present qualify under the Other Health Impairment category. Speech and language services may also be needed if language difficulties are present. Additionally, counseling as a related service may be needed to address the psychosocial aspects of the disorder. With early and appropriate medical, psychological, and academic intervention, individuals with Turner syndrome can live productive and fulfilling lives.

USHER SYNDROME

Usher syndrome is a rare autosomal-recessive disorder manifested primarily by sensorineural hearing loss and retinitis pigmentosa. Although others described the syndrome earlier, it is named for Charles Usher, a British ophthalmologist who emphasized the role of heredity in the disorder. The degree of hearing loss in most affected individuals is severe to profound. Retinitis pigmentosa causes deterioration of the retina and progressive loss of vision, usually to blindness. Disturbances of balance occur with some types of Usher syndrome. Recent MRI evidence has indicated decreased brain and cerebellum size in a sample of Usher syndrome patients, suggesting a broader impact of the disorder than on the visual, auditory, and vestibular systems alone.

Usher syndrome is actually a group of conditions identified as three major types, distinguished by age of onset and severity of symptoms. A fourth, X-linked type, is hypothesized. Although clinical symptoms present as three main types, gene localization studies have shown that one clinical type may be caused by any of several different genes located on different chromosomes. For example, seven different genes have been found that cause Usher syndrome.

There is no known cure for Usher syndrome. Cochlear implants have shown significant benefits in young children. A special form of vitamin A has been found to delay the progression of retinitis pigmentosa. Treatment of Usher syndrome primarily involves providing education and support services to optimize the functional ability of those affected by the condition. Prompt identification is important to allow initiation of treatment at the earliest opportunity.

Special education services are vital in helping individuals with Usher syndrome to cope with the often severe consequences of losing both vision and hearing. The progressive nature of the condition, coupled with onset in childhood, presents enormous challenges to successful adjustment. Treatment for the individual patient may include instruction in American Sign Language and tactile sign language; orientation and mobility training; Braille education; psychological, genetic, and career counseling; assistive devices; and support groups. Opportunities for children with the disorder to interact with successful adult Usher syndrome patients can be especially helpful.

The prognosis in Usher syndrome is variable depending on type and severity. However, with appropriate intervention, Usher syndrome patients may be able to attend college or receive vocational training and work in a wide variety of occupations. Loss of vision may progress sufficiently slowly that some individuals retain functional vision well into adulthood.

WEAVER SYNDROME

Weaver syndrome is an early overgrowth syndrome of unknown etiology. It is associated with accelerated development of bone and physical growth and is also accompanied by developmental delay, specific craniofacial manifestations, and bony abnormalities. It is also known as Weaver-Smith syndrome and WSS.

At present, there is no known cure for the underlying disorder. Therefore, treatment is symptomatic and supportive (e.g., orthopedic interventions may be used to correct foot deformities, physical therapy may be required to address symptoms such as hypertonia).

A student entering school with a diagnosis of Weaver syndrome will probably qualify for special services under the Individuals with Disabilities Education Act, within the other physical disability category. These students are likely to require extensive services, accommodations, and modifications. Physical therapy may be necessary, and transportation may be required. Students with Weaver syndrome may be developmentally delayed and may require accommodations to address this issue. Students may need extended periods of time away from school due to medical issues; therefore, arrangements may need to be made to help the student keep up with schoolwork. Because Weaver syndrome is associated with craniofacial abnormalities and other malformations of the bodily structure, students with this diagnosis may at various times require counseling (e.g., to come to terms with body image and identity).

WERNER SYNDROME

Werner syndrome (WS) is an autosomal recessive genetic disease that resembles premature aging. Although the disorder is not usually diagnosed until the third decade of life, the characteristic short stature and low body weight are present during childhood and adolescence. Individuals with WS display clinical features that are similar to features of progeria. However, WS is characterized by a later age of onset, and many symptoms of WS are not manifested in progeria.

Children with WS have an abnormally slow growth rate and may therefore become the object of teasing by their peers. This problem may lead the child to develop low self-esteem and become angry or lonely. The child's school performance could be negatively affected by these feelings, resulting in low academic achievement. If school personnel suspect that the child has a learning disability, they should consider whether the child's emotional problems better account for his or her low school achievement. Persons diagnosed with WS have a poor prognosis. They will probably experience gradual physical deterioration and early onset of age-related disorders. Although the clinical features of WS resemble premature aging, individuals with WS are not susceptible to some medical conditions, such as Alzheimer's disease and hypertension.

WILLIAMS SYNDROME

Williams syndrome (WS) is characterized by distinctive facial features, cardiovascular disease, a specific cognitive profile, unique personality, cognitive impairments, and developmental delay. Elevated blood calcium levels and connective tissue abnormalities are also common.

Many of these children are diagnosed failure to thrive. Feeding problems are often linked to low muscle tone, severe gag reflex, poor suck-swallow, and tactile defensiveness. Infants with WS often display an extended period of colic or irritability and developmental delays such as walking, talking, and toilet training are common.

Children with WS have similar facial features that become more apparent with age. These children also tend to look more like other WS children than relatives. Some of the common characteristics observed are broad brow, upturned nose, wide mouth, full lips, widely spaced teeth, small chin, puffiness around the eyes, small head, and depressed nasal bridge. Young children usually have full cheeks and small, widely spaced teeth, whereas adults tend to have long faces and necks. Children with blue or green eyes may also have a starlike pattern in the iris.

Children with WS are often described as being overly friendly or excessively social. This behavior may be due in part to the fact that they tend to be unafraid of strangers, despite other anxieties. WS children show a distinct cognitive profile, with strength in auditory rote memory and expressive language and weakness in visual-spatial skill. Approximately 75% of individuals with WS score in the mild mental retardation range but range from severely impaired to low average. Intellectual delays and adaptive problems often affect these individuals' ability to function independently in the community; therefore, most adults live with parents or in group homes.

The management of WS requires a multidisciplinary approach that includes regular medical checkups and developmental as well as psychological evaluations. Consultation with speech and language pathologists and with occupational and physical therapists is often necessary in order to provide the best service possible. Prognosis largely depends on early diagnosis and early treatment. Genetic testing may be helpful, but research is still needed to determine which services are more likely to help a child with WS adapt to the environment. Presently, most children with WS who require special education services are often provided these under the categories of Intellectual Disability, Learning Disability, and Other Health Impaired (OHI). Children who do not require special education are likely to need accommodations in the classroom, given the high rate of learning and social problems. Vocational training is also critical and should be provided as early as possible. Because WS is a lifelong (and complex) condition, counseling should be offered to the child and to his or her family.

WILSON DISEASE

Wilson disease (WD), or hepatolenticular degeneration, is a rare autosomal recessive metabolic disease linked to Chromosome 13. As a result of increased copper accumulation in the liver, brain, and corneal tissue, individuals with Wilson disease often suffer from cirrhosis of the liver, bilateral softening and degeneration of the basal ganglia, and brown pigmented rings in the periphery of the cornea, referred to as Kayser-Fleischer rings.

The disease is most commonly diagnosed in children, but symptoms can be manifested later on. In one third of all cases, the initial symptom is liver disease; however, the other two thirds present first with neurological or psychiatric symptoms. These problems, however, are all a result of accumulated excess copper due to the liver's failure to metabolize and store the copper.

Treatment typically consists of methods to reduce the amount of copper in the liver and other tissues. Although a low-copper diet is recommended, more often than not a copper-chelating agent has to be administered (e.g., D-penicillamine). The chelating agent, however, has been shown to have serious side effects in 20 to 25% of patients (e.g., systemic lupus and a nephrotic syndrome). Trietine is an alternate treatment to D-penicillamine, and it is the drug of choice when neurological symptoms are exhibited. Zinc salt has also been used but only as a supplement. In cases of progressive liver disease such as chronic hepatitis and organ failure, liver transplants may be necessary. Prognosis is generally good after treatment is instituted; however, about 20% of patients who have to have transplants die in the first year following surgery.

Children with Wilson disease may present with academic and behavioral symptoms before the diagnosis is actually made. These children may show a sudden deterioration in schoolwork, uncharacteristic and socially inappropriate behaviors, anxiety, and depression. Memory problems and lack of motor coordination may underlie some of these functional problems. In most cases, if accommodations are even needed, they are short term (e.g., providing the child with a homework manual or memory aide until treatment takes effect). These children should, however, be carefully evaluated by school psychologists and other ancillary staff (e.g., speech and language pathologists and occupational therapists) to determine the presence of persistent cognitive, motor, and behavior problems and to determine the need for services, including special education.

WOLFRAM SYNDROME

Wolfram syndrome is a neurodegenerative disorder of early onset and is often referred to as the acronym DIDMOAD (diabetes insipidus, diabetes mellitus, optic atrophy, and deafness).

The rate of severe mental disorders in patients with Wolfram syndrome is about 25% and most commonly presents as depression, aggression, or organic brain syndrome.

Currently, no cure exists for this neurological degenerative disorder, and treatment revolves around symptom management. The diabetes mellitus is generally treated with insulin.

Students with Wolfram syndrome will qualify for special education services under Section 504 of the Rehabilitation Act of 1973 and under the Individuals with Disabilities Act (IDEA). The individualized educational program planning team may recommend assistive technology devices to aid the student with auditory and visual impairments that interfere with learning. Furthermore, medical support for the treatment of the student's diabetes must be organized. Teachers should be sensitive to the possibility of urinary tract infections, and the school should provide appropriate accommodations. The school district may also need to consider educational supports for any associated cognitive difficulties.

6

State Acronym Lists Related to Special Education Terminology

SHARON HURST AND STEVE AXFORD

The following tables provide listings of special education–related acronyms and corresponding terminology for each of the 50 states representing the United States. The information was compiled by contacting state-level departments of education. These agencies were requested to provide official acronym lists for special education terminology used in their respective states. This project was initiated because of the well-known problem of states' using different terminology and corresponding acronyms related to individual state rules interpreting federal Individuals with Disabilities Education Act (IDEA) law. Of course, the use of different acronyms creates confusion for special education staff when receiving out-of-state individual education plans (IEPs). The tables of acronyms should then serve as a useful reference for clarifying transfer IEP documentation.

The acronym tables include educational disability categories but also other special education lexicon used by the various states. Sometimes this language mirrors federal (i.e., IDEA) or medical and *Diagnostic and Statistical Manual of Mental Disorders,* fourth edition (*DSM-IV*) language (e.g., Attention-Deficit/Hyperactivity Disorder), but often it does not (e.g., significant limited intellectual capacity [SLIC] in Colorado instead of "mental retardation"). In a number of cases, the same acronym has very different meanings for different states. For example, HI represents "hearing impaired" in Florida but "health impaired" in Illinois. The reader will note that the lists vary substantially in length. This raises the issue of the degree

The authors acknowledge the technical assistance of Kelley Maestas, administrative assistant and web site manager, District 49, Colorado Springs, Colorado.

to which the lists are comprehensive. Information provided in the lists is solely dependent upon information offered, generally in written form, by the various state-level departments of education. However, when limited information was provided, states were contacted again, sometimes repeatedly, to verify information. Also, to reiterate, only special education–related acronyms are provided.

ALABAMA

DB = Deaf Blindness
DD = Developmental Delay
ED = Emotional Disturbance
EI = Early Intervention
ESL = English as a second language
ESY = Extended School Year
FACE = Functional Assessment of the Classroom Environment
HI = Hearing Impaired
IEP = Individualized Education Program
LEA = Local Education Agency
LEP = Limited English Proficiency
LRE = Least Restrictive Environment
MD = Multiple Disabilities
MR = Mental Retardation
OHI = Other Health Impairment
OI = Orthopedic Impairment
OT = Occupational Therapy
PLOP = Present Level of Performance
PT = Physical Therapy
SES = Special Education Services
SLD = Specific Learning Disabilities
SLI = Speech Language Impairment
SSR = Student Services Review
TBI = Traumatic Brain Injury
VI = Visual Impairment

ALASKA

ABD = Antisocial Behavior Disorders
AD = Attachment Disorder
ADD = Attention-Deficit Disorder
ADHD = Attention-Deficit/Disorder
AI = Auditorily Impaired
APD = Antisocial Personality Disorder

APD = Auditory Processing Disorder
ASD = Autism Spectrum Disorder
AU = Autistic
AUT = Autism
BD = Behaviorally Disordered
BD = Brain Damaged
BI = Brain Injury
BIP = Behavior Intervention Plan
BMP = Behavior Management Plan
CAPD = Central Auditory Processing Disorders
CHI = Closed Head Injury
DB; DBL = Deaf-Blind
DCD = Development Coordination Disorder
D = Deaf
DD = Developmentally Delayed
EBD = Emotional and Behavioral Disorders
ED = Emotionally Disturbed
EMH = Educable Mentally Handicapped
EMR = Educable Mentally Retarded
FBA = Functional Behavior Assessment
HI = Health Impaired or Hearing Impaired
HOH = Hard of Hearing
IED = Intermittent Explosive Disorder
LD = Learning Disabled
M/ED = Mental or Emotional Disturbance
MH = Multiple Handicapped
MMR = Mild Mental Retardation
MHM = Multihandicapped Mainstream
MHMR = Mental Health Mental Retardation
MR/DD = Mentally Retarded/Developmentally Disabled
MR/MED = Mentally Retarded and Mentally or Emotionally Disturbed (refers to a dual diagnosis)
OH = Orthopedically Handicapped
OHI = Other Health Impairments
PCD = Perceptual Communicative Disability
PDD = Pervasive Development Disorder
PLI = Pragmatic Language Impairment
SPED = Special Education
TBI = Traumatic Brain Injury
TMH = Trainable Mentally Handicapped
TMR = Trainable Mentally Retarded
VI = Visually Impaired

ARIZONA

HI = Hearing Impairment
ID = Intellectual Disability
IEE = Individual Education Evaluation
IEP = Individual Education Program
IFSP = Individual Family Service Plan
LD = Learning Disability
LRBI = Least Restrictive Behavioral Interventions
LRE = Least Restrictive Environment
MD = Multi-Disability
MRDD = Division of Mental Retardation and Developmental Disabilities
OHI = Other Health Impaired
OI = Orthopedic Impairments
OT = Occupational Therapy
SC = Special Class
SED = Seriously Emotionally Disturbed
SH = Severely Handicapped
SID = Severe Intellectual Disability
SIT = Sensory Integration Therapy
SLD = Specific Learning Disability
SLP = Speech and Language Pathologist
SpEd = Special Education
SPED/LEP = Special Education/Limited English Proficiency
TBI = Traumatic Brain Injury
VH = Visually Handicapped

ARKANSAS

AU = Autism
DB = Deaf-Blindness
ED = Serious Emotional Disturbance
HI = Hearing Impaired
MD = Multiple Disabilities
MR = Mental Retardation
OHI = Other Health Impairments
OI = Orthopedic Impairments
PS = Developmental Delay
SI = Speech Language Impairment
SLD = Specific Learning Disabilities
TBI = Traumatic Brain Injury
VI = Visual Impairments

CALIFORNIA

ADD = Attention-Deficit Disorder
EH = Emotionally Handicapped
FEP = Fluent English Proficient
HI = Hearing Impaired
IEP = Individual Education Program
LD = Learning Disabled
LEP = English Learner
PH = Physically Handicapped
VI = Visually Impaired

COLORADO

ADD = Attention-Deficit Disorder
ADHD = Attention-Deficit/Hyperactivity Disorder
APE = Adapted Physical Education
BD = Behavior Disorder
CD = Cognitive Disability
D/HOH = Deaf/Hard of Hearing
DB = Deaf/Blindness
DD = Developmentally Delayed or Developmentally Disabled
ED = Emotional Disability
ESL = English as a Second Language
HI or HD = Hearing Impaired or Hearing Disabled
IEP = Individualized Education Plan
LD = Learning Disabled
LRE = Least Restrictive Environment
MR = Mentally Retarded
OCD = Obsessive-Compulsive Disorder
ODD = Oppositional Defiant Disorder
OT = Occupational Therapy
PCD = Perceptual or Communicative Disability
PD = Physical Disability
PT = Physical Therapy
SIED = Significant Identifiable Emotional Disorder
SL = Speech Language Disability
SLIC = Significant Limited Intellectual Capacity
TBI = Traumatic Brain Injury
VD = Visually Disabled
VI = Visually Impaired

CONNECTICUT

BIP = Behavior Intervention Plan
DD = Developmentally Delayed
FBA = Functional Behavior Assessment
ID = Intellectual Disability
IEP = Individualized Education Program
LD = Specific Learning Disability
LRE = Least Restrictive Environment
No acronyms for the following: Multiple Disability, Autism, Hearing Impairment, Visual Impairment
OHI = Other Health Impairment
PPT = Planning and Placement Team
SED = Serious Emotional Disturbance
SL = Speech Language
TBI = Traumatic Brain Injury

DELAWARE

ADD = Attention-Deficit Disorder
ADHD = Attention-Deficit/Hyperactivity Disorder
CP = Cerebral Palsy
CST = Child Study Team
EMD = Educable Mentally Disabled
IEP = Individual Education Program
LD = Learning Disabled
LRE = Least Restrictive Environment
OT = Occupational Therapy
PI = Physically Impaired
SED = Seriously Emotionally Disturbed
SMD = Severely Mentally Disabled
TBI = Traumatic Brain Injury
TMD = Trainable Mentally Disabled

FLORIDA

ADD = Attention-Deficit Disorder
ADHD = Attention-Deficit/Hyperactivity Disorder
APE = Adapted Physical Education
BD = Behavior Disorders
DB = Deaf/Blind
DD = Developmental Disabilities
DD = Developmentally Delayed

DHH = Deaf or Hard of Hearing
EBD = Emotional/Behavioral Disability
EH = Emotionally Handicapped
EMH = Educable Mentally Handicapped
HI = Hearing Impaired
LD = Learning Disabilities
LI = Language Impaired
OHI = Other Health Impaired
OI = Orthopedically Impaired
PI = Physically Impaired
PMH = Profoundly Mentally Handicapped
SED = Severely Emotionally Disturbed
SI = Speech Impaired
SLD = Specific Learning Disabled
TBI = Traumatic Brain Injured
TMH = Trainable Mentally Handicapped
VI = Visually Impaired

GEORGIA

ADD = Attention-Deficit Disorder
ADHD = Attention-Deficit/Hyperactivity Disorder
DHH = Deaf and Hard of Hearing
EBD = Emotional and Behavioral Disorder
LD = Learning Disability
MID = Mild Intelligence Disorder
MOID = Moderate Intelligence Disorder
OHI = Other Health Impaired
OI = Orthopedically Handicapped
PID = Profound Intellectual Disability
SDD = Significant Developmental Delay
SED = Severely Emotionally Disturbed
SLD = Specific Learning Disabilities
TBI = Traumatic Brain Injury
VI = Visual Impairment

HAWAII

ADD = Attention-Deficit Disorder
ADHD = Attention-Deficit/Hyperactivity Disorder
BL = Blind
DBL = Deaf-Blind

DF = Deaf
EBS = Effective Behavioral Support
EH = Emotionally Handicapped
FSC = Fully Self-Contained
HI = Hearing Impaired
ISC = Integrated Self-Contained
LI = Learning Impaired (preschool)
MIMR = Mild Mentally Retarded
MOMR = Moderate Mentally Retarded
MR = Mental Retardation
OH = Orthopedically Handicapped
OHI = Other Health Impaired
OHIA = Other Health-Impaired Autism
PMR = Profoundly Mentally Retarded
PS = Partially Sighted
SED = Severe Emotional Disability
SI = Speech Impaired
SLD = Specific Learning Disability
SLI = Speech Language Impaired
SMH = Severe Multiple Handicapped
SMR = Severely Mentally Retarded
VI = Visually Impaired

IDAHO

ADD = Attention-Deficit Disorder
ADHD = Attention-Deficit/Hyperactivity Disorder
AU = Autism
BIP = Behavior Intervention Plan
CI = Cognitive Impairment
DB = Deaf Blind
DD = Developmental Delay
ED = Emotional Disturbance
HI = Health Impairment
LD = Learning Disability
LI = Language Impairment
MD = Multiple Disabilities
OI = Orthopedic Impairment
SI = Speech Impairment
TBI = Traumatic Brain Injury
VI = Visual Impairment

ILLINOIS

ADD = Attention-Deficit Disorder
ADHD = Attention-Deficit/Hyperactivity Disorder
BD = Behavior Disorders
BIP = Behavior Intervention Plan
DB = Deaf Blindness
ED = Emotional Disturbance
HI = Health Impairment
LD = Learning Disabled
MD = Multiple Disabilities
MR = Mentally Retarded
OHI = Other Health Impaired
OI = Orthopedic Impairment
OT = Occupational Therapy
PH = Physically Handicapped
SPL = Speech Language
TBI = Traumatic Brain Injury
VI = Visual Impairment

INDIANA

ED = Emotional Disability
AUT = Autism Spectrum Disorder
CD = Communication Disorder
DB = Deaf-Blind
DD = Developmental Delay (early childhood)
HI = Hearing Impairment
LD = Learning Disability
MD = Mental Disability
MD = Multiple Disabilities
OHI = Other Health Impairment
OI = Orthopedic Impairment
TBI = Traumatic Brain Injury
VI = Visual Impairment

IOWA

ADD = Attention-Deficit Disorder
ADHD = Attention-Deficit/Hyperactivity Disorder
CC = Self-Contained Class
D/B = Deaf/Blind

DD = Developmentally Delayed
DD = Developmentally Disabled
DD/MR = Developmental Disabilities/Mental Retardation
ED = Emotional Disorder or Emotionally Disturbed
EMH = Educable Mentally Handicapped
EMR = Educable Mental Retardation
HI = Hearing Impaired
LD = Learning Disability or Learning Disabled
MD = Mental Disability or Mentally Disabled
MR = Mental Retardation
PD = Physically Disabled
S/L = Speech/Language Impaired
SCI = Self-Contained Class with Little Integration
SED = Severely Emotionally Disturbed
SLD = Specific Learning Disability
TBI = Traumatic Brain Injured
TMH = Trainable Mentally Handicapped
TMR = Trainable Mentally Retarded
VI = Visually Impaired

KANSAS

ADD = Attention-Deficit Disorder
ADHD = Attention-Deficit/Hyperactivity Disorder
AUT = Autism
BD = Behavior Disorder
BIP = Behavior Intervention Plan
CD = Cognitive Delay
D/B = Deaf and Blindness
DD = Developmentally Delayed
ED = Emotional Disturbance
HI = Hearing Impaired or Hearing Impairment
LD = Learning Disability or Learning Disabled
SLD = Specific Learning Disability
MD = Multiple Disabilities
MR = Mental Retardation
OHI = Other Health Impairment
OI = Orthopedic Impairment
PDD = Pervasive Development Disorder
S/L = Speech/Language
SED = Social and Emotional Disorder
SMD = Severe Multiple Disabilities
SP = Speech or Language Impairment

TBI = Traumatic Brain Injury
VI = Visual Impairment
YCDD = Young Child with a Developmental Delay

KENTUCKY

ADD = Attention-Deficit Disorder
ADHD = Attention-Deficit/Hyperactivity Disorder
AUT = Autism
D/B = Deaf/Blind
DD = Developmental Disability
EBD = Emotional Behavior Disability
FMD = Functional Mental Disability
HH = Home/Hospital Instruction
LD = Learning Disability
MD = Multiple Disabilities
MMD = Mild Mental Disability
OHI = Other Health Impaired
OI = Orthopedic Impairment
PD = Physically Disabled
S/L = Speech Language
SED = Seriously Emotionally Disturbed
SLD = Specific Learning Disability
TBI = Traumatic Brain Injury
VI = Visually Impaired

LOUISIANA

AUT = Autism
D/B = Deaf/Blind
DD = Developmental Delay
ED = Emotional Disturbance
HI = Hearing Impairment
LRE = Least Restrictive Environment
MD = Multiple Disabilities
MR = Mental Retardation
OHI = Other Health Impairment
OI = Orthopedic Impairment
SLD = Specific Learning Disability
SLI = Speech Language Impairment
TBI = Traumatic Brain Injury
VI = Visual Impairment
per IDEA Acronyms

MAINE

AUT = Autism
D/B = Deaf/Blind
DD = Developmental Delay
ED = Emotional Disturbance
HI = Hearing Impairment
LRE = Least Restrictive Environment
MD = Multiple Disabilities
MR = Mental Retardation
OHI = Other Health Impairment
OI = Orthopedic Impairment
SLD = Specific Learning Disability
SLI = Speech Language Impairment
TBI = Traumatic Brain Injury
VI = Visual Impairment
per IDEA Acronyms

MARYLAND

AUT = Autism
D = Deaf
DB = Deaf/Blind
DD = Developmentally Delayed (ages 3–5)
ED = Emotionally Disturbed
HI = Hearing Impaired
MD = Multiple Disability
MR = Mental Retardation
OHI = Other Health Impairment
OI = Orthopedically Impaired
S/L = Speech/Language
SLD = Specific Learning Disability
TBI = Traumatic Brain Injury
VI = Visually Impaired

MASSACHUSETTS

ABD = Antisocial Behavior Disorders
AD = Attachment Disorder
ADD = Attention-Deficit Disorder
ADHD = Attention-Deficit/Hyperactivity Disorder
AI = Auditorily Impaired
APD = Antisocial Personality Disorder

APD = Auditory Processing Disorder
ASD = Autism Spectrum Disorder
AU = Autistic
AUT = Autism
BD = Behaviorally Disordered
BD = Brain Damaged
BI = Brain Injury
BIP = Behavior Intervention Plan
BMP = Behavior Management Plan
CAPD = Central Auditory Processing Disorders
CHI = Closed Head Injury
D = Deaf
DB; DBL = Deaf-Blind
DCD = Development Coordination Disorder
DD = Developmentally Delayed
EBD = Emotional and Behavioral Disorders
ED = Emotionally Disturbed
EMH = Educable Mentally Handicapped
EMR = Educable Mentally Retarded
FBA = Functional Behavior Assessment
HI = Health Impaired or Hearing Impaired
HOH = Hard of Hearing
IED = Intermittent Explosive Disorder
LD = Learning Disabled
M/ED = Mental or Emotional Disturbance
MH = Multiple Handicapped
MHM = Multihandicapped Mainstream
MHMR = Mental Health Mental Retardation
MMR = Mild Mental Retardation
MR/DD = Mentally Retarded/Developmentally Disabled
MR/MED = Mentally Retarded and Mentally or Emotionally Disturbed (refers to a dual diagnosis)
OH = Orthopedically Handicapped
OHI = Other Health Impairments
PCD = Perceptual Communicative Disability
PDD = Pervasive Development Disorder
PDD-NOS = Pervasive Development Disorder—not otherwise specified
PLI = Pragmatic Language Impairment
SPED = Special Education
TBI = Traumatic Brain Injury
TMH = Trainable Mentally Handicapped
TMR = Trainable Mentally Retarded
VI = Visually Impaired

MICHIGAN

AI = Autistic Impaired
EI = Emotionally Impaired
H/H = Homebound/Hospitalized
HI = Hearing Impaired
IEP = Individualized Education Plan
LD = Learning Disabled
POHI = Physically or Otherwise Health Impaired
SLI = Severely Language Impaired
SXI = Severely Multiple Impaired
VI = Visually Impaired

MINNESOTA

ADD = Attention-Deficit Disorder
ADHD = Attention-Deficit/Hyperactivity Disorder
ASD = Autism Spectrum Disorder
AUT = Autism
BIP = Behavior Intervention Plan
BVI = Blind/Visually Impaired
CD = Cognitive Disability
DB = Deaf-Blind
DCD = Developmental Cognitive Disabilities
DD = Developmental Disabilities
DHH = Deaf/hard of hearing
EBD = Emotional and Behavior Disorders
ED = Emotional Disturbance
FBA = Functional Behavior Assessment
HI = Health Impaired or Hearing Impaired
LD = Learning disabled
MMR = Mild Mental Retardation
MSMI = Moderate to Severe Mental Impairment
OCD = Obsessive-Compulsive Disorder
OHI = Other Health Impairments
OT = Occupational Therapy
PD = Physical Disability
PT = Physical Therapy
SDD = Significant Developmental Delay
SED = Seriously Emotionally Disturbed
SPED = Special Education
TBI = Traumatic Brain Injury
VI = Visually Impaired

MISSISSIPPI

ADD = Attention-Deficit Disorder
ADHD = Attention-Deficit/Hyperactivity Disorder
APE = Adaptive Physical Education
AU = Autistic
AUT = Autism
BD = Behavior Disorder
BIP = Behavior Intervention Plan
DB/DBL = Deaf/Blind
DD = Developmentally Delayed
ED = Educational Disability
EHA = Education of the Handicapped
EMR = Educable Mentally Retarded
FBA = Functional Behavioral Assessment
HI = Hearing Impaired
IEE = Independent Education Evaluation
IEP = Individualized Education Program
L/S = Language/Speech
LD = Learning Disability
MH = Multiple Handicapped
MR = Mentally Retarded
OCD = Obsessive-Compulsive Disorder
ODD = Oppositional Defiance Disorder
OHI = Other Health Impairments
OT = Occupational Therapy
PT = Physical Therapy
SLD = Specific Learning Disability
SLI = Speech and Language Impaired
TBI = Traumatic Brain Injury
TBR = Trainable Mentally Retarded
VI = Visually Impaired

MISSOURI

AU = Autism
DB = Deaf-Blindness
ED = Emotional Disturbance
HI = Hearing Impairment
IEP = Individualized Education Program
LD = Specific Learning Disability
MD = Multiple Disabilities
MR = Mental Retardation

OHI = Other Health Impairments
OI = Orthopedic Impairment
SP = Speech or Language Impaired
TBI = Traumatic Brain Injury
VI = Visual Impairment
YCDD = Young Child with a Developmental Delay

MONTANA

AU = Autism
CD = Cognitive Delay (term used instead of "mental retardation")
CW = Child With A Disability (ages 3–5, inclusive)
DB = Deaf-Blindness
DE = Deafness
ED = Emotional Disturbance
HI = Hearing Impairment
LD = Learning Disabled
OH = Other Health Impairment
OI = Orthopedic Impairment
SL = Speech-Language Impairment
TB = Traumatic Brain Injury
VI = Vision Impairment

NEBRASKA

ADD = Attention-Deficit Disorder
ADHD = Attention-Deficit/Hyperactivity Disorder
BD = Behavior Disorder
DD = Developmental Delay or Developmental Disabilities
ED/BD = Emotionally Disturbed/Behavior Disordered
HI = Hearing Impairment
IEP = Individual Education Plan
LD = Learning Disability
MH = Mental Handicap
MR = Mental Retardation
OHI = Other Health Impairments
OI = Orthopedic Impairments
OT = Occupational Therapy
PT = Physical Therapy
SLD = Specific Learning Disabilities
SLI = Speech Language Impairment
TBI = Traumatic Brain Injury
VI = Visual Impairment

NEVADA

AH = Hearing Impaired
AU = Autism
DB = Deaf-Blind
DD = Developmentally Delayed
EH = Emotional Disturbance
HI = Health Impairment
LD = Learning Disabled
ME = Mentally Retarded
MU = Multiple Impaired
OI = Orthopedically Impaired
SLI = Speech/Language Impaired
TB = Traumatic Brain Injured
VH = Visually Impaired

NEW HAMPSHIRE

ADD = Attention-Deficit Disorder
ADHD = Attention-Deficit/Hyperactivity Disorder
D/B = Deaf/Blindness
DD = Developmental Delay
ED = Emotional Disturbance
EH = Emotional handicap
HI = Hearing Impaired
LD = Learning Disabled
MR = Mental Retardation
NVLD = Nonverbal Learning Disability
OHI = Other Health Impaired
OT = Occupational Therapy
PDD = Pervasive Developmental Disorder
SED = Serious Emotional Disturbance
SPL = Specific Learning Disability
TBI = Traumatic Brain Injury
VI = Visual Impairment

NEW JERSEY

AUT = Autism
DB = Deaf Blind
ED = Emotionally Disturbed
HI = Hearing Impaired

LI = Learning Impaired
MD = Multiple Disability
MR = Mental Retardation
OHI = Other Health Impairment
OI = Orthopedic Impairment
SLD = Speech Language Disability
TBI = Traumatic Brain Injury
VI = Vision Impairment
Uses IDEA Acronyms and Definitions

NEW MEXICO

AU = Autism
DB = Deaf Blind
DD = Developmentally Delayed
ED = Emotionally Disturbed
HI = Hearing Impaired
MD = Multiple Disability
MR = Mental Retardation
OHI = Other Health Impairment
OI = Orthopedic Impairment
SL = Speech Language Impaired
SLD = Speech Language Disability
TBI = Traumatic Brain Injury
VI = Vision Impairment

NEW YORK

AUT = Autism
DB = Deaf Blind
ED = Emotionally Disturbed
HI = Hearing Impaired
LI = Learning Impaired
MD = Multiple Disability
MR = Mental Retardation
OHI = Other Health Impairment
OI = Orthopedic Impairment
SLD = Speech Language Disability
TBI = Traumatic Brain Injury
VI = Vision Impairment
Uses IDEA Acronyms and Definitions

NORTH CAROLINA

AU = Autistic
DB = Deaf Blind
DD = Developmentally Delayed (ages 3–7)
EH = Behaviorally/Emotionally Disabled
EM = Educable Mentally Disabled
HI = Hearing Impaired
LD = Specific Learning Disabled
MU = Multihandicapped
OH = Other Health Impaired
OI = Orthopedically Impaired
SP = Severely/Profoundly Mentally Disabled
TB = Traumatic Brain Injury
TM = Trainable Mentally Disabled
VI = Visually Impaired

NORTH DAKOTA

ADD = Attention-Deficit Disorder
ADHD = Attention-Deficit/Hyperactivity Disorder
D = Deaf
DB = Deaf-Blind
ED = Emotionally Disturbed
HI = Hearing Impaired
IEP = Individualized Education Program
LRE = Least Restrictive Environment
MR = Mental Retardation
OHI = Other Health Impairment
OI = Orthopedic Impairment
SLD = Specific Learning Disability
TBI = Traumatic Brain Injury
VI = Visual Impairment

OHIO

ADD = Attention-Deficit Disorder
ADHD = Attention-Deficit/Hyperactivity Disorder
APE = Adaptive Physical Education
AUT = Autism
D/HOH = Deaf/Hard of Hearing
DB = Deaf/Blindness

DH = Developmentally Handicapped
ED = Emotional Disturbance
HI = Hearing Impaired
MD = Multiple Disabilities
MR = Mental Retardation
OHH = Other Health Handicapped
OI = Orthopedic Impairments
SL = Speech Language Impairment
SLD = Specific Learning Disabilities
TBI = Traumatic Brain Injury
VI = Visual Impairment

OKLAHOMA

AU = Autism
DB = Deaf-Blindness
DD = Developmental Delay
ED = Emotional Disturbance
HI = Hearing Impaired
MD = Multiple Disabilities
MR = Mental Retardation
OHI = Other Health Impaired
OI = Orthopedic Impairment
SLD = Specific Learning Disability
SLI = Speech and Language Impairment
TBI = Traumatic Brain Injury
VI = Visual Impairment

OREGON

ADD = Attention-Deficit Disorder
ADHD = Attention-Deficit/Hyperactivity Disorder
BD = Behavior Disorder
DD = Developmental Disability
ED = Emotionally Disturbed
HI = Health Impaired or Hearing Impaired
IEP = Individualized Education Program
LD = Learning Disabled
M/ED = Mental or Emotional Disturbance
MH = Multiply Handicapped
MR = Mental Retardation
MR/DD = Mental Retardation/Developmental Disabilities
MR/MED = Mentally Retarded and Emotionally Disturbed

SED = Seriously Emotionally Disabled
SLD = Specific Learning Disability
TBI = Traumatic Brain Injury
VI = Visual Impairment

PENNSYLVANIA

AUT = Autism
DB = Deaf/Blindness
DD = Developmental Delay (ages 3–5)
ED = Emotional Disturbance
HI = Hearing Impaired
MD = Multiple Disabilities
MR = Mental Retardation
OHI = Other Health Impairments
OI = Orthopedically Impaired
SL = Speech Language Impairment
SLD = Specific Learning Disability
TBI = Traumatic Brain Injury
VI = Visually Impaired

RHODE ISLAND

ASD = Autism Spectrum Disorder
BD = Behavioral Disordered
DD = Developmental Disabilities
LD = Learning Disability
LRE = Least Restrictive Environment
MR = Mental Retardation
PDD = Pervasive Development Disorder
SLD = Specific Learning Disability
SPL = Speech Language

SOUTH CAROLINA

DB = Deaf Blindness
ED = Emotional Disability
MD = Mental Disability or Multiple Disabilities
OHI = Other Health Impairment
OI = Orthopedic Impairment
SI/LI = Speech or Language Impairment
SLD = Specific Learning Disability

TBI = Traumatic Brain Injury
VI = Visual Impairment

SOUTH DAKOTA

HI = Hearing Impaired
MD = Multiple Disabilities
MR = Mental Retardation
OHI = Other Health Impairments
OI = Orthopedically Impaired
SL = Speech Language Impairment
SLD = Specific Learning Disability
TBI = Traumatic Brain Injury
VI = Visually Impaired

TENNESSEE

ADD = Attention-Deficit Disorder
AUT = Autism
D/B = Deaf/Blind
DD = Developmental Delay
ED = Emotional Disturbance
HI = Hearing Impaired
LRE = Least Restrictive Environment
MD = Multiple Disabilities
MR = Mental Retardation
OHI = Other Health Impairment
OI = Orthopedic Impairment
SLD = Specific Learning Disability
SLI = Speech Language Impairment
TBI = Traumatic Brain Injury
VI = Visual Impairment

TEXAS

AI = Auditory Impairment
AU = Autism
D/B = Deaf/Blind
DD = Developmental Delay
ED = Emotional Disturbance
LD = Learning Disability
MR = Mental Retardation

NEC = Noncategorical Early Childhood
OHI = Other Health Impairment
OI = Orthopedic Impairment
SI = Speech Impairment
TBI = Traumatic Brain Injury
VI = Visual Impairment

UTAH

ADD = Attention-Deficit Disorder
ADHD = Attention-Deficit/Hyperactivity Disorder
BIP = Behavior Intervention Plan
ED = Emotional Disturbance
HI = Hearing Impaired
ID = Intellectually Disabled
LD = Learning Disabled
LRE = Least Restrictive Environment
OHI = Other Health Impaired
TBI = Traumatic Brain Injury
VI = Visually Impaired

VERMONT

ADD = Attention-Deficit Disorder
ADHD = Attention-Deficit/Hyperactivity Disorder
DD = Developmental Delay (ages 3–5)
ED = Emotional Disturbance
IEP = Individualized Education Program
LD = Learning Disability
LI = Learning Impairment
LRE = Least Restrictive Environment
MD = Multiple Disabilities
OHI = Other Health Impairment
PDD = Pervasive Development Disorder
SLI = Speech Language Impairment
TBI = Traumatic Brain Injury
VI = Visual Impairment

VIRGINIA

ADD = Attention-Deficit Disorder
ADHD = Attention-Deficit/Hyperactivity Disorder

AUT = Autism
BIP = Behavior Intervention Plan
DB = Deaf Blindness
DD = Developmental Delay
ED = Emotional Disturbance
HI = Hearing Impairment
LRE = Least Restrictive Environment
MD = Multiple Disabilities
MR = Mental Retardation
OHI = Other Health Impairment
OI = Orthopedic Impairment
SD = Severe Disability
SLD = Specific Learning Disability
SLI = Speech Language Impairment
TBI = Traumatic Brain Injury
VI = Visual Impairment

WASHINGTON

ADD = Attention-Deficit Disorder
ADHD = Attention-Deficit/Hyperactivity Disorder
AU = Autism
BD = Behavior Disorder
BIP = Behavior Intervention Plan
DB = Deaf Blind
DD = Developmental Delay
DHH = Deaf and Hard of Hearing
DSI = Dual Sensory Impairment
E/BD = Emotional/Behavior Disorder
ED = Emotional Disturbance
EH = Emotionally Handicapped
FBA = Functional Behavior Assessment
HI = Hearing Impaired
LD = Learning Disability
LRE = Least Restrictive Environment
MD = Multiple Disabilities
MH = Mental Handicap or Multiply Handicapped
MI/mild = Mental Impairment (mild)
MI/mo = Mental Impairment (moderate)
MIMH = Mildly Mentally Handicapped
MMR = Mildly Mentally Retarded
MOMH = Moderate Mental Handicap

MR = Mental Retardation
OHI = Other Health Impairment
OI = Orthopedic Impairment
PD = Physical Disability
S/LP = Speech/Language
SMH = Severe Mental Handicap
TBI = Traumatic Brain Injury
TMR = Trainable Mentally Retarded
VH = Visually Handicapped
VI = Visual Impairment

WEST VIRGINIA

AU = Autism
BD = Behavior Disorders
CD = Speech/Language Impairments
DB = Deaf Blindness
HI = Deaf and Hard of Hearing
IEP = Individual Education Plan
LD = Specific Learning Disabilities
LRE = Least Restrictive Environment
MD = Moderately Mentally Impaired
MI = Mental Impairment
MM = Mildly Mentally Impaired
MP = Profoundly Mentally Impaired
MS = Severely Mentally Impaired
OH = Other Health Impaired
PH = Orthopedically Impaired
PS = Preschool Special Needs
SLD = Specific Learning Disabilities
TB = Traumatic Brain Injuries
VI = Blind and Partially Sighted

WISCONSIN

ADD = Attention-Deficit Disorder
ADHD = Attention-Deficit/Hyperactivity Disorder
BIP = Behavior Intervention Plan
CD = Cognitive Disability
EBD = Emotional Behavior Disability
FBA = Functional Behavior Assessment
LRE = Least Restrictive Environment

OHI = Other Health Impairment
OI = Orthopedic Impairment
SDD = Significant Development Delay
SLD = Specific Learning Disability

WYOMING

ADD = Attention-Deficit Disorder
ADHD = Attention-Deficit/Hyperactivity Disorder
BD = Behaviorally Disordered
DD = Developmentally Disabled
EMR = Educable Mentally Retarded
HI = Hearing Impaired
HOH = Hard of Hearing
IEP = Individual Education Plan
LRE = Least Restrictive Environment
MR = Mental Retardation
OHI = Other Health Impairment
OI = Orthopedic Impairment
S/L = Speech/Language Impaired
SED = Seriously Emotionally Disturbed
SLD = Specific Learning Disability
TMR = Trainable Mentally Retarded
VI = Visual Impairment

7

Special Education Case Law

KIMBERLY APPLEQUIST

This chapter is intended to provide background information about some of the key federal statutes, regulations, and cases that may be of interest to special educators and other members of the special education team. There may be additional state cases, statutes, and regulations that are relevant in your jurisdiction. The cases in this section are included for information purposes only and should not be substituted for legal advice from an attorney licensed to practice law in your jurisdiction.

This chapter provides summaries of a number of important legal cases that have had (or may have in the future) a significant impact on education in general and often on special education in particular. The cases are grouped by subject matter and are presented chronologically within each grouping to allow the reader to follow how court interpretations of relevant statutory and constitutional provisions have evolved over time.

DISCRIMINATION IN EDUCATION

Some of the earliest cases relating to public education deal with charges of discrimination on the basis of racial or ethnic background. Over time, the specific issues addressed in these cases have evolved as changes mandated by earlier cases have been incorporated by school systems and as the nature of discrimination has become more subtle. This is shown in the line of cases examined in this section. In the earliest case, *Brown v. Board of Education* (1954), the court dealt with blatant statutory segregation of students into separate schools based upon race. Over time, cases evolved to focus on inappropriate testing procedures resulting in

Box 7.A The U.S. Court System

Most of the court cases reviewed in this chapter involve rights or obligations under the U.S. Constitution or a variety of federal statutes. Consequently, most of the cases were heard in federal (as opposed to state) courts. The federal court system has three levels: the U.S. Supreme Court, the Courts of Appeals, and the District Courts.

The Supreme Court. The U.S. Supreme Court is the final arbiter on all matters relating to interpretation of the U.S. Constitution and federal statutes. It consists of nine justices who are appointed by the president with the approval of the U.S. Senate. The justices are appointed for life, serving until they retire or die, unless they are removed by Congress through the impeachment process. The U.S. Supreme Court hears appeals of decisions of the various Courts of Appeals and other cases that may reach it through other methods (e.g., appeals of state court decisions on federal constitutional or statutory grounds). Examples of U.S. Supreme Court cases included in this chapter are *Brown v. Board of Education* and *Board of Education v. Rowley.*

The U.S. Courts of Appeals. The Courts of Appeals consist of eleven circuits with jurisdiction over different geographical regions within the country, the D.C. Circuit (which hears appeals of cases in the District of Columbia and also hears Tax Court cases and cases involving federal administrative agencies) and the Federal Circuit (which hears cases involving patents, international trade, the U.S. Claims Court, and veterans' appeals). The Courts of Appeals hear, appropriately enough, appeals of District Court decisions and may hold rehearings pursuant to decisions of the U.S. Supreme Court.

U.S. District Courts. The District Courts are typically trial courts, where factual findings are made, expert testimony and witness testimony are heard, and decisions interpreting the facts and law are issued. They may also hear appeals from administrative agency decisions. The District Courts are the lowest-level courts in the federal system, but they issue the final ruling in a sizable percentage of cases (e.g., when no party appeals or when higher-level courts decline to hear an appeal). Not all decisions of the District Courts are officially published, but many are.

State Court Systems. State court systems are usually fairly similar to the federal system, though the state courts may go by different names. State court systems may include one or more additional levels, as well. Unlike federal judges, state court judges are not typically appointed for life, and many are elected and/or can be removed from office by a vote of state residents.

de facto segregation through tracking systems and disproportionate placement of members of ethnic minorities into special education.

Although cases dealing with the right of handicapped children to receive a free public education and to receive specific services in connection with that education raise some of the same issues that the discrimination cases raise, those subjects are dealt with under separate headings later in this chapter.

Brown v. Board of Education of Topeka et al.: 347 U.S. 483 (1954)

Factual Background: This landmark decision regarding discrimination in public education actually involves four separate state court cases, involving the states of Kansas, South Carolina, Virginia, and Delaware. In each state, laws either permitted or mandated segregated schools for children of different racial backgrounds.

Box 7.B Key Legal Terms Used in This Chapter

Plaintiff: The person bringing the lawsuit in a case. For the cases in this chapter, the plaintiff is typically the student or students complaining that his, her, or their rights are being violated by some school district action or policy.

Defendant: In a civil case, the party being sued. For the cases in this chapter, the defendant is typically a school district, state, or state education department, though it may also be a named individual sued in his or her capacity as an officer of a state.

Consent Decree: A court order giving force to an agreement between parties to a lawsuit, in effect ending the lawsuit so long as each party honors its obligations under the consent decree. Several of the cases discussed in this chapter were resolved via consent decrees.

Class Action: A case in which the named plaintiffs bring their suit in the name of all similarly situated individuals affected by a defendant's actions. Many of the cases in this chapter are class action lawsuits, where the plaintiffs sued on behalf of an entire class of individuals.

Remand: To send a case back to a lower-level court, usually for further findings of fact. The Supreme Court and Courts of Appeals frequently issue rulings relating only to key legal (as opposed to factual) matters at issue in a case, then remand the case to a lower court for further findings of fact to determine how the upper court's legal ruling should be applied.

In each state, children of African American ancestry sued after being denied admission to state public schools attended by Anglo-American children, asserting that the policy of racially segregating public schools violated their rights under the Equal Protection Clause of the Fourteenth Amendment to the Constitution.

The Fourteenth Amendment was one of several amendments to the U.S. Constitution adopted during the aftermath of the Civil War. It was adopted in part to protect the rights of the recently emancipated slaves, and it provides that no state may make or enforce any law that deprives any person of the equal protection of the laws. Prior to *Brown v. Board of Education,* segregated public schools had been presumed to be permitted under the "separate but equal" doctrine set forth in *Plessy v. Ferguson,* 163 U.S. 537 (1896), in which the Supreme Court found that the requirement for equality of treatment was met if the races were provided "substantially equal facilities," even though the facilities were separate.

The plaintiffs did not argue that the schools reserved for the different races were unequal—in fact, in all four cases, lower courts had expressly found that the schools either had been equalized or were in the process of being equalized with respect to buildings, curricula, teacher qualifications and salaries, and other tangible factors. Rather, the plaintiffs argued that the doctrine set forth in *Plessy v. Ferguson* should not apply in public education at all, that the very existence of separate schools for children of different races denied equal protection of the laws to children of minority status.

Court's Holding: After determining that a historical analysis of the intent behind the Fourteenth Amendment was unhelpful, given the relative lack of public schools at the time that it was adopted, the Supreme Court concluded that segregated schools, by their very existence, created irreparable harm to minority schoolchildren. This was a rare unanimous decision based in part upon psychological research that did not exist at the time it had heard *Plessy v. Ferguson,* that the doctrine of "separate but equal" in public schools was inherently *unequal.* The court

Box 7.1

"We conclude that in the field of public education the doctrine of 'separate but equal' has no place. Separate educational facilities are inherently unequal."

Chief Justice Earl Warren, *Brown v. Board of Education*
347 U.S. 483, 495

cited the lower court's decision in the Kansas case, which pointed out that segregation sanctioned by law is usually interpreted as denoting the inferiority of the minority group; in turn, a sense of inferiority affects children's motivation to learn. The Supreme Court held that modern psychological research supported this point, and expressly rejected any language from *Plessy v. Ferguson* to the contrary. It then ordered the integration of the previously segregated school systems that were the subject of this litigation.

Lasting Impact or Subsequent History: The consequences of this Supreme Court decision have been wide-ranging and long-lasting. In addition to forming the basis for subsequent school desegregation throughout the country, this case led the way for future court decisions prohibiting discrimination against children on the basis of race, sex, national origin, or disability or handicap.

Cross-References

- *Hobson v. Hansen*
- *Lau v. Nichols*
- Equal Protection Clause

Hobson v. Hansen: 269 F. Supp. 401 (D.C., 1967)

Factual Background: Prior to 1954, schools in the District of Columbia, as in many other parts of the country, were racially segregated under local law. In *Bolling v. Sharpe* (347 U.S. 497, 1954), a companion case to *Brown v. Board of Education,* the Supreme Court held that the system of segregation in use in the District of Columbia was a violation of students' rights under the Equal Protection Clause. The schools were desegregated, with the district adopting a "neighborhood schools" system in which children attended schools closest to their homes.

At the time this case was brought, over 90 percent of the children attending public schools in the District of Columbia were African American, with Anglo-American students heavily concentrated in one area of the city. The District Court found that the use of a neighborhood schools program resulted in a number of disparities among schools in predominantly Anglo-American neighborhoods compared to schools in predominantly African American neighborhoods: per-student expenditures were higher at predominantly Anglo-American schools; these schools were underpopulated, whereas schools that were predominantly African American were overcrowded; and a disproportionate share of students in the lower educational tracks were minority and disadvantaged children. Indeed, a number of the predominantly African American schools did not even provide access to the highest educational tracks, forcing students who were qualified for and interested in such

Box 7.2 The Equal Protection Clause

"No State shall . . . deny to any person within its jurisdiction the equal protection of the laws."

United States Constitution, Amendment 14, Section 1

"Not all classifications resulting in disparity are unconstitutional. If the classification is reasonably related to the purposes of the governmental activity involved and is rationally carried out, the fact that persons are thereby treated differently does not necessarily offend."

Judge Skelly Wright, *Hobson v. Hansen*
269 F. Supp. 401, 511

tracks to transfer to other schools—rendering such programs virtually inaccessible for many underprivileged students.

The issues relating to the tracking system, and the District Court's response to them, are of particular interest to special educators and school psychologists. The District of Columbia used a track system that assigned children to separate, self-contained curricula, with education in the lower tracks geared to what its creator (the Dr. Hansen identified in the case name) referred to as a "blue collar" student. Students were assigned to the various tracks largely based upon scores on group-administered aptitude tests that had been standardized primarily on Anglo-American middle-class children. Although individual tests were occasionally administered on a one-on-one basis, these were reserved almost exclusively for individuals considered for placement in the lowest academic track.

Court's Holding: As was the case in *Brown v. Board of Education,* the District Court's ruling turns on its interpretation of the Equal Protection Clause of the Fourteenth Amendment. The District Court found that the neighborhood schools system, as implemented in the District of Columbia, and the tracking system in place throughout the school district, amounted to de facto segregation in violation of the Equal Protection Clause.

Although the school district insisted that test scores were merely one factor used to determine track assignment, the District Court concluded, based upon the evidence presented by the parties, that they were "the most important consideration in making track assignments" (p. 475). The District Court indicated that the use of standardized aptitude tests that were standardized on (and relevant to) Anglo-American middle-class children was completely inappropriate when a large segment of the student body was African American, because "they produce inaccurate and misleading test scores when given to lower class and Negro students" (p. 514). As a result of using these tests, the court found that, rather than being classified according to ability to learn, students were actually being classified according to their socioeconomic or racial status, in violation of the Equal Protection Clause. Thus, in addition to other remedies addressing the problems associated with the neighborhood school approach, the District Court ordered the abolition of the tracking system used in the District of Columbia schools.

Lasting Impact or Subsequent History: Hobson v. Hansen was the first case, but by no means the last, in which federal courts examined racial issues related to placement in educational programs based upon the results of standardized tests. It should be noted that, while the District Court ordered the tracking system then in use in the District of Columbia to be abolished, it did not say that all such systems offended the principles set forth in the Equal Protection Clause and the Constitution, generally (see inset quotation.) Rather, it indicated that the basis for assigning individuals to academic tracks must not amount to classification on the basis of socioeconomic or racial status.

Cross-References

- *Brown v. Board of Education*
- Equal Protection Clause

Diana v. State Board of Education (1970) and *Guadalupe v. Tempe Elementary School District* (1972)

Factual Background: These two highly similar cases involving special education assessment were never actually brought to trial. In each case, civil rights groups filed suit on behalf of bilingual students who had been placed in classes for the mildly mentally retarded on the basis of intelligence tests administered in English to children who spoke primarily Spanish in the home. The plaintiffs argued that this practice was discriminatory and resulted in overrepresentation of bilingual children with Spanish surnames in programs for the mentally retarded.

Court's Holding: Neither case actually went to trial because they were resolved via consent decrees (agreements by the parties that were certified by courts in order to avoid further litigation). In *Diana,* the consent decree required assessment of the child's primary language. If the primary language was found to be other than English, any tests used to assess the child for placement in special education were required to be nonverbal, in the child's primary language, or administered through an interpreter. Unfair portions of any English-language test were required to be deleted, and more weight given to the results of nonverbal intelligence tests when making placement decisions.

The *Guadalupe* consent decree included the same provisions as the *Diana* consent decree, with four additional requirements: (1) standardized intelligence tests (IQ tests) could not be the exclusive or primary basis for a diagnosis of mild mental retardation; (2) adaptive behavior in nonschool settings was required to be assessed; (3) due process procedures were required to be instituted *before* individual assessment or any movement toward diagnosis and placement; and (4) special education was required to be provided in the most normal setting or environment (least restrictive environment) possible.

Lasting Impact or Subsequent History: While neither of these cases set legal precedent (because no judicial opinion was ever issued), both influenced subsequent state and federal legislation relating to placement of children in educational programs on the basis of IQ test results. Wording from the consent decrees is consistent with many state and federal statutes and regulations governing education for the handicapped (Reynolds, 2000).

Cross-References

- Education for All Handicapped Children Act of 1975
- *Lau v. Nichols*
- *Hobson v. Hansen*

Lau v. Nichols: 414 U.S. 563 (1974)

Factual Background: This case involves non-English-speaking students who brought suit against the San Francisco Unified School District seeking relief in connection with unequal educational opportunities that they claimed arose from the school district's failure to establish a program addressing the students' language issues.

San Francisco has a sizable Asian community, including many residents of Chinese ancestry. At the time this case was brought, there were several thousand students of Chinese ancestry who had only limited exposure to English prior to entering the school system. While some of these students were given supplemental courses in the English language, about 1,800 did not receive supplemental tuition.

Court's Holding: Although the case was argued in part on Equal Protection Clause grounds, as were both *Brown v. Board of Education* and *Hobson v. Hansen,* the Supreme Court did not feel it necessary to address that issue in the context of this case. Instead, it relied on Section 601 of the Civil Rights Act of 1964 (42 USCS 2000d), which prohibits entities that discriminate against racial groups from receiving federal financial assistance. The Supreme Court found that Chinese-speaking students by definition received fewer benefits than English-speaking students when a school system denied them a "meaningful opportunity to participate in the educational program" (p. 568), and ordered the case remanded to the lower court for appropriate relief. Although the Supreme Court did not specify an appropriate remedy for the Chinese-speaking students, it suggested that additional instruction to teach the students English was one appropriate remedy and that instructing the students in Chinese might be another.

Cross-References

- *Brown v. Board of Education*
- *Hobson v. Hansen*
- Civil Rights Act of 1964

Box 7.3

"Under [state-imposed standards] there is no equality of treatment merely by providing students with the same facilities, textbooks, teachers, and curriculum; for students who do not understand English are effectively foreclosed from any meaningful education.

"Basic English skills are at the very core of what these public schools teach. Imposition of a requirement that, before a child can effectively participate in the educational program, he must already have acquired those basic skills is to make a mockery of public education."

Justice William O. Douglas, *Lau v. Nichols*

"Simple justice requires that public funds, to which all taxpayers of all races contribute, not be spent in any fashion which encourages, entrenches, subsidizes, or results in racial discrimination."

Sen. Hubert Humphrey, during the floor debates on the Civil Rights Act of 1964

Mattie T. v. Holladay: 522 F. Supp. 72 (N.D. Miss., 1981)

Factual Background: This suit was filed on behalf of Mississippi school-age children who were handicapped or regarded by their schools as handicapped for failure to enforce students' rights under the Education for All Handicapped Children Act (P.L. 94-142). The suit alleged that the children were either excluded from school in segregated special programs or ignored in regular classes, or were non-handicapped minority students who had been misclassified as mentally retarded and inappropriately placed. Thus, the case combines elements of both the cases involving inappropriate placement of minority children in special education (e.g., *Hobson v. Hansen, Larry P. v. Riles*) and cases involving the right of handicapped children to receive a free appropriate public education (see section titled "Access to Special Education" later in this chapter).

Court's Holding: The District Court ruled that the defendants were, indeed, violating the plaintiffs' federal rights under P.L. 94-142, and ordered a comprehensive compliance plan. Subsequently, in 1979, the District Court approved a consent decree to force the schools to comply with the requirements of P.L. 94-142, requiring many of the same actions as other cases discussed in this section, including, specifically, (1) placement of students in the least restrictive environment, (2) redesign of the state's child evaluation procedures to eliminate discriminatory features, (3) compensatory education for students who had been misclassified and inappropriately placed (e.g., in classes for the educable mentally retarded), (4) elimination of school suspensions longer than 3 days, and (5) other procedures to improve compliance with the federal law.

Cross-References

- *Hobson v. Hansen*
- *Larry P. v. Riles*
- *Marshall v. Georgia*
- The Education for All Handicapped Children Act (P.L. 94-142)

Larry P. v. Riles: 495 F. Supp. 926 (N.D. Calif., 1979)

Factual Background: In another case involving students in the San Francisco school district, Larry P. and five other African American children sued the California state superintendent of public instruction (Wilson Riles) on behalf of African American children in California who were "wrongly placed and maintained in special classes for the 'educable mentally retarded'" (EMR; 495 F. Supp. 926, 931). The plaintiffs argued that the use of standardized individual intelligence tests (IQ tests) for the purpose of assigning children to this classification was inappropriate because the tests were biased and resulted in the disproportionate assignment of African American children to such classes.

Special classes for the EMR in the California schools focused on life and social skills, rather than on academic skills. As such, they were a virtual dead end for children, academically speaking, because the longer a child was enrolled in such special classes, the further behind academically he or she would fall compared to

Box 7.4

"The I.Q. tests must be recognized as artificial tools to rank individuals according to certain skills, not to diagnose a medical condition."

Judge Robert F. Peckham, *Larry P. v. Riles*
495 F. Supp. 926, 953

other children his or her age. Thus, inappropriate placement of a child in the EMR special classes had a particularly detrimental effect on the child's future.

Witnesses for the defendants (Riles and others associated with the California schools) testified that IQ tests were not the only factors considered when deciding whether to place children in the EMR program. In particular, they noted that classroom observation, academic performance, and behavioral assessment were also a part of any evaluation. However, the court concluded that IQ tests were one of the most important factors, perhaps the most important one, in any such evaluation.

Court's Holding: Based upon testimony presented by all sides in this case, the court made a number of findings about the nature of IQ tests and their ability to measure innate ability. The court noted that African American children score lower on average than Anglo-American children on the tests in use in California. If children were assigned to the EMR program based on IQ test scores, this would necessarily result in more African American children's receiving the EMR designation than Anglo-American children.

The court rejected the genetic and socioeconomic arguments regarding the difference in IQ test scores among Anglo-Americans and African Americans. Instead it concluded that the differences in test scores were primarily the result of cultural biases in the tests used to assess intelligence. Thus, it concluded, use of such tests to assign African American children to EMR classes was inappropriate and violated a number of state and federal statutes and constitutional provisions, including Title VI of the Civil Rights Act of 1964, Section 504 of the Rehabilitation Act of 1973, and the Education for All Handicapped Children Act of 1975 (P.L. 94-142), and equal protection provisions in both the federal and state constitutions. Furthermore, the court found that the defendants' conduct revealed an unlawful segregative intent, not necessarily to harm African American children but to place a "grossly disproportionate" number of them into EMR classes.

The court invalidated California's system of classification of African American children for EMR classes. It granted a permanent injunction preventing California public schools from using standardized intelligence tests for the purpose of identifying African American children for placement in EMR classes (or any subsequent equivalent of EMR classes). The court left room for approval of specific tests for these purposes, as long as certain conditions are met (see Box 7.5). The court also ordered the state to monitor and eliminate disproportionate placement of African American children in EMR classes.

Lasting Impact or Subsequent History: Despite its good intentions, the *Larry P.* case has not eliminated minority overrepresentation in special education programs of the type at issue in this case (Lambert, 2000). However, it does seem to have resulted in fewer children's being classified as mildly mentally retarded.

The court was careful to emphasize that its decision "should not be construed as a final judgment on the scientific validity of intelligence tests" (p. 989). Thus, it

Box 7.5 Requirements for Court Approval of Future Standardized Intelligence Tests to Identify African American Children for EMR or Similar Classes

- The State Board of Education must make a written request to the court for approval of the standardized intelligence test.
- The request must state the following:
  - The board has found that the test is not racially or culturally discriminatory.
  - The test will be administered in a nondiscriminatory manner.
  - The test has been validated for the purpose of determining EMR status or placement in EMR classes.
- The request must be accompanied by evidence supporting these statements, including
  - Statistics on the average scores of African American and Anglo-American children on the test
  - Statistics or other data forming the basis for the board's determination that the test is validated for the purpose(s) for which the board intends to use it
  - Certification that open public hearings were held on the proposed test

leaves open the possibility of using IQ tests that can be shown to lack the cultural biases of the tests in use at the time the decision was rendered to identify children who should be placed in special education programs like the EMR classes, though, as noted previously, any such use would require prior court approval.

Cross-References

- Cultural bias in testing
- Civil Rights Act of 1964
- Rehabilitation Act of 1973
- Education for All Handicapped Children Act of 1975 (P.L. 94-142)
- Equal Protection Clause

PASE v. Hannon: 506 F. Supp. 831 (N.D. Ill., E.D., 1980)

Factual Background: Like the *Larry P.* case, this case involves the use of standardized intelligence tests (IQ tests) for the purpose of classifying African American children for placement in special classes for the educable mentally handicapped (EMH)—a classification that seems more or less the equivalent of the educable mentally retarded designation in use in California (see Box 7.6 for the Illinois definition of educable mentally handicapped). The plaintiffs in this case were two African American children who suffered from remediable learning disabilities but were placed in EMH classes because of their low scores on IQ tests. They brought suit against the Chicago Board of Education on behalf of all African American children placed in EMH classes in Chicago after achieving low scores on IQ tests.

Court's Holding: Somewhat surprisingly, given this case's similarity to the *Larry P.* case (and the testimony of many of the same expert witnesses), the judge in *PASE v. Hannon* ruled in favor of the *defendants* rather than the plaintiff schoolchildren. The court engaged in a lengthy review of testimony regarding cultural biases in the Wechsler Intelligence Scale for Children (WISC), the revised WISC (WISC-R), and the Stanford-Binet tests, including question-by-question analyses

Box 7.6 Illinois Definition of Educable Mentally Handicapped

"[The educable mentally handicapped are Children] who because of retarded intellectual developed as determined by individual evaluation are incapable of being educated profitably and efficiently through ordinary classroom instruction but who may be expected to benefit from special education facilities designed to make them economically useful and socially adjusted."

Ill. Rev. Stat., ch. 122, § 14-1.04 (1977)

of many sections of these tests. The judge concluded that, while some biased items might exist in each test, the relative number of biased items was small and mostly confined to the upper limits of specific subtests. Thus, the judge concluded that the biased items were unlikely to result in the placement of an African American child in EMH classes who would not have been placed there anyway.

The court expressly rejected the reasoning set forth in the *Larry P.* case, finding that the judge in that case had merely accepted the contention that the tests used in California were culturally biased without delving into the specifics of the alleged biases. Instead, the judge in *PASE v. Hannon* concluded that the tests, when used in conjunction with other statutorily mandated criteria for determining an appropriate educational program for a child (for which the judge found evidence), did not discriminate against African American children in the Chicago public schools.

Lasting Impact or Subsequent History: The primary difference between this case and the *Larry P.* case was that the judge in *PASE v. Hannon* required the plaintiffs to establish a direct connection between the biased items on the various IQ tests in use in Chicago and the misclassification of African American students as EMH. Based on his evaluation, he concluded that the plaintiffs had failed to establish this connection, and accordingly he ruled in favor of the defendants.

Perhaps not surprisingly, given the contradiction between the judge's ruling and the *Larry P.* decision, the plaintiffs in this case elected to appeal the trial court's decision. However, the issue was rendered moot when the Chicago Board of Education banned the use of traditional IQ tests with African American students being evaluated for placement in EMH programs as part of a negotiated settlement in another court case relating to the desegregation of Chicago schools (Reschly, 2000).

Cross-References

- *Larry P. v. Riles*
- *Marshall v. Georgia*

Marshall v. Georgia (also known as *Georgia State Conference of Branches of NAACP v. Georgia*): 775 F.2d. 1403 (11th Cir., 1985)

Factual Background: Another in a series of cases relating to overrepresentation of African American children in programs for the EMR, this case, too, reached a very different conclusion than the *Larry P.* case. The plaintiffs were 35 African American schoolchildren who sued the Georgia State Board of Education and a number of local school districts, claiming that African American students were assigned to regular classes and EMR programs in a discriminatory manner. The District Court that originally heard the case found in favor of the defendants, and the plaintiffs appealed the case to the 11th Circuit Court of Appeals.

The plaintiffs asserted two claims: (1) that the use of ability or achievement grouping in public schools in Georgia either was intended to achieve or resulted in intraschool racial segregation, in violation of the Thirteenth and Fourteenth Amendments to the U.S. Constitution, Title VI of the Civil Rights Act of 1964, and the Equal Education Opportunities Act; and (2) that African American children were assigned to EMR programs in a discriminatory manner resulting in overrepresentation of African American students in EMR classes. The defendants argued that the ability or achievement grouping program used in Georgia schools was both appropriate and helpful to students at all levels, and that the overrepresentation of African American students in EMR classes was attributable to the effects of poverty rather than to any intentional or unintentional discrimination.

Court's Holding: The District Court accepted the defendants' arguments justifying the use of ability or achievement grouping. The court noted that a number of methods were used to determine group membership; that group membership was based upon actual performance; that assignment to groups was flexible, with periodic reconsideration of group assignment; and that changes to group assignments were made frequently based upon student performance. Grouping varied by subject matter (in direct contrast to the grouping found in *Hobson v. Hansen,* in which students were assigned to one of four separate curricula for all subjects); therefore, students were not forced into lower-level classes in areas of personal strength. Finally, the court noted that instruction in the various ability or achievement groupings was provided at the appropriate level for students in that grouping, creating a rational basis for the grouping (that is, students were not separated into different levels for the sake of being separated, then taught the exact same material at all levels). The court found that the remedial instruction provided at the lower academic grouping levels was a positive feature of the grouping program, rather than a negative feature that harmed students in those grouping levels.

With respect to the claim that African American students were overrepresented in EMR classes (and a concurrent claim that they were underrepresented in classes for the learning disabled), the District Court again sided with the defendants. While the plaintiffs argued that the schools used a number of practices in assigning children to EMR classes that the plaintiffs apparently assumed differentially harmed African American children, they presented no evidence that any of these practices were found more frequently with African American than with Anglo-American students, or that the changes in these practices advocated by the plaintiffs would result in reduction or elimination of the overrepresentation of African American students in EMR classes. The plaintiffs appealed the District Court's decision.

The Court of Appeals upheld the District Court's decision. With respect to the ability or achievement grouping claim, the Court of Appeals noted that the use of ability grouping in schools is not automatically unconstitutional. Even where a history of past discrimination exists, achievement grouping may still be permissible if the school district "can demonstrate that its assignment method is not based on the present results of past segregation *or* will remedy such results through better educational opportunities" (p. 1414). The Court of Appeals concluded that the District Court's finding that the ability grouping schemes in use in the various school districts would "remedy the consequences of prior segregation through better educational opportunities" (p. 1416), which was not challenged by plaintiffs on appeal, was not clearly erroneous. The Court of Appeals also upheld the District Court's decision with respect to the overrepresentation claim.

The Court of Appeals did note that the defendants had violated certain procedural regulations under the Rehabilitation Act of 1973, and remanded the case for relief on those claims.

Lasting Impact or Subsequent History: This case established certain guidelines concerning allegations of discrimination and the development of programs for the EMR.It clearly demonstrated that overrepresentation of one group in EMR classes was not, of itself, enough to prove discrimination. Rather, such overrepresentation must be accompanied by additional evidence of discrimination.

Cross-References

- Civil Rights Act of 1964
- Equal Education Opportunity Act
- Section 504 of the Rehabilitation Act of 1973
- *Larry P. v. Riles*
- *Hobson v. Hansen*

COMPETENCY TESTING

Debra P. v. Turlington: 474 F. Supp. 244 (M.D. Fla., 1979) 644 F.2d 397 (5th Cir., 1981) 564 F. Supp. 177 (M.D. Fla., 1983) 730 F.2d 1405 (11th Cir., 1984)

Factual Background: This case challenged a new Florida statute requiring all high school students in that state to pass a competency examination prior to graduation. The plaintiff, Deborah P., represented the class of students (of all ethnic backgrounds) in danger of failing the test. She made three separate claims with respect to the competency testing program: (1) that the testing program was racially biased and/or violated the Equal Protection Clause and various federal statutory provisions, including Title VI of the Civil Rights Act of 1964 and the Equal Education Opportunities Act; (2) that the program changed requirements for graduation without adequate notice or time to prepare for the examination, in violation of the Fourteenth Amendment; and (3) that the test was used as a mechanism for resegregating Florida public schools through the use of remedial classes for students failing the test, also in violation of the Fourteenth Amendment. Prior to the initial District Court case, the test had been administered to Florida students a total of three times. On all three occasions, the percentage of African American students failing one or both portions of the exam far exceeded the percentage of Anglo-American students similarly failing.

Court's Holding: The District Court found that, because a high school diploma was required for admission to the nine universities in Florida, the denial of a diploma that would result from failure to pass both portions of the exam had a disproportionate effect on college attendance by African American students. With respect to the claim that the program was racially discriminatory, the District Court noted that when the plaintiffs in this case started school, Florida schools were still segregated. There was ample evidence that schools attended by African American students prior to desegregation were inferior to the schools attended by Anglo-Americans in most, if not all, respects, with the result that the African American students who had attended those schools started their academic careers at a significant disadvantage compared to their Anglo-American classmates. Thus, although the state had a legitimate interest in implementing a test to evaluate students prior to graduation, the past purposeful discrimination affecting the African American students in the initial years of the testing program was effectively perpetuated by the requirement that they pass the test in order to receive their diplomas. It is important to note that the District Court did not find the test itself to be unduly biased with respect to any racial or ethnic group. It indicated that the professional testing companies that wrote the items for the test reviewed the items for possible racial and ethnic bias, and that the State Department of Education had also sought input from groups of teachers with respect to any racial bias in the questions.

With respect to the claim that the program changed requirements for graduation without adequate notice or time to prepare for the examination, the District Court again sided with the plaintiff students.

Given the nature of its findings with respect to both the lack of adequate notice and time for preparation and the racially discriminatory effects for African American plaintiffs who had begun their academic careers under the shadow of racial segregation, the District Court issued an injunction prohibiting the use of the test as a requirement for graduation until the 1982–83 school year. It felt that this would allow those African American students who had attended racially segregated schools time to graduate before the test became a graduation requirement, and would provide adequate notice and time to prepare to all future students, regardless of their racial background.

On appeal, the Fifth Circuit Court of Appeals upheld the District Court's injunction but sent the case back to the lower court for further findings on two issues potentially affecting use of the test as a "diploma sanction" after the injunction period expired. Specifically, the Court of Appeals required the state to demonstrate that the competency exam was a fair test of subjects taught in Florida public schools, and that the material tested was actually taught. On remand, the District Court concluded that the state had successfully shown that the test was a fair test of such subjects. With respect to the second issue, the District Court concluded that, although there were still vestiges of past segregation in the Florida schools, and although the test still had a racially discriminatory impact, there was "no causal link between the disproportionate failure rate of black students and those present effects of past segregation." On appeal of the second District Court decision, the 11th Circuit Court of Appeals affirmed the decision of the District Court.

Lasting Impact or Subsequent History: The courts involved in this matter did not prohibit the use of competency exams as a high school graduation requirement. Rather, they considered whether students had adequate notice prior to the implementation of penalties for failure to pass such exams, and whether past discrimination against a segment of the student body made the use of such exams unreasonable with respect to students who had experienced such discrimination.

ACCESS TO SPECIAL EDUCATION

Over the course of the last 30 years or so, handicapped students have brought their fight for access to a public education to the courts, resulting in a significant number of legal decisions. This portion of the chapter summarizes some of the most important federal cases relating to access to education.

Mills v. Board of Education of the District of Columbia: 348 F. Supp. 866 (D.C., 1972)

Factual Background: Another case involving the District of Columbia, *Mills* involves a lawsuit by seven school-aged children who sought to enjoin the school district from excluding them from District of Columbia public schools and/or denying them a publicly supported education. The children sought to compel the school district to provide them with education in the public schools or alternative educational placement at public expense. The student plaintiffs in the case claimed that they could benefit from an education, either in regular classrooms with supportive services or in special classes adapted to their needs, but that they had been labeled as "behavioral problems, mentally retarded, emotionally disturbed or hyperactive" and excluded from the public schools with no provision of alternative educational placement or periodic review.

There was no issue of material fact—that is, all parties agreed that the school district had an affirmative duty under the laws of the District of Columbia to provide the plaintiffs and similarly situated schoolchildren with a publicly supported education suited to their needs, with constitutionally adequate prior hearings and periodic review. Further, all parties agreed that the school district had failed to provide a publicly supported education and constitutionally adequate prior hearing and periodic review. Indeed, prior to the issuance of the final District Court decision, the parties had entered into a consent order requiring the school district to provide the plaintiffs with publicly supported education suited to the plaintiffs' needs by a date early in 1972. The school district failed to comply with the decree, and the plaintiffs brought the matter to the District Court on a motion to compel the school district to comply with its terms.

Court's Holding: The District Court ruled in favor of the students under the laws of the District of Columbia (which required the school district to provide education to any school-age child unless the child was found to be mentally or physically unable to profit from attendance at school), and the Equal Protection and Due Process Clauses of the Fourteenth Amendment. With respect to the Equal Protection Clause claim, the District Court noted that the school district's failure to comply with the terms of the consent order denied the students not just an *equal* publicly supported education but *all* publicly supported education. With respect to the Due Process Clause claim, the District Court indicated that many of the students in the case (and similarly situated students in the school district) had been suspended or expelled from regular schooling or specialized instruction without any prior hearing, and were given no periodic hearing thereafter, which denied the students due process under the law.

Box 7.7 The Due Process Clause

"Nor shall any State deprive any person of life, liberty, or property, without due process of law . . ."

United States Constitution, Amendment 14, Section 1

The District Court rejected the school district's contention that it was not possible to provide the relief requested by the plaintiffs (that is, a publicly supported education) because it did not have the financial resources to provide such services. It held that the school district's statutory and constitutional obligations to provide a publicly supported education to all school-age children who could benefit from one outweighed financial considerations.

Lasting Impact or Subsequent History: This case has had a lasting impact on the education of children with disabilities. It predated the Education for All Handicapped Children Act of 1975 (P.L. 94-142) by 3 years and clearly influenced its adoption and form. Today, all states are required by federal law to provide a free and appropriate public education to all children with disabilities. In addition, significant progress has been made in addressing the educational needs of children with disabilities.

Cross-References

- The Education for All Handicapped Children Act of 1975 (P.L. 94-142)
- Individuals with Disabilities Education Act
- Equal Protection Clause
- Due Process Clause

Pennsylvania Association for Retarded Citizens v. Pennsylvania: **334 F. Supp. 1257 (E.D. PA, 1972)**

Factual Background: This case, like the *Mills* case discussed previously, involves the educational rights of the handicapped. The plaintiffs were 13 mentally retarded students, suing on behalf of all similarly situated students in Pennsylvania. The students claimed that the state's policy of providing a free public education to some citizens while denying other students the right to attend state schools or receive an education at state expense denied students' rights under the Equal Protection Clause and the Due Process Clause of the Fourteenth Amendment.

Court's Holding: The District Court's decision—actually a combined order, injunction, and consent agreement—called for sweeping changes in the education system in Pennsylvania, many of which were incorporated in later state and federal statutes and regulations. Among the many significant changes required by the District Court was the requirement that the state provide "a free, public program of education and training appropriate to the child's capacity, within the context of a presumption that, among the alternative programs of education and training required by statute to be available, placement in a regular public school class is preferable to placement in a special public school class and placement in a special public school class is preferable to placement in any other type of program of education and training" (p. 1260). A full summary of all of aspects of the District Court's decision is beyond the scope of this work, but most, if not all, of the changes ordered by the District Court have since been incorporated in legislative enactments at the federal and state level.

Lasting Impact or Subsequent History: This case, together with the *Mills* case preceding it, was extremely influential with respect to special education as it is currently implemented in the United States. The two decisions prompted a rapid and sweeping change in American schools, bringing children with often profound disabilities into public schools, often for the first time. They were instrumental in passing state and federal legislation, like the Education for All Handicapped Children Act of 1975 (P.L. 94-142), assuring the rights of handicapped children to a free, appropriate public education.

Cross-References

- *Mills v. Board of Education of District of Columbia*
- Least Restrictive Environment
- The Education for All Handicapped Children Act of 1975 (P.L. 94-142)
- Individuals with Disabilities Education Act
- Equal Protection Clause
- Due Process Clause

RIGHT TO SPECIFIC SERVICES

Recent years have seen an increasing number of lawsuits demanding specific treatments or educational programs for children with special needs. Results in such cases have generally been mixed. While courts have generally insisted on flexibility in meeting the needs of handicapped students (e.g., by providing year-round schooling for certain students), they have stopped far short of demanding that all possible supplemental services be provided to students with disabilities. This section of the chapter summarizes some of the leading cases in this area, along with one recent case in which the court rejected the parents' demands for a specific course of treatment for their autistic child.

Battle v. Pennsylvania: 629 F. 2d 269 (3rd Cir., 1980)

Factual Background: Battle v. Pennsylvania is considered by many to be the lead case in the area of extended school years for handicapped children. The plaintiffs in the case were five handicapped children suing on behalf of all Pennsylvania children who might require "a program of special education and related services in excess of 180 days per year" (p. 271). The plaintiffs claimed that the state's policies, specifically the 180-day rule, and the school districts' refusal to fund the provision

Box 7.8

"We believe the inflexibility of the defendants' policy of refusing to provide more than 180 days of education to be incompatible with the Act's emphasis on the individual. Rather than ascertaining the reasonable educational needs of each child in light of reasonable educational goals, and establishing a reasonable program to attain those goals, the 180 day rule imposes with rigid certainty a program restriction which may be wholly inappropriate to the child's educational objective. This, the Act will not permit."

Judge Hunter, *Battle v. Pennsylvania*
629 F. 2d 269, 280

of more than 180 days of educational programming violated (1) the Education for All Handicapped Children Act, (2) the Due Process and Equal Protection Clauses of the Fourteenth Amendment, and (3) various state laws.

Court's Holding: The Court of Appeals noted that for some (but not all) special needs children, attainment of even the most basic objectives of special education, such as acquisition of self-help skills, can be negatively affected by breaks in the educational program created by the 180-day rule (e.g., summer vacations). As a result of such program interruptions, such children may lose significant skills and development. The time required to regain such skills and development might well be significant. The Court of Appeals concluded that the state's inflexible approach to the 180-day rule conflicted with the Education for All Handicapped Children Act's emphasis on the needs of the individual child, in violation of the act. The Court of Appeals did not rule on the Due Process Clause and Equal Protection Clause claims, having found for the plaintiffs on the basis of the federal statutory claim.

Lasting Impact or Subsequent History: Subsequent court cases have generally followed the court's decision in *Battle.* Subsequent litigation has turned to the issue of which individual handicapped children are eligible for extended-year services.

Cross-References

- *Board of Education v. Rowley*
- *Crawford v. Pittman*
- Due Process Clause
- Equal Protection Clause

Board of Education v. Rowley: 458 U.S. 176 (1982)

Factual Background: In this case, the plaintiff, Rowley, a deaf student, sued the New York Board of Education claiming that she was entitled to a sign-language interpreter in public school classes. In preparation for regular school, her parents (who were also deaf) had enrolled her in a regular kindergarten class in order to allow an assessment of what supplemental services would be necessary for her education. During the fall of her first-grade year, her school prepared an individualized educational program (IEP) for her, as required by the Education of All Handicapped Children Act of 1975 (the Act). The plan called for a number of accommodations for the plaintiff's condition, including use of a hearing aid that linked to a microphone worn by the teacher, instruction from a tutor for the deaf for one hour each day, and instruction from a speech therapist for three hours a week.

The Rowleys agreed with parts of the IEP but felt that their daughter should be provided with a sign-language interpreter in all her academic subjects, in lieu of other services proposed in the IEP. The Supreme Court notes in its opinion that a sign-language interpreter had been placed in the plaintiff's kindergarten class for the first 2 weeks she was there, but that the interpreter had reported that the plaintiff did not need the interpreter's services at that stage of her academic career. The school administrators at the plaintiff's elementary school had similarly concluded that she did not need such an interpreter at that stage of her academic career. They had consulted with the school district's committee on the handicapped, which in turn had received evidence from Amy's parents on the importance

Box 7.9

"A 'free appropriate public education' consists of educational instruction specially designed to meet the unique needs of the handicapped child, supported by such services as are necessary to permit the child 'to benefit' from the instruction."

Chief Justice William Rehnquist, *Board of Education v. Rowley*
458 U.S. 176, 188–189

of an interpreter, heard testimony from the plaintiff's teacher and others regarding her academic and social progress, and visited a school for the deaf.

The plaintiff's parents demanded (and received) a hearing before an independent examiner to appeal the school district's denial of their request for an interpreter. The examiner agreed with the school administrator's conclusion that an interpreter was not necessary at that time because the plaintiff was "achieving educationally, academically, and socially without such assistance" (p. 185). After exhausting their administrative appeals, the plaintiff's parents sued the school district in federal court.

The District Court concluded that, while the plaintiff was doing well socially and academically, she was not doing as well as she would without her handicap. This disparity between the plaintiff's achievement and her potential led the District Court to conclude that she was not receiving a free appropriate public education within the meaning of the Act, which the District Court interpreted as "an opportunity to achieve her full potential commensurate with the opportunity provided to other children" (pp. 185–186). The Second Circuit Court of Appeals affirmed the District Court's decision, and the school district appealed the case to the Supreme Court.

Court's Holding: The Supreme Court reversed the decisions of the lower courts, stating that the schools need not provide a sign-language interpreter for a deaf student when that student was already receiving an adequate education and personalized instruction and related services calculated by local school administrators to meet her educational needs.

The Supreme Court's decision turned on its interpretation of the statutory language relating to a free appropriate public education. It noted that the Act requires that such an education is required to be tailored to the "unique needs of the handicapped child" (p. 181) through an IEP developed through a meeting between "a qualified representative of the local educational agency, the child's teacher, the child's parents or guardian, and, where appropriate, the child" (p. 182) and reviewed and, where appropriate, revised at least annually. The Supreme Court concluded that so long as "personalized instruction is being provided with sufficient supportive services to permit the child to benefit from the instruction . . . the child is receiving a 'free appropriate public education' as defined by the Act" (p. 189).

Lasting Impact or Subsequent History: This case is significant primarily because it sets forth the Supreme Court's interpretation of what constitutes a "free appropriate public education." In the 20 or so years since this decision was articulated, the case has been cited extensively in other judicial opinions for that very purpose.

Cross-References

- Education for All Handicapped Children Act of 1975 (94-142)

Crawford v. Pittman: 708 F. 2d 1028 (5th Cir., 1983)

Factual Background: Another key case in the area of extended school years for certain handicapped children, *Crawford v. Pittman* is a class-action lawsuit that revolves around six mentally handicapped children from Mississippi who sued, arguing that the Mississippi policy of providing only 180 days of schooling per year violated their rights under the Education of All Handicapped Children Act of 1975 (P.L. 94-142). The IEPs prepared for the children did not specifically call for year-round schools, but the court noted that until 1980, the school that three of the six children attended had operated on a year-round basis, so that year-round schooling would have been an implicit (rather than explicit) feature in their IEPs. Following 1980, the school these students attended lost its federal funding and began receiving its funding from the Mississippi Department of Education, at which time the school began following the state policy of limiting IEPs to 9-month programs, prompting this lawsuit. The remaining three students also did not have anything in their respective IEPs regarding a need for year-round schools, although a memorandum prepared for one of the students by his teacher indicated that he needed a program that would "cover all his waking hours" (p. 1031), which would seem to imply that year-round schooling would be desirable and beneficial.

The plaintiffs argued that handicapped children regress significantly during extended breaks in their education program (e.g., summer vacations), potentially causing them to lose much or all of what they learned during the school year. Further, they argued that the regression suffered by handicapped children far exceeds any regression experienced by nonhandicapped children during the summer months.

The District Court upheld Mississippi's refusal to provide more than 180 days of special education services per year. It concluded that the Act governs only the kind and quality of services the states are required to provide, rather than the quantity or duration of such services. The plaintiffs appealed.

Court's Holding: Citing *Battle v. Pennsylvania,* the Fifth Circuit Court of Appeals pointed out that the defendants' adherence to a policy of restricting education to 180 days per year for all students, without regard to any individual student's special needs, was incompatible with the Act's emphasis on the individual student. It further cited *Rowley* for its interpretation of the Act's emphasis on the individual student. The Court of Appeals concluded that, while the Act did not require states to give handicapped children the means to achieve strict equality of opportunity or services, it did not permit the states to furnish handicapped children with "only such services as are available to nonhandicapped children" (p. 1034). Thus, Mississippi's adherence to the 180-day policy violated the Act. The Court rejected the argument that a lack of funds might relieve the state of its obligation to provide appropriate educational services to handicapped students more than it did the state's obligation to provide services to nonhandicapped children.

Lasting Impact or Subsequent History: The Court of Appeals stressed the importance of the IEP in determining the appropriateness of year-round education for handicapped children. For some children, such schooling is clearly appropriate, while for others, it may be no more necessary than it is for children without disabilities.

Cross-References

- The Education of All Handicapped Children Act of 1975 (P.L. 94-142)
- *Board of Education v. Rowley*
- *Battle v. Pennsylvania*

N.B. v. Warwick School Committee et al.: No. 03-1988 (1st Cir., March 18, 2004)

Factual Background: This case involves an attempt by parents to dictate the specific educational approach to be used by public schools in the education of their special-needs child under the Individuals with Disabilities Education Act (IDEA). The case revolves around N.B., a child with autism. His parents moved to Warwick, Rhode Island, in 2000, at which time they contacted the school district to find out what special education services would be available for their son in the district. The district called a meeting within 2 weeks, after reviewing materials relating to recent assessments at the child's former school, at which time an interim IEP was proposed, subject to revision after the school had time to observe N.B.'s progress under the interim IEP. Under the IEP, N.B. would be educated in a self-contained classroom established for autistic children of his age, where he would be instructed using a modified version of educational techniques known as Treatment and Education of Autistic and related Communication-handicapped CHildren (TEACCH). N.B.'s parents rejected the IEP and gave notice of their intent to enroll N.B. in a private school that used a different technique known as Discrete Trial Training (DTT).

N.B.'s parents requested a due process hearing. The hearing officer sided with N.B.'s parents, concluding that Warwick had violated its procedural obligations under the IDEA, and ordered the school district to reimburse N.B.'s parents for tuition costs and to pay future tuition at the private school where N.B. was enrolled. The parents proceeded to file suit in federal court for attorneys' fees, at which time the school district filed a countersuit, challenging the hearing officer's findings that it had committed procedural violations and denied N.B. a free appropriate public education.

Court's Holding: The District Court sided with the school district, finding that any procedural violations that may have existed were not sufficient to justify rejection of the IEP or to mandate tuition reimbursement, and that the IEP proposed by the school district did not deny N.B. a free and appropriate public education.

The First Circuit Court of Appeals upheld the decision of the District Court. Citing prior cases, including *Board of Education v. Rowley,* the Court of Appeals noted that the IDEA does not require a public school to provide what is "best" for a special-needs child, only that it provide an IEP that is "reasonably calculated to provide an appropriate education as defined in federal and state law." The Court of Appeals rejected an argument put forth by N.B.'s parents that the 1997 amendments to the IDEA changed this standard in a way that required school districts to provide the "maximum benefit" to special-needs children, noting that other courts had continued to apply the standard articulated in the *Rowley* decision subsequent to the enactment of the 1997 IDEA amendments.

Lasting Impact or Subsequent History: It is far too soon to speculate what the lasting impact of this case will be, if any. It does provide further evidence that parents do not have a right to demand that a particular educational approach be used with their learning-disabled or otherwise mentally impaired child.

Cross-References

- Individuals with Disabilities Education Act
- *Board of Education v. Rowley*

PROFESSIONAL STANDARDS FOR SCHOOL PSYCHOLOGISTS

The following case highlights the role of the professional obligations of school psychologists.

Forrest v. Ambach: 107 Misc. 2d 920 (Sup. Ct. New York, 1980)

Factual Background: This case arose from the termination of the part-time employment of a school psychologist named Muriel Forrest. The school district claimed she was terminated because her work was unsatisfactory and because she refused to follow orders directing her to change the way in which she prepared her reports regarding her evaluations of potentially handicapped or disabled children.

Forrest claimed that she was terminated for adhering to professional obligations to perform evaluations of handicapped children in the manner required under certain state and federal laws and regulations. Specifically, she claimed that she was fired because her thorough evaluations of children suspected of having handicapping conditions "tended to expose [the school district's] attempts to avoid their statutory obligations regarding such children." She further argued that her dismissal interfered with her constitutional right to free expression and with her performance of her duties under federal and state laws governing education for handicapped children. In addition, Forrest asserted that she was, in fact, a tenured employee, and thus could not be summarily dismissed.

Court's Holding: The New York court first rejected Forrest's claim that she was a tenured employee, noting that she had been specifically notified in 1978 that, as a part-time employee, she was ineligible for tenure. Thus, she was what is known as an "at-will" employee who could be terminated at the board's discretion. However, the court pointed out that there was an exception to this at-will employment, if the plaintiff could establish that her employment was terminated for a constitutionally impermissible purpose. The court found that professionals like school psychologists have levels of professional competence and "standards which must be recognized and respected, not only for the profession itself, but for the purpose of rendering the best service to the school board and ultimately to the students they serve" (p. 924). The court ruled that if Forrest truly was dismissed solely due to her professional standards as a psychologist, then her dismissal would indeed be "arbitrary, capricious and unconstitutional" (p. 924). The court remanded the case to the Commissioner of Education (Ambach) for further findings as to whether Forrest was, in fact, so dismissed.

Lasting Impact or Subsequent History: This decision emphasizes the impor-

Box 7.10

"The ethical standards of any professional employed by a school board cannot be cavalierly dismissed as irrelevant to the employer-employee relationship, and may indeed become quite relevant in certain circumstances."

Judge Lawrence E. Kahn, *Forrest v. Ambach*
107 Misc. 2d 920 (1980), 924

Box 7.11 Obtaining Full Text of Court Cases

There are a number of online sources available to those who wish to read the full text of the court decisions summarized in this chapter. One of the best free web sites for legal research is Findlaw (www.findlaw.com/casecode/index.html), which allows you to search through a variety of state and federal statutes, regulations, and cases. The major weakness of the Findlaw web site is that you have to know a bit about what you're looking for (e.g., party name, court, state, etc.) before you start searching, because if you look in the wrong place, you won't find anything. Its coverage is also limited primarily to upper-level federal court cases, so District Court and state court cases may be unavailable. Some schools have agreements with online providers of academic materials, which may include some access to legal databases like Lexis/Nexis. Such content is frequently expensive, however, and therefore generally unavailable even at secondary schools where students might be expected to do some online research. Sometimes merely entering a case's name into one of the popular web search engines, like Google (www.google.com) or Yahoo! (www.yahoo.com) will provide a link to the full text of the decision, as well.

tance of professional standards, providing important legal precedent for similar situations (Prasse, 2000).

REFERENCES

Lambert, N. M. (2000). Larry P. In C. R. Reynolds and E. Fletcher-Janzen (Eds.), *Encyclopedia of Special Education* (2nd ed., pp. 1058–1059). New York: Wiley.

Prasse, D. P. (2000). Forrest v. Ambach. In C. R. Reynolds and E. Fletcher-Janzen (Eds.), *Encyclopedia of Special Education* (2nd ed., pp. 762–763). New York: Wiley.

Reschly, D. J. (2000). PASE v. Hannon. In C. R. Reynolds and E. Fletcher-Janzen (Eds.), *Encyclopedia of Special Education* (2nd ed., pp. 1325–1326). New York: Wiley.

Reynolds, C. R. (2000). Deborah P. v. Turlington. In C. R. Reynolds and E. Fletcher-Janzen (Eds.), *Encyclopedia of Special Education* (2nd ed., p. 543). New York: Wiley.

8

Useful Web Sites for Special Educators

JOHN O. WILLIS AND RON DUMONT

This list of Uniform Resource Locators (URLs) that we have found helpful is necessarily subjective and limited by our experience. Omission of a Web address is more likely to reflect our ignorance than a decision to omit a site. All links were active as of July 2004 but, of course, may not remain online. Any list of URLs can turn out to be a moving target. For example, the Educational Resources Information Center (ERIC; http://www.eric.ed.gov/) "will introduce a new Web site on September 1, 2004."

Descriptions within quotation marks are taken from the listed web sites. The notation "membership" means that one may join the sponsoring organization, not that paid membership is required to access the site (although there may be members-only pages as well as open ones). However, free registration is required to access some listed sites. Some sites require paid membership to access members-only pages within the site, but all of the sites listed in this chapter provide some information at no cost. You should, of course, always exercise caution in sending personal information, especially credit card numbers, over the Internet.

We gratefully acknowledge the valuable assistance of A. Lynne Beal, PhD, Judith E. Bischoff, MEd, SAIF, Carol Anne Evans, MEd, Robin Peters Henne, MS, SAIF, Guy M. McBride, PhD, NCSP, and Susan Morbey, SAIF.

Disclosure: One of the web sites listed in this chapter, Dumont/Willis on the Web (http://alpha.fdu.edu/psychology), is operated by the authors. One or both of the authors have been compensated for consultation, examiner training, workshops, and/or service on an editorial board by the following publishers, whose web sites are listed in this chapter: American Guidance Service (AGS; http://www.agsnet.com/), Riverside Publishing (http://www.riverpub.com/), The Psychological Corporation (TPC; http://www.harcourtassessment.com), and John Wiley & Sons (http://www.wiley.com/).

Web site URLs are listed within each section in alphabetical order within categories. The categories are necessarily arbitrary, so, for example, a site listed under School Psychology might fit as well under Assessment. The "See also" lists at the ends of some categories refer to relevant addresses that are listed in other categories. The note at the beginning of each section suggests other sections with related content.

We have, in some cases, listed specific pages rather than the home pages of more general sites, because the specific page listed was more germane to special education. You may find it worthwhile to click on links to home pages (e.g., main, opening, title page for the site) and other pages listed on the side or top of the screen for the specific special education page we listed. If the page does not show a link to the home page, or if there is an error on the page that we provided here, try deleting the last (right-most) section of the address and hitting Enter or Return again. For example, http://trace.wisc.edu/resources/at-resources.shtml is the page for Selected Resources about Technology from the Trace Center of the College of Engineering at the University of Wisconsin. If you delete the last part of the address and hit Enter or Return, you will go to http://trace.wisc.edu/resources/, a broader, more general resources page. If you again delete the last part of the address (resources/), you will reach the home page for the Trace Center. Most sites contain much more information than we could cite here. You may find another page within the site more useful than the one that caught our attention. Also, a particular page within a site (possibly even the one we listed in this chapter) might become a dead link for some reason, but the rest of the site might still be active.

The notation "links" is especially important because it indicates that the web site includes one or more sets of links to other, related web sites. Those links are often the most valuable contribution offered by a web site, and were a major consideration in the selection of web sites for this chapter. The notation "downloadable" refers to articles, papers, PowerPoint presentations, Excel programs, and other documents that can be downloaded to your computer for later access, printing, or other uses permitted by the copyright holder. It is always a prudent habit to scan a potential download for viruses, even when you are taking it from a trusted source.

We have attempted to list only sites with information that appears to us to be useful, accessible, and trustworthy. Nonetheless, you must cautiously use your own good judgment in evaluating the information you find. See, for example, Stephen Barrett's warnings on his QuackWatch page at http://www.quackwatch.org/12Web/honviolators.html. Dr. Barrett notes concerns with some aspects of some of the sites listed in this chapter, although we decided they offered enough good information to justify keeping them in the list. We have generally excluded purely local and regional web sites unless they offered widely applicable information or links.

Many of the web sites offer bulletin boards, chat rooms, or listservs. These can be extremely valuable, but need to be used with caution. For example, a question about a test posted on the American Guidance Service (AGS) Psychological Forum (http://www.psychologicalforum.com/index2.asp) or Speech and Language Forum (http://www.speechandlanguage.com/) might elicit a reply from the author of the AGS test in question, but it might also elicit a reply from another member of the forum with unknown qualifications. You may wish to open a free electronic mail (e-mail) account (e.g., Yahoo or Hotmail) with a user name other than your own name and reserve it just for listservs, chat rooms, and bulletin boards. There may be times when your anonymity is essential, such as when your identity would be a clue to the identity of the carefully disguised student on whose behalf you are soliciting professional guidance, or when your boss is also a member of the same listserv. Anonymity can also be desirable if your reasonable and tactful opinion enrages another list member. You may also find it helpful to have separate accounts for personal e-mail and for listservs because some listservs have a high volume of e-mail. Bulletin boards and message centers do not send you e-mail, but let you visit and browse the postings when you wish. Many listservs offer options such as receiving each e-mail as it is posted, receiving a periodic digest of postings, or only visiting a web site to browse postings.

When typing Internet addresses, spelling counts. For example, http://www.disabilityresource.com/ and http://www.disabilityresources.org/ are two valuable but entirely different sites.

For information on effective use of special education web sites and Internet browsing, we highly recommend Sandra Steingart's *The Well-Connected School Psychologist: The Busy Person's Guide to School Psychology on the Internet (2004–2005 ed.)* (Longmont, CO: Sopris West, 2004). It is available in two versions, with and without a CD. These are print and electronic companions to Dr. Steingart's web site, http://www.schoolpsychology.net, listed below. In addition to a large collection of categorized and helpfully annotated Internet addresses for resources, the book includes a clear, detailed, practical tutorial for taking advantage of the Internet's resources, and a glossary.

ASSESSMENT

Information on assessment can also be found under Disabilities, Behavior Assessment and Intervention, Curriculum-Based Assessment and Curriculum-Based Measurement, General Sites for Special Education and School Psychology, School Psychology Pages, Special Education Law, Special Education and Psychology Organizations, Publishers, Speech and Language, and sections for specific disabilities. Publishers of tests often provide additional information and updates on the web sites about their tests.

http://espse.ed.psu.edu/spsy/Watkins/Watkins3.ssi Free download of Mountain Shadows Phonemic Awareness Scale. Watkins, M. W., & Edwards, V. A. (2004). Assessing early literacy skills with the Mountain Shadows Phonemic Awareness Scale (MS-PAS). *Journal of Psychoeducational Assessment, 22,* 3–14. Also a large number of downloadable statistics programs for evaluators and researchers.

http://gri.gallaudet.edu/~catraxle/reviews.html Review of tests for deaf and hard-of-hearing examinees. "Anne B. Spragins, Ph.D., and Lynne Blennerhassett, Ph.D. (both faculty members in the Psychology Department at Gallaudet University, 800 Florida Avenue NE, Washington, DC 20002), and Yvonne Mullen, Ed.D. (of the Division of Psychology, CLARKE School for the Deaf/Center for Oral Education, Round Hill Road, Northampton, MA 01060) have reviewed a variety of instruments for use with deaf and hard of hearing students. Anne Spragins developed these 1996 and 1998 Updates to the Four Test Reviews." Includes basic information about each test and a brief, critical review of each for use with examinees with hearing impairments.

http://gri.gallaudet.edu/Assessment/ Additional downloadable articles on "Assessment and Deaf Test Takers."

http://facpub.stjohns.edu/~ortizs/cross-battery/ "Official site of the CHC Cross-Battery Approach—Dawn P. Flanagan, Ph.D. & Samuel O. Ortiz, Ph.D. . . . CHC Cross-Battery Online is intended to serve as the central clearinghouse for dissemination of information, electronic resources, and downloadable materials regarding CHC Cross-Battery assessment, interpretation, and related issues (e.g., using the Cross-Battery approach in LD determination)." "Developed by Dawn P. Flanagan, Ph.D., Kevin S. McGrew, Ph.D., & Samuel O. Ortiz, Ph.D. and based on an integrated Cattell-Horn-Carroll (CHC) model of intelligence (formerly known as *Gf*-*Gc* theory), Cross-Battery assessment is an innovative and promising framework for significantly enhancing the reliability and validity of the measurement and interpretation of cognitive abilities." Includes downloadable resources, tutorials, library, and links.

http://pareonline.net/Home.htm *Practical Assessment, Research, and Evaluation,* a peer-reviewed electronic journal (ISSN 1531-7714). Articles may be downloaded and copied with acknowledgment, and you can sign up for notifications of new articles.

http://www.agsnet.com/calc/ Chronological age calculator for evaluators. Provided by American Guidance Service (AGS) for use online or to download.

http://www.apa.org/science/fairtestcode.html *Code of Fair Testing Practices in Education,* prepared by the Joint Committee on Testing Practices. The *Code* has been prepared by the Joint Committee on Testing Practices (American Counseling Association [ACA], American Educational Research Association [AERA], American Psychological Association [APA], American Speech-Language-Hearing Association [ASHA], National Association of School Psychologists [NASP], National Association of Test Directors [NATD], and National Council on Measurement in Education [NCME]).

http://www.cdc.gov/nchs/about/major/nhanes/growthcharts/clinical_charts.htm National Center for Health Statistics (Centers for Disease Control and Prevention [CDC]). Downloadable height, weight, body mass index charts. Lots of other information.

http://www.ed.gov/offices/OCR/archives/testing/contents *The Use of Tests as Part of High-Stakes Decision-Making for Students: A Resource Guide for Educators and Policy Makers.* Office of Civil Rights (OCR; December 2000). Extensive, downloadable report. "This resource guide has been developed by OCR in an effort to assemble the best information regarding test measurement standards, legal principles, and resources to help educators and policymakers ensure that uses of tests as a part of decision-making that has high-stakes consequences for students are educationally sound and legally appropriate. . . . This resource guide was developed by the U.S. Department of Education, in consultation with numerous stakeholders. . . . the primary drafters of this document: David Berkowitz, Barbara Wolkowitz, Rebecca Fitch, and Rebecca Kopriva (Consultant)." Includes detailed appendices.

http://www.ilstu.edu/~wjschne/tests.htm Psychological Tests and Test Interpretation Tools—W. Joel Schneider, PhD. Several, very useful Excel spreadsheets for scoring and interpreting several tests. Also includes "a suite of over 25 repeatable tests. For now, *none of them have been normed* [our emphasis] but they can be used for cognitive rehabilitation and qualitative assessment. The suite includes tests of attention, long-term and working memory, reasoning, reaction time, executive functions and visual-spatial processing."

http://www.natd.org/ National Association of Test Directors. Lots of links and information.

http://www.neuropsychologycentral.com/ Neuropsychology Central. Jeff Browndyke, Editor; Lee Ashendorf and Brandon Gavett, Webmasters. Many articles and links and a forum, all related to neuropsychology.

http://www.ssa.gov/disability/professionals/bluebook/ Disability Evaluation for Social Security (Blue Book—January 2003). "This edition of Disability Evaluation Under Social Security, (also known as the Blue Book), has been specially prepared to provide physicians and other health professionals with an understanding of the disability programs administered by the Social Security Administration. It explains how each program works, and the kinds of information a health professional can furnish to help ensure sound and prompt decisions on disability claims." Includes evidentiary requirements and listings of impairments.

http://www.unl.edu/buros/ Buros Institute of Mental Measurements. You can locate basic information on tests and purchase copies of reviews from the Mental Measurements Yearbooks for $15 each.

Please see also http://www.aph.org/, http://dibels.uoregon.edu, http://www.schoolpsychology.net, and most School Psychology Home Pages.

ATTENTION-DEFICIT/HYPERACTIVITY DISORDER (ADHD)

Additional resources for ADHD may be found under Assessment, Disabilities, General Sites for Special Education and School Psychology, Medical Information Not Listed Elsewhere, Parent, Advocacy, and Support Groups and Pages, Publishers, and School Psychology Pages.

http://www.chadd.org/ Children and Adults with Attention-Deficit/Hyperactivity Disorder. Membership; downloadable articles and fact sheets, free newsletter.

http://www.nichq.org/resources/toolkit/ National Initiative for Children's Healthcare Quality (NICHQ) ADHD Practitioners' Toolkit. "Sponsored by the American Academy of Pediatrics (AAP), the NICHQ set out to create a set of real-world tools for primary care practitioners to use in implementing the new AAP guidelines for treating ADHD. The documents available below are the product of this project. The Vanderbilt Tools are now available in Spanish. These newly translated tools are near the bottom of this page but are not part of the Toolkit. Note: also included in the Toolkit is a booklet for parents from the AAP entitled *Understanding ADHD: Information for Parents About Attention-Deficit/Hyperactivity Disorder.* This booklet is not available online but may be bought separately from the AAP." Free, downloadable information and checklists.

Please see also http://www.schoolpsychology.net.

AUTISM

Additional resources for autism, Pervasive Developmental Disorder, and Asperger syndrome may be found under Assessment, Disabilities, General Sites for Special Education and School Psychology, Medical Information Not Listed Elsewhere, Parent, Advocacy, and Support Groups and Pages, and School Psychology Pages.

http://info.med.yale.edu/chldstdy/autism/index.html Yale Child Study Center Developmental Disabilities Clinic. Information and links.

http://www.cdc.gov/nip/vacsafe/concerns/autism/autism-facts.htm Center for Disease Control. "Facts about Autism" with emphasis on the question of their viewpoint on immunizations; links.

http://www.health.state.ny.us/nysdoh/eip/autism/index.htm Downloadable Clinical Practice Guideline for Assessment and Intervention. "This guideline was developed by an independent panel of professionals and parents sponsored by the New York State Department of Health, Early Intervention Program."

http://www.nichd.nih.gov/autism/ National Institutes of Health, National Institute of Child Health and Development. Links to autism research.

http://www.udel.edu/bkirby/asperger/ Online Asperger Syndrome Information and Support (OASIS). Lots of downloadable information and many links, parent support, and message board.

Please see also http://www.schoolpsychology.net.

BEHAVIOR ASSESSMENT AND INTERVENTION

Additional resources for behavior assessment and intervention may be found under Assessment, Disabilities, General Sites for Special Education and School Psychology, Parent, Advocacy, and Support Groups and Pages, Publishers, and School Psychology Pages.

http://www.air-dc.org/cecp/ Center for Effective Collaboration and Practice. An array of downloadable papers, other resources, and links "related to emotional and behavioral problems in such areas as education, families, mental health, juvenile justice, child welfare, early intervention, school safety, and legislation." Safe Schools Guide is at http://www.air-dc.or/cecp/guide.

http://www.casel.org/ Collaborative for Academic, Social & Emotional Learning. Newsletters, publications, downloadable articles.

http://www.counseling.org/ American Counseling Association. Membership; bookstore, downloadable information, links.

http://www.pbis.org/ Office of Special Education Programs (OSEP). Technical Assistance Center on Positive Behavioral Interventions and Supports (PBIS). Downloadable articles, papers, forms, and tools, links.

Please see also http://www.interventioncentral.org/, and http://www.school psychology.net.

BLINDNESS AND VISUAL IMPAIRMENT

Additional resources for blindness and visual impairment may be found under Assessment, Books on Tape or CD, Disabilities, General Sites for Special Education and School Psychology, Parent, Advocacy, and Support Groups and Pages, Publishers, Medical Information Not Listed Elsewhere, School Psychology Pages, and Technology Not Listed Elsewhere.

http://cim.ucdavis.edu/eyes/eyesim.htm Eye Simulation "application simulates eye motion and demonstrates the effects of disabling one or more of the 12 eyes muscles and one or more of the 6 cranial nerves that control eye motion. The purpose of this simulator is to teach medical students and doctors how the eye motion will change with pathology of the eye muscles and cranial nerves and what to look for during a standard neurological eye exam."

http://www.aao.org American Academy of Ophthalmology. Information about vision, including papers on controversial "complementary therapies," such as vision therapy for learning disabilities.

http://www.acb.org/ American Council of the Blind. "The Council strives to improve the well-being of all blind and visually impaired people by: serving as a representative national organization of blind people; elevating the social, economic and cultural levels of blind people; improving educational and rehabilitation facilities and opportunities; cooperating with the public and private institutions and organizations concerned with blind services; encouraging and assisting all blind persons to develop their abilities and conducting a public education program to promote greater understanding of blindness and the capabilities of blind people." Membership; magazine (online in print, voice, and braille), store, links.

http://www.afb.org/ American Foundation for the Blind. Information and a specialized search engine.

http://www.aph.org/ American Printing House for the Blind. Links, large catalogue of books, software, and equipment, custom production services, information on Accessible Tests.

http://wwweb.org/oma/ Ocular motor apraxia home page. Information, message board, mailing list.

http://www.lea-test.fi/en/vistests/pediatric/pedtests.html Instructions for LEA pediatric vision tests. Some tests allow examiners to check near vision with symbols rather than letters—very important if school nurses do not check near vision. Cards can be purchased from https://www.schoolhealth.com/.

http://www.lowvision.org/ Low Vision Gateway. Discussion group and lots of information. Categorized lists of links for equipment and specialists.

http://www.nfb.org/ National Federation of the Blind. "The purpose of the National Federation of the Blind is two-fold—to help blind persons achieve self-confidence and self-respect and to act as a vehicle for collective self-expression by the blind. By providing public education about blindness, information and referral services, scholarships, literature and publications about blindness, aids and appliances and other adaptive equipment for the blind, advocacy services and protection of civil rights, development and evaluation of technology, and support for blind persons and their families, members of the NFB strive to educate the public that the blind are normal individuals who can compete on terms of equality." Membership; information, categorized links, publications, news.

https://www.schoolhealth.com/ School Health. Commercial site for school health programs, including vision and hearing screening and tests. For near vision screening cards: register, then click on vision and hearing screening, then visual acuity charts. LEA and other near vision symbol cards are among the options.

http://www.tsbvi.edu/index.htm Texas School for the Blind and Visually Impaired. Lots of general information and links.

Please see also http://www.rfbd.org/, http://www.schoolpsychology.net, and http://www.tsbvi.edu/Education/audioassisted.htm.

BOOKS ON TAPE OR CD

Additional resources for books on tape or CD may be found under Booksellers and Clearinghouses Online, Publishers, Reading, Teaching, and Technology Not Listed Elsewhere.

http://www.audiobookshelf.com/index.html Sales of unabridged books; information for use of audiobooks in school.

http://www.blackstoneaudio.com/ Commercial sales and rentals of unabridged books.

http://www.recordedbooks.com/ Commercial sales and rentals of unabridged books; resources for schools, including packages of audiobooks and books in print, equipment, variable-speed recordings, resources for teachers and librarians.

http://www.rfbd.org/ Recording for the Blind and Dyslexic. Paid membership required for recorded books and players. With sufficient notice, books can be recorded by request.

http://www.tsbvi.edu/Education/audioassisted.htm *Changing Channels—AudioAssisted Reading: Access to Curriculum for Students with Print Disabilities.* Carol Anne Evans. Paper explains how to make the best use of audiobooks and materials. Very useful.

BOOKSELLERS AND CLEARINGHOUSES ONLINE

Books are also available, of course, from sources listed under Publishers. Please see also Reading. Many web sites encourage you to purchase books online through a link between the site and Amazon (http://www.amazon.com) or another bookseller. These arrangements typically yield a small royalty for the web site for each sale. Even if you plan to purchase a book through your local independent bookstore, these sites allow you to look up information on the book.

http://www.amazon.com Amazon. Commercial bookseller of new and used books and other items.

http://www.any-book-in-print.com/index.htm Discount books for educators.

http://www.a-z-books.com/index.html A-Z Books. Searches for new and used books.

http://www.barnesandnoble.com Barnes and Noble. Commercial bookseller of new and used books and other items.

http://www.bestwebbuys.com/books/index.html Online comparison shopping for new and used books.

http://www.bookfinder.com/ BookFinder.com. Searches for new and used books.

CURRICULUM-BASED ASSESSMENT, CURRICULUM-BASED MEASUREMENT

Additional resources for curriculum-based assessment or measurement may be found under Assessment, General Sites for Special Education and School Psychology, Problem-Solving Model, Publishers, and School Psychology Pages.

http://education.umn.edu/CI/MREA/CBM/cbmMOD.html Minnesota Reading Excellence Act Progress Measures. Professor Stan Deno, University of Minnesota. "The purpose of this module is to provide participants with an introduction to procedures for monitoring student reading progress in the classroom based on Curriculum Based Measurement (CBM), and the steps required to implement a system for screening and monitoring students in the area of reading and summary of research on the effectiveness of these procedures. Throughout this module the focus is on students who are not making satisfactory progress and are at risk of failing to develop basic reading skills. This module is organized into fifteen sections. In addition, a study guide has been developed that complements the information and procedures outlined in this module."

http://www.aimsweb.com/ "AIMSweb® is a formative assessment system that 'informs' the teaching and learning process by providing continuous student performance data and reporting improvement to students, parents, teachers, and administrators to enable evidence-based evaluation and data-driven instruction. Based on over 25 years of scientific research, the AIMSweb® system consists of Standard Curriculum-Based Measurement (CBM) testing materials and web-based data management and reporting applications." Although it is a commercial site with materials for purchase, AIMSweb® also includes free, useful articles about curriculum-based measurement.

Please see also http://dibels.uoregon.edu, http://www.interventioncentral.org/, and most of Problem-Solving Model.

DEAFNESS AND HEARING IMPAIRMENT

Additional resources for deafness and hearing impairment may be found under Assessment, Disabilities, General Sites for Special Education and School Psychology, Parent, Advocacy, and Support Groups and Pages, Publishers, Medical Information Not Listed Elsewhere, School Psychology Pages, and Technology Not Listed Elsewhere. There is considerable controversy about the education of deaf children.

You will find some sites strongly advocating a purely oral approach to teaching and others strongly advocating the additional use of manual communication. Educators, parents, and deaf adults have many different viewpoints on these questions, cochlear implants, and other issues.

http://clerccenter.gallaudet.edu/ Gallaudet University. Many links and resources, including the one following.

http://clerccenter.gallaudet.edu/Literacy/ Laurent Clerc National Deaf Education Center, Gallaudet University. Many links and resources.

http://commtechlab.msu.edu/sites/aslweb/browser.htm Michigan State University Communication Technology Laboratory: alphabetized glossary of finger-spelled letters and signed words with a verbal description of each and a picture (which requires installation of Apple QuickTime).

http://home.inreach.com/torsi/frame.html Deaf Education: A Parents' Guide. "The purpose of this page and the various linking pages are an attempt to serve as a guide and provide information to parents and others with regard to issues related to deafness, the education of the deaf, and Deaf culture. This guide is not to be used as sole resource for information, but merely a starting point for further inquiry into other sources. The issues presented here are meant to inform in an unbiased way the various aspects of deaf education." Many pages of information and links.

http://www.agbell.org/ Alexander Graham Bell Association for the Deaf and Hard of Hearing. Membership; information, news, job search, and school search.

http://www.beginningssvcs.com/ Beginnings for Parents of Children Who are Deaf or Hard of Hearing. Articles, information, and links.

http://www.deafchildren.org/resources/resources.html American Society for Deaf Children. Membership; information, and links.

http://www.deafnation.com/ DeafNation Language and Cultural Pride. "DeafNation.com is on the Internet to become the on-line destination for Web surfers wanting to stay abreast of what's happening in the deaf and hard-of-hearing community. The Web site provides constantly updated news feed, video clips in sign language, and the latest in deaf sports accessed through www.deafnation.com." Includes advertisements and an online store.

http://www.gallaudet.edu/ Gallaudet University, Washington, DC. "Undergraduate and graduate programs for deaf, hard of hearing, and hearing students." Research papers (some online, some for purchase) are posted at http://gri.gallaudet.edu/.

http://www.hearmore.com Commercial products for persons who are deaf or hard-of-hearing.

http://www.lburkhart.com/elem/sssign.htm "This is a list of Web sites that have online Signs. Look up a sign for a word or learn to fingerspell. Some sites even offer a quiz feature so you can test your skills." Linda J. Burkhart.

http://www.nad.org/ National Association of the Deaf. Membership; news, advocacy, discussion forums, links.

http://www.shhh.org "Self Help for Hard of Hearing People is the nation's largest organization for people with hearing loss. SHHH exists to open the world of communication for people with hearing loss through information, education, advocacy and support." Membership; information, store, news, links.

Please see also http://gri.gallaudet.edu/, http://gri.gallaudet.edu/~catraxle/reviews.html, and http://www.schoolpsychology.net.

DISABILITIES

Each of the web sites in this section covers a wide range of disabilities. There are thousands of web sites devoted to specific disabilities. A few sections in this chapter (Autism, Blindness and Visual Impairment, Deafness and Hearing Impairment, Learning Disabilities and Dyslexia, Mental Retardation/Intellectual Challenge, and Speech and Language) list such sites, but they barely scratch the surface. To find web sites that focus on a particular disability, you can use the categorized links posted on many of the web sites following. An Internet search using one of the search engines listed in the Tools section of this chapter will find hundreds of additional web sites for most disabilities. The depth and accuracy of information provided in those sites vary tremendously, and the variation does not always follow the apparent qualifications of the person or group operating the web site. Some parent-run sites contain extremely valuable information, whereas others may reflect the unique personal experiences and conclusions of a parent whose circumstances may have been atypical. Similarly, a professional web site may contain current and generally accepted information or may exist to support a theory not shared by most experts in the field. Cautious skepticism is essential.

http://cpmcnet.columbia.edu/dept/nsg/PNS/ Columbia University Pediatric Neurosurgery Home Page. "This site is dedicated to providing families with information regarding various aspects of the field of pediatric neurosurgery. . . . This page is designed and written not for professionals, but rather for parents and friends looking for answers to common pediatric neurosurgical conditions. This page is maintained by Neil Feldstein MD, a pediatric neurosurgeon at Columbia-Presbyterian Medical Center in New York City. It does not necessarily reflect the opinions or sentiments of any governing body of neurosurgery. It does try to give a general synopsis of current surgical views. Obviously, any questions you have regarding this information and the specific care your child is receiving should be discussed with your neurosurgeon." Information is categorized by disabilities and is accessible by clicking on the topic.

http://familyvillage.wisc.edu/ Family Village, a Global Community of Disability-Related Resources. This site "integrates information, resources, and communication opportunities on the Internet for persons with cognitive and other disabilities, for their families, and for those that provide them services and support . . . includes informational resources on specific diagnoses, communication connections, adaptive products and technology, adaptive recreational activities, education, worship, health issues, disability-related media and literature, and much, much more!" The Library includes an alphabetical card file of many links to web pages devoted to specific diagnoses and to more general information. Links to chat rooms, resources for adaptive equipment, educational resources, books and articles, and so on. Waisman Center, University of Wisconsin-Madison.

http://seriweb.com/ Special Education Resources on the Internet. Lots of categorized links.

http://www.ahead.org/homepage.html Association on Higher Education and Disability. Membership; online information, notices of training.

http://www.biausa.org/ Brain Injury Association of America. Lots of information and links.

http://www.disabilityresource.com/ "The Disability Resource is dedicated to providing valuable information and resources of information to people with disabilities and the people who care for them." Central site for companies selling products for persons with disabilities. You can request "cardpacks" of postcards from their advertisers. There are also links to web sites of their advertisers and other manufacturers. You must select, copy, and paste the addresses into the address box in your browser to go to the manufacturer's web site.

http://www.disabilityresources.org/ Disabilities Resources Monthly Guide to Disability Resources on the Internet. Many categorized links.

http://www.hgmp.mrc.ac.uk/DHMHD/view_human.html MRC Rosalind Franklin Centre for Genomics Research. Alphabetical list of hundreds of genetic dysmorphic syndromes, listing the features of each.

http://www.miusa.org/ Mobility International USA. "Empowering people with disabilities around the world by ensuring their inclusion in international exchange and international development programs." Information about international exchange programs and development for persons with disabilities.

http://nichcy.org/resources/default.asp National Dissemination Center for Children with Disabilities (NICHCY). Searchable database with links for a wide variety of topics, including specific disabilities.

http://www.ninds.nih.gov/index.htm National Institute of Neurological Diseases and Stroke. Information on this branch of the National Institutes of Health, news, job information, and a very large, searchable, list of disorders, each with information and links to many web sites devoted to the disorder.

http://www.rarediseases.org/ National Organization for Rare Disorders (NORD). Huge database of information on low-incidence disorders. Some useful information can be viewed online and reports can be purchased. Also, news briefs and other information. Paid membership and subscriptions are available.

http://www.sath.org/ Society for Accessible Travel and Hospitality: lots of information and links regarding travel for persons with disabilities.

http://www.tash.org/ "TASH is an international association of people with disabilities, their family members, other advocates, and professionals fighting for a society in which inclusion of all people in all aspects of society is the norm." Paid membership. Some information available at the web site.

http://www.ucp.org/ United Cerebral Palsy. Paid membership. Lots of information on various related disabilities available at the web site.

Please see also http://health.nih.gov/, and http://www.schoolpsychology.net.

GENERAL SITES FOR SPECIAL EDUCATION AND SCHOOL PSYCHOLOGY

Most of these sites are relevant to most if not all of the other categories in this chapter and may serve as starting points for searches for information not included in the chapter.

http://alpha.fdu.edu/psychology Dumont/Willis on the Web. Articles, free downloadable software for interpreting tests, free downloadable forms, links. [Refer to disclosure at beginning of this chapter.]

http://www.apa.org/psychologists/ American Psychological Association. Many articles and fact sheets. See also http://www.indiana.edu/~div16/index.html.

http://www.apa.org/monitor/ American Psychological Association, *Monitor on Psychology.* Articles on psychological topics from 1998 to the present.

http://www.ed.gov/index.jhtml U.S. Department of Education home page. Links to articles and publications.

http://www.ed.gov/pubs/socialpromotion/index.html 1999 U.S. Department of Education Report. "Taking Responsibility for Ending Social Promotion: A Guide for Educators and State and Local Leaders." Includes specific recommendations.

http://www.edpubs.org/webstore/Content/search.asp To order publications from U.S. Department of Education.

http://www.ibwebs.com/canadian.htm Canadian Special Education. Canadian province-by-province links to Boards of Education and Departments of Education, and some resources, such as Hearing Associations.

http://www.indiana.edu/~div16/index.html American Psychological Association Division (16) of School Psychology. Membership; information, online editions of *The School Psychologist.*

http://www.interventioncentral.org/ Jim Wright's Intervention Central. This site "offers free tools and resources to help school staff and parents to promote positive classroom behaviors and foster effective learning for all children and youth. The site was created by Jim Wright, a school psychologist from Syracuse, NY." It includes articles, online tools, downloadable forms, and valuable links.

http://www.schoolpsychology.net Sandra Steingart's School Psychology Resources Online. Contains carefully classified links for psychologists, parents, and educators to hundreds of URLs for specific conditions and disorders, and dozens of categories of general information, as well as a bookstore, job listings, and other information.

http://www.thegateway.org/ "The Gateway to Educational Materials℠ is a Consortium effort to provide educators with quick and easy access to thousands of educational resources found on various federal, state, university, non-profit, and commercial Internet sites. GEM is sponsored by the *U.S. Department of Education.* Teachers, parents, administrators can search or browse The Gateway℠ and find thousands of educational materials, including lesson plans, activities, and projects from over 500 of the 700+ *GEM* Consortium members."

HISTORY

http://psychclassics.yorku.ca/ "An Electronic Resource Developed by Christopher D. Green, York University, Toronto, Canada ISSN 1492-3173." Very large, searchable, downloadable collection of more than 200 full-text primary sources in psychology (e.g., Aristotle, Broca, Descartes, Freud, James, Maslow, Pavlov, Rogers, Wertheimer, Witmer) with a link to York University History & Theory of Psychology Electronic Question & Answer Forum.

http://www.indiana.edu/%7Eintell/ "This site includes biographical profiles of people who have influenced the development of intelligence theory and testing, in-depth articles exploring current controversies related to human intelligence, and resources for teachers." Dr. Jonathan Plucker, Indiana University.

http://www.nyise.org/blind/ History of Reading Codes for the Blind from The New York Institute for Special Education.

Please see also http://www.iapsych.com/.

LEARNING DISABILITIES AND DYSLEXIA

Additional resources for learning disabilities and dyslexia may be found under Assessment, Disabilities, General Sites for Special Education and School Psychology, Medical Information Not Listed Elsewhere, Parent, Advocacy, and Support Groups and Pages, Publishers, School Psychology Pages, and Technology Not Listed Elsewhere.

http://www.allkindsofminds.org/ Mel Levine's institute for understanding learning differences. Membership; downloadable articles, discussion groups, and books and assessment tools for purchase.

http://www.interdys.org/index.jsp International Dyslexia Association. "The International Dyslexia Association (IDA) is a non-profit organization dedicated to helping individuals with dyslexia, their families and the communities that support them." Information, member forum, and links regarding dyslexia and reading.

http://www.ldanatl.org/ Learning Disabilities Association of America. Membership; information about learning disabilities, bookstore, links.

http://www.ldao.ca Learning Disabilities Association of Ontario. Information about learning disabilities, online resources including question-answer bulletin boards, links to online courses about LD, and LDAO projects, sponsors, events, and comments on political issues.

http://www.ldonline.org/ LDOnLine. Newsletter, news, lots of categorized information, many categorized links, listings for professionals, products, and schools.

http://www.nasponline.org/advocacy/ldreferences.html National Association of School Psychologists (NASP). Internet and print resources on the reauthorization of the Individuals with Disabilities Education Act (IDEA) and learning disabilities reforms.

http://www.nldline.com/ Nonverbal learning disabilities and related topics: links, chatrooms, news, and many articles.

http://www.nldontheweb.org/ Nonverbal learning disabilities and related topics: links, forum, news, and many articles.

http://www.nrcld.org/html/information/articles/digests/digest3.html National Research Center on Learning Disabilities (NRCLD) Information Digest #3: *Researcher Consensus Statement.* "As a follow up to the Learning Disabilities Summit: Building a Foundation for the Future, the Office of Special Education Programs (OSEP) in the U.S. Department of Education brought together a group of researchers for a meeting November 29–30, 2001." This is the digest of their agreements about learning disabilities.

http://www.schwablearning.org/index.asp Schwab Learning for learning "differences," not "disabilities." Designed for parents, but useful for professionals as well. Newsletter, articles, message boards, set up "my page."

Please see also http://www.aao.org, and http://www.schoolpsychology.net.

MEDICAL INFORMATION NOT LISTED ELSEWHERE

This section contains medical information not listed under the other categories.

http://aappolicy.aappublications.org/ American Academy of Pediatrics. Downloadable policy statements, clinical and technical reports, clinical practice guidelines (e.g., treatment of ADHD), and parent pages. Articles include links to other sources of information.

http://familydoctor.org/ American Academy of Family Physicians. Alphabetized, searchable information on many health conditions and issues, dictionary, drug information, search by symptoms.

http://www.health.org/ National Clearinghouse for Drug & Alcohol Information (Substance Abuse and Mental Health Services Administration [SAMHSA], an agency of the U.S. Department of Health & Human Services). Many related links available when you click on Resources near the top of the page.

http://www.healthfinder.gov Healthfinder®. This site was "developed by the U.S. Department of Health and Human Services together with other Federal agencies." Lots of information on health issues and disabilities. The directory of Healthfinder® organizations includes links to many health-related sites.

http://www.hon.ch Health On Net Foundation search engine. Produces huge numbers of links on disabilities and health issues.

http://www.mayohealth.org Mayo Clinic. Huge database of information on diseases and conditions and on medications, including controversial alternative therapies.

http://www.medscape.com Medscape™ from WebMD™. Requires membership for free newsletters and use of medical search engines.

http://health.nih.gov/ National Institutes of Health. Huge, searchable database of health information, including disabilities.

http://www.ncbi.nlm.nih.gov/entrez/query.fcgi Department of Health and Human Services. "PubMed, a service of the National Library of Medicine, includes over 14 million citations for biomedical articles back to the 1950's. These citations are from MEDLINE and additional life science journals.

PubMed includes links to many sites providing full text articles and other related resources."

http://www.neuroguide.com/ Neurosciences on the Internet. "A searchable and browsable index of neuroscience resources available on the Internet: Neurobiology, neurology, neurosurgery, psychiatry, psychology, cognitive science sites and information on human neurological diseases."

http://www.nlm.nih.gov/ National Library of Medicine. Tremendous amount of searchable medical information. Easy access site at http://www.nlm.nih.gov/medlineplus/ with interactive tutorials and other resources.

http://www.pediatricneurology.com/ Pediatric Neurological Associates. A selective set of "Best Bet Web Sites" links, a search engine, articles by their staff members, and links to purchase their books.

http://www.quackwatch.org/index.html Stephen Barrett, MD, Guide to Health Fraud. Warnings and articles about unproved and disproved therapies and related topics, some of which, such as "Nutritional Supplements for Down Syndrome" by Len Leshin, are directly germane to special education. Material reflects Dr. Barrett's and colleagues' opinions.

http://www.rxlist.com/ RxList, the Internet Drug Index. Searchable database of information on drugs; searchable medical definitions from Taber's Medical encyclopedia; searchable database of definitions of medical abbreviations; online pharmacy.

Please see also http://www.hgmp.mrc.ac.uk/DHMHD/view_human.html, https://www.schoolhealth.com/, and http://www.schoolpsychology.net.

MENTAL RETARDATION/INTELLECTUAL CHALLENGE

Additional resources for mental retardation and intellectual challenge may be found under Assessment, Disabilities, General Sites for Special Education and School Psychology, Parent, Advocacy, and Support Groups and Pages, Publishers, Medical Information Not Listed Elsewhere, School Psychology Pages, and Technology Not Listed Elsewhere.

http://nads.org/ National Association for Down Syndrome. Information, discussion group, products and publications, links.

http://www.aamr.org American Association on Mental Retardation. Membership; downloadable information, including their definition of mental retardation, bookstore, downloadable books, free access to archived issues of *Mental Retardation and American Journal on Mental Retardation.*

http://www.acf.hhs.gov/programs/pcpid/ President's Committee for People with Intellectual Disabilities. Information about the Committee and some links.

http://www.thenadd.org/ National Association for the Dually Diagnosed (developmental disabilities and mental health needs). Membership; information, discussion forum, links.

http://www.psychiatry.com/ Psychiatry.com is maintained by Mark J. Hauser; under "Resources," there are several pages of categorized links, including mental retardation and mental retardation and psychiatry. There are also student information and a discussion forum.

http://www.thearc.org/ "The Arc is the national organization of and for people with mental retardation and related developmental disabilities and their families. It is devoted to promoting and improving supports and services for people with mental retardation and their families. The association also fosters research and education." Membership; downloadable articles, some links.

Please see also http://www.schoolpsychology.net.

PARENT, ADVOCACY, AND SUPPORT GROUPS AND PAGES

Advocacy and support information for parents may also be found under Disabilities, sections for various specific disabilities, and Special Education Law. Many parent-oriented sites reflect extremely strong personal opinions.

http://groups.yahoo.com/group/IEP_guide/, http://groups.yahoo.com/group/iepguidefilesII Two web pages with extensive special education information for parents and advocates. A list of useful links is available to nonmembers. Access to archived messages and posted articles requires free membership.

http://www.al-anon.alateen.org/ Al-Anon and Alateen. Resources for adults and teenagers whose lives are affected by someone's drinking. Link to find a local meeting. You must click on "English" or "Spanish" to get past the opening page.

http://www.copaa.net/ Council of Parent Attorneys and Advocates. Restricted membership, but useful downloads are available to nonmembers.

http://www.fetaweb.com/help/states.htm Wrightslaw state-by-state listing of parent resources. See also http://www.wrightslaw.com.

http://www.our-kids.org/ Our-Kids for parents of children with disabilities: e-mail and chat room for members, articles, stories, poems, and links.

http://www.pacer.org/ Parent Advocacy Coalition for Educational Rights, a national center based in Minnesota. "The mission of PACER Center is to expand opportunities and enhance the quality of life of children and young adults with disabilities and their families, based on the concept of parents helping parents. Through its ALLIANCE and other national projects, PACER, a national center, responds to thousands of parents and professionals each year. . . . With assistance to individual families, workshops, materials for parents and professionals, and leadership in securing a free and appropriate public education for all children, PACER's work affects and encourages families. . . . Paula F. Goldberg, Executive Director." Articles, links.

http://www.selectivemutism.org/ Selective Mutism Group—Childhood Anxiety Network. Membership; forum, chat room, downloadable articles, FAQs, handout.

http://www.giftfromwithin.org/ Gift From Within, "An International Organization for Survivors of Trauma and Victimization is a private, non-profit organization dedicated to those who suffer post-traumatic stress disorder

(PTSD), those at risk for PTSD, and those who care for traumatized individuals; develops and disseminates educational material, including videotapes, articles, books, and other resources through its website; maintains a roster of survivors who are willing to participate in an international network of peer support; is designated by the Internal Revenue Service as 501(c)(3) public charity, eligible to receive tax-exempt grants, gifts, and donations." Articles, links, purchasable audiovisual resources, support groups.

Please see also http://familyvillage.wisc.edu/, http://home.inreach.com/torsi/frame.html, http://www.beginningssvcs.com/, http://www.proactiveparent.com, http://www.schoolpsychology.net, and http://www.wrightslaw.com.

PROBLEM-SOLVING MODEL

Please see also Curriculum-Based Assessment, Curriculum-Based Measurement, and Special Education Law.

http://tasponline.org/home.htm Tennessee Association of School Psychologists web site. Scroll down and right to *The Demise of IQ Testing for Children with Learning Disabilities,* a PowerPoint presentation by Robert H. Pasternack, PhD, a seminal presentation on Response to Intervention (RTI) and the Problem-Solving Model (PSM).

http://www.fcrr.org/staffpresentations/Joe/NA/Special%20Ed%20Directors—LDNA.ppt *Alternate Methods for Identifying Children with Learning Disabilities: Some Synergies with Reading First in Florida.* PowerPoint presentation by Joseph K. Torgesen, Association of Special Education Directors, Tampa, FL, Sept. 2002.

http://www.aea1.k12.ia.us/spedmanual/manual.html Manual (228 pages) from the Keystone, Iowa, Area Education Agency (AEA). Keystone has published its material on the Internet, addressing special education entitlement decisions in some depth. There are also some useful links.

http://www.cecdr.org/testimony/February25/Reschly.pdf Reschly, D. J. (2002). *Minority Students in Gifted and Special Education* (NRC, 2002). Presentation to the White House Commission on Excellence in Special Education, February 25. Discusses disparate impact and cites the PSM as a means for reducing disproportionality.

http://www.fsds.org/index.html Flexible Service Delivery, "a change effort supported by the Illinois State Board of Education is designed to deliver educational services that are more responsive to students." Membership; newsletter, information, downloadable PowerPoint and Pack And Go training packages, links to training sessions, and forum.

http://www.mpls.k12.mn.us/services/speced/resources/psm/Comparison_PSM_state.pdf Information about the Minneapolis Problem-Solving Model, often referenced in discussions of this topic and Response to Intervention. This link will take you to a search page. Enter "Problem-Solving Model" to be given a list of relevant pages.

http://www.nasponline.org/information/pospaper_rwl.html National Association of School Psychologists (NASP) Position Statement on Rights Without Labels.

http://www.nasponline.org/futures/horrycounty.html Barbour, C. B., & Schwanz, K. A. (2002). The Winds of Change: A Problem Solving Model in Horry County. National Association of School Psychologists (NASP) *Communiqué, 30,* 8. Description of Horry County's model with data.

http://www.nasponline.org/futures/psmbiblio.html Canter, A. (2002). *Introduction to Problem Solving: Resources for Educators.* National Association of School Psychologists (NASP) *Communiqué, 31,* 4. A useful bibliography compiled by Andrea Canter.

http://www.nasponline.org/publications/cq308minneapolis.html Marston, D., Canter, A., Lau, M., & Muyskens, P. (2002). Problem Solving: Implementation and Evaluation in Minneapolis Schools. National Association of School Psychologists (NASP) *Communiqué, 30,* 8.

http://nrcld.org/html/symposium2003/index.html Text and PowerPoint papers from the National Resource Center on Learning Disabilities (NRCLD) Responsiveness-to-Intervention Symposium, December 4–5, 2003, Kansas City, MO.

Please see also http://www.interventioncentral.org/, http://dibels.uoregon.edu, and http://www.nasponline.org/advocacy/ldreferences.html.

PUBLISHERS

It can be worthwhile to take time to explore a publisher's web site. There are often free tools, sign-ups for free newsletters, free downloads of articles and bibliographies, and discussion groups or bulletin boards. If you use tests, it is prudent to keep visiting the publisher's web site for new information about your tests. Some publishers invite submission of manuscripts or ideas for tests or teaching materials. Many test publishers solicit examiners to try out or norm new tests and compensate examiners with cash or purchase certificates. Additional resources may be found at Booksellers and Clearinghouses Online.

http://www.academictherapy.com/ Academic Therapy Publications. Assessments, curriculum materials, books.

http://www.aseba.org/index.html Achenbach System of Empirically Based Assessment (ASEBA). Assessment.

http://www.agsnet.com/ American Guidance Service (AGS). Assessment and instruction. Includes articles, several professional forums, newsletters, and a chronological age calculator.

http://www.psychologicalforum.com/index2.asp AGS Psychological Forum. Sign up for free discussion group addressing AGS psychological products and general topics of psychological practice. Incorporates the previous BASC Forum and Vineland forum. Featured articles and "Lighter Side" anecdotes.

http://www.speechandlanguage.com/ AGS Speech and Language Forum: sign up for free discussion group addressing AGS speech and language products and general topics of speech/language pathology. "Clinical Café" articles and "Lighter Side" anecdotes.

http://www.booksschool.com Interactive Books. Books for special needs children.

http://www.ctb.com/ CTB/McGraw-Hill. Assessment. Products, articles and publications; sign up for newsletter.

http://www.elsevier.com/homepage/ Elsevier. Books and journals.

http://www.epsbooks.com/ Educators Publishing Service. Includes free teaching resources. Assessment and instruction.

http://www.ets.org/ Educational Testing Service. Information on accommodations for students with disabilities is in the drop-down menu for "Services."

http://www.harcourtassessment.com Harcourt Assessment, including the Psychological Corporation. Assessment. Tests, books, PowerPoint presentations on tests, and links to bulletins, full-text articles and research reports. HarcourtAssessment.com/ScienceDirect includes "links to journals and articles from ScienceDirect, the world's leading resource for Scientific, Technical & Medical information. Through the partnership of PsychCorp and ScienceDirect, you can now access the peer-reviewed research related to PsychCorp assessments as well as other topical research areas directly from your desktop."

http://www.hmco.com/indexf.html Houghton Mifflin.

http://www.jkp.com/catalogue/ Jessica Kingsley Publishers. "Accessible professional and academic books in the social and behavioural sciences."

http://www.larcpublishing.com/ LARC Publishing. Reading instruction and related topics.

http://www.linguisystems.com/ LinguiSystems. "Speech, language, learning disabilities, reading." Products, sign-ups to be a test examiner or author, links.

http://www.mhs.com/ MHS (Multi-Health Systems). Assessment and practice- and treatment-management.

http://www.nap.edu/ National Academies Press. Books and Academy reports.

http://www.parinc.com/index.cfm Psychological Assessment Resources (PAR). Books and tests: assessment, counseling, career planning, speech/language, and so forth.

http://www.proedinc.com/ PRO-ED. Assessment, books, curriculum and therapy materials.

http://www.researchpress.com/ "Books and videos in School Counseling, Special Education, Psychology, Counseling and Therapy, Parenting, Death and Dying, and Developmental Disabilities."

http://www.riverpub.com/ Riverside Publishing. Psychological and educational assessment. Articles on legislation, tests, and testing issues; Assessment Service Bulletins; news, author comments, links. Much of the information can be found by selecting a product and then clicking on support or resources on the sidebar.

http://www.sattlerpublisher.com/ Jerome Sattler, publisher. Textbooks on assessment.

http://www.school-tools.com/Fearon.htm Fearon Educational School Supplies for Teachers and Parents. An extensive selection from the most popular vendors for preschool through secondary grades, with special emphasis on *No Child Left Behind* and *Reading First* programs.

http://www.slosson.com/ Slosson Educational Publications. "Educational materials in the areas of: Intelligence, Aptitude & Developmental Abilities,

School Screening & Achievement, Speech-Language & Assessment Therapy, Emotional/Behavior & Special Needs."

http://www.sopriswest.com/ Sopris West. Books, journals, newsletter, Q&A, Hot Topics in Education, and links related to teaching, assessment, behavior, and other educational topics.

http://www.stoeltingco.com/ Stoelting. Psychological and educational tests, biofeedback monitors, polygraphs, and hardware for physiological research.

http://www.testpublishers.org/ Association of Test Publishers. They are "a non-profit organization representing providers of tests and assessment tools and/or services related to assessment, selection, screening, certification, licensing, educational or clinical uses." Downloadable newsletter, journal, and papers, links.

http://www.wpspublish.com/Inetpub4/index.htm Western Psychological Services. Tests, books, software, and therapy tools.

http://www.wiley.com/ Wiley. Books, e-books, and journals on topics including education and psychology.

READING

Additional resources for Reading may be found under Assessment, Books on Tape or CD, Booksellers and Clearinghouses Online, Curriculum-Based Assessment and Curriculum-Based Measurement, General Sites for Special Education and School Psychology, Learning Disabilities and Dyslexia, Publishers, School Psychology Pages, and Technology Not Listed Elsewhere.

http://clerccenter.gallaudet.edu/Literacy/beginreader.html List of publishers of series of books written at a second- to fourth-grade reading level for middle school and high school beginning readers. Laurent Clerc National Deaf Education Center, Gallaudet University.

http://dibels.uoregon.edu The Official DIBELS Home Page. The Dynamic Indicators of Basic Early Literacy Skills (DIBELS) are a set of standardized, individually administered measures of early literacy development. They are designed to be short (1 minute) fluency measures used to regularly monitor the development of prereading and early reading skills. The site includes information, links, free, downloadable measures, and Benchmark and Progress Monitoring booklets (some free, some at nominal cost).

http://reading.uoregon.edu "This website is designed to provide information, technology, and resources to teachers, administrators, and parents across the country. Big Ideas in Beginning Reading focuses on the five Big Ideas of early literacy: phonemic awareness, alphabetic principle, fluency with text, vocabulary, and comprehension. The website includes definitions and descriptions of the research and theories behind each of the big ideas, describes how to assess the big ideas, gives information on how to teach the big ideas including instructional examples, and finally, shows you how to put it all together in your school." Articles, information, and links.

http://www.sunsite3.berkeley.edu/kidsclick!/ Search engine and web guide for children with many links to online books and other information, each rated by reading grade level.

http://www.auburn.edu/~murraba/ "Dr. Bruce Murray—the Reading Genie—an associate professor in the Department of Curriculum and Teaching at Auburn University." Lessons, materials, and links for teaching reading.

http://www.fcrr.org Florida Center for Reading Research. Articles, research reports, and bibliographic references on reading.

http://www.getreadytoread.org/ "Get Ready to Read! *(GRTR!)* is a national initiative to build the early literacy skills of preschool-age children. The initiative provides an easy-to-administer, research-based screening tool to early childhood educators, child care providers, and parents in order to help them prepare all children to learn to read and write." Screening tools, activities, and links to resources.

http://www.nifl.gov/readingprofiles/ "This website is based on the ARCS, a study that assessed the reading of 955 adult learners. Researchers tested participants individually on eleven skills (components) that contribute to reading ability. A list of scores for each learner became that individual's reading profile, illustrating his or her strengths and instructional needs. . . . On the "Match a Profile" track, you can enter scores for your learner and be matched to one of the 11 ARCS-based profiles. You will find suggestions for instruction as well as information about the ARCS learners in this group that may relate to your learner. . . . the "Mini-Course" offers an opportunity to learn more about reading. You will find extensive information on the major reading components and assessment as well as sections containing references and downloadable resources."

http://www.proactiveparent.com Information and links about reading for parents, but also useful for teachers. Susan L. Hall and Louisa C. Moats, EdD.

http://www.reading.org/ International Reading Association. Membership; many articles, links, discussion group, library.

SCHOOL PSYCHOLOGY PAGES

Additional resources for School Psychology may be found under Assessment, General Sites for Special Education and School Psychology, and Publishers.

http://facpub.stjohns.edu/~ortizs/spwww.html Samuel Ortiz's site. School psychology chat rooms and many categorized links for school psychology pages, assessment, media resources, legal resources, training programs, and a "miscellaneous" list with many special education links.

http://groups.yahoo.com/group/IAPCHC/ Kevin McGrew's Yahoo Groups home page for the Institute for Applied Psychometrics (IAP) and Cattell-Horn-Carroll (CHC) theory. "This is an unmoderated discussion list regarding theoretical, research, measurement & assessment issues related to the CHC theory of intelligence. It is also the FYI list for the Institute for Applied Psychometrics, llc (IAP)." See also http://www.iapsych.com/. [Note: Willis is listed as one of the official arbiters of any possible disputes on the list.]

http://www.bartow.k12.ga.us/psych/psych.html The School Psychologists' Home

Page, Bartow County School System, Cartersville, GA. Information for school psychologists and a large list of educational links.

http://www.dac.neu.edu/cp/consult/ "The Global School Psychology Network is an innovative Internet community for school psychologists. It is dedicated to professional development, peer support, problem-solving assistance, and research. Its main goal is to develop and improve a true community in which participants advance their professional knowledge, provide and receive peer support, and actively involve themselves in developing the community. . . . Support provided by: Massachusetts School Psychologists Association [and] Northeastern University." Membership; interviews, presentations, book reviews, and many links, including a section devoted to crisis management and terrorism.

http://www.iapsych.com/ Kevin McGrew's "Institute for Applied Psychometrics, llc (IAP) is devoted to the application of psychological, educational, measurement and statistical concepts and procedures to issues and problems in education and psychology. The goal of the IAP is to serve as a bridge between psychological, psychometric, measurement and statistical theory and methods and applied practice in psychology and education. The IAP has a special focus on the use of the Cattell-Horn-Carroll Theory of Cognitive Abilities (aka., Cattell-Horn Gf-Gc theory and/or the Carroll tri-stratum theory) in intelligence test development and interpretation." Includes a great deal of information, including PowerPoint presentations on various psychometric topics. See also http://groups.yahoo.com/group/IAPCHC/.

http://www.ispaweb.org/en/index.html International School Psychology Association. Membership; links, publications, colloquium, ISPA news.

http://www.mypsychologist.com/ Jack A. Naglieri's page, with information about the Cognitive Assessment System, Naglieri Nonverbal Ability Test, and other tests; ordering information, and some articles.

http://www.schoolpsychology.net Sandra Steingart's School Psychology Resources Online for psychologists, parents, and educators contains carefully classified links to hundreds of URLs for specific conditions and disorders and dozens of categories of general information as well as a bookstore, job listings, and other information.

Please see also http://www.psychologicalforum.com/index2.asp.

SPECIAL EDUCATION LAW

Additional resources for Special Education Law may be found under Assessment, General Sites for Special Education and School Psychology, School Psychology Pages, Special Education and Psychology Organizations, and Parent, Advocacy, and Support Groups and Pages.

http://128.146.206.233/glarrc/Resources/NSPD.cfm "Great Lakes Area Regional Resource Center National State Policy Database (NSPD). A collaborative project of the National Association of State Directors of Special Education and the Regional Resource & Federal Centers network. This work is funded in part by the U.S. Department of Education, Office of Special Education Programs (OSEP)." Links to documents are searchable by state and topic. The NSPD currently holds state department of education rules and regulations for Special Education.

http://nces.ed.gov/surveys/ National Center for Educational Statistics. Links to all NCES Survey/Program groups.

http://www.ed.gov/nclb/landing.jhtml Official U.S. Department of Education Web site for No Child Left Behind.

http://nclb.ecs.org/nclb/ Searchable Education Commission of the States database for No Child Left Behind. Current status of state NCLB policies and plans, other ECS publications.

http://nichcy.org/states.htm National Dissemination Center for Children with Disabilities (NICHCY). "State Resource Sheets of disability-related resources in each state . . . locate organizations and agencies within your state that address disability-related issues, including: governors and U.S. senators; state agencies serving children and youth with disabilities; state chapters of disability organizations and parent groups; and parent training and information projects."

http://search.ed.gov/csi/ "Search any or all web sites funded by the U.S. Department of Education via the Cross-site Indexing Project." Requires careful specification of search words or searching within a large number of hits on broad topics.

http://thomas.loc.gov/ "In the spirit of Thomas Jefferson, a service of the Library of Congress." Search for history, current status, and text of House and Senate bills. Search by bill number (e.g., for the IDEA reauthorization: h.r. 1350 or s. 1248) or word/phrase (e.g., Individuals with Disabilities Education Improvement Act of 2004). Bill numbers work better. Also: Congressional Record, summaries of bills and laws back to the 93rd Congress (e.g., 93-380), and other information. Very useful for tracking progress of pending legislation.

http://www.504idea.org/504resources.html Council of Educators for Students with Disabilities (CESD formerly known as TACHO). PDF files of information on Section 504 of the Rehabilitation Act.

http://www.ed.gov/about/offices/list/ocr/504faq.html Frequently asked questions about section 504 of The Rehabilitation Act (Public Law 93-112).

http://www.ed.gov/inits/commissionsboards/whspecialeducation/reports.html President's Commission on Excellence in Special Education. Microsoft Word and PDF downloads of 89-page report.

http://www.ed.gov/offices/OSERS/Policy/IDEA/index.html Official Individuals with Disabilities Education Act (IDEA) page. Updates, letters and memos, the text of the law (P.L. 105-17), regulations (please see the following), and other information.

http://www.ed.gov/offices/OSERS/Policy/IDEA/regs.html Final 1999 IDEA Regulations in HTML and PDF.

http://www.ed.gov/policy/rights/reg/ocr/edlite-34cfr104.html Regulations for nondiscrimination on the basis of handicap in programs or activities receiving federal financial assistance (Section 504 of the Rehabilitation Act of 1973).

http://www.findlaw.com/ Findlaw®. Legal web site with articles, information, and searchable database of court decisions and legal information.

http://www.gpoaccess.gov/cfr/index.html Code of Federal Regulations (CFR). Complete set of current federal regulations implementing federal laws, (e.g., 34CFR300 for 1999 regulations for the 1997 Individuals with Disabilities Education Act [IDEA]). Search by number, name, or topic. Also, "find, review, and submit comments on Federal rules that are open for comment and published in the Federal Register using Regulations.gov. Purchase individual CFR titles through the U.S. Government Online Bookstore. Find issues of the CFR (including issues prior to 1996) at a local Federal depository library."

http://www.hhs.gov/ocr/hipaa/, http://www.hhs.gov/ocr/hipaa/assist.html Links to information about National Standards to Protect the Privacy of Personal Health Information under HIPAA (Health Insurance Portability and Accountability Act of 1996 [Public Law 104-191]).

http://www.ideapractices.org/ "The ASPIIRE and ILIAD IDEA Partnership Projects have completed their five-year grant. Through the Council for Exceptional Children (CEC), the most informative and popular sections of the IDEAPractices Web site, Law & Regulations and the Professional Development Resources, will still be available." Wealth of information about IDEA, including downloadable text of regulations.

http://www.nichcy.org/Trainpkg/toctext.htm National Dissemination Center for Children with Disabilities (NICHCY) Training package for 1997 IDEA and 1999 Regulations. "The training package is comprised of 14 modules or chapters, plus a collection of more than 150 overheads in English. Spanish overheads are also available. As such, the training package is simply too large to be placed on-line in one Acrobat PDF file. We've broken down each module, and each section of each module, into separate PDF files. . . . The background text on the statute, addendum text on the Federal regulations, handouts, resources, training script, and overheads are presented in separate files."

http://www.splcenter.org/ Southern Poverty Law Center. Membership; information on anti-discrimination and Teaching Tolerance.

http://www.usdoj.gov/ U.S. Department of Justice Home Page. Includes, among many other things, information on complaints under the Americans with Disabilities Act http://www.usdoj.gov/crt/ada/adahom1.htm.

http://www.wrightslaw.com/ Wrightslaw by Peter and Pam Wright. Lots of downloadable information about special education law, free newsletter subscription, bookstore, links. Designed for parents, parents' attorneys, and advocates, but open to everyone.

Please see also http://alpha.fdu.edu/psychology/wisdom_of_guy_mcbride.htm, a collection of informative comments by Guy McBride. The opinions are Dr. McBride's, but he provides many extremely helpful links to laws, regulations, and legal opinions.

SPECIAL EDUCATION AND PSYCHOLOGY ORGANIZATIONS

Additional resources for these organizations may be found under General Sites for Special Education and School Psychology, Parent, Advocacy, and Support Groups and Pages, and School Psychology Pages.

http://www.apa.org/psychologists/ American Psychological Association. Membership and many articles and fact sheets. See also http://www.indiana.edu/~div16/index.html, the School Psychology Division.

http://www.cec.sped.org/ Council for Exceptional Children. Membership; discussion forums, publications and products, and a tremendous amount of downloadable information.

http://www.nea.org/ National Education Association (NEA).

http://www.cpa.ca/ Canadian Psychological Association (CPA). Information about joining CPA, CPA archives, publications, and workshops, careers in psychology.

http://www.cpa.ca/casp/ Canadian Association of School Psychologists. Canadian national organization representing "the needs, concerns, and interests of school psychologists across Canada." Members receive a subscription to the *Canadian Journal of School Psychology.*

http://nasponline.org/ National Association of School Psychologists (NASP). Membership; resources for parents, teachers, and principals, downloadable publications on safe schools and model programs, information on school crisis planning and intervention.

http://www.urbancollaborative.org/ Urban Special Education Leadership Collaborative, "a network of special and general education leaders working together to improve outcomes for students with disabilities in the nation's urban schools." Membership fee. Useful articles are available for nonmembers to download.

Please see also http://www.schoolpsychology.net.

SPECIAL EDUCATION RESEARCH AND PHILOSOPHY

Additional resources for special education research and philosophy may be found under Assessment, Disabilities, General Sites for Special Education and School Psychology, Publishers, School Psychology Pages, and Special Education Law.

http://cie.asu.edu/ *Current Issues in Education,* College of Education, Arizona State University, Tempe, AZ. Online journal offered at no cost. Searchable archive of complete text of current and past articles.

http://www.edexcellence.net/library/special_ed/ Thomas Fordham Foundation papers on *Rethinking Special Education for a New Century,* edited by Chester E. Finn, Jr., Andrew J. Rotherham, & Charles R. Hokanson, Jr., May 2001.

http://www.eric.ed.gov/ Educational Resources Information Center (ERIC). This has been an accessible repository of a huge amount of research reports and other information. The U.S. Department of Education has closed the separate Clearinghouse services and web sites, including the AskERIC service and toll-free numbers. The main ERIC site is still available. "ERIC will introduce a new Web site on September 1, 2004. The new centralized ERIC will provide users with a modernized system that is easy-to-use, comprehensive, and up-to-date, with many free-of-charge full-text resources."

http://www.natd.org/grants.htm Information on grants listed by National Association of Test Directors.

http://www.nichcy.org/researchinfo.asp National Dissemination Center for Children with Disabilities (NICHCY). Links organized by topic to databases for many research reports and summaries.

http://www.schoolgrants.org/ Information and links for grants for schools.

Please see also http://www.nrcld.org/html/information/articles/digests/digest3.html.

SPEECH AND LANGUAGE

Additional resources for speech and language may be found under Assessment, Disabilities, General Sites for Special Education and School Psychology, Medical Information Not Listed Elsewhere, Publishers, and School Psychology Pages.

http://familyvillage.wisc.edu/lib_capd.html Central Auditory Processing Disorder. Information, links to other sites, links to chat groups for parents and for professionals.

http://www.asha.org/public/ American Speech-Language-Hearing Association. Public page with information about speech, hearing, and language issues.

http://www.wordfinding.com/ "The purpose of this Word Finding Web site is to provide information about Word Finding for professionals, parents, and learners with word finding difficulties. Topics in this web site include definition, characteristics, assessment, intervention, and available course work. Student groups who might have word finding difficulties are highlighted. References and/or materials helpful in understanding word finding are presented in these sections. At the virtual help section viewers are invited to ask questions about a learner's word finding difficulties or about their own word finding difficulties. A final section lists other internet resources that may be useful to individuals interested in Word Finding. This site was created by Dr. Diane German, a professor in the Special Education Department at National-Louis University, Chicago. (http://nlu.nl.edu)"

Please see also http://www.schoolpsychology.net, and http://www.speechandlanguage.com/.

TEACHING

Additional resources for teaching may be found under Disabilities, General Sites for Special Education and School Psychology, Publishers, and School Psychology Pages.

http://www.teachers.net/lessons/ The Teachers.Net Lesson Bank. Large database of lesson plans.

http://www.aaamath.com/ Commercial site with lots of free online math practice exercises.

http://www.abcteach.com abcteach. Lots of free materials.

http://www.awesomelibrary.org/student.html Awesome Library for Kids. Lots of links.

http://www.educationworld.com Education World. Lots of categorized information for teachers.

http://www.enc.org/ "ENC Online [Eisenhower National Clearinghouse, Iowa State University] is a K–12 math and science teacher center. Visit *Classroom Calendar, Digital Dozen, ENC Focus,* or *Lessons & Activities.* Or just *Ask ENC.*" Includes links, curriculum resources, and education topics.

http://www.gameskidsplay.net/index.html Rules for hundreds of children's games by Geof Nieboer.

http://www.hellofriend.org/ Ennis William Cosby Foundation web site with lots of good information for teachers.

http://www.muskingum.edu/~cal/database/ Lots of learning strategies collected by Muskingum College.

http://www.nde.state.ne.us/SPED/iepproj/index.html Nebraska Department of Education IEP Technical Assistance Guide 9/98. Lots of information about writing Individualized Education Programs (IEPs).

http://www.nwrel.org/sky/index.asp "The Library in the Sky is a database of interesting and useful educational Web sites for those involved in education. Find the information you want through the Search, User Tabs, by Department, or Materials." Northwest Regional Educational Library.

http://www.pdkintl.org/kappan/kappan.htm *"Phi Delta Kappan,* the professional print journal for education, addresses policy issues for educators at all levels. Advocating research-based school reform, the *Kappan* provides a forum for debate on controversial subjects. Published since 1915, the journal appears monthly September through June." Selected articles available free online.

http://pics.tech4learning.com/ "Pics4Learning is a copyright-friendly image library for teachers and students. The Pics4Learning collection consists of thousands of images that have been donated by students, teachers, and amateur photographers. Pics4Learning is developed as part of the Partners in Education program by *Tech4Learning,* and the Orange County Public Schools *Technology Development Unit.*"

http://www.resourceroom.net/ The Resource Room. Downloadable articles, lesson plans, and so forth for multisensory learning with an Orton-Gillingham orientation. Links.

http://www.sitesforteachers.com/ Very large set of links for teachers.

Please see also http://www.interventioncentral.org/, and http://www.schoolpsychology.net.

TECHNOLOGY NOT LISTED ELSEWHERE

Additional resources for technology may be found under sections for specific disabilities, Disabilities, General Sites for Special Education and School Psychology, Publishers, and School Psychology Pages.

http://discovertechnology.com/ Discover Technology Inc. "Our mission is to create and administer adaptive technology labs for persons with disabilities, to encourage communication between persons with or without disabilities and to educate the general population about the disabled population." Lots of links, pen-pal connections, information.

http://jset.unlv.edu Online *Journal of Special Education Technology.* Free access to past volumes.

http://trace.wisc.edu/world/computer_access/ Trace Center, College of Engineering, University of Wisconsin-Madison. "This page represents cooperative efforts by many of the major computer and software developers towards making computers and software more usable—for all. This page is organized as an outline with four major topic areas. The first major area, *Computer and Software Developers,* has four subtopics; the second major area, *Computer Access Program at Trace,* has six subtopics; and the third major area, *Software Toolkits,* contains the history of, an outline of, and links to each of the five operating system related toolkits. The fourth area includes a listing of *Other Computer Access Resources* that are also relevant to computer access research."

http://www.abledata.com/ Abledata. Source for information on assistive technology. Huge set of links for equipment, lots of other links related to disabilities, reading room, consumers' forum, and so on.

http://www.aboutonehandtyping.com/ Information and sales related to one-handed typing.

http://www.alphasmart.com/ Sales of AlphaSmart portable word processors.

http://closingthegap.com/ Lots of information on computer technology in special education and rehabilitation.

http://www.lburkhart.com/elem/ Linda J. Burkhart. Lots of information on using the Internet for instruction.

http://www.mathtalk.com/ Metroplex Voice Computing, Inc. Speech recognition mathematics without the keyboard or mouse. Commercial sales.

http://www.readplease.com/ Text-to-speech software to read computer screens. Commercial sales.

http://www.resna.org/ Rehabilitation Engineering & Assistive Technology Society of North America. Information about assistive technology. Links.

http://www.tedpa.org/ Telecommunications Equipment Distribution Program Association. Click on State Programs and then a state for links.

http://www.texthelp.com/ "Texthelp Systems Inc. has developed software products which fall into many classes . . . accessibility software, dyslexia software, text to speech software, to name just three. Our solutions are suitable for individuals and corporate or government organisations, to overcome accessibility difficulties such as dyslexia or simply as language learning aids." Commercial sales.

TOOLS

Many of the web sites listed throughout this chapter include search engines, some general and some specific for the web site's topic.

http://babelfish.altavista.com/ AltaVista translation tool. Translates text or entire web sites from English into other languages and from other languages into English. The site offers other services. http://www.altavista.com/web/tools provides other useful tools.

http://espse.ed.psu.edu/spsy/Watkins/Watkins3.ssi A large number of downloadable statistics programs for evaluators and researchers. Also a free download of Mountain Shadows Phonemic Awareness Scale (Watkins, M. W., & Edwards, V. A. [2004]. Assessing early literacy skills with the Mountain Shadows Phonemic Awareness Scale [MS-PAS]. *Journal of Psychoeducational Assessment, 22,* 3–14).

http://ipl.sils.umich.edu/ Internet Public Library, University of Michigan. Ann Arbor, MI. Sponsored by Intel Sun Microsystems. Vast array of links.

http://www.ask.com/ Ask Jeeves. Plain language search engine.

http://www.britannica.com/ Concise version allows free online searches for brief articles. Membership required for more extensive articles.

http://www.eduhound.com/ EduHound. Everything for Education K–12. Categorized search engine for educational information and materials.

http://www.google.com/ Google. Popular general search engine.

http://www.hyperdictionary.com/ Hyperdictionary. Online English, computer, dream, and medical dictionaries and thesaurus. Fairly comprehensive, but lacking some obscure words. The dream dictionary is entertaining.

http://www.infoplease.com/ infoplease®. Searchable almanacs, atlas, encyclopedia, dictionary, and thesaurus.

http://members.aol.com/johnp71/javastat.html More than 600 links to "Web pages that perform statistical calculations" grouped into categories. John C. Pezzullo.

Please see also http://www.schoolpsychology.net.

9

Self-Determination for the Special Education Student

RANDALL L. DE PRY

Students with disabilities receive both short- and long-term benefits from being able to make choices, express preferences, set personal and educational goals, and work in meaningful ways to attain their goals. Choice, goal setting, and goal attainment are critical features of what is known as *self-determination*. Educators, parents, and disability advocates know that persons with disabilities often have limited opportunities and/or skills to fully express interests, preferences, and goals that are both meaningful and attainable. Because of this, educators and advocates have incorporated instructional strategies that promote self-determination into educational programs and practices since the 1960s.

A review of the self-determination research literature suggests several common constructs that are used to promote self-determination. They include (1) preference identification, (2) need and skill identification, (3) goal setting, (4) task initiation, (5) monitoring and self-evaluation, and (6) goal attainment and/or goal adjustment. These constructs are increasingly being incorporated into educational programs and curricula that special educators can use across a variety of educational and community settings. For example, student goal setting and goal attainment strategies are often used during transition planning, community-based programming, supported employment, student-directed IEP meetings, student-led conferences, student-directed functional assessments and behavior support planning meetings, and they have been embedded into general education academic and social skills instruction.

Use of self-determination strategies are supported by research that suggests that providing students with choices may (1) decrease disruptive classroom behav-

Box 9.1 General Guidelines for Helping a Student Become Self-Determined

- ❑ Teach Self-Determination Curriculum
- ❑ Identify Preferences
- ❑ Complete Skill and Needs Assessments
- ❑ Help Student Create Personal, Educational, and/or Vocational Goals
- ❑ Initiate Tasks to Meet Goals
- ❑ Monitor and Self-Evaluate Goal Attainment
- ❑ Adjust or Reevaluate as Necessary

Source: *Adapted from Martin, Huber-Marshall, and De Pry (2005)*

Box 9.2

Increasingly, educational professionals and families are helping students become more self-directed by providing opportunities for choice, opportunities to express preferences and goals, and using teaching strategies that help students attain their goals.

ior and increase learning, (2) increase productivity during vocational tasks, and (3) increase self-reports of task enjoyment by students with disabilities. Additionally, researchers have found that students who scored higher on self-determination measures prior to leaving high school had higher rates of employment when compared to students who had lower self-determination scores. Research also suggests that persons with disabilities who receive instruction in self-determination retained their jobs longer than peers who did not receive this type of instruction. More importantly, researchers have argued that self-determination is a central tenet of the normalization principle in that it helps students focus on attitudes and abilities that reduce external influence and encourage the learner to be the primary causal agent in her or his life.

Perhaps self-determination is best understood by using the example of the student-led IEP meeting. IDEA mandates that students who are 14 years old or older must be invited to attend their IEP meetings. However, researchers have learned that students who attend their meetings without prior knowledge of the IEP meeting expectations and process, and who have not learned how to express personal preferences and educational goals, did not benefit from the IEP meeting in terms of understanding and participation.

Curricula have been developed that teach students how to lead and actively participate in their IEP meetings. Students who have received this instruction learn to lead their IEP meeting, review their past goals and performance, learn how to solicit feedback from others, learn how to ask clarifying questions, learn to verbally communicate what supports they may need to meet current goals, and develop and implement strategies that will allow them to work on meeting their IEP goals for the coming school year. Research on this approach has demonstrated that students who received instruction and support related to leading their IEP meetings attended these meetings more frequently, shared their interests more effectively, expressed aspirations and job preferences for the future more readily, felt more ownership of the process and meeting outcomes, and expressed more confidence in meeting their IEP goals.

Students with disabilities receive support and services from caring and thought-

Box 9.3

. . . Self-determination is a central tenet of the normalization principle in that it helps students focus on attitudes and abilities that reduce external influence and encourage the learner to be the primary causal agent in their life.

Box 9.4

Reported Benefits from Teaching Self-Determination Skills

- ❑ Decreases in disruptive classroom behavior
- ❑ Increases in learning
- ❑ Increases in productivity during vocational tasks
- ❑ Increases in self-reports of task enjoyment by students

ful professionals on a daily basis. Yet, these same professionals may forget that self-determination is a learned set of behaviors that need to be taught and supported throughout the educational careers of their students. Increasingly, educational professionals and families are helping students become more self-directed by providing opportunities for choice, opportunities to express preferences and goals, and using teaching strategies that help students attain their goals. Self-determination, when seen in this light, is a critical method for increasing meaningful school and postschool outcomes for students with disabilities.

SELF-DETERMINATION RESOURCES

Books

Field, S., Martin, J., Miller, B., Ward, M., & Wehmeyer, M. (1997). *A practical guide for teaching self-determination.* Reston, VA: Council for Exceptional Children.

Martin, J. E., Marshall, L. H., & De Pry, R. L. (2005). Participatory decision-making: Innovative practices that increase student self-determination. In R. W. Flexer, T. J. Simmons, P. Luft, & R. Baer (Eds.), *Transition planning for secondary students with disabilities* (2nd ed., pp. 304–332). Columbus, OH: Merrill.

Curricula

ChoiceMaker, Self-Determination Materials, Sopris West Educational Services http://www.sopriswest.com

Internet Resources

Self-Determination Synthesis Project: http://www.uncc.edu/sdsp/home.asp

Center for Self-Determination, University of Colorado at Colorado Springs: http://web.uccs.edu/education/special/self_determination/index.html

Self-Determination Assessments

Hoffman, A., Field, S., & Sawilowsky, S. (1996). *Self-determination knowledge scale.* Austin, TX: PRO-ED.

Martin, J. E., & Huber-Marshall, L. H. (1996). *ChoiceMaker self-determination transition assessment.* Longmont, CO: Sopris West Educational Services.

Wehmeyer, M. L. (1995). The ARC's self-determination scale. (Available from the ARC of the United States, 500 E. Border Street, Suite 300, Arlington, TX 76010).

10

Special Education–Related Associations

RACHEL TOPLIS

AMERICAN ACADEMY FOR CEREBRAL PALSY AND DEVELOPMENTAL MEDICINE (AACPDM)

The American Academy for Cerebral Palsy and Developmental Medicine (formerly the American Academy of Cerebral Palsy) was founded in 1947. This is a professional organization of physicians, representatives of specialty boards, and other professionals concerned with diagnosis, treatment, and research in cerebral palsy and developmental disorders. AACPDM headquarters are located at 6300 N. River Road, Suite 727, Rosemont, IL 60018.

AMERICAN ASSOCIATION FOR THE ADVANCEMENT OF SCIENCE (AAAS)

The American Association for the Advancement of Science was founded in 1848. AAAS is dedicated to the advancement of the sciences and technology and to increase the general public's understanding of science and technology. AAAS draws members internationally and is composed of scientists, science educators, engineers, and other science-related professionals. AAAS publishes science books and references, including the weekly *Science*. AAAS has a website at www.aaas.org.

AMERICAN ASSOCIATION OF COLLEGES FOR TEACHER EDUCATION (AACTE)

The American Association of Colleges for Teacher Education is comprised of colleges and universities which offer undergraduate and higher level programs in the preparation of professional educators. AACTE is a major influence on state and federal policy: It advocates for teachers and advises the National Council for Accreditation of Teacher Education (NCATE) on issues of accreditation and standards.

AMERICAN ASSOCIATION FOR MARRIAGE AND FAMILY THERAPY (AAMFT)

Founded in 1942, the American Association for Marriage and Family Therapy is a national organization representing marriage and family therapists. AAMFT sponsors annual conferences and institutes and provides printed materials, reported recent research, and updates in the field. AAMFT seeks to advance family therapy by increasing understanding, research, and treatment; by establishing standards in education and training, and by promoting professional development. AAMFT headquarters are located at 1133 15th St., NW, Suite 300, Washington, DC 20005.

AMERICAN ASSOCIATION ON MENTAL RETARDATION (AAMR)

Founded in 1876, the American Association on Mental Retardation is composed of professionals from academic disciplines who are interested in the field of mental retardation, as well as nonprofessional individuals involved in the care and treatment of the mentally retarded. AAMR publishes journals disseminating the latest research. One of the goals of AAMR is to assist individuals with mental retardation to live fulfilled lives. It is located at 444 North Capitol St., NW, Suite 846, Washington, DC 20001-1512.

AMERICAN FOUNDATION FOR THE BLIND (AFB)

The American Foundation for the Blind is a nonprofit organization that offers resources such as talking books for the blind and visually impaired. AFB hopes to enable the blind and visually impaired to take advantage of opportunities and achieve success in their lives. AFB attempts to identify and resolve issues pertinent to the blind in the areas of educational access, employment opportunity, and legislation. AFB publishes books, videos, and materials about blindness for professionals, in an attempt to educate policymakers. AFB headquarters are located at 11 Penn Plaza, Suite 300, New York, NY 10001.

AMERICAN OCCUPATIONAL THERAPY FOUNDATION

Founded in 1965, the American Occupational Therapy Foundation raises money and resources for publications, research, and scholarship in the field of occupational therapy. The foundation attempts to increase public knowledge concerning the occupational profession. It also provides grants for research and information on scholarships. The foundation is located at 4720 Montgomery Lane, PO Box 31220, Bethesda, MD 20824.

AMERICAN ORTHOPSYCHIATRIC ASSOCIATION (Ortho)

Founded in 1924, the American Orthopsychiatric Association attempts to provide a forum for psychiatrists, psychologists, social workers, and others who are interested in human behavior. In particular, Ortho is interested in children with behavior problems such as Conduct Disorder. Ortho publishes the *American Journal of Orthopsychiatry* and addresses research concerning childhood mental disorders. Ortho can be contacted at 330 7th Ave., 18th Floor, NY, NY 10001-5010.

AMERICAN PHYSICAL THERAPY ASSOCIATION (APTA)

The American Physical Therapy Association supports physical therapists in the field as well as students of physical therapy. APTA offers workshops, continuing education, accredited programs, and employment opportunities. APTA also has a variety of resources for individuals who require physical therapy—for example, stroke victims, quadriplegics, or amputees. Headquarters of APTA are at 1111 North Fairfax St., Alexandria, VA 22314.

AMERICAN PSYCHIATRIC ASSOCIATION (APA)

Founded in 1844, the American Psychiatric Association is a national medical specialty society that represents physicians who specialize in the diagnosis and treatment of mental and emotional disorders. The APA publishes journals and books and organizes workshops and conferences in order to promote the advancement and care of people with mental illness, and to increase the general public's understanding and awareness of mental illness. APA headquarters are located at 1400 K St., NW, Washington, DC, 20005.

AMERICAN PSYCHOLOGICAL ASSOCIATION (APA)

The American Psychological Association was established in 1892, and currently is divided into 51 specialized subfields reflecting the diversity of the science and practice of psychology. APA publishes periodicals, books, journals, and pamphlets. It organizes an annual conference and works with the government to promote issues and concerns in the field of psychology. The APA is open to psychologists and students worldwide and is located at 750 First St., NE, Washington, DC 20002-4242. The APA web site is a valuable resource for parents, educators, and psychologists, and is found at www.apa.org.

AMERICAN SOCIETY FOR DEAF CHILDREN (ASDC)

The American Society for Deaf Children was founded in 1967. Its purpose is to support deaf individuals and their families. ASDC supports the use of sign language and encourages a positive attitude toward the deaf culture. ASDC advocates for educational and employment opportunities for deaf individuals and provides information concerning deafness and issues of concern to the deaf community. ASDC headquarters are located at 1820 Tribute Rd., Suite A, Sacramento, CA 95815.

AMERICAN SPEECH-LANGUAGE-HEARING ASSOCIATION (ASHA)

The American Speech-Language-Hearing Association consists of a variety of professions; for example, speech-language pathologists, audiologists, and speech-language and hearing scientists. ASHA supports high-quality services for people with communication disorders. The association is important in developing standards and licensing procedures for professionals in this field. ASHA is located at 10801 Rockville Pike, Rockville, MD 20852.

ASSOCIATION FOR CHILDHOOD EDUCATION INTERNATIONAL (ACEI)

The Association for Childhood Education International has as its objective the promotion of quality educational practices for children. Members include parents and professional educators, who participate in local and state meetings, workshops, and so on. The objective is to share ideas and to contribute to excellence in teaching in all areas, including child care, preschool, and kindergarten, to university-level teacher education programs. ACEI has many resources, including a library on childhood and elementary education, available at their head offices. ACEI is located at 17904 Georgia Ave., Suite 215, Olney, MD 20832.

ASSOCIATION FOR THE ADVANCEMENT OF BEHAVIOR THERAPY (AABT)

Founded in 1966 as the Association for Advancement of the Behavioral Therapies, the AABT is a nonprofit organization consisting of mental health professionals and students. Membership is interdisciplinary, including psychologists, psychiatrists, social workers, physicians, nurses, and other professionals who work with mental health patients. AABT supports training programs, workshops, and conferences in behavior therapy and cognitive behavioral therapy. AABT publishes printed materials to continue public education and to provide information on treatments and current research to practitioners, patients, and their families. AABT has a web site at www.aabt.org/aabt.

THE ASSOCIATION FOR THE GIFTED

The Association for the Gifted is one of the divisions of The Council for Exceptional Children. Its purpose is to promote the welfare and education of, and to improve educational opportunities for, gifted children. The Association for the Gifted also disseminates information, conducts research, and supports the professional preparation of educators. The Association for the Gifted can be contacted via The Council for Exceptional Children, 1920 Associations Dr., Reston, VA 20191.

ASSOCIATION OF BLACK PSYCHOLOGISTS (ABPsi)

Founded in 1968, the Association of Black Psychologists began as a way for the needs of Black psychologists to be addressed. One of the main purposes of the ABPsi is to have a positive impact on the mental health of the Black community through programs, services, and training. The ABPsi is not an international organization; its main headquarters are located at PO Box 55999, Washington, DC 20040-5999.

AUTISM SOCIETY OF AMERICA (ASA)

The Autism Society of America was founded in 1965. ASA attempts to promote lifelong access to opportunities for people within the autism spectrum. Members include people diagnosed with autism or on the autism spectrum, parents, family members, professionals, and caregivers. ASA attempts to increase public awareness and promote research relating to autism and advocacy. ASA publishes several informative newsletters and packets of information. Local chapters help families find trained service providers and professionals. The headquarters of ASA is located at 7910 Woodmont Ave., Suite 650, Bethesda, Maryland 20814-3015. Their web site is www.autism-society.org.

BRAIN INJURY ASSOCIATION (BIA)

Formerly the National Head Injury Association, the Brain Injury Association advocates for persons with head injuries and their families. BIA wants to increase awareness, education, and prevention of brain injury. BIA works closely with rehabilitation providers, physicians, attorneys, educators, and others. Their work has helped to increase awareness of safety belts, car seats, and the detriments of drinking and driving. BIA has information on brain injuries in the form of a magazine and other educational resources. BIA can be reached at 105 North Alfred St., Alexandria, VA 22314.

CHILDREN'S DEFENSE FUND (CDF)

The Children's Defense Fund was founded in 1973 as an advocacy organization for poor, minority, and handicapped children. CDF is a lobbying organization with an annual agenda in the U.S. Congress; they work with state and local child advocates and provide information, technical assistance, and support. CDF headquarters are located at 25 E. St., NW, Washington, DC 20001. Their web site is www.childrensdefense.org.

COUNCIL FOR CHILDREN WITH BEHAVIORAL DISORDERS (CCBD)

The Council for Children with Behavioral Disorders is a division of the Council for Exceptional Children. Members of CCBD include teachers, teacher educators, administrators, parents, and mental health professionals. The goals of CCBD include promoting educational opportunities for children with behavioral disorders, advocating for the needs of children and their families, disseminating information, and providing training programs and professional support. CCBD can be contacted via the Council for Exceptional Children, 1920 Association Drive, Reston, VA 20191-1589.

COUNCIL FOR EXCEPTIONAL CHILDREN (CEC)

The Council for Exceptional Children is dedicated to the welfare of children. It was founded in 1922; members include parents, educators, students, and others concerned with the welfare of children with disabilities, and with the gifted and talented. CEC is divided into special interest groups such as physically handicapped, behavioral disorders, learning disabilities, mental retardation, communication disorders, gifted and talented, and visually handicapped. CEC's goals are to increase educational opportunities for exceptional children and youth and to improve working conditions and opportunities. CEC headquarters are located at 1920 Association Drive, Reston, VA 20191.

COUNCIL FOR LEARNING DISABILITIES

See the Council for Exceptional Children.

COUNCIL OF ADMINISTRATORS OF SPECIAL EDUCATION (CASE)

The Council of Administrators of Special Education was founded in 1952; its members include administrators, directors, supervisors and coordinators of private and public special education programs, and schools and classes serving children with special needs. The purpose of CASE is to provide support, promote professional leadership, and encourage communication of issues relating to the administration of special education programs. CASE headquarters are located at 615 16th St. NW, Albuquerque, NM 87104.

EPILEPSY FOUNDATION OF AMERICA (EFA)

The Epilepsy Foundation of America is a voluntary health organization. The EFA is a national organization with many local chapters. The EFA publishes pamphlets and other publications addressing epilepsy treatment, education, and research. The national address for EFA is The Epilepsy Foundation of America, 1828 L St., NW, Washington, DC 20036.

FOUNDATION FOR CHILDREN WITH LEARNING DISABILITIES (FCLD)

The Foundation for Children with Learning Disabilities is a charitable foundation. The organization's goals are to educate the public and the legal system about links between learning disabilities and delinquency, as well as to educate people on the problems and issues faced by individuals with learning disabilities. It is located at 99 Park Ave., NY, NY 10016.

GIFTED EDUCATION RESOURCE INSTITUTE (GERI)

The Gifted Education Resource Institute has conducted research on giftedness; it trains teachers in gifted education at the masters and doctoral level. The institute provides summer and weekend programs for gifted students and makes psychological testing and counseling available for gifted youth. GERI attempts to disseminate information concerning identification and assessment of gifted students to schools and parents. It is based at Purdue University, West Lafayette, IN.

HELEN KELLER INTERNATIONAL

Helen Keller International is an association which offers courses for teachers of blind children and adults. The training focuses on prevention and treatment of blindness due to malnutrition, trachoma, cataracts, and other eye diseases. The organization also collects statistics on blindness throughout the world and attempts to disseminate information through annual reports, newsletters, and educational materials. Several other organizations are involved in the Helen Keller International organization. These associations include the Permanent Blind Relief War Fund, American Braille Press for War and Civilian Blind, and the American Foundation for Overseas Blind. The headquarters for Helen Keller International is at 15 West 16th St., NY, NY 10011.

INSTITUTION NATIONALE DES SOURDS-MUETS

The Institution Nationale des Sourds-Muets was founded in Paris in 1755 as the first public, nonpaying school for the deaf in the world. It was founded by Abbot Charles Michel de l'Epée, who was very influential in establishing a sign system as a recognized language. The Institution changed its name in 1960 to Institut National de Jeunes Sourds (INJS; National Institute for Young Deaf).

INSTITUT NATIONAL DE JEUNES SOURDS (INJS)

This organization attempts to revitalize deaf education. This institute, although presently housing only a day school, has recently moved progressively toward mainstreaming. Teachers are becoming more and more itinerant, in order to support pupils in ordinary school environments. The INJS also trains interpreters. The INJS is found in the heart of Paris, formerly the Institution Nationale Des Sourds-Muets.

INTERNATIONAL DYSLEXIA ASSOCIATION (IDA)

The International Dyslexia Association (formerly the Orton Dyslexia Society) is an international nonprofit organization. The IDA tries to help individuals with dyslexia and their families. The association attempts to promote effective teaching, supports and encourages interdisciplinary study and research, and disseminates research-based knowledge. More information on IDA can be found at their web site at www.interdys.org.

INTERNATIONAL READING ASSOCIATION (IRA)

The International Reading Association is a nonprofit professional organization. The IRA includes teachers, administrators, researchers, psychologists, parents, and other individuals interested in the field of reading instruction. The organization is closely involved with the worldwide literacy movement and advocates for better reading programs, teacher education, and the improvement of reading instruction. The IRA organizes local, national, and international conventions, and publishes several journals on reading-related topics.

LEARNING DISABILITIES ASSOCIATION (LDA)

The Learning Disabilities Association is a national volunteer organization that includes individuals with learning disabilities, families, and professionals. The LDA attempts to promote the education and well-being of children and adults with learning disabilities. This includes educating the general public about learning disabilities and informing individuals with learning disabilities of their rights. LDA works with regular education and special education teachers, and promotes early identification and improved services for students. The LDA is one of the largest nonprofit organizations for people with learning disabilities, and has extensive resources. The LDA is based at 4156 Library Rd. Pittsburgh, PA 15234. Their web site is http://ldanatl.org.

MUSCULAR DYSTROPHY ASSOCIATION (MDA)

The Muscular Dystrophy Association is an international, voluntary health organization. It promotes research and supports patient care, and is funded almost entirely by private contributions. MDA provide research grants, diagnostic services, and rehabilitation follow-up. It provides financial assistance toward orthopedic appliances, physical therapy, and transportation to and from clinics. MDA also sponsors self-help groups, summer camps for children, and educational seminars. MDA's web site is at www.mdausa.org/.

NATIONAL ASSOCIATION FOR GIFTED CHILDREN (NAGC)

The National Association for Gifted Children was founded in 1954, and supports and develops policies and practices that encourage expressions of giftedness in children and youth from all walks of life. NAGC believes that this population is underrecognized, and therefore attempts to advocate for research, professional communication, and development in this area. NAGC headquarters are at 1707 L St., NW, Suite 550, Washington, DC 20036.

NATIONAL ASSOCIATION FOR THE DEAF (NAD)

The National Association for the Deaf was founded in 1880 and is a private, nonprofit organization. The NAD promotes the rights of deaf and hard-of-hearing individuals in education, employment, health care, social services, and telecommunications. NAD provides programs and services such as captioned media, sign language professionals, and interpreters. NAD also offers free legal representation in areas related to civil rights, employment, and education. The NAD has a web site at www.nad.org/.

NATIONAL ASSOCIATION OF SCHOOL PSYCHOLOGISTS (NASP)

The National Association of School Psychologists strives "to promote educationally and psychologically healthy environments for all children and youth by implementing research based, effective programs that prevent problems, enhance independence, and promote optimal learning" (NASP, 1998). NASP was founded in 1969, and is composed mainly of practicing school psychologists. However, NASP is open to anyone working or credentialed as school psychologist, trained as a school psychologist and working as a consultant or supervisor of psychological services, and college- and university-based professors who train school psychologists. NASP organizes conferences and symposia, publishes books and articles of interest to school psychologists, professionals, and parents, and has a very practical, useful, and informative web site at www.naspweb.org.

NATIONAL ASSOCIATION OF STATE BOARDS OF EDUCATION (NASBE)

The National Association of State Boards of Education is a nonprofit, private organization. NASBE hopes to strengthen state leadership in educational policymaking, promote excellence in the education of all students, advocate for equal access to educational opportunity, and encourage citizen support for public education. Based in Alexandria, Virginia, NASBE communicates with Congress, federal executives, business and industry, and national associations and other state decision makers, to promote critical policy issues.

NATIONAL ASSOCIATION OF STATE DIRECTORS OF SPECIAL EDUCATION (NASDSE)

The National Association of State Directors of Special Education is an independent, nonprofit membership organization. The principle objective is to serve the informational and professional needs of the chief administrators of special education at the state level. NASDSE was founded in 1938 and is governed by a board of directors elected from the general membership. With offices located in Alexandria, Virginia, NASDSE provides information on national trends and activities, in-service training in program administration, and policy development. NASDSE also advocates on behalf of its members before state and federal level decision makers.

NATIONAL COUNCIL FOR ACCREDITATION OF TEACHER EDUCATION (NCATE)

Founded in 1954, the National Council for Accreditation of Teacher Education is a national body designed to develop and promote standards and review of accreditation for teacher preparatory colleges and programs. NCATE is a coalition of teachers, teacher educators, content specialists, and local and state policymakers, and is recognized by the U.S. Department of Education as the appropriate accrediting body in educational preparation. NCATE is located at 2010 Massachusetts Ave., NW, Suite 50, Washington, DC 20036-1023.

NATIONAL EASTER SEAL SOCIETY

The National Easter Seal Society was founded in 1919 with the purpose of helping children with physical disabilities. This society is a national volunteer health care organization that provides services to children and adults with disabilities and to their families. This includes early intervention programs, preschool and daycare programs, adult vocational training, and employment and medical rehabilitation services.

NATIONAL EDUCATION ASSOCIATION (NEA)

The National Education Association was founded in 1857 as the National Teacher Association. Its name was changed in 1876. The NEA is the largest and oldest organization of teachers in the United States. NEA advocates for public education and upholds the rights and welfare of teachers, including promoting professional development. NEA is also involved in government relations and political action. NEA organizes workshops, is involved in negotiating contracts, and lobbies government for need resources. NEA headquarters is located at 1201 16th St., NW, Washington, DC 20036.

NATIONAL FEDERATION OF THE BLIND (NFB)

The National Federation of the Blind was founded in 1940 and is designed to promote action and advocacy for the blind. NFB's objectives include educating the public, addressing legal, economic, and social discrimination, and promoting the rights of blind individuals. NFB is involved in employment programs and adaptive and assistive technology for the blind. NFB headquarters are located at 1800 Johnson St., Baltimore, MD 21230.

NATIONAL DISSEMINATION CENTER FOR CHILDREN WITH DISABILITIES (NICHCY)

The National Dissemination Center for Children with Disabilities is supported by the Office of Special Education Programs of the U.S. Department of Education. NICHCY provides information on disability related issues. Topics addressed include individualized education programs and educational rights. Services available through NICHCY include referrals to disability organizations, parent groups, information for databases and libraries, and various publications. NICHCY has a web site at http://nichcy.org.

NATIONAL INSTITUTES OF MENTAL HEALTH (NIMH)

The National Institutes of Mental Health is a federal agency that was founded in 1946. NIMH supports and conducts research into causes, treatment, and prevention of mental illness. NIMH also publishes bulletins and other printed materials addressing the diagnosis and treatment of mental disorders, as well as organizing and conducting educational campaigns. NIMH headquarters are located at 5600 Fishers Lane, Rockville, MD 20857. The NIMH e-mail address is nimhinfo@nih.gov.

NATIONAL INSTITUTE OF NEUROLOGICAL DISORDERS AND STROKE

The National Institute of Neurological Disorders and Stroke conducts and supports research into human neurological disorders such as traumatic brain injury (TBI) and spinal cord injuries, muscular dystrophy, Parkinson's disease, and others, as well as research investigating normal brain and nervous system development to compare with, and better understand, neurological disorders.

NATIONAL JOINT COMMITTEE ON LEARNING DISABILITIES (NJCLD)

Founded in 1975, the National Joint Committee on Learning Disabilities is comprised of representatives from other educationally based organizations. Members include the American Speech-Language-Hearing Association, the Council for Learning Disabilities, the Council for Exceptional Children, the International Reading Association, the National Association of School Psychologists, and others. The primary purpose of the NJCLD is to encourage communication among organizations to promote a forum for discussion and dissemination of issues related to learning disabilities. Publications relating to learning disabilities are available from NJCLD headquarters at 10801 Rockville Pike, Rockville, MD 20852.

NATIONAL MERIT SCHOLARSHIP CORPORATION

The National Merit Scholarship Corporation was founded in 1955 as an independent organization designed to solicit businesses to support scholarships for intellectually talented students. Recipients must be U.S. citizens. A separate program is available to increase educational opportunities for Black students. Approximately 6,500 awards are made annually. Headquarters are located at 1 American Plaza, Evanston, IL 60201.

NATIONAL ORGANIZATION FOR RARE DISORDERS (NORD)

The National Organization for Rare Disorders is a voluntary health organization that offers programs of education, advocacy, and research in the identification, treatment, and cure of rare disorders. A membership fee is required, and members receive newsletters, updates, and online searches of its databases (the Rare Disease Database or RDB). The RDB contains information on over 1,100 rare diseases. Information can also be found on organizations designed to serve people with rare diseases, and a drug designation database from the Food and Drug Administration. NORD headquarters are located at PO Box 8923, New Fairfield, CT 06812-8923. The NORD web site is www.rarediseases.org.

NATIONAL REHABILITATION ASSOCIATION (NRA)

Founded in 1925, the National Rehabilitation Association is composed of counselors, therapists, physicians, and other individuals interested in the rehabilitation of disabled people. The NRA has an annual conference and produces printed materials addressing such topics as legislation and specialized education.

NATIONAL SOCIETY FOR THE PREVENTION OF BLINDNESS (NSPB)

The National Society for the Prevention of Blindness has as its primary purpose the prevention of blindness and the conservation of sight. Since 1908 the NSPB has organized educational programs and research. Additionally, the NSPB provides a variety of services such as those to support glaucoma screenings, preschool vision tests, and industrial eye safety. Grants for medical research are available through NSPB, as are various printed and educational materials. NSPB headquarters are located at 500 E. Remington Rd., Schaumburg, IL 60173.

UNITED CEREBRAL PALSY (UCP)

United Cerebral Palsy is a voluntary association designed to provide direct services to individuals with cerebral palsy and their families. These services include special education, transitional services, and community living facilities. Beginning as a parent organization, UCP now supports professional education, promotes research, and increases public awareness and advocacy. UCP has a very informative web site at www.ucp.org.

WORLD FEDERATION OF THE DEAF (WFD)

The World Federation of the Deaf was founded in 1951 and encompasses societies or organizations acting for the deaf. WFD serves as a consultant to the World Health Organization; it has an extensive library and bestows awards for merit and special achievement in areas of education and social rehabilitation of the deaf. WFD consist of members representing the languages of English, French, and Italian, and is located in Rome, Italy. Its web site is at www.hearinglossweb.com/res/hlorg/wfd.htm.

11

Publishers of Special Education Materials

ELAINE FLETCHER-JANZEN

The following list of publishers of special education materials has been provided by the Council for Exceptional Children (CEC). For those readers who are unfamiliar with the CEC, this list is one of hundreds of wonderful, informative fact sheets, publications, and links to materials that directly enhance the teaching of exceptional children, including those who are gifted and talented.

The CEC web site is very useful for the practicing special educator. The web site includes information about careers, diversity, IDEA law, international programs, professional development, professional standards, public policy, a national clearinghouse for professions in special education, and numerous excellent journals and publications. The CEC home web site is at www.cec.sped.org/index.html. The editors of this Almanac gratefully acknowledge CEC's work and contribution to this volume.

A

Ablenet, Inc.
1081 10th Ave. SE
Minneapolis, MN 55414-1312
800.322.0956
www.ablenetinc.com

Ablex Publishing Company
355 Chestnut St.
Norwood, NJ 07648-2090
201.767.8450
www.ablexbooks.com

Academic Communication Associates
4149 Avenida de loc Plata
PO Box 4279
Oceanside, CA 92052-4279
760.758.9593; 888.758.9558
www.acadcom.com

Academic Therapy Publications
20 Commercial Blvd.
Novato, CA 94949-6191
415.883.3314; 800.422.7249
www.atpub.com

Addison-Wesley Publishing Co.
1 Jacob Way
Reading, MA 01867
781.944.3700; 800.447.2226
www.awl.com

Alexander Graham Bell Association for the Deaf
3417 Volta Pl. NW
Washington, DC 20007-2778
202.337.5220
www.agbell.org

Allyn & Bacon
Division of Pearson
160 Gould St.
Needham Heights, MA 02494
www.vig.abacon.com

American Counseling Association
5999 Stevenson Ave.
Alexandria, VA 22304-3300
703.823.9800; 800.347.6647
www.counseling.org

American Foundation for the Blind
11 Penn Plaza, Suite 300
New York, NY 10001
212.620.2000; 800.232.5463
www.afb.org

American Guidance Service
4201 Woodland Rd.
PO Box 99
Circle Pines, MN 55014-1796
800.328.2560
www.agsnet.com

Aspen Publishers
7201 McKinney Cir.
Frederick, MD 21704
301.417.7500; 800.638.8437
www.aspenpub.com

Attainment Company, Inc.
PO Box 930160
Verona, WI 53593-0160
800.327.4269
www.attainmentcompany.com

Autism Asperger Publishing Company
PO Box 23172
Shawnee Mission, KS 66283-0173
913.897.1004
www.asperger.net

B

Basic Educational Materials, Publishers
PO Box 36998
Rock Hill, SC 29732-0516
803.327.9396
www.bempub.com

Brookes Publishing Company
PO Box 10624
Baltimore, MD 21285-0624
301.337.9580; 800.638.3375
www.brookespublishing.com

Brookline Books
PO Box 381047
Cambridge, MA 02238-1047
617.558.8010; 617-558-8011 (fax)
www.brooklinebooks.com

Brooks/Cole Publishing Co.
Thomson Learning
7625 Empire Dr.
Florence, KY 41042
800.354.9706
www.brookscole.com

Brunner/Routledge
c/o Taylor & Francis
7625 Empire Dr.
Florence, KY 41042

800.634.7064
www.taylorandfrancis.com

Butte Publications
PO Box 1328
Hillsboro, OR 97123-1328
www.buttepublications.com

C

Charles C. Thomas Publishing
2600 South First St.
Springfield, IL 62794-9265
217.789.8980; 800.258.8980
www.ccthomas.com

Communication Skill Builders
PO Box 42050
Tucson, AZ 85733
800.866.4446
www.psychcorp.com

Corwin Press
Sage Publications
2455 Teller Rd.
Thousand Oaks, CA 91320-2218
www.corwinpress.com

The Council for Exceptional Children
1110 N. Glebe Rd.
Arlington, VA 22201-5704
888.232.7733
www.cec.sped.org

Curriculum Publications Clearinghouse
Horrabin Hall 46
Western Illinois University
1 University Circle
Macomb, IL 61455
800.322.3905
www.wiu.edu/CPC

D

Dawn Sign Press
6130 Nancy Ridge Dr.
San Diego, CA 92121

619.625.0600; 800.549.5350
www.dawnsign.com

E

Edmark Associates
6727 185th Ave. NE
PO Box 3903
Redmond, WA 98052
206.746.3900; 800.426.0856
www.edmark.com

Educational Press
4405 East West Hwy., Suite 405
Bethesda, MD 20814
301.913.5517

F

Facts on File
11 Penn Plaza, 15th Floor
New York, NY 10001-2096
212.290.8090; 800.363.7976

Fanlight Productions
4196 Washington St., Suite 2
Boston, MA 02131
617.469.4999; 800.937.4113
www.fanlight.com

Free Spirit Publishing Company
217 Fifth Ave. North, Suite 2000
Minneapolis, MN 55401-1299
612.338.2068; 800.735.7323
www.freespirit.com

G

Gallaudet University Press
800 Florida Ave., NE
Washington, DC 20002-3695
202.651.5488; 800.451.1073
http://gupress.gallaudet.edu

Garland Publishing Company
c/o Taylor & Francis

7625 Empire Dr.
Florence, KY 41042
800.634.7064
www.taylorandfrancis.com

Gifted Psychology Press
PO Box 5057
Scottsdale, AZ 85261
602.954.4200
www.giftedpsychologypress.com

Globe-Fearon
Pearson Education
PO Box 2649
Columbus, OH 42316-2694
800.848.9500
www.globefearon.com

Greenwood Publishing Group, Inc.
88 Post Rd. West, Box 5007
Westport, CT 06881
203.226.3571; 800.225.5800
www.greenwood.com/

Gryphon House
PO Box 207
Beltsville, MD 20704
301.595.9500; 800.638.0928
www.ghbooks.com

Guilford Publications, Inc.
72 Spring St.
New York, NY 10012
212.431.9800; 800.365.7006
www.guilford.com

H

Harcourt Health Science
11830 Westline Industrial Dr.
St. Louis, MO 63146
800.545.2522
www.mosby.com

HarperCollins
10 East 53rd St.
New York, NY 10022
212.207.7000
www.harpercollins.com

Haworth Press, Inc.
10 Alice St.
Binghamton, NY 13904-1580
607.722.5857; 800.429.6784
www.haworthpressinc.com

Heinemann Educational Books, Inc.
361 Hanover St.
Portsmouth, NH 03801-3912
603.431.7894; 800.793.2154
www.heinemann.com

Hope Publishing, Inc.
1856 North 1200 East
North Logan, UT 84321
435.752.9533
www.hopepubl.com

Houghton Mifflin
222 Berkley St.
Boston, MA 02116
617.351.5000
www.hmco.com

I

International Universities Press, Inc.
PO Box 1524
Madison, CT 06443-1524
203.245.4000; 800.835.3487
www.iup.com

J

Jai Press, Inc.
PO Box 168
Greenwich, CT 06836-1678
203.661.7602
www.jaipress.com

JayJo Books
PO Box 213
Valley Park, MO 63088-0213
636.861.1331
www.jayjo.com

J. Weston Walch
321 Valley St.

PO Box 658
Portland, ME 04104-0658
800.341.6094
www.walch.com

John Wiley & Sons, Inc.
1 Wiley Dr.
Somerset, NJ 08875-1272
732.469.4400; 800.225.5945
www.wiley.com

Jossey-Bass
A John Wiley & Sons Co.
350 Sansome St.
San Francisco, CA 94104
415.433.1740
www.josseybass.com

K

Krieger Publishing Co.
PO Box 9542
Melbourne, FL 32902-9542
www.krieger-publishing.com

L

L & A Publishing/Training
708 Young Forest Dr.
Wake Forest, NC 27587
www.lapublishing.com

Lexington Books
Rowman & Littlefield Publishing Group
4720 Boston Way
Lanham, MD 20706
717.794.3800; 800.462.6420
www.lexingtonbooks.com

Lighthouse International
111 East 59th St.
New York, NY 10022-1202
212.821.9200; 800.829.0500
www.lighthouse.org

LinguiSystems
3100 4th Ave.
East Moline, IL 61244-0747

309.755.2300; 800.776.4332
www.linguisystems.com

Little, Brown and Company
Time and Life Building
1271 Avenue of the Americas
New York, NY 10020
212.522.8068; 800.343.9204

Longman Publishing Group
Imprint of Addison-Wesley Longman
The Longman Building
1185 Avenue of the Americas
New York, NY 10036
212.782.3300
www.awlonline.com

Love Publishing Company
9101 E. Kenyon Ave., Suite 2200
Denver, CO 80237
303.221.7333
www.lovepublishing.com

LRP Publications
757 Dresher Rd.
PO Box 980
Horsham, PA 19044-0980
215.784.9639; 800.515.4577
www.lrp.com

M

Macmillan Publishing Company
Division of Pearson
201 West 103rd St.
Indianapolis, IN 46290
317.581.3500; 800.571.5840

Marcel Dekker, Inc.
270 Madison Ave.
New York, NY 10016-6602
212.696.9000; 800.228.1160
www.dekker.com

Mayfield Publishing Company
1280 Villa St.
Mountain View, CA 94014
415.960.3222; 800.433.1279
www.mayfield.com

Mosby Year Book, Inc.
11830 Westline Industrial Dr.
St. Louis, MO 63146
314.872.8370; 800.325.4177

N

National Association of the Deaf
814 Thayer Ave.
Silver Spring, MD 20910-4500
www.nad.org

National Professional Resources, Inc.
25 South Regent St.
Port Chester, NY 10573
800.453.7461
www.nprinc.com

O

Open Minds, Inc.
PO Box 21325
Columbus, OH 43221-0325
800.550.0242
http://openmindsinc.com

P

PCI Educational Publishing
PO Box 34270
San Antonio, TX 78265-4270
800.594.4263
www.pcicatalog.com

Plenum Publishers
233 Spring St.
New York, NY 10013-1578
212.620.8000; 800.221.9369

PRO-ED Publishers
8700 Shoal Creek Blvd.
Austin, TX 78758-6879
512.451.3246; 800.897.3202
www.proedinc.com

Prometheus Books
59 John Glenn Dr.
Amherst, NY 14228-2197

716.691.0133; 800.421.0351
www.prometheusbooks.com

R

Research Press
2612 N. Mathis Ave.
Champaign, IL 61822
217.352.3273; 800.519.2707
www.researchpresss.com

Riverside Publishing Co.
425 Spring Lake Dr.
Itasca, IL 60143-9921
800.323.9540
www.riverpub.com

S

Sage Publications, Inc.
2455 Teller Rd.
Thousand Oaks, CA 91320-2218
805.499.9774
www.sagepub.com

Singular Publishing Group, Inc.
Thomson Learning
401 West A St., Suite 325
San Diego, CA 92101-7904
619.521.8000; 800.521.8545
www.singpub.com

Slosson Educational Publications
PO Box 280
East Aurora, NY 14052-0280
888.756.7766
www.slosson.com

Sopris West
4093 Specialty Pl.
Longmont, CO 80504
800.547.6747
www.sopriswest.com

Springer-Verlag, NY, Inc.
175 Fifth Ave.
New York, NY 10010
212.460.1500; 800.777.4643
www.springer-ny.com

Sycamore Publishing Company
PO Box 133
Sycamore, IL 60178
815.756.5388

T

T.J. Publishers
817 Silver Spring Ave., Suite 206
Silver Spring, MD 20910-4617
301.585.4440; 800.999.1168

Taylor & Francis, Inc.
Book Customer Services for North America
10650 Toebben Dr.
Independence, KY 41051
800.634.7064
www.taylorandfrancis.com

Teachers College Press
Teachers College, Columbia University
1234 Amsterdam Ave.
New York, NY 10027
212.678.3929; 800.575.6566

W

Woodbine House
6510 Bells Mill Rd.
Bethesda, MD 20817
301.897.3750; 800.843.7323
www.woodbinehouse.com

Y

York Press, Inc.
PO Box 504
Timonium, MD 21094
410.560.1557; 800.962.2763
www.yorkpress.com

This list was compiled by:
ERIC Clearinghouse on Disabilities and Gifted Education
Last updated: March 25, 2003
Readers may send updates to: ericec@cec.sped.org or http://ericec.org

12

Biographies of Special Educators

RACHEL TOPLIS

Louise Bates Ames

AMES, LOUISE BATES (1908–1996)

Dr. Ames collaborated with Arnold Gesell, Frances Ilg, and Janet Learner to found the Gesell Institute in 1950. Louise Ames was also an assistant professor at Yale Medical School (1936–1950) and curator of the Yale Films of Child Development (1944–1950). Dr. Ames was instrumental in initiating an important developmental theory that suggests that predictable behaviors are associated with chronological age. This theory proposes that human development unfolds in discrete, recognizable stages. Louise Ames' career interests and research involved the development and behavior of normal children, which resulted in standardized references for psychologists working with children. Dr. Ames was a prolific author. Among her most well-known publications were *Infant and Child in the Culture of Today* (1940) and *School Readiness* (1956).

Recommended Reading

Ames, L. B. (1940). *Infant and child in the culture of today.* New York: Harper & Row.

Ames, L. B., & Chase, J. A. (1956). *School readiness.* New York: Harper & Row.

BARDON, JACK I. (1925–1993)

Dr. Bardon earned his MA in psychology in 1951 and a PhD in clinical psychology in 1956, both from the University of Pennsylvania. He worked as a school psychologist and served as a coordinator of special education services in the New Jersey schools from 1958–1960. Jack Bardon was Rutgers University director of doctoral programs in school psychology in 1960 and graduated to become head of the department by 1968. Dr. Bardon's program at Rutgers University was one of the pioneering programs in the field of school psychology, through which Dr. Bardon had an impact on the delivery of school psychology services nationally. Jack Bardon's aim was to apply psychological theory, methods, and techniques to improve schooling in general. Dr. Bardon was also instrumental in defining the role of the school psychologist. Jack Bardon was editor of the *Journal of School Psychology* from 1968 to 1971. In 1969, he was a president of the Division of School Psychology (APA), and he served on the board of the American Orthopsychiatric Association from 1981 to 1984.

BELL, TERREL H. (1921–1996)

Dr. Bell received his MA from the University of Idaho in 1954 and his PhD in educational administration from the University of Utah in 1961. Dr. Bell was the U.S. Commissioner of Education from 1974 to 1976. He was the secretary of the U.S. Department of Education from 1981 to 1984. Terrel Bell was an instrumental member of the group that wrote the national charter, which provided support and leadership for the National Commission on Excellence in Education. The commission found serious flaws in the American educational system and helped to begin the movement to overhaul education. Dr. Bell received numerous awards, including the Department of Defense Distinguished Public Service Medal. He authored several books and publications, including *How to Shape Up Our Nation's Schools: Three Crucial Steps for Renewing American Education* (1991).

BENDER, LAURETTA (1897–1987)

Dr. Bender received her MA from the University of Chicago in 1922. She earned her MD degree from State University of Iowa in 1926. Lauretta Bender held several psychiatric residency positions and received training in neuroanatomy, physiology, and pathology. Bender honed her skills during numerous appointments, such as senior psychiatrist at Bellevue Hospital (1930–1956), director of the Child Guidance Clinic at the New York City Infirmary (1954–1960), and principal research scientist of child psychiatry at New York State Department of Mental

Hygiene (1956–1960). Dr. Bender received numerous awards during her career. These include the Adolph Meyer Award in 1953 for the contributions she made in understanding schizophrenia in children. Dr. Bender has many publications to her name. However, she is best known for the Visual Motor Gestalt Test (1937) and her book, *Psychopathological Disorders of Children with Organic Brain Disease* (1956).

Recommended Reading

Bender, L. (1956). *Psychopathological disorders of children with organic brain disease.* Springfield, IL: C. Thomas.

BINET, ALFRED (1857–1922)

Alfred Binet is credited as the founder of French experimental psychology. In 1895 he was appointed as the director of the Laboratory of Physiological Psychology at the Sorbonne in Paris. In 1904, the minister of public instruction appointed him to a commission to devise a method to identify mentally retarded children in schools, in order to provide special education programs. Binet observed children and used questionnaires and interviews during his investigations. Out of this work the first scale for measuring intelligence was created. The scale was first published by Binet and Simon in 1905 and was subsequently revised several times. In the United States, L. M. Terman from Stanford University published the *Stanford Revision of the Binet Scales.* Many translations and revisions have taken place of the Stanford-Binet Scales, and they are still extensively used today.

BIRCH, JACK W. (1915–1998)

Dr. Birch began his career as an elementary school teacher. He went on to receive his MeD from Pennsylvania State University in 1941 and his PhD in psychology from the University of Pittsburgh (1951). Birch taught classes for the educable mentally retarded; he was a psychologist and supervisor of special education, and was director of special education for the Pittsburgh public schools (1948–1958). Jack Birch finished out his career at the University of Pittsburgh, first as a professor of psychology and education and finally as an associate dean in the School of Education. Dr. Birch became an emeritus professor in 1985. He was among the first to advocate the mainstreaming of students with handicaps. After reviewing the process of mainstreaming in a national sample of school systems in 1978 he concluded that the expansion of individualized education was a necessity. He recommended four essential ways to effectively implement mainstreaming: educators needed to be cognizant of the adaptation requirements of students with handicaps in regular class settings; teachers must learn to use specialized instructional materials for handicapped students; regular classroom teachers must be able to obtain help from special education teachers; and immediate assistance must be available for teachers if a crisis or individual management situation occurs. Dr. Birch was a prolific author—he published over 120 articles and books on various topics important in the special education field, including gifted and talented, speech issues, and blindness and deafness. Two of his major books are

Teaching Exceptional Children in All America's Schools, and *Reports on the Implementation and Effects of the Adaptive Learning Environments Model in General and Special Education Settings.*

Recommended Reading

Reynolds, M. C., & Birch, J. W. (1982). *Teaching exceptional children in all America's schools.* Reston, VA: Council for Exceptional Children.

Wang, M. C., & Birch, J. W. (1985). *Reports on the implementation and effects of the adaptive learning environments model in general and special education settings.* Pittsburgh, PA: University of Pittsburgh.

BLOOM, BENJAMIN S. (1913–1999)

Dr. Bloom earned his MS from Pennsylvania State University and his PhD from the University of Chicago in 1942. Bloom's career included positions as the Charles Swift Distinguished Service Professor of education at Northwestern University. He served as advisor to the governments of India and Israel with reference to educational issues. He was recipient of several awards, including the John Dewey award (1968) and the Teacher's College medal for distinguished service of Columbia University (1970). Dr. Bloom is held in high esteem for his work with taxonomies of educational objectives, the impact of environment and heredity on intelligence, and mastery learning. Bloom classified cognitive behaviors according to a hierarchy of domains, proving a framework for viewing the educational process, classifying goals of the educational system, and specifying objectives for learning experiences. The hierarchy includes knowledge, comprehension, application, analysis, synthesis, and evaluation. Bloom also demonstrated that there are changes in measured intelligence over time, and that environmental factors can have an effect upon these changes. Bloom's work resulted in an educational shift, with more emphasis on early development. Bloom was a prolific author, publishing many articles and books in his area of expertise. Some of his most well-known are *Taxonomy of Educational Objectives* and *Stability and Change in Human Characteristics.*

Recommended Reading

Bloom, B. S. (Ed.). (1956). *Taxonomy of educational objectives. The classification of educational goals–Handbook I, cognitive domain.* New York: McKay.

Bloom, B. S. (1964). *Stability and change in human characteristics.* New York: Wiley.

BROWN, ANN L. (1943–1999)

Dr. Brown earned her PhD in psychology from the University of London in 1967. During her career she held positions at the University of Illinois, and as professor of cognition and development in the Graduate School of Education at the University of California, Berkeley. Brown was a past president of the National Academy of Education and the American Educational Research Association. She was also editor and consulting editor of several scholarly journals, including *Experimental Psychology, Child Development,* and *Developmental Psychology.* Brown is considered a leader in the field of metacognition. Brown distinguished between knowledge (cognition) and how that knowledge is understood (metacognition). Brown highlighted the importance of attention to pertinent developmental issues and understanding transition from other-regulated to self-regulated thought. Her major works include *Knowing When, Where, and How to Remember* and *Metacognition Reconsidered* (with R. Reeve). Dr. Brown received the American Psychological Society James McKeen Cattell Fellow Award for Distinguished Service to Applied Psychology in 1997.

Recommended Reading

Brown, A. L. (1978). Knowing when, where, and how to remember: A problem in metacognition. In R. Glasser (Ed.), *Advances in instructional psychology* (pp. 77–165). Hillsdale, NJ: Erlbaum.

Reeve, R. A., & Brown, A. L. (1984). *Metacognition reconsidered: Implications for intervention research.* Champaign, IL: University of Illinois.

BUROS, OSCAR K. (1905–1978)

Oscar Buros earned his graduate degree from Teacher's College, Columbia University. He served on the faculty at Rutgers University until his retirement. Buros advocated for the critical analysis of educational and psychological tests. He published the *Buros Mental Measurements Yearbook Series* (MMY). The first was published in 1938, with several updates to follow. He also published the *Tests in Print* series (1961, 1974). In 1979 the Buros Institute of Mental Measurements moved to the University of Nebraska-Lincoln to continue printing the Tests in Print and Mental Measurement Yearbook Series. Buros received numerous awards and honors—for example, many citations from the American Educational Research Association and the American Psychological Association. In 1965 he received the Phi Delta Kappa research award and in 1973 the Distinguished Service to Measurement Award from the Educational Testing Service.

Recommended Reading

Buros, O. K. (1938). *The 1938 mental measurements yearbook.* Highland Park, NJ: Gryphon.

Buros, O. K. (1961). *Tests in print.* Highland Park, NJ: Gryphon.

BURT, SIR CYRIL (1883–1971)

In 1913, Sir Cyril Burt was hired by the London County Council (UK). It is generally thought that he was the first psychologist to be employed by a school district.

Sir Burt's interests generally centered on the applications of psychological theory, methods, and techniques to enhance the educational process in schools. He carried out influential studies in the areas of mental retardation, delinquency, and the genetics of intelligence. From 1931 until his retirement Burt was a professor at University College, London. He was knighted in 1946. Unfortunately, it appears Burt fabricated findings in several of his studies, which casts doubt on his research findings. However, he is still viewed as having made many contributions to the field of psychology and special education. Burt published the influential book *Factors of the Mind* in 1941, and he coauthored the *British Journal of Statistical Psychology.*

Recommended Reading

Burt, C. (1941). *The factors of the mind: An introduction to factor analysis in psychology.* New York: Macmillan.

CHALL, JEANNE S. (1921–1999)

Jeanne S. Chall

Dr. Chall earned her PhD in 1952 from Ohio State University; she taught at the City University of New York before joining the faculty at Harvard University. Dr. Chall became professor emeritus of education and director of the reading laboratory in the Harvard Graduate School of Education. Chall served on several government education agencies as well as on the editorial board of scholarly journals such as *Reading Research Quarterly* and the *Journal of Educational Psychology.* Chall's contributions to the field of special education centered on areas of reading and language development and the development of diagnostic tests of reading disorders. Chall published the *Roswell-Chall Diagnostic Reading Test of Word Analysis Skills,* as well as developed a readability measure of instructional materials known as the Dale-Chall formula. Chall authored many books and articles during her career. Some of the most well-known are *Learning to Read: The Great Debate* and *Qualitative Assessment of Text Difficulty: A Practical Guide for Teachers and Writers.* Chall received many honors for her achievements, including the American Psychological Association Edward L. Thorndike Award for Educational Psychology. Chall was also elected to the Reading Hall of Fame and the National Academy of Education in 1979.

Recommended Reading

Chall, J. S. (1967). *Learning to read: The great debate.* Fort Worth, TX: Harcourt Brace.

Chall, J. S., Bixxes, G., Conard, S., & Harris-Sharples, S. (1996). *Qualitative assessment of text difficulty: A practical guide for teachers and writers.* Cambridge, MA: Brookline Books.

Roswell, F. G., & Chall, J. S. (1997). *Roswell-Chall diagnostic test of word analysis skills* (4th ed.). Cambridge, MA: Educators Publishing Company.

CRISSEY, MARIE SKODAK (1910–2000)

Dr. Crissey earned her MA from Ohio State University in 1931 and her PhD in developmental psychology from the University of Iowa in 1938. During her career Crissey worked at the Child Guidance Center at Flint, Michigan, was director of school psychology and special education at Dearborn, Michigan, and also spent time in private practice. Crissey is well known for her research on the heredity-environment issue, which countered the idea of the genetically determined, fixed-IQ orientation of the time. Crissey's research indicated that both heredity and environment influence intelligence. Based upon this premise, she demonstrated that favorable home environments could raise levels of measured intelligence, and thus championed the potential effectiveness of environmental intervention programs. Dr. Crissey developed, among other things, special education programs, intervention programs for handicapped and deprived students, and vocational rehabilitation services for the handicapped. Crissey was honored with numerous awards, including the Joseph P. Kennedy International Award for research in mental retardation, and a citation for distinguished service from the American Psychological Association.

William M. Cruickshank

CRUICKSHANK, WILLIAM M. (1915–1992)

Dr. Cruickshank earned his MA from the University of Chicago in 1938, and his PhD from the University of Michigan in 1945. He was a distinguished professor and founder and director of the Division of Special Education and Rehabilitation at Syracuse University from 1946–1967. Dr. Cruickshank subsequently became the director of the Institute for the Study of Mental Health and Related Disabilities at the University of Michigan. Cruickshank was also the founder, first president, and executive director of the International Academy for Research in Learning Disabilities. He received six honorary degrees and taught in many countries. Dr. Cruickshank's areas of study centered on brain-injured children, the neurologically handicapped, and the neurophysiologic characteristics of learning disabled children. Dr. Cruickshank has published and edited many books and articles. His major contributions included *Teaching Methods for Brain-Injured and Hyperactive Children* (1961), *Learning Disabilities in Home, School, and Community* (1977), and *Psychoeducational Foundations of Learning Disabilities* (1973).

Recommended Reading

Cruickshank, W. M. (1977). *Learning disabilities in home, school, and community* (rev. ed.). Syracuse, NY: Syracuse University.

Cruickshank, W. M., Bentzen, F. A., Ratzeburg, F. H., & Tannhauser, M. T. (1961). *Teaching methods for brain-injured and hyperactive children.* Syracuse, NY: Syracuse University.

DECROLY, OVIDE (1871–1932)

Belgian-born Ovide Decroly was a physician who, through his work with handicapped children, devised a unique educational setting based on the needs of these children. Based on his method, known as "the center of interest," Decroly established a special school in 1901 for the "retarded and abnormal." The assumption was that children could learn if emphasis was placed on activities that draw on the individual's needs and interests. Centers of interest were designed around the four basic needs: food, protection from the elements, defense against dangers, and work. Decroly demonstrated that these methods work for handicapped and nonhandicapped children, and his work profoundly influenced the European concept of education at that time.

DE L'EPÉE, ABBÉ CHARLES MICHEL (1712–1789)

The *Institution Nationale des Sourds Muets,* the first public school for the deaf, was founded in Paris by Abbé Charles Michel de l'Epée. He developed a language system based on signs. This sign language was the basis for the instructional system in the first school for the deaf in America, and is still in use today in a modified form.

Abbé Charles Michel De l'Epée

Edgar A. Doll

DOLL, EDGAR A. (1889–1968)

Edgar Doll accepted an appointment in 1913 as a researcher and clinical psychologist at the Training School, Vineland Laboratory, New Jersey. After returning from armed service and obtaining his PhD from Princeton University and a teaching position at Ohio State University, Dr. Doll returned in 1925 to the Vineland Laboratory. The Vineland Laboratory was devoted solely to the study of mental retardation, and it was during this time that Dr. Doll's investigations of social competence led to the publication of the *Vineland Social Maturity Scale.* This scale provided the first objective measurement of social functioning. Dr. Doll served as president of several associations, including the American Association of Applied Psychology, the American Association on Mental Deficiency, and the American Orthopsychiatric Association.

EISENSON, JON (1907–2001)

Jon Eisenson earned his MA in 1930 and his PhD in 1935 from Columbia University. His major interests revolved around language and the brain. In particular, he wrote extensively about aphasia, stuttering, dyslexia, and communication. Dr. Eisenson was influential in the development of techniques for recovering reading skills after brain injury. Dr. Eisenson authored numerous articles and books; included in these is the influential *Is My Child's Speech Normal?*

Recommended Reading

Eisenson, J. (1997). *Is my child's speech normal?* (2nd ed.). Austin, TX: Pro-Ed.

FARRELL, ELIZABETH E. (1870–1932)

Elizabeth Farrell began her teaching career in rural New York state schools. These schools were ungraded, and she taught all grades in the same classroom. In 1890 she began work as an elementary school teacher in New York City. Observations of students struggling and failing in the elementary grades led Farrell to form an ungraded class for these students. This was the first special class in public schools. In 1906 Farrell became the director of the newly established Department of Ungraded Classes. In 1911, at the Maxwell Training School in New York she designed the first training programs for special educators, and taught university courses for special class teachers at the University of Pennsylvania in 1912. Through Farrell's efforts, the journal of the Ungraded Class Teachers Association, known as *Ungraded,* was founded. Farrell was the first editor. Farrell was also one of the educators who founded the International Council for Exceptional Children in 1922.

FENICHEL, CARL (1905–1975)

Dr. Fenichel earned his doctorate in education from Yeshiva University. He began work as a teacher and psychologist. Fenichel believed that it was possible to educate severely emotionally disturbed children in a day program supported by appropriate home management and care. He advocated intensive training for parents in order to provide the necessary care at home. Fenichel succeeded in this endeavor when he founded the League School for Seriously Disturbed Children in Brooklyn, New York, in 1953. Dr. Fenichel worked as professor of education at Teachers College, Columbia University, as well as lectured at the Downstate Medical College in Brooklyn. Fenichel's League School served as a model for future schools for severely emotionally handicapped students in the United States.

FROSTIG, MARIANNE (1906–1985)

Dr. Frostig was born in Vienna, Austria, where she received a degree as a children's social worker from the College of Social Welfare in 1926. Upon moving to the United States, she earned her MA from Claremont Graduate School in 1940 and her PhD from the University of Southern California in 1955. Dr. Frostig believed that people should be assessed and treated as individuals. She supported the idea that education should be adjusted to meet the needs of the student, and was therefore interested in finding the most appropriate educational program for each child. Frostig believed that "problem children" are those children whose needs are not being met. Dr. Frostig authored *Education for Dignity,* a book that presented her views and was intended as a practical guide to meeting individual children's needs in the classroom. Frostig also published the first visual perception test of its kind to segregate visual abilities (i.e., eye-motor coordination, figure ground, perceptual consistency, spatial relationships); this test is known as *The Marianne Frostig Developmental Test of Visual Perception.* Dr. Frostig received several honors and awards in her career. These include the *Los Angeles Times Woman of the Year Award* and the *Golden Key Award of the International Association for Children with Learning Disabilities.*

Recommended Reading

Frostig, M. (1976). *Education for dignity.* New York: Grune & Stratton.

Frostig, M., Lefever, D. W., & Whittlesey, J. R. B. (1964). *The Marianne Frostig Developmental Test of Visual Perception* (3rd ed.). Palo Alto, CA: Consulting Psychologist.

GALTON, FRANCIS (1822–1911)

Francis Galton, born in England, was the cousin of Charles Darwin. By all accounts, Galton came from a distinguished, highly intellectual family. Galton pioneered the development of psychological tests and formulated the genetic principle of segregation of inherited characteristics. His influential book, *Hereditary Genius,* published in 1869, argues for the genetic basis of individual differences in intelligence. During his research into the relationship of characteristics between parents and offspring, Galton discovered the phenomenon of regression to the mean and developed the concept of correlation. Galton was a prolific author, publishing over 300 articles and books covering a range of topics.

Recommended Reading

Galton, F. (1869). *Hereditary genius: An inquiry into its laws and consequences.* London: Macmillan.

GODDARD, HENRY H. (1866–1957)

Dr. Goddard earned his PhD in psychology at Clark University. He taught at the Pennsylvania State Teachers College, and was the director of the Training School at Vineland. In 1918 Goddard became the director of the State Bureau of Juvenile Research in Ohio. Subsequently, he was professor of abnormal and clinical psychology at Ohio State University. Dr. Goddard specialized in the study of atypical children. During his tenure at the Training School at Vineland he had a major influence on the education of mentally retarded children. He founded the first psychological laboratory devoted to the study of mentally retarded children. He developed and tested educational methods that were most suitable for instructing the mentally retarded. Dr. Goddard was responsible for translating and adapting the Binet-Simon intelligence scales for use in the United States. In 1912, Goddard published his influential study of mental retardation as an inherited trait, *The Kallikak Family: A Study in the Heredity of Feeblemindedness.*

Recommended Reading

Goddard, H. H. (1912). *The Kallikak family: A study in the heredity of feeblemindedness.* New York: Macmillan.

GOODENOUGH, FLORENCE LAURA (1886–1959)

Dr. Goodenough earned her PhD in psychology under Lewis M. Terman at Stanford University; she also worked as a teacher in public school and at the Training School at Vineland, New Jersey. Dr. Goodenough's skills lay in understanding, interpreting, and applying research methodology. She applied a variety of research techniques to diverse research questions; this work was the basis of her publication, *Experimental Child Study,* with John E. Anderson. This publication evaluated the pros and cons of numerous research methodologies. Dr. Goodenough also published the *Draw a Man* test in 1926 and the *Minnesota Preschool Scale.*

Recommended Reading

Goodenough, F. L., & Anderson, J. E. (1982). *Experimental child study.* Darby, PA: Arden Library.

GOWAN, JOHN C. (1912–1986)

Dr. Gowan earned his EdM and EdD at the University of California at Los Angeles. During his career he filled several overseas lecturing positions, and was a professor at California State University for over 25 years. Dr. Gowan's field of expertise was in the area of guidance for the gifted. He researched and wrote extensively about issues surrounding socialization and giftedness. He also focused on the use of developmental stage theory to enhance creativity in gifted children. Dr. Gowan authored several publications; his most well-known include *Trance, Art and Creativity,* and *Educating the Ablest.*

Recommended Reading

Gowan, J. C. (1971). *Educating the ablest: A book of reading on the education of gifted children.* Itasca, IL: Peacock.

Gowan, J. C. (1987). *Trance, art and creativity: A psychological analysis of the relationship between the individual ego and the numinous element in three modes—prototaxic, parataxic and syntaxic.* Buffalo, NY: Creative Education.

GROHT, MILDRED A. (1890–1971)

Mildred A. Groht

Mildred Groht graduated from Swarthmore College with an honorary doctorate from Gallaudet College. She worked as a teacher of the deaf for several years, and served as a principal at the Lexington School for the Deaf in New York City until her retirement. Groht's contribution to the field was the natural language method of teaching deaf children which she proposed and developed. This language method is based upon the assumption that deaf children best acquire language through activities that are a natural part of the child's life. She proposed that such real-life language development activities are more effective than the traditional grammatical or analytical approach. Many programs today use a variety of natural and analytical procedures. Groht described her natural approach in her book, *Natural Language for Deaf Children*. Groht was called "one of America's most distinguished teachers of the deaf" (O'Conner, 1958).

Recommended Reading

Groht, M. A. (1958). *Natural Language for Deaf Children*. Washington, DC: Alexander Graham Bell Association for the Deaf.

HALL, FRANK H. (1843–1911)

Frank Hall was a school supervisor and superintendent of the Illinois Institution for the Education of the Blind. Hall advocated for blind students to have the same opportunities as sighted students. To this end he invented the braillewriter, a typewriter that quickly replaced the time-consuming slate and handheld stylus of the time. This invention made the mass production of Braille materials feasible. Hall also persuaded the school authorities of Chicago to establish day classes for the blind, instead of a boarding school. This was the first public-school day classes for the blind.

HAVIGHURST, ROBERT J. (1900–1991)

Dr. Havighurst earned his doctorate from Ohio State University in 1924. He was a professor of education and psychology for over 40 years at the University of Chicago. One of Dr. Havighurst's major contributions to the field was his introduction of the theory of developmental tasks. Havighurst believed that skills, knowledge, functions, or attitudes are normally acquired by an individual during a specific time period. He coined the phrase "teachable moments" to mean periods when a person is most able and receptive to learning new skills. Havighurst believed that if skills are not acquired during this time, it is harder to develop them at a later time. During his career, Havighurst was director of the Rockefeller Foundation's European Rehabilitation Program. He was also involved as a codirector of the Brazilian Government's efforts to establish an elementary and secondary school system.

HOWE, SAMUEL GRINDLEY (1801–1876)

Samuel Howe was trained as a physician who later became superintendent of Massachusetts' first school for the blind. This school became known as the Perkins Institute and Massachusetts School for the Blind. Under Howe's leadership, this school championed programs to enable blind students to become academically competent, self-reliant, and competitively employable. Due to the renown of Howe's most famous student, Laura Bridgeman, who was a deaf-blind child, Helen Keller's father appealed to the Perkins Institute for help, and the famous relationship between Helen Keller and Anne Sullivan was made possible. Howe was also instrumental in the establishment of the American Printing House for the Blind in 1879. Through his work with the mentally retarded, Howe convinced the legislature that the education of the mentally retarded should be a public responsibility, and the Walter E. Fernald State School was established in 1855.

HUNT, JOSEPH MCVICKER (1906–1991)

Joseph McVicker Hunt

Dr. Hunt earned his MA in 1930 from the University of Nebraska and his PhD in 1933 from Cornell University. He held several lecturer positions and research positions during his career. His final position was as a professor of psychology at the University of Illinois. It was through this university that he was awarded professor emeritus status in 1974. Apart from his numerous studies in child psychology, Hunt was appointed chair of the White House Task Force on Early Childhood Education. It was through this task force that the report "A Bill of Rights for Children" was developed, which recommended extending Head Start programs and promoting follow-up programs that would extend the age limits of the Head Start program.

KIRK, SAMUEL A. (1904–1996)

Samuel A. Kirk

Dr. Kirk received his MA in psychology in 1931 from the University of Chicago and his PhD in 1935 from the University of Michigan. During his career, Kirk held a position at the University of Illinois as well as serving as director of the Federal Office of Education's Division of Handicapped Children. Kirk's major contributions to the field include developing methods to measure linguistic, perceptual, and memory abilities in young children. The *Illinois Test of Psycholinguistic Abilities (ITPA)* was published in 1968. A study published by Kirk in 1958, *Early Education of the Mentally Retarded,* is credited for influencing the establishment of the Head Start program. Kirk also contributed to early federal legislation that led to the Early Education Assistance Act of 1968 and the establishment of the Bureau for the Education of Handicapped Children. The work of this bureau culminated in PL 94-142, the Education for All Handicapped Children Act of 1975. Kirk is credited with coining the term "Learning Disabilities" in 1962, and is widely thought of as the father of learning disabilities. Dr. Kirk was a prolific author and the recipient of numerous awards, including the First International Award in Mental Retardation from the Joseph P. Kennedy Foundation.

Recommended Reading

Kirk, S. A. (1958). *Early education of the mentally retarded—an experimental study.* Urbana: University of Illinois Press.

Kirk, S. A., McCarthy, J. J., & Kirk, W. D. (1968). *The Illinois Test of Psycholinguistics Abilities.* Urbana: University of Illinois Press.

MCCARTHY, DOROTHEA (1906–1974)

Dr. McCarthy received her PhD in 1928 at the University of Minnesota. She was appointed associate professor and professor at Fordham University, where she served for 40 years. McCarthy was particularly interested in early childhood cognitive development and the means by which these abilities are measured. McCarthy developed the *McCarthy Scales of Children's Abilities,* which was published in 1972. These scales were designed to measure the mental and motor abilities of children aged 2 1/2 to 8 1/2. McCarthy also published two influential chapters on the language development of preschoolers and the vocalizations of infants. These chapters appeared in Murchison's *Handbook of Child Psychology* and Carmichael's *Manual of Child Psychology.* In 1967 she was awarded an honorary degree of doctor of sciences by the College of New Rochelle.

Recommended Reading

McCarthy, D. (1972). *Manual for the McCarthy Scales of children's abilities.* New York: Psychological Corporation.

MONTESSORI, MARIA (1870–1952)

Maria Montessori was Italy's first female physician. She is well known for her educational approach, known as the Montessori Method. Originally used for the instruction of mentally retarded students, the method incorporates nongraded classroom, individualization of instruction, sequential ordering of learning tasks, sensory and motor training, use of concrete materials, abolition of punishment, discovery learning, and freedom of activity and choice. Montessori soon discovered that her method was successful with nonhandicapped students. Montessori taught and lectured in many countries and her method was adopted by many schools. After visiting the United States in 1914 the American Montessori Society was founded, with Alexander Graham Bell as its president.

T. Ernest Newland

NEWLAND, T. ERNEST (1903–1992)

Dr. Newland earned his PhD at Ohio State University in 1931. After serving on the faculty at Bucknell University, Newland became chief of the Division of Special Education in the Pennsylvania Department of Special Education. Newland was also professor in the College of Education at the University of Illinois for 20 years. Newland's contributions to the field include increasing educators' understanding of testing as a part of the assessment process, furthering psychologists' understanding of intelligence as involving both product and process. He developed the *Blind Learning Aptitude Test* in 1980, and published *The Gifted in Socioeduca-*

tional Perspectives. Newland implemented the first statewide county supervisor of special education programs, he established the first mandatory state hearing test program for public school children, and was central in the decision to expand the state's definition of exceptional children to include the gifted. Ernest Newland was honored with awards from the Association for the Gifted, the Illinois Psychological Association, and the Division of School Psychology of the American Psychological Association.

Recommended Reading

Newland, T. E. (1976). *The gifted in socioeducational perspective.* Englewood Cliffs, NJ: Prentice Hall.

Newland, T. E. (1980). *Blind Learning Aptitude Test.* Champaign, IL: University of Illinois.

ORTON, SAMUEL T. (1879–1948)

Samuel Orton was trained as a physician; however, he is best known for his studies of children with severe reading disabilities. Although they were otherwise not handicapped, Orton noticed that the children he worked with experienced great difficulty acquiring the skills of reading, writing, spelling, or speech. Orton observed that these language difficulties were often accompanied with confusion in direction, time, and sequence. Orton called this syndrome *word blindness* and offered principles for its remediation. The Orton Society, formed after his death, continues the work he began.

PEREIRE, JACOB R. (1715–1780)

Jacob Pereire was an early educator of the deaf. He conducted schools for the deaf in Paris and Bordeaux, and his work influenced individuals such as l'Epée and Sicard. Pereire was the originator of lip reading and the first manual alphabet that used only one hand. Pereire also showed that speech can be understood using the vibrations and muscular movements of the vocal mechanisms. Pereire was awarded a pension by King Louis XV, he received an official commendation of the Parisian Academy of Science, and became a member of the Royal Society of London in recognition of his achievements.

PREHM, HERBERT J. (1937–1986)

Herbert J. Prehm

Dr. Prehm received his MS in 1962 and his PhD in 1964 from the University of Wisconsin, Madison. Dr. Prehm was trained as an elementary teacher and reading consultant with dyslexics; however, his main area of interest focused on effective teaching of mentally handicapped children. Prehm's research resulted in a model that allowed for controlled, formal investigation of relevant variables such as race, age, and handicapping condition. As a tool, this model was used in studying teaching methods. Among his contributions to the field, Prehm served as assistant executive director of the Department of Professional Development of the Council for Exceptional Children. He also served as president of the teacher education division of the Council for Exceptional Children. Prehm was awarded the TED-Merril Award for excellence in teaching education.

REDL, FRITZ (1902–1988)

Fritz Redl

Dr. Redl was born and educated in Austria. He received his PhD in philosophy and psychology in 1925 from the University of Vienna. For 11 years he trained as an analyst at the Weiner Psychoanalysis Institute. Dr. Redl held positions as clinical director of the University of Michigan Fresh Air Camp, chief of the Child Research Branch of the National Institute of Mental Health, and the president of the American Orthopsychiatric Association. Redl's interests and work focused on the exploration of children's behavior controls, their defenses, and how to prevent or treat the disorganization that results when behavioral controls are maladaptive (Redl 1966, 1975). Redl developed the "life space interview," which was designed to provide strategies and techniques for dealing with immediate crisis in children's lives. Redl also established Pioneer House, a residential program for the study and treatment of delinquent children. The Detroit Group Project was originated by Redl and was designed to provide clinical work with children and a summer camp for low-income families. Redl's book (coauthored with D. Wineman), *The Aggressive Child,* (1957) summarizes his work at Pioneer House.

Recommended Reading

Redl, F., and Wineman, D. (1957). *The aggressive child.* New York: Free Press.

Redl, F. (1966). *When we deal with children: Selected writings.* New York: Free Press.

Redl, F. (1975). Disruptive behavior in the classroom. *School Review, 83,* 569–594.

ROBINSON, HALBERT B. (1925–1981) AND ROBINSON, NANCY M. (1930–)

Nancy and Hal Robinson are important contributors to the field of mental retardation, early child care, and gifted children. In 1966, with Ann Peters, Hal Robinson founded the Frank Porter Graham Development Center at the University of North Carolina. After accepting a position at the University of Washington, Seattle, he served as the principal investigator of the Child Development Research Group (now the Halbert Robinson Center for the Study of Capable Youth). This center focused on the identification and development of curriculum for children with advanced intellectual and academic skills. Nancy and Hal Robinson have published in many important areas, including the counseling of highly gifted children. They have also coauthored an influential text defining the field of mental retardation, known as *The Mentally Retarded Child: A Psychological Approach* (1976). Additionally, they published the *International Monograph Series on Early Child Care* (1974).

Recommended Reading

Robinson, H. B., & Robinson, N. M. (1974). *International Monograph Series on Early Child Care.* London: Gordon, Breach.

Robinson, H. M., & Robinson, N. M. (1976). *The mentally retarded child: A psychological approach* (2nd ed.). New York: McGraw-Hill.

ROUSSEAU, JEAN J. (1712–1778)

Jean Rousseau was a French-Swiss philosopher and moralist who expounded on education in his novel *Emile.* This novel revolutionized child-rearing and educational practices, and has influenced major educational reform and influential theorists in the educational field, including Montessori, Froebel, and Dewey.

Recommended Reading

Rousseau, J. J. (1969). *Emile.* New York: Dutton.

SEGUIN, EDOUARD (1812–1880)

Edouard Seguin's influence on the early development of special education services is extensive. He studied under Jean Marc Gaspard Itard in Paris, began the first school in France for the mentally retarded, and moved to America in 1848. In the United States, Seguin practiced medicine, served as the director of the Pennsylvania Training School, and advised numerous state institutions. Seguin's methodology, which was found to be remarkably successful, was based upon five main principles. These are: observation of the child is the foundation of the educational program for that child; the educational program deals with the whole child (as a result, Seguin incorporated art, music, and gymnastics into his programs); the program should incorporate real life, concrete events, situations, and materials; perceptual training should precede the training of concepts; every child has some capacity for learning. Seguin was the founder and first president of the American Association on Mental Deficiency (previously known as the Association of Medical Officers of American Institutions for Idiotic and Feeble-minded Persons).

STRAUSS, ALFRED A. (1897–1957)

Alfred Strauss received his medical degree and subsequent training from his native country, Germany. After a period of time in Spain at the University of Barcelona, where he helped to establish Barcelona's first child guidance clinics, Strauss moved to the United States. Strauss worked in 1937 as a research psychiatrist and director of child care at Wayne County School in Michigan. In 1947 he founded the Cove School, the first residential facility for brain-injured children, at Racine, Wisconsin. During his tenure as president the school received international acclaim for its pioneering work. Some of Strauss's major contributions to the field include the development of tests for diagnosing brain injury and a systematic description of "minimally brain injured" children, which was a new clinical entity. Written with Laura Lehtinen, Strauss' book *Psychopathology and Education of the Brain-Injured Child* (1947) became a major guide for school programs during the 50s and 60s.

Recommended Reading

Strauss, A. A., & Lehtinen, L. E. (1947). *Psychopathology and education of the brain-injured child* (Vol. 1). New York: Grune & Stratton.

TERMAN, LEWIS M. (1877–1956)

Lewis M. Terman

Lewis Terman earned his PhD in education and psychology from Clark University, under the supervision of G. Stanley Hall. Dr. Terman was an experienced teacher, principal, and college instructor, but the majority of his career was spent at Stanford University, where he was the head of the psychology department. Dr. Terman's contributions to the field were numerous; however, he is best known for his work with mental tests. The most renowned is the Stanford-Binet tests of intelligence, which he adapted for the Binet-Simon Scales of Intelligence in 1916. Terman also developed the first group intelligence tests, known as the Army Alpha and Beta tests, which were designed to classify servicemen during the First World War. Terman made popular the term IQ (intelligence quotient) when he introduced the concept with the Stanford-Binet tests. Dr. Terman has also been credited with beginning the gifted and talented movement. He began the first comprehensive study of gifted children (classified as IQ of over 140) in 1921. This long-term study reported that contrary to popular belief at the time, children with higher IQs are often healthier, happier, more stable, and more successful in their personal and professional lives than children with average IQs. This study is ongoing, and the findings from this study have been used to promote the provision of special education programs for these students.

TORRANCE, ELLIS PAUL (1914–2003)

Ellis Paul Torrance

Dr. Torrance earned his MA at the University of Minnesota (1944) and his PhD at the University of Michigan. For an extensive part of his career, Torrance served as professor of educational psychology and as department chairman at the University of Georgia. Torrance is considered an influential theorist in the field of giftedness. His work identifying gifted people from all cultures and ages encouraged him to develop the Torrance Tests of Creative Thinking (TTCT), and the Thinking Creatively in Action and Movement (TCAM), among others. Dr. Torrance was also a prolific author, publishing over 40 books. These books include *Guiding Creative Talent* and *Making the Creative Leap Beyond.* Dr. Torrance, along with his wife Pansy, founded the Future Problem Solving Program in 1974, which teaches problem-solving skills to thousands of children.

Recommended Reading

Torrance, E. P. (1962). *Guiding creative talent.* Englewood Cliffs, NJ: Prentice Hall.

Torrance, E. P., & Safter, H. T. (1998). *Making the creative leap beyond.* Buffalo, NY: Creative Education Foundation.

VAN RIPER, CHARLES (1905–1991)

Charles Van Riper earned his MA from the University of Michigan in 1930, and his PhD from the University of Iowa in 1934. Van Riper's area of expertise is in the field of speech pathology and psychology. Dr. Van Riper served as a professor in the department of speech pathology and audiology of Western Michigan University and director of the Speech and Hearing Clinic at the university. Dr. Van Riper's major contributions included developing the theory of stuttering and methods for understanding, evaluating, and altering speech behavior. Van Riper was a strong believer in involving the family when addressing speech problems. Van Riper's most influential publications were *Your Child's Speech Problems* (1961) and *Speech Corrections: Principles and Methods* (1978).

Recommended Reading

Van Riper, C. (1961). *Your child's speech problems.* New York: Harper & Row.

Van Riper, C. (1978). *Speech correction: Principles and methods* (6th ed.). Englewood Cliffs, NJ: Prentice-Hall.

John Edward Wallace Wallin

WALLIN, JOHN EDWARD WALLACE (1876–1969)

Dr. Wallin was a pioneer in the field of special education and clinical psychology. He earned his MA in 1899 and his PhD in 1901 from Yale University. Wallin worked as an assistant to G. Stanley Hall at Clark University in Massachusetts. He also held numerous other positions, such as head of the psychology department and vice president of East Stroudsburg State Teachers College in Pennsylvania. From 1909 to 1910 he was head of the department of psychology and education at the Normal Training School at Cleveland, Ohio. During this time he developed the field of special education, psychoclinical examinations, and one of the first group intelligence tests. At the University of Pittsburgh in 1912 Dr. Wallin founded the first psychoeducational clinic. Dr. Wallin was affiliated with numerous clinics and universities during his illustrious career. He was a leading advocate for the use of clinical psychology in education, especially as used in the identification and diagnosis of handicapped children. Wallin was a prolific author; he published over 30 books and 350 articles. He was a political activist for policies, regulations, and change to ensure the appropriate education for handicapped children. He was a member of several professional organizations and held important positions on many committees, such as secretary of the committees on special education for the White House Conference on Child Health and Protection for 1929 to 1930.

WECHSLER, DAVID (1896–1981)

David Wechsler earned his MA from Columbia University in 1917, following which he worked with the armed forces in evaluating recruits. Toward the end of his army tour he studied with Charles Spearman and Karl Pearson in London and then with Henri Peron and Louis Lapique in Paris. Wechsler completed his PhD at Columbia University in 1925. Wechsler worked as a psychologist at New York City's newly established Bureau of Child Study. He worked as chief psychologist at New York's Bellevue Hospital, and during his 35-year tenure he developed numerous tests, including the Wechsler-Bellevue Intelligence Scale I (1939) and Scale II (1942), the Wechsler Intelligence Scale for Children (1949), the Wechsler Adult Intelligence Scale (1955), and the Wechsler Preschool and Primary Scale of Intelligence (1967). Dr. Wechsler authored *The Range of Human Capacities* in 1935. This, he felt, was his seminal work. He is also credited with the dissemination of the concept of the deviation IQ, used for reporting adult intelligence scores, instead of the mental age and ratio IQ. Dr. Wechsler received many honors, including the Distinguished Professional Contributions Award from the American Psychological Association, as well as awards from the Division of Clinical Psychology and the Division of School Psychology.

WITMER, LIGHTNER (1867–1956)

Lightner Witmer

Lightner Witmer succeeded James McKeen Cattell as director of the psychological laboratory at the University of Pennsylvania, where he moved psychology from the theoretical concerns of the laboratory to the applied study of the learning and behavior problems of children in the classroom. Proposing to merge the clinical methods of psychology and the diagnostic methods of teaching, Witmer established the world's first psychological clinic at the University of Pennsylvania in 1896. Witmer developed an interdisciplinary approach to education; his clinic trained psychologists, teachers, social workers, and physicians. He formed special classes that served as models for many of the programs established in the early 1900s. Lightner Witmer proposed that learning-disabled children would show the way for the education of all children, foreseeing special education's strong influence on mainstream education.

13

Positive Behavioral Support

RANDALL L. DE PRY

Historically, students with disabilities who engaged in chronic or persistent challenging behavior were placed in programs that excluded them from their general-education peers, and resulted in behavior reduction programs that were highly aversive and/or consequence based. In retrospect, we know that these strategies often did not respect the dignity of the student of concern, did not teach more appropriate alternatives to the problem behavior, and did not take into account the role that the environment (i.e., persons, events, settings) played in occasioning the problem behavior. Over the past 25 years, increased interest and research in this area has resulted in a greater understanding of why persons engage in challenging behaviors, and in the application of evidenced-based practices at the individual student level, as well as at the school and family systems levels.

Positive Behavioral Support (PBS), as applied to the individual student, seeks to understand the environmental events that may occasion or trigger the problem behavior, as well as the purpose or function that the problem behavior serves for the individual. This process, called functional behavioral assessment, results in a behavior support plan that, when fully implemented, provides a comprehensive level of support for the person of concern by teaching him or her positive alternatives to engaging in the problem behavior, and by creating more effective environments that will occasion the alternative behavior(s).

Researchers have found that PBS is also an effective method for producing systemic change in schools. Data suggest that schools that incorporate PBS as part of a proactive school-wide discipline model can reduce problem behavior by providing a continuum of academic and social/behavioral support within and across settings. A continuum of support includes (1) universal or primary interventions that

Positive Behavioral Support Systems

- School-Wide
- Classroom
- Non-classroom Settings
- Individual Student

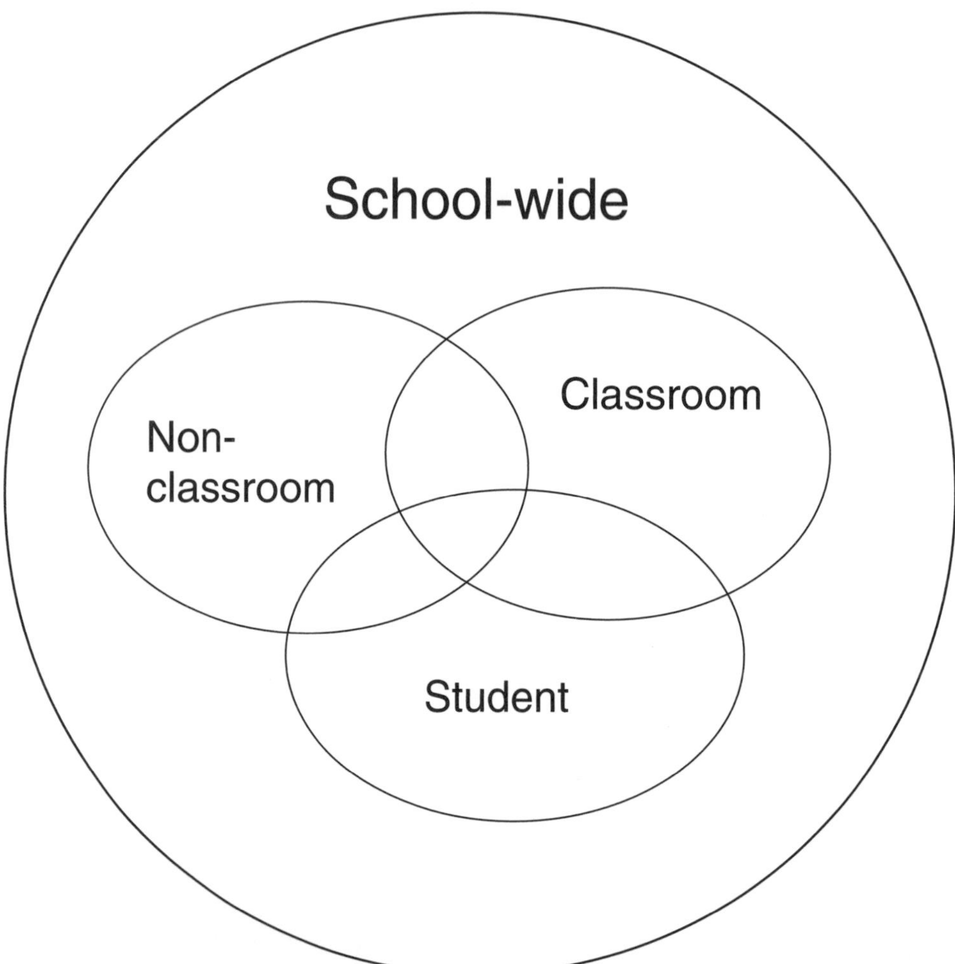

Figure 13.1 Systems of School-Wide Positive Behavior Supports
Source: OSEP Center for Positive Behavior Inteventions and Supports

are applied to all learners, (2) targeted or secondary interventions that are applied to learners who are at risk for academic or social failure, and (3) intensive or tertiary interventions that are applied to individual learners with chronic or persistent problem behavior.

Schools that have incorporated PBS into their proactive school-wide discipline model have several common features, including: (1) strong administrative leadership, (2) team-based implementation, (3) defined behavioral expectations that apply to all learners and are applicable across all settings, (4) effective methods for

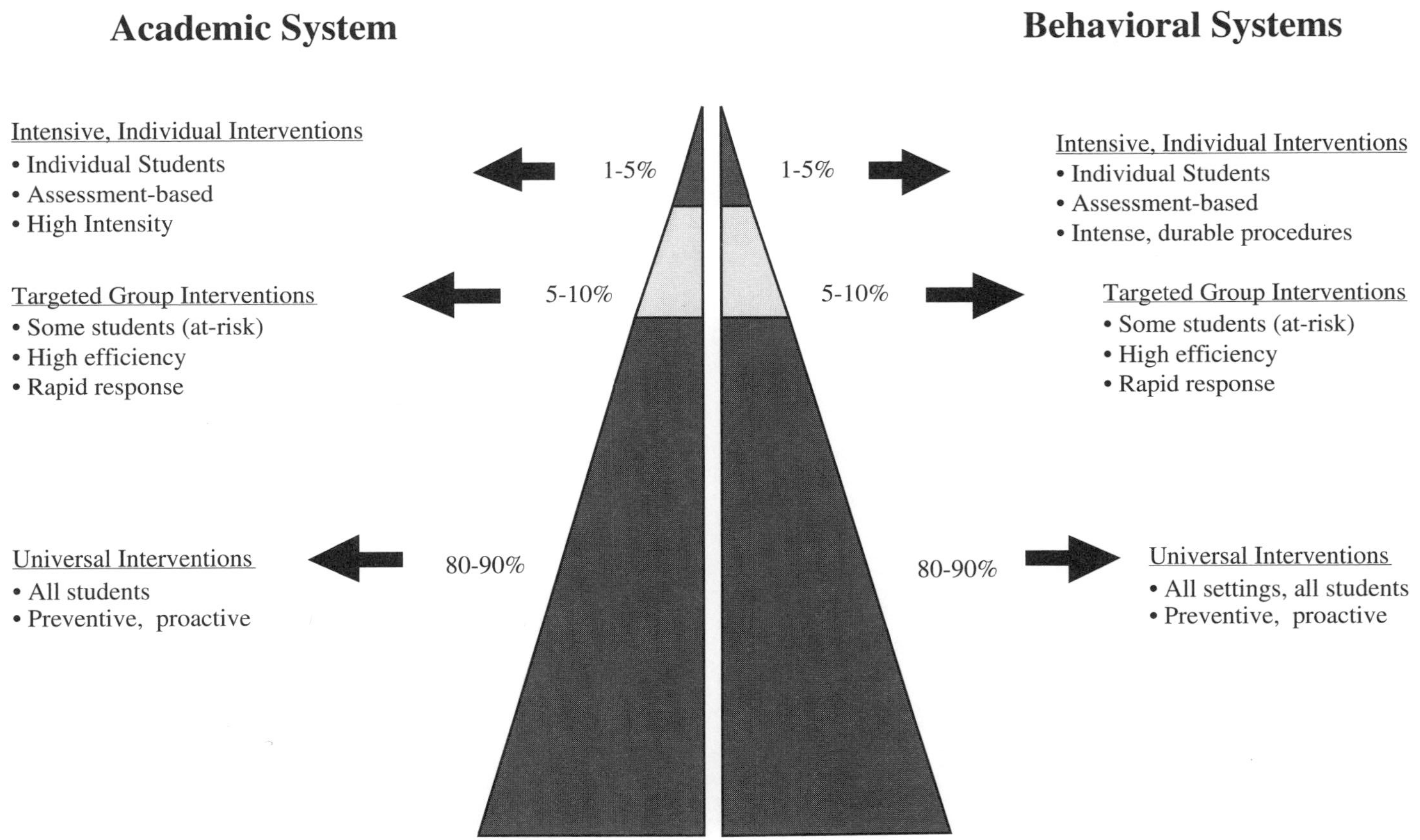

Figure 13.2 Designing School-Wide Systems for Student Success

School-wide PBS Implementation Features Checklist

- Expectations for student behavior are defined.
- Expectations for student behavior are taught.
- Student behavior is monitored.
- Faculty decisions are data driven.
- Positive behavior is acknowledged.
- Effective instruction is emphasized.
- Procedures are implemented consistently by all staff and across all settings.
- Problem behavior has clear and consistent consequences.

directly teaching the behavioral expectations to all learners, (5) acknowledgment and reinforcement of expected behaviors, (6) monitoring and correcting of behavioral errors, (7) use of discipline data to inform decision making, and (8) clearly delineated plans that encourage collaboration between school and home. In schools that use PBS, the preceding features are applied consistently by all faculty and staff within and across the four systems found in each school: school-wide systems, classroom management systems, non-classroom setting systems, and individual student systems.

Schools that have adopted PBS share several common features, including: a focus on strategies that are both proactive and preventative, application of strategies that are research based, use of teaching strategies for establishing behavioral expectations, and high levels of faculty and staff support for the initiative. Hundreds of schools in the United States and Canada are currently implementing PBS as their school-wide discipline model, with a high degree of faculty and staff satisfaction, as well as strong support from students and their families. In fact, many PBS schools report increases in academic engagement and decreases in disruptive problem behaviors when compared to baseline levels of performance prior to implementation.

Educators, families, and researchers are using Positive Behavioral Support as a method for creating more effective school, home, and community environments. This method holds promise for learners with challenging behavior by providing understanding of the contextual and learned nature of problem behavior and by providing effective and positive alternatives that support the person of concern. PBS also holds promise as an effective method for decreasing the exclusion that often results from chronic or persistent challenging behavior, by creating effective and efficient behavior support plans that increase opportunities for inclusion and meaningful participation in school, home, and community settings. Additionally, this method, when used as a model for proactive school-wide discipline, results in both academic and behavioral support for all learners.

PBS RESOURCES

Books and Journals

Koegel, L. K., Koegel, R. L., & Dunlap, G. (1996). *Positive behavioral support: Including people with difficult behavior in the community.* Baltimore: Paul H. Brookes.

O'Neill, R. E., Horner, R. H., Albin, R. W., Sprague, J. R., Storey, K., & Newton,

J. S. (1997). *Functional assessment and program development for problem behavior: A practical handbook* (2nd ed.). Pacific Grove, CA: Brooks/Cole.

Quinn, M. M., Osher, D., Warger, C. L., Hanley, T. V., Bader, B. D., & Hoffman, C. C. (2000). *Teaching and working with children who have emotional and behavioral challenges.* Longmont, CO: Sopris West.

Journal of Positive Behavior Interventions (ISSN: 1098-3007). PRO-ED, 8700 Shoal Creek Boulevard, Austin, TX 78757-6897. http://www.proedinc.com/journals.html

Internet Resources

OSEP Technical Assistance Center on Positive Behavioral Interventions & Supports. (English and Spanish Versions) http://www.pbis.org

The Association for Positive Behavior Support. PO Box 328, Bloomsburg, PA 17815. http://www.apbsinternational.org

Colorado Department of Education, *Colorado School-wide Positive Behavior Support Initiative.* http://www.cde.state.co.us/pbs

Florida Positive Behavior Support Project. http://www.fmhi.usf.edu/cfs/dares/flpbs

Positive Behavior Support Electronic Library at Northern Arizona University. http://www.nau.edu/ihd/positive/library

School Wide Information System (SWIS). http://www.swis.org

Online Academy Positive Behavior Support (PBS) modules. http://www.uappbs.lsi.ku.edu

Functional Behavioral Assessment Resources. http://interact.uoregon.edu/wrrc/Behavior.html#FBA

14

Creativity and the Special Education Student

JAMES C. KAUFMAN, JONATHAN A. PLUCKER, GAYLE T. DOW, JOHN BAER, CANDACE J. ANDREWS, ERICA R. MITCHELL, AND ALLISON B. KAUFMAN

WHAT IS CREATIVITY?

What is creativity, exactly? This question may seem a bit silly—we all know what creativity is, don't we? Yet many of the instant responses (such as "thinking outside the box," "being different," or "doing your own thing") aren't particularly useful. What does it really *mean* to think outside the box, to be different, or to do your own thing? Many academic psychologists focus their research studies on creativity, and much of this work can be applied to the classroom.

The first person to study creativity on a wide-scale basis was J. P. Guilford. His Structure of Intellect model placed creativity within a larger framework of intelligence, and attempted to organize all of human cognition along three dimensions. The first dimension, "operations," meant the mental gymnastics needed for any kind of task. The second dimension, "content," referred to the general subject area. Finally, the third dimension, "product," represented the actual products that might result from different combinations of thinking styles and subject matters. With five operations, four contents, and six products, Guilford's model had an amazingly complex 120 different possible mental abilities (Guilford, 1967). Indeed, he later expanded the model to include 180 different abilities, although the 120-abilities model is the one more often studied (Guilford, 1988). One of Guilford's operations (sometimes called *thought processes*) was divergent thinking—how you respond to questions that have no obvious, singular answer (e.g., "What would happen if we didn't need sleep?"). Divergent thinking is one way that creativity is conceptualized.

Most research and theory-based definitions of creativity boil down to two components. First, creativity must represent something different, new, or innovative (Baer, 1997). This part begs a few questions (e.g., how new? Different in what ways?) that will be addressed later. However, unlike originality, simply being novel isn't enough to qualify in the larger picture as being creative. If we ask you to show a proof for the transitive property in algebra, and you answer, "a herring!," this response is clearly *different*—but we wouldn't call it creative. We'd be more inclined to want to measure your mental health than your creativity.

So it isn't enough to just be different—creativity must also be appropriate to the task at hand. A creative response is useful and relevant. There are some circumstances (such as if you were doing a stand-up comedy routine) where "a herring" *might* be an appropriate response to an algebraic proof. But there are not many. A certain level of high quality is often linked with appropriateness—you not only fulfill task demands, but you do it well (Sternberg, 1999; Sternberg, Kaufman, & Pretz, 2002).

If there appears to be some consensus about the basic definition of creativity, the path is less smooth when it comes to its measurement.

ASSESSING CREATIVITY

How Does One Assess Creativity?

Assessing creativity is generally considered to be quite difficult, and it is considered to be difficult for one important reason: Creativity is many things to many people. As discussed elsewhere in this section, creativity is a complex, multifaceted construct, and any attempt to measure complex human behaviors and capacities is going to be difficult and often controversial.

However, researchers and educators have been addressing this challenge for several decades, and a variety of strategies are currently being used to assess children's creativity. In this section, we review basic approaches to creativity assessment and discuss the attributes of the most widely used instruments and strategies. A more detailed, academic treatment of this topic is available in Plucker and Renzulli (1999).

Approaches to Measuring Creativity

Creativity scholars have developed three general approaches to assessing creativity: historiometric, biometric, and psychometric. Of these three, only psychometric approaches are widely used in educational settings and will receive most of our attention in this section, although the other two approaches are described briefly.

In the *historiometric approach,* researchers assess biographical and historical data about eminent creators and leaders. For example, Dean Keith Simonton, a leading historiometrician, investigated the role between acquired expertise and creative development of classical composers (Simonton, 1989). He examined factors such as age of first operas, age of first compositions, and age of first lessons. He compared these data to creative products (genre-specific operas, all operas, all vocal compositions, and all compositions). He concluded that creative musical ability is predicted by overtraining in the specific field and versatility cross-training in other fields. Due to the need to study relatively unambiguous examples of creative accomplishment, this approach has little utility for assessing children's creativity.

Researchers employing the *biometric* approach are concerned with biological assessment of creativity. For example, Bekhtereva et al. (2000) examined brain function, using advanced scanning equipment while participants completed creativity tasks. Results suggest that, contrary to conventional wisdom about creativity being a right brain activity, creative thinking tasks require the contribution of many parts of the human brain. The high cost and limited practical applications of biometric measurement currently prevent meaningful applications to education, although this may change over time.

Researchers employing *psychometric* methods generally investigate one or more of the "Four P's": creative processes, creative personality, creative products, or creative press (e.g., environmental and contextual aspects of creativity; as they do not focus on individual children, we do not discuss them further). A majority of creativity tests used with children focus on creative processes. For example, J. P. Guilford researched and developed a wide variety of psychometric tests to measure creativity. In his Unusual Uses Test (Guilford, Merrifield, & Wilson, 1958), test takers are asked to produce as many substitute uses for common items, such as a "brick," as they can. Responses can be scored for fluency (number of responses), originality (uniqueness of responses), flexibility (the variety of responses), and elaboration (amount of detail in the responses). In the following section, we describe the major process, product, and personality assessments.

Creativity Assessments

The four specific areas in which psychometric methods are applied to creativity research comprise investigations into creative processes, personality and behavioral correlates of creativity, characteristics of creative products, and attributes of creativity-fostering environments.

Creative Process

Tests of creative process are often found to be the most widely used creativity assessments in educational settings, with a majority of those process assessments focusing on divergent thinking. Divergent thinking (DT) tests require individuals to produce several responses to a specific prompt, in sharp contrast to most standardized tests of achievement or ability that require one correct answer (i.e., convergent thinking tests). This emphasis upon fluency, also referred to as ideational fluency or ideation, is seen as an important yet not sufficient component of creative processes. Among the first tests of divergent thinking were Guilford's (1967) Structure of the Intellect divergent production tests and Torrance's (1974) Tests of Creative Thinking, versions of which both remain in wide use in creativity research and education.

The Structure of the Intellect (SOI) battery (Guilford, 1967) consists of several tests on which subjects are asked to exhibit evidence of divergent production in several areas, including divergent production of semantic units (e.g., listing consequences of people no longer needing to sleep), of figural classes (finding as many classifications of different sets of figures as is possible), and of figural units (taking a simple shape such as a circle and elaborating and adding onto it as often as possible). The entire SOI divergent production battery consists of several dozen such tests, corresponding to the various divergent thinking components of Guilford's Structure of the Intellect model. Factors representing several types of fluency, flexibility, originality, and elaboration of ideas have been established for the SOI tests. Although the SOI tests are no longer widely used in educational settings, Meeker and colleagues (e.g., Meeker & Meeker, 1982) developed a version of the SOI, the Structure of the Intellect–Learning Abilities Test (SOI-LA) to diagnose weaknesses in divergent thinking (among other areas) which can then be addressed by remedial services.

The *Torrance Tests of Creative Thinking* (Torrance, 1974), which are based upon many aspects of the SOI battery, are the most commonly used tests of divergent thinking in schools (Hunsaker & Callahan, 1995). Torrance (1974) refined the administration and scoring of the TTCT over several decades, which may account for its enduring popularity. The Torrance tests are available in two forms: figural and verbal. The Figural TTCT presents the child with an abstract figure (such as three wavy, parallel lines). The child is instructed to "list all the things this figure could be." The student might then respond with "a river, ocean waves, dancing snakes" and so on. Much like Guilford's divergent thinking test described earlier, TTCT scores are calculated for fluency, originality, flexibility, and elaboration, and additional scores can be calculated for other aspects of the test (amount of detail in the response) and the level of abstractness in the title. Children completing the Verbal TTCT are instructed to improve a particular product, such as laundry soap, or to brainstorm possible outcomes to a hypothetical scenario.

A related, nonverbal DT assessment is the *Thinking Creatively with Sounds and Words* (TCSW; Torrance, Khatena, & Cunnington, 1973). Children are presented with abstract sounds and onomatopoeias (e.g., pow, bang, crunch) and are instructed to "list all the things this sound could be." Scores are again reported for fluency, originality, flexibility, and elaboration.

In general, evidence of reliability for DT tests is impressive, but predictive validity evidence is less convincing. Part of the problem may be that DT tests appear susceptible to administration and scoring effects. In other words, how the tests are administered to students and subsequently scored may influence a student's results.

Another measure of creativity that addresses both divergent and convergent thinking (this distinction will be analyzed in more detail later in this chapter) is the Remote Associations Test (RAT; Mednick & Mednick, 1967). Based on the view that creativity consists of forming new associations of preexisting information, Mednick developed the RAT to assess the ability to form ideas into new combinations. The Remote Associations Test presents the child with a triad of three words; the child is instructed to answer with the single, correct word that connects all three of the words together. For example, the child may be presented with RAT: BLUE: COTTAGE and is asked to think of another word that is associated with all three words. In this example the correct answer is "cheese." The RAT is not commonly used in schools, but is still used occasionally because of its unique attributes.

Creative Products

A second category of creative assessments involves evaluation of student work. Students produce a wide range of products while in school, thereby making evaluation of products an important aspect of creativity assessment. Most product assessments provide teachers with scales on which they can rate the creativity of specific student work on various dimensions. For example, the Creative Product Semantic Scale (Besemer & O'Quin, 1993) allows raters to judge the novelty, problem resolution, and elaboration and synthesis attributes of products, and the Student Product Assessment Form (Reis & Renzulli, 1991) provides ratings of nine product traits (e.g., problem focusing, appropriateness of resources, originality, action orientation, audience). Westberg (1996) designed an instrument to evaluate student inventions, with scores provided for product originality, technical goodness, and aesthetic appeal. Each of these instruments is associated with evidence of reliability, although validity issues remain to be addressed. In the one available comparison of teachers' and parents' ability to evaluate children's ideas, the two groups were similarly successful (Runco & Vega, 1990), suggesting that parents may be able to use product evaluation instruments to provide a complementary set of data to teacher ratings.

Creative Personality

The third area of creativity assessment that is common in schools addresses personality issues. This is a rough categorization, in that many of these measures address aspects of creativity that can be interpreted as processes or products (e.g., observations of creativity-related behaviors). But the common characterization of the measures discussed in this personality section is that the instruments all involve self-, teacher-, or parent-reports of creativity-related attitudes, personality characteristics, or behaviors. The *Alpha Biological Inventory* (Taylor & Ellison, 1966) is an example that was constructed to measure an individual's creative capacity based on traits such as "openness to experiences," "adventurous," and "risk taking."

Self-reports are more common in research than in educational applications, but a handful of instruments exist. The self-report tests typically include a checklist of questions completed by the child that address his or her creative activities and creativity behavior. For example, the *Creative Attitude Survey* (Schaeffer, 1971) is designed for children in grades 4 through 6, and assesses imagination, interest in art and writing, desire of novelty, and attraction to the abstract and magical. Children are presented with statements such as "I get bored easily" and are instructed to rate themselves on a 5-point scale that ranges from strongly disagree to strongly agree. Another self-report test is the *Khatena-Torrance Creative Perception Inventory,* in which older children (age 12+) rate themselves on a variety of personality characteristics, such as their level of initiative, intellectuality, individuality, artistry, self-confidence, inquisitiveness, and imagination.

A second category of personality measures requires teachers or parents to rate a child on specific dimensions. For example, the Preschool and Kindergarten Interest Descriptor (Rimm, 1983) is a measure of creativity of 3- to 6-year-olds that is completed by the child's parents or teachers. The adult responds to a list of statements such as "my child asks a lot of questions" and responds to a 5-point scale ranging from "not at all" to "very much." This scale provides scores related to a child's level of playfulness, humor, curiosity, and originality, for placement in a creativity or gifted program.

Teacher rating scales are a component of most gifted education program identification systems. In recent years, a number of high-profile scales have been published or substantially revised, and nearly all of the major scales include at least

> "Imagination is cheap if we don't have to bother with the details."
>
> —Daniel Dennett

one creativity subscale. For example, the Scales for Rating the Behavioral Characteristics of Superior Students (SRBCSS; Renzulli et al., 2002) is widely used in schools, and it includes scales for learning, motivation, creativity, leadership, art, music, dramatics, planning, and communication. Similarly, the Scales for Identifying Gifted Students (SIGS; Ryser & McConnell, 2004) includes scales on general intellectual ability, four specific content areas, creativity, and leadership (both teacher and parent versions are available). The Gifted Rating Scales (GRS; Pfeiffer & Jarosewich, 2003) consist of scales for intellectual ability, academic ability, creativity, artistic talent, and motivation, on the preschool/kindergarten form; these same scales, with the addition of a leadership scale, are on the school form for students in grades 1 to 8. Other, similar scales include the Gifted and Talented Evaluation Scales (Gilliam, Carpenter, & Christensen, 1996), Gifted Evaluation Scale (McCarney & Anderson, 1989), and Purdue Secondary Ratings Scales (Feldhusen, Hoover, & Sayler, 1990). All of these scales are generally easy to complete and score, but technical quality varies. The newest instruments and revisions, the SRBCSS, SIGS, and GRS, are associated with the most impressive evidence of reliability and validity.

OTHER CREATIVITY ASSESSMENTS FOR THE CLASSROOM

Although psychometric tests and published scales or instruments are the most commonly used way of assessing creativity, particularly by creativity researchers, they are not the only way. There are some methods that can be conducted very quickly and easily in the classroom. These methods include self-ratings, peer-ratings, looking at past creative behavior, and assessing actual creative work.

The simplest way to assess someone's creativity is to just ask. This method can be as basic as a question, such as "On a scale from 1 to 10, with 1 being the lowest and 10 being the highest, rate your own creativity." The results are often more valid and reliable than one might think (e.g., Furnham, 1999). But like any type of self-report, this method is very easy to fake (especially if there are any kind of high stakes associated with the result). People, including children, may also have over-inflated views of their own creativity. One solution is to ask students to informally give feedback on which classmates they consider the most creative, or to rate peers on their creativity. A whole new set of problems, of course, can arise with this situation, ranging from personal feelings disrupting the pureness of the ratings to the risk of children's feelings being hurt.

Another possibility is looking at a person's past creativity by asking them to report on accomplishments, creative work, and life events. In studies of eminent creative people, variables such as awards (Kaufman, 2001), career length (Crozier, 1999), age at different accomplishments (Simonton, 1988), influence, international recognition, and productivity (Ludwig, 1995) have all been used as measures of creativity. Obviously, most students won't have any Pulitzer Prizes to report, but you can ask them how many poems or stories they write in an average month, about any awards or honors they have won, or similar questions. One inherent problem in this method, of course, is that you're limited to what the student tells you (for example, what counts as a poem?).

The final common way that creativity is measured is through the Consensual Assessment Technique (CAT), developed by Amabile (1996). With the CAT, raters are solicited for their experience in an area and provide independent judgments about the creativity of a product. The judgments compare products against each other, rather than against an absolute standard or ideal, and the products are judged in a random order (Amabile, 1985; Amabile, Hennessey, & Grossman, 1986; Conti, Coon, & Amabile, 1996). Experts can include teachers (e.g., Besemer & O'Quin, 1986) or peers (e.g., Kaufman, Gentile, & Baer, in press). The products rated can range from inventions or devices (Finke, Ward, & Smith, 1992), collages (Amabile, Hennessey, & Grossman, 1986), haikus (Hennessey, 1994), musical compositions (Hickey, 2001), pictures drawn based on a suggested topic (Sternberg & Lubart, 1995), storytelling (Baer, 1994), to longer poems, stories, and personal narratives (Baer, Kaufman, & Gentile, 2002). Using expert judges is very common in educational settings (e.g., at science fairs, art contests, writing contests), but these judges rarely use formal assessment strategies associated with reliability and validity evidence.

RESEARCH ON CREATIVITY IN SPECIAL EDUCATION POPULATIONS

Several studies have examined creativity as it applies to special education populations. In this section, we review those that illustrate the relationship between creativity and students with special education needs. The disorders presented in this section include learning disabilities, dyslexia, Asperger's syndrome, Down syndrome, and Williams' syndrome.

One study examined how elementary students with learning disabilities (LD) compared on the Torrance Tests of Creative Thinking (TTCT) to students without impairments. The data revealed that children with LD engaged in less task persistence than children without LD and, as a result, scored lower on the elaboration section of the TTCT. What is more significant however, is the fact that on the other three components of the TTCT, the children with LD scored as well as the group of children without LD (Argulewicz, Mealor, & Richmond, 1979). Another study of children with LD used a naming task (in which students are asked to name things to eat). The children with LD were found to produce more original responses than a matched group of children without LD, while the matched group was more flexible on a similar task on naming things to wear (Kaufman & Kaufman, 1980).

In a study of children with mild learning disabilities (MLD), Cox and Cotgreave (1996) studied three groups of children: 10-year-olds with MLD, 10-year-olds without MLD, and 6-year-olds. They measured creativity by examining human figure drawings the children had completed, and then compared the results between the different groups. They found that the drawings by the MLD children were easily distinguished from the other 10-year-olds, but not from the group of 6-year-old children. The implication is that while the children with MLD may develop artistic and creative abilities at a slower rate, their development still approaches a normal pattern. Another study of gifted children with and without LD found that there were no significant differences between the two groups on measures of verbal creativity (Woodrum & Savage, 1994). These findings, taken together, demonstrate that for students with LD or MLD who receive lower scores on ability or achievement tests, creativity tests may demonstrate ways in which these students perform at the same level as their peers.

Considering creativity can also lend insight to individuals with dyslexia. LaFrance (1997), for example, points to creative thinking as being a good way of distinguishing gifted dyslexic students from nongifted dyslexic students. Additionally, Burrows and Wolf (1983) suggest creativity as a way of reducing frustration and improving how dyslexic children view themselves and their abilities. The importance of creativity is consistent with other findings that show dyslexic children frequently excel at divergent thinking (Vail, 1990). It is also interesting to note that case studies have been noted of individuals with dyslexia who were very creative in the literary domain—the very area of their learning disability (Rack, 1981).

Another learning disability with a strong connection to creativity is Attention-Deficit Hyperactivity Disorder (ADHD). Several scholars have proposed that the behaviors and characteristics associated with ADHD are highly similar to creative behaviors (Cramond, 1994; Leroux & Levitt-Perlman, 2000). Traits such as sensation, stimulation seeking, and high usage of imagery, for example, are associated with both children with ADHD and highly creative children (Shaw, 1992). Children with ADHD who have high IQs scored higher on tests of figural creativity than high-IQ children who did not have ADHD (Shaw & Brown, 1990, 1991). Students with ADHD showed specific creativity strengths in fluency, originality, and elaboration on the TTCT (Gollmar, 2001).

Indeed, a study of undergraduates found that having a wider breadth of attention was correlated with writing poems that were judged to be more creative, and distracting noise disrupted creative performance more in those students with a wide breadth of attention (Kasof, 1997). In other words, the same aspects of ADHD that may make students more prone to be creative may also make them more prone to being distracted and, in some situations, produce lower-quality work.

Creativity also can be analyzed with students that have even more severe disabilities. Children with autism and Asperger's syndrome were able to generate changes to an object as part of the TTCT. These children made fewer changes than a sample of children without impairment, and their changes were more reality based than imagination based (Craig & Baron-Cohen, 1999). The very fact that creativity assessment is able to add information about this population's abilities is encouraging. An additional study compared children with autism and children with Asperger's syndrome (Craig & Baron-Cohen, 2000). They found that while both groups showed less imaginative events in a storytelling exercise than children without impairment, children with Asperger's syndrome were better able to demonstrate imagination than children with autism. This finding was also demonstrated by using a drawing task (Craig, Baron-Cohen, & Scott, 2001). Although similar to the earlier findings, Craig et al. (2001) found that children with autism produced fewer changes and less imaginative changes than did a group of age-matched controls. The authors also found, however, that there were no differences between children with autism and children with MLD on a task in which children were asked to draw an "impossible" man.

Other studies have explored the relationship between creativity (particularly imaginative play) and autism. Sherratt (2002) and Stahmer (1995) demonstrated that children with autism could be taught to use symbolic acts and pretend play. Both studies had a small number of children participating (five and seven, respectively), but the results are promising. Stahmer's study found that after training, children with autism were able to engage in creative play at the same level of

> "Imagination is more important than knowledge."
>
> —Albert Einstein

language-matched controls. Lewis and Boucher (1995) asked 15 children with autism to generate actions with a car and with a doll. The children generated fewer changes with the car than both a control group and children with learning disabilities. There was no difference, however, in the ability to generate possible actions with a doll.

In a related fashion, researchers studied human figure drawings in children with Down syndrome (Cox & Maynard, 1998). While Down syndrome children scored lower than both same age and younger children, it is interesting to note that their drawings did not differ when drawn from a model or drawn from imagination, whereas both groups of non-Down syndrome children improved when drawn from a model. This finding indicates that creative processes may be a comparative strength for children with Down syndrome.

One particular learning disability, Williams Syndrome (WS), is caused by a lack of genetic material that produces the protein elastin. Children with WS are developmentally delayed and often have profound disabilities in spatial cognition (Bellugi, Lichtenberger, Jones, Lai, & St. George, 2000). Yet children with WS have exceptional narrative skills for their cognitive ability level. Although their syntax was simpler and they were more likely to make errors in morphology than children without WS, they also used more evaluative devices, and—of most interest for creativity studies—used much more elaboration in their narratives (Losh, Bellugi, Reilly, & Anderson, 2000). This tendency toward elaboration combined with the hypersociability associated with WS results in frequent storytelling (Jones et al., 2000). Although their stories use less complex syntax compared to children without WS, they are much more complex (and more expressive) than children with similar cognitive abilities with Down syndrome (Reilly, Klima, & Bellugi, 1990).

These various research findings demonstrate that there do exist relationships that can be strong and unique between creativity and different learning disabilities. With many newer theories (e.g., Carroll, 1993; Sternberg, 1996) incorporating creativity as an aspect of intelligence, it makes sense to look to creativity as a source of new information. For children who do not perform strongly on traditional IQ tests, creativity measures may represent a way of gaining new insights into thinking and learning styles and of encouraging and evaluating academic success and progress.

APPLYING MAINSTREAM CREATIVITY RESEARCH IN THE SPECIAL EDUCATION CLASSROOM

Divergent Thinking

One common research finding is an association between divergent-thinking skill and creativity (Albert & Runco, 1999; Baer, 1993, 1997a; Nickerson, 1999; Plucker & Renzulli, 1999; Runco, 1991, 1992; Taber, 1983, 1985). Increasing a student's divergent-thinking abilities tends to lead to increased creativity, especially if the activities used for training match the area in which improved creative perfor-

How many uses can you think of for a brick?

To build a house? As a paperweight? As a weapon?

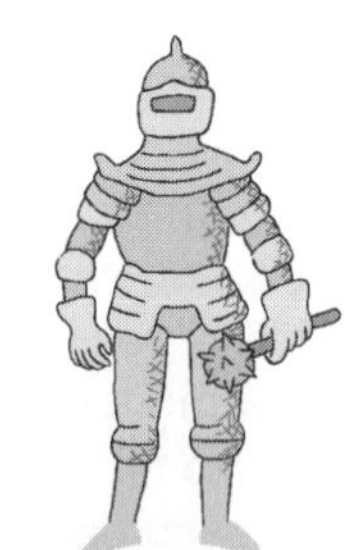

As a parking brake?

As a doorstop?

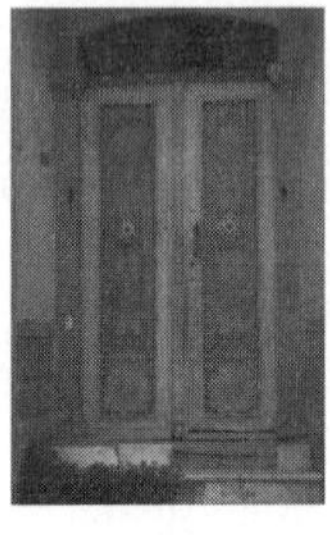

Figure 14.1 How many uses can you think of for a brick?

mance is desired (Baer, 1996). Unfortunately, because divergent-thinking tasks (and tests) are often fun and even silly (e.g., "Think of as many uses as you can for a brick") they are sometimes dismissed as not serious or appropriate educational activities. Such a judgment misses the many ways in which divergent-thinking training can not only enhance creative performance, but also improve academic skills and the acquisition of knowledge.

First, what is divergent thinking? As discussed earlier, divergent thinking was first proposed by Guilford (1956, 1967) in his Structure of the Intellect model. Divergent thinking is a kind of thinking that aims not at producing correct answers, but rather at coming up with a variety of unusual, original, or even off-the-wall ideas; it can be thought of as the ability to produce many (not necessarily correct) ideas, to produce unusual and original (but, again, not necessarily workable) ideas, and to take an idea and spin out elaborate variants of the idea.

Divergent thinking is often contrasted to convergent thinking, which refers to thinking that focuses (or converges) on a single correct answer. Convergent thinking is what is tested on most intelligence and achievement tests. Guilford was the first major theorist to argue that divergent thinking was every bit as important as convergent thinking. Convergent thinking produces correct answers, but divergent thinking produces interesting, imaginative, and potentially creative ideas.

As discussed earlier, divergent thinking has four components:

- *Fluency* refers to the number of different ideas one can produce.
- *Flexibility* refers to the variety among the ideas one produces.
- *Originality* refers to how unusual are the ideas one produces.
- *Elaboration* refers to richness of detail in the ideas one produces.

Teaching divergent thinking begins with fluency—getting students to produce many ideas—and then trying to push them for more varied, unusual, or elaborate responses.

Brainstorming is the most common (and probably most effective) method to promote divergent thinking. Here are the rules for brainstorming:

- Defer judgment.
- Avoid ownership of ideas. When people feel that an idea is theirs, egos sometimes get in the way of creative thinking. They are likely to be more defensive later, when ideas are critiqued, and they are less willing to allow their ideas to be modified.
- Feel free to "hitchhike" on other ideas. This means that it's okay to borrow elements from ideas already on the table, or to make slight modifications of ideas already suggested.
- Wild ideas are encouraged. Impossible, totally unworkable ideas may lead someone to think of other, more possible, more workable ideas. It's easier to take a wildly imaginative bad idea and tone it down to fit the constraints of reality than to take a boring idea and make it interesting enough to be worth thinking about.

It's the first rule—deferring judgment—that is perhaps most important. When we think our ideas will be judged, we are more careful, more cautious, and often less creative. The goal of brainstorming is to produce lots of ideas, both good and bad. If we are brainstorming as part of a problem-solving process, we may later judge the ideas (remember, the rule said "defer judgment," not "never judge"), but to produce many diverse (and potentially creative) ideas, we need to temporarily relax judgment in order to allow intellectual risk taking.

Using brainstorming to encourage and produce divergent thinking can be helpful in many different situations. The big question is how and when to use brainstorming in a special education classroom. Here are some appropriate times:

- *At the beginning of a unit of study, or any time you are introducing a new topic, it can be helpful to brainstorm what students already know about the topic.* For example, if you are about to study the Civil War, ask students to brainstorm anything they know about it. This actually achieves several goals: it activates prior knowledge, it creates interest in the topic, and it alerts you to both what students may already know and what misconceptions they may have. When using brainstorming for this purpose, remember to follow the rules, especially the one about deferring judgment. If a student says that George Washington was president during the Civil War, there will be time later to correct this misconception.

- *To review something you have been studying, ask students to brainstorm interesting facts that they remember about the topic.* For example, if your students have been studying mammals, ask them how many mammals they can name. You might want to have groups brainstorm together to see which group can create the longest list. After they finish brainstorming, *then* ask them to judge their ideas (and remove any that the group thinks might not be mammals).
- *To help students develop a skill, have them brainstorm applications of the skill.* For example, to help develop phonemic awareness, have students brainstorm all the words they can think of that begin with a particular sound (e.g., words that begin with an "f" sound, as in "fire"). Or to help students improve their skills at prediction when reading a story, ask, "What things *might* the author do next at this point in the story?"
- *To liven up the class, have students brainstorm something just for fun.* Here are some sample topics:
  - In what ways might one improve the rules of baseball (or other sport) to make it more exciting (or to make it more challenging, easy, interesting, fair, etc.)?
  - In what ways might one use whole numbers and the processes of addition and subtraction to reach a total of 12?
  - In what ways might one improve the design of automobiles (or houses, classrooms, schools, bookbags, food containers, desks, computer keyboards, etc.) to make them more efficient (or more user-friendly, environment-friendly, attractive, etc.)?
  - In what ways might one use a computer that most people would never think of?
  - In what ways might one convince one's parents to buy an iguana for a household pet?

Special education students enjoy these kinds of activities as much as any of us, and can be quite good at brainstorming, once they get the hang of it. Learning disabilities often don't interfere with divergent thinking, so this is a kind of activity—and an important component of creativity—at which they may show real talent.

Intrinsic Motivation

One cartoon shows how *not* to teach for creativity. A student is daydreaming some delightful and very creative things in the middle of a lesson. The student's thinking is related to the topic of the lesson, but it is clearly not the kind of thinking that is likely to produce a correct answer to the teacher's question. The teacher interrupts to remind the student that "Creativity Time" is not for another hour.

It was clear that this teacher didn't know much about creativity. And yet, she was doing *something* right. It's very important to know what your goals are for a

> "An essential aspect of creativity is not being afraid to fail."
>
> —Isaac Newton

Brainstorming

Brainstorming is a useful tool in generating creative ideas. In your classroom have students generate a list of items for things such as the following.

1. A new snack food.
2. A new kind of toy.
3. Names for a class pet.
4. New types of games to play at PE.
5. A new dinner dish, including ingredients.

given lesson regarding creativity. Sometimes the goal is to encourage creativity in the work students are doing right now. Other times, that's not what's wanted at all. Instead, what we want is for students to learn the right answer (for example, we don't generally want students to produce "creative" math facts). Or we want them to learn some skill, even at the expense of limiting their creative options to the activity at hand. The key is to be clear about our goals, so we can set up the most appropriate motivational constraints for the current goal.

We all know that people will do things for rewards. Rewards motivate people to do things they wouldn't otherwise do. The giving and receiving of rewards is a regular part of human interaction, both in and out of the classroom.

What many people don't know is that rewards can also make behaviors *less* likely to occur—they can actually *decrease* the frequency of the desired and rewarded behavior—under certain conditions. This is called the hidden cost of reward. For example, most preschool children enjoy drawing. Given the opportunity, drawing is one of many activities preschool children will spontaneously choose to do. In one preschool, it was observed that during time when children could choose their own activities, they spent, on average, about 16% of their time drawing. Rewards were then offered for drawing during this free-choice period. Children were still free to choose whatever activity they wanted to do, but if they chose drawing, they would earn a reward (a certificate with a gold seal and ribbon).

Did the amount of time spent drawing increase? It certainly did—preschool children love rewards, just like the rest of us, and they were happy to spend more time drawing in order to receive them.

So where's the problem? It came later, after the reward for drawing was taken away. Now conditions were just like before the reward was introduced: Drawing was one of several activities children could choose, with no inducement offered for picking any particular activity.

When researchers observed the children in the preschool a week or two later, they found the students now chose drawing only about 8% of the time—far less than the 16% rate before rewards had been briefly introduced (and subsequently discontinued). In a matched control group observed during the same period of time, the average amount of time spent drawing did not change throughout the entire time the study was being conducted.

How does this relate to creativity? Researchers have also found that people are more creative when they are intrinsically motivated (i.e., performing a task for enjoyment), and less creative when they are extrinsically motivated (i.e., performing a task for a reward; Amabile, 1983, 1996; Baer, 1997a, 1997b, 1997c, 1998; Hennessey & Amabile, 1988). Doing things to earn rewards, or doing things that we believe will be evaluated, leads to lower creativity. And, as the hidden cost of reward

> "Creativity is a type of learning process where the teacher and pupil are located in the same individual."
>
> —Arthur Koestler

research shows us, rewards tend to undermine our interest in activities. For teachers who want to encourage their students' interest in schoolwork and their students' creativity, these findings are quite frightening. They suggest that one of our most useful and widely used tools—rewards—is harmful to students, and that evaluation of students' work also has negative effects.

Many readers may now be hoping we have something like a magic wand that we will wave to show that we really don't need to be so worried about rewards and evaluations. How bad could such common practices really be? But there is no such wand, no way to make these negative consequences disappear. We do have some advice on how to use this information effectively to promote student learning, intrinsic motivation, and creativity, however, and also ways that minimize the possible damage rewards and evaluation can cause.

We can't simply decide to stop evaluating students' work or to cease offering rewards of any kind. It would make it difficult—probably impossible—to do much of what we know we must do as teachers, including teaching our students the skills and content that we know they need to learn. Students need feedback on their performance to improve their skills, and they often need some kind of extrinsic motivation, like rewards, to keep working when they otherwise would simply stop. So they very often *need* extrinsic motivation to learn. But at other times extrinsic motivation may be unnecessary, and these are times we should avoid using it.

There is an important distinction between short-term and long-term impact on creative performance. Doing something for a reward, or doing something in the anticipation of receiving an evaluation of some sort, is likely to diminish students' creativity at whatever it is they're working on. Skills and knowledge can be acquired by continuing to practice or study, even when one's level of intrinsic motivation is low. However, extrinsically motivated study may provide the very knowledge and skills one will need in the future to do something in a more creative way than would be possible at present. Similarly, the skills acquired by receiving feedback on (or evaluation of) one's performance on a task like writing an essay or designing an experiment may help one do a more competent revision.

There are some things one can do to avoid this problem, but in many cases they aren't easy. The first thing we need to keep in mind is our goal or objective for a given lesson. We can't have it both ways, at least not at the same time. If our goal in a particular lesson is skill development or knowledge acquisition, then we need to give ourselves permission to do some things that we know make extrinsic motivation salient and therefore depress creativity. And if our goal is to encourage creativity, then we need to avoid doing things that will increase extrinsic motivation and try to do whatever we can to increase intrinsic motivation.

As much as we value creativity, we recognize that skill development and acquisition of knowledge are our primary goals as teachers, and so, much of the time, we should use rewards to motivate our students and evaluate their work to help them learn. But for all students, and especially special education students, lack of intrinsic motivation is a real problem. We can't act as if trying to interest our students in their work (however difficult that may be some days) and encouraging their creativity are luxuries we can simply do without. We need to do both things—teach for skill and knowledge acquisition, and teach for intrinsic motivation and creativity. But we will be wise if we keep those goals, and those lesson plans, separate.

Here's an example. When teaching writing, we want students to learn a number of skills, and we (sometimes) want them to write imaginatively and find writing interesting. These goals are at odds, because one requires an emphasis on extrinsic motivation—evaluation, in this case, and possibly rewards also, in order to get them to participate in something they may find uninteresting—and the other requires an emphasis on intrinsic motivation, which would require us to avoid evaluation. If we try to do a little of each, it won't work, because extrinsic motivation will tend to drive out intrinsic motivation. But we *can* do both if we do them at different times. When working on skill development in writing, we can let students know that their work will be evaluated, let them know the criteria that will be applied, and then evaluate using those criteria. Other times we can tell them that although they must do the writing assignment, they'll get credit simply for doing it—there will be no further evaluation.

When you do this, you can let your students know you're looking forward to reading their stories, or whatever it is they're writing, but at the same time promise them you won't evaluate. And then keep your promise. Don't praise or criticize; don't correct or point out any errors; and don't suggest any changes, or things they might try next time. What you need to do is simply not comment at all, beyond showing that you enjoyed reading what they wrote. After a while, students will come to believe you. This will allow them, when you tell them you will be evaluating their work, to concentrate on skills and focus on doing things right; and it will free them up to write more imaginatively, if with less technical correctness, when you tell them that their work won't be evaluated. And this way their interest in writing won't get buried beneath a constant expectation of evaluation.

Will some kids abuse the license that a no-evaluation promise confers? Of course they will. Sometimes we need to allow the students who want to do as little as possible to get away with it, in order not to punish those students who have the kind of intrinsic motivation that we wish all our students had.

Here's another guideline, one that is fairly easy to state but will require much creativity on your part to apply. Use rewards *only when necessary* to get students to do things they wouldn't otherwise do, and avoid rewarding students for doing things they would do anyway. There are two reasons for this rule. First, using rewards (bribing students) to do things that they already find interesting is likely to diminish their interest in the activity. And second, finding rewards that will actually entice students to do things they don't like is hard enough, so why waste them?

Many special education students have experienced a great deal of failure at school and may exhibit little intrinsic motivation to engage in many of the learning activities we need them to do. In these cases, by all means use rewards. There is little to lose—that is, they have very little intrinsic motivation—and the practice provided by the activities will help them learn important skills and content.

> "Creativity requires the courage to let go of certainties."
>
> —Erich Fromm

And as they acquire skills and content knowledge in some area, they may actually find it less onerous—and even somewhat interesting—to do those activities and thereby become more intrinsically motivated.

But special education students also have diverse interests, some of which relate to school activities. In those cases, we are far wiser to avoid rewards and simply show interest in the students' activities. One way that teachers often misuse rewards has to do with extra credit projects. A student shows interest in learning about the solar system, so we tell him or her we'll give extra credit for a project on the solar system. Far better to use the extra credit reward for something the student doesn't like doing, and provide simple encouragement and support (but no unnecessary bribes) as he or she explores his or her own interest in space.

One way this becomes complicated is in providing different reward structures for different students. If a class knows that we will offer rewards for reading books to the students in the class who hate reading, but not to students who like reading, it is likely that students who used to claim they liked reading will suddenly develop a real antipathy to books, unless they are rewarded for reading them. We all like rewards, and it may seem unfair that some students are rewarded for an activity for which other students earn no reward.

The answer is to make sure that rewards are available to *all* students. In special education it is in many ways easier to individualize reward structures, and this can even be part of an IEP.

Will doing these things—using brainstorming activities to introduce, practice, and review skills and content knowledge, and providing ungraded activities to promote intrinsic motivation and creativity—take time away from learning content? Perhaps. But probably not as much as one might fear. Spending a few hours each week doing content-related activities that will not be evaluated but which will be likely to increase students' intrinsic motivation (or at least help counterbalance

More Brainstorming!

Another idea for brainstorming is to take a simple tool or an everyday item and think of different uses for it.

Examples of items:

A cardboard box
Pencils
A hammer
Old newspapers
A candle
A plastic bag
A piece of paper

Another possibility would be to come up, as a class, with ways to make an item better.

For example:

1. Having a house telephone that is voice activated, so that no one needs to dial the number.
2. Having bicycles and cars in which you can program the directions and they take you there.
3. Having tires on a car or bike that, when pricked with a nail, push the nail out, plug the hole, and release more air into the tire.

> "All children are artists. The problem is how to remain an artist once he [or she] grows up."
>
> —Pablo Picasso

the diminishment of such motivation that tends to occur in schools) won't take a large amount of time away from other kinds of class activities, and brainstorming activities can easily be part of teaching important skills and content knowledge. These kinds of activities can help students acquire content knowledge and skills, even without evaluations or rewards, simply because these activities allow and encourage students to think about that content knowledge and apply those skills in different, and sometimes even original, ways.

LOOKING FORWARD

This section on creativity and special education began with the question, "What is creativity?" and ends with a discussion of ways one might apply what we know about creativity from mainstream creativity research to teaching in special education classrooms. The goal has been to introduce readers with an interest in special education to the field of creativity research in ways that will make that new knowledge both accessible and useful.

Creativity is an undeniably complex phenomenon. As suggested earlier, even defining it is more easily said than done. However, creativity theorists, researchers, and trainers have made great progress in coming to consensus on what is a useful definition; "creativity refers to anything someone does in a way that is original to the creator and that is appropriate to the purpose or goal of the creator" (Baer, 1997a, p. 4) will work in most situations. This definition is similar to the way creativity is understood in a wide variety of contexts, ranging from creativity research and theory to child development to educational psychology (see, e.g., Berk, 2003; Sternberg, Kaufman, & Pretz, 2002; Woolfolk, 2004). In the area of the measurement of creativity there is also an emerging consensus focusing on two very different kinds of assessment; psychometric assessment (and especially divergent thinking tests; e.g., Torrance, 1990; Plucker, 1999) and the consensual assessment of creative products (e.g., Amabile, 1996; Baer, Kaufman, & Gentile, 2004).

A great deal has been learned about creativity since J. P. Guilford's 1950 presidential address to the American Psychological Association, when he first challenged psychologists to take creativity seriously as a field of study. As a direct result of that speech, creativity research, which had received almost no attention in mainstream psychology, finally took off, and much has been learned in the more than 5 decades since Guilford's challenge (Barron, 1988; Kaufman & Baer, in press). There is a great deal more still to be discovered, of course, but there is much that we can do today with all that we already know about creativity. Knowledge gained from creativity research can be put to excellent use in more fully assessing the abilities of special education students, and in designing more effective learning environments for those students. We hope that readers will try out some of the ideas presented earlier in this section, adapt them to their individual situations, and refine and improve those techniques.

Some things that promote creativity:

- Choice
- Interest
- Open-ended tasks
- Freedom from judgment

Some things that hinder creativity:

- Evaluation
- Rewards
- Criticism
- Right-answer fixation

A few words of explanation—or perhaps one should say words of encouragement—are appropriate about efforts to adapt, refine, and improve the ideas and techniques discussed in this section. Nothing in education is "One size fits all," and nowhere is that more true than in the field of special education. Every child is different, and every special need is part of a unique constellation of abilities and interests, and therefore no single technique, applied uniformly, will work uniformly well with all children. For some children, a greater focus on the development of their creativity, perhaps through an exploration of ideas and possibilities by means of divergent-thinking activities, or by an emphasis on intrinsic motivation and a de-emphasis on rewards and evaluation, will be appropriate. For other children, some or all of these ideas may be less productive (and less in line with the individual child's needs). And even for children who will profit from the approaches aforementioned, there will be times to emphasize creativity-relevant techniques and times to emphasize other techniques. It is therefore to be expected that some IEPs will stress creativity more than others, and that even among IEPs in which creativity is a principal element, different students' IEPs will focus on different creativity-enhancing strategies. It is also certain that developing a student's creativity will not be the *only* element one will find in any student's IEP. But it may be one part, and in many cases it may be a very important part, of helping a given special needs child reach his or her fullest potential.

As special educators use more of the ideas from creativity theory, assessment, and research that have been discussed in this section, we anticipate that they will reflect on how these ideas work (and work best) in different situations and with different kinds of students, and that they may also design research of their own to help answer questions that will be important both to special educators and to creativity researchers. Both special education journals and creativity research journals are excellent venues for research about innovative ways one might adapt ideas to help students with special needs reach their learning and other goals more effectively. We would like to encourage teachers to actively follow and participate in this learning community. There is a great deal of research waiting to be conducted that can demonstrate ways in which the education of students with specific learning disabilities can be helped by such techniques as divergent thinking training, or by better understanding of the effects of intrinsic versus extrinsic motivation on performance. This is research that will both help special educators in their work, and creativity researchers and theorists in theirs.

REFERENCES

Albert, R. S., & Runco, M. A. (1999). A history of research on creativity. In R. J. Sternberg (Ed.), *Handbook of creativity* (pp. 16–31). New York: Cambridge University Press.

Amabile, T. M. (1983). *The social psychology of creativity.* New York: Springer-Verlag.

Amabile, T. M. (1985). Motivation and creativity: Effects of motivational orientation in creative writers. *Journal of Personality and Social Psychology, 48,* 393–397.

Amabile, T. M. (1996). *Creativity in context: Update to the social psychology of creativity.* Boulder, CO: Westview.

Amabile, T. M., Hennessey, B. A., & Grossman, B. S. (1986). Social influences on creativity: The effects of contracted-for reward. *Journal of Personality and Social Psychology, 50,* 14–23.

Argulewicz, E. N., Mealor, D. J., & Richmond, B. O. (1979). Creative abilities of learning disabled children. *Journal of Learning Disabilities, 12,* 21–24.

Baer, J. (1993). *Creativity and divergent thinking: A task-specific approach.* Hillsdale, NJ: Erlbaum.

Baer, J. (1994). Divergent thinking is not a general trait: A multi-domain training experiment. *Creativity Research Journal, 7,* 35–46.

Baer, J. (1996). The effects of task-specific divergent-thinking training. *Journal of Creative Behavior, 30,* 183–187.

Baer, J. (1997a). *Creative teachers, creative students.* Boston: Allyn and Bacon.

Baer, J. (1997b). Gender differences in the effects of anticipated evaluation on creativity. *Creativity Research Journal, 10,* 25–31.

Baer, J. (1997c). The hidden costs of rewards and evaluation: Who gets hurt, and what teachers can do. *Focus on Education, 41,* 24–27.

Baer, J. (1998). Gender differences in the effects of extrinsic motivation on creativity. *Journal of Creative Behavior, 32,* 18–37.

Baer, J., Kaufman, J. C., & Gentile, C. A. (2004). Extension of the consensual assessment technique to nonparallel creative products. *Creativity Research Journal, 16,* 113–117.

Barron, F. (1988). Putting creativity to work. In R. J. Sternberg (Ed.), *The nature of creativity* (pp. 76–98). New York: Cambridge University Press.

Bekhtereva, N. P., Starchenko, M. G., Klyucharev, V. A., Vorob'ev, V. A., Pakhomov, S. V., & Medvedev, S. V. (2000). Study of the brain organization of creativity: II. Positron-emission tomography data. *Human Physiology, 26,* 516–522.

Bellugi, U., Lichtenberger, E. O., Jones, W., Lai, Z., & St. George, M. (2000). The neurocognitive profile of Williams syndrome: A complex pattern of strengths and weaknesses. *Journal of Cognitive Neuroscience, 12,* 7–29.

Berk, L. E. (2000). *Infants, children, and adolescents* (4th ed.), Boston: Allyn & Bacon.

Besemer, S. P., & O'Quin, K. (1986). Analyzing creative products: Refinement and test of a judging instrument. *Journal of Creative Behavior, 20,* 115–126.

Besemer, S. P., & O'Quin, K. (1993). Assessing creative products: Progress and potentials. In S. G. Isaksen, M. C. Murdock, R. L. Firestien, & D. J. Treffinger (Eds.), *Nurturing and developing creativity: The emergence of a discipline* (pp. 331–349). Norwood, NJ: Ablex.

Burrows, D., & Wolf, B. (1983). Creativity and the dyslexic child: A classroom view. *Annals of Dyslexia, 33,* 269–274.

Carroll, J. B. (1993). *Human cognitive abilities.* New York: Cambridge University Press.

Conti, R., Coon, H., & Amabile, T. M. (1996). Evidence to support the componential model of creativity: Secondary analyses of three studies. *Creativity Research Journal, 9,* 385–389.

Cox, M. V., & Cotgreave, S. (1996). The human figure drawings of normal children and those with mild learning difficulties. *Educational Psychology, 16,* 433–438.

Cox, M. V., & Maynard, S. (1998). The human figure drawings of children with Down syndrome. *British Journal of Developmental Psychology, 16,* 133–137.

Craig, J., & Baron-Cohen, S. (1999). Creativity and imagination in autism and Asperger syndrome. *Journal of Autism & Developmental Disorders, 29,* 319–326.

Craig, J., & Baron-Cohen, S. (2000). Story-telling ability in children with autism or Asperger syndrome: A window into the imagination. *Israel Journal of Psychiatry, 37,* 64–70.

Craig, J., Baron-Cohen, S., & Scott, F. (2001). Drawing ability in autism: A window into the imagination. *Israel Journal of Psychiatry, 38,* 242–253.

Cramond, B. (1994). Attention-Deficit Hyperactivity Disorder and creativity: What is the connection? *Journal of Creative Behavior, 28,* 193–210.

Crozier, W. R. (1999). Age and individual differences in artistic productivity: Trends within a sample of British novelists. *Creativity Research Journal, 12,* 197–204.

Feldhusen, J. F., Hoover, S. M., & Sayler, M. F. (1990). *Identifying and educating gifted students at the secondary level.* Monroe, NY: Trillium Press.

Finke, R. A., Ward, T. B., & Smith, S. M. (1992). *Creative cognition.* Cambridge: MIT Press.

Furnham, A. (1999). Personality and creativity. *Perceptual and Motor Skills, 88,* 407–408.

Gilliam, J. E., Carpenter, B. O., & Christensen, J. R. (1996). *Gifted and talented evaluation scales.* Waco, TX: Prufrock Press.

Gollmar, S. M. (2001). An investigation of Attention Deficit/Hyperactivity Disorder, creativity, and cognitive style: Interaction and impact on school success. *Dissertation Abstracts International Section A: Humanities and Social Sciences, 61,* 34–64.

Guilford, J. P. (1956). The structure of intellect. *Psychological Bulletin, 53,* 267–293.

Guilford, J. P. (1967). *The nature of human intelligence.* New York: McGraw-Hill.

Guilford, J. P. (1988). Some changes in the structure-of-intellect model. *Educational and Psychological Measurement, 48,* 1–4.

Guilford, J. P., Merrifield, P. R., & Wilson, R. C. (1958). *Unusual Uses Test.* Orange, CA: Sheridan Psychological Services.

Hennessey, B. A. (1994). The consensual assessment technique: An examination of the relationship between ratings of product and process creativity. *Creativity Research Journal, 7,* 193–208.

Hennessey, B. A., & Amabile, T. M. (1988). Conditions of creativity. In R. J. Sternberg (Ed.), *The nature of creativity* (pp. 11–38). New York: Cambridge University Press.

Hickey, M. (2001). An application of Amabile's consensual assessment technique for rating the creativity of children's musical compositions. *Journal of Research in Music Education, 49,* 234–244.

Hunsaker, S. L., & Callahan, C. M. (1995). Creativity and giftedness: Published instrument uses and abuses. *Gifted Child Quarterly, 39,* 110–114.

Jones, W., Bellugi, U., Lai, Z., Chiles, M., Reilly, J., Lincoln, A., & Adolphs, R. (2000). Hypersociability in Williams syndrome. *Journal of Cognitive Neuroscience, 12,* 30–46.

Kasof, J. (1997). Creativity and breadth of attention. *Creativity Research Journal, 10,* 303–315.

Kaufman, J. C. (2001). Genius, lunatics, and poets: Mental illness in prize-winning authors. *Imagination, Cognition, and Personality, 20,* 305–314.

Kaufman, J. C., & Baer, J. (in press). Creativity research in English-speaking countries. In J. C. Kaufman & R. J. Sternberg (Eds.), *International Handbook of Creativity.* New York: Cambridge University Press.

Kaufman, J. C., Gentile, C. A., & Baer, J. (in press). Do gifted student writers and creative writing experts rate creativity the same way? *Gifted Child Quarterly.*

Kaufman, N. L., & Kaufman, A. S. (1980). Creativity in children with minimal brain dysfunction. *Journal of Creative Behavior, 14,* 73.

LaFrance, E. B. (1997). The gifted/dyslexic child: Characterizing and addressing strengths and weaknesses. *Annals of Dyslexia, 47,* 163–182.

Leroux, J. A., & Levitt-Perlman, M. (2000). The gifted child with attention deficit disorder: An identification and intervention challenge. *Roeper Review, 22,* 171–176.

Lewis, V., & Boucher, J. (1995). Generativity in the play of young people with Autism. *Journal of Autism and Developmental Disorders, 25,* 105–121.

Losh, M., Bellugi, U., Reilly, J., & Anderson, D. (2000). Narrative as a social engagement tool: The excessive use of evaluation in narratives from children with Williams syndrome. *Narrative Inquiry, 10,* 265–290.

Ludwig, A. M. (1995). *The price of greatness.* New York: Guilford.

McCarney, S. B., & Anderson, P. D. (1989). *Gifted evaluation scale* (2nd ed.). Columbia, MO: Hawthorne Educational Services.

Mednick, S. A., & Mednick, M. T. (1967). *Remote Associations Test examiner's manual.* Boston: Houghton Mifflin.

Meeker, M., & Meeker, R. (1982). *Structure-of-Intellect Learning Abilities Test: Evaluation, leadership, and creative thinking.* El Segundo, CA: SOI Institute.

Nickerson, R. S. (1999). Enhancing creativity. In R. J. Sternberg (Ed.), *Handbook of Creativity* (pp. 392–430). New York: Cambridge University Press.

Pfeiffer, S. I., & Jarosewich, T. (2003). *Gifted rating scales.* San Antonio, TX: The Psychological Corporation.

Plucker, J. A. (1999). Is the proof in the pudding? Reanalysis of Torrance's (1958 to present) longitudinal data. *Creativity Research Journal, 12,* 103–114.

Plucker, J. A., & Renzulli, J. S. (1999). Psychometric approaches to the study of human creativity. In R. J. Sternberg (Ed.), *Handbook of Creativity* (pp. 35–61). New York: Cambridge University Press.

Rack, L. (1981). Developmental dyslexia and literary creativity: Creativity in the area of deficit. *Journal of Learning Disabilities, 14,* 262–263.

Reilly, J., Klima, E. S., & Bellugi, U. (1990). Once more with feeling: Affect and language in atypical populations. *Development and Psychopathology, 2,* 367–391.

Reis, S. M., & Renzulli, J. S. (1991). The assessment of creative products in programs for gifted and talented students. *Gifted Child Quarterly, 35,* 128–134.

Renzulli, J. S., Smith, L. H., White, A. J., Callahan, C. M., Hartman, R. K., & Westberg, K. L. (2002). *Scales for rating the behavioral characteristics of superior students. Technical and administration manual* (rev. ed.). Mansfield, CT: Creative Learning Press.

Rimm, S. B. (1983). *Preschool and Kindergarten Interest Descriptor.* Watertown, WI: Educational Assessment Service.

Runco, M. A. (1991). *Divergent thinking.* Norwood, NJ: Ablex.

Runco, M. A. (1992). *Creativity as an educational objective for disadvantaged students.* Stoors, CT: National Research Center on the Gifted and Talented.

Runco, M. A., & Vega, L. (1990). Evaluating the creativity of children's ideas. *Journal of Social Behavior and Personality, 5,* 439–452.

Ryser, G. R., & McConnell, K. (2004). *Scales for identifying gifted students: Ages 5 through 18.* Waco, TX: Prufrock Press.

Schaefer, C. E. (1971). *Creative Attitude Survey.* Yonkers, NY: Author.

Shaw, G. A. (1992). Hyperactivity and creativity: The tacit dimension. *Bulletin of the Psychonomic Society, 30,* 157–160.

Shaw, G. A., & Brown, G. (1990). Laterality and creativity concomitants of attention problems. *Developmental Neuropsychology, 6,* 39–56.

Shaw, G. A., & Brown, G. (1991). Laterality, implicit memory and attention disorder. *Educational Studies, 17,* 15–23.

Sherratt, D. (2002). Developing pretend play in children with Autism: A case study. *Autism: The International Journal of Research and Practice, 6,* 169–79.

Simonton, D. K. (1988). Age and outstanding achievement: What do we know after a century of research? *Psychological Bulletin, 104,* 251–267.

Simonton, D. K. (1989). Age and creative productivity: Nonlinear estimation of an information-processing model. *International Journal of Aging and Human Development, 29,* 23–37.

Stahmer, A. C. (1995). Teaching symbolic play skills to children with Autism using Pivotal Response Training. *Journal of Autism and Developmental Disorders, 25,* 123–141.

Sternberg, R. J. (1996). *Successful intelligence.* New York: Simon and Schuster.

Sternberg, R. J. (1999). A propulsion model of creative contributions. *Review of General Psychology, 3,* 83–100.

Sternberg, R. J., Kaufman, J. C., & Pretz, J. E. (2002). *The creativity conundrum.* New York: Psychology Press.

Sternberg, R. J., & Lubart, T. I. (1995). *Defying the crowd.* New York: Free Press.

Taber, T. H. (1983). The effects of creativity training on learning disabled students' creative expression. *Journal of Learning Disabilities, 16,* 264–265.

Taber, T. H. (1985). Effect of instruction for creativity on learning disabled students' creative expression. *Perceptual and Motor Skills, 61,* 895–898.

Taylor, C. W., & Ellison, R. L. (1966). *Alpha Biological Inventory.* Salt Lake City, UT: Institute for Behavioral Research.

Torrance, E. P. (1974). *Torrance Tests of Creative Thinking.* Bensenville, IL: Scholastic Testing Service.

Torrance, E. P. (1990). *The Torrance Tests of Creative Thinking: Norms-technical manual.* Bensenville, IL: Scholastic Testing Service.

Torrance, E. P., Khatena, J., & Cunnington, B. F. (1973). *Thinking creatively with sounds and words.* Bensenville, IL: Scholastic Testing Service.

Torrance, E. P., & Khatena, J. (1998). *Khatena-Torrance Creative Perception Inventory.* Bensenville, IL: Scholastic Testing Service.

Vail, P. L. (1990). Gifts, talents, and the dyslexias: Wellsprings, springboards, and finding Foley's rocks. *Annals of Dyslexia, 40,* 3–17.

Westberg, K. L. (1996). The effects of teaching students how to invent. *Journal of Creative Behavior, 30,* 249–267.

Woodrum, D. T., & Savage, L. B. (1994). Children who are learning disabled/gifted: Where do they belong? *Educational Research, 36,* 83–89.

Woolfolk, A. (2004). *Educational psychology* (9th ed.). Boston: Pearson.

15

Special Education–Related Journals

RACHEL TOPLIS

AMERICAN PSYCHOLOGIST

The American Psychologist is the official journal of the American Psychological Association. It is published monthly and is the most widely circulated psychological journal in the world. It is a valuable source of information on cutting-edge issues in psychology. It publishes empirical, theoretical and practical articles on a wide range of topics relevant to psychology.

Contact: 750 First St. NE, Washington, DC 20002-4242

APPLIED PSYCHOLINGUISTICS

Applied Psycholinguistics publishes articles on the psychological processes involved in language. Topics covered in the journal include the development, use, and impairment of language in all its modalities—spoken, signed, and written.

Contact: Harvard Graduate School of Education, Larsen Hall, 3rd Floor, Cambridge, MA 02138

ARCHIVES OF CLINICAL NEUROPSYCHOLOGY

Archives of Clinical Neuropsychology (ACN) is the official journal of the National Academy of Neuropsychology. The journal was founded in 1985 and was originally a quarterly journal, but now it publishes eight times a year. ACN publishes research addressing the etiology, diagnosis, and treatment of disorders arising out of dysfunctions of the nervous system. ACN also reviews books and texts and includes a section that provides in-depth information about individuals or small groups of patients with unique, unusual, or low-incidence disorders.

Contact (editor): Wm. Drew Gouvier, PhD, Director, Psychological Services Center, Louisiana State University, Department of Psychology, 236 Audubon Hall, Baton Rouge, LA 70803 or http://authors.elsevier.com/JournalDetail.html

BEHAVIOR THERAPY

Behavior Therapy is the journal of the Association for Advancement of Behavior Therapy. It is published in four issues (winter, spring, summer, and fall). The journal deals with theories, practices, and evaluation of cognitive behavioral therapy, behavioral therapy, or behavior modification.

Contact (editor): David A. F. Haaga, PhD, Department of Psychology, Asbury Building, American University, Washington, DC 20016-8062

BUROS MENTAL MEASUREMENT YEARBOOKS

The Buros *Mental Measurement Yearbooks* (MMYs) are published by the Buros Institute of Mental Measurements at the University of Nebraska, Lincoln. The purpose of the MMYs is to provide a forum in which tests can be reviewed to facilitate consumer choice. The yearbooks contain diverse information such as factual information on all known tests or revised tests, test reviews, extensive listings of test references and reviewer references, and more.

Contact: Buros Institute of Mental Measurements, Department of Educational Psychology, University of Nebraska, Lincoln, NE

DEVELOPMENTAL PSYCHOLOGY

Developmental Psychology is a publication of the American Psychological Association. It was founded in 1968 and publishes articles pertaining to developmental psychology. It addresses growth and development from various perspectives such as chronological age, physical growth, sex, and socioeconomic status.

Contact: American Psychological Association, 1200 Seventeenth St. NW, Washington, DC 20036

EDUCATIONAL AND PSYCHOLOGICAL MEASUREMENT

Educational and Psychological Measurement is a bimonthly journal. Articles published in the journal are divided into sections. The first section addresses articles reporting the results of research investigations into problems in the measurement of individual differences in education and psychology. The second section reports on validity studies on new or existing tests for measuring individual differences. The third section reports on computer studies—for example, programs used for carrying out statistical analyses when assessing the measurement of individual differences.

Contact (editor): Xitao Fan, University of Virginia, Charlottesville, VA

EDUCATION WEEK

Education Week is a weekly newspaper published 42 times during the academic year. It is published by Editorial Projects in Education. This paper carries news commentaries and editorials of interest to professional educators and researchers in the field. Classified ads and listings of job openings are also included.

Contact: http://www.edweek.org/

EXCEPTIONAL CHILDREN

Exceptional Children (EC) is the official journal of the Council for Exceptional Children (CEC). It was first published in 1934 and is published quarterly. Articles include data-based research, major research projects, and research that illustrates practical applications within the educational setting.

Contact (editor): Steve Graham, University of Maryland, Department of Special Education, 1308 Benjamin Building, College Park, MD 20742

GIFTED CHILD QUARTERLY

Gifted Child Quarterly is published by the National Association of Gifted Children and was first published in 1958. Articles are of interest to educational researchers, administrators, teachers, and parents of gifted children. The *Gifted Child Quarterly* publishes articles that offer new and creative insights into giftedness and talent development in school, at home, and in the wider society; it also offers information pertaining to policy and policy implications.

Contact: Center for Gifted Education Policy, American Psychological Foundation, 750 First St. NE, Washington, DC 20002 (phone: 202-336-5923)

GIFTED AND TALENTED INTERNATIONAL

Gifted and Talented International is a journal published by the World Council for Gifted and Talented Children. This journal publishes theory and research and promotes discussions concerning the problems and practices of gifted education from around the world.

Contact: World Council for Gifted and Talented Children, 18401 Hiawatha St., Northridge, CA 91325 (phone: 818-368-7501), worldgt@earthlink.net

HARVARD EDUCATIONAL REVIEW

Harvard Educational Review was first published in 1931 as the *Harvard Teachers Record*. This journal consists of opinions and research related to the field of education. Each journal, which is published quarterly, contains on average three manuscripts.

Contact: Harvard Graduate School of Education, Harvard University, 8 Story St., 5th Floor, Cambridge, MA 02138

INTELLIGENCE: A MULTIDISCIPLINARY JOURNAL

Intelligence is published quarterly. This journal is designed to address exclusively research into human intelligence. Papers published attempt to further our understanding of the nature and function of intelligence and include studies on Mental Retardation, early childhood development, measurement of individual differences, and issues of cultural bias.

Contact: Douglas K. Detterman, Case Western Reserve University, Department of Psychology, 10900 Euclid Avenue, Cleveland, OH 44106-7123 (phone 216-368-2680)

JOURNAL FOR EDUCATION OF THE GIFTED

Journal for Education of the Gifted (JEG) is the official journal of the Association for the Gifted (TAG), a division of the Council for Exceptional Children. JEG provides a forum for the analysis and communication of knowledge about the gifted and talented, as well as the exchange of ideas and diverse points of view regarding this special population. JEG is published by Prufrock Press, PO Box 8813, Waco, TX 76714-8813.

JOURNAL OF ABNORMAL CHILD PSYCHOLOGY

This is the official publication of the international society for research in child and adolescent psychopathology. The journal focuses on child and adolescent psychopathology with an emphasis on empirical studies of the major childhood disorders. Its articles cover a variety of topics including epidemiology, assessment, diagnosis, outcome, and treatment of childhood disorders. For more information, see http://journals.kluweronline.com/

JOURNAL OF APPLIED BEHAVIOR ANALYSIS

This journal is published quarterly by the Society for the Experimental Analysis of Behavior (SEAB). *The Journal of Applied Behavior Analysis* (JABA) publishes research relevant to applied behavior analysis, including research on behavior therapy and behavior control. Its articles include pilot research, case studies, and analogue studies, as well as technical articles addressing research methodology, data analysis, and instrumentation, plus article and book reviews.

Contact (editor): Wayne Fisher, Marcus Institute, 1920 Briarcliff Rd., Atlanta, GA 30329 (phone: 404-419-4454), JABA@Marcus.ORG

JOURNAL OF AUTISM AND DEVELOPMENTAL DISORDERS

This journal publishes material with a direct relevance to the understanding and remediation of Autism, childhood psychoses, and related developmental disorders. Professionals interested in this journal come from many fields, including medicine, psychology, neuroscience, biochemistry, physiology, and education. The multidisciplinary nature of this journal is designed to advance the understanding and remediation of Autism, childhood psychoses, and related developmental disorders. For more information, see http://journals.kluweronline.com/

JOURNAL OF CLINICAL CHILD PSYCHOLOGY

The *Journal of Clinical Child Psychology* (JCCP) is the official journal of the section on clinical child psychology (section 1) of the Division of Clinical Psychology (Division 12) of the American Psychological Association. It publishes research reviews and articles on child advocacy, training, and professional practice in clinical child psychology.

Contact: Wendy K. Silverman, Florida International University, Miami, FL

JOURNAL OF COMMUNICATION DISORDERS

This journal contains original articles related to speech, language, and hearing disorders, and attempts to address the prevention and treatment of communication disorders. Information in this journal relates to the assessment, diagnosis, and treatment of communication disorders. This journal is of interest to professionals from a variety of fields, including speech-language pathologists, audiologists, psychotherapists, and otolaryngologists.

Contact (editor): Theodore J. Glattke, Department of Speech and Hearing Sciences, University of Arizona, Tucson, AZ 85721

JOURNAL OF CONSULTING AND CLINICAL PSYCHOLOGY

This journal is published by the American Psychological Association. It publishes articles on topics such as the development and use of diagnostic techniques in the treatment of disordered behaviors, studies of personality (its assessment and development relating to consulting and clinical psychology), and cross-cultural and demographic studies of interest for behavioral disorders.

Contact: American Psychological Association, Journals Department, 750 First St. NE, Washington, DC 20002-4242

JOURNAL OF EMOTIONAL AND BEHAVIORAL DISORDERS

This journal publishes articles on research, practice, and commentary related to children and adolescents with emotional and behavioral disorders. Articles published are relevant to professionals from a variety of backgrounds, including counseling, social work, education, early childhood, psychiatry, psychology, juvenile corrections, mental health, rehabilitation, and special education. It is published by PRO-ED (8700 Shoal Creek Blvd., Austin, TX 78757-6897).

JOURNAL OF FLUENCY DISORDERS

The *Journal of Fluency Disorders* is the official journal of the International Fluency Association. It provides comprehensive coverage of clinical, experimental, and theoretical aspects of stuttering, including the latest remediation techniques, research and clinical reports, methodological articles, and reviews. The target audience includes clinicians and researchers in universities, hospitals, and community clinics.

Contact (editor): Edward G. Conture, PhD, edward.g.conture@vanderbilt.edu

JOURNAL OF FORENSIC NEUROPSYCHOLOGY

This journal publishes articles involving legal aspects of the practice of clinical neuropsychology. Special educators may be interested in the head injury and litigation of head injury cases, which involve the schooling and education of brain-injured children. It is published by Haworth Press.

Contact (editor): Jim Hom, PhD, jfn@neuropsych.com

JOURNAL OF INTELLECTUAL DISABILITY RESEARCH

This is the official journal of the International Association for the Scientific Study of Intellectual Disability and the European Association for Mental Health and Mental Retardation. It began publication as the *Journal of Mental Deficiency Research* and was renamed in 1992. It publishes papers reporting original observations, including clinical case reports, pathological reports, biochemical investigations, and genetic, psychological, educational, and sociological studies. For more information, see http://www.ingenta.com/

JOURNAL OF LEARNING DISABILITIES

The *Journal of Learning Disabilities* (JLD) contains reports of empirical research, opinion papers, and discussions of issues that are of concern in all disciplines in the field. JLD provides knowledge and research relevant to academic and professional disciplines from educational, social, and health settings.

Contact (editor): Bob Gates, Thames Valley University, UK, http://www.sagepub.com/Home.aspx

JOURNAL OF POSITIVE BEHAVIOR INTERVENTIONS

This journal deals exclusively with principles of positive behavior support in school, home, and community settings for people with challenges in behavioral adaptation. Articles published address such topics as program descriptions, commentaries, research reports, and discussion of family supports. It is edited by Glen Dunlap, PhD, and Robert L. Koegel, PhD, and published by PRO-ED (8700 Shoal Creek Blvd., Austin, TX 78757-6897).

JOURNAL OF PSYCHOEDUCATIONAL ASSESSMENT

This journal publishes current information regarding psychological and educational practices, legal mandates, and instrumentation; it includes topics such as cross-cultural assessment practices, differential diagnoses, and dynamic assessment neuropsychology. The *Journal of Psychoeducational Assessment* is published by the Psychoeducational Corporation. Subscriptions can be ordered by writing to R. Steve McCallum, The Psychoeducational Corp., 505 22nd St., Knoxville, TN 37916.

JOURNAL OF SCHOOL PSYCHOLOGY

The *Journal of School Psychology* (JSP) publishes "articles on research practice related to the development of school psychology as both a scientific and applied specialty." JSP also reviews tests and books and publishes brief reports and commentaries.

Contact: JSP, The Curry Programs in Clinical and School Psychology, University of Virginia, 405 Emmet St. South, PO Box 400270, Charlottesville, VA 22904-4270

JOURNAL OF SPECIAL EDUCATION

The *Journal of Special Education* (JSE) includes critical commentaries, intervention studies, and integrative reviews on areas relevant to special education, such as families, transitions, technology, general and special education interface, and legislation and litigation. JSE also publishes traditional, ethnographic, and single-subject research. It is published by PRO-ED (8700 Shoal Creek Blvd., Austin, TX 78757-6897).

JOURNAL OF SPEECH AND HEARING DISORDERS

This journal is published by the American Speech, Language and Hearing Association. Each issue is divided into three major categories: Language, Speech, and Hearing. Articles address the process and disorders of speech, language, and hearing, and the diagnosis and treatment of such disorders. Topics include screening, assessment, treatment techniques, prevention, and professional issues. For more information, see http://www.asha.org/default.htm/

JOURNAL OF VISUAL IMPAIRMENT AND BLINDNESS

The *Journal of Visual Impairment and Blindness* (JVIB) is published by the American Foundation for the Blind. Articles cover all aspects of visual impairment, including international news, short reports, research, innovative practice techniques, evaluation of new products and publications, educational issues, and language development. For more information, see http://www.afb.org/jvib.asp/

LEARNING DISABILITY QUARTERLY

Learning Disability Quarterly is the official journal of the Council for Learning Disabilities. This journal publishes articles designed to enhance the education and development of people with learning disabilities. Articles address identification, assessment, remediation, and programming considerations, as well as reviews of relevant literature, discussions of pertinent issues, and research with an applied focus.

Contact address: Council for Learning Disabilities, P.O. Box 4014, Leesburg, VA 20177, http://www.cldinternational.org/

PSYCHOLOGICAL ABSTRACTS

Psychological Abstracts (PA) provides a non-evaluative summary of over 950 of the world's journals in psychology and related disciplines. Since 1967, abstracts of articles from these journals have been entered into machine-readable tapes that now provide an automated search and retrieval service. This service is known as Psychological Abstracts Information Services (PsychINFO).

Contact: American Psychological Association, 750 First Street NE, Washington, DC 20002-4242, http://www.apa.org/

PSYCHOLOGICAL REPORTS

Psychological Reports is published bimonthly. This journal attempts to encourage scientific originality and creativity in the field of general psychology. It carries experimental, theoretical, and speculative articles, comments, special reviews, and a listing of new books.

Contact: Ammons Scientific, Ltd., P.O. Box 9229, Missoula, MT 59807-9229, http://www.ammonsscientific.com/

PSYCHOLOGY IN THE SCHOOLS

Psychology in the Schools attempts to meet the practical needs of professionals in the field and therefore has an applied orientation. Articles address a variety of areas, including theoretical papers and interpretive reviews of the literature; treatment and remediation approaches; evaluation of treatments; social groups; effects on adjustment and development; educational, intellectual, and personality assessment; etiology and diagnosis; and case studies.

Contact (editor): LeAdelle Phelps, Psychology in the Schools, 409 Baldy Hall, Department of Counseling and Educational Psychology, State University of New York, Buffalo, Buffalo, NY 14260, http://www3.interscience.wiley.com/cgi-bin/home

SCHOOL PSYCHOLOGY QUARTERLY

School Psychology Quarterly is the official journal of Division 16 of the American Psychological Association. This journal is intended as a forum for professional school psychologists and promotes the effective delivery of school psychology services. Articles address diverse issues such as the delivery and evaluation of services, ethical and legal considerations, and innovative professional procedures. *School Psychology Quarterly* is published by Guilford Publishers.

Contact (editor in chief): Rik Carl D'Amato, PhD, Division of Professional Psychology and Office of the Dean, College of Education, McKee 125, Campus Box 106, University of Northern Colorado, Greeley, CO 80639

TEACHING EXCEPTIONAL CHILDREN

Teaching Exceptional Children (TEC) is a professional journal published jointly by the Council for Exceptional Children Information Center and the Instructional Materials Centers Network for Handicapped Children and Youth. TEC attempts to "disseminate practical and timely information to classroom teachers working with exceptional children and youth." TEC is published quarterly, and articles cover interests such as practical classroom procedures for the gifted and handicapped, educational diagnostic procedures, evaluation of instructional materials, and new research findings. Readers are encouraged to provide feedback through features such as the Teacher Idea Exchange, Questions and Answers, and letters to the editor.

Contact: Dr. Alec Peck, Lynch School of Education, Campion 108, Boston College, Chestnut Hill, MA 02467-3813

TECHNIQUES: A JOURNAL FOR REMEDIAL EDUCATION AND COUNSELING

Techniques provides multidisciplinary articles concerned with the treatment and education of the exceptional individual. The orientation is primarily clinical and educational and is organized into various areas of interest such as educational and psychological materials, research studies, practical approaches in the field, parent education, reviews of books, and what's new in the field.

TOPICS IN EARLY CHILDHOOD SPECIAL EDUCATION

Topics in Early Childhood Special Education (TECSE) is published quarterly. Articles are of interest to those who provide services to infants, toddlers, and preschoolers. Issues addressed include problem identification, trends, and areas of concern and importance to early intervention. It is published by PRO-ED (8700 Shoal Creek Blvd., Austin, TX 78757-6897).

TOPICS IN LANGUAGE DISORDERS

Topics in Language Disorders is an interdisciplinary journal that is published quarterly. Contributors and target audience include speech and language pathologists, psycholinguists, pediatricians, neurologists, and special educators. This journal tries to meet the need for published interactions across the professional boundaries. The editor is Katharine G. Butler, PhD. For more information, see http://www.lww.com/index.html

16

Individualized Education Programs

RANDALL L. DE PRY

The Education for All Handicapped Children Act (P.L. 94-142) became law in 1975 and is viewed by many as one of the most important educational acts ever legislated by Congress. This legislation has resulted in increased inclusion, participation, and educational opportunities for students with disabilities. The passage of P.L. 94-142 can be traced back to two landmark Supreme Court cases (*Brown v. Board of Education,* 1954; *Pennsylvania Association for Retarded Children v. Pennsylvania,* 1971, 1972) that examined equal access and equal rights for students of color and students with disabilities. These Supreme Court decisions, along with strong parental and societal advocacy, contributed to the passage of P.L. 94-142 and resulted in critical safeguards that ensure that students with disabilities will always have equal access and support in public educational programs.

All schools in the United States must provide students with disabilities a free, appropriate public education (FAPE), in the least restrictive environment (LRE), which results in the provision of special education services that are based on the student's individual learning needs. These mandated provisions are outlined in the Individuals with Disabilities Education Act (IDEA), formerly the Education for All Handicapped Children Act, which was amended and reauthorized by Congress in 1990 and 1997.

Students can receive special education services if they meet the following statutory requirements: (1) the student is between the ages of 3 and 21, (2) the student has an identifiable disability, and (3) it has been determined that the student requires special education and related services. When these requirements are met the student's educational program is developed and outlined in the individualized education program (IEP).

Procedural safeguards are also included as part of IDEA to protect the rights of

IEP Objective Features and Example

1. Learner (who)
2. Condition (where)
3. Behavior (what)
4. Criterion (how much and when)

William (*learner*) will share materials with peers (*behavior*) during math cooperative learning groups (*condition*) during 80% of opportunities by April 30 (*criterion*).

students and their parents. For example, IDEA stipulates that parental consent must be obtained prior to evaluation and assessment, prior to making the initial placement, and prior to changing a student's educational placement. Additional safeguards include (1) parental participation in the development of the IEP, (2) a review of the IEP at least annually, (3) a reevaluation of the IEP at least every 3 years, and (4) making all confidential records available to the parents. If parents disagree with an evaluation, they can obtain an independent evaluation of their child. If parents disagree with decisions related to the evaluation, identification, or placement of their child they can participate in a due process hearing and may resolve the matter through third-party mediation.

An IEP is a written educational program that includes present levels of performance, annual goals, short-term objectives, and delineation of special education and related services that are designed to ensure that the student receives a reasonable educational benefit in the least restrictive educational environment at no cost to the student or parents. Additionally, IEPs may include a statement of progress monitoring, statements of participation or nonparticipation with nondisabled students, and specific plans that outline programs that are intended to meet the specific learning needs of the student (e.g., behavior plans, assistive technology, communication support). The IEP team includes the child's parents (or surrogate), the child when appropriate (must be invited if 14 or older), general and special education teachers, a representative from the local education agency, and other qualified professionals who collaboratively develop the IEP in accordance with IDEA requirements and state laws.

The IEP process first includes the determination of whether the student has a disability as outlined in IDEA. Evaluation must include all domains related to the child's suspected disability and must be given in the child's primary language or other mode of communication. The evaluation must provide information that will allow the team to determine if the student meets IDEA disability criteria and if the student needs special education and related services. If the team determines that these standards have been met, then the student's educational program can be developed. The student's IEP must include the features outlined here and all special education and related services that are needed to ensure that the student receives a FAPE. Once the IEP has been developed, the IEP team will review and determine an appropriate placement. All placement decisions are based on the IEP and must result in a learning environment that is appropriate for the student and ensures that the student is educated and/or participates with nondisabled students to the maximum extent possible.

The IEP is best understood as a legally mandated and prescribed process that results in meaningful educational program plans that are designed to ensure that all students with disabilities can and will receive a reasonable educational benefit from their public school education. The IEP process can be time consuming. How-

Statement of Measurable Annual Goals, Including Benchmarks or Short-Term Objectives—34 CFR §300.347(a)(2)

"The IEP for each child with a disability must include . . . a statement of measurable annual goals, including benchmarks or short-term objectives, related to

"(i) Meeting the child's needs that result from the child's disability to enable the child to be involved in and progress in the general curriculum (i.e., the same curriculum as for nondisabled children), or for preschool children, as appropriate, to participate in appropriate activities; and

"(ii) Meeting each of the child's other educational needs that result from the child's disability."

ever, some of the paperwork burden has been mitigated by the use of computerized IEP programs that reduce paperwork and help educators and students monitor progress on the IEP. Congress is also exploring other program enhancements as part of its deliberations for the next reauthorization of IDEA. As a program plan, the IEP informs educators and related support personnel on what needs to be accomplished and where these services are best provided to ensure both educational benefit and the full participation of all students with disabilities. Because of this, the IEP has become the guiding principle that distinguishes special education from other educational initiatives and a major part of what makes special education so special and important for families and students with disabilities.

BOOKS ON IEP

Bateman, B. D., & Linden, M. A. (2000). *Better IEPs: How to develop legally correct and educationally useful programs* (3rd ed.). Longmont, CO: Sopris West Educational Services.

Osborne, A. G., Jr., & Russo, C. J. (2003). *Special education and the law: A guide for practitioners.* Thousand Oaks, CA: Corwin Press.

INTERNET RESOURCES

U.S. Department of Education, *Guide to the Individualized Education Program:* http://www.ed.gov/parents/needs/speced/iepguide/index.html

National Information Center for Children and Youth with Disabilities (NICHCY):

P.O. Box 1492

Washington, DC 20013

(800) 695-0285 (Voice/TTY); (202) 884-8200 (V/TTY)

E-mail: nichcy@aed.org

Web: www.nichcy.org

Electronic Disability Law Library:

http://www.edlaw.net/publications/epubs.html

Resources on Individualized Education Programs (IEPs):

http://ericec.org/minibibs/eb27.html

http://www.ideapractices.org/resources/topic.php?subcatID=86

17

Medications and the Special Education Student

ELAINE FLETCHER-JANZEN AND JULIE WILLIAMS

INTRODUCTION

Many children and adolescents in special education take prescription medications to help them meet the demands of everyday living in the home, schools, and community. Psychoactive medications have many functions. They can enhance attention; reduce psychotic symptoms such as hallucinations; lessen depressive ideas, thoughts, and feelings; reduce debilitating anxiety; and increase positive social and learning behaviors in the classroom, to name just a few.

Sometimes children come to special education with conditions that require medical intervention and maintenance, and other times children need pharmaceutical intervention to help them cope with the secondary problems associated with having a disability. Regardless of the etiology for medication intervention, there are many things that special educators and other professionals on the special education team can do to help with the evaluation and maintenance of medications and their possible side effects. It is very important to welcome well-planned medication interventions into the child's individual treatment plan. It is also important to make sure that the interventions are appropriate and that school personnel assist in the evaluation of the effectiveness of the medication intervention.

How do we go about helping evaluate a medication intervention? There are basically three things that special education personnel (special education teachers, speech language pathologists, school psychologists, special education aides, and other supportive personnel) can do to help the child who is taking medications:

1. Be aware of the medications that the child is taking and be aware of changes in dosage or type of medication.
2. Be aware of untoward effects or negative side effects of the medications that are common or severe, or that need immediate attention from medical personnel.
3. Be aware of the expected positive outcomes that are intended for the child with respect to the efficacy of the medication. In other words, does the medication do what it was intended to do?

In many cases, school personnel spend more time with children in an objective setting that anyone else in the child's life. It is a perfect environment to gather information about how a child is meeting the demands of everyday living. Personnel can set target behaviors and see if they increase or decrease with targeted medications, and they can measure these behaviors in many ways that provide objective information for the parents, physician, and teachers. Of course, this all depends on having a well-functioning special education team that has detailed and open communication with the parents and physician.

Many times, psychoactive medications that are used with children to help with psychological, social, cognitive, emotional, and behavioral adjustment are not tested on children (Green, 2001). Although some medication patents are extended by the Food and Drug Administration to drug companies who wish to do clinical studies with children, most medication trials are fraught with medical ethical problems associated with trying medications on young subjects, the long-term effects of which are not known. The fact still remains, however, that there are many children with disabilities that need help, and with the appropriate support from the physician, parents, and school, they can take medications that lessen daily discomfort on many levels.

CLINICAL DIAGNOSIS AND THE PRESCRIPTION OF MEDICATION

Green (2001) outlines the appropriate procedures for placing children on medications. The first step is to conduct a comprehensive assessment to understand the etiology of the problems, the types of physical issues that might be present, the type of support that medication therapy will receive, and the medical and psychological monitoring indicators to measure treatment success or failure. Table 17.1 outlines the constituents of a comprehensive medication assessment and the treatment evaluation that follows.

To summarize the table's contents, the appropriateness of any medication prescription is based on a thorough analysis of the child's history, medical condition, psychological diagnosis, target treatments, and professional management of the course of treatment. This is a difficult task that requires the cooperation of the child, family, physician, and school in a combined effort that is ever vigilant.

ETHNOPSYCHOPHARMACOLOGY

It is important to be aware of possible reactions to (or lack of effectiveness of) certain psychoactive drugs because individuals of various ethnicities may absorb,

Table 17.1 Elements of a comprehensive medication assessment

Diagnosis

Determination of the diagnosis may be dependent on family history, medical history, age of child, presenting symptoms, and other pertinent information—and must be accurate and verified.

Previous response to clinical and psychopharmacological treatments should be noted.

Target symptoms

Target symptoms must be clearly identified and related to diagnosis.

Target symptoms must be of sufficient severity to warrant risk associated with medications.

Baseline Assessments Before Administration of Medications

Physical examination.

Laboratory tests and diagnostic procedures. Routine tests should include (but not be limited to) the following: complete blood cell count (CBC), differential and hematocritp; urinalysis; blood urea nitrogen (BUN) level; serum electrolyte levels for sodium, potassium, chloride, calcium, phosphate, and carbon dioxide content; liver function tests; serum lead level determination in children under 7 years of age and older children when indicated; screening of urine or blood for substance abuse where necessary.

Other tests that might be warranted depending on known interactions are pregnancy, thyroid function, kidney function, prolactin levels, electrocardiogram for cardiovascular functioning, and electroencephalogram for patients with histories of seizures or high risk of seizures.

Baseline assessments of psychological domains and behaviors are essential. Various multidimensional instruments are available that gain information from teachers, parents, and the child.

Maturational and Developmental Issues

Children may respond differently than adults to medications for many reasons.

Developmental stage-specific efficacy and neurotoxicity are concerned with drug-induced biochemical or physiological changes, morphological manifestations, and behavioral symptoms.

Young children are not capable of giving feedback to the clinician in temporal and reliable ways; therefore, the clinician has to determine feedback from multiple sources.

Relationship with the Child's Family

Families should understand that psychoactive medications are rarely the single line of treatment.

Comprehensive treatment plans provide for other modalities of treatment to support medication therapy, and also treatments that involve the family system as an action agent for change.

Treatment Compliance

Parents and family are interposed between the physician and child; therefore, compliance is more complex than with adult patients.

Family members should be educated as to the anticipated effects, side effects to look for, symptoms of toxicity or that require immediate medical attention, and negative consequences of unplanned withdrawal.

Children old enough to understand elementary concepts of treatment compliance should be brought into the treatment regime.

Communication with the family about the costs and attainability of the medications is important.

Informed Consent

Where possible, the child should be drawn into the treatment plan to assist in informed consent and to give the child a sense of control and responsibility for the medications, maintenance, and evaluations of treatment.

Monitoring of Treatment Plan

Family should be aware of a schedule of maintenance for checkups and physical tests to prevent toxicity or untoward effects.

School should be aware of negative side effects and side effects that require immediate medical attention.

School should have arrangements in place for appropriate administration of medications that need to be taken during school hours.

continued

Table 17.1 *Continued*

School should provide baseline objective clinical assessments of targeted symptoms.
School should provide broad-based objective clinical assessments to pick up behaviors that might be side effects induced by medication.
School should keep record of changes in medications with concomitant objective assessments.
School should update individualized education plan with changes in medical treatment if positive or negative effects are noted.

Source: Adapted from Green (2001).

respond to, and assimilate medications differently. There are many biological, physiological, and genetic factors involved in responses to psychoactive drugs. An example is the cytochrome P450 system, a group of enzymes that are pertinent in rates of psychotropic medication metabolism and have great genetic variation (Lin & Poland, 2002; Ruiz, 2002).

Although information on ethnic differences and psychopharmacology is limited and general, some differences and a few specific drugs have been studied and documented. According to Ruiz (2002), African American patients have a high risk of toxicity and other side effects when taking tricyclic antidepressants and lithium. This group also has a high risk of developing tardive dyskinesia and other side effects with antipsychotics as well as atypical neuroleptics and antipsychotics, such as clozapine and olanzapine.

Hispanic patients also show differential responses to tricyclic antidepressants and antipsychotics: they may experience greater incidence of side effects and may need lower doses of medications. Clinical studies have shown that most Asians are prescribed lower doses of medications, including antidepressants, antipsychotics, and benzodiazepines, possibly because of slower metabolism (Lin & Poland, 2002; Lin, Poland, & Nakasaki, 1993).

Detailed analysis of this subject is not appropriate for this section. However, pharmacy databases and drug company literature increasingly speak to ethnic responses to medications. The reader is referred to the annotated reference list for further information on ethnic response differences to psychoactive medications.

DESCRIPTION OF MEDICATION ENTRIES

This section of the *Almanac* is designed to be a quick and handy reference on psychoactive medications commonly used to help children with exceptionalities. Many times educators are presented with lists of medications that a child is taking, and it is difficult to know what the medications do, what they help with, or how they can hurt a child if negative side effects are present. This section also has a standardized layout for a list of over 100 medications. The standardized layout is present to help the reader locate the type of information that he or she wants at a glance. Although we have made much effort to be thorough, the list may not be complete, as it contains only a small proportion of the myriad of the total medications that are on the market. In addition, there are many new drugs that are not yet available or are still in development for use in the United States.

The template used for each drug is designed to offer important information in a concise and straightforward way. The following sections describe the individual parts of each entry.

Name: Each drug is listed by brand name followed by the pharmaceutical name. There are some drugs with more than one popular or brand name, in which case we have listed the name most frequently used. Table 17.2 provides a cross-referenced list where the pharmaceutical name is listed first, in alphabetical order, followed by the brand name(s), just in case the reader is looking for a medication by the pharmaceutical name.

Category: This is the class of drugs that the medication belongs to (e.g., antipsychotic, antidepressant, antianxiety). Some drugs have more than one category listed because they are a special type of drug or have a specific function within a class of drugs. For example, an antidepressant may work by inhibiting reuptake of serotonin, in which case it would be labeled as both an antidepressant and a selective serotonin reuptake inhibitor (SSRI).

Used For: We have named the primary and some secondary diagnostic conditions for the use of the drug. For example, Wellbutrin is primarily used as a treatment for depression; however, it can also be used as a treatment for Attention-Deficit/Hyperactivity Disorder (ADHD).

Function: The exact neurological mechanisms of how a specific drug works are often unknown. There are times when the general idea of how a drug functions is known, and it is usually associated with blocking or supporting various neurotransmitters in the brain or working with the central nervous system. We have listed the general functions as they are generally described by the drug manufacturer.

Side Effects: Every medication has many side effects, and we have listed the effects that are most common and severe, as well as instances in which to seek medical attention.

Attention: Some drugs carry high risks of serious conditions—neuroleptic malignant syndrome, for example, which is a rare but potentially fatal medication reaction involving a range of symptoms (described elsewhere in this chapter). These high-risk conditions should be watched for and reported immediately.

Drug Interactions: Most drugs have many possible interactions, including other medications, diet, and herbal supplements. We have listed what is known to affect a specific drug, but there is much additional information that is beyond the scope of this document. Please refer to the resources mentioned in this chapter for more information.

Dosage: Many medications only list recommended dosages for adults because the medication has not been subjected to clinical studies with children. Therefore, the physician usually starts off with a low dose and makes educated changes as therapy progresses.

Therapeutic Levels: If information is available, we have listed a time range to attain therapeutic levels, as well as peak blood levels with each administration. *Note:* time for therapeutic levels and dosages are often different between children and adults, because children metabolize medications differently.

Use with Children: Many medications have not been tested on children, so

Table 17.2 Pharmaceutical names and brand names of medications

Pharmaceutical name	Brand name(s)
Alprazolam	Xanax
Amitriptyline HCL	Elavil, Endep
Adderall, amphetamine	Dextroamphetamine
Amoxapine	Asendin
Aripiprazole	Abilify
Atomoxetine HCL	Strattera
Benztropine mesylate	Cogentin
Bupropion HCL	Wellbutrin, Zyban
Buspirone HCL	BuSpar
Carbamazepine USP	Tegretol
Chlordiazepoxide HCL	Libruim, Libritabs, Mitran, Reponsans-10, Sereen
Chlordiazepoxide and Amitriptyline HCL	Limbitrol
Chlorpromazine HCL	Thorazine
Citalopram	Celexa
Clomipramine HCL	Anafranil
Clonazepam	Klonopin
Clonidine HCL	Catapres, Catapres-TTS
Clorazepate dipotassium	Tranxene, ClorazeCaps, ClorazeTabs, GenENE
Clozapine	Clozaril
Diazepame	Valium, Valrelease
Desipramine HCL	Norpramin, Pertofane
Desmopressin	DDAVP, Concentriad, Stimate
Dexmethylphenidate HCL	Focalin
Dextroamphetamine sulfate	Dexedrine
Diphenhydramine HCL	Benadryl, Benylin
Doxepin HCL	Sinequan, Adapin
Duloxetine	Cymbalta
Ethosuximide	Zarontin
Felbamate	Felbatol
Fluoxetine HCL	Prozac, Sarafem
Fluphenazine HCL	Prolixin, Permitil
Flurazepam HCL	Dalmane
Fluvoxamine maleate	Luvox
Gabapentin	Neurontin
Guanfacine HCL	Tenex
Haloperidol	Haldol
Hydroxyzine HCL	Atarax, Vistaril
Imipramine HCL	Tofranil
Lamotrigine	Lamictal
Lithium carbonate	Lithium, Cibalith-S, Eskalith CR, Lithane, Lithobid, Lithonate, Lithotabs
Lorazepam	Ativan
Loxapine succinate	Loxitane
Mecamylamine	Inversine
Mephobarbital	Mebaral
Meprobamate	Equanil, Mesprospan, Miltown, Neuramate
Mesoridazine besylate	Serentil
Methamphetamine HCL	Desoxyn
Methsuximide	Celontin
Methylphenidate HCL	Concerta, Metadate CD, Metadate ER, Methyline, Methyline ER
Methylphenidate HCL	Metadate, Concerta, Ritalin, Methylin
Metoprolol tartrate	Lopressor, Toprol XL
Mirtazapine	Remeron, Remeron SolTab
Modafinil	Provigil
Molindone HCL	Moban
Naltrexon	ReVia
Nefazodone HCL	Serzone
Nortriptyline HCL	Pamelor, Aventyl
Olanzapine	Zyprexa
Oxazepam	Serax
Oxcarbazepine	Trileptal
Paroxetine HCL	Paxil
Pemoline	Cylert
Perphenazine	Trilafon
Perphenazine with Amitriptyline HCL	Etrafon, Triavil
Phenelzine sulfate	Nardil
Phenobarbital	Phenobarbital, Sulfoton
Phenytoin	Dilantin, Dilanton infatab, Dilantin kapseals
Pimozide	Orap
Primidone	Mysoline
Prochlorperazine	Compazine
Propranolol HCL	Inderal, Betachron ER, Inderal LA
Protriptyline HCL	Vivactil
Quazepam	Doral
Quetiapine fumarate	Seroquel
Risperidone	Risperdal
Selegiline HCL	Eldepryl
Sertraline HCL	Zoloft
Temazepam	Restoril
Thiothixene HCL	Navane

Pharmaceutical name	Brand name(s)	Pharmaceutical name	Brand name(s)
Thioridazine	Mellaril	Topiramate	Topamax
Tiagabine HCL	Gabitril	Valproic acid	Depakene, Depakote, Divalproex sodium
Tranylcypromine sulfate	Parnate	Valsartan	Diovan
Trazodone HCL	Desyrel	Venlafaxine HCL	Effexor
Triazolam HCL	Halcion	Ziprasidone HCL	Geodon
Trifluoperazine HCL	Stelazine	Zolpidem	Ambien
Trihexyphenidyl HCL	Artane		
Trimipramine maleate	Surmontil		

there is no information about their safety or effectiveness with children. Those medications that have been tested with children are cited with dosages related to known studies.

Special warnings, notes, and Attention boxes: There are primarily three types of warnings that the reader may note in the text of the entries: tardive dyskinesia, agranulocytosis, and neuroleptic malignant syndrome.

Tardive dyskinesia is described by Rothenberg and Chapman (1994) as an

> abnormal condition characterized by involuntary and repetitious movements of muscles of the face, trunk, and limbs; most often occurring as a side effect in people treated with phenothiazine drugs for parkinsonism, or in patients taking antipsychotic medications. (p. 469)

This condition is usually only seen in individuals months or years after treatment begins. It may be irreversible or severely disabling and is clearly the most significant and common long-term effect of antipsychotic medications (Green, 2001). Interestingly, in children tardive dyskinesia may disappear over the course of weeks or as late as 3 years (Green, 2001).

Emotional distress typically worsens the symptoms of tardive dyskinesia, and tiredness and sleep cause them to diminish or stop completely. Green (2001) suggests that antipsychotic medications should only be given to children when no potentially less harmful drug will suffice.

Agranulocytosis, according to Rothenberg and Chapman (1994), is

> an acute blood disorder, often resulting from radiation or drug therapy, characterized by a severe decrease in granulocytes (a type of white blood cells). Rarely asymptomatic, agranulocytosis is usually accompanied by fever, prostration, and ulcers of the mucous membrane of the mouth, rectum, and vagina. (p. 16)

Agranulocytosis is usually seen early in treatment and should gain immediate attention from a physician.

Neuroleptic malignant syndrome (NMS) is life threatening and usually occurs early in treatment. It is characterized by severe muscular rigidity, altered consciousness, stupor, catatonia, hyperpyrexia, labile pulse and blood pressure, and occasionally myoglobinemia (Green, 2001). NMS can continue for several weeks even if the medication is discontinued. If NMS is detected, usually the medication is immediately withdrawn and hospitalization is necessary (Green, 2001).

The reader will note that there are other cautionary warnings or notes in the entries that pertain to the potential for a medication to be addictive and at high risk for substance abuse, the use of stimulants with individuals who may have Tourette syndrome, or the negative consequences of abrupt or unplanned withdrawal. These are general warnings and notes, and they are not exhaustive.

In every case, the text of these entries does not propose to supplant good, sound medical advice and supervision. This section of the *Almanac* is designed only to provide basic supplementary information to educators who wish to understand the needs of the children they serve. It is strongly suggested that the reader seek out expert medical advice for any questions arising from this text.

Annotated Resources

Facts and Comparisons, 2004 (http://www.factsandcomparisons.com), is a resource that is used by most pharmacies. It is a searchable database that gives complete information about any medication. Use of the database is by subscription only, but it is also possible to receive a 30-day free trial subscription. University libraries with pharmacy programs may subscribe to this database.

Medline Plus, 2004 (http://www.medlineplus.org), is an online resource that provides basic factual information about medications but also provides literature searches about the different research studies done with the medications.

The Physician's Desk Reference (http://pdr.net) is another popular searchable database partially accessed through subscription and contains most drug company information about the medication. This resource is also in print form.

Annotated References

Green, W. (2001). *Child and adolescent clinical psychopharmacology* (3rd ed.). Philadelphia: Lippincott Williams and Wilkins.
This book is a rare work written by a psychiatrist who references the *Diagnostic and Statistical Manual of Mental Disorders,* fourth edition (*DSM-IV*) diagnoses that can be assigned to children and adolescents and the medications used for the diagnoses. In its third edition, the book outlines clear and detailed objectives for assessing the use of medications, and it also has detailed chapters on the different classes of medications and supporting research studies.

Konopasek, D. (2003). *Medication facts sheets: A behavioral medication reference guide for the education professional.* Longmont, CO: Sopris West.
This book is written primarily for persons working in education. It an easy-to-read resource book that allows for quick reference information about different medications that are used with children.

Lin, K.M., & Poland, R.E. (2002). *Ethnicity, culture, and psychopharmacology.*

Common Pharmaceutical Terms

Route

IM: intramuscular
IV: intravenous
PO: by mouth
PR: per rectum
SG: sublingual (dissolves in mouth)
SQ: subcutaneous

Frequency

Qd: once daily
Qod: every other day
Bid: twice daily
Tid: three times daily
Qid: four times daily
Pid: five times daily
Qw: every week

Form

Gtt: drop
Oin: ointment
Ung: ointment

Other

Q: every, per (q)
Hs: bedtime
Pc̄: with food
Ac̄: after food
c̄: with
s̄: without
PM: night
AM: morning
H, h, o: hour
PRN: as needed
UD: use as directed
D, d: day
A: ear
Ad: right ear
As: left ear
Au: both ears
O: eye
Od: right eye
Os: left eye
Ou: both eyes

Retrieved October 27, 2004, from the American College of Neuropsychopharmacology web site: http://www.acnp.org.
This article gives detailed information on mechanisms affecting drug responses and factors that affect drug metabolism, including ethnicity. The web site is a good source of information, offering articles, journals, and links to neuropsychopharmacology.

Lin, K.M., Poland, R.E., & Nakasaki, G. (1993). *Psychopharmacology and psychobiology of ethnicity.* Washington, DC: American Psychiatric Press.
This book is one of the first published works on medication's relationship to ethnic differences. It is a compilation of studies that have been done on differences in psychopharmacology to date. Although additional information has come to light since this book has been published, the information is useful and is a marker of progress made.

Rothenberg, M.A., & Chapman, C.F. (1994). *Dictionary of medical terms* (3rd ed.). Hauppauge, NY: Barron's Educational Series.
This is an excellent quick reference guide to medical terms and conditions.

Ruiz, P. (2002). *Ethnicity and psychopharmacology.* Washington, DC: American Psychiatric Press.
This book is one of few that give information about ethnic differences in psychopharmacology. It has an informative introduction to ethnopsychopharmacology, and each chapter is specific to a different group's genetic variation, metabolism, and response to some medications. It references the results of many specific studies that have been done.

Guide to Psychoactive Medications

■ ABILIFY/ARIPIPRAZOLE

Category: Antipsychotic
Used For: Schizophrenia
Alternate uses: None
Function: Decreases positive and negative psychotic symptoms by blocking dopamine and serotonin
Side Effects:

Common
- headache
- nervousness
- difficulty falling asleep or staying asleep
- drowsiness
- lightheadedness
- weakness
- restlessness
- upset stomach
- vomiting
- constipation
- weight gain
- coughing
- runny nose
- shaking hands
- rash
- dry skin
- itchy eyes
- ear pain
- loss of appetite

Severe (none listed)

Seek immediate attention for:
- dizziness
- fainting
- blurred vision
- slow, fast, or irregular heartbeat
- chest pain
- swelling of hands, feet, ankles, or lower legs
- depression
- seizures
- difficulty swallowing
- trouble breathing
- urgent need to urinate
- high fever
- muscle stiffness
- confusion
- sweating
- abnormal excitement
- tardive dyskinesia (see explanation in introduction)
- neuroleptic malignant syndrome (see explanation in introduction)

Drug Interactions: Alcohol, carbamazepine, fluoxetine, paroxetine, quinidine, ketoconazole
Dosage: Adults: 10–30 mg/day
Therapeutic levels: 14 days; peak blood levels 3–5 hours
Use with Children: Safety and efficacy not established

■ ADDERALL/AMPHETAMINE AND DEXTROAMPHETAMINE

Category: Stimulant
Used For: As part of a treatment program for Attention-Deficit/Hyperactivity Disorder (ADHD)
Alternate uses: Narcolepsy, obesity, Panic Disorder
Function: Stimulates the central nervous system and has paradoxical effect of improving behaviors associated with ADHD

Side Effects:

Common

- nervousness
- restlessness
- difficulty falling or staying asleep
- false feeling of well-being
- feeling of unpleasantness
- dizziness
- tremor
- difficulty coordinating movements
- headache
- in males, inability to have or maintain an erection
- changes in sex drive
- dry mouth
- diarrhea
- constipation
- loss of appetite
- weight loss
- bad taste in mouth

Seek immediate attention for:

- fast or irregular heartbeat
- fast or irregular breathing
- hallucinations
- red, itchy skin rash

Severe (none listed)

Attention:

- This medicine may be habit forming with a potential for abuse.
- Fatigue, depression, and sleep disorders can occur if this medicine is stopped suddenly.
- Stimulants may bring on or intensify some of the symptoms of Tourette syndrome.

Drug Interactions: Adrenergic blocking agents, antihistamines, antihypertensives, chlorpromazine, haloperidol, lithium, methenamine, ethosuximide, furazolidone, ascorbic acid, fruit juices, glutamic acid, guanethidine, reserpine, sodium bicarbonate, meperidine, norepinephrine, monoamine oxidase inhibitors (MAOIs), phenobarbital, phenytoin, propoxyphene, tricyclic antidepressants, ammonium chloride, sodium acid phosphate, acetazolamide

Dosage: Children 3–6 years: start with 2.5 mg/day.
Children 6 years: start with 5 mg/day.
Adolescents: start with 10 mg/day.

Therapeutic levels: Peak blood levels 2 hours.

Use with Children: Safety and efficacy have not been established in children under 3 years. Adderall XR has not been tested on children under 6 years.

■ AMBIEN/ZOLPIDEM

Category: Sedative/hypnotic

Used For: Short-term treatment for Insomnia

Alternate uses: None

Function: Sedative effect on the brain

Side Effects:

Severe
- drowsiness
- upset stomach
- vomiting
- constipation
- diarrhea
- headache
- dry mouth
- muscle aches

Seek immediate attention for:
- skin rash
- itching
- fast or irregular heartbeat
- chest pain
- difficulty breathing
- fever
- behavior changes
- mental confusion
- abnormal thinking or dreams
- depression

Drug Interactions: Some foods, ritonavir
Dosage: Adults: 5 mg/day
Therapeutic levels: Blood peak levels 15 minutes
Use with Children: Safety and effectiveness for children under 18 not established

■ AMOXAPINE/ASENDIN

Category: Tricyclic antidepressant
Used For: Depression in individuals with neurotic or reactive depressive disorders as well as psychotic depressions; also indicated for depression accompanied by anxiety or agitation
Alternate uses: Chronic pain
Function: Inhibits reuptake of neurotransmitters norepinephrine and serotonin and may block the effect of dopamine
Side Effects:

Common
- upset stomach
- drowsiness
- weakness or tiredness
- excitement or anxiety
- insomnia
- nightmares
- dry mouth
- skin more sensitive to sunlight
- changes in appetite or weight

Severe
- constipation
- difficulty urinating
- frequent urination
- blurred vision
- excessive sweating

Seek immediate attention for:
- jaw, neck, and back muscle spasms
- slow or difficult speech
- shuffling walk
- persistent fine tremor or inability to sit still
- fever
- difficulty breathing or swallowing
- severe skin rash
- yellowing of the skin or eyes
- irregular heartbeat
- tardive dyskinesia (see explanation in introduction)
- neuroleptic malignant syndrome (see explanation in introduction)

Drug Interactions: Barbiturates, charcoal, cimetidine, fluoxetine, clonidine, central nervous system depressants, monoamine oxidase inhibitors (MAOIs)
Dosage: Adults: 200–300 mg/day
Therapeutic levels: 2 weeks; peak blood level 90 minutes
Use with Children: Safety and efficacy not established in children under 16 years

■ ANAFRANIL/CLOMIPRAMINE HCL

Category: Tricyclic antidepressant
Used For: Obsessive-Compulsive Disorder
Alternate uses: Attention-Deficit/Hyperactivity Disorder (ADHD), Autism, Enuresis, school phobia/separation anxiety, Panic Disorder, chronic pain
Function: Reduces symptoms of Obsessive-Compulsive Disorder and depression by inhibiting reuptake of serotonin and norepinephrine
Side Effects:

Common
- drowsiness
- dry mouth
- upset stomach
- vomiting
- diarrhea
- constipation
- nervousness
- decreased memory or concentration
- headache
- stuffy nose
- change in appetite or weight

Severe (none listed)

Seek immediate attention for:
- tremor
- seizures
- fast, irregular, or pounding heartbeat
- difficulty urinating or loss of bladder control
- depression
- delusions or hallucinations
- eye pain
- shakiness
- difficulty breathing or fast breathing
- severe muscle stiffness
- unusual tiredness or weakness

Drug Interactions: Anticholinergics, barbiturates, charcoal, cimetidine, fluoxetine, haloperidol, phenothiazine antipsychotics, oral contraceptives, clonidine, central nervous system depressants, guanethidine, monoamine oxidase inhibitors (MAOIs)
Dosage: Adults: 25–250 mg/day
Children under 11 years: 25–200 mg/day
Therapeutic levels: 2–3 weeks; peak blood levels 2–6 hours
Use with Children: Not recommended for children under 10 years

■ ARTANE/TRIHEXYPHENIDYL HCL

Category: Antispasmodic
Used For: To reduce tremors and other symptoms associated with Parkinson's disease, and side effects of some antipsychotic medications
Alternate uses: None
Function: Inhibits parts of central nervous system and relaxes smooth muscles
Side Effects:

Common
- drowsiness
- dizziness or blurred vision
- dry mouth
- upset stomach
- vomiting
- diarrhea
- constipation
- increased eye sensitivity to light
- difficulty urinating

Severe (none listed)

Seek immediate attention for:
- skin rash
- fast, irregular, or pounding heartbeat
- fever
- confusion
- depression
- delusions or hallucinations
- eye pain

Drug Interactions: Haloperidol, phenothiazines

Dosage: Adults: 5–15 mg/day
Therapeutic levels: Peak blood levels 1–1.5 hours
Use with Children: Safety and effectiveness not established

■ ATARAX/HYDROXYZINE HCL

Category: Antipsychotic/antihistamine
Used For: Allergies, preoperative sedation, motion sickness
Alternate uses: Short-term treatment for anxiety disorders and agitation
Function: May suppress activity in subcortical area of central nervous system (CNS) to have a relaxing effect on skeletal muscles
Side Effects:

Common
- dry mouth, nose, and throat
- upset stomach
- drowsiness
- dizziness
- chest congestion
- headache
- reddening of skin

Severe (none listed)

Seek immediate attention for:
- difficulty breathing
- muscle weakness
- increased anxiety

Drug Interactions: Alcohol, CNS depressants
Dosage: Adults: 50–100 mg/day, titrated
Children over 6 years: 50–100 mg/day, titrated
Children under 6 years: 50 mg/day, titrated
Therapeutic levels: Peak blood levels 15–30 minutes
Use with Children: As prescribed by physician

■ ATIVAN/LORAZEPAM

Category: Antianxiety/benzodiazepines/central nervous system (CNS) depressant
Used For: Anxiety Disorders, anxiety associated with depression and hypertension
Alternate uses: Insomnia
Function: Increases neural inhibition and has tranquilizing effect
Side Effects:

Common
- drowsiness
- dizziness
- tiredness
- weakness
- dry mouth
- diarrhea
- upset stomach
- changes in appetite

Severe
- restlessness or excitement
- constipation

Seek immediate attention for:
- shuffling walk
- persistent fine tremor or inability to sit still
- fever
- difficulty breathing or swallowing
- severe skin rash
- yellowing of the skin or eyes
- irregular heartbeat

- difficulty urinating
- frequent urination
- blurred vision

Drug Interactions: Alcohol, central nervous system depressants, digoxin, oral contraceptives, rifampin, scopolamine, theophyllines
Dosage: Adults: 1.0–1.6 mg/day, divided
Therapeutic levels: Peak blood levels 2 hours
Use with Children: Safety and efficacy not established in children under 12 years

■ BENADRYL/DIPHENHYDRAMINE HCL

Category: Antihistamine
Used For: Allergies
Alternate uses: Motion sickness, tremors, and other symptoms associated with Parkinson's disease; Anxiety Disorders and agitation; side effects of antipsychotic medications; Insomnia
Function: Antihistamine has anticholinergic and sedative effects
Side Effects:

Common
- dry mouth, nose, and throat
- drowsiness
- upset stomach
- chest congestion
- headache

Seek immediate attention for:
- vision problems
- difficulty urinating
- muscle weakness
- excitement (especially in children)
- nervousness

Severe (none listed)

Drug Interactions: Alcohol, central nervous system depressants, monoamine oxidase inhibitors (MAOIs)
Dosage: Adults: 25–50 mg/4 hours (300 mg/day max)
Children 6–12 years: 12.5–25 mg/4 hours (150 mg/day max)
Children under 6 years: 6.25–12.5 mg/4 hours (25 mg/day max)
Therapeutic levels: Peak blood levels 1–4 hours
Use with Children: Children may be excited rather than sedated. Overdose in infants may cause hallucinations, convulsions, or death.

■ BUSPAR/BUSPIRONE HCL

Category: Antianxiety
Used For: Generalized Anxiety Disorder
Alternate uses: Reduce or eliminate violent angry outbursts
Function: Unknown; possible effects with neurotransmitters serotonin, dopamine, norepinephrine; does not exert anticonvulsant or muscle relaxant effects
Side Effects:

Common
- drowsiness
- upset stomach
- vomiting
- constipation

Seek immediate attention for:
- skin rash
- itching
- fast or irregular heartbeat
- blurred vision

- diarrhea
- stomach pain
- headache
- dry mouth
- depression
- excitement
- fatigue
- nervousness
- difficulty sleeping
- lightheadedness
- weakness
- numbness
- unusual movements of the head or neck muscles

Severe (none listed)

Drug Interactions: Diazepam, fluoxetine, haloperidol, carbamazepine, dexamethasone, phenobarbital, phenytoin, rifampin, diltiazem, erythromycin, grapefruit juice, itraconazole, ketoconazole, nefazodone, ritonavir, verapamil, monoamine oxidase inhibitors (MAOIs), nefazadone, trazodone

Dosage: Adults: 15–60 mg/day, divided

Therapeutic levels: 1–2 weeks; peak blood levels 40–90 minutes

Use with Children: There are no long-term safety or efficacy data with this population.

■ CATAPRES/CLONIDINE HCL

Category: Antihypertensive

Used For: Anxiety and hypertension

Alternate uses: Attention-Deficit/Hyperactivity Disorder (ADHD), Tourette syndrome, other uses

Function: Inhibits release of norepinephrine; reduces blood pressure, pulse rate, and central nervous system (CNS) stimulation

Side Effects:

Common

- dry mouth
- drowsiness
- dizziness
- constipation
- tiredness
- headache
- nervousness
- upset stomach
- vomiting
- rash

Severe (none listed)

Seek immediate attention for:

- fainting
- increased or decreased heartbeat
- irregular heartbeat
- swollen ankles or feet

Drug Interactions: Alcohol, central nervous system depressants, beta blockers, local anesthetics, narcotic analgesics, tricyclic antidepressants

Dosage: Adults: 0.2–0.6 mg/day, divided

Therapeutic levels: Peak blood levels 3–5 hours

Use with Children: Safety and efficacy not established in children under 12 years

■ CELEXA/CITALOPRAM

Category: Antidepressant/selective serotonin reuptake inhibitor (SSRI)
Used For: Depression
Alternate uses: None
Function: selective serotonin reuptake inhibitor (SSRI): inhibits or blocks the reuptake of the neurotransmitter serotonin
Side Effects:

Common
- upset stomach
- drowsiness
- weakness, tiredness, or anxiety
- excitement
- difficulty falling or staying asleep
- nightmares
- dry mouth
- changes in appetite or weight

Severe
- constipation
- difficulty urinating
- frequent urination
- blurred vision
- excessive sweating

Seek immediate attention for:
- jaw, neck, and back muscle spasms
- slow or difficult speech
- shuffling walk
- persistent fine tremor or inability to sit still
- fever
- difficulty breathing or swallowing
- severe skin rash
- yellowing of the skin or eyes
- irregular heartbeat

Drug Interactions: Beta blockers, cimetidine, cyproheptadine, lithium, monoamine oxidase inhibitors (MAOIs), sumatriptan, metoprolol
Dosage: Adults: 20–40 mg/day
Therapeutic levels: 2–3 weeks; peak blood levels 4 hours
Use with Children: Safety and effectiveness not established

■ CELONTIN/METHSUXIMIDE

Category: Anticonvulsant
Used For: Absence seizure disorder
Alternate uses: None
Function: Depresses abnormal neuronal discharges in the central nervous system; depresses motor cortex of brain and therefore inhibits seizures
Side Effects:

Common
- drowsiness
- upset stomach
- vomiting
- constipation
- diarrhea
- stomach pain
- loss of taste and appetite
- weight loss
- irritability
- mental confusion
- depression

Seek immediate attention for:
- difficulty coordinating movements
- joint pain
- red, itchy skin rash
- easy bruising
- tiny purple-colored skin spots
- bloody nose
- unusual bleeding
- yellowing of the skin or eyes
- dark urine
- fever
- sore throat

- insomnia
- nervousness
- headache

Severe (none listed)

Drug Interactions: Hydantoins, phenobarbital, lamotrigine

Dosage: Adults: 300–1200 (max) mg/day

Therapeutic levels: Peak blood levels 1–4 hours

Use with Children: As prescribed by physician

■ CLOZARIL/CLOZAPINE

Category: Antipsychotic—atypical

Used For: Schizophrenia when individual is treatment resistant or when individual is unable to tolerate effects of other antipsychotic medications

Alternate uses: None

Function: Decreases psychotic symptoms by inhibiting dopamine receptors in the limbic area

Side Effects:

Severe

- drowsiness
- dry mouth
- diarrhea
- constipation
- restlessness
- headache

Seek immediate attention for:

- tremor
- seizures or convulsions
- difficulty urinating or loss of bladder control
- confusion
- eye pain
- shakiness
- chest pain
- severe muscle stiffness
- sore throat
- unusual bleeding or bruising
- upset stomach
- vomiting
- loss of appetite
- yellowness of the skin or eyes
- tardive dyskinesia (see explanation in introduction)
- neuroleptic malignant syndrome (see explanation in introduction)

Attention: Because of a significant risk of agranulocytosis, a potentially life-threatening adverse event, clozapine is reserved for use in the treatment of severely ill patients with Schizophrenia who fail to show an acceptable response to adequate courses of standard antipsychotic drug treatment, or for reducing the risk of recurrent suicidal behavior in patients with Schizophrenia or Schizoaffective Disorder who are judged to be at risk of reexperiencing suicidal behavior. Patients being treated with clozapine must have a baseline white blood cell (WBC) and differential count before initiation of treatment as well as regular WBC counts during treatment and for 4 weeks after discontinuation of treatment.

Drug Interactions: Agents that suppress bone marrow, anticholinergics, antihypertensives, barbiturates, nicotine, phenytoin, rifampin, caffeine, cimetidine,

erythromycin, ritonavir, selective serotonin reuptake inhibitors (SSRIs), central nervous system drugs, propafenone, flecainide
Dosage: Adults: 25 mg at bedtime (900 mg/day max)
Therapeutic levels: Peak blood levels 2.5 hours
Use with Children: Safety and efficacy not established

■ COGENTIN/BENZTROPINE MESYLATE

Category: Anticholinergic
Used For: Parkinsonian symptoms/extrapyramidal effects associated with side effects of antipsychotic medications
Alternate uses: None
Function: Inhibits parts of central nervous system, creating a relaxing effect on muscles
Side Effects:

Common
- drowsiness
- dry mouth
- difficulty urinating
- constipation

Severe (none listed)

Seek immediate attention for:
- skin rash
- fast, irregular, or pounding heartbeat
- fever
- confusion
- depression
- delusions or hallucinations
- eye pain

Drug Interactions: Amantadine, digoxin, haloperidol, phenothiazines
Dosage: Adults: 0.5–6.0 mg/day as needed
Therapeutic levels: Information not available
Use with Children: Safety and efficacy not established

■ COMPAZINE/PROCHLORPERAZINE

Category: Antipsychotic
Used For: Schizophrenia, Psychotic Disorders
Alternate uses: Control of nausea or vomiting, generalized nonpsychotic anxiety, migraines
Function: Appears to block dopamine action and helps reduce psychotic symptoms
Side Effects:

Common
- drowsiness

Severe (none listed)

Seek immediate attention for:
- jaw, neck, and back muscle spasms
- fine wormlike tongue movements
- rhythmic face, mouth, or jaw movements
- slow or difficult speech
- difficulty swallowing
- restlessness and pacing
- tremors
- shuffling walk
- skin rash

- yellowing of the skin or eyes
- tardive dyskinesia (see explanation in introduction)
- neuroleptic malignant syndrome (see explanation in introduction)

Drug Interactions: Alcohol, central nervous system depressants, anticholinergics, barbiturate anesthetics, beta blockers, cisapride, sparfloxacin, guanethidine, metrizamide, paroxetine

Dosage: Adults: 15–40 mg/day, divided
Children 40–85 pounds: 7.5–10 mg/day
Children 30–39 pounds: 2.5–7.5 mg/day
Children 20–29 pounds: 2.0–5.0 mg/day

Therapeutic levels: Large individual differences

Use with Children: Do not give to children under 9 kg (20 lbs.) or 2 years.

■ CONCERTA/METHYLPHENIDATE HCL

Category: Stimulant

Used For: Part of treatment for Attention-Deficit/Hyperactivity Disorder (ADHD)

Alternate uses: Narcolepsy

Function: Unknown; activates cortical arousal and paradoxically reduces symptoms associated with ADHD

Side Effects:

Common

- nervousness
- difficulty falling asleep or staying asleep
- dizziness
- drowsiness
- upset stomach
- vomiting
- headache
- loss of appetite

Severe (none listed)

Seek immediate attention for:

- seizures or convulsions
- blurred vision
- agitation
- skin rash
- heart palpitations or irregular heartbeat
- fever
- sore throat
- unusual bleeding or bruising

Attention:

- Can be habit forming.
- May exacerbate or initiate symptoms of Tourette syndrome.

Drug Interactions: Anticonvulsants, selective serotonin reuptake inhibitors (SSRIs), tricyclic antidepressants, coumarin anticoagulants, guanethidine, monoamine oxidase inhibitors (MAOIs)

Dosage: Adults: 18–54 mg/day

Therapeutic levels: Peak blood levels 6–8 hours

Use with Children: Safety and efficacy have not been established in children under 6 years. Carefully monitor children on long-term therapy, especially for growth in height and weight.

■ CYLERT/PEMOLINE

Category: Stimulant
Used For: Attention-Deficit/Hyperactivity Disorder (ADHD; not a first-line treatment due to associated risks)
Alternate uses: Narcolepsy
Function: Unknown; acts as central nervous system stimulant but with little sympathomimetic effects
Side Effects:

Severe
- insomnia
- weight loss
- upset stomach
- diarrhea

Seek immediate attention for:
- hallucinations
- excitement
- agitation
- restlessness
- fast heartbeat
- seizures
- dizziness

Attention:
- Risk of life-threatening liver failure.

Drug Interactions: Not well documented
Dosage: Adults: 56.25–75 (112.5 max) mg/day
Therapeutic levels: 3–4 weeks; peak blood levels 2–4 hours
Use with Children: Safety and efficacy in children under 6 years not established

■ CYMBALTA/DULOXETINE HCL

Category: Antidepressant
Used For: Major Depressive Disorder
Alternate uses: None
Function: Unknown; may inhibit reuptake of norepinephrine and serotonin
Side Effects:

Common
- dizziness
- insomnia
- somnolence
- decreased appetite
- constipation
- diarrhea
- dry mouth
- nausea
- fatigue

Severe (none listed)

Seek immediate attention for:
- anxiety
- agitation
- panic attacks
- hostility
- impulsivity
- akathisia
- hypomania
- mania
- worsening of depression
- suicidal ideation

Attention: As this is a new drug, some side effects may not be known. See physician for any adverse reactions.
Drug Interactions: monoamine oxidase inhibitors (MAOIs); tentative evidence of interactions with fluvoxamine, quinolone antibiotics, fluoxetine, quinidine, fle-

cainide, phenothiazines, propafenone, tricyclic antidepressants, thioridazine, alcohol, central nervous system–acting drugs, drugs highly bound to plasma protein (e.g., warfarin); may be other interactions still unknown
Dosage: Adults: 40–60 mg/day, divided
Therapeutic levels: 3 days; peak blood levels 6–10 hours
Use with Children: Safety and efficacy in children have not been established.

■ DALMANE/FLURAZEPAM HCL

Category: Benzodiazapines/central nervous system (CNS) depressant/sedative and hypnotic
Used For: Short-term treatment of Insomnia
Alternate uses: None
Function: Increased neural inhibition; blocks arousal of higher cortical brain processes
Side Effects:

Common
- headache
- heartburn
- diarrhea
- hangover effect (grogginess)
- drowsiness
- dizziness or lightheadedness
- weakness
- dry mouth

Severe
- constipation
- difficulty urinating
- frequent urination
- blurred vision

Seek immediate attention for:
- jaw, neck, and back muscle spasms
- slow or difficult speech
- persistent fine tremor or inability to sit still
- fever
- difficulty breathing or swallowing
- severe skin rash
- yellowing of the skin or eyes
- irregular heartbeat

Attention:
- Should be discontinued after 28 days

Drug Interactions: Alcohol, central nervous system depressants, cimetidine, disulfiram, oral contraceptives, isoniazid, omeprazole, digoxin, phenytoin, rifampin, theophyllines
Dosage: Adults: 15–30 mg/day
Therapeutic levels: Peak blood levels 30–60 minutes
Use with Children: Not recommended in children under 15 years

■ DDAVP/DESMOPRESSIN

Category: Posterior pituitary hormone
Used For: Enuresis, specific types of diabetes insipidus
Alternate uses: Chronic autonomic failure
Function: Antidiuretic, decreases urinary volume and increases urine osmolality

Side Effects:

Severe (none listed)

Seek immediate attention for:
- upset stomach
- headache
- stuffy or runny nose
- reddening of the skin
- stomach cramps
- pain in the external genital area (in women)

Drug Interactions: Carbamazepine, chlorpropamide

Dosage: Adults: 0.1–1.2 mg/day, divided.
Children 3–12 years: begin with .05 mg/day.

Therapeutic levels: Peak blood levels 1 hour

Use with Children: Infants and children require careful fluid intake restriction to prevent possible hyponatremia and water intoxication. Safety and efficacy of intranasal form have not been established in children less than 11 months. Safety and efficacy of parenteral form for control of diabetes insipidus have not been established for children less than 12 years.

■ DEPAKENE/VALPROIC ACID

Category: Anticonvulsant

Used For: Seizure disorders

Alternate uses: Manic phase of Bipolar Disorder, Borderline Personality Disorder, prevention of migraine headaches

Function: Suppresses the spread of abnormal or diffuse electrical discharges in the brain

Side Effects:

Severe
- drowsiness
- headache
- indigestion

Seek immediate attention for:
- skin rash
- easy bruising
- tiny purple-colored skin spots
- bloody nose
- unusual bleeding
- dark urine
- fever
- sore throat

Attention:
- Risk of severe, sometimes fatal, liver toxicity

Drug Interactions: Alcohol, central nervous system depressants, amitriptyline/nortriptyline, barbiturates, diazepam, ethosuximide, carbamazepine, hydantoins, charcoal, cholestyramine, chlorpromazine, cimetidine, erythromycin, rifampin, salicylates, clonazepam, felbamate, lamotrigine, meropenem, zidovudine

Dosage: Adults: 60 mg/day

Therapeutic levels: Peak blood level 1–4 hours

Use with Children: Use with extreme caution in children under 2 years. Safety and efficacy for various treatments have not been established for children under 18 years.

DESOXYN/METHAMPHETAMINE HCL

Category: Central nervous system (CNS) stimulant
Used For: Short-term treatment for obesity
Alternate uses: Attention-Deficit/Hyperactivity Disorder (ADHD)
Function: Noradrenergic activation stimulates central nervous system and respiratory system.
Side Effects:

Common

- dizziness
- restless mood
- overstimulation
- exaggerated sense of well-being
- sleeplessness
- headache
- motor tics
- diarrhea
- constipation
- dry mouth
- unpleasant taste
- upset stomach
- hives

Severe (none listed)

Seek immediate attention for:

- pounding in the chest
- increased heartbeat
- bizarre behavior
- growth suppression in children
- tremor

Attention:

- High abuse potential
- May initiate or exacerbate symptoms of Tourette syndrome

Drug Interactions: Guanethidine, monoamine oxidase inhibitors (MAOIs), furazolidone, tricyclic antidepressants, urinary acidifiers, urinary alkalinizers
Dosage: Children over 5 years: 20–25 mg/day, divided
Therapeutic levels: Rapid absorption
Use with Children: Not recommended as anorectic agent in children under 12 years

DESYREL/TRAZODONE HCL

Category: Antidepressant
Used For: Depression
Alternate uses: Anxiety, Insomnia
Function: Unknown; may block reuptake of the neurotransmitter serotonin
Side Effects:

Common

- dry mouth
- sedation
- nausea
- dizziness
- fainting
- excitement or anxiety
- insomnia

Seek immediate medical attention for:

- excessive sweating
- jaw, neck, and back muscle spasms
- slow or difficult speech
- shuffling walk
- persistent fine tremor or inability to sit still
- dizziness or lightheadedness

- nightmares
- skin more sensitive to sunlight than usual
- changes in appetite or weight

Severe

- constipation
- difficulty urinating
- frequent urination
- blurred vision
- blood in urine
- fever
- difficulty breathing
- shortness of breath
- severe skin rash
- yellowing of the skin or eyes
- irregular heartbeat
- prolonged erection

Drug Interactions: monoamine oxidase inhibitors (MAOIs), carbamazepine, fluoxetine, hypotensive agents, phenothiazines, selective serotonin reuptake inhibitors (SSRIs), herbal supplements

Dosage: Adults: 15–400 (600 max) mg/day, divided

Therapeutic levels: 2–4 weeks; peak blood levels 1 hour

Use with Children: Safety and efficacy for use in children under 18 years of age have not been established.

■ DEXEDRINE/DEXTROAMPHETAMINE SULFATE

Category: Stimulant/amphetamines

Used For: Part of the treatment for Attention-Deficit/Hyperactivity Disorder (ADHD)

Alternate uses: Obesity, narcolepsy

Function: Central nervous system stimulant that has a paradoxical effect of reducing Attention-Deficit/Hyperactivity Disorder (ADHD) symptoms; releases the neurotransmitter norepinephrine

Side Effects:

Common

- changes in appetite or weight
- insomnia
- irritability or anxiety
- decreased growth rate

Severe / seek immediate attention for:

- worsening of tics or Tourette syndrome
- pounding in chest
- fast heartbeat
- tremor
- difficulty moving
- psychotic episodes

Attention:

- May intensify symptoms of Tourette syndrome
- May be habit forming with potential for abuse

Drug Interactions: Guanethidine, monoamine oxidase inhibitors (MAOIs), furazolidone, tricyclic antidepressants, ammonium chloride, ascorbic acid, acetazolamide, sodium bicarbonate

Dosage: Adults: 10–60 mg/day, divided
Children over 6 years: 5–60 mg/day, divided
Children 3–5 years: 0.1–0.5 mg/kg/dose

Therapeutic levels: Peak blood levels 2 hours

Use with Children: Do not use as anorectic agent in children under 12 years. This drug is not recommended for Attention-Deficit/Hyperactivity Disorder (ADHD) in children under 3 years.

■ DILANTIN/PHENYTOIN

Category: Anticonvulsant
Used For: Seizure disorders
Alternate uses: Control arrhythmias (irregular heartbeat), migraine headaches, facial nerve pain
Function: Appears to act at motor cortex in inhibiting spread of seizure activity
Side Effects:

Common

- drowsiness
- redness, irritation, bleeding, and swelling of the gums
- upset stomach
- vomiting
- constipation
- stomach pain
- loss of taste and appetite
- weight loss
- difficulty swallowing
- mental confusion
- blurred or double vision
- insomnia
- nervousness
- muscle twitching
- headache
- increased hair growth

Seek immediate medical attention for:

- difficulty coordinating movements
- skin rash
- easy bruising
- tiny purple-colored skin spots
- bloody nose
- slurred speech
- unusual bleeding
- yellowing of the skin or eyes
- dark urine
- swollen glands
- fever
- sore throat

Drug Interactions: Cyclosporine, disopyramide, enteral nutritional therapy, folic acid, metyrapone, mexiletine, nondepolarizing muscle relaxants, phenobarbital, sodium valproate, valproic acid, primidone, sympathomimetics, theophyllines
Dosage: Adults: 300–400 mg/day, divided
Children: 300 (max) mg/day
Therapeutic levels: Peak blood levels 4–12 hours
Use with Children: As prescribed by physician

■ DIOVAN/VALSARTAN

Category: Hypertension
Used For: High blood pressure
Alternate uses: Treatment of heart failure in patients who are intolerant of angiotensin-converting enzyme (ACE) inhibitors
Function: Reduces constriction of blood vessels, lowers blood pressure, and stabilizes heart rate
Side Effects:

Common

- dizziness
- lightheadedness

Severe / seek immediate attention for:

- swelling of the face, eyes, lips, tongue, arms, or legs

- congestion
- cough
- diarrhea
- trouble sleeping
- headache
- muscle aches
- fever
- sore throat
- runny nose
- excessive tiredness

- difficulty breathing or swallowing
- fainting
- rash

Drug Interactions: Lithium
Dosage: Adults: 80–320 mg/day
Therapeutic levels: Peak blood levels 6 hours
Use with Children: Safety and efficacy have not been established for use in children under 18 years.

■ DORAL/QUAZEPAM

Category: Antianxiety/benzodiazepines
Used For: Insomnia (short-term)
Alternate uses: None
Function: Increased neural inhibition, blocking arousal of higher brain processes and assisting sleep
Side Effects:

Common
- headache
- drowsiness
- dizziness
- dry mouth
- stomachache
- vision changes
- diarrhea
- constipation
- appetite loss
- nervousness
- irritability
- memory loss
- ringing in the ears
- sore throat
- joint pain

Severe / seek immediate attention for:
- irregular heartbeat
- chest pain
- yellowing of the skin or eyes
- rash
- unusual bleeding or bruising

Drug Interactions: Alcohol, central nervous system depressants, cimetidine, disulfiram, omeprazole, digoxin, theophylline
Dosage: Adults: 7.5–12 mg/day
Therapeutic levels: Peak blood levels 2 hours
Use with Children: Safety and efficacy have not been established for use in children under 18 years.

■ EFFEXOR/VENLAFAXINE HCL

Category: Antidepressant
Used For: Depression
Alternate uses: Generalized Anxiety Disorder
Function: Inhibit reabsorption of neurotransmitters serotonin and nerepinephrine
Side Effects:

Common
- nausea
- sweating
- constipation
- twitching
- dry mouth
- anxiety
- drowsiness
- dizziness
- headache
- chest pain
- fast heartbeat
- itching
- agitation
- confusion
- abnormal thinking
- personality changes
- depression
- impaired urination
- sleeplessness
- weakness
- appetite/weight loss
- diarrhea
- blurred vision
- vomiting
- abnormal dreams
- muscle stiffness
- mood changes
- taste change
- ringing in the ears

Severe / seek immediate attention for:
- seizures

Attention: Venlafaxine should not be taken if taking or have taken any monoamine oxidase inhibitor (MAOI; e.g., Nardil Parnate) within the last 2 weeks.
Drug Interactions: Desipramine, haloperidol, monoamine oxidase inhibitors (MAOIs), St. John's wort, sibutramine, sumatriptan, trazodone.
Dosage: Adults: 75–225 mg/day, divided
Therapeutic levels: 3 days
Use with Children: Safety and efficacy for use in children under 18 years of age have not been established.

ELAVIL/AMITRIPTYLINE HCL

Category: Tricyclic antidepressant
Used For: Depression
Alternate uses: Anxiety associated with depression
Function: Inhibits the reuptake of transmitters norepinephrine and serotonin
Side Effects:

Common

- upset stomach
- drowsiness
- weakness or tiredness
- excitement or anxiety
- insomnia
- nightmares
- dry mouth
- skin more sensitive to sunlight than usual
- changes in appetite or weight

Severe

- constipation
- difficulty urinating
- frequent urination
- blurred vision
- changes in sex drive or ability
- excessive sweating

Seek immediate attention for:

- jaw, neck, and back muscle spasms
- slow or difficult speech
- shuffling walk
- persistent fine tremor or inability to sit still
- fever
- difficulty breathing or swallowing
- severe skin rash
- yellowing of the skin or eyes
- irregular heartbeat

Drug Interactions: Barbiturates, charcoal, cimetidine, fluoxetine, clonidine, central nervous system depressants, monoamine oxidase inhibitors (MAOIs)
Dosage: Adults: 75–150 mg/day, divided
Adolescents: 10 mg 3 times/day with 20 mg at bedtime
Therapeutic levels: Up to 30 days
Use with Children: Not recommended for children under 12 years

ELDEPRYL/SELEGILINE HCL

Category: Antidepressant/monoamine oxidase inhibitor (MAOI)
Used For: Parkinson's disease
Alternate uses: None
Function: Inhibits reuptake of neurotransmitters serotonin and noepinephrine
Side Effects:

Common

- dizziness
- dry mouth
- upset stomach
- vomiting
- loss of appetite
- heartburn
- constipation

Seek immediate attention for:

- severe headache
- chest pain
- fast, irregular, or pounding heartbeat
- tremors
- confusion
- involuntary movements of hands or face
- nightmares
- difficulty breathing
- difficulty urinating

Drug Interactions: Fluoxetine, meperidine
Dosage: Adults: 10 mg/day, divided
Therapeutic levels: Reduce dose after 2–3 days
Use with Children: Effects have not been evaluated.

■ EQUANIL/MEPROBAMATE

Category: Antianxiety
Used For: Short-term (less than 4 months) treatment of Anxiety Disorders and hypertension in individuals older than 6 years
Alternate uses: None
Function: Acts on limbic system and thalamus to relax skeletal muscles
Side Effects:

Common

- drowsiness
- clumsiness
- dizziness
- slurred speech
- headache
- feeling of whirling motion
- weakness
- abnormal skin sensations
- vision problems
- exaggerated sense of well-being
- overstimulation
- excitement
- nausea
- vomiting
- diarrhea
- pounding in the chest
- fast heartbeat
- irregular heartbeat
- fainting
- rash

Seek immediate attention for:

- severe uncontrollable fever
- chills
- facial swelling
- breathing problems
- infrequent urination
- inability to urinate
- severe allergic reaction (itching, redness, swelling, hives, difficulty breathing)
- skin inflammation
- inflammation of the mouth and rectum
- dependence

Attention:

- May support drug dependence and abuse.
- Medicine should be gradually reduced over a period of 1 to 2 weeks

Drug Interactions: Alcohol, central nervous system depressants
Dosage: Adults: 400 mg/day, 3–4 times
Children 6–12 years: 200–600 mg/day, divided
Therapeutic levels: Peak blood levels 1–3 hours
Use with Children: Do not administer to children under 6 years of age because of a lack of documented evidence of safety and efficacy. The 600 mg tablet is not intended for use in children.

■ ETRAFON/PERPHENAZINE WITH AMITRIPTYLINE HCL

Category: Antidepressant (effects of amitriptyline) combined with tranquilizer (effects of perphenazine)
Used For: Anxiety/agitation with depressed mood
Alternate uses: Treatment of Schizophrenia with associated depression
Function: Blocks reuptake of neurotransmitters serotonin and norepinephrine and appears to block dopamine receptors
Side Effects:

Common
- upset stomach
- drowsiness
- weakness or tiredness
- excitement or anxiety
- insomnia
- nightmares
- dry mouth
- skin more sensitive to sunlight than usual
- changes in appetite or weight

Severe
- constipation
- difficulty urinating
- frequent urination
- blurred vision
- changes in sex drive or ability
- excessive sweating

Seek immediate attention for:
- jaw, neck, and back muscle spasms
- slow or difficult speech
- shuffling walk
- persistent fine tremor or inability to sit still
- fever
- difficulty breathing or swallowing
- severe skin rash
- yellowing of the skin or eyes
- irregular heartbeat
- tardive dyskinesia (see explanation in introduction)
- neuroleptic malignant syndrome (see explanation in introduction)

Drug Interactions: Amphetamines, anticholinergics, barbiturates, carbamazepine, charcoal, cimetidine, fluoxetine, haloperidol, clonidine, central nervous system depressants, guanethidine, lithium, monoamine oxidase inhibitors (MAOIs), metrizamide, sympathomimetics
Dosage: Adults: do not exceed 8 tablets of any strength.
Therapeutic levels: Not documented
Use with Children: Not recommended for use in children

■ FELBATOL/FELBAMATE

Category: Anticonvulsant
Used For: Seizure disorders
Alternate uses: Lennox-Gastaut syndrome; rarely used due to risks of developing aplastic anemia
Function: Reduces abnormal or diffuse brain cell electrical charges; increases seizure threshold
Side Effects:

Severe
- fever
- fatigue
- weight loss
- pain

- drowsiness
- sleeplessness
- nervousness
- headache
- abnormal thinking
- clumsiness
- urinary problems
- mood swings
- small pupils
- rash
- loss of appetite
- vomiting
- constipation
- hiccups
- nausea
- indigestion
- hives
- upper respiratory tract infection
- constipation
- coughing
- sore throat
- ear infection

Attention:

- Significant risk of developing serious and potential fatal condition of aplastic anemia.

Drug Interactions: Antiepileptic drugs

Dosage: Adults: 45 (max) mg/kg/day, divided
Children 2–14 with Lennox-Gastaut syndrome: 45 (max) mg/kg/day

Therapeutic levels: Not documented

Use with Children: Safety and efficacy have not been established other than for adjunctive therapy of Lennox-Gastaut syndrome.

■ FOCALIN/DEXMETHYLPHENIDATE HCL

Category: Stimulant

Used For: Part of the treatment for Attention-Deficit/Hyperactivity Disorder (ADHD; effectiveness beyond 6 weeks undetermined)

Alternate uses: None

Function: Inhibit reuptake of neurotransmitters norepinephrine and dopamine

Side Effects:

Common

- stomach pain
- fever
- loss of appetite
- upset stomach
- vomiting
- difficulty falling asleep or staying asleep

Seek immediate attention for:

- fast or pounding heartbeat
- muscle twitching
- blurred vision
- seizures
- abnormal thinking
- seeing things or hearing voices that do not exist (hallucinations)

- dizziness
- nervousness
- weight loss
- skin rash
- headache
- motion tics
- verbal tics

Severe (none listed)

Attention:

- Dexmethylphenidate can be habit forming.
- Taking too much dexmethylphenidate can cause abnormal behavior, including violence.
- Do not stop taking dexmethylphenidate without talking to your doctor.

Drug Interactions: Antihypertensive agents, pressor agents (e.g., dopamine), oumarin anticoagulants (e.g., warfarin), anticonvulsants (e.g., phenytoin), tricyclic antidepressants (e.g., amitriptyline), selective serotonin reuptake inhibitors (SSRIs; e.g., fluoxetine), monoamine oxidase inhibitors (MAOIs)

Dosage: Children over 6 years: 5–20 mg/day, divided

Therapeutic levels: Peak blood level 1–1.5 hours

Use with Children: Safety and efficacy in children under 6 years of age have not been established. Long-term effects in children have not been well established

■ GABITRIL/TIAGABINE HCL

Category: Anticonvulsant

Used For: Adjunctive treatment for partial seizure disorders

Alternate uses: None

Function: May block reuptake of neurotransmitter gamma-aminobutyric acid (GABA) to help inhibit neural activity in parts of the brain

Side Effects:

Common

- dizziness
- fatigue
- depression
- confusion
- impaired concentration
- speech or language problems
- lack of energy
- weakness
- upset stomach
- nervousness
- tremor
- stomach pain

Seek immediate attention for:

- rash
- change in vision
- seizures following one after another without a break

Severe (none listed)

Drug Interactions: Carbamazepine, phenytoin, primidone, phenobarbital

Dosage: Adults: 4–56 mg/day, divided
Adolescents: 4–32 mg/day, divided

Therapeutic levels: 2 days; peak blood levels 45 minutes

Use with Children: Safety and efficacy in children under 12 years not established

■ GEODON/ZIPRASIDONE HCL

Category: Antipsychotic
Used For: Psychotic Disorders, Schizophrenia
Alternate uses: None
Function: Decreases abnormal brain activity and psychotic symptoms by blocking neurotransmitters serotonin and dopamine
Side Effects:

Common
- drowsiness
- weakness
- upset stomach
- constipation
- diarrhea
- dry mouth
- loss of appetite
- muscle pain
- restlessness
- runny nose
- sneezing
- cough
- weight gain

Seek immediate attention for:
- dizziness
- rapid, irregular, or pounding heart beat
- fainting
- rash or hives
- fever
- muscle rigidity
- confusion
- sweating
- puckering of the lips and tongue
- writhing of the arms or legs
- painful erection of penis that lasts for hours
- breast enlargement
- irregular menstrual periods
- vision problems
- tardive dyskinesia (see explanation in introduction)
- neuroleptic malignant syndrome (see explanation in introduction)

Drug Interactions: Alcohol, central nervous system–acting drugs, amiodarone, dofetilide, dolasetron, droperidol, levomethadyl, moxifloxacin, pimozide, quinidine, sotalol, sparfloxacin, tacrolimus, thioridazine, antihypertensive agents, carbamazepine, ketoconazole, dopamine agonists, levodopa
Dosage: Adults: 20–80 mg/day, divided
Therapeutic levels: 1–3 days; peak blood levels 6–8 hours
Use with Children: Safety and efficacy with children not established

■ HALCION/TRIAZOLAM

Category: Benzodiazapines
Used For: Insomnia (short-term treatment)
Alternate uses: None
Function: Increases neuronal inhibition and central nervous system (CNS) depression
Side Effects:

Common
- headache
- heartburn

Seek immediate attention for:
- jaw, neck, and back muscle spasms
- slow or difficult speech

- diarrhea
- hangover effect (grogginess)
- drowsiness
- dizziness or lightheadedness
- weakness
- dry mouth

Severe

- constipation
- difficulty urinating
- frequent urination
- blurred vision
- persistent fine tremor or inability to sit still
- fever
- difficulty breathing or swallowing
- severe skin rash
- yellowing of the skin or eyes
- irregular heartbeat

Drug Interactions: Alcohol, central nervous system depressants, cimetidine, disulfiram, omeprazole, oral contraceptives, digoxin, theophylline

Dosage: Adults: 0.125–0.25 mg/day

Therapeutic levels: Peak blood levels 2 hours

Use with Children: Not for use in children under 18 years

■ HALDOL/HALOPERIDOL

Category: Antipsychotic

Used For: Psychotic Disorders, Tourette syndrome, severe behavioral problems in children, short-term treatment of hyperactivity

Alternate uses: None

Function: Blocks neurotransmitter dopamine receptors, decreases psychotic symptoms

Side Effects:

Common

- drowsiness
- dry mouth
- constipation
- restlessness
- headache
- weight gain

Seek immediate attention for:

- tremor
- restlessness or pacing
- fine wormlike tongue movements
- unusual face, mouth, or jaw movements
- shuffling walk
- slow, jerky movements
- seizures or convulsions
- fast, irregular, or pounding heartbeat
- difficulty urinating or loss of bladder control
- confusion
- eye pain or discoloration
- difficulty breathing or fast breathing
- fever
- skin rash
- severe muscle stiffness
- unusual tiredness or weakness
- unusual bleeding or bruising
- yellowing of the skin or eyes

- tardive dyskinesia (see explanation in introduction)
- neuroleptic malignant syndrome (see explanation in introduction)

Drug Interactions: Anesthetics, opiates, alcohol, anticholinergics, azole antifungal agents, carbamazepine, lithium, rifamycins

Dosage: Adults: 3 to 5 mg/2–3 times/day
Children 3–12 years: 0.05–0.075 mg/kg/day

Therapeutic levels: After 3–4 doses

Use with Children: Do not use in children under 3 years. Safety and efficacy of IM/injection form have not been established.

■ INDERAL/PROPRANOLOL HCL

Category: Beta-adrenergic blocker, antihypertensive

Used For: Hypertension

Alternate uses: Long-term management of cardiac arrhythmias, rage reactions associated with brain injuries; prevention of migraine headaches and tremors

Function: Blocks certain neuropathways in brain, lowers blood pressure and heart rate, stabilizes cardiac functioning

Side Effects:

Common

- dizziness or lightheadedness
- difficulty sleeping
- excessive tiredness
- upset stomach
- vomiting
- rash
- diarrhea
- constipation

Severe (none listed)

Seek immediate attention for:

- difficulty breathing
- sore throat
- unusual bleeding
- swelling of the feet or hands
- unusual weight gain
- chest pain
- slow, irregular heartbeat

Attention:

- Do not stop taking propranolol without talking to your doctor. If stopped suddenly, it may cause chest pain or heart attack.

Drug Interactions: Barbiturates, cimetidine, clonidine, epinephrine, ergot derivatives, hydralazine, insulin, lidocaine, nonsteroidal anti-inflammatory drugs (NSAIDs), phenothiazines, prazosin, methimazole, propafenone, propylthiouracil, quinidine, rifabutin, rifampin, theophylline, verapamil

Dosage: Adults: 120–240 mg/day, divided
Children: not above 16 mg/kg/day

Therapeutic levels: Peak blood levels 1–2 hours

Use with Children: Safety and efficacy have not been established. Intravenous (IV) use is not recommended, but oral propranolol has been used.

■ INVERSINE/MECAMYLAMINE

Category: Antihypertensive
Used For: Hypertension
Alternate uses: None
Function: Ganglionic blocking agent
Side Effects:

Common
- urinary retention
- dizziness
- lightheadedness
- constipation
- vomiting
- nausea
- loss of appetite
- inflammation of the tongue
- dry mouth
- blurred vision
- enlarged pupils
- weakness
- tiredness
- drowsiness

Severe (none listed)

Seek immediate attention for:
- fainting
- tremors
- abnormal movements
- convulsions
- abnormal thinking

Drug Interactions: Anesthetics, other antihypertensives, alcohol, antibiotics, sulfonamides
Dosage: Adults: initial does of 2.5 mg/day
Therapeutic levels: Not documented
Use with Children: Safety and efficacy not established

■ KLONOPIN/CLONAZEPAM

Category: Anticonvulsant/benzodiazepines/central nervous system (CNS) depressant
Used For: Seizure disorders, Panic Disorders
Alternate uses: Anxiety, Obsessive-Compulsive Disorder
Function: Unknown; possible suppression of spike and wave discharge intensity in seizure activity
Side Effects:

Common
- drowsiness
- dizziness
- tiredness
- weakness
- dry mouth
- diarrhea
- upset stomach
- changes in appetite

Severe
- restlessness or excitement
- constipation

Seek immediate attention for:
- seizures
- shuffling walk
- persistent fine tremor or inability to sit still
- fever
- difficulty breathing or swallowing
- severe skin rash
- yellowing of the skin or eyes
- irregular heartbeat

- difficulty urinating
- frequent urination
- blurred vision

Drug Interactions: Alcohol and CNS depressants, carbamazepine, phenytoin, rifampin, cimetidine, oral contraceptives, disulfiram, digoxin, theophyllines

Dosage: Adults: 20 mg/kg/day (max)
Children: 0.2 mg/kg/day (max), divided

Therapeutic levels: Blood peak levels 1–4 hours

Use with Children: The initial dose should be small and dosage increments made gradually, in accordance with the response of the individual, to preclude ataxia or excessive sedation. For treatment of Panic Disorder, safety and efficacy have not been established.

LAMICTAL/LAMOTRIGINE

Category: Anticonvulsant

Used For: Seizure management, Lennox-Gastaut syndrome

Alternate uses: Bipolar Disorder

Function: Unknown; may inhibit release of excitatory amino acids

Side Effects:

Common

- drowsiness
- upset stomach
- vomiting
- diarrhea
- changes in balance
- loss of taste and appetite
- headache
- irritability
- insomia

Severe (none listed)

Seek immediate attention for:

- fever
- swollen lymph nodes
- redness of skin
- swelling

Attention:

- Can cause serious rashes that can be fatal (toxic epidermal necrolysis) and Stevens-Johnson Syndrome

Drug Interactions: Acetaminophen, carbamazepine, phenytoin, oral contraceptives, oxcarbazepine, phenobarbital, primidone, progestins, rifamycins, methsuximide, carbamazepine, folate inhibitors, valproic acid

Dosage: Adults: 150–500 mg/day, divided

Therapeutic levels: Peak blood levels 1–4 hours

Use with Children: For the treatment of partial seizures and for generalized seizures of Lennox-Gastaut syndrome, safety and efficacy have not been established for children under 2 years. For other uses in seizure disorders, safety and efficacy have not been established in children under 16 years. Safety and efficacy have not been established in patients under 18 years with Bipolar Disorder.

LIBRIUM/CHLORDIAZEPOXIDE HCL

Category: Antianxiety/central nervous system (CNS) depressant/Benzodiazepines

Used For: Anxiety, tension

Alternate uses: Irritable bowel syndrome

Function: Appears to increase neural inhibition

Side Effects:

Common

- drowsiness
- dizziness
- tiredness
- weakness
- dry mouth
- diarrhea
- upset stomach
- changes in appetite

Severe

- restlessness or excitement
- constipation
- difficulty urinating
- frequent urination
- blurred vision

Seek immediate attention for:

- shuffling walk
- persistent fine tremor or inability to sit still
- fever
- difficulty breathing or swallowing
- severe skin rash
- yellowing of the skin or eyes
- irregular heartbeat

Drug Interactions: Alcohol and CNS depressants, azole antifungal agents (e.g., itraconazole, ketoconazole), fluvoxamine, isoniazid, nefazodone, protease inhibitors (e.g., indinavir), cigarette smoking, theophyllines, cimetidine, oral contraceptives, disulfiram, omeprazole, digoxin, rifamycins

Dosage: Adults: 100 (max) mg/day
Children over 6 years: 10–30 mg/day, divided

Therapeutic levels: 1–2 days; peak blood levels 0.5–4 hours

Use with Children: Not recommended for children under 6 years

LIMBITROL/CHLORDIAZEPOXIDE AND AMITRIPTYLINE HCL

Category: Psychotherapeutic combination/anti-anxiety (chlordiazepoxide) and tricyclic antidepressant (amytriptyline)

Used For: Depression associated with moderate to severe anxiety

Alternate uses: None

Function: Increases neural inhibition and blocks reuptake of neurotransmitter norepinephrine

Side Effects:

Common

- vivid dreams
- impotence
- tremors
- confusion
- stuffy nose
- loss of appetite

Seek immediate attention for:

- jaundice (yellowing of the skin or eyes)

- tiredness
- weakness
- restlessness
- lack of energy

Severe (none listed)

Drug Interactions: Cimetidine, fluoxetine, haloperidol, phenothiazine antipsychotic compounds, oral contraceptives, cimetidine, disulfiram, fluoxetine, isoniazid, ketoconazole, metoprolol, propoxyphene, propranolol, valproic acid, clonidine, central nervous system depressants, alcohol, digoxin, guanethidinem, monoamine oxidase inhibitors (MAOIs), oral anticoagulants

Dosage: Adults: 3–4 tablets/day, divided

Therapeutic levels: Not documented

Use with Children: Not recommended in children under 12 years

■ LITHIUM/LITHIUM CARBONATE

Category: Antipsychotic

Used For: Bipolar Disorder

Alternate uses: Episodic anger/aggression, Schizophrenia, alcoholism, Depressive Disorders, migraine headaches, premenstrual tension, bulimia, tardive dyskinesia, hyperthyroidism, postpartum affective psychosis, corticosteroid-induced psychosis, neutropenia (cancer-induced and in AIDS patients receiving zidovudine)

Function: Unknown; appears to increase reuptake of neutrotransmitters serotonin and norepinephrine; diminishes manic symptoms

Side Effects:

Common

- weakness
- hand tremors
- diarrhea
- vomiting
- drowsiness
- muscle weakness
- incoordination
- dizziness
- muscle twitching
- feeling of a whirling motion
- rapid eye movement
- loss of bladder and bowel control
- restlessness
- confusion
- stupor
- drying and thinning of the hair; hair loss
- psoriasis
- blurred vision
- dry mouth
- dehydration
- loss of appetite

Seek immediate attention for:

- blackouts
- seizures
- slurred speech
- severe slow heartbeat

- nausea
- decreased urination

Severe (none listed)

Drug Interactions: Acetazolamide, osmotic diuretics, theophyllines, urinary alkalinizers, angiotensin-converting enzyme (ACE) inhibitors, fluoxetine, loop diuretics, nonsteroidal anti-inflammatory drugs (NSAIDs), thiazide diuretics, carbamazepine, haloperidol, methyldopa, iodide salts neuromuscular blocking agents, tricyclic antidepressants, phenothiazines, verapamil

Dosage: Adults: 900–1800 mg/day, divided
Children over 12 years: 15–20 mg/kg/day, divided

Therapeutic levels: 1–3 weeks; peak blood levels 3 hours

Use with Children: Safety and efficacy not established in children under 12 years

■ LOPRESSOR/METOPROLOL TARTRATE

Category: Antihypertensive/beta-adrenergic blocker

Used For: High blood pressure, angina, heart arrhythmias

Alternate uses: Panic attacks, aggressive behavior

Function: Blocks beta receptors, lowers blood pressure and heart rate, stabilizes cardiac functioning

Side Effects:

Common

- dizziness or lightheadedness
- excessive tiredness
- upset stomach
- vomiting
- diarrhea
- constipation
- rash
- cold hands and feet

Severe (none listed)

Seek immediate attention for:

- difficulty breathing
- sore throat and fever
- unusual bleeding
- swelling of the feet or hands
- unusual weight gain
- chest pain
- slow, irregular heartbeat

Attention:

- Do not stop taking metoprolol without talking to your doctor. If stopped suddenly, it may cause chest pain or heart attack.

Drug Interactions: Barbiturates, cimetidine, clonidine, Hydralazine, lidocaine, nonsteroidal anti-inflammatory drugs (NSAIDs), prazosin, methimazole, propafenone, propylthiouracil, quinidine, rifampin, verapamil

Dosage: Adults: 100–450 mg/day

Therapeutic levels: Peak blood levels within an hour

Use with Children: Safety and efficacy not established in children

■ LOXITANE/LOXAPINE SUCCINATE

Category: Antipsychotic/tranquilizer

Used For: Psychotic Disorders/Schizophrenia

Alternate uses: None

Function: Unknown; has calming effect and reduces aggressive behavior

Side Effects:

Common

- drowsiness
- dizziness
- blurred vision
- dry mouth
- upset stomach
- vomiting
- diarrhea
- constipation
- headache
- *Severe* (none listed)

Seek immediate attention for:

- tremor
- restlessness or pacing
- fine wormlike tongue movements
- unusual face, mouth, or jaw movements
- slow or difficult speech
- difficulty swallowing
- seizures
- fever
- yellowing of the skin or eyes
- tardive dyskinesia (see explanation in introduction)
- neuroleptic malignant syndrome (see explanation in introduction)

Drug Interactions: Lorazepam

Dosage: Adults: 60–100 mg/day, divided

Therapeutic levels: Peak blood levels 1.5–3 hours

Use with Children: Safety and efficacy not established in children

■ LUVOX/FLUVOXAMINE MALEATE

Category: Antidepressant

Used For: Obsessive-Compulsive Disorder

Alternate uses: Depression, Tourette syndrome

Function: Blocks the reabsorption of neurotransmitter serotonin

Side Effects:

Common

- drowsiness
- dry mouth
- upset stomach
- headache
- diarrhea
- constipation
- indigestion
- nervousness
- tremor
- weakness
- difficulty sleeping
- *Severe* (none listed)

Seek immediate attention for:

- rapid heartbeat
- sweating
- skin rash
- hives
- seizures or convulsions

Drug Interactions: Cisapride, pimozide, cyproheptadine, lithium, tryptophan, monoamine oxidase inhibitors (MAOIs), smoking, amphetamine, St. John's wort, warfarin, clozapine, tricyclic antidepressants, benzodiazepines, carbamazepine, methadone, metoprolol, propranolol, theophylline, tacrine, cyclosporine

Dosage: Adults: 50–300 mg/day, divided
Children over 8 years: 50–200 mg/day, divided

Therapeutic levels: 1 week; peak blood levels 3–8 hours
Use with Children: Safety and efficacy in patients less than 8 years have not been established.

■ MEBARAL/MEPHOBARBITAL

Category: Barbiturate/sedative/hypnotic/anticonvulsant
Used For: Insomnia; epilepsy
Alternate uses: None
Function: Depresses sensory activity in brain, decreases motor activity
Side Effects:

Common

- agitation
- confusion
- hyperactivity
- clumsiness
- nightmares
- nervousness
- sleeplessness
- anxiety
- dizziness
- abnormal thinking
- fainting
- nausea
- vomiting
- constipation
- headache
- fever
- drowsiness
- *Severe* (none listed)

Seek immediate attention for:

- hallucinations
- severe allergic reaction (rash, itching, difficulty breathing, tightness in the chest, severe diarrhea)
- yellowing of the skin or eyes
- breathing difficulties

Drug Interactions: Alcohol, central nervous system depressants, anticoagulants, beta-blockers, doxycycline, felodipine, griseofulvin, methadone, metronidazole, nifedipine, quinidine, theophyllines, verapamil, anticonvulsants, estrogens, estrogen-containing oral contraceptives, monoamine oxidase inhibitors (MAOIs), methoxyflurane, phenytoin
Dosage: Adults: 400–600 mg/day, divided
Children over 5 years: 32–64 mg/day, 3–4 times
Children under 5 years: 16–32 mg/day, 3–4 times
Therapeutic levels: Peak blood levels 30–60 minutes
Use with Children: As prescribed by physician

■ MELLARIL/THIORIDAZINE

Category: Antipsychotic
Used For: Psychotic Disorders, Schizophrenia
Alternate uses: None
Function: Appears to block dopamine receptors and diminishes psychotic symptoms

Side Effects:

Common
- drowsiness
- dizziness
- blurred vision
- dry mouth
- upset stomach
- vomiting
- diarrhea
- constipation
- restlessness
- headache
- weight gain

Severe (none listed)

Seek immediate attention for:
- cardiac irregularities
- tremor
- restlessness or pacing
- fine wormlike tongue movements
- unusual face, mouth, or jaw movements
- difficulty swallowing
- shuffling walk
- seizures or convulsions
- difficulty urinating or loss of bladder control
- yellowing of the skin or eyes
- tardive dyskinesia (see explanation in introduction)
- neuroleptic malignant syndrome (see explanation in introduction)

Attention:
- May cause life-threatening irregular heartbeat
- Should only be used in cases where there has been poor response to other antipsychotic medications

Drug Interactions: Alcohol and other central nervous system depressants, anticholinergics, barbiturate anesthetics, beta blockers, cisapride, fluoxetine, paroxetine, propranolol, pindolol, epinephrine, lithium

Dosage: Adults: 200–800 mg/day, divided
Children 2–12 years: 0.5–3.0 (max) mg/kg/day, divided

Therapeutic levels: Not documented

Use with Children: As prescribed by physician

■ METADATE/METHYLPHENIDATE HCL

Category: Stimulant

Used For: Part of treatment for Attention-Deficit/Hyperactivity Disorder

Alternate uses: Narcolepsy

Function: Unknown; may activate brain stem arousal system and have paradoxical calming effect

Side Effects:

Common
- nervousness
- difficulty falling alseep or staying asleep
- dizziness
- drowsiness
- upset stomach
- vomiting
- headache
- loss of appetite

Severe (none listed)

Seek immediate attention for:
- seizures or convulsions
- blurred vision
- agitation
- skin rash
- heart palpitations or irregular heartbeat
- fever
- sore throat
- unusual bleeding or bruising

Attention:
- May be habit forming
- May exacerbate or initiate symptoms of Tourette syndrome

Drug Interactions: Anticonvulsants, selective serotonin reuptake inhibitors (SSRIs), tricyclic antidepressants, coumarin anticoagulants, guanethidine, monoamine oxidase inhibitors (MAOIs)
Dosage: Adults: 20–60 mg/day
Children over 6 years: 5–60 mg/day, divided
Therapeutic levels: Peak blood levels 2 hours
Use with Children: Do not give to children under 6 years because safety and efficacy are not established. Carefully monitor children on long-term therapy, especially for growth in height and weight.

■ METHYLIN/METHYLPHENIDATE HCL

Category: Stimulant
Used For: Part of treatment for Attention-Deficit/Hyperactivity Disorder
Alternate uses: Narcolepsy
Function: Unknown; may activate brain stem arousal system and have paradoxical calming effects
Side Effects:

Common
- nervousness
- difficulty falling asleep or staying asleep
- dizziness
- drowsiness
- upset stomach
- vomiting
- headache
- loss of appetite

Severe (none listed)

Seek immediate attention for:
- seizures or convulsions
- blurred vision
- agitation
- skin rash
- heart palpitations or irregular heartbeat
- fever
- sore throat
- unusual bleeding or bruising

Attention:
- May be habit forming
- May exacerbate or initiate symptoms of Tourette syndrome

Drug Interactions: Anticonvulsants, selective serotonin reuptake inhibitors (SSRIs), tricyclic antidepressants, coumarin anticoagulants, guanethidine, monoamine oxidase inhibitors (MAOIs)
Dosage: Adults: 20–30 mg/day, divided
Children over 6 years: 60 (max) mg/day, divided
Therapeutic levels: Peak blood levels 2 hours
Use with Children: Do not give to children under 6 years because safety and efficacy are not established. Carefully monitor children on long-term therapy, especially for growth in height and weight.

■ MOBAN/MOLINDONE HCL

Category: Antipsychotic
Used For: Psychotic Disorders, Schizophrenia
Alternate uses: None
Function: Appears to block neurotransmitter dopamine and diminishes psychotic symptoms; acts as tranquilizer
Side Effects:

Common

- drowsiness
- dry mouth
- upset stomach
- vomiting
- diarrhea
- constipation
- restlessness
- headache

Severe none listed

Seek immediate attention for:

- tremor
- restlessness or pacing
- fine wormlike tongue movements
- unusual face, mouth, or jaw movements
- shuffling walk
- slow, jerky movements
- seizures or convulsions
- fast, irregular, or pounding heartbeat
- difficulty urinating or loss of bladder control
- eye pain or discoloration
- difficulty breathing or fast breathing
- unusual tiredness or weakness
- unusual bleeding or bruising
- yellowing of the skin or eyes
- tardive dyskinesia (see explanation in introduction)
- neuroleptic malignant syndrome (see explanation in introduction)

Drug Interactions: None well documented
Dosage: Adults: 30–100 mg/day
Therapeutic levels: Blood peak levels 1.5 hours
Use with Children: Safety and efficacy not established in children under 12 years

■ MYSOLINE/PRIMIDONE

Category: Anticonvulsant
Used For: Seizure disorders
Alternate uses: Tremors
Function: Unknown; raises seizure threshold and alters seizure patterns
Side Effects:

Common

- drowsiness
- incoordination
- irritability
- excitement (in children)
- upset stomach
- tiredness

Seek immediate attention for:

- seizures
- sore throat
- fever
- severe skin rash
- yellowing of the skin or eyes
- dark urine

- headache
- changes in appetite

Severe

- restlessness or excitement
- hair loss
- swollen eyelids or legs
- double vision
- blurred vision
- bloody nose
- unusual bleeding
- tiny purple skin spots
- easy bruising

Drug Interactions: Anticoagulants, beta blockers, carbamazepine, corticosteroids, doxycycline, estrogens, oral contraceptives, ethanol, felodipine, griseofulvin, hydantoins, valproic acid, methadone, methoxyflurane, metronidazole, nifedipine, quinidine, succinimides, theophyllines

Dosage: Adults: 750–1000 mg/day, divided
Children over 8 years: 750–1000 mg/day, divided
Children under 8 years: 375–750 mg/day, divided

Therapeutic levels: Blood peak levels 3 hours

Use with Children: As prescribed by physician

■ NARDIL/PHENELZINE SULFATE

Category: Monoamine oxidase inhibitors (MAOIs)/antidepressant

Used For: Atypical depression

Alternate uses: Depression when unresponsive to other antidepressants, bulimia, Panic Disorder with Agoraphobia

Function: Increases neurotransmitters serotonin and norepinephrine by inhibiting breakdown and reuptake

Side Effects:

Common

- upset stomach
- drowsiness
- weakness or tiredness
- excitement or anxiety
- insomnia
- nightmares
- dry mouth
- skin more sensitive to sunlight than usual
- changes in appetite or weight

Severe

- constipation
- difficulty urinating
- frequent urination
- blurred vision
- excessive sweating

Seek immediate attention for:

- severe headache
- jaw, neck, and back muscle spasms
- neck stiffness or soreness
- swelling of legs or arms
- fever, chills, sore throat, or flulike symptoms
- difficulty breathing or swallowing
- severe skin rash
- yellowing of the skin or eyes
- irregular heartbeat
- hypertensive crisis

Drug Interactions: Amine-containing foods, anorexiants, central nervous system (CNS) depressants, dextromethorphan, fluoxetine, paroxetine, sertraline, trazodone, guanethidine, insulin, sulfonylureas, levodopa, meperidine, sympathomimetics, tricyclic antidepressants, buspirone, cyclobenzaprine, carbamazepine, maprotiline, guanethidine, central nervous system stimulants, tyramine

Dosage: Adults: 60–90 mg/day, divided
Therapeutic levels: 4 weeks; blood peak levels 2–3 hours
Use with Children: Not recommended in children under 16 years

■ NAVANE/THIOTHIXENE HCL

Category: Antipsychotic
Used For: Psychotic Disorders, Schizophrenia
Alternate uses: None
Function: Blocks neurotransmitter dopamine receptors
Side Effects:

Common
- drowsiness
- dizziness or blurred vision
- dry mouth
- upset stomach
- vomiting
- diarrhea
- constipation
- restlessness
- headache
- weight gain

Severe (none listed)

Seek immediate attention for:
- tremor
- restlessness or pacing
- fine wormlike tongue movements
- unusual face, mouth, or jaw movements
- shuffling walk
- seizures or convulsions
- fast, irregular, or pounding heartbeat
- difficulty urinating or loss of bladder control
- yellowing of the skin or eyes
- tardive dyskinesia (see explanation in introduction)
- neuroleptic malignant syndrome (see explanation in introduction)

Drug Interactions: Alcohol, other central nervous system depressants, anticholinergics, guanethidine
Dosage: Adults: 20–30 mg/day
Therapeutic levels: Blood levels peak at 2–3 hours; absorption can be erratic and can vary.
Use with Children: Not recommended in children under 12 years

■ NEURONTIN/GABAPENTIN

Category: Anticonvulsant
Used For: Adjunctive therapy for partial seizure disorders
Alternate uses: None
Function: Unknown; binding sites found in neocortex and hippocampus of the brain
Side Effects:

Common
- drowsiness
- headache
- fatigue
- blurred vision

Seek immediate attention for:
- itching
- difficulty moving or breathing
- clumsiness
- fever

- tremor
- anxiety
- irregular eye movements
- flulike symptoms
- irregular, pounding, or fast heartbeat
- seizures

Severe (none listed)

Drug Interactions: Antacids, cimetidine

Dosage: Adults: 900–1800 mg/day, divided
Children 5 years and older: 25–35 mg/kg/day, divided
Children 3–4 years: 40 mg/kg/day, divided

Therapeutic levels: Not documented

Use with Children: Safety and efficacy in children under 3 years not established; safety and efficacy in management of postherpetic neuralgia in pediatric patients not established

■ NORPRAMIN/DESIPRAMINE HCL

Category: Tricyclic antidepressant

Used For: Depression

Alternate uses: Panic Disorders, Eating Disorders

Function: Appears to inhibit reuptake of neurotransmitters norepinephrine and serotonin

Side Effects:

Common

- upset stomach
- drowsiness
- weakness or tiredness
- excitement or anxiety
- insomnia
- nightmares
- dry mouth
- skin more sensitive to sunlight than usual
- changes in appetite or weight

Severe

- constipation
- difficulty urinating
- frequent urination
- blurred vision
- excessive sweating

Seek immediate attention for:

- jaw, neck, and back muscle spasms
- slow or difficult speech
- shuffling walk
- persistent fine tremor or inability to sit still
- fever
- difficulty breathing or swallowing
- severe skin rash
- yellowing of the skin or eyes
- irregular heartbeat

Drug Interactions: Barbiturates, carbamazepine, charcoal, cimetidine, fluoxetine, haloperidol, quinidine, oral contraceptives, phenothiazine antipsychotics, clonidine, central nervous system (CNS) depressants, monoamine oxidase inhibitors (MAOIs)

Dosage: Adults: 100–200 mg/day
Adolescents: 25–100 mg/day

Therapeutic levels: 2–4 weeks; rapid absorption

Use with Children: This medication is not recommended in children under 18 years, because efficacy has not been established with this group.

■ ORAP/PIMOZIDE

Category: Antipsychotic
Used For: Treatment of motor and vocal tics in Tourette syndrome when unresponsive to standard treatments
Alternate uses: Schizophrenia
Function: Blocks neurotransmitter dopamine receptors
Side Effects:

Common
- sleepiness
- headache
- weakness
- dry mouth
- diarrhea
- constipation
- unusual hunger or thirst
- muscle tightness
- changes in posture
- difficulty falling or staying asleep
- nervousness
- changes in behavior
- changes in taste
- eyes sensitive to light
- changes in vision
- decreased sexual ability
- rash

Seek immediate attention for:
- unusual movements of body or face that cannot be controlled
- high fever
- muscle stiffness
- confusion
- sweating
- fast heartbeat
- shuffling walk
- restlessness
- difficulty moving any part of body
- difficulty speaking
- tardive dyskinesia (see explanation in introduction)
- neuroleptic malignant syndrome (see explanation in introduction)

Severe (none listed)

Drug Interactions: Central nervous system depressants, amphetamine, methylphenidate, pemoline, aprepitant, azole antifungal agents, macrolide antibiotics, nefazodone, phenothiazines, protease inhibitors, sertraline, tricyclic antidepressants, voriconazole, zileuton, ziprasidone, grapefruit juice
Dosage: Adults: 1–10 mg/day; dosages greater than 10 mg/day or 0.2 mg/kg/day not recommended
Therapeutic levels: Peak blood levels 6–8 hours
Use with Children: There is limited information regarding use, efficacy, and safety in patients under 12 years.

■ PAMELOR/NORTRIPTYLINE HCL

Category: Tricyclic antidepressant
Used For: Depression
Alternate uses: Anxiety Disorders, Attention-Deficit/Hyperactivity Disorder (ADHD)
Function: Inhibits reuptake of neurotransmitters norepinephrine and serotonin
Side Effects:

Common
- upset stomach
- drowsiness
- weakness or tiredness

Seek immediate attention for:
- jaw, neck, and back muscle spasms
- slow or difficult speech
- shuffling walk

- excitement or anxiety
- insomnia
- nightmares
- dry mouth
- skin more sensitive to sunlight than usual
- changes in appetite or weight

Severe
- constipation
- difficulty urinating
- frequent urination
- blurred vision
- excessive sweating
- persistent fine tremor or inability to sit still
- fever
- difficulty breathing or swallowing
- severe skin rash
- yellowing of the skin or eyes
- irregular heartbeat

Drug Interactions: Anticoagulants, carbamazepine, cimetidine, fluoxetine, central nervous system (CNS) depressants, clonidine, guanethidine, monoamine oxidase inhibitors (MAOIs), sympathomimetics.

Dosage: Adults: 75–100 mg/day, divided; doses above 150 mg/day not recommended

Adolescents: 30–50 mg/day, divided

Therapeutic levels: Not documented

Use with Children: Safety and efficacy not established

■ PARNATE/TRANYLCYPROMINE SULFATE

Category: Monoamine oxidase inhibitor (MAOI)/antidepressant

Used For: Reactive depression; used when unresponsive to other antidepressants

Alternate uses: Bulimia, Panic Disorder with Agoraphobia

Function: Increases neurotransmitters serotonin and norepinephrine by inhibiting breakdown and reuptake

Side Effects:

Common
- upset stomach
- drowsiness
- weakness or tiredness
- excitement or anxiety
- insomnia
- nightmares
- dry mouth
- skin more sensitive to sunlight than usual
- changes in appetite or weight

Severe
- constipation
- difficulty urinating
- frequent urination
- blurred vision
- excessive sweating

Seek immediate attention for:
- severe headache
- jaw, neck, and back muscle spasms
- neck stiffness or soreness
- swelling of legs or arms
- fever, chills, sore throat, or flulike symptoms
- difficulty breathing or swallowing
- severe skin rash
- yellowing of the skin or eyes
- irregular heartbeat

Drug Interactions: Amine-containing foods, anorexiants, central nervous system (CNS) depressants, dextromethorphan, fluoxetine, fluvoxamine, nefazodone,

paroxetine, sertraline, trazodone, venlafaxine, guanethidine, levodopa, meperidine, sympathomimetics, tricyclic antidepressants, busipirone, carbamazepine, central nervous system stimulants, cyclobenzaprine, maprotiline, tyramine
Dosage: Adults: 30 mg/day, divided
Therapeutic levels: 1–3 weeks; blood peak levels 3 hours
Use with Children: Not recommended for children under 16 years

■ PAXIL/PAROXETINE HCL

Category: Antidepressant/selective serotonin reuptake inhibitors (SSRIs)
Used For: Obsessive-Compulsive Disorder, Panic Disorder, Major Depressive Disorder
Alternate uses: Posttraumatic Stress Disorder (PTSD), Generalized Anxiety Disorder
Function: Inhibits reabsorption of neurotransmitter serotonin.
Side Effects:

Common
- upset stomach
- drowsiness
- weakness or tiredness
- excitement or anxiety
- insomnia
- nightmares
- dry mouth
- changes in appetite or weight

Severe
- constipation
- difficulty urinating
- frequent urination
- blurred vision
- excessive sweating

Seek immediate attention for:
- jaw, neck, and back muscle spasms
- slow or difficult speech
- shuffling walk
- persistent fine tremor or inability to sit still
- fever, chills, sore throat, or flulike symptoms
- difficulty breathing or swallowing
- severe skin rash
- yellowing of the skin or eyes
- irregular heartbeat

Drug Interactions: Cimetidine, cyclosporine, cyproheptadine, CYP2D6 system, digoxin, hemostatic agents, monoamine oxidase inhibitors (MAOIs), phenobarbital, phenytoin, procyclidine, protein bound agents, sibutramine, St. John's wort, sympathomimetics, amphetamine, theophylline, thioridazine, tricyclic antidepressants, tryptophan, warfarin, zolpidem
Dosage: Adults: 20–50 mg/day
Therapeutic levels: 2 weeks; peak blood levels 5–6 hours
Use with Children: Safety and efficacy not established

■ PHENOBARBITAL

Category: Central nervous system (CNS) depressant/barbiturate/sedative and hypnotic
Used For: Seizure disorders; emergency of acute convulsive episodes
Alternate uses: Anxiety Disorders, insomnia (short-term)
Function: Decreases sensory cortex and motor activity, produces sedation

Side Effects:

Common
- drowsiness
- headache
- dizziness
- depression
- excitement (especially in children)
- upset stomach
- vomiting

Severe
- nightmares
- increased dreaming
- constipation
- joint or muscle pain

Seek immediate attention for:
- seizures
- mouth sores
- sore throat
- easy bruising
- bloody nose
- unusual bleeding
- fever
- difficulty breathing or swallowing
- severe skin rash

Attention: Large doses of naltrexone may cause liver failure; doctor should be notified if patient has liver or kidney disease.

Drug Interactions: Alcohol, central nervous system depressants, anticoagulants, beta blockers, doxycycline, metronidazole, quinidine, theophyllines, verapamil, anticonvulsants, corticosteroids, estrogens, estrogen-containing oral contraceptives, phenytoin

Dosage: Adults: 60–200 mg/day
Children: 3–6 mg/kg/day

Therapeutic levels: Peak blood levels 1 hour

Use with Children: As per physician recommendation

■ PROLIXIN/FLUPHENAZINE HCL

Category: Antipsychotic

Used For: Psychotic Disorders, Schizophrenia

Alternate uses: Tourette syndrome

Function: Blocks neurotransmitter dopamine receptors and reduces psychotic symptoms

Side Effects:

Common
- upset stomach
- drowsiness
- weakness or tiredness
- excitement or anxiety
- insomnia
- nightmares
- dry mouth
- skin more sensitive to sunlight than usual
- changes in appetite or weight

Severe
- constipation
- difficulty urinating

Seek immediate attention for:
- jaw, neck, and back muscle spasms
- slow or difficult speech
- shuffling walk
- persistent fine tremor or inability to sit still
- fever, chills, sore throat, or flulike symptoms
- difficulty breathing or swallowing
- severe skin rash
- yellowing of the skin or eyes
- irregular heartbeat
- tardive dyskinesia (see explanation in introduction)

- frequent urination
- blurred vision
- changes in sex drive or ability
- excessive sweating
- neuroleptic malignant syndrome (see explanation in introduction)

Drug Interactions: Alcohol and other central nervous system (CNS) depressants, anticholinergics, barbiturate anesthetics, beta blockers, bromocriptine, cisapride, sparfloxacin, guanethidine, hydantoins lithium, metrizamide, paroxetine
Dosage: Adults: 2–10 mg/day, frequently administered as an injection
Therapeutic levels: Not documented
Use with Children: Not recommended in children under 12 years

PROVIGIL/MODAFINIL

Category: Central nervous system (CNS) stimulant
Used For: Narcolepsy
Alternate uses: Attention-Deficit/Hyperactivity Disorder (ADHD)
Function: Unknown; effects similar to those of other stimulant medications
Side Effects:

Common
- headache
- upset stomach
- nervousness
- difficulty falling asleep or staying asleep
- dizziness
- depression
- diarrhea
- runny nose
- dry mouth
- loss of appetite
- vomiting
- neck pain or stiffness
- confusion or forgetfulness

Severe (none listed)

Seek immediate attention for:
- chest pain
- fast, pounding, or irregular heartbeat
- shortness of breath
- rash or hives
- fever, sore throat, chills, and other signs of infection

Drug Interactions: Certain tricyclic antidepressants, clomipramine, contraceptives, oral, cyclosporine, monoamine oxidase inhibitors (MAOIs), methylphenidate, phenytoin
Dosage: Adults: 200 mg/day
Therapeutic levels: Peak blood levels 2–4 hours
Use with Children: Safety and efficacy in children under 16 years not established

PROZAC/FLUOXETINE HCL

Category: Antidepressant/selective serotonin reuptake inhibitor (SSRI)
Used For: Depression
Alternate uses: Panic attacks, Obsessive-Compulsive Disorder, bulimia, obesity, Premenstrual Dysphoric Disorder (PMDD)

Function: Inhibits reabsorption of neurotransmitter serotonin
Side Effects:

Common
- upset stomach
- drowsiness
- weakness or tiredness
- excitement or anxiety
- insomnia
- nightmares
- dry mouth
- skin more sensitive to sunlight than usual
- changes in appetite or weight

Severe
- constipation
- difficulty urinating
- frequent urination
- blurred vision
- excessive sweating

Seek immediate attention for:
- jaw, neck, and back muscle spasms
- slow or difficult speech
- shuffling walk
- persistent fine tremor or inability to sit still
- fever, chills, sore throat, or flulike symptoms
- difficulty breathing or swallowing
- severe skin rash or hives
- yellowing of the skin or eyes
- irregular heartbeat

Drug Interactions: Naratriptan, rizatriptan, sumatriptan, zolmitriptan, benzodiazepines, beta blockers, buspirone, carbamazepine, clozapine, cyclosporine, cyproheptadine, haloperidol, hydantoins, lithium, monoamine oxidase inhibitors (MAOIs), amphetamine, tricyclic antidepressants
Dosage: Adults: 20–60 (80 max) mg/day
Children: 8–18 years: 10–60 mg/day
Therapeutic levels: 4–8 weeks; peak blood levels 6–8 hours
Use with Children: Safety and efficacy not established

■ REMERON/MIRTAZAPINE

Category: Antidepressant
Used For: Major depression
Alternate uses: None
Function: Unknown; may enhance neurotransmitter noradrenergic and serotonergic activity
Side Effects:

Common
- drowsiness
- dizziness
- anxiousness
- confusion
- increased weight and appetite
- dry mouth
- constipation
- upset stomach
- vomiting

Severe (none listed)

Seek immediate attention for:
- flulike symptoms, fever, chills, sore throat, mouth sores, or other signs of infection
- chest pain
- fast heartbeat
- seizures
- agranulocytosis

Drug Interactions: Alcohol, central nervous system depressants, monoamine oxidase inhibitors (MAOIs)

Dosage: Adults: 15–45 mg/day
Therapeutic levels: 1 week; peak blood levels 2 hours
Use with Children: Safety and efficacy not established

■ RESTORIL/TEMAZEPAM

Category: Central nervous system (CNS) depressant/benzodiazepines/sedative
Used For: Insomnia (short-term treatment)
Alternate uses: None
Function: Increases neural inhibition and blocks arousal of higher brain processes
Side Effects:

Common
- headache
- heartburn
- diarrhea
- hangover effect (grogginess)
- drowsiness
- dizziness or lightheadedness
- weakness
- dry mouth

Severe (none listed)

Seek immediate attention for:
- jaw, neck, and back muscle spasms
- slow or difficult speech
- persistent fine tremor or inability to sit still
- fever
- difficulty breathing or swallowing
- severe skin rash
- yellowing of the skin or eyes
- irregular heartbeat

Drug Interactions: Alcohol, other central nervous system depressants, digoxin, theophylline
Dosage: Adults: 7.5–30 mg/day
Therapeutic levels: Peak blood levels 90 minutes
Use with Children: Not for use in children under 18 years

■ REVIA/NALTREXONE

Category: Opiate agonist
Used For: Alcoholism; substance addiction
Alternate uses: Eating Disorders
Function: Blocks opioid receptors; markedly attenuates or completely blocks, reversibly, the subjective effects of intravenously administered opioids
Side Effects:

Common
- alcoholism
- nausea
- headache
- dizziness
- nervousness
- drowsiness
- sleeplessness
- vomiting
- anxiety
- substance abuse

Seek immediate attention for:
- stomach pain for more than a few days
- white bowel movements
- dark urine
- yellowing of the skin or eyes

- difficulty sleeping
- stomach pain or cramps
- vomiting
- low energy
- joint and muscle pain
- appetite loss
- diarrhea
- constipation
- increased thirst
- increased energy
- irritability

Severe
- depression
- thoughts of suicide; suicide attempt

Attention:
- Large doses of naltrexone may cause liver failure, which may be life threatening.

Drug Interactions: Disulfiram, opioid-containing medication, thioridazine
Dosage: Adults: 25–50 mg/day
Therapeutic levels: Not documented
Use with Children: Safety and efficacy not established in children under the age of 18 years

RISPERDAL/RISPERIDONE

Category: Antipsychotic/benzisoxdole derivative
Used For: Psychotic Disorders, Schizophrenia, bipolar mania
Alternate uses: Aggression, tics associated with Tourette syndrome, behavioral problems with Autism
Function: Apparently blocks neurotransmitters dopamine's and serotonin's receptors, reduces psychotic symptoms, improves negative psychotic symptoms
Side Effects:

Common
- drowsiness
- dizziness
- upset stomach
- diarrhea
- constipation
- heartburn
- weight gain
- stomach pain
- increased dreaming
- anxiety
- agitation
- difficulty falling asleep or staying asleep
- decreased sexual interest or ability
- heavy bleeding during menstrual periods

Seek immediate attention for:
- fever
- muscle stiffness
- confusion
- fast or irregular pulse
- sweating
- unusual movements of face or body that cannot be controlled
- slow or difficult speech
- faintness
- weakness or numbness in an arm or leg
- seizures
- difficulty swallowing
- slow movements or shuffling walk
- shortness of breath
- rash

- runny nose
- cough
- sore throat
- muscle pain
- dry or discolored skin
- dry mouth
- difficulty urinating

Severe (none listed)

- painful erection of the penis that lasts for hours
- tardive dyskinesia (see explanation in introduction)
- neuroleptic malignant syndrome (see explanation in introduction)

Drug Interactions: Alcohol, central nervous system depressants, antihypertensives, carbamazepine, clozapine, fluoxetine, paroxetine, levodopa, and other dopamine agonists

Dosage: Adults: 4–6 mg/day, divided doses

Therapeutic levels: 1 week; peak blood levels 1 hour

Use with Children: Safety and efficacy not established with children under the age of 15 years

■ RITALIN/METHYLPHENIDATE HCL

Category: Stimulant

Used For: Part of treatment of Attention-Deficit Hyperactivity Disorder ADHD, Narcolepsy

Alternate uses: Depression in elderly patients and in patients who have cancer, brain injury, HIV, or stroke

Function: Unknown: activates brain stem arousal, paradoxically having calming effects

Side Effects:

Common

- nervousness
- difficulty falling asleep or staying asleep
- dizziness
- drowsiness
- upset stomach
- vomiting
- headache
- loss of appetite

Severe (none listed)

Seek immediate attention for:

- seizures or convulsions
- blurred vision
- agitation
- skin rash
- heart palpitations or irregular heartbeat
- fever
- sore throat
- unusual bleeding or bruising

Attention:

- May be habit forming
- May exacerbate or initiate symptoms of Tourette syndrome

Drug Interactions: Anticonvulsants, selective serotonin reuptake inhibitors (SSRIs), tricyclic antidepressants, coumarin anticoagulants, guanethidine, monoamine oxidase inhibitors (MAOIs)

Dosage: Adults: 20–30 mg/day
Children 6 years and older: 5–60 mg/day

Therapeutic levels: Peak blood levels 1–2 hours

Use with Children: This drug is not recommended for children under 6 years because safety and efficacy are not established. Carefully monitor children on long-term therapy, especially for growth in height and weight.

■ SERAX/OXAZEPAM

Category: Antianxiety/central nervous system (CNS) depressant
Used For: Anxiety Disorders (short-term treatment), also Anxiety Disorders associated with depression
Alternate uses: Alcohol withdrawal symptoms, irritable bowel syndrome
Function: Increased neural inhibition, blocking arousal of higher brain processes
Side Effects:

Common
- drowsiness
- dizziness
- tiredness
- weakness
- dry mouth
- diarrhea
- upset stomach
- changes in appetite

Severe
- restlessness or excitement
- constipation
- difficulty urinating
- frequent urination
- blurred vision

Seek immediate attention for:
- shuffling walk
- persistent fine tremor or inability to sit still
- fever
- difficulty breathing or swallowing
- severe skin rash
- yellowing of the skin or eyes
- irregular heartbeat

Drug Interactions: Alcohol, central nervous system depressants, digoxin, theophyllines
Dosage: Adults: 45–120 mg/day, 3–4 times
Therapeutic levels: Peak blood levels 3 hours
Use with Children: Dosage and efficacy not established in children under 6 years; absolute dosage not established for patients 6 to 12 years

■ SERENTIL/MESORIDAZINE BESYLATE

Category: Antipsychotic
Used For: Schizophrenia, organic brain disorders
Alternate uses: Alcoholism, Personality Disorders
Function: Appears to block neurotransmitter dopamine receptors
Side Effects:

Common
- drowsiness
- dry mouth
- upset stomach
- vomiting
- diarrhea
- constipation
- restlessness
- headache
- weight gain

Severe (none listed)

Seek immediate attention for:
- dizziness or seizures
- lightheadedness or fainting
- tremor
- jaw, neck, or back muscle spasms
- restlessness or pacing
- fine wormlike tongue movements
- unusual face, mouth, or jaw movements
- shuffling walk
- slow, jerky movements

- seizures or convulsions
- difficulty urinating or loss of bladder control
- eye pain or discoloration
- difficulty breathing or fast breathing
- skin rash
- yellowing of the skin or eyes
- cardiac arrhythmias
- tardive dyskinesia (see explanation in introduction)
- neuroleptic malignant syndrome (see explanation in introduction)

Attention:

- May cause serious heart problems that are life threatening.
- Should only be given to patients who have not responded to other medications appropriately.

Drug Interactions: Alcohol, central nervous system depressants, anticholinergics, drugs that prolong the QT interval, guanethidine, paroxetine

Dosage: Adults: 50–400 mg/day

Therapeutic levels: Not documented

Use with Children: Safety and efficacy not established

■ SEROQUEL/QUETIAPINE FUMARATE

Category: Antipsychotic (atypical)

Used For: Schizophrenia

Alternate uses: None

Function: Appears to block dopamine, serotonin, and other neurotransmitters; reduces psychotic symptoms

Side Effects:

Common

- dizziness
- lightheadedness
- dry mouth
- constipation
- upset stomach
- stomach pain
- headache
- tiredness
- excessive weight gain
- runny nose
- rash
- ear pain
- flu symptoms
- swollen ankles
- blurred vision

Severe (none listed)

Seek immediate attention for:

- fainting
- seizures
- increased body temperature (fever)
- muscle stiffness
- difficulty thinking clearly
- fast or irregular heartbeat
- muscle spasms
- fine wormlike tongue movements
- tremors
- shuffling walk
- inability to sit still
- jerky movements
- tardive dyskinesia (see explanation in introduction)
- neuroleptic malignant syndrome (see explanation in introduction)

Drug Interactions: Alcohol, central nervous system (CNS)–acting drugs, anti-

hypertensive agents, dopamine agonists, levodopa, hepatic enzymem, ketoconazole, itraconazole, fluconazole, fluoxetine, erythromycin, lorazepam, thioridazine
Dosage: Adults: 150–750 mg/day, divided
Therapeutic levels: 1–2 days: peak blood levels 1–2 hours
Use with Children: Safety and efficacy not established for children under the age of 17 years

■ SERZONE/NEFAZODONE HCL

Category: Antidepressant
Used For: Depression
Alternate uses: None
Function: Inhibits reuptake of neurotransmitters serotonin and norepinephrine
Side Effects:

Common
- upset stomach
- drowsiness
- weakness or tiredness
- excitement or anxiety
- insomnia
- nightmares
- dry mouth
- skin more sensitive to sunlight than usual
- changes in appetite or weight

Severe
- constipation
- difficulty urinating
- frequent urination
- blurred vision
- excessive sweating

Seek immediate attention for:
- jaw, neck, and back muscle spasms
- slow or difficult speech
- shuffling walk
- persistent fine tremor or inability to sit still
- fever
- difficulty breathing or swallowing
- severe skin rash
- irregular heartbeat
- seizures
- painful erections of the penis lasting more than 4 hours

Attention:
- May cause liver failure, which can be life threatening

Drug Interactions: Benzodiazepines, buspirone, carbamazepine, cisapride, digoxin, haloperidol, simvastatin, monoamine oxidase inhibitors (MAOIs), pimozide, propranolol, St. John's wort, sibutramine, sumatriptan, trazodone
Dosage: Adults: 300–600 mg/day, divided
Therapeutic levels: 4–5 days; peak blood levels 1 hour
Use with Children: Safety and efficacy in children under 18 years not established

■ SINEQUAN/DOXEPIN HCL

Category: Tricyclic antidepressant
Used For: Depression; anxiety associated with depression
Alternate uses: Enuresis, insomnia

Function: Appears to block reuptake of neurotransmitter norepinephrine
Side Effects:

Common
- upset stomach
- drowsiness
- weakness or tiredness
- excitement or anxiety
- insomnia
- nightmares
- dry mouth
- skin more sensitive to sunlight than usual
- changes in appetite or weight

Severe
- constipation
- difficulty urinating
- frequent urination
- blurred vision
- excessive sweating

Seek immediate attention for:
- jaw, neck, and back muscle spasms
- slow or difficult speech
- shuffling walk
- persistent fine tremor or inability to sit still
- fever
- difficulty breathing or swallowing
- severe skin rash
- yellowing of the skin or eyes
- irregular heartbeat

Drug Interactions: Cimetidine, clonidine, guanethidine, monoamine oxidase inhibitors (MAOIs), selective serotonin reuptake inhibitors (SSRIs), dopamine, epinephrine, propafenone, flecainide
Dosage: Adults: 75–150 mg/day
Therapeutic levels: 2–8 days
Use with Children: Not recommended for children under 12 years

■ STELAZINE/TRIFLUOPERAZINE HCL

Category: Antipsychotic
Used For: Schizophrenia
Alternate uses: Anxiety (short-term treatment)
Function: Blocks neurotransmitter dopamine receptors, reduces psychotic symptoms
Side Effects:

Common
- drowsiness
- dizziness or blurred vision
- dry mouth
- upset stomach
- vomiting
- diarrhea
- constipation
- restlessness
- headache
- weight gain

Severe (none listed)

Seek immediate attention for:
- tremor
- restlessness or pacing
- fine wormlike tongue movements
- unusual face, mouth, or jaw movements
- shuffling walk
- seizures or convulsions
- fast, irregular, or pounding heartbeat
- difficulty urinating or loss of bladder control
- yellowing of the skin or eyes
- tardive dyskinesia (see explanation in introduction)

- neuroleptic malignant syndrome (see explanation in introduction)

Drug Interactions: Alcohol, central nervous system depressants, anticholinergics, barbiturate anesthetics, beta blockers, cisapride, sparfloxacin, guanethidine, metrizamide, paroxetine
Dosage: Adults: 15–20 mg/day
Children over 6 years: 1–15 mg/day, based on weight
Therapeutic levels: 2–3 weeks; peak blood levels 2–4 hours
Use with Children: When drug is used in children with acute illnesses, there is susceptibility to neuromuscular reactions. Avoid use of drug in children and adolescents with signs and symptoms suggestive of Reye syndrome. This drug is not generally recommended for children under 12 years.

■ STRATTERA/ATOMOXETINE HCL

Category: Psychotherapeutic Attention-Deficit/Hyperactivity Disorder (ADHD) treatment
Used For: Part of treatment for Attention-Deficit/Hyperactivity Disorder (ADHD)
Alternate uses: None
Function: Unknown; thought to block reuptake of neurotransmitter norepinephrine
Side Effects:

Common
- heartburn
- upset stomach
- vomiting
- loss of appetite
- stomach pain
- constipation
- dry mouth
- excessive tiredness
- difficulty falling asleep or staying asleep
- dizziness
- headache
- mood swings
- irritability
- weight loss
- decreased sex drive or ability
- difficulty urinating
- painful menstrual periods
- cough
- runny nose
- violent behavior
- crying
- fever
- chills

Seek immediate attention for:
- pounding heartbeat
- swelling of the face, throat, tongue, lips, eyes, hands, feet, ankles, or lower legs
- hoarseness
- difficulty swallowing or breathing
- hives
- rash

- muscle pain
- sweating
- hot flashes

Severe (none listed)

Drug Interactions: Albuterol, fluoxetine, quinidine, monoamine oxidase inhibitors (MAOIs), pressor agents

Dosage: Adults: 40–100 (max) mg/day

Children under 70kg: 0.5–1.4 mg/kg/day or 100 mg, whichever is less

Therapeutic levels: Peak blood level 1–2 hours

Use with Children: Safety and efficacy not established in children under 6 years

■ SURMONTIL/TRIMIPRAMINE MALEATE

Category: Tricyclic antidepressant

Used For: Depression

Alternate uses: Nerve pain, Insomnia, enureses, ulcers

Function: Unknown; appears to block reuptake of neurotransmitters norepinephrine and serotonin

Side Effects:

Severe

- upset stomach
- vomiting
- diarrhea
- stomach pain
- drowsiness
- weakness or tiredness
- excitement or anxiety
- confusion
- dizziness
- headache
- difficulty falling asleep or staying asleep
- nightmares
- dry mouth
- changes in appetite or weight
- constipation
- difficulty urinating
- frequent urination
- blurred vision
- excessive sweating
- ringing in the ears
- painful, burning, or tingling feeling in the hands or feet

Seek immediate attention for:

- jaw, neck, and back muscle spasms
- slow or difficult speech
- shuffling walk
- persistent fine tremor or inability to sit still
- fever and sore throat
- difficulty breathing or swallowing
- severe skin rash
- yellowing of the skin or eyes
- seizures
- seeing things or hearing voices that do not exist (hallucinating)
- chest pain
- pounding or irregular heartbeat

Drug Interactions: Alcohol, central nervous system depressants, catecholamines/anticholinergics, cimetidine, amiodarone, fluoxetine, quinidine, monoamine oxidase inhibitors (MAOIs)

Dosage: Adults: 75–150 mg/day

Adolescents: 50–100 mg/day, divided

Therapeutic levels: 2–4 weeks
Use with Children: Safety and efficacy not established

■ TEGRETOL/CARBAMAZEPINE USP

Category: Anticonvulsant
Used For: Seizure disorders
Alternate uses: Aggression, chorea, facial nerve pain, restless leg syndrome
Function: Unknown; appears to depress thalamus and lower neuronal stimulation threshold
Side Effects:

Common
- drowsiness
- upset stomach
- vomiting
- stomach pain
- loss of appetite
- constipation
- diarrhea
- hallucinations
- insomnia
- agitation
- irritability (especially in children)
- drowsiness
- mental confusion
- headache
- difficulty coordinating movements
- speech problems
- dry mouth
- mouth or tongue irritation

Seek immediate attention for:
- red, itchy skin rash
- easy bruising
- tiny purple-colored skin spots
- bloody nose
- unusual bleeding
- yellowing of the skin or eyes
- fever
- sore throat
- mouth sores
- irregular heartbeat
- joint pain
- faintness
- swelling of the feet or lower legs
- seizures

Severe (none listed)

Attention:
- Risk of blood disorder agranulocytosis
- Risk of aplastic anemia

Drug Interactions: Acetaminophen, benzodiazepines, bupropion, clozapine, cyclosporine, olanzapine, succinimides, tiagabine, topiramate, ziprasidone, anticoagulants, azole antifungal agents, diltiazem, verapamil, danazol, propoxyphene, macrolide antibiotics (except azithromycin), barbiturates, charcoal, activated, cimetidine, contraceptives, oral, doxycycline hyclate, felbamate, felodipine, haloperidol, hydantoins, isoniazid, lamotrigine, lithium, monoamine oxidase inhibitors (MAOIs), voriconazole, nondepolarizing muscle relaxants, primidone, protease inhibitors, selective serotonin reuptake inhibitors (SSRIs), theophylline, tricyclic antidepressants, valproic acid
Dosage: Adults: 600–1200 mg/day
Children 6–12: 400–800 mg/day
Children under 6 years: 35 mg/kg/day
Therapeutic levels: Not documented
Use with Children: Management of epilepsy in children is derived from clinical investigations in adults; dosage in children is at physician's discretion.

■ TENEX/GUANFACINE HCL

Category: Antihypertensive
Used For: High blood pressure
Alternate uses: Migraine headaches, withdrawal symptoms
Function: Appears to stimulate central alpha 2-adrenergic receptors; relaxes and dilates blood vessels
Side Effects:

Common
- dry mouth
- drowsiness
- dizziness
- constipation
- tiredness
- headache
- upset stomach
- vomiting

Severe (none listed)

Seek immediate attention for:
- fainting
- increased or decreased heartbeat
- irregular heartbeat
- swollen ankles or feet

Drug Interactions: Alcohol, central nervous system depressants, barbiturates, phenytoin
Dosage: Adults: 1.0–3.0 mg/day
Therapeutic levels: 4 days; peak blood levels 1–4 hours
Use with Children: Safety and efficacy in children younger than 12 years not established

■ THORAZINE/CHLORPROMAZINE HCL

Category: Antipsychotic/tranquilizer
Used For: Psychotic Disorders
Alternate uses: Severe behavioral problems, severe hiccups, nausea and vomiting
Function: Blocks neurotransmitter dopamine receptors
Side Effects:

Common
- dry mouth
- drowsiness

Severe (none listed)

Seek immediate attention for:
- skin discoloration (yellowish-brown to greyish-purple)
- jaw, neck, and back muscle spasms
- pacing
- fine wormlike tongue movements
- rhythmic face, mouth, or jaw movements
- slow or difficult speech
- difficulty swallowing
- shuffling walk
- skin rash
- tardive dyskinesia (see explanation in introduction)
- neuroleptic malignant syndrome (see explanation in introduction)

Drug Interactions: Alcohol, central nervous system depressants, anticholinergics, barbiturate anesthetics, beta blockers, cisapride, sparfloxacin, epinephrine, norepinephrine, guanethidine, lithium, meperidine, metrizamide, paroxetine

Dosage: Adults: 200–800 (1000 max) mg/day, divided
Children: 0.25 mg/lb every 4–6 hours (to manage behavioral problems)

Therapeutic levels: Not documented

Use with Children: Do not use in children under 6 months unless considered life saving. This drug is not used in conditions for which a specific children's dosage is not established.

■ TOFRANIL/IMIPRAMINE HCL

Category: Tricyclic antidepressant

Used For: Depression

Alternate uses: Enuresis, Panic Disorder, Attention-Deficit/Hyperactivity Disorder (ADHD), chronic pain, Eating Disorders

Function: Inhibits reuptake of neurotransmitter norepinephrine

Side Effects:

Common
- upset stomach
- drowsiness
- weakness or tiredness
- excitement or anxiety
- insomnia
- nightmares
- dry mouth
- skin more sensitive to sunlight than usual
- changes in appetite or weight

Severe
- constipation
- difficulty urinating
- frequent urination
- blurred vision
- excessive sweating

Seek immediate attention for:
- jaw, neck, and back muscle spasms
- slow or difficult speech
- shuffling walk
- persistent fine tremor or inability to sit still
- fever
- difficulty breathing or swallowing
- severe skin rash
- yellowing of the skin or eyes
- irregular heartbeat

Drug Interactions: Carbamazepine, cimetidine, fluoxetine, clonidine, central nervous system depressants, dicumarol, guanethidine, monoamine oxidase inhibitors (MAOIs), sympathomimetics

Dosage: Adults: 50–150 mg/day
Children over 6 years: 25–100 mg/day, before bed; not to exceed 2.5 mg/kg/day

Therapeutic levels: 1–3 weeks; peak blood level 2–4 hours

Use with Children: Safety and efficacy as temporary adjunctive therapy for nocturnal enuresis in pediatric patients under 6 years have not been established; effect of long-term use in patients younger than 11 years has not been established

■ TOPAMAX/TOPIRAMATE

Category: Anticonvulsant
Used For: Adjunctive treatment for seizure disorders
Alternate uses: Cluster headaches, infantile spasms
Function: Unknown: appears to control spread of neuronal stimulation
Side Effects:

Common

- can cause hypoglycemia, especially in children

Severe

- slow thinking or movements
- difficulty concentrating
- speech problems, especially difficulty thinking of specific words
- memory problems
- lack of coordination
- trouble walking
- confusion
- nervousness
- aggressive behavior
- irritability
- mood swings
- depression
- headache
- extreme tiredness
- drowsiness
- weakness
- extreme thirst
- weight loss
- constipation
- diarrhea
- gas
- heartburn
- change in ability to taste food
- swelling of the tongue
- overgrowth of the gums
- dry mouth
- increased saliva
- trouble swallowing
- nosebleed
- teary or dry eyes
- back, muscle, or bone pain
- missed menstrual periods
- excessive menstrual bleeding
- skin problems or changes in skin color
- dandruff
- hair loss
- growth of hair in unusual places

Seek immediate attention for:

- blurred vision
- eye pain
- double vision
- tingling in fingers or toes
- shaking hands that cannot be brought under control
- restlessness, inability to sit still
- crossed eyes
- worsening of seizures
- slow heart rate
- pounding or irregular heartbeat
- chest pain
- trouble breathing
- fast, shallow breathing
- inability to respond to things going on around the patient
- upset stomach
- vomiting
- stomach pain
- loss of appetite
- excessive hunger
- unintentional loss of urine
- difficult or painful urination
- unusual bruising or bleeding
- sore throat, fever, chills, and other signs of infection
- muscle weakness
- bone pain

- runny nose
- difficulty falling or staying asleep

Drug Interactions: Alcohol, central nervous system depressants, carbamazepine, carbonic anhydrase inhibitors, oral contraceptives, phenytoin, valproic acid
Dosage: Adults: 200–400 mg/day, divided
Children 2–16: 5–9 mg/kg/day, divided
Therapeutic levels: 4 days; peak blood levels 2 hours
Use with Children: Safety and efficacy in children under 2 years of age not established

■ TRANXENE/CLORAZEPATE DIPOTASSIUM

Category: Antianxiety/central nervous system depressant/benzodiazepines
Used For: Anxiety Disorders, adjunct treatment for seizure disorders
Alternate uses: Alcohol withdrawal symptoms, irritable bowel syndrome
Function: Increases neural inhibition, reduces arousal of higher brain processes
Side Effects:

Common
- drowsiness
- dizziness
- tiredness
- weakness
- dry mouth
- diarrhea
- upset stomach
- changes in appetite

Severe
- restlessness or excitement
- constipation
- difficulty urinating
- frequent urination
- blurred vision

Seek immediate attention for:
- seizures
- shuffling walk
- persistent fine tremor or inability to sit still
- fever
- difficulty breathing or swallowing
- severe skin rash
- yellowing of the skin or eyes
- irregular heartbeat

Drug Interactions: Azole antifungal agents, fluvoxamine, isoniazid, erythromycin, nefazodone, delavirdine, efavirenz, indinavir, cimetidine, oral contraceptives, disulfiram, digoxin, omeprazole, rifamycins, theophyllines
Dosage: Adults: 30 mg/day, divided (max 90 mg/day)
Children 9–12: 60 (max) mg/day, divided
Therapeutic levels: 2 days; 1–2 hours
Use with Children: Initial dose should be small and gradually increased. This drug is not recommended in children under 9 years.

■ TRILAFON/PERPHENAZINE

Category: Antipsychotic
Used For: Psychotic Disorders
Alternate uses: Severe nausea and vomiting; hiccups; anxiety
Function: Blocks neurotransmitter dopamine receptors

Side Effects:

Common
- drowsiness
- dizziness
- blurred vision
- dry mouth
- upset stomach
- vomiting
- diarrhea
- constipation
- restlessness
- headache
- weight gain

Severe (none listed)

Seek immediate attention for:
- tremor
- restlessness or pacing
- fine wormlike tongue movements
- unusual face, mouth, or jaw movements
- shuffling walk
- seizures or convulsions
- fast, irregular, or pounding heartbeat
- difficulty urinating
- yellowing of the skin or eyes
- tardive dyskinesia (see explanation in introduction)
- neuroleptic malignant syndrome (see explanation in introduction)

Drug Interactions: Alcohol, central nervous system depressants, anticholinergics, barbiturate anesthetics, cisapride, sparfloxacin, guanethidine, metrizamide, paroxetine

Dosage: Adults: 8–24 mg/day
Children over 12 years: 4–12 mg/day

Therapeutic levels: Peak blood levels 1–3 hours

Use with Children: Not recommended in children younger than 12 years

■ TRILEPTAL/OXCARBAZEPINE

Category: Anticonvulsant

Used For: Seizure disorders

Alternate uses: None

Function: Unknown; appears to stabilize and reduce overactive electrical impulses in brain

Side Effects:

Common
- dizziness
- drowsiness
- headache
- vision changes
- double vision
- excessive tiredness
- upset stomach
- vomiting
- stomach pain
- tremors
- difficulty coordinating movements
- speech problems
- nervousness
- difficulty concentrating
- confusion

Severe (none listed)

Seek immediate attention for:
- red, itchy skin rash
- seizures
- shortness of breath
- rash with fever, swollen lymph nodes, and joint pain

Drug Interactions: Carbamazepine, oral contraceptives, felodipine, lamotrigine, Phenobarbital, phenytoin, valproic acid, verapamil
Dosage: Adults: 600–2400 (max) mg/day
Children 4–16 years: 900–1800 mg/day based on weight
Therapeutic levels: 2–3 days; peak blood levels 3–13 hours
Use with Children: Safety and efficacy have not been determined in patients under 4 years.

■ VALIUM/DIAZEPAM

Category: Central nervous system depressant/benzodiazepines
Used For: Anxiety Disorders; muscle relaxant
Alternate uses: Seizure disorders, muscle spasms, panic attacks, irritable bowel syndrome; also used as preoperative medication
Function: Increased neural inhibition
Side Effects:

Common
- drowsiness
- dizziness
- tiredness
- weakness
- dry mouth
- diarrhea
- upset stomach
- changes in appetite

Severe
- restlessness or excitement
- constipation
- difficulty urinating
- frequent urination
- blurred vision

Seek immediate attention for:
- seizures
- shuffling walk
- persistent fine tremor or inability to sit still
- fever
- difficulty breathing or swallowing
- severe skin rash
- yellowing of the skin or eyes
- irregular heartbeat

Drug Interactions: Azole antifungal agents, diltiazem, fluvoxamine, isoniazid, erythromycin, nefazodone, delavirdine, efavirenz, indinavir, cimetidine, oral contraceptives, disulfiram, digoxin, omeprazole, rifamycins, theophyllines
Incompatibilities: Diazepam interacts with plastic containers and IV tubing, significantly decreasing availability of drug delivered. Do not mix or dilute with other solutions or drugs in a syringe or infusion container.
Dosage: Adults: 40 mg/day
Children over 6 months: 10 (max) mg/day, divided
Therapeutic levels: Peak levels 0.5–2 hours
Use with Children: Oral form not recommended in patients younger than 6 months; parenteral form not recommended in infants younger than 30 days

■ VIVACTIL/PROTRIPTYLINE HCL

Category: Tricyclic antidepressant
Used For: Depression
Alternate uses: Obstructive sleep apnea, Panic Disorder

Function: Inhibits reuptake of neurotransmitters norepinephrine and serotonin

Side Effects:

Common

- lightheadedness
- confusion
- anxiety
- restlessness
- agitation
- nightmares
- incoordination
- weakness
- numbness
- tingling
- abnormal skin sensations
- fever
- urinary retention
- delayed urination
- dilation of the urinary tract
- blurred vision
- dry mouth
- sensitivity to sunlight
- nausea
- vomiting
- loss of appetite
- stomach pain
- diarrhea
- stomach cramps
- constipation
- headache

Seek immediate attention for:

- irregular heartbeat
- fast heartbeat
- pounding in the chest
- hallucinations
- disorientation
- delusions
- worsening of bizarre behavior
- panic attacks
- seizures
- tremors
- increased pressure in the eye
- black tongue

Severe (none listed)

Drug Interactions: Cimetidine, fluoxetine, central nervous system depressants, clonidine, dicumarol, guanethidine, monoamine oxidase inhibitors (MAOIs), sympathomimetics, norepinephrine, phenylephrine, sympathomimetics, dopamine, ephedrine

Dosage: Adults: 15–40 mg/day
Adolescents: three doses of 5 mg/day

Therapeutic levels: 2–3 weeks; peak blood levels 8–12 hours

Use with Children: Not recommended for use in children under 12 years of age

■ WELLBUTRIN/BUPROPION HCL

Category: Antidepressant

Used For: Depression

Alternate uses: Attention-Deficit/Hyperactivity Disorder, smoking cessation treatment

Function: Unknown; thought to block reuptake of neurotransmitters sertotonin, norepinephrine, and dopamine

Side Effects:

Common
- drowsiness
- weakness or tiredness
- excitement or anxiety
- dry mouth
- insomnia
- nightmares
- change in appetite or weight

Severe
- frequent urination
- difficulty urinating
- constipation
- blurred vision
- excessive sweating
- headaches

Seek immediate attention for:
- seizures or tremors
- loss of coordination
- fever
- severe skin rash
- itching
- hives
- chest pain
- shortness of breath
- muscle or joint pain
- yellowing of the skin or eyes
- irregular heartbeat

Attention:
- Can cause seizures when taken in large doses

Drug Interactions: Alcohol, amantadine, levodopa, antidepressants, antipsychotics, systemic steroids, theophylline, carbamazepine, monoamine oxidase inhibitors (MAOIs), selegiline, ritonavir, tricyclic antidepressants

Dosage: Adults: 300 mg/day, divided

Therapeutic levels: 4 weeks; peak blood levels 2 hours

Use with Children: Safety and efficacy not established in children under the age of 18 years

■ XANAX/ALPRAZOLAM

Category: Antianxiety/central nervous system (CNS) depressant/benzodiazepines

Used For: Anxiety, high blood pressure, Panic Disorder

Alternate uses: Anxiety associated with depression, irritable bowel syndrome, premenstrual syndrome, Agoraphobia

Function: Increased neural inhibition

Side Effects:

Common
- drowsiness
- dizziness
- tiredness
- weakness
- dry mouth
- diarrhea
- upset stomach
- changes in appetite

Severe
- restlessness or excitement
- constipation
- difficulty urinating
- frequent urination
- blurred vision

Seek immediate attention for:
- shuffling walk
- persistent fine tremor or inability to sit still
- fever
- difficulty breathing or swallowing
- severe skin rash
- yellowing of the skin or eyes
- irregular heartbeat

Attention:

- Long-term use not recommended
- May cause psychological and physiological dependence

Drug Interactions: Alcohol, central nervous system depressants, cimetidine, oral contraceptives, disulfiram, digoxin, diltiazem, fluvoxamine, grapefruit juice, erythromycin, nefazodone delavirdine, efavirenz, indinavir, itraconazole, ketoconazole, omeprazole, rifamycins, theophyllines

Dosage: Adults: 1.0–4.0 mg/day, divided

Therapeutic levels: 12 hours; peak blood level 1–2 hours

Use with Children: Safety and efficacy in children under 18 years not established

■ ZARONTIN/ETHOSUXIMIDE

Category: Anticonvulsant

Used For: Seizure disorders

Alternate uses: None

Function: Elevates seizure threshold and suppresses certain brain wave activity indicative of short lapses of consciousness

Side Effects:

Common

- drowsiness
- upset stomach
- vomiting
- constipation
- diarrhea
- stomach pain
- loss of taste and appetite
- weight loss
- irritability
- mental confusion
- depression
- insomnia
- nervousness
- headache

Seek immediate attention for:

- difficulty coordinating movements
- joint pain
- red, itchy skin rash
- easy bruising
- tiny purple-colored skin spots
- bloody nose
- unusual bleeding
- yellowing of the skin or eyes
- dark urine
- fever
- sore throat

Severe (none listed)

Drug Interactions: Hydantoins, primidone

Dosage: Adults: 500 mg/day
Children over 6 years: 500 (max) mg/day
Children 3–6 years: 250 mg/day

Therapeutic levels: Peak blood levels 3–7 hours

Use with Children: As prescribed by physician

■ ZOLOFT/SERTRALINE HCL

Category: Antidepressant/ selective serotonin reuptake inhibitor (SSRI)

Used For: Depression

Alternate uses: Obsessive-Compulsive Disorder, Panic Disorder, Posttraumatic Stress Disorder, social anxiety

Function: Inhibits or blocks reabsorption of neurotransmitter serotonin

Side Effects:

Common
- upset stomach
- drowsiness
- weakness or tiredness
- excitement or anxiety
- insomnia
- nightmares
- dry mouth
- skin more sensitive to sunlight than usual
- changes in appetite or weight

Severe
- constipation
- difficulty urinating
- frequent urination
- blurred vision
- excessive sweating

Seek immediate attention for:
- jaw, neck, and back muscle spasms
- slow or difficult speech
- shuffling walk
- persistent fine tremor or inability to sit still
- fever, chills, sore throat, or flulike symptoms
- difficulty breathing or swallowing
- severe skin rash
- yellowing of the skin or eyes
- irregular heartbeat

Drug Interactions: Naratriptan, rizatriptan, sumatriptan, zolmitriptan, alcohol, central nervous system depressants, cimetidine, clozapine, phenytoin, monoamine oxidase inhibitors (MAOIs), pimozide, St. John's wort, amphetamine, fenfluramine, tolbutamide, tricyclic antidepressants, propafenone, flecainide, zolpidem

Dosage: Adults: 50 (200 max) mg/day
Children 6–12 years: 25 mg/day

Therapeutic levels: 1 week; peak blood levels 4–8 hours

Use with Children: Safety and efficacy not established

■ ZYPREXA/OLANZAPINE

Category: Atypical antipsychotic

Used For: Schizophrenia

Alternate uses: Short-term treatment of acute mixed or manic episodes

Function: Unknown; may block neurotransmitter dopamine and serotonin receptors

Side Effects:

Severe
- headache
- agitation
- drowsiness
- constipation
- dry mouth
- upset stomach
- vomiting
- diarrhea

Seek immediate attention for:
- seizures
- uncontrollable jerking movements
- fever
- very stiff muscles
- excess sweating
- fast or irregular heartbeat

Drug Interactions: Antihypertensive drugs, carbamazepine, fluvoxamine, levodopa and other dopamine agonists, sedating drugs, alcohol

Dosage: Adults: 10–15 mg/day

Therapeutic levels: 1 week; peak blood levels 6 hours

Use with Children: Safety and efficacy not established for children under 17 years of age

18

Instruction and Assessment of Culturally and Linguistically Diverse Students

A Systematic Approach for English Language Development and Nondiscriminatory Assessment, Intervention, and Teaching

SAMUEL O. ORTIZ

INTRODUCTION

Few tasks facing teachers, administrators, and school professionals are more complex and misunderstood than those that relate to either providing an appropriate educational and instructional program to culturally and linguistically diverse students or evaluating and assessing their capabilities and achievement. As the nation's school-age population continues to become more and more diverse, schools are realizing that dealing with these issues, and dealing with them well, is unavoidable and often difficult. It was largely on the basis of the ever-growing training needs of school districts that the pages in this chapter were developed.

Perhaps the most important realization to come out of this attempt to provide training regarding issues involving the instruction or evaluation of diverse students was that it was impossible to stay within traditionally defined professional boundaries. It is not appropriate to teach school psychologists, for example, how to properly evaluate the achievement or cognitive abilities of culturally and linguistically diverse students if they do not understand language development and its relationship to various types of instruction and English language development methods. Likewise, it is nearly pointless to try and help special education teachers develop appropriate methods for instruction if they do not understand the impact of second language acquisition and cultural differences on expectations of classroom performance and current levels of functioning, particularly when tested. Consequently, the material contained in the pages that follow begins with concepts and information that span various disciplines, including those that generally fall under the province of general education (English as a second language [ESL] services, English language development, instructional strategies for English learners, etc.), those that are more identified with speech-language training (first and second language acquisition, bilingualism, language proficiency and development, etc.), and those that relate to assessment or evaluation (achievement or psychological testing, learning disability [LD] evaluations, speech-language evaluations, etc.).

It will become quickly apparent that the format of this chapter is very different than what is ordinarily encountered in other texts—in that there is no actual narrative or continuous discourse to follow. Instead, the reader is presented with vignettes or snapshots that are deliberately intended to provide information in a way that is clear and readily accessible. Each page covers a particular concept, idea, step, or procedure that has significant relevance in the teaching or assessment of individuals from culturally and linguistically diverse backgrounds.

The reason for such a format comes from the fact that these pages were designed specifically as tools for inservice training and formal workshop instruction. That is, they were developed primarily to facilitate the education of professionals within the context of professional development workshops and continuing education sessions. Unfortunately, the accessibility in comprehension that is gained by the brevity and to-the-point text is tempered by the lack of oral explanation that would ordinarily accompany each of the pages that follow. Although the vast majority of the pages are readily understood and mostly self-explanatory, there is no question that the reader's understanding would benefit more from the dialogue that normally accompanies them; consequently, references and resources have been added to support that end. Nonetheless, one of the primary purposes of this Almanac is to provide pages that are clear and easy to follow and understand, even without the aid of explanation. Accordingly, many of the pages contain enjoyable graphics, figures, and other materials that are designed to promote clarity and convey meaning as efficiently as possible.

For these and other practical reasons, the pages have been ordered somewhat in a way that mirrors the experience of students who are English-language learners, and is organized into five sections: (1) language and language development; (2) instruction and educational practices; (3) pre-assessment considerations; (4) assessment; and (5) intervention and special education.

The initial section focuses on basic language development, first language acquisition, and second language acquisition. Information regarding some common misconceptions about language is also included, and may prove surprising to many. The following section provides some basic strategies and guidance related to providing linguistically appropriate instruction to English learners, including the application of Vygotsky's Zone of Proximal Development (ZPD) and its relationship to cognitive and linguistic development. The next section, pre-assessment, is intended to guide educators and evaluators regarding issues that need to be considered when planning to conduct formal evaluations of English learners. This is followed by an extensive section on issues, methods, and procedures for conducting nondiscriminatory assessment that is couched within a 10-stage comprehensive framework for evaluation. The final section provides information on issues relevant to special education teachers and other educators, such as the development of culturally and linguistically appropriate IEP goals and objectives, as well as recommendations for instructional strategies that are helpful in remediation efforts with English learners.

Mixed in with the information are additional resources for educators, including some enjoyable tasks such as a quiz on special education law, interesting quotes about culture, humorous examples and illustrations regarding processing abilities used in reading, and other material that is intended to further explain and highlight many of the more salient points. In addition, the information is provided in a thematic manner that emphasizes a deliberate and decidedly transdisciplinary focus. This is done to further reinforce the notion that language, education, and evaluation all interact and influence each other in reciprocal, not linear ways.

LANGUAGE

Stages of Language Acquisition

Comprehensible input is essential in order to progress through these stages

Preproduction/Comprehension (no BICS)

Sometimes called the silent period, where the individual concentrates completely on figuring out what the new language means, without worrying about production skills. Children typically may delay speech in L2 from one to six weeks or longer.

listen **point** **match** **draw**
move **choose** **mime** **act out**

Early Production (early BICS)

Speech begins to emerge naturally but the primary process continues to be the development of listening comprehension. Early speech will contain many errors. Typical examples of progression are:

yes/no questions **lists of words**
one word answers **two word strings & short phrases**

Speech Emergence (intermediate BICS)

Given sufficient input, speech production will continue to improve. Sentences will become longer, more complex, with a wider vocabulary range. Numbers of errors will slowly decrease.

three words and short phrases **dialogue**
longer phrases **extended discourse**
complete sentences where appropriate **narration**

Intermediate Fluency (advancedBICS/emerging CALP)

With continued exposure to **adequate** language models and opportunities to interact with fluent speakers of the secondlanguage, second language learners will develop excellent comprehension and their speech will contain even fewer gramatical errors. Opportunities to use the second language for varied purposes will broaden the individual's ability to use the language more fully.

give opinions **analyse** **defend** **create**
debate **evaluate** **justify** **examine**

Figure 18.1 Language: Stages of Language Acquisition.
Source: Krashen, S. D. (1982). *Principles and Practice in Second Language Acquisition.* New York: Pergamon.

Language

Issues in Second Language Acquisition

Basic Interpersonal Communication Skills (BICS)

- *Ability to communicate basic needs and wants*
- *Ability to carry on basic interpersonal conversations*
- *Takes 1–3 years to develop*
- *Insufficient to facilitate academic success*

Cognitive Academic Language Proficiency (CALP)

- *Ability to communicate thoughts and ideas with clarity and efficiency*
- *Ability to carry on advanced interpersonal conversations*
- *Takes at least 5–7 years to develop, possibly longer*
- *Required for academic success*

Cummins' Developmental Interdependence Hypothesis

- *BICS is the small, visible, surface level of language.*
- *CALP is the larger, hidden, deeper structure of language ability.*
- *Each language has a unique and Separate Underlying Proficiency (SUP).*
- *Proficiency in a first language (L1) is required to develop proficiency in a second language (L2).*
- *Common Underlying Proficiency (CUP) facilitates transfer of cognitive skills.*

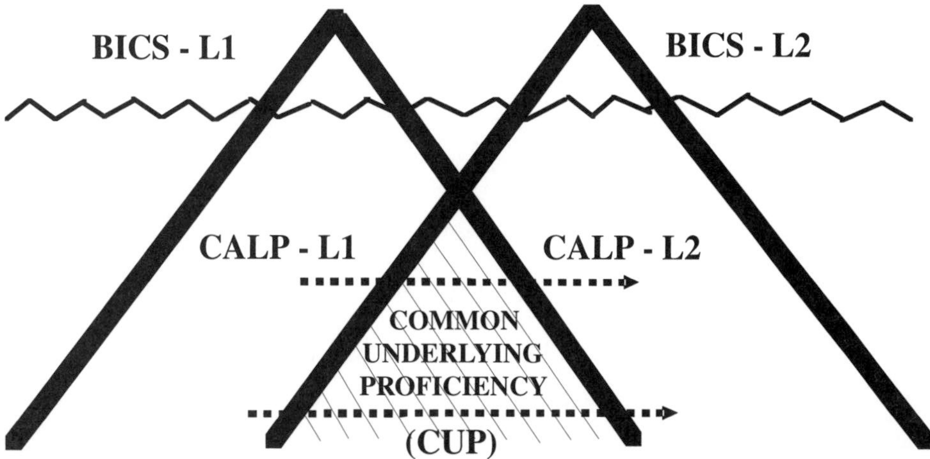

Figure 18.2 BICS—LI.

Source: Cummins, J. C. (1984). *Bilingual and Special Education: Issues in Assessment and Pedagogy.* Austin, TX: Pro-Ed.

LANGUAGE

Dimensions of Bilingualism and Relationship to Generations

Type	Stage	Language Use
		First generation—foreign born
A	Newly arrived	Understands little English. Learns a few words and phrases.
Ab	After several years of residence—type 1	Understands enough English to take care of essential everyday needs. Speaks enough English to make self understood.
Ab	Type 2	Is able to function capably in the work domain where English is required. May still experience frustration in expressing self fully in English. Uses immigrant language in all other contexts where English is not needed.
		Second generation—U.S. born
Ab	Preschool age	Acquires immigrant language first. May be spoken to in English by relatives or friends. Will normally be exposed to English-language TV.
Ab	School age	Acquires English. Uses it increasingly to talk to peers and siblings. Views English-language TV extensively. May be literate only in English if schooled exclusively in this language.
AB	Adulthood—type 1	At work (in the community) uses language to suit proficiency of other speakers. Senses greater functional ease in his first language in spite of frequent use of second.

Type	Stage	Language Use
A**B**	Adulthood—type 2	Uses English for most everyday activities. Uses immigrant language to interact with parents or others who do not speak English. Is aware of vocabulary gaps in his first language.
		Third generation—U.S. born
A**B**	Preschool age	Acquires both English and immigrant language simultaneously. Hears both in the home although English tends to predominate.
a**B**	School age	Uses English almost exclusively. Is aware of limitation sin the immigrant language. Uses it only when forced to do so by circumstances. Is literate only in English.
a**B**	Adulthood	Uses English almost exclusively. Has few opportunities for speaking immigrant language. Retains good receptive competence in this language.
		Fourth generation—U.S. born
Ba	Preschool age	Is spoken to only in English. May hear immigrant language spoken by grandparents and other relatives. Is not expected to understand immigrant language.
Ba	School age	Uses English exclusively. May have picked up some of the immigrant language from peers. Has limited receptive competence in this language.
B	Adulthood	Is almost totally English monolingual. May retain some receptive competence in some domains.

Source: Valdès, G., & Figueroa, R. A. (1994). *Bilingualism and testing: A special case of bias.* Norwood, NJ: Ablex.

Language

Popular Misconceptions about Acquisition, Learning, and Development

- *Accent is an indicator of proficiency*—no, it is only a marker that indicates when an individual first began to hear and/or learn the language.
- *Children learn languages faster and better than adults do*—no, they only seem to, because they have better pronunciation, but the Common Underlying Proficiency between languages aids adult learners considerably.
- *Language development can be accelerated*—no, but having developed one language to a high degree (i.e., developed Cognitive Academic Language Proficiency) does help in learning a second language more easily.
- *Learning two languages leads to a kind of linguistic confusion*—no, there is no evidence that learning two or more language simultaneously produces any type of cognitive interference whatsoever.
- *Learning two languages leads to poor academic performance*—no, on the contrary, students who learn two languages very well (have Cognitive Academic Language Proficiency in both) tend to outperform their monolingual peers in school.
- *Code-switching is an example of a language disorder and poor grammatical ability*—no, it is only an example of how bilinguals use whatever words may be necessary to communicate their thoughts as precisely as possible, irrespective of the language.

INSTRUCTION

Strategies for English Language Development

CONTENT-BASED ESL

This approach utilizes content, or subject-area material, as a vehicle for language acquisition and development. The content is modified to match the language proficiency of the students and is best used within a comprehensive English language development (ELD) program.

Content-based ELD does not replace content area instruction. In this way, it differs from Specially Designed Academic Instruction in English (SDAIE) or Sheltered English. Content-based ESL has language acquisition as its goal, whereas SDAIE has content mastery as its goal.

INSTRUCTION

Strategies for Development of Academic and Content Area Knowledge

There are three types of programs that can be used to ensure that English language learners have access to the core content-area curriculum. They include:

Primary Language Instruction

Research tells us that this is the most effective method for developing language and literacy in both L1 and L2, particularly for students in the earliest stages of language acquisition. It requires a greater commitment of resources and personnel, along with high-level administrative support, to ensure success. English language development is built into the curriculum.

Specially Designed Academic Instruction in English

SDAIE is also called "Sheltered English" and is an approach that utilizes special strategies to ensure understanding. It is most appropriate for students who have already reached the intermediate fluency level. It bridges between primary language instruction and mainstream instruction, providing access to core curriculum for a wide variety of English learners.

Mainstream (Grade-Level) Classroom Instruction

This is the instruction that all English learners will and should eventually receive. It is most effective for students whose language proficiency is beyond the intermediate fluency stage (advanced fluency) and who no longer require any additional language support. CALP must be in place in order for this type of instruction to be successful.

Instruction

Strategies for Development of Academic and Content Area Knowledge

The Zone of Proximal Development

Effective teaching, including use of SDAIE, requires that instruction be delivered at a level that is just above what a student can do independently. The range of performance between what the child can already do without any help and what the child can actually accomplish with help or assistance is known as the Zone of Proximal Development (ZPD). Vygotsky developed the phrase, ZPD, as a way to more accurately describe the nature of learning and intellectual functioning as consisting of both independently displayed abilities as well as assisted performance. Effective instruction, then, is that which involves what the student is ready to learn next, not material that is beyond that level.

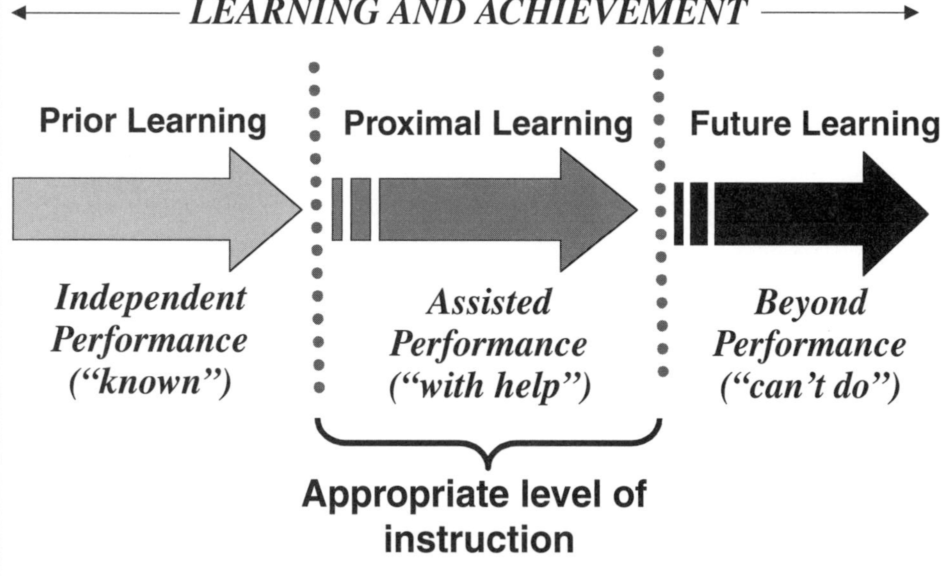

Figure 18.3 Learning and Achievement.

INSTRUCTION

Strategies for Teaching English Learners

Matching Instruction to Development

- Don't be afraid to provide the cognitively-linguistically appropriate level of instruction, regardless of current *age* or *grade.*
- Teach within the zone of proximal development—essentially what comes *next*—because instruction that is beyond what comes next will be ineffective and impede development even further.
- Don't try to alter cognitive or linguistic development, because you *can't.* Alter the curriculum, because you *can.*
- Provide access to core curriculum and focus on developing thinking and literacy skills from the *current* developmental level.
- Use metacognitive strategies that help students think about, plan, monitor, and evaluate learning at their *current* level.
- Use cognitive strategies that help engage students in the learning process and that involve interacting with or manipulating the material mentally or physically, and applying a specific technique to learning tasks at their *current* developmental level.
- Use social-affective strategies that help students interact with another person, accomplish a task, or that assist in learning.

TEST YOURSELF

Nondiscriminatory Assessment under IDEA

1. No child, including one who is culturally and linguistically diverse, may be placed in special education solely on the basis of identified academic need in the absence of a disability related to educational performance. (34CFR 300.7) T F
2. Information about the child's language proficiency in both the primary language and in English must be considered in determining how to conduct the evaluation of a pupil with limited English proficiency. (34CFR 300.532) T F
3. Lack of familiarity with the English language does not preclude a child from being eligible for special education services. (34CFR 300.534b2) T F
4. Cultural difference ("disadvantage") is not a sufficient condition with which eligibility for special education services can be questioned. (34CFR 300.7b10ii and 300.541b4) T F
5. Environmental or economic disadvantage that adversely affects a pupil's academic achievement may be used to form the basis of a disability or establish eligibility for special education services. (34CFR 300.7b10ii and 300.541b4) T F
6. The normal process of second-language acquisition, as well as manifestations of dialect and sociolinguistic variance may be diagnosed as a handicapping condition. (34CFR 300.533a and 300.534b) T F
7. Tests and procedures that are culturally discriminatory cannot be used to qualify a pupil for special education services. (34CFR 300.532a1) T F
8. Tests and other assessment materials need not be provided in the pupil's primary language or other mode of communication. (34CFR 300.532a2) T F
9. Psychological assessment of a pupil in his or her native language by a bilingual psychologist meets the requirements under the law for assessment in the primary language. (34CFR 300.136 and 300.533a) T F
10. The written assessment report must contain a determination regarding the effects of cultural or linguistic difference on the functioning of the pupil only when a child is found to have a specific learning disability. (34CFR 300.543a7) T F

ANSWERS:

1. T—it is illegal to put a child without an identified and primary disability into special education solely on the basis of need.
2. T—it would be difficult to evaluate a child fairly without knowledge of current language proficiency.
3. T—students with LEP who also have a disability that is the primary reason for their academic difficulties can receive services.
4. F—if a student's difficulties are primarily due to cultural difference, not a disability, the student is not disabled.
5. F—just because a student is poor doesn't mean he or she is automatically disabled.
6. F—normal regional variations in language usage, pronunciation, vocabulary, and such are not considered evidence of disability.
7. T—but impossible to comply with, because *all* procedures, methods, and tools are discriminatory to some extent.
8. F—however, if there is no competent and/or qualified professional available in the student's county of residence, alternatives are allowed.
9. F—because assessors must also have knowledge regarding how culture affects test performance and interpretation of results.
10. F—the report must in all cases contain a determination regarding the effects of culture and language on performance.

PRE-ASSESSMENT

Considerations in Nondiscriminatory Assessment

Comparison of Traditional versus Alternative Models of Assessment

Traditional model	Alternative models
Based on medical model, where the learning problem is identified as being an internal flaw within the child	Based on ecosystems model, where the learning problem is identified as being due to dysfunctional transactions between the child and the learning environment
Focus is on measuring performance on tests and comparing results to provide relative standing against performance of other age- and grade-level peers	Focus is on assessing environmental and systemic factors that may be affecting child's ability to learn
Intent of assessment is to identify disabilities in isolation rather than generate intervention strategies or modifications	Intent of assessment is to identify problem situations in context in order to develop intervention strategies or modifications
Children are given labels corresponding to their measured performance and are classified by disability category	Strengths and weaknesses of the situation and the child are identified regardless of disability
Child's abilities and potential are innate, static, immutable, and unchangeable	Child's abilities are experiential, dynamic, modifiable, and changeable
Assessment is conducted by a multidisciplinary team of experts who evaluate learning difficulties relatively independently	Assessment is conducted by a team of people familiar with the child who collaborate in a transdisciplinary approach
Parents and general education teachers are not active participants in the assessment process	Parents and general education teachers are key participants in the assessment and intervention planning process
Standardized testing provides little useful information that can assist in the development of instructional approaches for the classroom	Alternative and authentic methods of assessment provide information directly applicable to the development of instruction for the classroom

Sources: Cook-Morales, V. J. (1995). *Ecosystems service delivery: Assessment and intervention.* Selected readings for CSP 710A, Ecosystems. San Diego State University, Department of Counseling and School Psychology; Henning-Stout, M. (1994). *Responsive assessment.* San Francisco: Jossey-Bass; and Lidz, C. S. (1991). *Practitioner's guide to dynamic assessment.* New York: Guilford.

PRE-ASSESSMENT

Considerations in Nondiscriminatory Assessment

Contrasting Paradigms

	Psychometric	Ecosystemic
Orientation	Individual child	Ecosystem of the child
Role of Home and Culture	Background information	Foreground of hypothesis generation and central to interpretations
Role of Parents	Source of information	Collaborators
Problem Definition	Internal individual differences	Situations
Process	Identification of child's deficits	Differentiation of functional and dysfunctional transactions and settings and identification of potential resources
Intervention	Remediation	Mediation Liaison Consultation
Goal	Fix the child	Alter transactions

Source: Cook-Morales, V. J. (1994). The Cultural and Linguistic Diversity Project. A preservice professional training grant funded by the Office of Bilingual Education and Minority Language Affairs. Washington, DC: U.S. Department of Education.

PRE-ASSESSMENT

Considerations in Nondiscriminatory Assessment

Potential bias	Approach	Techniques/procedures
Failure to consider cultural and linguistic implications of background experiences	**Transactional**	• Cultural knowledge bases • Culture-appropriate processes • Parent and child involvement • Cultural advocates
Failure to view behavior or performance within context of learning environment or ecology	**Ecological**	• Ecosystems assessment • Culture-based hypotheses • Ecological assessment • Adaptive behavior evaluation
Failure to measure both performance and achievement via informal and direct methods	**Alternative**	*Authentic* (skill focused) • CBA/M, portfolio (work samples) • Criterion-referenced tests/procedures • Contextual-participant observation *Process* (cognition focused) • Dynamic assessment • Clinical observations • Piagetian assessment (Ordinal Scales)
Failure to reduce potential bias and discrimination in the use of standardized tests	**Psychometric**	• Underlying theory • Cultural and linguistic bias • Test adaptations • Test selection • Test interpretation
Failure to collaborate across disciplines in evaluation and decision making	**Interdisciplinary**	• Establishing a professional assessment team • Inclusion of parent in the assessment process

Sources: Adapted from Flanagan, D. P., & Ortiz, S. O. (2001). *Essentials of cross-battery assessment.* New York: Wiley; and Cook-Morales, V. J. (1995). *Ecosystems service delivery: Assessment and intervention.* Selected readings for CSP 710A, Ecosystems. San Diego State University, Department of Counseling and School Psychology.

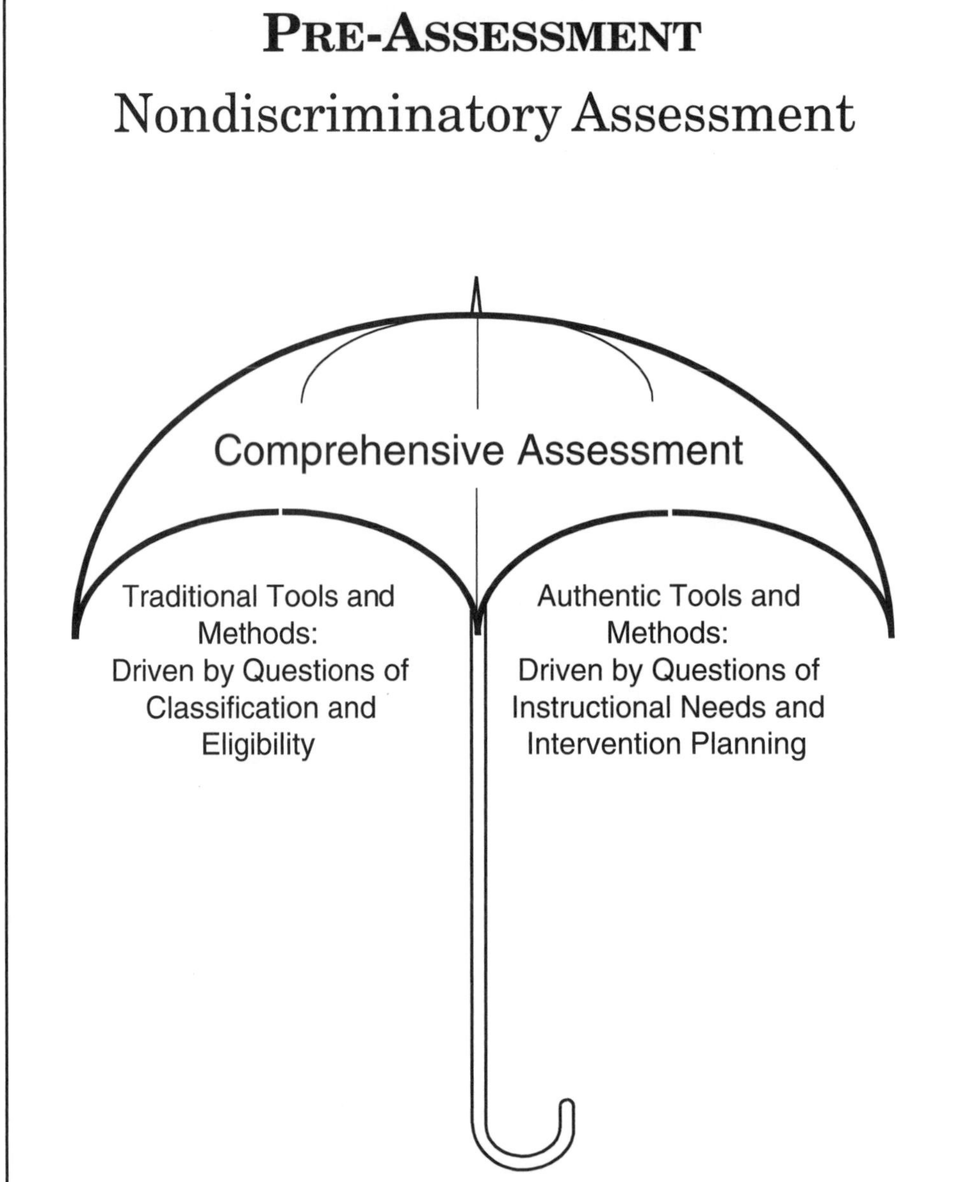

Figure 18.4 Pre-Assessment: Considerations in Nondiscriminatory Assessment.

NONDISCRIMINATORY ASSESSMENT

Comprehensive Framework for Evaluation of Diverse Students

1. *Develop Cultural and Linguistic Hypotheses.*
2. *Assess Language Development and Proficiency.*
3. *Assess Cultural and Linguistic Differences.*
4. *Assess Environmental and Community Factors.*
5. *Evaluate, Revise, and Retest Hypotheses.*
6. *Determine Need for and Languages of Assessment.*
7. *Modify and Adapt Traditional Practices.*
8. *Utilize Nondiscriminatory Practices.*
9. *Evaluate All Data within Cultural / Linguistic Context.*
10. *Link Assessment with Intervention.*

Prereferral procedures (1–5).
Postreferral procedures (6–10).

Nondiscriminatory Assessment

Comprehensive Framework for Evaluation of Diverse Students

1. ASSESS AND EVALUATE THE LEARNING ECOLOGY

Begin with the assumption that there exists an infinite number of reasons for why any given child is having learning difficulties and that a given disability only represents one of those reasons. In other words, try first to eliminate all other potential reasons for learning difficulties, particularly those related to culture or the process of second language acquisition, before entertaining the idea of testing for the presence of a suspected internal disability. Utilize ecological and ecosystems approaches to frame the child's school performance within the context of any cultural, linguistic, or other external factor that may be affecting the learning process. Sample starter hypotheses regarding why a child may be having academic difficulties include the following.

- The school curriculum does not provide cultural relevance and meaning for the student.
- The student is not receiving or has not received instruction in a linguistically appropriate manner.
- The school environment does not affirm the student's native language or culture.
- The student's attendance has not been consistent and regular.
- The student has not had sufficient experience with the school system.
- The home-school relationship does not support the student's learning.
- The family environment is not supportive and conducive to the student's learning.
- The student's basic survival needs (e.g., food, clothing, shelter) have not been adequately met.
- The match between current or previous teacher's teaching style and the student's learning style is not or has not been satisfactory.

- The current or previous school or classroom environments are not or have not been conducive to learning.
- The student's cultural learning style is not and has not been accommodated to promote learning.
- Standardized group achievement scores are comparable to other children of the same age, grade, and cultural or linguistic experience.
- Student's grades are comparable to other children of the same age, grade, and cultural or linguistic experience.
- Current work samples and classroom performance are comparable to other children of the same age, grade, and cultural or linguistic experience.

TYPICAL PERFORMANCE CHARACTERISTICS AND BEHAVIORS OF ENGLISH LEARNERS

Characteristics and behaviors often associated with various disorders and cognitive deficits	Common manifestations of English Language Learners (ELLs) during testing situations or classroom instruction hat may mimic various tdisorders or cognitive deficits
Slow to begin tasks	ELLs may have limited comprehension of the test instructions or classroom language, so that they are not always clear on how to properly begin tasks or what must be done in order to start them or complete them correctly.
Slow to finish tasks	ELLs, especially those with very limited English skills, often need to translate material from English into their native language in order to be able to work with it and then must translate it back to English in order to demonstrate it. This process extends the time for completion of speeded and other time-limited tasks found on tests or expected in the classroom.
Forgetful	ELLs cannot always fully encode information as efficiently into memory as monolinguals because of their limited comprehension of the language, and will often appear to be forgetful, when in fact the issue relates more to their lack of proficiency with English.
Inattentive	ELLs may not fully understand what is being said to them during testing or in the classroom; consequently, they don't know when exactly to pay attention or what exactly they should be paying attention to.
Hyperactive	ELLs may appear to be hyperactive because they are unaware of conduct expected during testing, situation-specific behavioral norms, or classroom rules and other rules of social behavior.
Impulsive	ELLs may lack the ability to fully comprehend instructions, so they display a tendency to act impulsively in their work rather than following test or classroom instructions systematically.
Distractible	ELLs may not fully comprehend the language being used to explain test instructions or what is being spoken in the classroom, and therefore will move their attention to whatever they can comprehend, appearing to be distractible in the process.
Disruptive	ELLs may exhibit disruptive behavior, particularly excessive talking—often with other ELLS, due to a need to try and figure out what is expected of them or to frustration about not knowing what to do or how to do it.
Disorganized	ELLs often display strategies and work habits that appear disorganized, because they don't comprehend instructions on how to organize or arrange materials and may never have been taught efficient strategies.

NONDISCRIMINATORY ASSESSMENT

Comprehensive Framework for Evaluation of Diverse Students

2. ASSESS AND EVALUATE LANGUAGE DEVELOPMENT AND PROFICIENCY

Knowledge of a child's language proficiency and language dominance forms the basis of any assessment and guides the appropriate collection of information and data. Language proficiency in both languages must be assessed and determined, as such information is crucial to the interpretation of any assessment data that is gathered. Broadly speaking, there are essentially four general combinations of bilingual ability that can be identified and evaluated through testing. In general, children referred for evaluation will come from the Type 2 and Type 4 categories.

	High L1 (CALP)	**Low L1 (BICS)**
High L2 (CALP)	Type 1 Equal Proficiency "true bilingual"	Type 3 Atypical Second Language Learner "acceptable bilingual"
Low L2 (BICS)	Type 2 Typical Second Language Learner "high potential"	Type 4 At-risk Second Language Learner "difference vs. disorder"

General Guidelines for Distinguishing Language Differences from Disorders

- *The disorder must be present in the child's native language (L1) and English (L2) but this condition may occur for other reasons.*
- *Testing must be conducted in the native language (L1) and/or both the native language and in English (L2).*
- *Assessments must be conducted using both formal and informal measures.*
- *Language must be assessed in a variety of speaking contexts.*
- *Patterns of language usage must be described.*
- *Error patterns must be determined.*
- *The child's language performance must be compared to that of other bilingual speakers who have had similar cultural and linguistic experiences, that is, the child should be compared to members of the same cultural group who speak the dialect and who have had similar opportunities to hear and use the language.*
- *Factors which may be contributing to the interruption of development in the native language must be identified.*

Sources: Adapted from Hamayan, E. V., & Damico, J. S. (1991). *Limiting bias in the assessment of bilingual students.* Austin, TX: Pro-Ed; Mattes, L. V., & Omark, D. R. (1984). *Speech and language assessment for the bilingual handicapped.* San Diego, CA: College-Hill; and Ortiz, A. A., & Maldonado-Colón, E. (1986). Recognizing learning disabilities in bilingual children: How to lessen inappropriate referral of language minority students to special education. *Journal of Reading, Writing, and Learning Disabilities International, 43,* 47–56.

NONDISCRIMINATORY ASSESSMENT

Comprehensive Framework for Evaluation of Diverse Students

3. ASSESS AND EVALUATE OPPORTUNITY FOR LEARNING

The more a child's or their parent's culture differs from the dominant culture in which they live, the greater the chances that learning will be adversely affected. Likewise, the more a child's or parent's language differs from the dominant language in which they live, the greater the chances that learning will be adversely affected. The following factors are to be viewed as starter hypotheses that suggest whether or not and to what extent each one may or may not contribute to a child's observed academic difficulties. They must be carefully examined to determine the extent that any such cultural and linguistic differences are present that could be inhibiting a child's learning.

- Current language(s) of the home
- Student's initial/primary language (L1)
- Student's total informal experience with L1 and L2
- Student's fluency in L1 and L2
- Student's birth order/sibling influence
- Parent's fluency in L1 and L2
- Parent's level of literacy in L1 and L2
- Parent's level of acculturation
- Parent's level of education
- Parent's socioeconomic status

General Characteristics Associated with Different Learning Patterns

Slow Learner[a]	Under-motivated	Culturally different	Linguistically different	Learning disabled
		Cognitive ability		
Achievement is commensurate with potential. Pupil is deficient in academic areas but about equal across all other areas.	Achievement is usually far below potential, but fairly even across most areas. A particular interest may be evident.	Achievement should be commensurate with cognitive ability, motivation, quality and quantity of instruction.	Achievement in primary language is commensurate with measured cognitive ability and length of school experience. Pupils generally score better on nonverbal sections of cognitive tasks.	Achievement is often far below potential in some areas. Usually has a very uneven learning profile.
		Progress		
Even with additional assistance, progress is slow. Probably will make less than one year's progress per year regardless of placement in regular or special class.	When attending, often learns new material with ease. May be the first person finished with a task. May be receiving low grades, but standardized achievement tests indicate good progress (underachiever).	As with all other pupils, progress is dependent upon quality and quantity of instruction.	Progress in primary language is contingent upon adequacy of language of instruction. Academic progress in English will be dependent upon the quality and quantity of English instruction. During the transition period, English performance may lag.	May show remarkable progress in some areas when tasks are analyzed, taught sequentially, and include higher extent of teach-pupil interaction. Skills may jump 1–2 years in 1 year.
		Productivity		
In a lesson or task involving many concepts, may focus on only one. May need assistance with words or directions. May require graphic explanation. May have just begun a task when time is called. May be unable to switch from task to task.	May understand directions, be able to read some of the words, yet rarely completes task. Often appears disinterested.	Verbal and written directions are generally understood. Productivity, as with all other students, would depend on motivation and other factors.	Verbal and written directions may not be understood due to insufficient English development. This may lead to pupils not beginning tasks, or switching tasks without assistance.	Verbal directions may be too complex. May be unable to read written directions. May want to do task, be embarrassed about lack of skill, not be able to concentrate. May not begin task without assistance. Often unable to switch from task to task.

Slow Learner[a]	Under-motivated	Culturally different	Linguistically different	Learning disabled
		Health		
May have mild delay in developmental milestones.	May have dysfunctional family, frequent family moves, nutritional and financial problems.	No significant health characteristics for this group, but consider developmental factors in cultural context.	No significant health characteristics for this group but consider developmental factors in cultural context.	May have a history of risk at infancy, ear infections/hearing problems, sleep/eating disturbances, incontinence, and family incidence of learning disability.
		Peer interaction		
Will often be a follower in peer group.	May be rejected due to antisocial tendencies, or accepted as a leader. This leadership may be negative.	Pupil may tend to interact with more students from own cultural group.	Pupils may experience social isolation because of unfamiliarity with social and linguistic rules and may be likely to be followers rather than leaders in the English group. Pupil may tend to interact with more pupils from own cultural group.	May have frequent fights or arguments. Others may complain of clumsiness. May be a class isolate. May play with younger pupils. Occasionally pupils will be socially adequate.
		Language		
Similar to that of Learning Disabled child but may be at a lesser degree. Takes longer to learn a concept but will usually retain it once learned.	Usually language-adequate, but fails to apply skills consistently in the classroom.	Receptive and expressive language is similar to all other pupils. However, may exhibit some sub-group dialectional differences.	Primary language is appropriate for age level while English skills are still in the acquisition stage. The nonverbal communication skills are appropriate for age level, i.e., eye contact, response to speaker, clarification of response, turn taking, etc. Pupil does not know specific vocabulary although is familiar with item or concept. Sentence structure and grammar is in highly transitional stage that follows similar patterns of normal language development. Student may pass though predictable periods, i.e., silent period, speech emergence, etc.	Auditory processing is usually at a low skill level. Vocabulary and word-finding skills usually delayed. Sentences are simplified and lack complexity. Commonly cannot transfer skills learned in the classroom into everyday usage.

[a]Not to be confused with mild retardation.

Note: These categories are not mutually exclusive. Culturally different = Native and nonnative English speakers who identify with nonmainstream culture. Linguistically different = Nonnative English speakers who lack native-like skills in English.

Source: Adapted from Special Edge, California Department of Education, September/October/November, 1996.

NONDISCRIMINATORY ASSESSMENT

Comprehensive Framework for Evaluation of Diverse Students

4. ASSESS AND EVALUATE RELEVANT CULTURAL AND LINGUISTIC FACTORS

In order for a child to benefit from instruction, the language of instruction must be fully comprehensible to the child, the instruction must draw upon the child's existing cultural and linguistic foundations, the child must be able to identify and relate to the content of the curriculum, and the child must be made to feel that her or his personal language and culture are assets, not liabilities. Failure to accommodate these learning needs leads to the creation of a learning environment that can significantly inhibit academic achievement. Again, the following factors are to be viewed as starter hypotheses that suggest whether or not and to what extent each one may or may not have contributed to a child's observed academic difficulties. They must be carefully examined in order to determine the extent to which any such environmental factor is present that could inhibit a child's learning.

- Attendance and experience with school setting
- Match between child's L1 and language of instruction
- Parent's ability to support language of instruction
- Years (duration) of instruction in L1 and L2
- Quality of L1/L2 instruction or bilingual program
- Cultural relevance of the curriculum
- Consistency in location and curriculum
- Teaching strategies, styles, attitudes, expectations
- System attitude regarding dual language learners
- Socialization with peers versus isolation from peers

As stated previously, the more a child's culture differs from the dominant culture in which she or he lives, the greater the chances that learning will be adversely affected. In order for a child to benefit from instruction, the community or neighborhood in which the family of the child lives must affirm, value, and allow for the expression of their native culture. Lack of support for cultural practices and beliefs can lead to the development of social interactions that can significantly inhibit academic achievement. Once more, the following factors are to be viewed only as starter hypotheses that suggest whether or not and to what extent each one may or may not contribute to a child's observed academic difficulties. As with cultural, linguistic, and environmental factors, they must be carefully examined in order to determine the extent to which any such community factor is present that could inhibit a child's learning.

- General demographic diversity within the community
- Parent's role/position in the community
- Match between parent/student's culture and surrounding community
- Community's attitude toward student's culture or language
- Opportunity and support for primary language within the community (friends, neighbors, and others)
- Opportunity and support for expression of cultural practices and beliefs within the community
- Availability of community groups/agencies for assistance with acculturation processes
- Availability of community groups/agencies for assistance with home-school communication

NONDISCRIMINATORY ASSESSMENT

Comprehensive Framework for Evaluation of Diverse Students

5. EVALUATE, REVISE, AND RETEST HYPOTHESES

Ensure that all potential factors that might be related to the child's learning difficulties have been thoroughly evaluated and ruled out as the primary cause of the observed learning problems. Except in cases where there are obvious physical disabilities, in general it is only when you feel confident that there are no plausible or demonstrable external factors that can account for the child's learning difficulties would a referral for special education assessment be appropriate.

- Analyze prereferral data to identify patterns of referral that differentiate between the needs of teachers, the needs for programs, and the individual needs of children.
- Lack of knowledge, skills, confidence, or objectivity to teach culturally and linguistically diverse (CLD) students effectively has been eliminated as primary cause of learning problems.
- Cultural and linguistic differences as well as environmental and economic disadvantage have been eliminated as primary causes of learning problems.
- Lack of school experience or poor attendance have been eliminated as primary causes of learning problems.
- Parent(s) and general education teacher(s) continue as equal partners in the problem definition and assessment process.
- Refer for special education assessment when external factors have been ruled out.
- Student Study Team easily reconstitutes itself into Assessment Team.

NONDISCRIMINATORY ASSESSMENT

Comprehensive Framework for Evaluation of Diverse Students

6. DETERMINE NEED FOR AND LANGUAGE(S) OF ASSESSMENT

The legal system recognizes that assessors need to consider the child's primary language ability (in addition to his or her ability in English). The interpretive validity of assessment data rests squarely on the proper identification and understanding of the child's entire linguistic history, as well as other factors influencing the development of both languages. The language or languages of assessment are determined collaboratively by the Assessment Team, which selects appropriate tools and techniques on the basis of prereferral data. The development of an appropriate assessment plan forms the transition from prereferral to special education evaluation. However, up to this point, all activities could and should have been accomplished within the context of the prereferral process. The following statements represent only the most general guidelines applicable to all children. There is simply no way to make specific guidelines to cover even a large majority of cases, since each assessment must be made on the basis of the unique and individual circumstances of each child.

- All children who are Limited English Proficiency (LEP) *must* be assessed in their primary language, in addition to any English language testing that may be appropriate.
- Children who are Fluent English Proficient (FEP) *may* be assessed in their primary language in addition to any English language testing that may be appropriate.
- All LEP and FEP children *must* be assessed by an assessor competent in both the language and culture of the pupil, in order to ensure that results are evaluated in a nondiscriminatory manner.

Bilingual Assessment or Assessment of Bilinguals?

Bilingual Assessment

- *Refers to the assessment of bilinguals by bilingual school psychologists.*
- *The bilingual school psychologist is in a position to conduct assessment activities in a manner (that is, bilingually) that is not available to the monolingual school psychologist, even with the aid of an interpreter.*
- *A competent and qualified bilingual school psychologist proficient in the same language of the student is the best option in the assessment of bilinguals.*
- *Bilingual assessment is a relatively new research tradition with little empirical support to guide appropriate practice.*
- *There are no truly "bilingual" tests or assessment protocols and not much is yet known about the performance of bilinguals on monolingual tests administered in the primary language.*

Assessment of Bilinguals

- *Refers to the assessment of bilinguals by monolingual English-speaking school psychologists.*
- *There is considerably more research about the performance of bilinguals as a group on tests given monolingually in English than in the native language.*
- *Use of instruments, whether or not designed or standardized for use with bilinguals, must be conducted in a manner that seeks to reduce the discriminatory aspects in the use of such instruments to the maximum extent possible.*
- *The emphasis on bias reduction applies equally to tests given in the native language as well as in English.*
- *A monolingual psychologist properly trained in nondiscriminatory assessment and competent in cultural and linguistic issues is the second best option for assessment when using a trained interpreter for communication.*
- *An untrained psychologist, whether monolingual or bilingual, who possesses no training in nondiscriminatory assessment or cultural and linguistic knowledge regarding test performance of bilinguals is the last option for assessment.*

Nondiscriminatory Assessment

Comprehensive Framework for Evaluation of Diverse Students

7. REDUCE BIAS IN TRADITIONAL TESTING PRACTICES

Because there is no research regarding test performance of individuals on modified or adapted test administrations, it is generally best to administer tests in a standardized way first, so that the data can be analyzed against known performance patterns of other similar individuals. Whereas adaptation of traditional tools and practices is rarely done in a systematic way, the validity and reliability of obtained results is questionable. Because there are no standardized tests that are truly appropriate for students who are culturally or linguistically diverse (due mainly to acculturation and language proficiency issues) maintaining standardization may seem unnecessary. But the goal isn't to eliminate all bias or find unbiased tests—this is unlikely and impractical. Rather, the goal is toward reduction of bias to the maximum extent possible. One established method for doing this is the Cattel-Horne-Carroll (CHC) Culture-Language Matrix that is a part of the CHC Cross-Battery approach. This method balances the need to measure specific areas of functioning with attempts to reduce the biasing effects of acculturation and linguistic demands. By giving tests in a standardized manner, determination of the primary versus contributory effects of culture and language may be accomplished. After such data are collected, examiners may then adapt and modify standardized tests in order to secure additional *qualitative* information about functioning that is extremely useful in instructional planning. In general, examiners should

- Utilize best available tools with respect to the child's native and second languages.
- Remember that direct test translation is poor practice and is psychometrically indefensible.
- Recognize that norming samples are not stratified on the basis of bilingual ability and are rarely applicable to the majority of CLD students being assessed, thus invalidating scores.
- Adapt test items, content, stimuli, administration, or performance criteria as necessary to ensure more valid responding by the student only after administering the test first in a standardized way.
- Recognize that use of an interpreter can assist in collecting information

and administering tests; however, score validity remains low even when the interpreter is highly trained and experienced.

- Use systematic methods based on established literature for collecting and interpreting data in a nondiscriminatory way (e.g., CHC Culture-Language Matrix).

In addition to the difficulties associated with interpreting the validity and reliability of standardized test results with culturally and linguistically diverse children, the use of common classification schemes tends to accentuate misconceptions regarding the true meaning of this type of score. The following is an alternative classification scheme that provides a less technical and more positive description of performance.

Classification	Standard score	Percentile rank range
Highly proficient	Standard score = 116 or higher	Percentile rank = 86th percentile or higher
Proficient	Standard score = 85 to 115	Percentile rank = 16th percentile to 85th percentile
Emergent	Standard score = 80 to 84	Percentile rank = 9th percentile to 14th percentile
Problematic	Standard score = 79 or lower	Percentile rank = 8th percentile or lower

NONDISCRIMINATORY ASSESSMENT

Comprehensive Framework for Evaluation of Diverse Students

8. UTILIZE AUTHENTIC AND ALTERNATIVE ASSESSMENT PROCEDURES

Standardized methods of assessment are largely symbolic in nature, because they evaluate only a sample of what should have been taught or exposed to an individual. They cannot, however, cover adequately the entire scope of information covered by all the various curricula used in the schools. Nonstandardized, alternative assessment strategies are often less discriminatory because they provide information regarding the true difference between what an individual has actually been taught and what she or he has actually learned. It is, therefore, a more authentic form of assessment that can provide crucial information that assists in determining the presence or absence of a disability for any student. Moreover, authentic measures have the advantage of providing information that readily translates into psychoeducational interventions and modifications. Assessment for special education involves not only the identification of a qualifying disability but the development of an appropriate instructional program to meet the disabled child's specific needs. Therefore, whether or not any standardized testing is done, appropriate assessment of diverse children should include authentic and alternative forms of assessment.

- Curriculum Based Assessment—authentic measures of academic skills
- Portfolio Assessment—developmental documentation of skills learning and academic progress
- Symbolic Dynamic Assessment—assess learning potential, cognitive strengths and weaknesses
- Authentic Dynamic Assessment—assess learning style and instructional needs

Authentic versus Symbolic Assessment

The Importance of Authentic Assessment

Assessment of a child's academic skills and abilities must directly examine the child's skills and abilities with respect to the actual materials and content used to instruct that child. Thus, authentic assessment seeks to uncover whether learning difficulties can be ascribed to experiential differences rather than ability differences. Not only does this ensure greater validity of the assessment, it provides valuable information necessary to develop specific and effective instructional strategies. In general, evidence of lack of opportunity for learning, ineffective prior instruction, and linguistically inappropriate curricula are all factors that increase the likelihood that no disability exists.

NONDISCRIMINATORY ASSESSMENT

Comprehensive Framework for Evaluation of Diverse Students

9. EVALUATE AND INTERPRET DATA WITHIN CONTEXT OF LEARNING ECOLOGY

Once an assessment is completed, it is imperative that knowledge of both the individual's cultural and linguistic experiences be used to frame the patterns seen in the data. Frequently, in bilingual assessment, only linguistic considerations are made and cultural considerations are all but ignored. Remember, linguistically appropriate assessment is only a small part of the equation. Cultural knowledge, on the other hand, forms the necessary context for understanding performance. With respect to standardized testing:

- Evaluate cultural and linguistic differences (large differences = more adverse effect on performance).
- Evaluate inhibiting factors (many inhibiting factors = more adverse effect on performance).
- Evaluate nondiscriminatory data (is child capable of learning normally if given the chance?).
- Evaluate opportunity for learning (less opportunity = lower probability of disability).
- Base all decisions on all available data.

The following figure provides an illustration that can help distinguish between difference or disorder. It is important to note that the probability or likelihood of one versus the other is based primarily on data regarding cognitive functioning generated from standardized tests compared against the information regarding the relative influence of cultural or linguistic differences and the presence of inhibitory factors (environmental and community). Decisions concerning difference versus disorder must ultimately be supported by other information including that derived from direct observation, interviews with people familiar with the child, informal or authentic assessment, and analysis of actual work samples. These figures should not be used for making definitive conclusions about performance; rather, they should be viewed only as a guide for evaluating data.

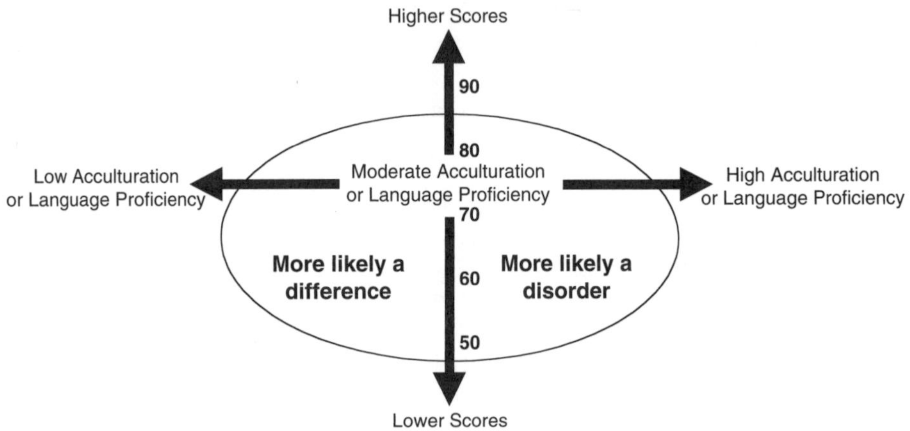

Figure 18.5 The Cultural Context of Performance.

The Cultural Context of Performance

The Importance of Culture

Of all the factors that affect an individual's behavior or performance on a given task, none are more likely to be greater than culture. Virtually everything that an individual knows, does, feels, thinks, believes, or says can be traced to the interaction between the cultural roots of the home, the community, and the society in which the individual is raised. In order to understand the functioning of an individual on a measured task, we must first understand the influences that caused the individual to perform in the manner observed. When we fail to account for such culturally based behavior we run the greatest risk of identifying simple differences as serious deficits, when in fact they are not.

Cultural Effects on Listening Comprehension and Receptive Language Abilities

> "I pledge a lesson to the frog of the United States of America, and to the wee puppet for witches hands. One Asian, under God, in the vestibule, with little tea and just rice for all."
>
> *Source:* Lord, B. B. (1986). *In the Year of the Boar and Jackie Robinson.* New York: HarperTrophy.

Children who are learning a second language hear and interpret sounds in a manner that conforms to words that already exist in the vocabulary. This is a natural part of the first and second language acquisition process and should not be considered abnormal in any way. It represents the brain's attempt to make sense and meaning of what it perceives by connecting this information to what is already known. But this phenomenon goes both ways. Consider the following:

> Jose Feliciano's "Feliz Navidad," often heard by English speakers as "Police naughty dog" or "Fleas on the dog," or the song "Guantanamera," often heard by English speakers as "One-ton tomato."

These types of errors, sometimes referred to as "Mondegreens" (a term coined by writer Sylvia Wright), are probably most common in music—which is one reason why music is not really an effective way of learning a language. For example, "Gladly the cross I'd bear" is a well-known hymn often sung as "Gladly, the cross-eyed bear," particularly by children. "There's a bathroom on the right" is often the meaning taken from the Creedence Clearwater Revival song where the wording is in fact "There's a bad moon on the rise." The Jimi Hendrix song "Purple Haze" contains the line "Excuse me while I kiss the sky," which is often heard as "Excuse me while I kiss this guy." Crystal Gayle once sang "Don't it make my brown eyes blue," which was frequently heard as "Doughnuts make my brown eyes blue." And the early '70s song "Midnight at the Oasis" by Maria Mulduar was sometimes thought to be "Midnight after you're wasted." There are many other classic examples of this linguistic phenomenon, and it serves to highlight the fact that teachers need to be very aware of the meaning that students are constructing as they learn English.

Cultural Effects on Reading Comprehension and Phonological Processing Abilities

Read the following passage:

'Twas brillig, and the slithy toves
Did gyre and gimble in the wabe:
All mimsy were the borogoves,
And the mome raths outgrabe.
("Jabberwocky" by Lewis Carroll)

Now answer the following questions:

1. What things were slithy?
2. What did the toves do in the wabe?
3. How were the borogoves?
4. What kind of raths were there?

The fact that it is very easy for mature readers to answer these questions regarding comprehension demonstrates the fact that meaning in print is not derived solely from word knowledge or lexical ability. As readers advance and become more fluent in reading they tend to discard decoding as a primary means for developing reading abilities in favor of processing letters, words, sentences, and grammatical structure, in an orthographic manner. The orthographic process and the structural context in which the meaning is embedded is bound by cultural experiences, and thus meaning can often be inferred simply from our cultural knowledge and experience with the language—even in the absence of actual word understanding. More experience equals clearer meaning.

Cultural Effects on Reading Comprehension and Orthographic Processing Abilities

Read the following passage:

I cdnuolt blveiee taht I cluod aulaclty uesdnatnrd waht I was rdgnieg—the phaonmneal pweor of the hmuan mnid. Aoccdrnig to a rscheearch at Cmabrigde Uinervtisy, it deosn't mttaer in waht oredr the ltteers in a wrod are, the olny iprmoatnt tihng is taht the frist and lsat ltteer be in the rghit pclae. The rset can be a taotl mses and you can sitll raed it wouthit a porbelm. Tihs is bcuseae the huamn mnid deos not raed ervey lteter by istlef, but the wrod as a wlohe. Amzanig huh? Yaeh, and I awlyas tohguht slpeling was ipmorantt!

The fact that you are able to read the passage above again demonstrates that for more mature readers meaning is constructed primarily by orthographic representations and not by simple phonological processing abilities. Semantic meaning is derived from access to vocabulary, which is triggered by first and last letter positions and by other contextual support, such as short words that are not scrambled, particularly conjunctions, articles, and pronouns.

Consider how much more difficult the task would be to read the passage if the word order were completely random and you get a sense about how important grammatical structure alone is to comprehension in reading.

Read the following sentence and count how many "f's" it contains:

"FINISHED FILES ARE THE RESULT OF YEARS OF SCIENTIFIC STUDY COMBINED WITH THE EXPERIENCE OF YEARS."

In this case, your orthographic processing abilities are confounded by the intensity of the phonological processing requirement of finding the letters that make the "f" sound. The phonological matching of the sound for "f" (or "eff") causes your orthographic processing to ignore letters that do not make this sound. As such, most people will "see" about three to four "f's" in the sentence. In fact, there are six. Really! The task to match the phonetic sound of "f" causes people to miss "f's" that are pronounced with more of a "v" sound, as in the word "of." The word "of" appears three times in the sentence and is often overlooked because of these processes. Once again, the task shows how orthographic processing remains unimpaired and facilitates comprehension in mature readers, while phonological processing is rendered largely irrelevant. These points are important in the instruction and development of intervention strategies for English learners in that they need to develop such orthographic abilities in order to become more efficient and fluent readers.

Nondiscriminatory Assessment

Comprehensive Framework for Evaluation of Diverse Students

10. LINK ASSESSMENT TO INTERVENTION

The final step in nondiscriminatory assessment is also the most important; link results from assessment with intervention. Once assessment is completed, the child is not going to be "cured" of his or her learning problems merely because a diagnosis or label has been applied. Therefore, the role of assessment should not be limited to identification only; rather, it should be extended to inform appropriate instructional interventions, modifications, and program development.

- Utilize collected data to guide instructional interventions, modifications, and program development.
- Ensure that instructional goals and objectives are culturally and linguistically appropriate.

Linguistically appropriate goals and objectives have the following characteristics.

- They are appropriate for the cognitive level of the student.
- They are appropriate for the linguistic level of the student.
- They match the developmental level of the student's primary (L1) or secondary (L2) language.
- They match the student's general education transition criteria and redesignation policy (i.e., from LEP to FEP).

Culturally appropriate goals and objectives have the following characteristics.

- They access the student's prior knowledge and experiences.
- They incorporate culturally relevant materials and experiences.
- They affirm the student's cultural heritage.

The following rubric needs to be followed in order to ensure that any given goal or objective meets the definition of being linguistically appropriate as previously specified.

- It states specifically in what language (Spanish, Vietnamese, Tagalog, etc.) the particular goal and objective will be accomplished.
- It is appropriate to the student's level of linguistic development and proficiency in that language.
- It is consistent with the known developmental structure of that language.
- It provides cultural relevance in the curricular framework.

INTERVENTION

Strategies for Teaching English Learners

Provide Comprehensible Input and Output

1. Use contextual references (visuals, realia).
2. Implement listening activities to assist students in developing the sounds of English.
3. Allow for an initial listening (or silent period) for students at the preproduction level.
4. Use a variety of questioning strategies and activities to meet the needs of individuals at varying stages of language acquisition.
5. Expose students to higher levels of comprehensible language.
6. Link new vocabulary and language to previously learned information.
7. Provide activities and opportunities for increased student talk as students develop English.
8. Tap into and access student's prior knowledge.

Source: Walter, T. (1996). *Amazing English: How-to handbook.* New York: Addison-Wesley.

INTERVENTION

Strategies for Teaching English Learners

Negotiate Meaning

1. Monitor student comprehension through interactive means, such as checking for comprehension and clarification, utilizing questioning strategies, having students paraphrase, define, and model.
2. Modify instruction as needed, using strategies such as scaffolding, expansion, demonstration, and modeling.
3. Encourage students to communicate in English, using familiar vocabulary and structures.
4. Modify teacher-talk to make input comprehensible.
5. Use extralinguistic clues (e.g., gestures, facial expressions) to emphasize or clarify meaning.
6. Match language with experience.
7. Model the language with natural speech and intonation.
8. Provide opportunities for students to use English with varied audiences and for a variety of purposes.
9. Verify that all students comprehend before moving on.

Source: Walter, T. (1996). *Amazing English: How-to handbook.* New York: Addison-Wesley.

INTERVENTION

Strategies for Teaching English Learners

Shelter the Core/Content Instruction

1. Modify the language input according to the needs of the students (e.g., rate of speech, added definitions and examples, controlled vocabulary, and careful use of idioms).
2. Review main topic, key vocabulary, and ideas.
3. Check frequently for understanding.
4. Bridge new unknown material to known—what students have already learned.
5. Organize instruction around themes and content appropriate to students' grade level.
6. Engage students in active participation activities and responses.
7. Integrate culture and content instruction.
8. Use added resources and strategies to help students access core curriculum.

Source: Walter, T. (1996). *Amazing English: How-to handbook.* New York: Addison-Wesley.

INTERVENTION

Strategies for Teaching English Learners

Develop Thinking Skills

1. Ask questions, give directions, and generate activities to advance students to higher levels of thinking (from recalling to evaluating).
2. Elicit student questions and encourage them to support their answers.
3. Allow ample wait time after asking questions.
4. Guide students through learning using varied groupings and configurations.

Source: Walter, T. (1996). *Amazing English: How-to handbook.* New York: Addison-Wesley.

INTERVENTION

Strategies for Teaching English Learners

Give Appropriate Error Correction

1. Practice sensitive error correction, focusing on errors of meaning rather than form.
2. Accept appropriate student responses.
3. Encourage taking risks in English.
4. Develop classroom activities to address recurring or systematic errors.
5. Allow for flow of uninterrupted student thought.

Source: Walter, T. (1996). *Amazing English: How-to handbook.* New York: Addison-Wesley.

INTERVENTION

Strategies for Teaching English Learners

Control Classroom Climate

1. Use relevant material.
2. Ensure that displays of student work are evident.
3. Utilize (and demonstrate respect for) students' home language and culture.
4. Nurture a positive climate.
5. Reward all attempts at language.

Source: Walter, T. (1996). *Amazing English: How-to handbook.* New York: Addison-Wesley.

INTERVENTION

Culturally and Linguistically Appropriate IEP Goals and Objectives

Basic Definitions

- A *goal* is a long-term plan for improving academic performance.
- An *objective* is a short-term method of instruction used to reach the goal.

Philosophy

For any student receiving special education services and designated as LEP, goals and objectives must reflect the individual's cognitive and linguistic development and her or his language of instruction in order to be appropriate.

Reminder: Students in special education who are designated as LEP must continue to receive English language development (ELD) instruction.

Linguistic Considerations

Linguistically appropriate goals and objectives have the following characteristics:

- They are appropriate for the cognitive level of the student.
- They are appropriate for the linguistic level of the student.
- They match the developmental level of the student's primary (L1) or secondary (L2) language.
- They match the student's general education transition criteria and redesignation policy (i.e., from LEP to FEP).

Cultural Considerations

Culturally appropriate goals and objectives have the following characteristics:

- They access the student's prior knowledge and experiences.
- They incorporate culturally relevant materials and experiences.
- They affirm the student's cultural heritage.

General Rubric

The following rubric needs to be followed in order to ensure that any given goal or objective meets the definition of being linguistically appropriate as specified earlier.

- It states specifically in what language (Spanish, Vietnamese, Tagalog, etc.) the particular goal and objective will be accomplished.
- It is appropriate to the student's level of linguistic development and proficiency in that language.
- It is consistent with the known developmental structure of that language.
- It provides cultural relevance in the curricular framework.

INTERVENTION

Sample IEP Goals and Objectives

The goals and objectives shown on this and the following pages were developed by Julie Esparza Brown, MEd, and Samuel O. Ortiz, PhD.

Language Goal/Objective (preproduction stage)

Goal: To increase comprehension of the _____ (L2/English, Spanish, Tagalog, etc.) language.

Objective: By _____ (date) when shown visual stimuli (e.g., pictures, real objects, etc.) _____ (student) will respond *nonverbally* (e.g., point, nod, shake her head, clap hands, act out, etc.) to preproduction stimuli with _____ (%) accuracy as measured by _____ (teacher observation, records, etc.).

Examples of preproduction stimuli:

1. "Nod your head when I point to the pencil."
2. "Clap your hands when I touch a farm animal."

Language Goal/Objective (early production stage)

Goal: To be able to give one-word responses in _____ (L2/English, Spanish, Tagalog, etc.) to questions asked with comprehensible input.

Objective: By _____ (date) when shown visual stimuli (e.g., pictures, real objects, etc.) _____ (student) will respond with a *one-word response* to questions with comprehensible input with _____ (%) accuracy as measured by _____ (teacher observation, records, etc.).

Examples of questions with comprehensible input:

1. "Are you hot [teacher pantomimes wiping perspiration from forehead] or cold?" (teacher pantomimes shivering and bundling up)
2. "Is this a dog?" (teacher points to a cat in a picture)
3. "How many flowers [teacher points] are in the vase?"

Language Goal/Objective (speech emergence stage)

Goal: To respond to literal questions with short phrases which may or may not be grammatically correct.

Basic Objective: By _____ (date) when given comprehensible input, _____ (student) will respond to (who, what, where, when, how, and why) questions using short phrases with _____ (%) accuracy as measured by _____ (teacher observation, records, etc.).

Examples of basic questions with comprehensible input:

1. "Where is the dog?" (sample student response: "By the tree")
2. "Who is walking the dog?" (sample student response: "The man")
3. "Why is the cat frightened?" (sample student response: "Sees the dog")

Advanced Objective: By _____ (date) in a natural environment _____ (student) will be able to articulate and express on his or her own initiative basic ideas and requests with _____ (%) accuracy as measured by _____ (teacher observation, records, etc.).

Examples of advanced student ideas and requests:

1. "I am cold."
2. "I go to the bathroom?"
3. "I like it!"

Language Goal/Objective (intermediate fluency stage)

Goals:

1. To be able to respond to questions in writing in _____ (L2/English, Spanish, Tagalog, etc.) to questions with a level of quality comparable to their level of written language skills in _____ (L1/native language).
2. To be able to read _____ (L2/English, Spanish, Tagalog, etc.) at a comparable level to their reading proficiency in native language.
3. To be able to respond in either writing or orally in _____ (L2/English, Spanish, Tagalog, etc.) to stimuli that prompts critical and creative thinking with a response that shows elaboration and complex sentence structures.

Basic Objective: By _____ (date) after reading a story at his or her readability level _____ (student) will respond to writing task with _____ (%) accuracy as measured by _____ (teacher observation, records, etc.).

Examples of basic student responses:

1. answering comprehension questions after reading a story
2. writing a friendly letter
3. writing a creative story

Intermediate Objective: By _____ (date) _____, (student) will be able to comprehend reading selection at his or her readability level as measured by grade level curriculum assessment.

Advanced Objective: By _____ (date) _____, (student) will be able to articulate responses to questions that require critical and creative thinking in the following four main areas: (1) synthesis, (2) evaluation, (3) analysis, and (4) application as measured by the following criteria: (1) descriptive vocabulary, (2) ability to elaborate, and (3) use of complex sentence structures within their response.

Reading Goal/Objective

Goal: To increase reading comprehension in _____ (English, Spanish, Tagalog, etc.).

Objective: By _____ (date), _____ (student) will identify two common themes/main ideas and two differences in stories after reading _____ (independently, with modifications, listening, etc.) four folk tales from different countries with _____ (%) accuracy as measured by _____ (teacher observation, work samples, task-based criteria, etc.).

Written Language Goal/Objective

Goal: To increase writing fluency in _____ (English, Spanish, Tagalog, etc.).

Objective: By _____ (date), _____ (student) will respond by _____ (dictating, writing a sentence, writing a paragraph, etc.) and share his or her personal responses to an open-ended question that draws upon his or her life experiences, culture, and perceptions after listening/reading to a story from core/supplemental curriculum with _____ (%) accuracy as measured by _____ (teacher observation, work samples, task-based criteria, etc.).

Math Goal/Objective

Goal: To increase understanding of multiplication concepts taught in _____ (English, Spanish, Tagalog, etc.).

Objective: By _____ (date), _____ (student) will be able to use an array of _____ (graph paper, multilink cubes, other manipulatives, etc.) to demonstrate her or his comprehension of the multiplication process after comparing and contrasting Mexican and Egyptian methods of multiplication as measured by _____ (teacher observation, work samples, task-based criteria, etc.).

Cognitive Development Goal/Objective

Goal: To increase _____ (student's) ability to use systematic exploratory strategies when approaching new tasks.

Objective 1: When presented with an assignment, _____ (student) will scan the assignment, including a sample provided by the teacher, and describe the goal of the assignment with _____ (%) accuracy as measured by _____ (teacher observation, work samples, task-based criteria, etc.).

Objective 2: When presented with an assignment, _____ (student) will produce a list of steps required in order to complete the assignment with teacher assistance with _____ (%) accuracy as measured by _____ (teacher observation, work samples, task-based criteria, etc.).

Psycholinguistic Development Goal/Objective

Objective 1: When presented with 10 symbols of meaningful objects, _____ (student) will differentiate them using verbal labels in _____ (English, Spanish, Tagalog, etc.) with _____ (%) accuracy as measured by _____ (teacher observation, work samples, task-based criteria, etc.).

Objective 2: When presented 10 signs associated with the previously chosen symbols, _____ (student) will differentiate them using verbal labels with _____ (%) accuracy as measured by _____ (teacher observation, work samples, task-based criteria, etc.).

SELECTED BIBLIOGRAPHY ON ASSESSMENT

Ambert, A. M., & Dew, N. (1982). *Special education for exceptional bilingual students: A handbook for educators.* Milwaukee, WI: Midwest National Origin Desegregation Assistance Center.

Baca, L. M., & Almanza, E. (1991). *Language minority students with disabilities.* Reston, VA: The Council for Exceptional Children.

Cummins, J. C. (1984). *Bilingual and special education: Issues in assessment and pedagogy.* Austin, TX: Pro-Ed.

Flanagan, D. P., & Ortiz, S. O. (2001). *Essentials of cross-battery assessment.* New York: Wiley.

Flanagan, D. P., & Ortiz, S. O. (2002). Best practices in intellectual assessment: Future directions. In A. Thomas & J. Grimes (Eds.), *Best practices in school psychology IV* (pp. 1351–1372). Washington, DC: National Association of School Psychologists.

Flanagan, D. P., Ortiz, S. O., Alfonso, V., & Mascolo, J. (2002). *The Achievement Test Desk Reference (ATDR): Comprehensive assessment and learning disability.* Boston: Allyn & Bacon.

Hamayan, E. V., & Damico, J. S. (1991). *Limiting bias in the assessment of bilingual students.* Austin, TX: Pro-Ed.

Krashen, S. D. (1985). *Inquiries and insights: Second language teaching: Immersion and bilingual education, literacy.* Englewood Cliffs, NJ: Alemany Press.

Mattes, L. J., & Omark, D. R. (1984). *Speech and language assessment for the bilingual handicapped.* San Diego, CA: College-Hill Press.

Ortiz, A. A., & Maldonado-Colon, E. (1986). Recognizing learning disabilities in bilingual children: How to lessen inappropriate referral of language minority students to special education. *Journal of Reading, Writing, and Learning Disabilities International, 43,* 47–56.

Ortiz, S. O. (2001). Assessment of cognitive abilities in Hispanic children. *Seminars in Speech and Language, 22,* 17–37.

Ortiz, S. O. (2002). Best practices in nondiscriminatory assessment. In A. Thomas & J. Grimes (Eds.), *Best practices in school psychology IV* (pp. 1321–1336). Washington, DC: National Association of School Psychologists.

Ortiz, S. O. (2004). Use of the WISC-IV with culturally and linguistically diverse populations. In D. P. Flanagan and A. S. Kaufman (Eds.), *Essentials of WISC-IV assessment.* New York: Wiley.

Ortiz, S. O., & Flanagan, D. P. (1998a). *Gf-Gc* cross-battery interpretation and selective cross-battery assessment: Considering referral concerns and the needs of culturally and linguistically diverse populations. In K. S. McGrew & D. P. Flanagan (Eds.), *The Intelligence Test Desk Reference(ITDR):* Gf- Gc *cross battery assessment* (pp. 401–444). Needham Heights, MA: Allyn & Bacon.

Ortiz, S. O., & Flanagan, D. P. (1998b). Enhancing cognitive assessment of culturally and linguistically diverse individuals: Application and use of selective *Gf-Gc* cross-battery assessment. *The School Psychologist, 52,* 6–9.

Ortiz, S. O., & Flanagan, D. P. (2002). Best practices in working with culturally diverse children and families. In A. Thomas & J. Grimes (Eds.), *Best Practices in School Psychology IV* (pp. 337–351). Washington, DC: National Association of School Psychologists.

Sanchez, G. I. (1934). Bilingualism and mental measures: A word of caution. *Journal of Applied Psychology, 18,* 756–772.

Scarr, S. (1978). From evolution to Larry P., or what shall we do about IQ tests? *Intelligence, 2,* 325–342.

Valdés, G., & Figueroa, R. A. (1994). *Bilingualism and testing: A special case of bias.* Norwood, NJ: Ablex.

SELECTED BIBLIOGRAPHY ON INSTRUCTION

Ambert, A. M., & Dew, N. (1982). *Special education for exceptional bilingual Students: A handbook for educators.* Milwaukee, WI: Midwest National Origin Desegregation Assistance Center.

Asher, J. (1982). *Learning another language through actions: The complete teacher's guidebook.* Los Gatos, CA: Sky Oaks.

Baca, L. M., & Almanza, E. (1991). *Language minority students with disabilities.* Reston, VA: The Council for Exceptional Children.

Bogomaz, B., & McMillan, S. (1995). *English Learner Achievement Project (ELAP) Training Handbook.* San Diego, CA: San Diego City Schools.

California State Department of Education, Office of Bilingual Bicultural Education (1991). *Schooling and language minority students: A theoretical framework.* Los Angeles: Evaluation, Discrimination and Assessment Center, CSULA.

Chamot, A. U., & O'Malley, J. M. (1986). *A cognitive academic language learning approach: An ESL content-based curriculum.* Washington, DC: National Clearinghouse for Bilingual Education.

Cummins, J. C. (1984). *Bilingual and special education: Issues in assessment and pedagogy.* Austin, TX: Pro-Ed.

Hakuta, K. (1986). *Mirror of language: The debate on bilingualism.* New York: Basic Books.

Hamayan, E. V., & Damico, J. S. (1991). *Limiting bias in the assessment of bilingual students.* Austin, TX: Pro-Ed.

Krashen, S. D. (1985). *Inquiries and insights: Second language teaching: Immersion and bilingual education, literacy.* Englewood Cliffs, NJ: Alemany Press.

Krashen, S., & Terrell, T. (1983). *The natural approach.* Hayward, CA: Alemany Press.

Mattes, L. J., & Omark, D. R. (1984). *Speech and language assessment for the bilingual handicapped.* San Diego: College-Hill Press.

McMillan, S. (1995). *English Learner Achievement Project (ELAP) Training Handbook.* San Diego, CA: San Diego City Schools.

Ortiz, A. A., & Maldonado-Colon, E. (1986). Recognizing learning disabilities in bilingual children: How to lessen inappropriate referral of language minority students to special education. *Journal of Reading, Writing, and Learning Disabilities International, 43,* 47–56.

Ortiz, A. A., & Wilkinson, C. Y. (1991). Assessment and Intervention Model for the Bilingual Exceptional Student (AIM for the BESt). *Teacher Education and Special Education, 14,* 35–42.

Samuda, R. J., Kong, S. L., Cummins, J., Pascual-Leone, J., & Lewis, J. (1991). *Assessment and placement of minority students.* Lewiston, NY: C. J. Hogrefe/Intercultural Social Sciences Publications.

Short, D. J. (1991). *Integrating language and content instruction: Strategies and techniques.* Washington, DC: National Clearinghouse for Bilingual Education.

Thomas, W., & Collier, V. (1997). *Language minority student achievement and program effectiveness.* Washington, DC: National Clearinghouse for Bilingual Education.

Valdés, G., & Figueroa, R. A. (1994). *Bilingualism and testing: A special case of bias.* Norwood, NJ: Ablex.

Walter, T. (1996). *Amazing English: How-to handbook.* New York: Addison-Wesley.

19

Special Education Legislation

KIMBERLY APPLEQUIST

SPECIAL EDUCATION LEGISLATION

This chapter provides summaries of a number of important federal constitutional provisions, statutes, and regulations that have had (or may have in the future) a significant impact on education in general and often on special education in particular. The statutes and regulations are presented chronologically to allow the reader to follow how relevant statutory and constitutional provisions have evolved over time. No attempt has been made to group statutes by subject matter, because many of the statutes cover a multitude of subjects. Because of the profound and wide-ranging importance of the Individuals with Disabilities Act (IDEA), it has been assigned its own section at the end of the chapter. However, it should be noted that, as this chapter was going to press, the IDEA was up for reauthorization, so the reader should anticipate some changes to the material in that section of the chapter.

This chapter is intended to provide background information about some of the key federal statutes and regulations that may be of interest to special educators and other members of the special education team. There may be additional state or federal statutes and regulations that are relevant to your situation or in your jurisdiction. The statutes and regulations included in this chapter are included for information purposes only, and should not be substituted for legal advice from an attorney licensed to practice law in your jurisdiction.

FEDERAL CONSTITUTIONAL PROVISIONS

A number of court cases (e.g., *Brown v. Board of Education*) and later statutes that deal with discrimination in the provision of educational services or deprivation of rights relating to a public education have their origins in two federal constitutional provisions: the Equal Protection Clause and the Due Process Clause. Both clauses are part of the Fourteenth Amendment—one of the post-Civil War era amendments intended to redress the wrongs done to former slaves in the southern states and to prevent future discrimination against them. The full text of the relevant section of the Fourteenth Amendment is:

> Section 1. All persons born or naturalized in the United States, and subject to the jurisdiction thereof, are citizens of the United States and of the State wherein they reside. No State shall make or enforce any law which shall abridge the privileges or immunities of citizens of the United States; nor shall any State deprive any person of life, liberty, or property, without due process law; nor deny to any person within its jurisdiction the equal protection of the laws.

A full discussion of the implications of this section of the Fourteenth Amendment is beyond the scope of this chapter. Indeed, entire books have been written on the subject. What follows is a very brief explanation of the significance of these two important constitutional provisions.

Equal Protection Clause

As indicated earlier, the Equal Protection Clause prohibits states from denying any person or class of persons equal protection of the laws. Though it has not been interpreted by the courts as meaning that all people be treated equally at all times, it does generally require that any classification made by a law, regulation, or other government action must (1) be a reasonable one, (2) further a legitimate government purpose, and (3) treat the classification's subject groups or classes equally. In addition, if the classification relates to a fundamental right or "suspect criteria," as defined subsequently, the classification must be *necessary* to promote a *compelling* state interest, and it must be the *least burdensome* alternative available to further that compelling state interest. *Suspect criteria* include, but are not necessarily limited to, race, religion, sex, country of national origin, alien/residency status, and socioeconomic status. Suspect criteria also include criteria that are statistically related to membership in any of the foregoing classifications.

In special education, the Equal Protection Clause is implicated when any classification, such as a placement proceeding, is made that could result in a child being treated differently than other children in his or her cohort (Reynolds, 2000). Courts have relied on the Equal Protection Clause in a number of cases that affect student rights (see cases cross-referenced following). In essence, courts have found that schools may not discriminate among groups of people without a substantial and legitimate purpose. The Equal Protection Clause has been invoked in a number of cases relating to children who were classified by schools as handicapped, who argued that they were not in fact handicapped and that, by placing them in special education programs, the schools were impermissibly discriminating against them under the Equal Protection Clause. The doctrine is also seen in the cases predating the Education for All Handicapped Children Act of 1975 (P.L. 94-142), in which courts held that handicapped children had a right to attend public schools.

Cross-references

- *Brown v. Board of Education*
- *Hobson v. Hansen*
- *Larry P. v. Riles*
- *Mattie T. v. Holladay*
- Education for All Handicapped Children Act of 1975 (P.L. 94-142)

Due Process Clause

The Due Process Clause requires that any government entity (including schools) that seeks to deprive an individual of some important right or privilege must follow certain procedural requirements prior to taking such an action, in order to ensure that the entity is not arbitrarily or capriciously depriving the individual of such right or privilege. In the school setting, actions by the school or local education agency that could potentially have a detrimental effect on a child (e.g., expelling the child, assigning the child to a special education program) trigger the right of due process.

It should be noted that many statutes and regulations relating to special education also have due process requirements. For example, procedural safeguard and due process provisions in the Individuals with Disabilities Education Act (IDEA), provide parents with the right to participate in decisions potentially affecting their children's placement in special education programs. For additional information about these provisions, see the discussions of the relevant statutes in this chapter.

Cross-references

- Individuals with Disabilities Education Act
- *Pennsylvania Association for Retarded Citizens v. Pennsylvania*
- *Battle v. Pennsylvania*

FEDERAL LEGISLATION

This section summarizes a number of key federal statutes from the past 40 years that relate, directly or indirectly, to special education or to cases that are themselves related to special education.

Civil Rights Act of 1964 (P.L. 88-352)

The Civil Rights Act of 1964 (CRA) was perhaps the most important piece of civil rights legislation in the last 50 years. Growing out of the civil rights movement from that period of our nation's history, the CRA addresses voting rights and discrimination in the provision of public accommodations or the enforcement of any law or regulation. With respect to the latter, the CRA provides generally that "All persons shall be entitled to be free, at any establishment or place, from discrimination or segregation of any kind on the ground of race, color, religion, or national origin, if such discrimination or segregation is or purports to be required by any law, statute, ordinance, regulation, rule, or order of a State or any agency or political subdivision thereof" (Civil Rights Act of 1964, § 202). Although individuals with disabilities are not included as a protected category under the CRA, the principles behind the CRA can be seen in later legislation that does affect the rights of individuals with disabilities, and the statute was cited in early cases that had an impact on the placement of individuals in protected categories into special education programs.

Cross-references

- *Lau v. Nichols*
- *Larry P. v. Riles*
- *Marshall v. Georgia*

Elementary and Secondary Education Act of 1965 (P.L. 89-10)

The Elementary and Secondary Education Act (ESEA) of 1965 instituted the first major program of federal assistance to local school districts (Ricciuti, 2000). Title 1 of this statute, which was later amended and restated as Chapter 1 of the Education Consolidation and Improvement Act of 1981, provided grants to school districts based upon the poverty levels in the district, to be used in providing compensatory educational services to children from deprived backgrounds (Ricciuti, 2000). In early 2002, the ESEA was reauthorized, amended, and renamed the No Child Left Behind Act of 2001 (see discussion of the new statute elsewhere in this chapter).

The ESEA also included a precursor to a portion of the Education for All Handicapped Children Act of 1975 (P.L. 94-142), which in turn was a precursor of the Individuals with Disabilities Education Act. This precursor authorized the Chapter 1 state agency program for disabled children in public schools (or state-supported schools; Ricciuti, 2000), providing grants to states for the provision of supplemental educational services for handicapped children, mostly in institutional settings.

Cross-references

- Education of All Handicapped Children Act of 1975
- Individuals with Disabilities Education Act
- No Child Left Behind Act

Handicapped Children's Early Education Assistance Act (P.L. 90-538)

The Handicapped Children's Early Education Assistance Act (HCEEAA) was enacted in 1968 to create the Handicapped Children's Early Education Program. The HCEEAA was intended to provide assistance for the development of educational programs for young children with disabilities. Initially, the HCEEAA provided grants for the establishment of "demonstration projects" at the preschool and early education levels for children with various disabilities, so that such programs could be evaluated for their usefulness in providing educational services for young children with disabilities and, where successful, serve as a model for other programs and entities providing services to young children with disabilities. In 1971, a Technical Assistance Development System was funded to provide assistance with demonstration projects (Button, 2000). The Handicapped Children's Early Education Program later provided funds for outreach services to allow successful demonstration projects to communicate their successes to others, and state implementation grants to help state agencies increase their ability to provide early intervention services to young children with disabilities. In 1977, four research institutes were funded to carry out longitudinal research in areas such as social, emotional, physical, cognitive, and behavioral aspects of children with disabilities (Button, 2000). In 1982, additional research institutes were funded to research problems relating to services for children with autistic-like disorders. One more institute was funded in 1985 to evaluate program outcomes for various forms of early intervention for children with disabilities (Button, 2000). Information collected through these research institutes has greatly expanded scientific knowledge about early intervention techniques for young handicapped children (Davis & Warren, 2000).

Cross-references

- Individuals with Disabilities Education Act

Title IX of the Education Amendments of 1972 (P.L. 92-318)

Title IX of the Education Amendments of 1972 was designed to reduce discrimination against girls and women in the field of education. It provided, with certain exceptions, that "no person in the United States shall, on the basis of sex, be excluded from participation in, be denied the benefits of, or be subjected to discrimination under any education program or activity receiving federal financial assistance" (20 U.S.C. Sections 1681(a)). In other words, educational programs and institutions that prevented students from attending or participating in educational programs and activities are ineligible to receive financial assistance from the federal government.

Cross-references

- Civil Rights Act of 1964

Rehabilitation Act of 1973 (P.L. 93-112)

The Rehabilitation Act of 1973 (sometimes also known as the Vocational Rehabilitation Act of 1973) authorizes vocational rehabilitation services to improve the employability of physically and/or mentally handicapped individuals or, in the case of severely disabled individuals, to improve the ability of such individuals to live independently. In addition to authorizing state grants in furtherance of these goals, the Rehabilitation Act also provides federal funding for such grants, on a matching basis with state funding.

Section 504 of the Rehabilitation Act of 1973 was an important precursor to the Education of All Handicapped Children Act of 1975 (P.L. 94-142), which in turn was superseded by the Individuals with Disabilities Education Act. Among other things, Section 504 protects the rights of disabled children and precludes discrimination in employment and education (Kamphaus, 2000). These requirements were later incorporated into the requirements of the Americans with Disabilities Act. Section 504 was important in many early court cases relating to discrimination with respect to special education, and was cited by the District Court in the famous *Larry P. v. Riles* decision regarding the use of intelligence tests when making decisions about the placement of a child into a special education program.

Cross-references

- *Larry P. v. Riles*
- *Marshall v. Georgia*
- Americans with Disabilities Act
- Education of All Handicapped Children Act of 1975 (P.L. 94-142)
- Individuals with Disabilities Education Act

Child Abuse Prevention and Treatment Act (CAPTA) (P.L. 93-247)

The Child Abuse Prevention and Treatment Act (CAPTA) was enacted in 1974 to provide federal funding to states, public agencies, and nonprofit organizations to support child abuse prevention, assessment, prosecution, investigation, and treatment, and to create demonstration projects relating to child abuse prevention and treatment. CAPTA also sets forth a minimum definition of child abuse and neglect, although states remain free to enact more extensive or detailed definitions, so long as the basic requirements of the federal definition are met. The act has been amended several times since it was originally enacted, and has recently been renamed and reenacted as the Keeping Children and Families Safe Act of 2003 (P.L. 108-36).

Cross-references

- Keeping Children and Families Safe Act of 2003

Family Educational Rights and Privacy Act (P.L. 93-380)

The Family Educational Rights and Privacy Act (FERPA), also known as the Buckley Amendment, was enacted in 1975 and gives parents and eligible students (students who have reached the age of 18 or who are attending school beyond the high school level) certain rights with respect to student educational records, though the specific rights have been added to and modified in the years since the statute was originally enacted. FERPA applies only to public schools and state and local educational agencies, and under the terms of the statute, schools and agencies that do not comply with its record-keeping procedures are not eligible for federal funds. Portions of the FERPA regulations were later incorporated into the Education for All Handicapped Children Act of 1975 (P.L. 94-142), now known as the Individuals with Disabilities Act (Lowe & Reynolds, 2000b).

FERPA was enacted due to often wildly inconsistent record-keeping policies and procedures in the nation's public schools. For example, it was not unheard of for schools to deny parents access to their children's educational records, yet to provide those same records to other third parties, including government agents and prospective employers (Lowe & Reynolds, 2000b). Parents often could not challenge the accuracy of information contained in their child's records (Lowe & Reynolds, 2000b). Furthermore, prior to FERPA's enactment, rights of access to student educational records varied from state to state, and sometimes from district to district, creating confusion and inconsistencies.

FERPA gives parents or eligible students the right to inspect the student's educational records and the right to have medical and psychological portions of the record reviewed by appropriate professionals acting on their behalf. However, schools are not required to give parents or eligible students copies of the records unless it is impossible for them to review the records (i.e., due to great distance). In such instances, schools are permitted to charge parents or eligible students a reasonable fee for photocopying the records.

Parents and eligible students may also request that a school correct educational records that they believe are misleading or inaccurate, though they cannot *require* a school to do so. However, if a school refuses to make requested changes to a student's records, the parents or eligible student may request a formal hearing on the matter, and may place a statement with the record regarding the disputed information.

The statute also limits disclosure of information in the student's educational records without parental consent (see Box 19.1) though it does permit schools to disclose "directory" information (i.e., a student's name, address, telephone number, date and place of birth, honors and awards, and dates of attendance), after

When May a School Disclose Information from a Student's Education Record?

Ordinarily, a school must have written permission from a parent or the eligible student prior to disclosing information from the student's educational record. However, under certain circumstances, a school may disclose such information without the student's consent. Under the provisions of 34 CFR § 99.31, schools may disclose information:

- To school officials with a legitimate educational interest in the information
- To another school to which a student is transferring
- To certain specified officials for audit or evaluation purposes
- To certain parties in connections with financial aid for a student
- To organizations conducting certain types of studies for or on behalf of the school
- To accrediting organizations
- In compliance with a judicial order or lawfully issued subpoena (e.g., for a court hearing or trial, or pursuant to the USA PATRIOT Act)
- To appropriate officials in the event of health and safety emergencies
- To state and local authorities within a juvenile justice system in accordance with the requirements of specific state law

(U.S. Department of Education, n.d.)

first notifying the parents or eligible student and allowing a reasonable period of time for the parents or eligible student to request nondisclosure of this information. The statute imposes penalties on parties who inappropriately release personally identifiable information from a student's educational records, so it is appropriate to exercise caution in their disclosure.

The statute applies only to a student's "education records," which are defined in the implementing regulations as "any records maintained by an educational agency or institution or by a person acting for such agency or institution that contains information directly related to a student" (34 CFR § 99.3). It is important to note that such records may take a variety of forms, including handwritten, print, computer and other electronic media, videotape, audiotape, film, microfilm, and/or microfiche (Lowe & Reynolds, 2000b). It is also important to remember that they may include a student's individualized education program, psychological assessment results, and juvenile court or social service agency reports that a school maintains in its files (Lowe & Reynolds, 2000b). Certain records are also *excluded* from a student's education records, such as the law enforcement records of school-based law enforcement units that are both maintained separately from the student's education records and used for law enforcement purposes only (Lowe & Reynolds, 2000b). Similarly, medical and psychological records of eligible students (that is, students who are 18 or older or who are attending postsecondary institutions) are excluded if they are made or used in connection with the provision of treatment, *unless* that treatment consists of remedial education or instructional programming, in which case the records are not excluded (Jacob-Timm & Hartshorne, 1995).

Finally, it should be noted that schools must maintain a record indicating requests for access to a student's education record, including the name of the individual seeking access, the purpose for which access was requested, and the date access was provided. Requests from, and disclosures to, parents, eligible students, and school officials with a legitimate educational interest are exempt from this record-keeping requirement. This record must be kept with the student's education record. However, to the extent that access to the student's education record was granted pursuant to a court order obtained as part of an investigation under the Uniting and Strengthening America by Providing Appropriate Tools Required to Intercept and Obstruct Terrorism Act of 2001 (USA PATRIOT Act), no such record is required.

Additional Sources of Information

The following web sites provide additional information about the Family Educational Rights and Privacy Act and its implementing regulations:

- U.S. Department of Education web site: http://www.ed.gov/policy/gen/guid/fpco/ferpa/index.html
- http://www.healthinschools.org/focus/2003/no1.htm

Cross-references

- Education of All Handicapped Children Act of 1975 (P.L. 94-142)
- Individuals with Disabilities Education Act

Education of All Handicapped Children Act of 1975 (P.L. 94-142)

The Education of All Handicapped Children Act of 1975 (P.L. 94-142) was enacted following several significant state and federal cases relating directly or indirectly to the education of children with disabilities. Three key cases were *Brown v. Board of Education, Pennsylvania Association for Retarded Children v. Commonwealth of Pennsylvania,* and *Mills v. Board of Education.* In *Brown,* the United States Supreme Court ordered the integration of schools in four states that had previously been segregated along racial lines. The Supreme Court's decision in *Brown* eventually led parents of children with disabilities to file suits against their local school districts to fight denial of educational services to their children. In *PARC,* a federal District Court found an obligation for the state to provide "a free, public program of education and training appropriate to the child's capacity" (334 F. Supp. 1257, 1260). In *Mills,* a federal District Court found an obligation to provide a publicly supported education to all school-age children who could benefit from one, relying on federal constitutional provisions and the laws of the District of Columbia, where the case took place. These three cases, as well as others like them, prompted the wide-scale filing of legal actions against school districts on behalf of children with disabilities (Martin, 1979), and provided the impetus for congressional action with respect to prevention of discrimination against students on the basis of physical or mental disabilities (Jacob-Timm & Hartshorne, 1995).

Earlier statutes helped lay the groundwork for the Education of All Handicapped Children Act, as well. In particular, the Elementary and Secondary Education Act and the Handicapped Children's Early Education Assistance Act influenced the Education of All Handicapped Children Act. Section 504 of the Rehabilitation Act of 1973 was another significant precursor to this statute.

With the enactment of P.L. 101-476, in 1990, amending the statute, the Education of All Handicapped Children Act was expanded, updated, and renamed the Individuals with Disabilities Education Act. The reader is referred to the discussion of the renamed statute later in this chapter for the particulars of the current law.

Cross-references

- *Brown v. Board of Education*
- *Mills v. Board of Education*
- *Pennsylvania Association for Retarded Children v. Commonwealth of Pennsylvania*
- Elementary and Secondary Education Act
- Handicapped Children's Early Education Assistance Act
- Rehabilitation Act of 1973
- Individuals with Disabilities Education Act

Gifted and Talented Children's Education Act of 1978 (P.L. 95-561)

The Gifted and Talented Children's Education Act of 1978 describes gifted and talented children who are entitled to special educational services and/or activities due to recognized or potential abilities for above-average performance in intellectual, creative, or particular academic areas, leadership, or the visual and performing arts. The statute also provides for financial assistance to state educational agencies to develop, plan, and operate programs for gifted and talented children, and to eligible public or private organizations, agencies, or other institutions for research, training, or demonstration projects relating to special educational programs and activities for gifted and talented children.

Americans with Disabilities Act of 1990 (P.L. 101-336)

The Americans with Disabilities Act of 1990 (ADA) is a civil rights law intended to "provide a clear and comprehensive national mandate for the elimination of discrimination against individuals with disabilities" (42 U.S.C. § 12101 Sec. 2(b)(1)). It was passed in response to evidence that individuals with handicaps faced a large number of obstacles in daily life, some of which could best be addressed legislatively on a national level. Though the substance and intent of the statute borrow heavily from Section 504 of the Rehabilitation Act of 1973, the actual procedures set forth in the ADA are drawn from the Civil Rights Act of 1964.

The five titles of the ADA, summarized in greater detail subsequently, address discrimination in employment, public services, public accommodations and services operated by private entities, and telecommunications. As employers and providers of public services (in the case of public schools) or public services operated by private entities (in the case of private schools), educational institutions are required to comply with the terms of the statute and its implementing regulations. Following is a brief description of the key requirements of the statute's various titles:

- *Title I—Employment.* Title I of the ADA generally prohibits discrimination against "a qualified individual with a disability *because of the disability* in regard to job application procedures, the hiring, advancement, or discharge of employees, employee compensation, job training, and other terms, conditions, and privileges

Who Is a "Qualified Individual with a Disability" under the ADA?

Both Title I and Title II of the ADA make reference to the "qualified individual with a disability." The definition of a qualified individual with a disability varies slightly depending upon the applicable title. Under Title I, which pertains to employment relationships, a qualified individual with a disability is an individual with a disability who can perform the essential functions of the employment position that such individual holds or desires, either with or without reasonable accommodation (42 U.S.C. 12111(8)). Under Title II, which is applicable to the delivery of education services in the public school environment, the term means an "individual with a disability who, with or without reasonable modifications to rules, policies, or practices, the removal of architectural, communication, or transportation barriers, or the provision of auxiliary aids and services, meets the essential eligibility requirements for the receipt of services or the participation in programs or activities provided by a public entity" (42 U.S.C. 12115(2)).

In both instances, a "disability" is broadly defined, with respect to an individual, as (1) a physical or mental impairment that substantially limits one or more major life activities, (2) a record of such an impairment, or (3) *being regarded as* having such an impairment (42 U.S.C. 12102).

of employment" (42 U.S.C. 12112(a), emphasis added). Under the terms of Title I, a number of behaviors can constitute prohibited discrimination, including (but not limited to) failure to make reasonable accommodations that would allow the qualified individual with a disability to perform any essential job functions (42 U.S.C. 12112(b)(5)(A)). It "may be" a defense to charges of discrimination under the act if the employer can show that the qualification standards, tests, or selection criteria that tend to screen out an individual with a disability can be shown to be job-related and consistent with business necessity, and that performance of the job functions by the job applicant cannot be accomplished with reasonable accommodations (42 U.S.C. 12113(a)). In other words, an employer is required to make reasonable accommodations to otherwise qualified employees or applicants, unless undue hardship (such as excessive expense) would result.

- *Title II—Public Services.* Title II generally prohibits the exclusion of any qualified individual with a disability from participation in the services, programs, or activities of a public entity, or the discrimination against such an individual by such an entity (42 U.S.C. 12132). School districts are required, under this title, to furnish appropriate assistance or aids to qualified individuals with disabilities to allow them to participate in available programs and services. These may include after-school activities and social events, public entertainment or lectures sponsored by a district, field trips, and other services provided for students and staff (Office of Civil Rights, 1996). The nondiscrimination requirements of Section 504 of the Rehabilitation Act of 1973 relating to a school district's obligation to provide a free, appropriate public education to school-aged children with disabilities are incorporated into the general provisions of Title II, as well. Title II also requires that school facilities be made physically accessible to individuals with disabilities, with different standards applying for existing facilities and newly constructed facilities, though there are limitations on the extent of this latter requirement.

- *Title III—Public Accommodations and Services Operated by Private Entities.* Title III is similar in many respects to Title II, except that it applies to services provided by private, rather than government, entities. Private schools at all levels, from nursery school through the postgraduate level, fall within the definition of "public accommodations" described in this portion of the ADA (42 U.S.C. 12181(7)(J)). Broadly speaking, Title III prohibits discrimination against any individual on the basis of a disability "in the full and equal enjoyment of the goods, services, facilities, privileges, advantages, or accommodations of any place of public accommodation" by any person who owns, leases, or operates a place of public accommodation (42 U.S.C. 12182).

- *Title IV—Telecommunications.* Title IV relates to expanding the availability of telecommunications and closed-captioning services for hearing-impaired and speech-impaired individuals. Under Title IV, schools are required to ensure effective communication with disabled individuals on the same basis as non-disabled individuals (Lowe & Reynolds, 2000a).

- *Title V—Miscellaneous Provisions.* Title V of the ADA addresses a variety of issues, including the interaction of the ADA with federal statutes and regulations that were already in existence at the time the ADA was passed, and the prohibition of retaliation against and coercion of individuals who make claims or otherwise pursue their rights under the ADA.

Additional Sources of Information

The following web sites provide additional information about the Americans with Disabilities Act and its implementing regulations:

- U.S. Department of Justice ADA web site: http://www.usdoj.gov/crt/ada/adahom1.htm
- U.S. Equal Employment Opportunity Commission ADA web site: http://www.eeoc.gov/facts/fs-ada.html
- DisabilityResources.org web site: http://www.disabilityresources.org/ADA.html

Cross-references

- Civil Rights Act of 1964
- Rehabilitation Act of 1973

Health Insurance Portability and Accountability Act of 1996 (P.L. 104-191)

The Health Insurance Portability and Accountability Act of 1996 (HIPAA) was enacted by Congress in order to protect health insurance coverage for individuals with preexisting health conditions when they change jobs and health insurers. HIPAA also includes a number of important provisions relating to the confidentiality of medical information that are potentially relevant in the educational setting. To the extent that a school provides health care services to its students and receives funding for such services from a federal program like Medicaid, the school may be held to the confidentiality standards of HIPAA, at least to some degree (Whelley, Cash, & Wrobel, 2002).

A complete discussion of the provisions of HIPAA relating to the confidentiality of medical records (which might in some circumstances include student education records or a child's individualized education program under the IDEA) is beyond the scope of this chapter. Briefly, HIPAA prohibits disclosures of individually identifiable health information except in certain circumstances (e.g., disclosures necessary to the provision of treatment to the covered individual) or to certain entities (e.g., disclosures made to an insurer or other third-party payor in order to obtain payment for services provided to the covered individual) unless the individual or entity making the disclosure first obtains the consent of the individual whose protected health information is to be disclosed. The statute and its implementing regulations define individually identifiable health information as any information, including demographic information, collected from an individual that (1) is created or received by a health care provider, health plan, employer, or health care clearinghouse, (2) relates to past, present, or future physical or mental health condition of an individual, the provision of health care to an individual, or the payment for the provision of health care to an individual, and (3) identifies the individual or could reasonably believed to be usable to identify the individual. The key question, then, is whether a school that is providing covered health care (which could include mental health care services) is a covered health care provider within the meaning of the statute. While most often a school will not fall within this designation, there may be instances when it will. Fortunately there are a number of tools available on the Internet to help determine whether one is a covered health care provider, including one available on the web site of the Centers for Medicare and Medicaid Services (see Additional Sources of Information, following).

It is important to remember that, even if one can conclude that one's school is not a covered health care provider under HIPAA, the school is still subject to other statutes and regulations that may impose obligations with respect to the confidentiality of information about a student, such as the Family Educational Rights and Privacy Act (discussed earlier) and the Individuals with Disabilities Education Act (discussed following). Maintaining the confidentiality and physical security of a student's education record or individualized education program should always be an important consideration for school psychologists and special educators.

Additional Sources of Information

- Centers for Medicare and Medicaid Services web site: http://www.cms.hhs.gov/hipaa/
- National Association of School Psychologists web site: http://www.nasponline.org/publications/cq314hipaa.html

Cross-references

- Family Educational Rights and Privacy Act
- Individuals with Disabilities Education Act

No Child Left Behind Act (2002) (P.L. 107-110)

The No Child Left Behind Act, enacted in 2002, is intended to improve education by providing "accountability for results; an emphasis on doing what works based on scientific research; expanded parental options; and expanded local control and flexibility" (U.S. Department of Education, n.d.b). This mammoth statute (the full text of the statute is 670 pages) provides resources for early childhood education, and calls for increased accountability through testing of students' reading and math skills on an annual basis from grades 3 through 8, and at least once in grades 10 through 12. The statute also imposes requirements for teacher education and competency, demonstration of adequate yearly progress in a school's students, use of evidence-based educational interventions, and provisions allowing parents some measure of school choice for their children. Given the length and sweeping nature of this statute, a detailed discussion of all its provisions far exceeds the scope of this chapter, and only provisions of particular interest to school psychologists and special educators will be discussed here. See Box 19.3 for a brief listing of areas covered by the No Child Left Behind Act.

As noted above, schools must demonstrate "adequate yearly progress" in their students' proficiency in math, reading, and science, and students in special education programs are not generally exempted from this requirement. Thus of particular interest to school psychologists and special educators are recent guidelines issued by the Education Department regarding how to include students with disabilities in annual assessments required by the statute. The guidelines, issued in December 2003, allow states and school districts to assess up to 1 percent of their total student population using alternate standards when determining whether

Key Provisions of the No Child Left Behind Act

- Annual testing in reading and math for children in grades 3 through 8
- Biennial testing of a sample of children in grades 4 through 8 using the National Assessment of Educational Progress test (used as an independent benchmark to judge state standards of accountability)
- A requirement that schools show "adequate yearly progress" toward the goal of 100 percent student proficiency in reading, math, and science, for all students
- Public school choice provisions that require schools that fail to show adequate yearly progress in 2 consecutive years to offer parents of students in such schools to transfer to another public school (does not apply if applicable state law prohibits school choice)
- A requirement that school districts provide "supplemental instructional services" (tutoring, after-school classes, and summer classes) to students who attend schools that fail to show adequate yearly progress for 3 consecutive years
- A requirement that school districts provide "corrective actions" if a school fails to show adequate yearly progress in 4 consecutive years
- A requirement that school districts implement plans for significant changes to how a school is run if the school fails to show adequate yearly progress in 5 consecutive years
- A requirement that states develop a plan to ensure that all teachers will be "highly qualified" by the end of the 2005–2006 school year
- Provision for two new reading programs: Reading First, which will distribute grants to states for reading programs that service children in kindergarten through third grade; and Early Reading First, which will provide competitive grants to school districts and private organizations to develop and implement preschool reading programs
- Fiscal flexibility provisions that allow state and local education agencies to reallocate a portion of federal funds received under the act to permitted programs
- State and local demonstration projects
- Financial and technical assistance to school districts to improve student achievement at low-performing schools
- Other provisions relating to bilingual education, innovative education programs, technology education, after-school programs, safe and drug-free schools, and certain immunity provisions relating to teachers and school officials acting within the scope of their duties relating to providing educational services and in compliance with applicable laws and regulations, so long as any harm was not the results of willful or criminal misconduct or gross negligence

(Council for Exceptional Children, 2004)

such students meet state proficiency requirements. Students who exceed the 1 percent cap generally must be included in the state count as nonproficient (assuming their test scores indicate this). States and local education agencies may seek a waiver of the 1 percent cap if they can show data necessary to support this. The guidelines say that the 1 percent cap is intended only to apply to students "with the most significant cognitive disabilities" but does not elaborate on what this might mean.

The statute appropriates funds for a variety of educational purposes, including between $13.5 billion and $25 billion in each year from 2002 to 2007, for the purpose of improving basic programs operated by local educational agencies, with additional amounts for a variety of specific programs, although it should be noted that for many of these additional programs, either no amount is specifically authorized, or funds are only specifically authorized for the first year, raising the possibility that in future years these programs might not be funded at the same level as they were in their first year, let alone enough to account for any necessary growth of those programs over time.

The No Child Left Behind Act has been controversial, for a variety of reasons. The National Education Association suggests that the statute actually creates obstacles to helping students and strengthening public schools because it focuses on, in their words, "punishments rather than assistance, mandates rather than support for effective programs, [and] privatization rather than teacher-led, family-oriented solutions" (National Education Association, n.d.). While it is too soon to ascertain the long-term effects of the No Child Left Behind Act, at press time a number of organizations were advocating the repeal or substantial revision of either the entire act or specific provisions within the act, and the 2004 legislative session saw at least one bill introduced, the NCLB Fairness Act of 2004, that would have made significant changes to the "adequate yearly progress" provisions of the No Child Left Behind Act.

Additional Sources of Information

- Education Department's No Child Left Behind Act web site: http://www.ed.gov/nclb/landing.jhtml
- White House No Child Left Behind Act web site
- National Education Association's position on the No Child Left Behind Act: http://www.nea.org/esea/
- Council for Exceptional Children technical assistance document on the No Child Left Behind Act: http://www.cec.sped.org//pp/OverviewNCLB.pdf

Keeping Children and Families Safe Act of 2003 (P.L. 108-36)

The most recent iteration of the Child Abuse Prevention and Treatment Act, the Keeping Children and Families Safe Act of 2003 provides a national clearinghouse for data relating to child abuse, and grants for research and development of programs to prevent child abuse. It also includes provisions regarding adoption, abandoned infants, and family violence prevention and services.

INDIVIDUALS WITH DISABILITIES EDUCATION ACT

The Individuals with Disabilities Education Act (IDEA, P.L. 101-476, as amended by P.L. 105-17) grew out of the earlier Education of All Handicapped Children Act of 1975 (P.L. 94-142), discussed elsewhere in this chapter. It was initially enacted in 1990, amended and restated in 1997, and amended as this book goes to press in December 2004. The law was renamed (H.R. 1350, P.L. 108-446) The Individuals with Disabilities Education Improvement Act of 2004 (IDEIA).

A summary of IDEIA 2004 is provided by the U.S. Congressional web site, (Thomas, http://thomas.loc.gov/home/thomas.html) and is as follows:

> Individuals with Disabilities Education Improvement Act of 2004—Title I: Amendments to the Individuals with Disabilities Education Act—(Sec. 101) Amends the Individuals with Disabilities Education Act (IDEA) to revise and reauthorize its programs.

What Must State Plans Include under the IDEA?

In order for a state to receive federal funds, its state plan must include the following components (discussed more fully in the accompanying text):

- Free appropriate public education
- Full educational opportunity goal
- Child find
- Individualized education program
- Least restrictive environment
- Procedural safeguards
- Confidentiality
- Transition from infant and toddler program to preschool program
- Children in private schools
- State educational agency responsibility
- Ensuring services
- Comprehensive system for personnel development
- Personnel standards
- Performance goals and indicators
- Participation in assessments
- Establishment of a state advisory panel
- Examination of suspension and expulsion rates of disabled and nondisabled children
- Public comment prior to adoption of new policies and procedures

(Lowe & Reynolds, 2000c)

Revises IDEA part A general provisions, including definitions. Revises requirements for assistive technology devices and related services to eliminate coverage of surgically implanted medical devices or their replacement. Allows a State or local educational agency (LEA), with respect to children ages three to nine, to include any subset of that age range for purposes of determinations that an individual is experiencing development delays and needs special education and related services as a child with a disability. Provides definitions of core academic subject, highly qualified teacher, and limited English proficient individual to conform with requirements under the Elementary and Secondary Education Act (ESEA), as amended by the No Child Left Behind Act (NCLBA). Includes interpreting services and school nurse services under related services.

Sets forth requirements relating to State administration, policies, and rulemaking under IDEA.

Provides for a paperwork reduction demonstration program. Authorizes the Secretary of Education to grant waivers of statutory or regulatory requirements, other than civil rights requirements, under part A for up to four years to up to 15 States, based on State proposals to reduce excessive paperwork and noninstructional time burdens that do not assist in improving educational and functional results for children with disabilities. Prohibits such waiver program from being construed to: (1) affect the right of a child with a disability to receive a free appropriate public education (FAPE) under part A; and (2) permit a State or LEA to waive specified procedural safeguards. Directs the Secretary to include in certain annual reports to Congress information related to the effectiveness of such waivers, including any specific recommendations for their broader implementation.

Revises IDEA part B assistance for education of all children with disabilities.

Authorizes appropriations for part B programs, in specified increasing amounts for FY 2005 through FY 2011, and in necessary sums for FY 2012 and succeeding fiscal years. (Provides a separate authorization of appropriations for preschool grants under part B.)

Sets forth a formula for determining the maximum amount to be available for awarding grants to States under part B for any fiscal year. Bases the FY 2005 and FY 2006 formula on the number of children with disabilities in the State who are receiving special education and related services. Bases the formula for FY 2007 and subsequent fiscal years on the number of such children who received such education and services in the 2004–2005 school year. Provides for such numbers to be multiplied by 40 percent of the national average per pupil expenditure, and adjusted by the rate of annual change in the sum of 85 percent of a State's population of children and 15 percent of a State's population of children living in poverty.

Provides allocation formulas for grants to States (with subgrants to LEAs), outlying areas and freely associated States, and the Secretary of the Interior for programs for Indian children. Includes population and poverty components of the specified permanent formula in determining the amount available for States' maximum grants. Provides for continued funding of outlying areas and freely associated States at the FY 2003 level.

Makes State expenditure of administrative funds contingent upon its certification that agreements to establish public agency responsibilities for providing and financing part B services within a State are current. Revises the formula for determining the amount States may use for State administration and other State activities. Includes enforcement among required State activities, as well as the currently required monitoring, complaint investigation, and mediation system. Includes among optional State activities: support for paperwork reduction; positive behavioral interventions and supports and mental health services; technology; transition programs; alternate programming for those expelled from school, in correctional facilities, or in State-operated or State-supported schools; appropriate accommodations and alternate assessments; and technical assistance and direct services, including supplemental educational services.

Requires States to reserve a specified portion of part B funds to establish a risk pool fund to assist LEAs in serving high-need children with disabilities or unanticipated special education costs. Requires placement-neutral policies for settings of high-need students that: (1) do not favor public, nonpublic or out-of-district placements; and (2) provide the services to which children are entitled in a setting that is consistent with their individualized education plan (IEP). Prohibits risk pool funds from being used to pay costs that otherwise are reimbursable as medical assistance for a child with a disability under a State Medicaid program.

Provides that public charter schools that operate as LEAs are entitled to subgrants as LEAs.

Removes certain procedural and reporting requirements for State eligibility. Requires States to provide assurances that they have the appropriate policies and procedures in place to ensure that they have met part B requirements.

Revises requirements for LEAs to oblige proportional amounts of funds for parentally-placed private school children with disabilities, under certain conditions. Requires LEAs to: (1) provide direct services to such children to the extent practicable; (2) provide data on the number of students evaluated, found to have a disability, and served under part B; (3) conduct the child-find process for such children in a time period comparable to that for students attending public schools; (4) not consider the cost of such child-find and individual evaluations in meeting their proportional obligations; and (5) consult with private school officials on the child-find process, determination of proportional share of Federal funds, provision of services, alternative delivery mechanisms, and third party providers. Allows private schools to appeal if such consultation does not take place. Requires such special education and related services to be secular, neutral, and nonideological. (Continues requirements for: (1) no cost to parents for State or LEA placement of a child in a private school to receive required special education and services; and (2) reimbursement for the parents' placing the child in a private school for such education and services, if a court or hearing officer orders it upon finding that the public agency had not made a free appropriate public education available to the child prior to that enrollment.)

Revises personnel standards to direct States to adopt policies that require LEAs to take measurable steps to recruit, hire, and retain highly qualified personnel.

Requires all special education teachers in an elementary, middle or secondary school to be highly qualified no later than the end of the 2005–2006 school year.

Eliminates a requirement that States develop a comprehensive system of personnel development. Requires State standards governing the qualifications of related service personnel serving children with disabilities to be consistent with any State-approved or State-recognized certification or licensing or other comparable requirement applicable to the specific professional discipline of such personnel. Requires States to ensure that such personnel have not had their certification or licensure requirements waived on an emergency, temporary, or provisional basis. Provides that such provisions shall not: (1) be construed to create a right of action on behalf of an individual student for the failure of a particular SEA or LEA staff person to be highly qualified; or (2) prevent a parent from filing a State complaint regarding staff qualifications with the SEA.

Revises requirements for academic achievement and functional performance of children with disabilities to conform IDEA to the State and LEA accountability system established under NCLBA, with school and LEA disaggregation of data to examine the results of children with disabilities and ensure that such subgroup is making adequate yearly progress (AYP) towards reaching proficiency.

Includes provisions relating to AYP among State performance goals and indicators for children with disabilities.

Revises requirements for participation in assessments. Requires alternate assessments to be a part of State and LEA assessment programs and accountability systems. Sets forth additional requirements for developing and administering alternate assessments aligned with the State's academic content and achievement standards, and for developing alternate standards for those children with significant cognitive disabilities. Requires States and LEAs to develop and use universally designed assessments to the extent feasible.

Prohibits States from having funding mechanisms that distribute funds based upon the type of setting in which a child is served. Requires States to revise any such current policies or procedures.

Prohibits States from using part B funds to satisfy State-law mandated funding obligations to LEAs, including funding based on student attendance or enrollment, or inflation, in complying with part B requirements relating to: (1) supplementation of State, local, and other Federal funds; and (2) maintenance of State financial support.

Establishes requirements for accessibility of instructional materials. Allows SEAs to opt not to coordinate with the National Instructional Materials Access Center in adopting a national instructional materials accessibility standard, if they assure the Secretary that they will provide instructional materials to blind persons or other persons with print disabilities in a timely manner. Requires, within two years after enactment of this Act, those SEAs that opt to coordinate with the Center to enter into contracts with publishers of print instructional materials to: (1) require the publisher to prepare and supply to the Center electronic files with such materials' contents using such standard; or (2) purchase from the publisher instructional materials that are produced, or may be rendered, in specialized formats.

Requires State policies and procedures to prevent overidentification or disproportionate representation by race and ethnicity of children as children with disabilities, including identification of children as children with a particular impairment.

Requires SEAs to prohibit SEA and LEA personnel from requiring a child, as a condition of attending school or receiving IDEA evaluations or services, to obtain a prescription for a substance covered by the Controlled Substances Act.

Removes certain procedural and reporting requirements for LEA eligibility. Requires LEAs to submit plans with assurances to SEAs that they have in effect policies, procedures, and programs that meet specified part B requirements.

Includes among allowable uses of part B funds by LEAs: (1) services that also benefit nondisabled children; (2) early intervening educational services; (3) high cost education and services; and (4) administrative case management, including related technology.

Revises provisions relating to public charter schools to: (1) authorize LEAs to distribute IDEA funds to charter schools based on relative enrollment and proportional distribution; and (2) direct LEAs to provide supplemental and related services on site at the charter school to the same extent as to other public schools.

Revises provisions regarding early intervening services. Authorizes LEAs to use up to 15 percent of their IDEA funds to develop and implement coordinated, early intervening educational services for students who are not receiving special education services but who require additional academic and behavioral support to succeed in a regular education environment, and who may be likely referrals to special education programs and services at a later time. Includes among such allowable services: (1) professional development for teachers and other school staff to deliver scientifically-based academic and behavioral interventions; and (2) providing educational and behavioral evaluations, services, and supports, including scientifically-based literacy instruction.

Eliminates provisions for a School-Based Improvement Plan.

Sets forth provisions for SEA flexibility to allow adjustments in State fiscal effort under certain conditions.

Revises requirements for evaluations, eligibility determinations, IEPs, and placements. Provides that a parent, SEA, other State agency, or LEA has a right to request an initial evaluation to determine whether a child qualifies for IDEA services. Provides that an LEA does not violate the FAPE requirement by failing to provide special education and related services to a child with a disability as long as these are refused by the parent. Includes academic information among the information the LEA is required to gather in the evaluation process of a child.

Revises additional requirements for LEA procedures in selecting and administering tests and other evaluations to determine a child's eligibility under IDEA. Requires tests and evaluations to be provided and administered, to the extent practicable, in the language and form most likely to yield accurate information on what the child knows and can do academically, developmentally, and functionally.

Revises a special rule for eligibility determination to provide that a lack of scientifically based reading instruction cannot be the determinant factor for deciding whether the child is a child with a disability. Provides that LEAs, in determining whether or not a student has a specific learning disability, shall not be required to take into consideration whether there is a severe discrepancy between achievement and intellectual ability in specified skills. Allows LEAs, as part of evaluation procedures, to use a process that determines if a child responds to scientific, research-based intervention.

Revises exit evaluation requirements. Provides that such evaluations before termination of IDEA eligibility are not required upon: (1) graduation from secondary school with a regular diploma; or (2) exceeding age eligibility for a free appropriate public education under State law. Requires LEAs, in such cases, to provide students with a summary of their academic achievement and functional performance, including recommendations on how to assist them in meeting their postsecondary goals.

Requires individualized education programs (IEPs) to include a statement of the child's present levels of academic achievement and functional performance (currently educational performance). Requires the statement of measurable annual goals to include academic goals and functional goals.

Eliminates requirements for benchmarks and short-term objectives in IEPs. Requires IEPs to contain descriptions of: (1) how the child's progress toward meeting the annual goals will be measured; and (2) when periodic progress reports will be provided. Requires progress updates to provide parents with specific, meaningful, and understandable information on the progress children are making.

Revises requirements for accommodations and alternate assessments. Provides for testing of some children that includes certain necessary accommodations, an alternate assessment, or an alternate assessment based upon alternative standards for those children with significant cognitive disabilities. Requires a statement of appropriate accommodations to be made for State or districtwide assessments. Requires the IEP team, if it determines that a child shall take an alternate assessment, to state why the child cannot participate in the regular assessment and why the particular alternate assessment selected is appropriate for that child.

Revises requirements for transition services. Requires IEPs, beginning not later than the first IEP to be in effect when the child is 16, and updated annually thereafter, to contain: (1) appropriate measurable postsecondary goals based upon age appropriate assessments related to training, education, employment, and, where appropriate, independent living skills; and (2) the transition services the child needs to reach those goals.

Provides that nothing in IDEA regarding IEPs shall be construed to require that additional information be included in an IEP beyond what is explicitly required.

Allows a member of the IEP team to be excused from an IEP meeting if: (1) no modifications are being made to that member's area of curriculum or service; or (2) when a relevant modification is made, if the member provides input prior to the meeting. Requires the IEP team member, the parent, and the LEA to agree to the member's being excused. Directs LEAs to encourage consolidation of IEP meetings and reevaluation meetings. Includes the academic, developmental, and functional needs of the child among factors the IEP team must consider in developing a child's IEP.

Requires IEP teams to provide positive behavioral interventions and supports for children with disabilities whose behavior impedes their learning or the learning of others.

Authorizes the Secretary to approve up to 15 proposals from States to carry out a demonstration program allowing parents and LEAs the option of developing a comprehensive multiyear IEP, of up to three years, designed to coincide with natural transition points.

Allows parents and LEAs to agree to participate in IEP Team and placement meetings via means such as video conferences and conference calls.

Revises procedural safeguards to provide that LEAs, as well as parents, have the right to present complaints. Requires the party filing a due process complaint to send the complaint to the other party, as well as to the State agency. Requires, in the case of a homeless child or youth, the parent's notice to the LEA to contain contact information for the child and the name of the school the child is attending. Prohibits a due process hearing unless the requesting party has filed a complaint that meets specified notice requirements. Requires States to develop a model form to assist parents in filing due process complaint notices and complaints. Requires the school to provide a parent with a prior written notice, when learning of a parent's dispute for the first time in a parent's due process complaint. Requires parents to receive the procedural safeguards notice generally only once a year, but also upon: (1) initial referral or parental request for an evaluation; (2) a parent's registration of a due process complaint; or (3) request by the parent. Allows an LEA to place a current copy of the procedural safeguards notice on its Internet website. Requires the procedural safeguards notice to inform parents regarding specified matters, including: (1) the time period in which parents can file complaints; (2) the school district's opportunity to resolve a complaint before a due process hearing; and (3) the time period in which a party can appeal a hearing officer's decision to court.

Provides that: (1) parents may request mediation before filing a complaint; and (2) a written mediation agreement is enforceable in court. Authorizes a State agency to establish procedures to offer parents, as well as schools, that choose not to use the mediation process an opportunity to speak with a disinterested party regarding the benefits of mediation.

Provides for a resolution session to give parents and LEAs an opportunity to resolve the complaint before a due process hearing.

Establishes a two-year timeline for requesting a hearing on claims for reimbursed or ongoing compensatory education services, unless there is an applicable State timeline.

Requires hearing officers to make decisions on due process complaints on substantive grounds based upon a determination of whether the child in question received a FAPE. Authorizes hearing officers, in matters alleging a procedural violation, to find that a child did not receive a FAPE only if the procedural inadequacies: (1) impeded the child's right to a FAPE; (2) significantly impeded the parents' opportunity to participate in the decisionmaking process regarding FAPE provision; or (3) caused a deprivation of educational benefits.

Prescribes requirements for administrative and judicial review. Provides for a 90-day-period, or the period provided by State law, for a party to appeal a due process hearing decision to State or Federal district court. Prohibits the award of attorneys' fees for services performed subsequent to a written offer of settlement, under specified conditions. Provides for reduction of award of attorneys' fees under certain circumstances, including where the parent or parent's attorney unreasonably protracted the final resolution of the controversy.

Sets forth types of disciplinary actions that an LEA may take under IDEA.

Authorizes schools to consider any unique circumstances on a case-by-case basis when determining whether to order a change in placement for a child with a disability who violates a code of student conduct.

Authorizes schools to order, for children with disabilities who violate student conduct codes, changes of placement to an appropriate interim educational setting, another setting, or suspension, for up to ten consecutive school days, to the same extent such alternatives would apply to children without disabilities, without making a manifestation determination.

Authorizes schools, upon determining that the violation in question was not a manifestation of the child's disability, to apply beyond that ten-day period the same disciplinary procedures as for a child without a disability, provided that FAPE requirements are met, with the option of providing such FAPE in an interim alternative educational setting.

Requires, within 10 school days of such a disciplinary decision to change placement, a review of all relevant informant by LEA, parent, and IEP Team to determine if the child's behavior was a manifestation of disability. Bases such determination on whether the conduct: (1) was caused by, or had a direct and substantial relationship to, the child's disability; or (2) was the direct result of the LEA's failure to implement the IEP. Requires the IEP Team, if the conduct is such a manifestation, to: (1) conduct a functional behavioral assessment and implement a behavioral intervention plan, if the LEA has not done so; (2) if such a plan has been developed, review and modify it to address the behavior; and (3) (except in cases involving weapons, drugs, or infliction of serious bodily injury) return the child to the placement from which the child was removed, unless the parent and LEA agree to a change of placement as part of the modification of the behavioral intervention plan.

Authorizes a school, in cases involving weapons or drugs, or when a child has committed serious bodily injury, to remove the child from the regular classroom setting for up to 45 school days, regardless of whether the child's behavior was a manifestation of disability. Requires that such children receive continued educational services and appropriate functional behavioral assessments and behavioral intervention services and modifications.

Directs the IEP team to determine the child's alternative educational setting.

Sets forth circumstances in which a party may request a hearing regarding disciplinary decisions or proposed disciplinary actions. Allows requests for such hearings by: (1) parents who disagree with LEA decisions regarding disciplinary actions, placements, or manifestation determinations, with the hearing officer to determine if the LEA decision is appropriate; and (2) LEAs that believe that maintaining the child's current placement is substantially likely to result in injury to the child or others.

Requires the child, during a parent's appeal, to remain in the interim alternative educational setting chosen by the IEP team pending the hearing officer's decision or until the time period for the disciplinary action expires, whichever occurs first, unless the parent and public agency agree otherwise. Requires the hearing to occur within 20 days of the hearing request, and to result in a determination within 10 days after the hearing.

Allows assertion of IDEA protections for a child not determined eligible for special education and related services who has violated a code of student conduct, if the LEA had knowledge that the child had a disability before the behavior that precipitated the disciplinary action occurred. Deems an LEA as knowing about a child's disability if: (1) the parent has expressed concern in writing; (2) the parent has requested an evaluation; or (3) a teacher or other school personnel has expressed concern about a pattern of behavior to either the special education director, or to other administrative personnel. Provides that an LEA will not be deemed to know that the child has a disability if the child's parent has not agreed to allow an evaluation requested by the LEA.

Revises provisions relating to transfer of parental rights at age of majority to allow a parent of a child with a disability to elect to receive required notices by e-mail communication, if the public agency makes such option available.

Provides for monitoring, technical assistance, and enforcement of part B programs. Directs the Secretary to: (1) monitor IDEA implementation through oversight of States' supervision and a system of performance indicators focused on improving educational results and functional outcomes for all children with disabilities; (2) enforce State compliance in making satisfactory progress toward improving educational results using certain indicators and benchmarks; and (3) require States to monitor and enforce LEA compliance.

Requires the primary focus of Federal and State monitoring activities to be on improving educational results and functional outcomes for all children with disabilities, while ensuring compliance with program requirements, with a particular emphasis on requirements relating to improving educational results for children with disabilities.

Sets the following monitoring priorities: (1) provision of a FAPE in the least restrictive environment; (2) State exercise of general supervisory authority; and (3) disproportionate representation of racial and ethnic groups in special education and related services, to the extent the overrepresentation is the result of inappropriate identification. Requires States to develop State performance plans, including targets to measure progress in priority areas.

Provides for various enforcement measures in cases of State needs for assistance, intervention, or substantial intervention.

Requires SEAs to prohibit LEAs from reducing their maintenance of effort if they are not meeting IDEA part B requirements.

Directs the Secretary to develop model forms for certain plans and notices.

Revises data collection requirements to require States to: (1) make data available to the public, as well as the Secretary; (2) provide the number and percentage of children in various categories; (3) collect information on the categories of gender and limited English proficiency status; (4) collect additional information in relation to certain disciplinary actions, due process complaints and hearings, and mediations; and (5) report data so as not to result in the disclosure of data identifiable to individual children. Authorizes the Secretary to permit States to obtain data through sampling.

Continues the preschool grants program under IDEA part B. Provides among State-level activities for early intervention any services which include an educational component that promotes schools' readiness and incorporates preliteracy, language, and numeracy skills.

Revises IDEA part C (Infants and Toddlers with Disabilities) programs of early identification and intervention.

Includes: (1) sign language and cued language services among part C early intervention services; and (2) vision specialists, ophthalmologists, and optometrists among listed qualified personnel who may provide such services. Allows States to include under part C certain children eligible for services under part B preschool grants.

Requires eligible statewide systems to have a rigorous definition of developmental delay to appropriately identify infants and toddlers with disabilities in need of part C services. Includes those who are homeless and those who are wards of of the State among all the infants and toddlers with disabilities and their families who are to receive part C services.

Allows part C statewide systems to include a State policy under which parents of children with disabilities who are eligible for part B preschool services and previously received part C services may choose the continuation of early intervention services for such children under this part until such children enter, or are eligible under State law to enter, kindergarten. Requires such continued services to include an educational component that promotes school readiness and incorporates preliteracy, language, and numeracy skills. Requires States that opt for such a policy to comply with certain requirements, including notice and information on options for parents and reports to the Secretary.

Requires the Individualized Family Services Plan (IFSP) to include a description of services for the child in transition from part C early intervention services to part B preschool services. Includes transition services among the service coordinator's responsibilities. Requires justification of the extent, if any, that early intervention services will be provided in a setting other than a natural environment. Require IFSPs to include: (1) measurable outcomes, including appropriate preliteracy and language skills; and (2) information on the frequency, intensity, and method of delivery of services. Provides that only services for which consent was obtained will be provided, when a parent does not provide written consent for all services on an IFSP.

Requires a public agency that initially fails to provide or pay for special education and related services, but is required to do so under a State's current system of arrangements, to meet its financial responsibilities by reimbursing the LEA or SEA that provided or paid for such education and services.

Includes a representative from the State Medicaid agency as a required member of the State Interagency Coordinating Council under part C.

Eliminates a requirement that the Secretary establish a Federal Interagency Coordinating Committee.

Extends through FY 2010 the authorization of appropriations for IDEA part C.

Revises IDEA part D National Activities to Improve Education of Children with Disabilities. Renames and replaces the current subpart 1 State Program Improvement Grants with a program of State Personnel Preparation and Professional Development Grants. Requires the State to: (1) continue, as under current law, to identify and address State and local needs for the preparation of personnel serving children with disabilities; and (2) use all subpart 1 grant funds to recruit, train, and retain highly qualified teachers and other special education personnel.

Requires grants to SEAs under the new program: (1) on a competitive basis, if the remaining funds are less than a specified amount for a fiscal year; and (2) on a formula basis, if such funds are equal to or greater than such amount.

Authorizes the Secretary to give priority in awarding such competitive grants to States that: (1) have the greatest personnel shortages; or (2) demonstrate the greatest difficulty in meeting part B requirements for personnel standards (which include the deadline for having highly qualified special education teachers by the end of the 2006–2007 school year). Directs the Secretary to make certain minimum competitive grants to all States.

Provides for formula grant allotments. Directs the Secretary to make certain minimum allotments for States that received competitive grants.

Directs the Secretary to reserve specified subpart 1 funds for any necessary continuation awards for multiyear grants to SEAs under such replaced program.

Allows SEAs to apply for a subpart 1 grant for a grant period of between one and five years. Requires an SEA, in order to be considered for such a grant, to: (1) establish a professional development partnership (PDP) with LEAs and other State agencies involved in, or concerned with, the education of children with disabilities, including institutions of higher education and the State agencies responsible for administering part C, child care, and vocational rehabilitation programs; (2) work in partnership with other persons and organizations involved in, and concerned with, the education of children with disabilities, which may include specified entities; and (3) include in the partnership any individual, entity, or agency other than the SEA that State law assigns responsibility for teacher preparation and certification, and ensure that such partner carries out any subpart 1 activities within that partner's jurisdiction.

Requires SEA grant applications to include a State personnel preparation and professional development plan with specified elements.

Revises part D subpart 2 requirements for personnel preparation, research, technical assistance, model demonstration projects, and dissemination of information. Sets forth provisions for personnel development to improve services and results for children with disabilities.

Revises technical assistance and demonstration projects to require such activities to be rooted in scientifically based research. Gives priority to applications that propose to: (1) serve teachers and school personnel directly in the school environment; or (2) strengthen the capacity of States and LEAs to improve instruction practices of personnel serving children with disabilities. Directs the Secretary to support certain activities concerned with, among other things: (1) inappropriate behavior of students; (2) valid and reliable yearly progress assessments; (3) different learning styles of children with disabilities; and (4) effective transition to post-school settings.

Establishes: (1) a beginning special educators program, which adds a fifth-year clinical learning opportunity; and (2) a program to assist general educators (including principals and administrators) in having the skills, knowledge, and leadership training to meet the needs of children with disabilities. Authorizes appropriations for FY 2005 through 2010 for these programs as well as for the leadership preparation program and other programs for personnel development.

Directs the Secretary to delegate to the Director of the Institute of Education Sciences (IES) responsibility for studies and evaluations (including the national assessment) of activities under IDEA (with the exception of the following by the Secretary: (1) an annual summary report to Congress; and (2) a study of the extent to which States adopt policies for statewide systems and the effect of such policies). Requires a national study or studies on alternate assessments and ensuring accountability for students with significant disabilities. Authorizes support for research on: (1) the impact of professional development and educational evaluation programs on student outcomes; (2) economic benefits to special education service delivery through more effective pre-referral services, and (3) teacher recruitment and retention.

Sets forth provisions relating to interim alternative educational settings, behavioral supports, and systemic school interventions. Authorizes the Secretary to make grants, contracts, and cooperative agreements for various activities to: (1) improve interim alternative educational settings; and (2) provide increased behavioral supports and research-based, systemic interventions in schools. Makes eligible individual LEAs as well as consortia of LEAs with community-based organizations with a proven record of helping children with disabilities with behavioral problems, community mental health providers, institutions of higher education, or educational service agencies.

Extends through FY 2010 the authorization of appropriations for certain subpart 2 programs.

Revises part D subpart 3 provisions for supports to improve results for children with disabilities. Directs the Secretary to: (1) make an award to at least one parent training and information center (PTIC) in each State; or (2) in the case of a large State, make awards to multiple PTICs, but only if the centers demonstrate that coordinated services and supports will occur among them. Requires parent organizations that are PTICs, and local parent organizations that support community parent resource centers (CPRCs), to have as their mission serving families of children and youth with a full range of disabilities. Authorizes the Secretary to make an award to one parent organization to provide technical assistance for developing, assisting, and coordinating programs carried out by PTICs and CPRCs. Requires such national technical assistance grantee to: (1) establish regional centers selected from PTICs and CPRCs; and (2) with such regional centers, develop collaborative agreements with geographically appropriate Regional Resource Centers.

Revises, and extends through FY 2010 the authorization of appropriations for, provisions for technology development, demonstration, and utilization, and for media services. Directs the Secretary to support video description, open captioning, and closed captioning of television programs, videos, or other materials that are appropriate for use in the classroom setting. Allows such support only when such services: (1) are not provided by the producer or distributor of such materials; or (2) have not been fully funded by other sources. Allows support for news programming only until September 30, 2006. Provides that visually impaired and print disabled students in postsecondary and graduate schools, as well as in elementary and secondary schools, may continue to be provided with free educational materials.

Directs the Secretary to establish and support, through the American Printing House for the Blind, a National Instructional Materials Access Center to facilitate collection and dissemination of instructional materials for blind and print-disabled students. Requires the Secretary to establish a national instructional materials accessibility standard.

Extends through FY 2010 the authorization of appropriations for subpart 3 programs.

Directs the Secretary, under subpart 4 general provisions, to develop and implement a comprehensive plan for activities under subparts 2 and 3, and report annually on such activities. Authorizes the Secretary to make grants to, or contracts or cooperative agreements with, eligible entities to carry out purposes of such subparts in accordance with such plan. Requires such entities to demonstrate in their application how they will address the needs of children with disabilities from minority backgrounds. Directs the Secretary to reserve a specified portion of funds for such subpart for outreach and technical assistance involving historically Black colleges and universities and institutions of higher education with minority enrollments of at least 25 percent.

Title II: National Center For Special Education Research—(Sec. 201) Amends the Education Sciences Reform Act of 2002 to establish the National Center for Special Education Research.

Requires the Center to: (1) sponsor research to expand knowledge of the needs of children with disabilities and improve IDEA services and implementation; (2) evaluate IDEA implementation and effectiveness; and (3) carry out appropriate research activities. Directs the Center's Commissioner to: (1) ensure that such research activities meet specified standards; and (2) propose to the Director of the Institute of Education Sciences (IES Director) a research plan developed in collaboration with the Assistant Secretary for Special Education and Rehabilitative Services. Authorizes the IES Director to award grants or enter into contracts or cooperative agreements with eligible entities in carrying out Center duties. Requires the Center to: (1) synthesize and disseminate findings and results from research it conducts or supports; and (2) assist the IES Director in preparing the IES biennial report.

Authorizes appropriations for FY 2005 through 2010 carry out Center activities.

(Sec. 202) Subjects to sunshine provisions of Federal law meetings of the National Board for Education Sciences.

(Sec. 203) Requires regional advisory committees to submit their assessments to the IES Director (formerly known as the Director for the Academy of Education Sciences).

Title III: Miscellaneous—(Sec. 301) Amends the Children's Health Act of 2000 to include the Department of Education among the Federal agencies required to be represented in a consortium involved in a long-term child development study authorized under such Act. Requires such study to be conducted in compliance with specified provisions of the General Education Provisions Act, including the requirement of prior parental consent for the disclosure of any education records, except without the use of authority or exceptions granted to authorized representatives of the Secretary of Education for the evaluation of federally-supported education programs or in connection with the enforcement of the Federal legal requirements that relate to such programs.

(Sec. 304) Repeals specified IDEA provisions relating to a Federal Interagency Coordinating Council.

(Sec. 306) Amends Federal copyright law to allow publishers of print instructional materials for elementary or secondary schools, under specified conditions, to create and distribute to the National Instructional Materials Access Center copies of certain electronic files to be used to reproduce or distribute contents of such materials in specialized formats for use by blind or other persons with disabilities.

REFERENCES

Button, J. (2000). Handicapped Children's Early Education Assistance Act (Public Law 90-538). In C. R. Reynolds and E. Fletcher-Janzen (Eds.), *Encyclopedia of Special Education* (2d ed., pp. 858–859). New York: Wiley.

Council for Exceptional Children (2004). *No Child Left Behind Act of 2001: Reauthorization of the Elementary and Secondary Education Act: A technical assistance resource.* Retrieved October 15, 2004, from http://www.cec.sped.org//pp/OverviewNCLB.pdf

Davis, J., & Warren, S. A. (2000). Handicapped Children's Early Education Program (HCEEP). In C. R. Reynolds and E. Fletcher-Janzen (Eds.), *Encyclopedia of Special Education* (2d ed., p. 859). New York: Wiley.

Jacob-Timm, S., & Hartshorne, T. (1995). *Ethics and law for school psychologists.* Brandon, VT: Clinical Psychology Publishing.

Kamphaus, R. W. (2000). Rehabilitation Act of 1973, Section 504 of. In C. R. Reynolds and E. Fletcher-Janzen (Eds.), *Encyclopedia of Special Education* (2d ed., p. 1519). New York: Wiley.

Lowe, P. A., & Reynolds, C. R. (2000a). Americans with Disabilities Act. In C. R. Reynolds and E. Fletcher-Janzen (Eds.), *Encyclopedia of Special Education* (2d ed., pp. 97–102). New York: Wiley.

Lowe, P. A., & Reynolds, C. R. (2000b). Family Educational Rights and Privacy Act (FERPA). In C. R. Reynolds and E. Fletcher-Janzen (Eds.), *Encyclopedia of Special Education* (2d ed., pp. 733–737). New York: Wiley.

Lowe, P. A., & Reynolds, C. R. (2000c). Individuals with Disabilities Education Act (IDEA), PL 105-17. In C. R. Reynolds and E. Fletcher-Janzen (Eds.), *Encyclopedia of Special Education* (2d ed., pp. 940–948). New York: Wiley.

Martin, R. (1979). *Educating handicapped children: The legal mandate.* Champaign, IL: Research Press.

National Clearinghouse on Child Abuse and Neglect Information (DHHS) (2003). *About the Federal Child Abuse Prevention and Treatment Act.* Retrieved September 26, 2004, from http://nccanch.acf.hhs.gov/pubs/factsheets/about.cfm

National Education Association (n.d.). 'No Child Left Behind' Act/ESEA. Retrieved September 30, 2004, from http://www.nea.org/esea/

Office of Civil Rights (1996). *Compliance with the Americans with Disabilities Act: A self-evaluation guide for public elementary and secondary schools.* Washington, DC: U.S. Government Printing Office.

Reynolds, C. R. (2000). Equal protection. In C. R. Reynolds and E. Fletcher-Janzen (Eds.), *Encyclopedia of Special Education* (2d ed., pp. 700–701). New York: Wiley.

Ricciuti, J. R. (2000). Elementary and Secondary Education Act (ESEA). In C. R. Reynolds and E. Fletcher-Janzen (Eds.), *Encyclopedia of Special Education* (2d ed., pp. 679–680). New York: Wiley.

U.S. Department of Education (n.d.a). *Family Educational Rights and Privacy Act (FERPA)*. Retrieved September 30, 2004, from http://www.ed.gov/policy/gen/guid/fpco/ferpa/index.html

U.S. Department of Education (n.d.b). *Introduction: No Child Left Behind.* Retrieved September 30, 2004, from http://www.ed.gov/nclb/overview/intro/index.html

Whelley, P., Cash, G., & Wrobel, G. (2002). Are you hip to HIPAA? *NASP Communiqué.* Retrieved October 10, 2004, from http://www.nasponline.org/publications/cq314hipaa.html